The Study of Ethnomusicology

Thirty-one Issues and Concepts

NEW EDITION

BRUNO NETTL

UNIVERSITY OF ILLINOIS PRESS

Urbana and Chicago

© 1983, 2005 by the Board of Trustees
of the University of Illinois
All rights reserved.
First edition published 1983
Manufactured in the United States of America

1 2 3 4 5 C P 5 4 3 2

♾ This book is printed on acid-free paper.
Library of Congress Cataloging-in-Publication Data

Nettl, Bruno, 1930–
The study of ethnomusicology : thirty-one issues and concepts /
Bruno Nettl.— 2nd ed.
p.   cm.
Includes bibliographical references (p.   ) and index.
ISBN-13: 978-0-252-03033-8 (cloth : alk. paper)
ISBN-10: 0-252-03033-8 (cloth : alk. paper)
ISBN-13: 978-0-252-07278-9 (paper : alk. paper)
ISBN-10: 0-252-07278-2 (paper : alk. paper)
1. Ethnomusicology. I. Title.
ML3798.N47   2005
780'.89—dc22   2005011181

The University of Illinois Press
is a founding member of the
Association of American University Presses.

University of Illinois Press
1325 South Oak Street
Champaign, IL 61820-6903
www.press.uillinois.edu

The Study of Ethnomusicology

For Wanda

Contents

Preface

This is my attempt to revise, bring up to date, and hopefully improve a work that was first begun in 1979, and published in 1983, giving an account of ethnomusicology as a field of research.

More than twenty-five years ago, I undertook, with some trepidation, to write a series of essays on concepts and issues that I considered central to ethnomusicology, essays that would help to explain informally and from a personal perspective—mainly to colleagues in ethnomusicology, but also to those in other disciplines such as historical musicology and anthropology and areas further afield, and of course to graduate students—what this field of study, as I saw it, was all about. In those long-ago days I received encouragement from colleagues and friends whose help I am now happy to acknowledge again—Larry Gushee, Dan Neuman, Charlie Capwell, Steve Slawek, Nazir Jairazbhoy (who later wrote a comprehensive review in *JAMS*), and the late Alan Merriam and Alexander Ringer. *The Study of Ethnomusicology* was received kindly, though also critically, but as time went by, some of its perspectives seemed to me increasingly remote, as ethnomusicology took off to establish a large and diverse body of literature. "Revision" usually means some rewriting and "updating," and when I began to think, about 2001, of preparing a new edition, I was continually reminded of the fact that in our academic discourse, in classes and at conferences, virtually all of the literature about which we talk has been published since the time of writing the first edition. Works that had seemed to me to be the recently established classics by authors with whom I frequently interacted—Merriam's *Anthropology of Music* (1964), Lomax's *Folk Song Style and Culture* (1968), Blacking's *How Musical Is Man?* (1973)—gradually took on the status of "old" and maybe even obsolete literature.

At the same time, some of the problems that stimulated me to write the first edition have receded in significance. For example, although ethnomusicologists still don't agree on just what their field is, the academic public and the world of music now know that there is such a thing; we no longer seem so strange. And there is considerable unity in at least North America on perspectives and training.

I finally decided upon the writing of a revision despite—or maybe even because of—the amount of change that our field has undergone. The original version struck me increasingly as an unrealistic presentation. And so the present offering, while in essence and in the majority of its content still the 1983 work, is devoted in considerable measure to describing the changes that have come about, and the relationship of our present and our recent past to the ways we worked and thought before 1980. The changes—and all chapters have been to an extent rewritten, some much more than others, and there are some new chapters—incorporate ideas and literature of the last twenty-five years and cast the material that was previously presented in a more historical perspective. This revised edition continues to look at ethnomusicology in terms of the ideas and concepts about which we argue. It continues to combine attempts to synthesize what scholars of the earlier and recent past have said, combining this with presentation of my personal ideas and reactions, and illustrating from my fieldwork in northern Plains, Persian, South Indian, and Western classical music.

There are some minor though significant organizational changes: The first of the four parts, on the study of the world's musics, is now followed by the chapters on fieldwork, after which come the more interpretive parts on the study of music in culture and of music in all its variations. Most chapters have new sections and have been rearranged, but there are four new (or newish) chapters: chapter 14, on fieldwork in one's own culture; chapter 17, on the writing of ethnography; chapter 26, on organology, and chapter 28, a very brief survey of women's music and women in musical culture and ethnomusicology. Four of the original chapters largely on European folk music have been reduced and combined into two (now chapters 9 and 25). There is at least somewhat more, throughout, on questions involving power relations, ethics, minorities, diasporas, scholarship in non-European nations, nationalism, globalization, and other issues of current interest. Many chapters, but particularly chapters 28–31, have been substantially reoriented. I have tried, throughout, to avoid redundancy; but the repeated use of an illustration in different contexts has often been maintained, as I wish to make it convenient for readers to use individual chapters without necessarily digesting the entire book. I have tried to make it easier to find things by a more explanatory (if less whimsical) table of contents and a more comprehensive index.

One important feature of revision is the bibliography, which consists only of works to which the text refers. The 1983 edition had around 600 items, while the one at hand has around 960. It has been possible to refer in appropriate places to much of the literature on which present-day thought in ethnomusicology depends, trying to integrate it with the earlier works that provide the historical perspective.

The first edition tries frequently to justify what we do, perhaps with a bit of a chip on the shoulder; I hope I've thrown out the chip, as we are now far better established. One thing I haven't changed is what I hope continues to be seen as a lighthearted tone, in my chapter and subdivision titles, in occasional anecdotes, little parables, jests, sarcasms, provided for making a point, or a change of pace, or comic relief. I hope they also transmit my feeling that research in ethnomusicology, often difficult and even frustrating, has usually also been a lot of fun, for myself and my colleagues. I beg forgiveness, as before, for these moments of levity, reminding the reader that the study and teaching of ethnomusicology is what I have been most serious about in fifty years of academic work.

I continue to be grateful to the colleagues and students who helped me in the preparation of the first edition, and to the University of Illinois Research Board, which provided grants to make possible the appointment of research assistants in the late 1970s. For suggestions regarding the revision specifically, I am grateful to Steve Blum, Tony Seeger, Vicki Levine, Phil Bohlman, Steve Slawek, Donna Buchanan, and Tom Turino for suggestions. Thanks to Marie Rivers for help with the index, and to my wife, Wanda, for proofreading. The readers for the University of Illinois Press provided helpful criticism and recommendations. I am grateful, finally, to Martha Ramsey for a superb job of copyediting, and to Judy McCulloh, friend and colleague of many years standing, whose contribution to the publication of scholarship in ethnomusicology and American music has been truly extraordinary, for putting up with my complaints and my eccentric ideas and seeing yet another of my projects through the University of Illinois Press.

PART 1

The Musics of the World

1

The Harmless Drudge:
Defining Ethnomusicology

Definitions

For years, people have been asking me the question: "You're an ethnomusicologist?" Shortly after 1950 it was likely to be accompanied by expressions of wonder and of the belief that I was somehow involved with "folk" music, with "primitive music," and particularly with "ancient music," and also that I must have a great deal of companionship with a tape recorder. By 1960 the questioner would likely bring up participation in an Indonesian gamelan, or perhaps an ability to play many of the world's odd instruments. In the 1970s, the conversation might well include the term "ethnic" music or even the etymologically outrageous "ethnomusic," and in the eighties and nineties, free association might lead to "diversity" and "world music."

I have always found it hard to come to a precise, concise, and readily intelligible definition. Dictionaries differ considerably but espouse limited views. In the 120 years in which modern ethnomusicology can be said to have existed, since pioneer works such as those of Ellis (1885), Baker (1882), and Stumpf (1886), attitudes and orientations have changed greatly, and so has the name, from something very briefly called *Musikologie* (in the 1880s), to "comparative musicology" (through about 1950), then to "ethno-musicology" (1950–ca. 1956), quickly to "ethnomusicology" (removing the hyphen actually was an ideological move trying to signal disciplinary independence), with suggestions such as "cultural musicology" (Kerman 1985) and "socio-musicology" (Feld 1984) occasionally thrown in. The changes in name paralleled changes in intellectual orientation and emphasis.

It is difficult to find a single, simple definition, to which most people in this field would subscribe, and thus ethnomusicologists have been perhaps excessively concerned with defining themselves. Alan P. Merriam, the scholar in the history of ethnomusicology most concerned with definition and the associated problems of basic orientation, frequently (Merriam 1960, 1964: 3–36, 1969b, 1975) cited the need for ethnomusicologists to look carefully at what they had done and wished to do in order to move in concerted fashion toward their goals. In a major essay discussing the history of definitions, Merriam (1977a) actually brought together a large number of separate statements defining the limits, the major thrust, the practicality, and the ideology of ethnomusicology (see also Myers 1992: 3, 7–9; Simon 1978).

There are various types of definitions: Some tell what each ethnomusicologist must do or be in order to merit the title, and some synthesize what the entire group does. Others focus on what has transpired in terms of research activity, or on what should in fact have been done, or what must eventually be done. They define in terms of a body of data to be gathered and studied, or of activities undertaken by typical scholars, or again by the questions that are asked of the raw data. Some seek to broaden limits, including within the scope of ethnomusicology all sorts of things also claimed by other fields or disciplines, while others envision narrow specialization. A scholar finding order among all of these definitions (Merriam cites over forty, but he stopped in 1976) would surely become what Samuel Johnson called (referring to himself, the lexicographer) a "harmless drudge." It's not, lest you've been misinterpreting the title of this chapter, the ethnomusicologists who claim or deserve that title.

What, specifically, are some of these definitions, and how can one group them? In their briefest form, without elaboration or commentary: Those who seek—or sought—to define ethnomusicology by the material that is contemplated have opted for one of these alternatives: (1) folk music, and music that used to be called "primitive," that is, tribal, indigenous, or possibly ancient music; (2) non-Western and folk music; (3) all music outside the investigator's own culture; (4) all music that lives in oral tradition; (5) all music of a given locality, as in "the ethnomusicology of Tokyo"; (6) the music that given population groups regard as their particular property, for example, "black" music of the United States; (7) all contemporary music (Chase 1958); and (8) all human music. Those focusing on type of activity might choose among the following: (1) comparative study (of musical systems and cultures), a basically musicological activity; (2) comprehensive analysis of the music and musical culture of one society—essentially anthropological; (3) the study of musics as systems, perhaps systems of signs, an activity related to linguistics or semi-otics; (4) the study of music in or as culture, or perhaps music in its cultural context, with techniques derived from anthropology, often called "anthro-pology of music"; and (5) historical study of musics outside the realm of West-ern classical music, using approaches of historians, area studies specialists, and folklorists. Definitions that look at our ultimate goals might include (1) the search for universals; (2) the description of "*all* factors which generate the pat-tern of sound produced by a single composer or society" (Blacking 1970: 69); and even (3) a "science of music history," aiming at the establishment of laws governing musical development and change. This sampling provides an idea of the number and variety of definitions and approaches. Beyond this, how-ever, the disciplinary identity of ethnomusicology is often the subject of de-bate. Opinions: Ethnomusicology is (1) a full-fledged discipline; (2) a branch of musicology, or (3) of anthropology; (4) an interdisciplinary field; (5) the kind of all-encompassing discipline that "musicology" ought to be, but hasn't become.

No wonder that preoccupation with identity has been a major activity. When attending meetings of the Society of Ethnomusicology, the largest or-ganization of the field, I used to be struck by the number of specialized pa-pers that began with statements giving the speakers' definition of and gen-eral orientation toward the field. Since about 1985, however, the obsession with defining ethnomusicology has declined, and some have decided to stop wor-rying about it while others have come to agree on a mainstream of thrusts and emphases. One might also define a field of research by the kinds of things about which its people argue and debate; in a sense, this series of essays is itself a somewhat clumsy attempt to define ethnomusicology in terms of some of its abiding issues, concepts, questions, and problem areas of general concern.

Who They Are and What They Actually Do

There may be many definitions, but what those who call themselves ethno-musicologists or who otherwise associate themselves with this field actually do has been fairly clear. Who are they? The Society for Ethnomusicology has been conducting a survey as yet incomplete at the time of this writing. De-scriptions of the ethnomusicological population between around 1950 and 1980 may be found in Myers (1992) and Hood (1971). Let me try an impres-sionistic overview of the present. Of those working in this field since about 1980, many have an initial background in academic music, as students of performance, theory, or composition; in North America, this may culminate in a bachelor's degree in music. But increasingly, they have also come from backgrounds in popular music, and some are motivated by prolonged residence—perhaps as teenagers—abroad. A good many also come to this field from exposure to third-world cultures as members of the Peace Corps, as teachers of English abroad, in missionary work. Typically, they seem to me to have been turned on to the field by the love of or fascination with some music. There usually soon follows some kind of exposure to a culture or society, and then often more formal study of culture, broadly speaking, perhaps including graduate study of anthropology, or of a field of area studies such as South Asia, Africa, the Middle East. Some turn to ethnomusicology after a period of living in a non-Western culture as teachers of Western music. Many students of ethnomusicology very quickly form a specialized allegiance to the music of a particular culture or area, and even a particular genre of music—Plains Indian powwow dances, Javanese gamelan music, North Indian classical instrumental music, Moroccan rai.

Most ethnomusicologists, in any event, undertake graduate study in this field; there aren't many (though there once were) scholars in other disciplines—music history, anthropology—who, in midcareer as professionals, switched lanes and moved to ethnomusicology. Graduate curricula in ethnomusicology vary considerably. Some of the leading ones are free-standing programs in their universities, many are attached to music departments and may be considered one of a number of specializations within musicology, and a few are in anthropology, popular culture, media studies, and folklore departments or programs. But while the orientations of these programs in North America varied greatly when they first came into existence in the 1950s and 1960s, and they still differ considerably, there has gradually developed a kind of mainstream, a central core of preparation, that includes some study of performance of the music in which one plans to undertake research—and perhaps incidentally also performance of other noncanonic musics that may be available—and considerable reading and study of anthropology, and of anthropologically related theory. Near the end of one's graduate study one ordinarily undertakes field research in a society or culture or subculture, or perhaps a genre or repertory in which one later becomes known as a specialist. This dissertation fieldwork, which is preceded by cultural and linguistic preparation, usually involves a year or more of residence in the field venue. Analysis of collected data used to include automatically the transcription of recordings into musical notation, and this is still important, though the arsenal of techniques has been widened. Arriving at musical insights, and—more difficult—developing a procedure for the analysis of human activities and attitudes revolving about the musical sounds, should follow, and the final stage in this research process is the interpretation of data in accordance with certain defined theoretical approaches or positions.

Most ethnomusicologists, Ph.D. in hand, seek teaching positions in higher education, though other kinds of work—librarianship, museology, the recording industry, public service of various sorts, publishing—are also available. Ethnomusicologists appointed to teaching positions are almost always assigned a course in "musics of the world," or at least something going far beyond the scope of their specialized research, along with something more in their particular line of expertise. Advanced courses may be devoted to world areas—for example, South Asia, sub-Saharan Africa—or they may be topical (e.g., world perspectives of children's music, improvised music around the world, or the study—on a global basis—of musical change). Interestingly, it seems that in middle age, many ethnomusicologists add a second world area to their fields of expertise; for myself, I started with Native American music and, at the age of thirty-nine, added the classical music of Iran. Among my colleagues, Thomas Turino, first an Andeanist, added the music of East Africa, and Charles Capwell added Indonesia to South Asia. Paul Berliner, an authority on East African mbira music, became, as well, an authority on jazz. I wish I could assert that elderly ethnomusicologists become wiser and more inclined to take broad and long views of the world of music, but I'm not so sure.

A typical ethnomusicologist's profile? Despite all diversity, a good many of my colleagues will recognize themselves here. As for the definitions cited above, there may be a lot of them, but ethnomusicologists really aren't all that different from each other. There is often a gap between what ethnomusicologists do and what, by their own definition, they claim to do or hope some day to accomplish.

What most of them actually do is to carry out research about non-Western, folk, popular, and vernacular music, taking into account both the music itself, as sound, and how it interacts with other things that people do—that's really what we mean by "music in culture." However we define these terms, they are what authors in such journals as *Ethnomusicology, World of Music,* and *Asian Music* actually write about. The definition of ethnomusicology as the study of non-Western and folk music, although widely criticized, is descriptively correct. On the other hand, the definition as study of music outside one's own culture is not, for Asian and African scholars who call themselves ethnomusicologists typically do study their own music (see chapter 14 for what "own" may mean), but when they study the European music that is outside their own culture, they prefer avoiding the term, instead calling themselves music historians or just musicologists.

Ethnomusicologists are supremely interested in music as a component of culture. For some time—perhaps the period between 1950 and 1970 is the most indicative—they tended to divide themselves into two groups, frequently at odds, one concentrating on the music "itself," the other on the cultural context. The first typically felt that they were properly studying the main point of focus, the music itself, in its cultural context, looking down on these other "contextualists" as amateurs unable to deal directly with music, while the others, espousing an anthropological approach, considered their opposite numbers to be naive, unable even to understand the musical artifact because they could not approach it as a product of culture, and unwilling to deal with musical concepts, attitudes, or forms of behavior other than the piece of music itself. After about 1980, the two groups tended to merge, but even in earlier times, I do not know of any ethnomusicologists who did not, in their total commitments, have a major interest in music as an aspect of human culture. Anthropologists, as a basic technique of their profession, know how to analyze the interaction of various domains in culture; musicologists are distinguished by their fundamental ability to make sophisticated analyses of musical artifacts. Most ethnomusicologists try to be both.

Most academic ethnomusicologists in North America associate themselves with music schools and departments; but many of the intellectual leaders come from anthropology. Yet, as the following chapters examine principal issues that ethnomusicologists confront, it will become evident that this is a field which frequently asks questions that are actually fundamental to musicology, the discipline that encompasses all kinds of music scholarship. Of course, many scholars concerned with music quite justly see themselves not as musicologists at all, but as anthropologists, folklorists, sociologists, linguists; and yet, when engaging in ethnomusicological work, they are contributing to this central core of musicological activity (see the essays in Blum 1987; Cook and Everist 1999). To be sure, they are at the same time making contributions to their home disciplines, such as anthropology and folklore, but typically their findings are not as central to these fields as they are to musicology. Ethnomusicology may function well as an independent field, and surely it has multiple disciplinary associations, but I strongly believe that ethnomusicological findings, insights, and theories, no matter to whatever other disciplines they may also contribute, have made their greatest contributions to musicology.

The first generations of ethnomusicologists, from around 1900 to maybe 1970, were seen as academic oddballs involved in an arcane subject of no interest outside the academy (or even inside). After 1960, they tried to make their musics known by issuing records and promoting concerts (of, say, Indian, Japanese, Arabic, West African musics), and I would assert that they played a role in the rapidly increasing interchanges of musics that led to the styles and the culture of "world music" as a category in the listening habits of Western society. So now, while few outsiders actually know exactly what it is that they do in their lives, ethnomusicologists are a concept and a term known to all levels of education, in the mass media, in areas of government. The world of music has changed incredibly since the 1980s, and ethnomusicologists are recognized as having contributed to these changes, and sought as interpreters of what has happened. Their work has contributed greatly to what is now taught in public school music programs, to the variety of musics available on recordings to all, and to the resources used by composers of concert music.

But ethnomusicology is actually not all that easily separated conceptually from historical musicology—what is usually called "musicology." All musicologists actually deal in some respects with music as sound and in culture. And all dictionary definitions of musicology include the work that ethnomusicologists do. There are two main attitudes that really distinguish ethnomusicologists in what they actually do from other musical scholarship.

One is the centrality of fieldwork. It wasn't always so. We began in the nineteenth century with a tendency to speculate on the basis of little supporting evidence, moving around 1900 to "armchair" research, in which the ethnomusicologist analyzed materials collected and recorded in the field by others—usually anthropologists and missionaries. But as the twentieth century progressed, fieldwork became increasingly essential and, after World War II, a sine qua non of the ethnomusicologist's own style of life and study. Of course face-to-face investigation of exotic music and musicians was known earlier, and even in the "armchair" period most ethnomusicologists did venture into the "field" or at least recognized the desirability of doing so.

Today it is taken for granted that each ethnomusicologist must have *some* field research experience, and that most studies are based on the researcher's own fieldwork. But considering economic and political developments since 1980, the difficulty of doing research in many parts of the world, and the fact that the world's societies produce recordings and publications of their own, it is possible that in the future the armchair will become part of our furniture.

The kind and quality of fieldwork on which given research is based have a profound effect on the conclusions, but ethnomusicological publications—

particularly those from before 1990—rarely tell much about the procedures used in the field (see chapters 10–11). They may give data such as names of informants and teachers, machinery used to record or film, questionnaires, but rarely the whole story of how it really felt. There is something curious about the combination of centrality and mystery in this hallmark of ethnomusicological life. As the primary technique for data gathering, fieldwork also has broader significance as the ethnomusicologist's bridge to the cultural "other" (which includes distant lands as well as societies close to home). It's a truism: Exposure to another culture stimulates empathy with both the strangeness and the common humanity, of another society of people, and incidentally with the complexity of the music and musical life in what may from a distance seem a simple situation. We believe that this understanding, once it has been gained in a particular culture, will carry over to further work not based on field research, that it will help to evaluate publications by others that may be based on fieldwork and provide insights necessary for guiding the fieldwork of students who investigate societies with which the teacher is not directly acquainted. All of this is, of course, tied to the fact that most ethnomusicologists study cultures outside their own, and to the resulting assumption that there is a dichotomy between one's own culture and all others, the latter in a certain sense all alike. This position has been widely critiqued in recent literature (going back to positions of the philosopher Antonio Gramcsi 1971, and summarized by Slobin 1992a; see chapter 15 here). Epistemologically our approach to foreign cultures initially lumps them into a single category; we begin by dividing the world into categories of "ours" and "not ours," into "familiar" and "strange." Later we try to overcome this simplistic view.

The second central attitude is the maintenance of an interculturally comparative perspective. Ethnomusicologists don't spend their time comparing the musics of different societies, and they certainly don't compare in order to determine who is better at this or that aspect of music-making. But they look at each musical culture from a viewpoint that relates it to the world of music, a world comprised of a multitude of musical cultures that are alike in some ways and different in others, and they believe that insight can be gained from comparison. A comparative perspective, yes; but when it comes to brass tacks, what kinds of comparison are significant, and whether there is a good method for comparing musics, these are questions the literature has generally avoided. The validity of comparative study has been debated (and the debates are followed in chapter 6). But to me, an interculturally comparative perspective is, like fieldwork, a hallmark of ethnomusicology.

Coming to Terms

Merriam (1977a: 192–93) believed that the terminological change to "ethnomusicology," around 1950, came from the recognition that this field is no more comparative than others, that comparison can be made only after the things to be compared are well understood in themselves, and that, in the end, comparison across cultural boundaries might be impossible because the musics and cultures of the world are unique. In his classic book *The Anthropology of Music* (1964: 52–53) he also pointed out that most of the general publications of ethnomusicology do not deal with methods and techniques of comparative study (Wiora 1975 and many essays in the *Garland Encyclopedia* from ca. 2000 notwithstanding). At the same time, it is difficult to find specialized studies that do not in some way, at least by implication, make use of intercultural comparison as a way of gaining and presenting insights. The proponents of comparative study, accepting the criticisms given here, nevertheless appear to consider the benefits of the comparative view so great that they feel it worth their while to indulge it.

But the adoption of the term "ethnomusicology" as a replacement for "comparative musicology" may have causes additional to those suggested by Merriam. I don't question the reasoning of Jaap Kunst, who is generally regarded as the first to have used the new term prominently in print (Kunst 1950: 7); he did so, he says, because comparative musicology is not *especially* comparative. But why then was the new term adopted so quickly, and particularly by Americans, who seem to have been the first to adopt it officially?

The participation of a number of anthropologists in the American leadership of comparative musicology seems likely to have favored the use of a term paralleling the names of several anthropological subfields: ethnolinguistics and ethnohistory, with others, such as ethnobotany and ethnoscience, coming later. Among the academic disciplines around 1950, anthropology had greater prestige than did musicology, itself often misunderstood even in midcentury. Musicologists, after all, were seen as the academic Simon Legrees for students of musical performance, and musicological study was frequently regarded as the refuge of the unsuccessful player or composer. The new term attractively symbolized association with anthropology or something that sounded anthropological. Nationalism too may have played a part. Americans were proud of their significant contributions to non-Western and folk music research between 1930 and about 1955, in comparison to their more modest work as historians of Western music. They might have needed a term that expressed their special role, that was not simply a translation of the established German term "vergleichende Musikwissenschaft." The fact that one was dealing with a special kind of music, low in the hierarchy of musics with which the conventional musicologist dealt, may also have stimulated the need for a special term, a whole word, "ethnomusicology," instead of a term merely designating a subfield of musicology that dealt, by implication, with "submusics" worthy only of being compared with the great art music of Europe.

But whatever the attitude toward comparison and its role in the development of a self-image, ethnomusicologists use it to generalize about world music. They are moderately effective here; before their advent, the same generalizations were made by philosophers and sociologists and historians of European music, and they could often be falsified by mere reference to standard descriptions of non-European cultures. Most of the comparisons found in the ethnomusicological literature involve observations of change and its processes, or questions of origin, and thus we may conclude that most of the generalizing done in this field has some kind of relevance to history. The ultimate contribution of comparative study of musics provides central insights into the understanding of the world of music—how it exists in the present and how it came to be.

A Credo

I have talked about the multiplicity of definitions, the different ways of defining a discipline, the history of the term "ethnomusicology," the principal activities of ethnomusicologists, and the kinds of people who eventually find themselves in this field. Time for me to try my hand at my own definition, or at least give the one that is central to this book. It's a two-pronged definition, to which are added two corollaries, and I think it is probably acceptable to at least some of my colleagues, and so I should like to tie it to certain beliefs and understandings that might be considered a kind of credo.

1. *For one thing, ethnomusicology is the study of music in culture.* A concept that has its problems, when examined carefully (as by Martin Stokes in *The New Grove Dictionary of Music and Musicians* 2001, 8:386–88), but in the end I think it holds up. Ethnomusicologists believe that music must be understood as a part of culture, as a product of human society, and while many pieces of research do not directly address the problem, we insist on this be-

lief as an essential ingredient of our overall approach. We are interested in the way in which a society musically defines itself, in its taxonomy of music, its ideas of what music does, how it should be, and also in the way a society changes its music, relates to, absorbs, and influences other musics. We stress the understanding of musical change, less in terms of the events than in the processes.

2. *Just as important, ethnomusicology is the study of the world's musics from a comparative and relativistic perspective.* We endeavor to study total musical systems and, in order to comprehend them, follow a comparative approach, believing that comparative study, properly carried out, provides important insights. But we study each music in its own terms, and we try to learn to see it as its own society understands it. Our area of concentration is music that is accepted by an entire society as its own, and we reserve a lesser role for the personal, the idiosyncratic, the exceptional, differing in this way from historians of music. We are most interested in what is typical of a culture.

3. *Principally, ethnomusicology is study with the use of fieldwork.* We believe that fieldwork, direct confrontation with musical creation and performance, with the people who conceive of, produce, and consume music, is essential, and we prefer concentration on intensive work with small numbers of individual informants to surveys of large populations. And we hope that this association will lead to some kind of benefit for the people from whom we learn.

4. *Ethnomusicology is the study of all of the musical manifestations of a society.* Although we take into account a society's own hierarchy of its various kinds of music, and its musicians, we want to study not only what is excellent but also what is ordinary and even barely acceptable. We do not privilege elite repertories, and we pay special attention to the musics of lower socio-economic classes, colonized peoples, oppressed minorities. We believe that we must in the end study all of the world's music, from all peoples and nations, classes, sources, periods of history. We just haven't yet got around to all of it.

These four areas of belief (though not in this order) are the basis of my organization of these essays, and they function here as both definition and fundamental understandings of what we do. Are they a kind of credo? Many of my colleagues, typical nonconformists among musicians and music scholars, are unlikely to accept any doctrine. And there are also some other, perhaps more fundamental beliefs that define the core of ethnomusicological thinking and should somehow be appended to a credo.

Ethnomusicologists seem to be driven by two major but apparently conflicting motivations. They search for universals, hoping to generalize intelligently about the way in which the world's cultures construct, use, conceive of music. They try to understand human music in the context of human culture as a unitary phenomenon. And yet they never cease to marvel at the incredible variety of manifestations of music. They delight in imparting to the world the strange facts uncovered by musical ethnography and analysis: that among the Sirionó of Bolivia, each person may at one time have sung only one tune all of his or her life, identifying the individual with a personal musical stamp (Key 1963; Stumpf 1886: 411); that in the classical music of India there is an almost incredibly complex interaction of melody and rhythm maintained over a sustained period by a musician who manipulates the rhythmic cycle in juxtaposition to improvised rhythmic units; that oppressed minorities have special uses for music in their struggles for improvement. Despite their interest in human universals, ethnomusicologists revel in their knowledge that most generalizations about structure and use of music can be overturned by reference to this or that small society. They vacillate between a view of music as a unified human phenomenon and as an emblem of the infinite variety of human cultures.

Fundamentally, ethnomusicologists are egalitarians. They become attached to cultures which they study and with which they identify themselves, they have special loves, obligations toward the musics they regard as ethnic or family heritage. They may consciously or tacitly believe in the intellectual, technical, aesthetic, or artistic superiority of certain musics and be able to make a good case for this belief, preferring the classical music of Europe or Asia because of its complexity, or the music of "simple" folk because of its presumably unspoiled nature. But, at the bottom line, at some level of conceptualization, they regard all musics as equal. Each music, they believe, is equally an expression of culture, and each culture and each music must be understood first and foremost in its own terms. They consider all musics worthy of study, recognizing that all, no matter how apparently simple, are in themselves inordinately complex phenomena. And they believe that all musics are capable of imparting much of importance to the peoples to whom they belong, and to the world, and thus naturally also to the scholars who study them.

But there is also a sense in which ethnomusicologists are usually not relativists. Taking a sympathetic view of the music of all peoples, they come to believe in the right of each society to determine its own way of life, and they are likely to become dedicated to the improvement of life for the people with whose music they are concerned. They may be impelled to social and political activism in opposition to colonialism or neo-colonialism and in support of minorities, and perhaps more typically, of a kind of musical activism which insists that the musics of the world's peoples must be protected, preserved, taught, and the musicians treated fairly and with respect. Although they may wish to study their subject dispassionately, they are in the end often unable to avoid the results of extended contact with humans and their works in a foreign society. They try to bring an understanding of their musics to their own society, believing that the teaching of their subject will in a small way promote intercultural—maybe even international—understanding, that it will combat ethnocentrism and build respect for the traditions of the world's societies. Intellectually neutral in their quest for knowledge of musical cultures, they nevertheless have a passion for showing that the music of the oppressed people of the world, of lower classes in rigidly stratified societies, of isolated, indigenous, technically developing peoples, is something innately interesting, something worthy of attention and respect—indeed, something truly magnificent. These attitudes are not a prerequisite of graduate study or a teaching position, not part of the definition of the field; and they are surely also found among members of other professions. But there are few ethnomusicologists who do not share them.

2

The Art of Combining Tones:
The Music Concept

The Cocktail Party

"The art of combining tones." This is how some dictionaries begin their definitions of music. But in American society, beyond the "harmless drudges," few people can actually define music, and they certainly differ greatly in what they think is significant about music. Let me reconstruct a cocktail party conversation about 1975 that began when I confessed to working in ethnomusicology. "Studying American Indian music!" says one amazed person. "I didn't know they even had music." I try patiently to explain. "Oh yes, I knew they had chants, but is that really music?" From an elderly gentleman: "I spent a year in Africa, heard a lot of singing and drumming, but that isn't music, is it? After all, they don't write it down, maybe they just make it up as they go along, they don't really know what they are doing." More explanation. A lady joins in the conversation: "A few days ago, I heard some ancient music from the Middle East which didn't sound at all unpleasant. The commentator said it sounded good because, after all, it is from the cradle of our own civilization." A young man has added himself. "But these sounds that some peoples in Asia make with their instruments and voices, or the Indian chants, can you call them music? To me, they don't sound like music. For example, they don't have harmony." And the old gentleman: "My teenage grandsons play their records all day, but hardly any of them sound like music to me."

(Time for that second Scotch.)

For the reader of these pages I don't have to repeat my answers. Actually, twenty years later, the guests would have been a bit more broad-minded.

They might have heard a good bit of "world music" emanating from their teenagers' bedroom and they would have heard the didjeridu in Australian films. They might have questioned whether the motor in George Antheil's "Airplane Sonata" was music and expressed doubts about the musicness of rap. Their increased tolerance would please me, but they wouldn't have solved the ethnomusicologist's first problem.

We claim to study music, and if we've become sufficiently broad-minded, all societies have something that sounds to us like music, but the point is that there is no interculturally valid conceptualization or definition of music. Very few societies have a concept (and a term) parallel to the European "music." They may instead have taxonomies whose borders cut across the universe of humanly organized sound in totally different ways from those of Western societies. Studying any musical culture should surely require an understanding of its definition and conceptualization of music, but for a long time that issue was not frequently brought out into the open, at least before Merriam (1964: 27–28) attacked it. Before making a quick survey, let's look at some difficulties into which we run even at home.

Imagine yourself coming from a foreign culture, or that you're an ethnomusicologist from Venus or Mars, the absolute outsider. You might quickly discover that in a complex society one can find definitions of important concepts in at least three ways: by asking the society's own "expert," who has thought about it long and hard (or perhaps you could look in the dictionary); by asking members of the society at large in order to determine whether there is a consensus (possibly using a questionnaire and distributing it widely); and by observing what people do, and listening to what they say to each other (for example, by going to concerts and record stores, or maybe attending cocktail parties).

Many music dictionaries published in Europe and North America avoid the definition of music in its most fundamental sense. Wisely, perhaps, their authors assume that the readers know what they, and the people with whom they associate, think music is. The editors of the 1980 edition of *The New Grove Dictionary of Music and Musicians* omitted it, but thought better of it in the 2001 (i.e., second) edition, presenting an article that looks at the concept from the perspective of different cultures but begins somewhat lamely by just designating music as "the principal subject of this [encyclopedia]." The old *Harvard Dictionary* (Apel 1969: 548) under "Music" discusses the phenomenon without giving a definition, and the 1986 edition, maybe to avoid a can of worms, dropped it again.

Language dictionaries can't escape so easily. In the *Oxford English Dic-*

tionary, music is "that one of the fine arts which is concerned with the com-bination of sounds with a view to beauty of form and the expression of thought or feeling." A work directed to young students, *Webster's Interme-diate Dictionary,* says that it is "the art of combining tones so that they are pleasing, expressive, or intelligible." In these and other dictionaries, includ-ing those of other European languages, music is discussed in terms of tones (which Western thinkers on music consider to be its basic building blocks), beauty and intelligibility (relating to music as art and as science), and ex-pressiveness (giving the sense that music is a kind of communication). This appears to be a consensus of the intelligentsia of Western culture, but there are societies and musics where these criteria make no sense at all.

So much for "authorities." What now do people in a typical American town or city who have not made a specialty of this field consider music to be? I have no systematic surveys to cite, but here's what I learned from some informal interviews of urban Americans who were not musicians, in the 1960s (Nettl 1963) and the 1980s. They weren't ready with outright definitions, but when pushed, they appeared to believe that almost any sound is potentially musi-cal. They quickly started telling me what was "good" or "boring" music, and what they liked (see also Russell 1993). It may seem fatuous to point this out, but since some cultures see it differently, music seems to Americans to be in-nately a "good" thing, and therefore it is probably good for a sound or even silence to be accepted potentially as a component of music. Sounds that are "good" are sounds that may be included in the music concept. Thus the sound of coins about to be paid is "music to my ears," a person whose speech one likes is said to have a "musical voice," and a language whose sound one dis-likes is called "unmusical."

At the same time, Americans think of music as something associated with particular social contexts, such as concerts, and thus any sound produced in a concert is likely to be considered music. If asked to consider the matter, many people accept any sound as music, including animal sounds, indus-trial noises, and of course any of a vast number of humanly produced sounds made on instruments, with the body, and with the voice, including speech. Twentieth-century Americans like music, and they like to feel that much of their world can somehow be related to music.

For the third approach to studying definitions, let's return to the cocktail party, this time masquerading as fieldworkers, trying to use what we hear to construct some idea of the conceptualization of music that this society holds when its members are not being asked artificially to consider the matter care-fully. I had to defend my interest in non-Western music because my friends wondered whether it was actually music. There is a curious disparity in what people include under the heading of music when given time to consider the question (when they exhibit broad tolerance) and what they will accept when giving quick reactions (when they are more narrow-minded). Fieldworkers early on learn this major lesson: They may get one kind of answer when asking a question that would normally have no place in the culture and another when observing the society's behavior. And we may note rather different approaches from formal statements by authorities, informal interviews, and observing ordinary conversations. Of the three, the cocktail party conversation may give us the most reliable perspective of the way urban, middle-class Americans actually use the concept of music in their lives.

They weren't interested in defining music, but in their questions, my friends divulged some of the criteria they ordinarily use by telling me what characteristics the activity and sounds they call "music" should have in order to be accepted as true and proper music. "Indians have only chants, not music," suggests that a certain level of complexity, as it is perceived by these listeners, is a necessary feature. What my friends colloquially called "chants" have only a few pitches and no harmony, and that kind of sound is not fully acceptable to them as music. Western urban society can conceive of music without a background of chords, or without two or more simultaneous sounds, but considers this texture as clearly exceptional. "Normal" music must have harmony, or at least some kind of rhythmic accompaniment. Here is another component in our exercise: Music must have certain traits in order to be acceptable, but some of them need be present only in the mainstream of a repertory. Minority repertories (e.g., traditional folk singing, Gregorian chant) in which they are absent are nevertheless accepted. In some societies the components are reversed. Thus, in certain Native American musics there were evidently some few songs that had harmony (Keeling 1992; Nettl 1961). While these were accepted as part of the musical material of the culture, the use of harmony was not extended to the mainstream of what these peoples themselves called "Indian music."

The idea that music is intrinsically good and pleasant was suggested in my interviews and in some of the dictionary definitions, and, indeed, my friends at that party brought it up as well, expecting music to be pleasing. Music is in itself a good and positive value, and with this goes the belief that we should enjoy its sound. Confronted with something whose sound they disliked, my friends tended to question whether it could even be music. Music critics have reacted thus to experiments in Western music. As a related point, the dictionaries implied that music must normally be composed and notated by individuals who are trained and who give thought to their work. The idea of preconceived structure, of music being something created by people who know what they are doing, was also important to my friends, and is tied to the more formal definition of music as a science. The significance of this criterion explains much of how Western urban society understands musical structure and activity of the past and present. Among other things, it explains at least in part why Western polite society considers "composition" to be nobler than "improvisation," which, in music dictionaries, is more craft than art.

Perhaps most intriguing is the skepticism that my friends at the cocktail party displayed over the possibility of another culture having music at all. They were not surprised at the existence of sounds such as singing, but they had second thoughts about calling it "music." This reaction has several possible implications. First, it is conceivable that my friends, and our society, regard music as so important to our way of life that they cannot see quite how another society could also have it. We are, after all, a rather ethnocentric lot. Music, being a priori a "good" thing, must belong exclusively to ours, the only truly "good" culture. Second, our tendency in Western society is to feel that other peoples do not know how to do anything properly if they have not adopted our way of doing it. In our technology we require computers; in agriculture, crop rotation; in political structure, democracy of a sort; in marriage, monogamy. Slash-and-burn agriculture, theocracy, polygamy may not really count as proper cultural systems. And, in the case of music, the implication would be that if a society does not have at least the central components of our kind of music, it may not truly have music, just as a society would not be considered to have marriage in a sense acceptable to us (North American "Anglos") if it permitted polygamy or incest. My friends, who love their own music, may know better; but they could not get themselves to quite admit that other cultures have something so close to their hearts as music. Or, to put it more bluntly, they may have doubted that the world's "savages" can have created something which is so valuable as music. To be sure, this viewpoint played more of a role in 1975 than it would thirty years later, and it has been rapidly receding in the last few decades, the result of tourism, concerts by musicians from everywhere, and the "world music" movement.

There are some obvious contradictions between the formal conceptualizations of music in our society and these that were informally derived. Dictionaries stress tones, but my friends stress harmony. The dictionaries imply that music is somehow a universal language, whereas my friends hold that it is culture-specific. But the definitions agree in some respects. Music is "pleasant" to my friends, "expressive" to the authorities; it is an art and a science in the dictionaries, and to my friends, something in which one must be skilled and therefore produce something complicated.

Amazing, what one can learn at a cocktail party.

Do They Really Have Music?

If we have trouble defining and conceptualizing music in our own culture, it's even harder to analyze the concept in cultures to which we are strangers. Even within one society a particular sound may be regarded as musical in one context and nonmusical in another (see, e.g., Robertson 1977: 35–40). But not so fast: European languages too have differences in terminology which indicate a variety of ways of seeing the shape of music. In German, *Musik* means "music" in general, but *Tonkunst,* glossed as "musics," is used to refer to classical music (typically, though, music of the German-, French-, and Italian-speaking nations). In Czech, though the terms overlap, *muzika* means vernacular music, mainly instrumental; *hudba* means classical or academic music. Actually, most languages of the world don't have a term to encompass music as a total phenomenon. Instead, they often have words for individual musical activities or artifacts such as singing, playing, song, religious song, secular song, dance, and many more obscure categories. Until recently, most ethnomusicological studies did not speak to the question of the definition or conception of music in any one society, taking for granted the existence of the concept, even in the absence of an actual term for music. Merriam (1967a: 3, 1964: 3–84) discusses this matter at length, and there are some classic studies of the terminology and taxonomy of individual cultures by Zemp (1979), Feld (1982), Al-Faruqi (1985–86), and Rowell (1992).

The absence of a general term for music doesn't necessarily mean that there's no music concept, but the way in which terms appear in discourse about music may tell us about the configuration of the concept. According to Ames and King (1971: ix; also Ames 1973b: 132), the Hausa of Nigeria have no term for music; there is a word, *musika,* derived from the Arabic and ultimately the Greek word, which is used for a very restricted body of music. But evidently many musical activities in which the Hausa engage are more important as components of a variety of cultural contexts, and thus verbally more associated with these, than understood as a complex of structurally similar phenomena. The same seems to be true of Native American societies that have no word to tie together all musical activities. The Blackfoot have a word, *paskan,* that can roughly be translated as "dance," which includes music and ceremony and is used to refer to religious and semireligious events that comprise music, dance, and other activities; but this word would not include certain musical activities, such as gambling, that have no dancing at all. They have a word for "song" but not one for instrumental music. A similar attitude, incidentally, may have been traditional in India; the word *sangit* or a derivative of it is used to translate "music" rather accurately, but the term may also include dance. According to McAllester (1954: 4), the Navajo have no word for music or for musical instruments. Keil (1979: 27–29) searched in vain for a specific term for music in a dozen languages of West Africa.

Although a society has a word roughly translatable as music, that word may include things we in Western urban society, despite our own loose definition, do not include as musical, and it may specifically exclude other phenomena that we regard as music. For example, the Persian term now generally used to translate "music" is *musiqi,* borrowed from Arabic. It refers, though, primarily to instrumental music, yet includes certain vocal music. But vocal music in general is mainly called *khāndan,* a word translated as "reading," "reciting," and "singing." The singing of the Koran, whose structure and sound are not very different from the singing of secular classical and folk music, is not admitted as belonging to *musiqi,* nor is the recitation of prayer or the muezzin's call to prayer. The reason for excluding the most specifically religious singing from the main category of "music" has to do with the opinion in Muslim law that music is in certain ways an undesirable and even sinful activity and that as a concept it must be kept separate from religion. One of the first acts of the Ayatollah Khomeini upon proclaiming the Islamic Republic of Iran in 1979 was to outlaw certain kinds of secular music. On the other hand, the singing of the nightingale, a paradigm of beauty, is regarded by Persians as at least closely related to human singing and, indeed, as a model for it. The Iranian classification (which coincides generally with others in the Islamic Middle East) is therefore overlapping. Instrumental music is *musiqi,* Koran singing and prayer are *khāndan,* and folk song, popular song, classical vocal music, and the nightingale are in both categories. The barking of dogs is in neither (see Farhat 1990: 121; Al-Faruqi 1985–86; Shiloah 1995).

According to Merriam (1964: 64–65), the Basongye of Zaire include as music what Westerners regard as singing, exclude bird song, and are not sure about the status of whistling and humming. Keil, on the other hand (1979: 28–30), questions the possibility of deriving such a definition where, as among the Basongye, there are no terms to correspond to "music," "sound," and "noise" and points out that, among the Tiv of Nigeria, a large set of specific terms substitute for our holistic idea of music.

By the same token, Western society, in its Anglo-American form, may appear quite arbitrary in what it includes as music. Birds sing, we say, but not donkeys and dogs (although the latter, to a dog lover, might well produce "music to my ears," reinforcing our contention that music symbolizes goodness and happiness). The sounds made by dolphins, acoustically as similar to human music as is bird song, are said to be "language" (see Truitt 1974: 387–92, also Sebeok 1977: 794–808, and several essays in Wallin, Marker, and Brown 2000), but the sound of birds, which also acts as communication, is not. Among the sounds produced by humans, it is clear that we are similarly arbitrary. The sound of a machine is not music unless it is produced in a concert with a program that lists its "composer" and with an audience which applauds (or at least boos). In the academic "new music" culture, even the presentation of art works on slides, in a concert listed as a general musical event, may be treated as musical composition by an audience. Examples are legion; but clearly, each society has its unique conception of music and a terminology to reflect the conception.

What Is This Thing Called Music?

Here are a couple of thoughts relevant but somewhat tangential to the definition of music per se. First, the value of music in a society may be a major factor in determining the breadth of its definition of music. Second, the widely held view of music as merely a kind of sound is a basis of operations too narrow for acceptance by ethnomusicologists.

Obviously, all cultures regard music as at least minimally valuable, but to some it is supremely valuable, and to others a more or less necessary evil. For example, the Blackfoot people traditionally believed that they could not live without their songs, for these were a major component in the relationship of humans to the supernatural. Members of certain Muslim societies in the Middle East like music but may worry that there is something wrong with that state of affairs and thus relegate much of it to low status (see, e.g., Engel 1987; Shiloah 1995; Zonis 1973: 7). The Basongye value music itself but then proceed to degrade its practitioners (Merriam 1973: 268), something also true of the Hausa of Nigeria, who accord musicians low social status while allowing some of them a high standard of living (Ames 1973b: 155–56). Modern urban Americans, as I have said, typically consider music a good thing but not, at least theoretically, as something essential to life. Certain societies regard music as something specific to humans (Blacking 1971: 37, 71; Merriam 1964: 64), while others such as the Havasupai (Hinton 1967–68, 1984) would

assert that other beings, spirits, the supernatural, or animals, may also produce music. To the Blackfoot, mythical animals sing, but animals in real life
do not (Nettl 1989a: 58–65).

These may be interesting observations, but one may ask what they have
to do with defining and delimiting the concept of music. As a hypothesis, I
suggest that a society which considers music to be valuable may include a great
deal within its conception of music, but it places ceremonial activities and
dance in the same category of thought, unafraid to put things with music that
might, to a member of another society, appear to be not obviously musical.
Unlike stereotypical Middle Easterners, people in such a society regard music
as a good thing and do not fear for the integrity and reputation of whatever
else is included. In Western society music is associated with good and with
happiness. Sounds that somehow symbolize happiness to us (e.g., bird song)
are called musical, while those we consider unhappy or neutral (again the
barking dogs) are not. But the concept of music is metaphorically extended
by Europeans to the whistling wind, musical speech, and the orchestration
of political strategy, and by some American Indian peoples to the supernatural sources of creation. By contrast, Middle Eastern Muslims, according
music lower value, appear to wish to restrict the concept by excluding its religious forms. The point to be contemplated is that perhaps societies do not
first develop the concept of music and then decide upon its attributes but,
rather, faced with the existence of musical sound, accord it function and thus
value, and then proceed to build a definition of the concept, using value as a
criterion.

Members of Western society often define music with specific reference
only to the sounds one hears and to their representation in written notation.
But ethnomusicologists have reason to define music more broadly. Merriam,
asserting that "music" is more than just sound, provided a model grouping
of three areas equally central to ethnomusicological work, labeling them concept, behavior, and sound (Merriam 1964: 32–33). Concept involves the way
people think about music in the broadest terms, considering, for example,
what power it has, what value, what fundamental function; behavior includes
the musical and nonmusical acts of musicians, the activities that precede,
follow, and accompany the production of sound; thus sound, which we usually call the music "itself," is in this context no more the primary focus of attention than the other parts of the tripartite model. Merriam regarded the
three components as equally deriving from and feeding into each other; but
I'm inclined to think that "concept" is primary, in the sense that the ideas
people have determines what they do, which in turn determines the nature

of the sonic product. But for sure, the way we in ethnomusicology conceptualize music determines in part the definition of ethnomusicology.

The Gluttonous Ethnomusicologist

Despite all of these definitional problems, musicologists and ethnomusicologists seem to have little trouble agreeing on the things that are within their purview for study. Defining the concept of music is basic to any understanding
and study of the subject, but it is not, after all, the ultimate aim of the ethnomusicologist. The task is more properly one of studying the definitions provided by the world's musical cultures in order to shed light on their way of con-
ceiving of music. Even so, we need a working definition that states with what
phenomena we should deal. In practical terms, ethnomusicologists seem to
have arrived at such a definition from two assumptions: (1) All societies have
music. (2) All humans can identify music—though not necessarily understand
it—when they hear it. So what do ethnomusicologists consider fair game?
Maybe the rules are these: When they find that a "musical" sound is considered speech, ethnomusicologists nevertheless include it in their area of study.
When the concept of music does not appear to exist in a culture, or when it is
extremely restricted so that certain phenomena considered to be music by the
ethnomusicologist's own culture fall outside it, these phenomena are accepted
as music too. When a society includes in its purview of music something that
Western ethnomusicologists do not recognize as music, they also accept this
for study, perhaps with certain reservations.

Having frequently served on the program committees of ethnomusicological societies, I do not remember that a paper was ever considered as unacceptable simply because the committee did not think that it was about music. Ethnomusicologists as a group take a broad view, accepting everything conceivable
into their scope of study. Having decided that one must look at the conceptualization of music in each culture and consider the possibility that such a thing
is not even extant in some societies, they have nevertheless decided for themselves that all cultures have music. They have discovered that all cultures have
forms of sound communication other than their spoken language, and much
of this is arbitrarily accepted as music. Defining music as human sound communication outside the scope of spoken language makes it possible for us to include, for musical study, such "nonmusical" events as Koran reading, African
drum signaling, whale and dolphin sounds, and Mexican Indian whistle speech,
all of which have appeared in the journal *Ethnomusicology.*

There's a bit of gluttony here, its function maybe to avoid ethnocentrism, but the avoidance turns out to be only partial. Insisting that they know what music is, ethnomusicologists then automatically include in their work anything that sounds to them like music, yet they may only grudgingly include sounds that don't fit the model their own culture provides them. Wachsmann said it more elegantly (1971b: 384): "I could say to myself that those phenomena outside my own immediate culture to which I now attach the label 'music' because I recognize and acknowledge them to be music, are merely so labeled because, rightly or wrongly, they seem to me to *resemble* the phenomena which I am in the habit of calling music in my home ground."

It may be sad to realize that it's almost impossible to get away from ethnocentrism, that it's in the nature of culture to be ethnocentric. Ethnomusicology as understood in Western culture is in fact a Western phenomenon. We will have occasion to talk about the world's "ethnomusicologies," but they are varieties of a species united by its background in Western. Ironically, non-Western musical scholarship, such as the theoretical traditions of India, Japan, China, and so on, and the theoretical systems in the oral traditions of all culture are regarded as material for ethnomusicological research rather than ethnomusicology in itself; but traditionally, Western musical scholarship has normally not been similarly considered. With all of its pejorative connotations, ethnocentrism has its uses. To respect all cultures and to study them on their own terms is desirable, but to strive for an interculturally valid approach *equally* derived from all of the world's societies may not work. To regard all languages as equally expressive is a valuable view, to which I readily subscribe. But it does not necessarily lead to the adoption of Esperanto.

Each society divides the world it knows into realms, domains, and categories. In Western society we recognize language, literary art, music, dance, and drama as more or less separable domains for which we have developed independent scholarly disciplines: linguistics, literary scholarship, musicology, art history, choreology. If there are societies that draw the lines at different points or not at all, they have or will have developed other intellectual ways of viewing their culture, ways that correspond to their conceptual classifications, and, like ethnomusicologists in the West, they see the rest of the world through their own eyes, hoping that some insights will come to them from what is also inevitably an essentially ethnocentric approach. Thus, if ethnomusicologists have developed a definition of music for themselves, one that doesn't necessarily correspond to the definitions used by other realms of thought, that definition must nevertheless be part and parcel of the Western background of the field.

3

Inspiration and Perspiration:
The Creative Process

Three Continuums

How does new music come into existence? Schubert is said to have composed a song while waiting to be served at a restaurant, quickly writing it on the back of the menu; Mozart turned out some of his serenades and sonatas almost overnight; and Theodore Last Star, a Blackfoot singer and medicine man, had visions in each of which, in the space of a minute or two, he learned from a guardian spirit a new song. But Brahms labored for years on his first symphony; Beethoven planned and sketched ideas for his Ninth for over two decades; and William Shakespear, an Arapaho, said that when he took a motif from one song, something from another, and a phrase from a third, thus making up a new Peyote song, it might take him a good part of an afternoon. The xylophonist of a Chopi orchestra made up music as he went along, but he was constrained by rules articulated by his leader (Tracey 1948: 109). The great North Indian sitarist sits down before his audience and creates a performance of new music on the spot, but he can only do this because for hours every day he practices exercises that he has memorized, and he maintains in his mind a musical vocabulary on which he can draw, and a group of rules that tell him, once he has selected a raga, what he must, may, or cannot do. A Kentucky mountaineer in about 1910 sang "The Two Sisters" in a tavern, his friends admiring a new twist in the refrain but insisting that only he can sing the song correctly. And the overjoyed Bach-lover after the cello recital exclaims, "She's never played like this before, she makes the Suite live as does no one else."

In some sense, each of these musicians has created music, but music scholars actually know very little about the way in which music comes about, especially in its innovative aspect, which is what they most admire. They believe that when music is produced (in any sense of the word), something new is being created. There is innovation in the composition of a symphony, the jazz improvisation of a new version of a well-known show tune, the unique rendition of a Japanese chamber work that has been handed down with little change for generations, the reading of a string quartet. Ethnomusicologists must deal with what is new, new in a sense generally understood by them and new also within the specific cognitive framework and understanding of its culture.

Speaking cross-culturally, what may be heard as new composition in one culture might be regarded as simple variation of something already extant in another. Judging the degree of innovation is a tricky business. The Persian improvisor who by the standards of European composition gives his audience something different each time he performs may not be, in his own manner of musical thought, doing something really new, but simply "playing a particular mode." By contrast, the Blackfoot singer who learned a song in a vision may have thought of it as a new song, even if it sounded identical to a song that had been received by one of his friends in another vision. The South Indian musician with a penchant for giving her audience unexpectedly strange vocalizations runs the risk of rendering something outside the realm of propriety and being criticized for not knowing her basic material. The American composer who wrote a piece inspired by Hindemith or Stravinsky might once have been criticized for presenting something belonging in the past and thus not properly innovative.

Rather than probing the essential nature of musical creation, ethnomusicologists ordinarily examine the ways in which various societies conceive of and evaluate musical creation. Considering the lack of terminology in most languages for discussing creativity, and the incompatibility of the concepts, comparison is a particularly thorny problem with a large body of relevant though not definitive literature, expertly surveyed by Blum (in his article "Composition" in *The New Grove Dictionary of Music and Musicians* 2001). Surveys of the world's musics may give examples of concepts and techniques known in different societies. Rather than summarizing, I suggest some further ways of examining the problem. It seems convenient, initially, to think of it in terms of three intersecting continuums.

1. *To some extent music is inspired, in the sense that we cannot analyze the way in which it finds its way into the thinking of a musician; but perhaps more*

important, it is also the result of the manipulation and rearrangement of the units of a given vocabulary, of hard work and concentration. The concepts of inspiration, of genius, and of acquiring music directly from supernatural sources are very widespread among human societies, simple and complex. Haydn worked regular hours and depended on some kind of inspiration; when it did not come, he prayed for it (Nohl 1883: 173), rather like the Native American seeking a vision who is also, in effect, praying for songs. At the other end of the line is the concept of composition as an essentially intellectual activity, in which one consciously manipulates the materials of music, organizing them carefully in ways that will make it possible for the listener to comprehend the structure, or even arranging them in ways that satisfy certain principles not audible and perceived only through careful analysis of a score.

A twentieth-century Western serialist composer is careful to include all units in a predetermined vocabulary, being precise in their manipulation so that they remain intact, following elaborate rules set by himself or herself. The listener may be unaware of all the care that has gone into the preparation of this complex structure. But such an approach is not limited to societies with written notation and music theory texts. Native American composers of Peyote songs may be equally careful, using and abiding by general structural principles that govern the song, musically making clear a number of intricate interrelationships, deriving new phrases from earlier ones, all within a rather rigidly defined formal framework. But it seems unlikely that the typical Native American listener understands the details of the structure. These two ends of the continuum merge: Mozart's music sounds divinely inspired and was often composed quickly yet has incredible consistency and complexity. The songs of the Yahi of California, sung by Ishi, the last "wild" Indian, ten seconds long and using only some three or four tones, exhibit considerable sophistication in their internal interrelationships, with a logic not totally unlike that of Mozart. An Iranian musician says that his improvised performance comes "from the heart," but analysis shows us highly structured and sophisticated patterns unique to the performer. An Indian improvisor learns a vast repertory of melodic and rhythmic units that can and must be interrelated in many ways, exhibiting her skill in showing the multitude of combinations she can control; yet in her culture this music is considered spiritual and may be related to another level of consciousness. Each case confronts us with aspects of both ends of the continuum, obviously in different proportions.

2. Improvisation and composition are frequently regarded as completely separate processes, but they are also two versions of the same (Nettl 1974b; Nettl and Russell 1998). The phenomenally quick though by no means careless way in which Schubert seems to have composed a sonata may well be comparable to the rapid combination and rearrangement of materials in an Indian improvisation, and the fact that Schubert used paper and pen could actually be incidental. On the other hand, the gigantic labor involved in the careful composition of a symphony by nineteenth-century composers, with the use of sketches and planning diagrams, is not totally unrelated to technique of the Yahi Indian composer who, within the strictest possible limits, nevertheless found a large number of ways of relating to each other the two short phrases that make up a song. For that matter, the many readings of a Beethoven sonata by a Horowitz are comparable to the twenty different ways in which an Arabic musician may render a maqam in the *taqsim* form in the period of a year, or in the course of his life. It may be rewarding to consider improvisation and composition as opposite aspects of the same process.

3. *The third continuum involves us in the course of events in the creation of a piece of music or of a performance.* We can consider a model in which all composition shares, in one way or another, in this sequence: precomposition, composition, and revision. In Western academic practice, what musicians first write down or fix in their minds might be a finished product, but is more likely to be something like a draft or plan. Eventually, a form that the composer considered reasonably satisfactory emerges, but it is subjected to correction and revision. I suggest that this sequence may be played out over months or years in some cases, and in other cases, in a few minutes. While this model is taken by some to be relevant only to formally composed music, distinguishing it from improvisation and from composition in oral/aural tradition, I suggest that it may also apply to all types of musical creation. The role of notation in the process of composition is in any event sometimes misunderstood and overestimated. There are, to be sure, composers for whom work with pen and paper is an intrinsic part of creation; one can hardly see how *The Art of Fugue, Meistersinger,* or *Wozzeck* could have been put together otherwise. But there are also Western composers who work things out in their minds (or at the keyboard, as reputedly did Haydn and Stravinsky) and then write down a relatively finished product. While many non-Western societies have musical notation systems (see Ellingson 1992a; Kaufmann 1967), these seem mostly to have or have had an archival or preservative role, perhaps serving as mnemonic devices for performers rather than as aids to composers in controlling and manipulating their structural building blocks. (For examples of studies of composition in so-called oral cultures, see Rice 1994; Tenzer 2000.)

The widespread belief that there is a difference, in essence, between composing art music, with its notation or at least a background of theory, and the music of folk and indigenous societies is probably misplaced. "Folk" composition is often, improperly, labeled as improvisation, as for instance by Knepler (in Brook, Downes, and Van Sokkema 1972: 231), who regarded true composition as the "synthesis" or "the linking together of musical elements stemming from different spheres." The difference between "art" music and others has been a major paradigm in musicology, and earlier ethnomusicologists insisted on its significance. Thus Bartók: "Whether peasants are individually capable of inventing quite new tunes is open to doubt" (1931: 2). Yet to me there seems no reason to regard composition in cultures with oral and written traditions as different species. The precomposition-composition-revision model, while most readily applied to Western academic composers who depend heavily on notation, also works for those who have none. In classical Indian music, for example, improvisors learn the ragas and the talas, the materials for and ways of dealing with melody and rhythm, and certain kinds of pieces that enable them to internalize techniques for improvisation. In the context of Indian performance, this would be the precomposition, and so also is a group of decisions as to what raga and what tala to perform on any given occasion, as well as some completely mental but nevertheless specific planning. Composition itself takes place during performance, and only what is performed constitutes the complete work. But revision is also there, the improvisor who sometimes moves away from an intended goal and makes constant accommodation to return to what was in mind in the first place, paralleling the Western composer with his manuscript. Mistakes must be covered up, quick adjustments made, unexpected slips absorbed in the structure that the musician has determined in advance; revising as one goes along. These continuums may be useful for comparative study of the creative processes in music. It seems that in most cultures, and perhaps everywhere, there is the interface of inspiration and "perspiration," and a decision-making process that involves the kind of thinking that goes into improvisation along with a systematic methodology including preparation, execution, and revision.

The Given and the Added

As already suggested, all kinds of music creation everywhere, including composition, improvisation, and performance, may have important things in common, but different societies have quite different views of just what constitutes musical creation. In many cases, there is the recognition that something already exists, in the most general sense of the word, and that the composer has the job of translating this "something" into acceptable musical sound. There is lots of variation. In Pima tradition, all songs exist already, somewhere in the cosmos, and it is the task of the composer to "untangle" them (Herzog 1936a: 333). In an Inuit song there's the text "All songs have been exhausted. He picks up some of all and adds his own and makes a new song" (Merriam 1964: 177), suggesting all songs already exist, and the singer creates by recombining material from them. In quite a different way traditional Western composers learn a basic body of music theory, comprising a kind of vocabulary and the rules for its use, and they draw on this for composing new music. Iranian musicians begin their careers by studying and memorizing the *radif,* a large body of music that they then use as inspiration for improvisation and composition, referring to it and avoiding going beyond its bounds. In each culture the musician is "given" something and then has the job of adding something else, but there are many different kinds of "given" and "added."

It may be helpful to look at the balance between them. Innovation itself has received considerable attention from anthropologists, beginning with a classic work by Barnett (1953), but as a concept it is usually treated as helpful in understanding culture change. Historical musicologists deal constantly with innovation; just as Western musicians accord highest value to doing something "new," music scholars typically concentrate on what is new in each period, style, and composer's opus (see, e.g., Meyer 1967: pt. 2). The issues inherent in identifying what is new have not frequently been touched upon. In their verbal and behavioral responses to music, most other cultures place less value on innovation than does the European-derived West. Given the difficulty of distinguishing what is in fact new and what may be perceived as "new" in any society, it nevertheless seems that there are many societies in which musical innovation is very restricted. For them, in terms of practical music-making, this may be interpreted to mean that what is "given" accounts for a very large proportion of the universe of music, and what is "added" for little.

The older Anglo-American and many European folk music traditions fit the latter model. A song, once composed, remained intact, as indicated for instance by the broad similarity of tunes collected in places and at times far apart (Bronson 1959: 72). People learned songs from their parents and friends and sang them, introducing minor variations and gradually developing variants that were still clearly recognizable as forms of the original. New songs might be composed, but they were cast in the rhythmic, melodic, and formal mold of songs already known. The repertory of songs—kritis—of the classical tradition of South India has similar characteristics: New songs are composed using models developed before the nineteenth century, and each singer develops an easily recognizable personal version. There are lots of songs that are relatively alike, lots of variants of each. There's more given than added. Still, something new has been made of something old.

Another illustration: It seems likely that in the better old days—before 1850 perhaps—the musical forms of Blackfoot and Arapaho music were quite varied, but at that time new songs came into existence rather infrequently. By contrast, in more recent times the forms available for use, the "given" materials, have shrunk in scope, but at the same time the number of new songs constantly appearing has increased, particularly in the powwow repertory. In European art music of the nineteenth century it would seem that what is given, including the quantity of harmonic materials, modulatory techniques, and forms, is vast. Composers similarly take upon themselves a huge set of vocabulary-like elements and characteristics on which they draw over long periods. Innovation in the sense of departure from these given traits, seen on a worldwide basis, may not really be very great. In nineteenth-century music one can very quickly recognize styles and composers—a few notes or chords may suffice—testifying to the consistency of what is "given." In each piece the proportion of this seems to me very great, and departure in the course of a piece seems less when viewed in intercultural comparison, even though we extol the value of radical innovation to be found in each composition. And the performer (as creator) is given a score, a blueprint much more detailed than that handed down in oral tradition or in earlier periods of Western music history when the available vocabulary was more compact.

It is not only the quantity but also the nature of what is "given" that varies among the world's cultures. In some Native American societies, it may be simply all music that a composer has already heard. One is not given the components in separately packaged form. Elsewhere, the basic materials for composition may be separated from the music itself. In Western culture this is in part a practical theory of music that one is supposed to learn before being permitted to compose, a vocabulary of materials and analytically derived rules for its use. In the jazz community (see Berliner 1994), it includes audible materials that are not in themselves music but that composers abstract from music they have heard. Native American composers of Peyote songs appear informally to have learned rules for separating a song into its component phrases and then recombining them. In the art music culture of South India, the building blocks for improvising and composing include the nature of ragas and talas, and the exercises that juxtapose the two, etude-like pieces called *varnams*, which are said to contain the grammar of a raga. In Persian classical music it is the *radif* and its constituent components, traditional "old" material that musicians vary and combine and recombine innovatively; but musicians in all cultures are also given options of all sorts, such as optimum lengths and socially acceptable ways of combining large and small units. What is "given" to the creator of music is the building blocks and the rules of what may be done with them; innovation consists of how the options are exercised.

For any culture, ethnomusicologists would wish to know about ways in which music is created, and is conceived as being created—whether it is the result of inspiration, which musicians sometimes ascribe to influences of supernatural forces, or simply the result of hard, disciplined work. It's such a central issue in the understanding of music, and of music in culture, that one might be surprised that it really received only tangential attention through most of the history of the field. This neglect, which characterized the history of our field before 1980, has a number of factors. Here are two. For one thing, we felt that as outsiders to a musical culture, we could probably not do more than to examine the music itself and try to draw conclusions on how it had been created by analyzing transcriptions. Thus, when George Herzog suggested that there were basically three types of musical form—progressive, iterative, and reverting—he meant that there were basically three kinds of decision-making in compositional practice, at least when it came to overall structure. Whether two societies might come up with the same form type but mean entirely different things by it—that we couldn't divine. Second, while music historians had for a long time delved into the creative process of composers by putting together musical, personal, and cultural components to shed light on such questions as why J. S. Bach so excelled at fugues, and what about French culture made Debussy write as he did, ethnomusicologists felt that the examination of culture via the study of outstanding and unique individuals was not in their purview.

The more recent history of our field shows more comprehensive attempts at explaining composition, relating the musical processes to social relations and factors; I'll mention the works of Charry (2000) on West Africa, Bakan (1999) and Tenzer (2000) on Bali, Turino (1993) on Peru, and Browner (2000) on North American powwows as exemplars. These publications show us that, in their fieldwork, ethnomusicologists depend and have always depended on extensive study of one person at a time—their teacher, "key" informant, culture broker—and so they really aren't all that far from the historian who is a Beethoven, Bach, or Schoenberg specialist. Both kinds of scholars have a deep interest in understanding the interface between inspiration and perspiration, between the composer as genius and as disciplined worker.

Two kinds of research, particularly—developed mainly after 1980—were important in helping ethnomusicologists to make progress in their understanding of the ways music is created, the ways this creative work is seen in some of the world's cultures, and how musical creativity is related to concept and values central to a culture. They concern the analysis of improvisation, and the ethnomusicological study of Western art music. In one case, it's a matter of watching as music unfolds; in the other, it's more a matter of analyzing myths about how it comes into existence.

In the Course of Performance

So how do creators of music work decide "what to do next"? For the likes of Beethoven, who made elaborate sketches which they gradually worked into completed compositions, one studies these sketches and, if lucky, can show how the composer progressed from one way of dealing with a musical idea on to others and to a final form (see, e.g., Kinderman 1989, 2003). For late twentieth-century composers, interviews and oral histories have shed light on the issue (see Cameron 1996 for an anthropological perspective). For Mozart, though there are plenty of close analyses of his works, and he did make a few sketches, we have maybe come closest to where we just throw up our hands and say, "We'll never be able to explain how he knew just what to do to make this work perfect."

When scholars first turned their attention to musical improvisation—the first to do so on a large scale was the Hungarian musicologist Ernst Ferand (1938)—they didn't do much to identify just what improvisers did, being satisfied with a "Mozart" approach identifying the fact of improvisation of some sort. The idea, still around in 1950, that improvisation just couldn't be explained, and widespread skepticism that there could even be such a thing, went hand in hand, perhaps, with ideas to the effect that oral transmission of music was a strange and unproductive form of enculturation. By the late twentieth century, the situation had changed enormously, as a large body of ethnomusicological literature had been developed.

Two types of study predominated. One sought to find the "model" on which improvisation was based. The term "model," used in the 1960s and 1970s, has given way to a variety of more or less satisfactory terms, from "point of departure," what you know or use to improvise "upon" (called PoD or just "pod" by my skeptical students), to the postmodern-sounding "catalytic referent" suggested in a seminar by Tom Paynter (see Nettl 1992; Nettl and Russell 1998). Among the PoDs most easily identified, and agreed upon by musicians in their cultures, are the Persian *radif,* and the kinds of things used by jazz musicians, and so it's not surprising that studies in jazz and Persian music have been in the forefront of this area of interest. But just how you get from *radif* or chord changes to real music, that's been the subject of other kinds of study, including, for example, the identification of jazz improvisation as political gesture by Monson (1996), and the concept of ecstasy as an area of negotiation between audience and musician by Racy (2003).

The second important area of improvisational study concerns the learning of improvisation. Importantly, it involves social and musical relationships between teacher and student. My teacher in Iran told me that he taught the *radif,* and that it itself would teach a student to improvise. He also said that the better you know the *radif,* the PoD, the more you had a right to depart from it in improvisation. In Madras/Chennai, I learned that the most improvisatory genre, alapana, though technically perhaps less difficult than the razzle-dazzle of *tanam* and *kalpana swaram,* was the one musicians could be trusted to execute properly only after they had been at it a long time. The most significant work along these lines, however, has been that of Paul Berliner, who, following his studies of musicians in Zimbabwe (1978), produced a detailed study of jazz musicians (1994), concentrating on how they learned to improvise through extensive interviews, observation of sessions, and analyses of recordings.

But as improvisation received more attention, ethnomusicologists also began to see it as a complex syndrome of behaviors. It was defined as "the creation of music in the course of performance," but just what "creation," and "performance" was might not be clear (see, e.g., Blum 1998). Didn't someone like Mozart, writing down quickly what came into his head, work like an improvisor? And didn't the Carnatic musician who felt required by tradition and audience expectation to go through many stages and, as it were, exercises, need to have a rather detailed plan of procedure in mind before sitting down on the stage? And then, what are we to make of the significance of improvisation in the world of European composition? Here, in the early nineteenth century, we see the development of genres such as rhapsody, impromptu, moment musical, which are composed and written but are intended to make the listener think that they are improvised, or at least somehow connected with an immediacy and spontaneity of creation. They should *sound* improvised. And at the same time, beginning earlier, to be sure, there's the practice of improvising pieces in complex forms—fugues come to mind most readily—in which the quality of musicianship is judged by the degree to which the improvised piece *sounds* as if it were *not* improvised.

Improvisation has begun to play a major role in ethnomusicological literature of the last twenty-five years (Lortat-Jacob 1987, Bailey 1992, and Berliner 1994 are important landmarks); but this literature has mainly added to our appreciation of the complexity of the issue. It has questioned the familiar taxonomy of composition-performance-improvisation as interculturally valid. It hasn't done much to explain mental and creative processes, and so we continue to see the world's improvisors as the Svengalis or Houdinis of the arts, yet in Western culture, lovers of art music continue to see improvisation as a skill and a craft deserving not quite the same respect as composition.

Culture Heroes

"Musical genius." What names does the term bring to mind? I'll wager many readers will instinctively say "Mozart and Beethoven." At one time, ethnomusicologists would have left them to others to contemplate, but lately these and other masters have come to play an important role in ethnomusicological thought, not as historical figures, which they certainly are, but as figures that also play a major role in our contemporary culture. They are culture heroes of a sort—one reason ethnomusicologists take an interest in them—representing two significant sides of our conception of creation. Mozart (says the myth) is the hero of inspiration, his music sounds as if he had composed it without effort, it's always perfect, and he composed so much in his life that it must have been easy for him. He could even compose great works when he was still a boy. And he was a rather crude, brash person, sometimes full of himself, a personality one wouldn't associate with such perfect music. He is Amadeus, the man loved by God, and this myth followed him from his death into the end of the twentieth century. Never mind that he was really a workaholic who devoted himself to solving difficult musical problems, had enormous knowledge and a stupendous memory, and basically worked himself to death.

Beethoven is the opposite, a man devoted to contemplation of the ethical (sometimes a bit of a scold), with a lot of bad luck in his life, but above all an enormously hard worker who labored over his compositions for years, making sketches and improving, quite unlike the Mozart who got it right the first time. These are the popular culture's conceptions of the two great composers, not historically correct, and in this way the ethnomusicologist, looking at what roles M and B play in our culture, provides a very different perspective from the historians, who want to know what M and B were really like. The same applies of course to Schubert, Wagner, and others. And don't forget to take into account the fact that people in this society may have definite ideas—involving such things as aesthetics, society, class, nation, sexuality—about these composers even if they are ignorant of their music and know them only by name or from a bust on a piano.

What I've just said illustrates the study of music and musicians who could be considered culture heroes because they reflect important societal values. If Mozart and Beethoven fill this role in contemporary Europe and North America, they have counterparts in the world of Carnatic music (see, e.g., Ayyangar 1972). The so-called music season in Madras/Chennai, in December and early January, is a period not unlike the festivals of European cities such as Salzburg, which possibly served as models. Some 200 concerts of Carnatic music are presented, sung, and played by scores of highly competent musicians. No European music is heard, but the Indian music is presented in public concerts, large and small, sponsored by societies or clubs. Of all this music, about half is improvised, and half consists of composed songs, mainly a genre called kriti, a complex form of monophonic, metric music with devotional words addressing the Hindu deities. Some of these songs are by twentieth-century musicians, but the most respected are by composers who lived in the late eighteenth and early nineteenth centuries. It is a situation not unlike concert life in Europe and the Americas.

Among these composers, the most significant were a trinity who lived from the late eighteenth century into the nineteenth: Syama Sastri (1762–1827); Muttuswami Dikshitar (1775–1835); and the greatest of the three, Tyagaraja, often called Saint Tyagaraja (1767–1847). These composers are the central figures in past and present, their role somewhat analogous to that of the great European composers—including the "trinity" of Mozart-Beethoven-Haydn—whose names are on our music halls and conservatories. Tyagaraja's creativity could not be analyzed but had to be ascribed to divine beneficence. Some Indian musicologists take their beliefs of Hinduism very seriously, believing in the efficacy of horoscopes and divine intervention, and so the significance of these parallels, coming at roughly the same time in history, was not lost on them.

According to P. Sambamoorthy (1967), Tyagaraja lived modestly with his family, and with some of his students and musical associates, on land inherited from his father, in a household devoted to music and the deities, living by teaching, mendicancy, and occasional patronage of performance. The master thus had something of a miniature court of his own, as a musician and holy man of great fame, being visited frequently by other musicians, looking after his disciples and guests. Indians compared him to Beethoven, his almost exact contemporary and, to the British living in India, the greatest, but he could also be compared to Haydn, seen today as the most human of the Viennese trinity, concerned with looking after and supporting the musicians he directed.

But, to me, in his role in the musical culture of modern Madras, Tyagaraja is the Carnatic Mozart. His songs sound as if he had composed them quickly, and the logic of the successive sections is unmistakable, yet there is nothing labored—in contrast to some of Dikshitar's kritis, which sound as if he might have made mental sketches and worked them out carefully over time. The mythology dwells on Tyagaraja's incredible creativity. According to legend he composed 24,000 songs, and in fact there are some 400. He worked hard, with the Indian musician's habit of long daily practice, called riaz, but also benefited from timely intercession of the deities, especially Rama. Like Mozart, he is the composer whose creativity came directly from the divine, who hardly had to try hard to solve his musical problems. And, like the supremely versatile Mozart, who claimed to control "any style and kind of composition," Tyagaraja was said to have composed songs in more ragas than other musicians.

In contrast to the Mozart myths, with their tragic overtones, the Tyagaraja legends have him and his contemporaries in benevolent relationships, living under the direction of the Hindu deities who intervened in times of difficulty and provided humans with very definite ideas of how to live the good life. Anecdotes of conflict hardly get worse than the account of students complaining that their dinner was delayed because the master and a distinguished guest were engrossed in discussing ragas and thus couldn't be interrupted to eat.

Despite the great accomplishments of musicians such as Zubin Mehta, and the significant participation of Ravi Shankar in Western music, one cannot claim that there is very much Western classical music to be heard in India, especially the South. Supported by the social and religious system, the Indian musical culture has been too powerful to be dislodged. During my stay in Madras, concerts of Western music took place only at foreign venues such as the German or American consulates. In contrast to the Western classical music culture of nations in East Asia, there was at most some token representation in cursory appendices of books on Western music, and in the curricula of music conservatories. I had the feeling that to the extent the educated Indian public was aware of Western music, Mozart was not even one of its greatest masters of European music, possibly a result of the British tastes (preferring Handel, Haydn, and Beethoven), which dominated nineteenth-century Anglo-Indian musical life.

But then, one day in Madras in 1982, I was surprised to see a performance, by a company of actors from Bangalore, of Peter Shaffer's play *Amadeus,* in the large auditorium of the Music Academy, venue of the grandest Carnatic concerts. Not a great performance. The pianist playing the musical background pieces by Mozart made mistakes at crucial points, but I doubt that anybody cared. I had occasion to speak to members of the audience, educated people interested in English-language theater and well versed in the works of Shakespeare. They didn't know what to make of the specifically musical issues raised in the play, or the characterizations of Mozart and Salieri. To them, instead, this was a play elucidating the abstract values of hard work and inspiration. It was about a composer so loved by God that his genius outweighed the undesirable sides of his personality, about another composer whose love of God was unrequited, and most of all about the inability of people to understand artistic genius and the acts of deities in bestowing it on a few humans. The play's interactions of composers with God were readily intelligible in the culture of Carnatic music.

I explained that to many Europeans and Americans, Mozart was the greatest of all composers, that there were stories about his ability to compose great music without effort, about his incredible inspiration, which almost seemed like the result of divine intervention. In illustrating the singularity of Mozart in the view of Western musicians, I could have quoted Kierkegaard's declarations of love, Rossini's assertion that Mozart is the only composer, the theologian Karl Barth's widely quoted speculation that when the angels play music, it is Bach in public but Mozart *en famille* (see Nettl 2001: 53). Unnecessary. "He is your Tyagaraja!" exclaimed a musician colleague who had probably never heard a note of Mozart. I told him that most of the Western world's classical musicians are at some point drawn to visit Salzburg. He replied by inviting me, the following week, to join the pilgrimage of hundreds of south Indian musicians who would gather at Tanjore and Tiruvaiyaru where, over several days, they would sing, in unison, the complete works of the culture hero Tyagaraja.

Despite a lot of speculation, little about the concept of genius and the aspect of musical creation we're calling "inspiration" is well understood. It seems to consist of the ability to do something significantly innovative, and to do it very well. But whether something is truly "new"—or whether it is so new as to be outside the cultural system and thus unacceptable is an issue negotiated between musician and audience. While the notion of musical stardom seems to be a specialty of Western culture, a specialty in which some other societies also participate, there certainly are many cultures that share the concept of musical genius in one way or another. The star system was there in the classical music of Iran of the mid–twentieth century, where the line between stars and others was even more pronounced than in Europe, star performers being accorded relatively more status, artistic license, and money. The nonstars were readily ranked from acceptable to incompetent. What distinguishes the "stars" among the improvisors, the most significant creative musicians in Iran, is their ability to do something new within strict confines.

Clearly, an understanding of the nature of musical creation is a major issue in the world of music, a problem largely unsolved in scholarship. There was a time when ethnomusicologists characterized the so-called traditional societies as having no musical culture heroes, but obviously they were wrong. But the world's societies differ greatly in their ways of evaluating and recognizing special musical achievement, and ethnomusicology can bring some insight into these enormously varied ways that the cultures of the world perceive musical creativity, and into what human cultures may hold in common.

4

The Universal Language: Universals of Music

Ethnomusicologist's Backlash

"Music is the universal language of mankind," Longfellow had written. But when I asked a new graduate student "What do you expect to do as an ethnomusicologist?" and she said, without hesitation, "To study universals," I was a bit dumbfounded—not only because I had always questioned whether there was such a thing as universals, but more because it hadn't occurred to me ever to give them pride of place in our discipline. In 1970, this student's statement sounded anachronistic, for in my college years, about 1950, the idea that there was much that all cultures shared was presented as ancient and abandoned history. If universals were here again, rearing their heads, anthropology and ethnomusicology must have come full circle.

Belief in universal traits of music was characteristic of nineteenth-century scholarship. Wilhelm Wundt, one of the last to have tried his hand at a complete culture history of the world, said that all "primitive" peoples have monophonic singing and use intervals rather like those of nineteenth-century Western music, major and minor seconds and thirds, singing that came from speech in which the duration of unwavering pitch, the note, became sufficiently long to be perceived and repeated (1911: 4:464–66). Most musicians of Wundt's time and later, too, were probably attracted to such a view, and even some teachers of music appreciation in North America as late as the 1980s might have been quite prone to consider music as a "universal language." In contrast to the languages of the world, which were mutually unintelligible, musics of all kinds were thought intelligible to anyone. So, in the

Western world, we developed books called *The History of Music* and courses called "Introduction to *the* Art of Music," which dealt with only one kind of music or treated all other kinds as true relatives, if distant, of the Western canon. The assumption seemed to be that the basic principles of Western music were universally valid, because it was the only "true" music, of which all other musics represented generative stages, or perhaps degenerations.

Simultaneously but contrastively with the music establishment, comparative musicologists (and the anthropologists who supported them) from the early twentieth century on saw it as their job to cry out against this unified view of world culture. Their principal motivation seems to me to have been a fascination with the diversity of human culture at large, with the many sounds, systems, and uses of music developed by humans. And so, when I was a graduate student, had I been asked what I wished to do, I would surely not have said "To study universals," but rather "To discover musical diversity while insisting that all musics, at some level, are equally good." Later, by the 1990s, it had again become difficult to view the world of music without admitting that there might be something about the notion of universals. But things had changed: The early believers in universals equated them with certain traits of Western music; the later ones looked to other cultures for guidance.

Surely, in the development of a general methodology of ethnomusicology as promulgated by the founding fathers of our discipline (and their successors, like Merriam and Hood), the nonuniversality of music looms as a major point of agreement. All musics were not alike, and the approaches used to understand Western music surely did not suffice for other societies; it was to show this, after all, that they were all in business. In a backlash against musical ethnocentrism, ethnomusicologists practiced gamesmanship, answering generalizations about music with a parody of the well-known "not in the South," insisting that it was "not so among the Cherokee" or "different in Japan." The task was to prove that facile generalizations were wrong, even immoral. When not engaged in gamesmanship at late-night graduate student bull sessions, ethnomusicologists tried seriously to show, in teaching and writing, that musics, like languages, were not universal; music, the "nonuniversal language," became in effect a battle cry (Herzog 1939).

The return to an interest in universals began in the late 1960s. Panels and special issues of periodicals (e.g., *Ethnomusicology,* vol. 15, no. 3, 1971; *The World of Music,* vol. 19, nos. 1–2, 1977) were devoted to the subject, and some of the leading scholars of the field (Blacking 1977b; Harrison 1977; Harwood 1976; Hood 1977; McAllester 1971; C. Seeger 1971; Wachsmann 1971b) had significant things to say on it. They had distinguished models in other fields, as a number of disciplines had developed new culture heroes who once again demonstrated interest in what tied humans together. Particularly, there were such trends in linguistics and anthropology. Noam Chomsky showed the underlying structure of all human languages and developed the idea that a deep structure, an ability to learn language, was present in all humans (Lyons 1977: 131–33). Lévi-Strauss asserted that all mythologies are basically alike, as are all customs involving basic human needs, their task to bridge the universal contrast between humans and animals, men and women, parents and children, us and them, nature and culture (Leach 1970: 53–86; Lévi-Strauss 1963: 208).

Chomsky and Lévi-Strauss may have been right, but in the 1940s it had really been important for ethnomusicologists to point out that music is indeed not a universal language. And nonuniversality became widely accepted, and eventually maybe even overstated, particularly by those opposed to comparative study, but it again became important to find ways in which the various musics of the world are alike. It seems to me that for some twenty years after about 1940, musics—as conceived in Western academia—had to be liberated, as it were, from Western ethnocentrism; ethnomusicology had to make clear their mutual independence, had to urge the acceptance of each on its own terms and not simply as evolutionary way stations to something greater and more perfect. This mission accomplished, ethnomusicology had to return to seeing the world's musics as part of a single whole. But seeking universals suggests two approaches—a search for specific features that musics ("a" music being a body of sound, a system of ideas, or a complex of events) have in common, and the discovery of a conceptual framework for analysis broad enough to subsume all imaginable differences. This chapter follows the first of these approaches.

Three Kinds of Universals

In the context of this discussion, just what is "everywhere"? I wish to ask whether there are musical traits present in every instant of musical sound, or some found in every musical utterance, or in the musical experience of every human, in the musical life of every human community or culture, or in every musical repertory. Let's examine three types, which might give us a hierarchy of universals.

Anything present in every instant of music: That would be tantamount to a definition of music. If we know what music is, we would expect to identify it instantly when we encounter it, distinguishing it immediately from all other kinds of sound—speech, weeping, animal sounds, random noise, wind, machinery. But there does not appear to be an interculturally valid definition of music, so this approach to a discussion of universals may be at most theoretically fruitful. One surely cannot distinguish certain kinds of speech from singing even after hearing a total performance—or certain electronic music from factory sounds—except on the basis of social context.

The typical view of ethnomusicologists provides for a cultural explanation for the musical choices made by humans; they decide what to do musically as a result of responses to environmental and cultural events, and on the basis of what they have learned from other humans. But near the end of the twentieth century, some ethnomusicologists, notably Blacking (1992, discussing the work of others as well) began to move closer to scholarship in psychology and biology of music-making (as presented, e.g., by Sloboda 1985), taking into account the possibility of biological determinants (see especially Wallin, Merker, and Brown 2000). This was not a return to any notions to the effect that the music of a particular society is genetically determined or has biological bases, but perhaps the growth of a willingness to entertain the idea that music as a whole—the universals of music, if you will—has biological bases.

In a second approach, the requirements are less stringent, as we ask whether there is anything that is present in every musical utterance, hypothesizing that this concept of "musical utterance" is itself a universal phenomenon. It would be a song (long or minuscule), a piece, an opera, a symphony, a march, a raga performance, a bugle call—some kind of culturally accepted unit of musical thought, long and complex or short and simple. One begins to make music, continues or repeats, and, at some point, comes to an end, by design or because the context has ceased to exist. Now, are there characteristics that all (or maybe almost all) such musical utterances have in common? Here are some suggestions. There is a more or less clearly marked beginning and ending. There is some redundancy, some repetition, balanced by some variety, articulated through rhythmic, melodic, textural means. There is a level of simplicity and there are levels of complexity beyond which the overwhelming majority do not extend. Music must evidently fall within some kind of perceptual band, even if one could imagine that it could go further. The musical utterance consists of smaller units—building blocks— which are fairly well marked, and for which one may substitute others from a given cultural repertory in order to produce new utterances—for example, tones, motifs, chords, phrases, sequences. In a sense they are comparable to phonemes and morphemes in language, a lexicon from which, given certain rules, a music-maker may draw to create old and new musical utterances. A musical utterance always consists of more than one minimal unit. These are examples; others would no doubt be equally general. But this second category of universals still does not tell us *how* humanity has chosen to structure its music; like the first type, it mainly tells us simply *that* humans have music.

For a third and somewhat more realistic approach, we ask whether there is anything that is found in each musical system, in the music of each society; whether, thus, there is a way in which all musics are (rather than saying that all music is) in some way alike, whether there are any characteristics or traits present somewhere in all of them.

First the sound of music, with the caveat of incomplete data. All cultures have singing, and some (if sometimes very rudimentary) instrumental music. In the vast majority of vocal musics, the chief melodic interval appears to be something in the very general range of a major second. Intervals of that general scope, including anything from three to five quarter tones, surely make up the bulk of the world's melodic progressions. Progressing consistently by half or quarter tones is exceedingly rare, as is progression mainly by thirds and fourths (found, though, here and there, as in some Andean musics).

In the vast majority of cultures most musical utterances tend to descend at the end, but they are not similarly uniform at their beginnings. All cultures make some use of internal repetition and variation in their musical utterances, and all have a rhythmic structure based on distinction among note lengths and among dynamic stresses. All of the mentioned features are universals in the sense that they exist practically everywhere, but significant universals also in another sense: They would *not* have to be present in order for music to exist, and thus are *not* simply a part of the definition of music. It would, for example, be conceivable for a musical system to use only perfect fourths, or only notes of equal length, but actually such a music doesn't exist. Evidently humanity has decided not only to make music but, despite the vast amount of variation among the musics of the world, to make music in a particular set of ways. There is, in other words, some kind of a universal grammar or syntax of music, perhaps somewhat like that of language.

Universals in the conceptualization of music and in musical behavior are harder to isolate, but let me try a short list. Surely significant among them must be the association of music with the supernatural. All known cultures accompany religious activity with music. McAllester (1971: 380) sounded a similar note when he said that everywhere "music transforms experience." Further, there is the conception of music as an art that consists of distinct units of creativity, which can be identified, by place in ritual, by creator or performer, by opus number. One does not simply "sing" but one sings *something* that has an identity. Thus, music is composed of artifacts, although cultures differ greatly in their view of what constitutes such an artifact. Also in this category of universals is the musical association with dance and speech. I can think of no culture that does not have *some* dance with musical accompaniment, nor one whose singing is completely without words, without poetry.

Viewed as self-contained systems, the musics of the world have common properties. They include the conception of musicality, the existence of tradition-carrying networks, the ubiquity of distinct repertories of children's music. It seems likely also that musics—the musical systems of cultures—have things in common, that is, share overall structural characteristics. For example, it goes without saying that in each society, limits are placed on musical creativity. Certain sounds are accepted as being proper music and others excluded. But possibly each music has its gray area, a group of pieces or musical utterances, if you will, that reside at or beyond the boundaries of music. Do people everywhere tolerate a limited amount of intolerable music-making? All musics seem to have a wide band of relatively exceptional materials at their borders, and, as indicated in chapter 2, some of it is only arguably accepted as music. In contemporary Western culture there is a good deal of electronic and synthesized music that is highly significant to its cognoscenti but not used or tolerated by the majority. Older Native American music was generally monophonic, but a few polyphonic utterances, for specific social purposes, were evidently permitted here and there (Keeling 1992; Nettl 1961). Even Bach seems to have written the occasional tabooed set of parallel fifths. The exceptional material often has certain special and significant social uses and functions. But each repertory also has a mainstream, a unified style clustering in the center, composed of a large number of songs or pieces that are very much alike. There may be a universal or at least a typical repertory structure in world music. What is best or greatest—either as music or because it has special social or religious significance—is also often somehow exceptional.

In each culture, there may be a different immediate reason for the value of the exceptional. In Western art and popular music, there is the value of innovation and originality (but see the discussion of originality in Shona culture by Turino 2000: 181–83). In Iran, the value of individualism and surprise is significant, and among the traditional Blackfoot, the association of songs with a few men's personal power over the supernatural. The similarity of these repertory structures again suggests that there is no difference in essence between Western and non-Western, urban and indigenous, musical repertory structure.

Let's Be Practical

A fourth approach to the study of universals is less problematic than the first three, and more practical. It asks, simply, whether there are features shared not by all but by a healthy majority of musics. We look for what is extremely common, substituting the concept of "statistical" universals for what may be described as a "true" universal, avoiding cultures that do not share in the worldwide mainstream. We (ethnomusicologists) know a great deal about a few musics, a bit about many, hardly anything about some others, and of course nothing about an unknown number from the past. We can satisfy our quest for specifying ways in which humans as a whole have chosen to make music and establish conceptual and sonic boundaries for their music-making that are not the result of physical conditions or necessities, or other essentially nonmusical factors. Following this argument, one need not even account for those cultures that do not share these "limited" universals, taking them to be historical accidents or aberrations. This "statistical" type of universal is not concerned, as are the others, with physiological or perceptual limitations to which all humans are subject (see Harwood 1976: 525–28). It is a bit like finding a musical consensus of the world's societies.

Examples: tetratonic and pentatonic scales composed of unequal intervals, often major seconds and minor thirds; men, women, and children singing in octaves; stanzaic structure of songs and pieces; the use of idiophones and of those sound tools called by Curt Sachs (1940: 63) the "oldest" layer of musical instruments. And there is the concept of musicianship itself, as most cultures recognize musical specialists who, for whatever reasons—religious, aesthetic, social, biological—know music better and are able to produce it more adequately and in larger quantity than others.

We have moved from the components of the definition of music itself to the essential characteristics of the musical utterance, on to the characteristics of total musical cultures or musics, and then on to traits generally typical of the world's musics; we can think of this as a set of concentric circles. It remains to ask, to speculate, what it means that such phenomena exist. Why, for instance, are there such "universals" of the fourth type? Demands of human physiology and anatomy do not provide a very convincing argument. The theory that there is a unilinear cultural evolution from which a few societies diverge, like mutations, or perhaps remain behind, seemingly reasonable, is not really tenable because it can be falsified by so many instances. Closest to being convincing is the argument that most human societies have, for millennia, been in some kind of direct and indirect contact with each other, and that there is a single world of music, rather like a single superfamily of language that has spawned many variants (Lyons 1977: 145). If so, it is interesting, when contemplating the structure of the entire world of music, to interpret it as a macrocosmic musical repertory with a structure not so different from that of the musics associated with individual societies mentioned above: a mainstream (the many repertories characterized by statistical universals such as pentatonic scales) and borders of material that the mainstream societies might not even consider proper music—as for instance the quantitatively simplest, and the most outrageously experimental.

While we're at it, let's make a whimsical excursion to conjectural history. There's a chance that at one time, the world's musics were more alike than they are now, that they might all have been somewhat like that of today's indigenous peoples. To the (imaginary) ethnomusicologist of that time, universals might have been very obvious. There's a presumed period in between, in which the world's societies developed individualized cultures and musics. But a period in which the world's musics are more alike, in which the world's peoples share many traits, may be upon us again, with the widespread acceptance of certain features of European, African, and Middle Eastern musical features in the body of music known as "world music."

Music is not the universal language, but musics are not as mutually unintelligible as languages. Significantly, before one spoke explicitly of universals, and before one used the expression "musics" of the world, rather than speaking of the "music" of the world, George Herzog (1939), putting forward the view that one should study the music of each society in its own terms and learn it individually, referred to "music's dialects" rather than "music's languages." Musical systems, "musics," do exist as separable units. But they are more readily connected with each other, and also more readily understood at least in certain respects, by foreigner or novice, than are true languages. Despite the enormous variety of musics, the ways in which people everywhere have chosen to sing and play are more alike than the boundaries of the imaginable might suggest.

5

The Nonuniversal Language: Varieties of Music

A World of Musics

One of the most influential concepts in the history of ethnomusicology, bimusicality, was developing in the late 1950s under the leadership of Mantle Hood (1960), and in North America and Europe one began to hear concerts of Javanese, Japanese, Indian music. Some listeners had trouble accepting these as belonging to the realm of music. At about the same time, concerts of electronic music were beginning to surface on campuses and at musicologists' conferences, and some in the audience had the same problem, asking "Is this really music?" Typically, those in the Asian concerts decided they liked what they heard, and were inclined to say "Yes, this is music"; the electronic music listeners might at first have been less inclined that way but determined to try again, to see if it made more sense next time. The student emerging from the gamelan concert saying "Wow, I loved it, it was so—so—exotic" and the professor coming out of the electronic concert saying "Ugh" had each crossed a musical border, and neither may actually have understood the new musical experience, despite the fact that they liked one and not the other. It's hard to know just what constitutes understanding in music, but the approach to the issue taken by many in ethnomusicology sees the world of music as a series of discrete musics. Indeed, uniqueness of musical style and incompatibility with the music of neighbors is an important feature of music as marker of a group's identity.

Most musicological studies deal with individual bodies of music as self-contained units. Not only the music of a people or nation or culture but also that of a period, a school of composers, a genre, a composer are dealt with as if they were systems somewhat analogous to languages. This widespread view, however, has rarely been the basis of an explicit theory (but see C. Seeger 1953a). Without pretending that language and music are of the same cloth, there are sufficient similarities to have permitted ethnomusicologists to take certain cues from the study of language in its structure and as a symbolic system to gain insight into the world of music (see Bright 1963; Feld 1974; H. Powers 1980).

If we are to find the typical characteristics of a music, we should first ask how one goes about defining what comprises it, identifying its boundaries. What it is that belongs to a language is determined by linguists in various ways. One is the recognition of the existence of units known as speech communities (Bloomfield 1951: 42), groups of people who communicate with each other regularly and consistently. The body of vocal sounds they use is a language, a dialect, or some unit that can be studied by linguists as a self-contained system. At the same time the total linguistic inventory of an individual person may also be a unit worthy of study. Known to linguists as "idiolect," it too is a way in which the content of language can be circumscribed. In contrast to these essentially social definitions of language, structural approaches view a language as consisting of a phonology and a grammar. A language can further be defined in terms of its content, a set of words, or perhaps of culturally or structurally acceptable statements. In a certain sense the content of a dictionary is the content of a language, and all of the words of a language, a kind of definition and circumscription of the language.

Linguists, like musicologists, have had to deal with the problem of boundaries, asking whether a traveler across India moves imperceptibly from one language to another, uncertain at what point he or she has made the transition from Tamil to Telugu country, and whether Old English changed rather suddenly or gradually to Middle English. Taking an essentially historical perspective for the study of separate languages, some linguists, interpreting languages as limited by sharp boundaries, insist that the speech of one community can be obviously classed as belonging to Language A, and that of a neighboring community to the related but separable Language B, that languages that seem to border on each other on the map, such as Czech, the Moravian variant of Czech, Slovak, and Polish, really can be clearly distinguished. Others, by contrast, believe that "every word has its own history," implying a gradual merging of one language into its geographical or chronological neighbor, the boundary for words at different points on the map (Anttila 1972: 291).

The most widely accepted way for establishing genetic language relationships and so-called language families is with the use of sound shifts that result in cognates, enabling us to prove, for example, that Persian, Latin, Czech, and English are related because of the closeness of words such as *barodar, frater, bratr,* and *brother.* But languages also exhibit relationships other than genetic. For example, some 50 percent of Persian words are loan-words from Arabic, a genetically unrelated language, and thus Arabic qualifies as a kind of relative of Persian. Hindi and Telugu, respectively Indo-European and Dravidian, have influenced each other consistently and share features of phonology. Languages from different families share systems of writing, vocabulary, and a kind of linguistic worldview, sometimes derived from common religion.

Some of the ways of finding language boundaries and defining language relationships can be suggestive for music scholars. Certainly musics can be shown to be related in the multiplicity of ways just mentioned for languages. The idea of a music community, for example, is well developed. A large proportion of ethnomusicological work claims to report upon the repertories of communities of people in which there is frequent exchange and communication of musical material. As a matter of fact, while there is no reason to doubt the validity of the concept, the typical collection of the music from one small society, group, or village is a collection made with a very small sampling of musicians or consultants, sometimes only one, and broader questions such as the degree to which the repertory is evenly distributed throughout the society, or the music community, are often ignored (but see Brailoiu 1960, the classic study of a village repertory; Hungarian Academy of Sciences 1992; and A. Seeger 1988). But the unit of music in most ethnomusicological publications is determined by a social group that communicates in ways other than musical, such as a group of people who also share a language. Musical communication within the group is normally assumed rather than proved.

"A music" may be the musical repertory of a society, and we are interested in how it is distributed through the population, but the music of a single individual, the musical idiolect, may also be "a music" (see Crafts, Cavicchi, and Keil 1993). In field research before around 1960, the concepts of a music and a musical idiolect were sometimes conflated by ethnomusicologists because of the limited availability of informants or consultants. Thus, the use of a single individual's repertory to determine the content of a music has been more widely accepted by music scholars than has the linguistic analogue. There are ways of approaching and defining a musical idiolect. We can ask what music one individual "knows," but first we had better define "knowledge," whether it means ability to perform, recognition, some kind of identification with self, admitted liking, or claimed understanding. The concepts of active and passive repertories, developed in folklore, would be useful to musicologists. The study of individual musicians not simply as typical representatives of a homogeneous society but as distinct persons has increased in the period since 1980, and the examination of personal repertories (as in Vander 1988) is a kind of byproduct of this development.

But what is "the" music of an in some way typical American around 1990? Let's use our imagination. We begin by inquiring into "musical understanding." If you, dear reader, are an American born around 1940 and have some academic pretensions, you might claim that you understand "Barbara Allen," a Beethoven symphony, records by Louis Armstrong and Elvis Presley, and a Gregorian mass. No matter if your professor of music history denies you the privilege unless you can make a thorough analysis; and no matter if specialized aficionados of jazz, rock, and early music believe that you lack true understanding. You claim a certain degree of insight. But are you likely to accept all of these kinds of music as somehow belonging truly to yourself? Some careful contemplation, or a listening quiz, might show your musical persona to be a pretty complex structure. Let's imagine such a middle-aged person. She identifies with Armstrong and Presley, loves the Beatles and Springsteen (but he's a bit new), claims some affinity with Beethoven, somewhat less with medieval and African music, and no affinity, though maybe attraction, to Indian and Chinese music, and in the end she throws up her hands at the electronic excerpt. Concentric circles—if this model doesn't fit you, something similar probably would. The structure of the given grouping might give us some important insights. Thus: Electronic and synthesized music in the context of Western culture is a new music, a new musical language, and society is being asked to learn it but has not yet done so. African music has a long-standing affinity with Western music, as long ago suggested by Richard Waterman (1952). The musical building blocks of Armstrong, Presley, and Beethoven are actually in important ways the same.

Our little exercise has defined a music, that person's music; or imagines that it has. Now, whether one society produces vastly different musical personas in its population, while in another most people know the same music, that's a question for detailed future study. It was once an article of faith among folklorists that in a typical folk or indigenous culture, musical experience was homogeneous and thus most people could sing most of the songs of the tribe. But such generalizations pale in the face of enormous cultural variety: thus the Sirionó were described in precisely the opposite terms (Key 1963: 18), as each person was observed to sing all of his or her songs to a single, personal tune. Somewhat similarly, an Iranian folk singer may sing only one song type and one melody type, constructing an entire performing life on one tune and its variants. Again in contrast, the men of the people of Yirkalla in northern Australia (R. Waterman 1956) appeared to learn the same songs, the idiolect of each man being essentially the same, but they learned the songs gradually, and only old men seem to have at their command the entire repertory. In the way they develop idiolects, the musics of the world differ widely in scope, size, and internal interrelationship.

Content and Style

The musics of the world have customarily been described by their style—the typical procedures used in music-making, the building blocks of pitch, note, rhythm, phrase, the accepted timbres and singing styles; in other words, in terms of their grammar and syntax. In music history one may learn, very simplistically, things like "Baroque music—counterpoint; the classical period—homophony," the most bare-bones descriptions of the musical styles of repertories. This approach—more sophisticated, one would hope—is so standard that it does not need further discussion here, except to provide background for a less commonly used approach to giving and accounting of a repertory or "a" music, which I'll call description of a music by its *content*.

If "style" is, using the linguistic analogue, the "phonology" of music, then let's consider themes, motifs, lines, tunes, in music as the equivalents of words or concepts in a language, and therefore the "content." Difficult to pin down, and hardly a perfect analogy. But if a tune retains its integrity through changes of scale, mode, meter, form, and singing style, that aspect of it that remains constant, that's the content. We could imagine a musical culture that might define as "new," and therefore as extraneous, any material not related to the musical content it already has. A new word, after all, does not enter a language, even though it may fit the phonology, unless there is a way in which the culture can make use of its meaning or conceptualization. In music, too, rather than accepting just anything that conforms to its style, a culture might not consider a newly introduced tune to be part of its music unless it also can be related to specific extant musical works such as songs.

Circumscribing, defining, or enumerating the content of a music hasn't often been tried. A few publication types qualify as attempts, although this wasn't their main purpose. Thematic catalogues (e.g., by Koechel for Mozart, or Schmieder for Bach) of the works of individual composers are a case in point, as might be W. Haas's (1932) attempt to put into musically logical order all of the themes by Beethoven, or, for folk music, attempts to make inventories of this sort, such as Bartók's listing of motifs in Romanian bagpipe tunes (1967). A listing of this content in some kind of systematic form would be the musical equivalent of a dictionary or lexicon. Otherwise, there are brief statements indicating recognition of the problem, like Samuel Bayard's (1953: 130–32) assertion that the overwhelming majority of American folk songs belongs to a very limited number of tune families, perhaps only forty tunes, that comprise this music.

A music may be defined by its style or by its content. "That's not our music, it sounds too weird" and "That song may sound okay but it's not one of ours" are two ways of stating these boundaries.

Musicality and Multi-musicality

"How musical is man?" asked John Blacking, rhetorically, in the title of his best-known book (1973). Writing today, he would likely have asked, "How musical are humans?" Yes, but the "is" played a significant role, because he wanted the reader to think of all humans as some kind of unit or unity. Saying "rhetorically," I am reminded of a paper by Nazir Jairazbhoy whose title asked, "How Indian Is Indian Film Music?" after which the speaker rose, said "very," and sat down again. (Then he proceeded to read his paper.) Blacking basically gave the same answer, adding a moral spin. He recognized the world as a group of musics, though he personally was always more interested in their borderlands than the centers, but he wanted to make sure that his readers understood a major point: In the end, all musics are equally valuable, or, let's put it this way, all musics are to an equal degree music. He would not have agreed with Kurt Weill (Taylor 1991), who famously said—his thinking not so far from Blacking's because he too wanted to discourage the snobbery of art-music lovers vis-à-vis popular music—that there was only "good" and "bad" music. I think Blacking thought some music supremely good, and the rest, fundamentally, good—a good thing for humanity. And so he considered all humans to be fundamentally musical, arguing that musicality is an inherently human quality. It's an attitude that most ethnomusicologists share: There is some great music, Blacking would have asserted, and in any case we need to know what each society considers great, and why. But all music is worthy of attention, and so are the musical utterances of each human. Just as humans have certain qualities relating to life functions, and all have a hard-wired quality of being able to learn to speak, so are they innately musical, Blacking would have said. To be sure, in Western culture, we have the concept of musicality and talent not shared by all (discussed by Kingsbury 1988), but in other cultures this notion may have different implications. Whether some individuals are more musical than others, having a sense of rhythm, or absolute pitch, or an excellent memory, that's a culture-specific matter. I have known superb Indonesian musicians who couldn't learn some simple musical concepts from Iran.

I love Blacking's egalitarian sentiment, but I'm not so sure about the equal musicality of humans, not because I scorn the student who can't "play his way out of a paper bag" but because there really is no interculturally accepted definition of music, or appropriate terminology, and thus of musicality. We can't visit all of the world's societies and ask them, "What do you think music is?" many would say, "Music? Whazzat?" I do agree with Blacking's definition of "humanly organized sound," at least to the extent that music is human-specific. Biologists and speech-communication experts (see the essays by Peter Marler and Thomas Geissmann in Wallin, Merker, and Brown 2000) have made a good case for the existence of something like music in other species—not because it sounds like human music, that would be ridiculous, but because it seems to have similar functions and can be distinguished from another, more everyday-like form of communication analogous to speech.

Is music human-specific? It's a question that member of other societies have asked themselves. Havasupai mythology has all beings, humans, spirits, animals, communicating by singing before the beginning of human culture. In Blackfoot tradition, songs are taught to humans by animals, in visions, but these animals sing with human voices, and when I asked whether the Blackfoot people think that the bears and wolves and beavers in Glacier National Park sang, they laughed at me. Music is a human activity, and all humans have music in some sense, but the musics of human societies are not alike and should not be judged by the same standards.

There's a concept widely used in ethnomusicology that is curiously both related and unrelated to that of musicality: bimusicality (see Hood 1960) and multimusicality. On the surface, it's also analogous to language; some people, and even some peoples, are bi- or multilingual, and by the same token, an ethnomusicologist can become expert in jazz and gamelan music, and a community such as the Blackfoot people of Browning, Montana, can be equally at home in Plains and Anglo-American musical styles. But such situations are exceptional, often the result of colonialism. People tend to absorb the fundamental grammars of their own language and their own music very early, to know very quickly whether a word belongs to their own language, and whether a particular interval or chord is proper in their own music. The suggestion that there are different "intelligences," including a "musical intelligence" sometimes held by persons who are otherwise not very intelligent, a respected contribution by Howard Gardner (1983), may not have cross-cultural validity, as the musical intelligence of one culture may be of little help in crossing musical boundaries. These considerations, too, tell us that music is a cultural universal, but not a universal "language," and that all humans are musical, but this musicality cannot really be tested with the use of concepts—intervals, rhythms—that are supposedly derived from no single culture's music and thus culturally neutral.

The Centers and the Borders

But the question of boundaries, and the converse of that concept—centers—is actually one of the major difficulties in dealing with the world of music as a group of musics. Take a geographical analogue. The development of musical areas analogous to culture areas in North America and Africa (Merriam 1959; Nettl 1954a) was a practical application of the concept of musics. In these areas it has been relatively easy to find central points in which the main characteristics of music are concentrated, but difficult to find the precise points on the map between an area and another where one "area" changes to another (Nettl 1969). Anthropologists have dealt with this problem in a broader context (see, e.g., Barth 1969; Driver 1961).

Chronological boundaries present problems similar to those of geographical borders. Historians of European music also use the analogy of language to establish their "musics" or, better in this case, musical dialects, as the division of their time-line into stylistically coherent "periods" continues to be an issue for them. Actually, the standard periodization in the history of European music now generally accepted (as in the highly respected text by Donald Jay Grout 1960) was once not at all taken for granted. There was much variety. Thus Guido Adler (1930) provided a scheme with four periods, and Einstein (1947b), Lorenz (1928), Sachs (1946), and Clark (1956), to name a few authors, all had different opinions of when the languages of music changed dramatically—and the issue has arisen again (see, e.g., the work of Daniel Heartz 2003). Moving from one period to another is rather like moving from one area on the map to another. A music may belong to an ethnic group, a nation, an individual person; even musical systems whose borders far exceed conventionally recognized cultural units have also been proposed, as for example by Lachmann (1929), who regarded North African, Middle Eastern, and South Asian musics as a unit on the basis of their method of improvising on modal models.

Let me return for a moment to the concept of bimusicality, which came out of the development of fieldwork in which a scholar would learn to participate—as performer and maybe composer—in the music he or she was studying, developing competence somewhat analogous to being bilingual. But the fact is that many cultures have been and are themselves natively bimusical (or polymusical), recognizing and keeping separate two or more musics in the same way bilingual people handle two languages. In India some musicians seem to have managed to keep classical and folk musics separate, obeying the rules of each. Some of the folk singers of northern Iran, specialists in two or three rather rigidly circumscribed repertories or genres of song, seem to keep these systems from affecting each other. In the nineteenth and twentieth centuries, Western music has come to be known to the members of most societies, leading to a variety of ways of dealing with the matter of musical boundaries.

Multimusicality has resulted in major changes in the musical map of the world. In West Africa, there has emerged a single, new musical language—with lots of genres, including juju and highlife (see Askew 2002; C. Waterman 1990)—resulting from the compatibility of Western and traditional African. This compatibility has also been a major concept in explanations for the growth of an essentially discrete African American music, with its emphasis on those elements that are shared by traditional West Africa and Europe. The Blackfoot people consider themselves bimusical, speaking of "white" and "Indian" musics, and keeping these socially separate, despite the fact that the "Indian" music has been importantly affected by Western music (Nettl 1985; Vennum 1989; Witmer 1973). Bimusicality here accompanies and symbolizes a bicultural society.

The view of the world as a system of musics with centers and boundaries must also take into account the rapidly increased accessibility to most people of a large variety of music, much more than was available before. The result of enormous changes in communications technology, significant already around 1900 with the spread of radio and records, was, by 2000, through the ubiquity of computers, the establishment of a kind of musical life beyond the imagination of earlier generations. The increased ease of travel, too, has provided totally unprecedented opportunities for societies to share music, as has the development of multiethnic nation-states, the neo-colonialist developments particularly after 1990, and the increased use of English as the world's "second language." This change is particularly significant in non-Western societies, which now have access to Western music along with their older traditions, giving them a larger spread of national or regional styles, but the musical profile of Europe and North America has changed markedly as well, with the availability and adoption of musics, presented intact, and of individual components of music such as rhythmic patterns and instruments.

This multimusical culture as we experienced it around 2000 might be interpreted as a world society learning more music, becoming multimusical, acquiring second, third, fourth musical languages, vastly increasing its musical tolerance, symbolic of the greater cultural diversity found in most societies; alternatively, maybe more realistically, it could be seen as the expansion of a single musical system that is enriched (or, some would say, polluting itself) by adding materials and styles, a kind of musical neo-colonialism reflecting social and political developments (see Keil and Feld 1994 and Stokes 1994 for discussion).

The idea of the world of music consisting of a large number of discrete systems, more or less acceptable for the past, becomes less practical as a norm for ethnomusicologists seeking a perspective for the twenty-first century. For the moment, however, having no clear alternative, it seems useful to continue with this concept, to take into account the reality of a society or culture unit with several musics, to continue in the belief that a given group of people will typically regard one music as being intrinsically its own, and also to claim to share others, and that a music is both a body of sound accepted by a group of people and a system with internal logic and consistency of style and a corpus of content. These considerations, as demonstrated in significant publications of the 1990s (e.g., Askew 2002; Stokes 1992; Turino 2000), play a special role in an era in which many kinds, degrees, and levels of social, ethnic, national, and class identity, increasingly important to our understanding of the social and political world, are inevitably tied to their musical analogues.

6

Apples and Oranges: Comparative Study

A State of Conflict

We've devoted five chapters now to defining and laying the groundwork—defined ethnomusicology and music, examined the concepts of creating music, and looked at the world of music in terms of its unity and its diversity—and are now ready to look at some of the things that ethnomusicologists—as ethnomusicologists—actually do. In chapter 1, the first clause of the definition of ethnomusicology stated that it is the study of any music from a comparative perspective, which sees each music as part of a world of musics.

Attitudes about the usefulness, efficacy, and even ethics of comparative study have changed. In 1953 I tried to present a panorama of Native American musical styles with a few examples for a class of students. There was a dearth of readily available records, but I tried to compare those that I had and surprised the students with the interesting variety of styles, showing that sharply descending contours characterized the songs of the Plains peoples, the use of the "rise" (an ascending phrase in the middle) was typical of some Yuman-speaking people's songs of the Southwest, and antiphonal songs of peoples of the Southeast. Although they had at most heard some songs of the Plains peoples, they took this exercise at face value, as it was clear to them that its purpose was simply to exhibit the variety, which struck them as important, and which could only be illustrated through comparison.

Twenty-five years later I tried the same thing, for another class of more knowledgeable and sophisticated students who had heard much more Native

American music. With a different attitude, they questioned the purposes of the comparison, wanted to know what valid conclusions one would draw from it, whether we were looking for differences or for similarities, had adequate samplings, were talking about the same historical period. They criticized the parameters upon which comparison was made and wondered whether a comparative examination of thirty examples was at all a good way to provide an introduction to this music. They were suspicious of making comparisons of what they claimed were "apples and oranges." Then, twenty-five years further on, a half-century after my first attempt, the students had become more accepting of comparison again, and they were interested, too, in how the various Native American musics related to those of Central Asia, South America, Native Australia.

My experience suggests agreement with Alan Merriam's (1977a) article outlining the history of definitions of the field, which argues that there has been a gradual trend from the concept of ethnomusicology as an essentially comparative field to an attitude in which comparative study is criticized, avoided, postponed. Beginning with Guido Adler (1885: 14), who in the first outline of the subdivisions of musicology stated that the purpose of this branch was to compare in order to provide groupings and classifications of the world's music, Merriam goes on to cite Hood (1963: 233, and in Apel 1969: 299) to the effect that comparisons are premature until satisfactorily accurate descriptions of musical systems are available, also quoting Meyer (1960: 49–50) and Blacking (1966: 218), who believed that comparison may result in the improper interpretation of similarities and differences. Most recently, there's a bifurcation between scholars who show a greater interest in comparative work and others who find it useless. Thus, we're frequently faced (on Internet discussion groups, for example) with students asking whether this or that kind of music, or behavior, found in one culture, is also known elsewhere, and at the same time, we have to note that the vast majority of recent ethnomusicological publications are in no way interculturally comparative studies. Whether ethnomusicology is in principle a comparative field or not, there is no doubt that the nature and the role of comparison have all along been central issues. They will arise many times in these essays, in specific contexts, and I wish here only to address the question in general.

Of course the concept of comparison is problematic. To note that two things are in one way alike does not mean that they are otherwise similar, spring from the same source, or have the same meaning. There are some respects in which no two creations of humankind can really be compared. On the other hand, I would maintain that even apples and oranges can very well be compared; they turn out to be alike in being fruit, round, and about the same size but different in color, taste, and texture. The fact that, to itself, an apple may not feel the least bit like an orange and doesn't know how it is to feel like an orange may be irrelevant for certain considerations, though crucial for others. The question is whether we can find systematic, elegant, and reliable ways to carry out the comparison, and whether, having done so, we find that it has been worth the effort. Actually, there is little discussion in the literature of ethnomusicology about comparative method. Many of the studies that use comparison do so by implication rather than explicitly, and the conclusions based on comparative work have their great limitations.

The usefulness and social and intellectual acceptability of comparative study hinges on several questions. Is the purpose of comparison to provide a convenient way of systematically setting forth a mass of diverse data, or to reconstruct history, to make possible interpretations about the nature of society and music, to show broad correlations of one sort or another, to illuminate social inequalities, or to make aesthetic judgments? Let's first look at the rather convoluted history of comparison in ethnomusicology. Described in Wiora's small but definitive book (1975) and more recently by A. Seeger (in Nettl and Bohlman 1991 and in Myers 1992), this history includes distinguished studies carefully executed, with criteria, method, and purpose clearly laid out. At the same time, there are unsupportable random comparisons made for capricious reasons or with an ideological agenda, such as relating Tibet to Portugal, but these make even the most devoted comparative musicologists cringe. While the concept of comparison appears basic to the early development of the field, it is also true that ethnomusicologists have not often set out systematically to make comparisons. Adler, in his classic article (1885), presumably felt that the immediate need was to classify the musics of the world in an ethnographic, that is, descriptive manner, in order to see what the universe of music contained, something best done through a series of comparisons.

To a certain extent the early period of ethnomusicology, through the early twentieth century, is marked by a general if not systematically controlled comparative approach, let's call it a comparative flavor, in contrast to earlier publications on non-Western music, such as those of Amiot (1779), Kiesewetter (1842), and Villoteau (1809), which approach their subjects with particularist zeal. Beginning at the turn of the twentieth century, E. M. von Hornbostel did not engage very much in comparison as such, but nevertheless provided a series of studies covering many parts of the world all based on a single analytical model, suggesting that comparative study was the ultimate purpose to which these descriptions would be put. His career, encompassing studies of the music of five continents, is itself an exercise in comparative method. Later scholars coming out of Hornbostel's circle also sustained an interest in comparative study (see also Bingham 1914). There are, for example, the comparison of Pima and Pueblo musics in George Herzog's dissertation (1936a), that of Yurok and Papago music in Schinhan's thesis (1937), and Helen Roberts's comparison of the styles and instruments in North American Indian culture areas (1936). And comparison saturates the many works of Curt Sachs (e.g., 1953, 1962).

The comparative approach of the early ethnomusicologists goes hand in hand with that of anthropologists of the same period. Around 1900 the purpose of anthropologists' comparisons appears to have been primarily that of historical reconstruction, and the notion of *a* comparative method, though hardly ever defined, runs deep in the literature. In an important statement of the history of comparative anthropological study, Oscar Lewis (1956: 260) very simply said: "Most anthropological writings contain comparisons," something one could equally maintain for ethnomusicological writings. But the broad comparisons and generalizations of early ethnomusicology, based inevitably on a small sample of evidence, may have made later scholars hesitant to pursue comparative method. A period of specialization followed. Spurred by greater opportunities for extended and efficient field research, the typical ethnomusicologist became more involved in one culture. Lengthier exposure instilled a respect for the intrinsic value of non-Western musics, particularly those of the Asian civilizations, which would only be satisfied by lifetime devotion to one culture, and this kind of study showed that the musics of the world are indeed in certain respects not comparable. While one can compare those elements of a music that are basically alike, each music also has elements so distinct as to make comparison a matter of methodological and conceptual difficulty. The comparative techniques that had been established by Hornbostel and his school—counting tones and intervals in scales, providing typologies of rhythmic units, and so forth—went only so far. It became clear that we must also study each music in terms of the theoretical system that its own culture provides for it, whether an explicitly articulated, written system or one that must be derived from interview and analysis; and that one must study musical behavior in terms of the underlying value structure of the culture from which it comes. Thus the period after 1940 showed a marked decline in concern for comparative work in ethnomusicology. But some forty years later it began again to rear its head, and about 2000, it is clearly here again, though without an explicit methodology, and usually without being named.

Anthropology, which had in many cases served as a model for ethnomusicology and preceded it in approach and method by a decade or two, experienced a similar fate. A discipline that in the nineteenth and early twentieth centuries thrived on comparison, particularly for the purpose of theoretically determining historical processes, it began to move in the direction of specialized ethnography early in the 1900s. But by the middle 1950s, and later even more, it again began to stress a comparative approach, as shown by the renewed emphasis on comparative study in some of the recent summaries of the field (e.g., Andre Beteille in Ingold 1994: 1010–39; Keesing 1976; Naroll and Cohen 1973) and the development of a specialized literature on (Sarana 1975) and criticism of comparative method. On the other hand, some the major theoretical works of the period after 1980, taking it for granted that one looks at the world broadly by comparing the various phenomena one observes (see, e.g., Geertz 2000: 251), don't go further to suggest a general methodology.

Kinds of Comparative Study

Anthropology can provide various broad kinds of classification for types of comparative study. Let's look at one published about the time ethnomusicologists began to turn away from comparison. In his bibliographical and analytical study of comparative research, Oscar Lewis (1956) surveyed 248 publications relevant (almost entirely of American and British origin) from between 1950 and 1954. Of these, 28 deal with the theory and methodology of comparison. Lewis did not try to guess the proportion of the comparative studies in the total anthropological corpus of his five-year period. But it is reasonable to assume that these 248 publications occupy a fairly substantial slice of the whole, and that some of the 28 theoretical and methodological pieces are among the important works of theory of the period.

Lewis classifies the studies further, finding six dominant aims: (1) establishing general laws or regularities, (2) documenting the range of variation of a phenomenon or (3) distribution of a trait, (4) reconstructing culture history, and (5) testing hypotheses derived from Western and (6) from non-Western societies. Furthermore, 34 studies involved global or random comparisons; 33, comparisons between continents and nations; 31, comparisons within one continent; 31, within one nation; 70, within one culture area; and 34, within one group or culture. Considerably more than half involved the Western hemisphere.

How did comparison fare in a similar period in the history of ethnomusicology? The prominence of the journal *Ethnomusicology* within its field possibly makes it a reliable sample for following Lewis's approach. A survey of volumes 2–17 (1958–73) reveals a total of approximately 270 articles. While it is difficult for us (as it must have been for Lewis) to segregate the "comparative" studies, it seems that only 43 of the articles are clearly (though not in all cases even primarily) addressed to the question of comparison of repertories or of segments of repertories, or of cultures. Of these, 13 articles are primarily theoretical. Nineteen contain comparisons within one culture area, and 11 are in some sense historical, comparing repertories from different periods or of different areas (such as African and African American) with the purpose of providing historical insight. All of this is perhaps curious in a discipline that has been greatly influenced by anthropology with its comparative orientation, a discipline that long called itself "comparative musicology," and particularly in a field within anthropology that lends itself, perhaps better than many others, to statistical examination of components and to quantification (Freeman and Merriam 1956: 465). Given the resurgence of comparison in American higher education, as demonstrated in the increase in topical courses and seminars that deal with a variety of cultures, it may be surprising that the editor of *Ethnomusicology* from 1998 to 2002 reported (*EM 46/2*, frontmatter) that of 164 articles submitted during the period, only 9 could be classed as principally comparative.

Wiora (1975: 19–25) also tried to classify comparative studies through the history (to ca. 1972) of ethnomusicology, dividing them into eight "centers or directions": (1) the holistically comparative Berlin school of Hornbostel and Sachs, (2) the somewhat more biologically oriented Vienna school of R. Lach and W. Graf, (3) European folk music scholarship, (4) comparative study of Jewish and Christian liturgies, (5) scholarship involving comparisons of closely neighboring areas, (6) American research concentrating on musical areas, (7) comparative study of European classical and folk music, and (8) comparative study of national styles of art music in Europe.

Instead of adopting a single agreed-upon comparative method, as for a time did linguists and anthropologists, ethnomusicologists engaged, for most of the twentieth century, in a variety of comparative studies. A number of models for comparison of musical styles, repertories, and individual pieces were established, with varying degrees of success. Hornbostel, in following a single method of stylistic description in many of his studies, provided a template for comparison. The analytical systems of Kolinski (e.g., 1956, 1959, 1961, 1965a, 1965b) tried to provide frameworks for the comparison of repertories in accordance with individual elements of music such as scale, melodic movement, rhythm, and tempo. Bartók's approach to analysis of Eastern European folk song (e.g., 1931, 1935, 1959) provides guidelines for comparison as well, and so does the method for comparing English folk tunes developed by Bayard (e.g., 1950, 1954) and Bronson (1959, 1959–72) and further developed by Cowdery (1990). The voluminous work dealing with classification of folk songs in one repertory, beginning early in the century (Koller 1902–3; Krohn 1902–3—see also chapter 9 here) and continuing through several decades (e.g., Bayard 1942; Elschekova 1966; Herzog 1950; Hustvedt 1936), and the comparative work in the field of African American music studies—as indicated in the publications of Herskovits (1945), R. Waterman (1952), Merriam (1955b), and Jackson (1943)—are also significant here. But these kinds of methodologies seem to have run their course, as the last important attempt in this direction was the system of cantometrics developed by Alan Lomax (1968, 1976; discussed further in chapters 8 and 24).

The Opposition

Ethnomusicologists seem not to have become very much involved in the epistemology of comparison and rarely ask whether it is possible to deal interculturally with music without, in some sense, systematically carrying out comparative study. Yet the importance of the question is suggested by the ubiquitous discussion of the identity of the field, with the presence or absence of comparative components as a major criterion. Some assert that ethnomusicology comprises the study of music or musical culture outside the investigator's own purview. The identity of investigators vis-à-vis their subject matter is here a major factor, and the fact that it should be accorded such significance is epistemologically significant. In several publications, Mantle Hood (1963: 233–34, 1971: 349) maintained that comparison is not a primary goal of the field and cannot, at the present time or perhaps for a long time in the future, be carried out properly. Even so, he states that the American (or European) ethnomusicologist, "because of *who* he is, is capable of insights and evaluations which no Javanese, even with training . . . in Western methods, could ever duplicate" (374). While this statement shows Hood to be perhaps of two minds, the view of ethnomusicology as essentially comparative is questioned by many non-European scholars who concentrate on their own musical traditions, feeling that only the "insider" is truly qualified for scholarship and, by implication, that comparison is not truly possible.

The many criticisms of comparative work revolve around the difficulty of

comparing cultures of which one has varying kinds and degrees of understanding, personal contact, data; and the problem of knowing any culture or
music in sufficient depth and breadth to carry out meaningful comparison.
There is fear of unwarranted conclusions. There is the allegation that the purpose of comparison is to make value judgments, detrimental to some whose
music is being compared. One is in awe of the complexity of musical systems, which itself can make them inherently incomparable. There is suspicion of the quantitative techniques inevitably used in comparative study, and
the belief that in a field devoted to this kind of work, data gathering will be
prejudicial in favor of materials that lend themselves to comparison. But let's
look at a few of these objections a bit more.

Are musics indeed comparable? In a widely cited discussion, John Blacking (1978: 75–76) suggested that superficial similarities may not be worth noting. To find the same intervals in the scales of two cultures, he contends, may
be of no interest at all if these intervals have different meanings in the two systems. Well and good, if one is also concerned at the moment about meanings.
The argument sounds weaker when Blacking gives its opposite number: "Statistical analyses may show that the music of two cultures is very different but
analysis . . . may reveal that they have essentially the same meaning, which
has been translated into the different 'languages' of the two cultures" (1966:
218). The latter finding would seem to be highly significant and interesting,
but how would one ever come up with it if one had not made the comparison in the first place? What Blacking is objecting to is the drawing of unwarranted conclusions, and he seems to have in mind certain studies that go no
further than making statistical comparisons. No one can take exception to
this critique, but the prescription would seem to be not avoidance of comparative study but more and better comparative study.

Western traditional harmony has become a major component of the modernized sector of traditional music in twentieth-century sub-Saharan Africa
and the Middle East. A comparison yields the broad conclusion that Africans do better with it, that is, conform more closely to European practices.
If one can assign a broad meaning to the use of harmony in the two cultures,
it is, grossly speaking, the same: a major musical symbol of modernization.
The fact that the Africans use it differently and, from European perspective,
"better" than Middle Easterners may tell us something about the relative
compatibility of the two sets of systems. Considering the longstanding use
of other harmonic systems in parts of Africa, it may also show something
about the effect of one harmonic system on the adoption of another and also
about the role of somewhat successful (in Africa) versus less successful (in

the Middle East) Christian missionary efforts, as well as many other things (see R. Waterman 1948, 1952).

The question of comparability of entire musics—and, for that matter, of components of musics such as tune variants—is closely related to the political and social relationships between field investigators and consultants, between Western scholars and those of developing nations. The growing skepticism of comparison goes hand in hand with a viewpoint characteristic of some scholars from the latter areas, its basis the deep conviction that a musical system can be properly understood only by its own people. It's not the simple act of making comparison that is itself unacceptable. Rather, one objects to the way in which it has been, or threatens to be, carried out. Thus, for example, non-European scholars may have a point in saying that if ethnomusicology is the study of music outside one's culture, it can hardly be taken seriously, for this definition seems like an excuse for superficiality. And it is undignified for anyone to study a musical system if the purpose is *only* to compare it to others.

On the issue of dignity: Is looking for differences or similarities a political gesture? In simply making a comparison, ethnomusicologists would appear to be neutral, though they have been criticized—particularly in Africanist studies—to have emphasized homogeneity over diversity (Agawu 1995b, 2003). Quite true, the conclusions that have been drawn are overwhelmingly based on similarities—among musics, among genres and pieces—for such observations lend themselves more readily to positive interpretation. Identifying historical strata, as was done by Curt Sachs for instruments (1929, 1940), establishing musical areas (Merriam 1959; Nettl 1954b), identifying tune relationships among Spain, England, and Hungary (Wiora 1953)—these are conclusions, justified or not, that came about as scholars at work found similarities persuasive enough to lead them at least to tentative conclusions. Whatever differences they found seem to have played a small role. So the suspicion has foundation: Comparativists, not so neutral as all that, are impressed by similarity, and seek it out.

A major purpose of comparative study has always been an understanding of history. We compared musics to see how they have developed, whether they have a common origin, and so on (Wiora 1975: 81–90). Conclusions at best will always be conjecture. Whether it was worth doing or whether, as John Blacking said, speculative history is a complete waste of effort (1973: 56) depends on the value one places on historical knowledge. If an understanding of history is accorded enormous importance, then, I would think, any way in which one can gain insight, however tentative, in situations lacking solid verifiable data is worth a lot of effort. If it is a matter of only secondary or, as Blacking puts it, "encyclopedic" interest, then one is better off devoting one's energy to other pursuits, for even a great deal of effort at comparison will indeed produce only the most tentative results.

A related objection came from certain students of the complex classical musics of Asia. They accepted the ethnomusicologist's comparative approach to tribal and folk musics, which they saw as simple and inferior systems (Danielou 1973: 28–33). But greater dignity, they would assert, must be accorded to classical systems, because they are in the same league as Western classical music, closer to unique. Western scholars should treat these classical systems as they have dealt with European classical music, which has hardly been the object of *primarily* comparative study. Thus it is sometimes put.

Comprehensive knowledge of non-Western musics and the admonitions of Asian musicians (e.g., Becker 1986; Shankar 1999) are supposed to rid us of the kind of prejudice that always places Western music and its values at the top. But then we shouldn't substitute the insistence that classical music systems in general—those of India, China, Japan, Indonesia, the Middle East, and Europe—constitute a musical elite. The old line privileging the elite musics would still be there, just moved over a few inches on the map. All musics are obviously worthy of more than merely comparative study. And if comparative study is helpful and even essential for understanding indigenous and folk musics, it can be so also for more complex systems. At some point of conceptualization all musics are equal. Beyond that, a careful look at the historiography of Western music indicates that comparison, among regions of Europe, periods of history, composers, pieces has been a major activity. In historical musicology, as in ethnomusicology, one would wish for better development of comparative method.

A Comparative Method?

Comparative study pervades the academy. We have comparative anatomy, comparative psychology, linguistics, law, religion all found as terms in encyclopedias, as titles of courses and books. In all cases, separate systems, usually defined as belonging to different populations, cultures, or societies, are somehow compared. It seems that scholars are attracted more by similarities than differences, trying to draw conclusions regarding function and history from them. There have been some attempts to draw together the many venues and uses of the concept of comparison (Warwick and Osherson 1973), and there are even departments of "comparative study" in some universities, with the implication that this represents a particular disciplinary focus. We also encounter the idea that comparative study is circumscribed by particular methods and limitations that go beyond the subject matter of an established discipline. Thus Myrdal (in Warwick and Osherson 1973: 98) suggests that—contrary to Hood—comparison should precede detailed examination of a phenomenon in its own terms, that "generalizations about reality, and their organization within an abstract framework of presumed interrelations, precede specification and verification." But a "comparative method" valid for many fields may not amount to much more than Merriam's very general admonition that "the approach must be cautious, that like things must be compared, that the comparisons must have some bearing upon a particular problem and be an integral part of the research design" (1964: 53).

On the other hand, individual disciplines have had specific, and in many cases unique, purposes for comparative study. The general purpose of comparative psychology is simply to ascertain the similarities and differences in behavioral organization among living beings, with a large variety of specific aims. Comparative law, while encompassing historical and anthropological interests, seems to have as its major aim the articulation of various legal systems and the improvement of the world's legal security, in the character of an applied field. Comparative literature deals with themes and motifs of literary content across linguistic boundaries, while linguists have reserved the name "comparative method" specifically for a way of reconstructing earlier languages or earlier stages in language by structurally comparing similar words, with identical or related meanings, in different languages and dialects. Linguists engage in comparison for other purposes, such as the establishment of cognitive systems or the solution of problems in the interrelationship of language and culture, but *the* comparative method tries to establish the history of genetic language relationships. In ethnomusicology the purpose of comparison is—or perhaps the major and even first purpose of comparative musicology was—also to contribute to an understanding of history. Linguists have established a clear-cut method, and its results are generally accepted by the profession and the public at large. The existence of proto-Germanic, proto-Indo-European, proto-Algonquian is not seriously questioned, although these languages are simply constructs (Anttila 1972: 65–66).

There has been no similar comparative method to deal with the reconstruction of musical forms. While comparison of widely separated cultures, or of variants of a song in a restricted area, has provided insights analogous to those of the comparative linguist, their significance is not agreed upon and often denied. Ethnomusicologists have rarely tried to adopt the methods of comparative and historical linguistics directly, and Gilbert Chase's suggestion that "the term 'comparative musicology' should be revived . . . but as it is used in linguistics" (quoted in Brook, Downes, and Van Solkema 1972: 219) fell on deaf ears. Comparison in ethnomusicology has been more a combination of attitude (e.g., "a comparative approach provides insight") with a group of techniques used ad hoc to deal with specific problems. Ethnomusicology has never had *a* comparative method.

But if no single comparative method has been accepted, there are approaches that have, by implication, tried to claim such a title—the analytical approaches of Hornbostel, Bartók, and Kolinski and the various approaches to stating geographic distribution of styles all seem at one point or another to have been informally considered as filling this role. The most recent—though it's actually pretty old—is Alan Lomax's cantometrics (1959, 1962, 1968, 1976), which provides a system of describing musical style within a comparative framework, valuable because it includes for the first time a number of aspects of music such as timbre and ways of using the voice.

While the main value of cantometrics seems to me to be its system of describing singing style, Lomax and his staff carried out comparisons of music and culture type in major culture areas, largely for the purpose of identifying cultural determinants of musical style. Large culture areas (e.g., American Indian, sub-Saharan Africa, the Pacific Islands, Australia, Europe, the "old high cultures" of Asia) were involved, and culture groups that contrast in some significant way, as in the fundamentals of social and political organization, type of subsistence economy, and child-rearing. Certainly the matching of culture types and musical styles is a venerable habit in ethnomusicology; M. Schneider (1957: 12–14) asserted that hunters, gatherers, and agriculturists have different styles of music, and Sachs (1937: 31–33) tried to distinguish patriarchal and matriarchal peoples. Lomax differs from them in large measure by his use of a more formal technique for comparison.

The musical discipline that is most concerned with establishing methodologies for comparison is music theory, a field that was once considered a minor subdivision of musicology, then a component (with psychology of music and acoustics) of "systematic musicology," and eventually, especially in the English-speaking world, a field with greater independence focusing on issues in the analysis and comprehension of music. Music theorists have tried to establish templates that would make possible the analysis of any music (Rahn 1983, 1996), and they have tried to apply concepts and methods engendered by studies of Western music to a broader scope (e.g., D. Temperley 2000), with varying degrees of success. In general, music theorists deal with music without major consideration of cultural context, but while this may have its problems, many theorists have the countervailing advantage of experience as composers. A number of scholars from theory, for example, Michael Tenzer, Jay Rahn, and John Rahn, have found themselves attracted to ethnomusicological subject matter and found ways to combine the approaches of both fields.

While almost all of the work touched upon in this chapter involved the comparison of musics because musical styles lend themselves to statistical analysis, there is a trend, exemplified early on by the rather formal juxtaposition of Ibo and Hausa musicians by David Ames (1973a), to provide comparisons of cultures in terms of musical behavior aside from the sounds that are produced. This too is evident in Lomax's work, as his parameters include aspects of the social roles and interrelationships of musicians. Another recent trend is the use of explicit comparisons within a repertory or a single musical culture to identify norms and deviations.

Some publications of the 1970s foresaw a bright future for comparative study. John Blacking, often skeptical, nevertheless acknowledged its uses and felt that its problems could be solved by such concepts as the relationship of "deep structures" and "surface structures," borrowed again from linguistics. We need, he wrote, "a unitary method of musical analysis which can be applied to *all* music," and which takes into account and explains sound itself and musical behavior as well (1971: 93). A number of attempts to develop such a method have been made and are described in chapter 8. Only when a satisfactory one is established, Blacking implied, will we be in a position to make acceptable comparisons, which are our ultimately efficacious technique (1972: 108). Wiora (1975), who did not simply equate comparative study with ethnomusicology, nevertheless showed dozens of examples successfully carried out. Porter (1977) considered a renewed interest in comparative work to be the last, best hope for research in European folk music.

In the period after 1980, comparative study as a concept does not appear very much in the literature, but comparisons nevertheless abound. One relevant area of study is the musical cultures of immigrant societies compared with the traditional homeland, a type of study begun fifty years earlier but now a standard, often labeled with the catchword "diasporas." Important studies include those of Sugarman (1997) on Albanians outside Albania in Europe and the United States, Myers (1998) on Hindu culture in Trinidad and its antecedents, Manuel (2000) on the various ways Indian music has been preserved in the Caribbean, Turino (1994) on Aymara musical culture in a village, a middle-size town, and the capital of Peru, and Reyes (1999) on the music of Vietnamese at home, and in the Philippines and eventually United States exile. Another kind of evidence for the strength of comparative study and the degree to which it is accepted is the vast number of edited volumes that have appeared since 1980, works in which a number of authors speak to the same problem or issue from the perspective of different cultures. It's almost embarrassing to try to pick examples from the many, but Koskoff (1987), on women's music, Moisala and Diamond (2000), on issues involving gender, Barz and Cooley (1996), on fieldwork in a variety of cultures, Nettl and Russell (1998), on improvisation in the world's cultures, and Radano and Bohlman (2000), on issues involving race, illustrate the genre and its popularity in the ethnomusicological academy. It seems that ethnomusicologists still believe Kolinski (1971: 160) when he said that the avoidance or indefinite postponement of the comparison of musics "deprives the discipline of an essential tool in its quest for a deeper insight into the infinite multifariousness of the universe of music."

7

I Can't Say a Thing until
I've Seen the Score: Transcription

A Difficult and Intricate Task

Western urban society has a special view of music. We may say that folk singers deviate from the way a song is "written" when we really mean from the particular forms in which they have learned it. We use the term "writing music" broadly, substituting it for "composing"—significantly in popular music—whether notation is involved or not. We think of a piece of music as existing in its truest form on a piece of paper. The academics among us can hardly conceive of discussing music without knowledge of a single, authoritative, visible version. "I can't say a thing until I've seen the score," critics may say upon hearing a new piece, because the true representation of music is the written form; but they ought perhaps to be saying, when seeing a new score, "I can't say a thing until I've heard it." Dealing with the written music is the classical musician's ideal. "Can you read music?" is the question used to separate musical sheep from goats, to establish minimum musical competence.

I am making a bit of fun of a segment of Western society for being so tied to notation. It equates composing with writing and accepts the creation of music on paper even when the composer can barely imagine its sound until he or she has heard it, of music that contains devices that can only be appreciated by the eye. Given that in all societies music is created and transmitted—entirely or to a large degree—aurally, the culture of Western classical music seems to represent a serious departure from the norm. But departure or not, this central characteristic of Western academic musical culture has had major impact on ethnomusicology. Concerned with a study of music that lives largely in oral tradition, ethnomusicologists have spent a great deal of their energy finding ways of reducing it to visual form. Like those critics, ethnomusicologists faced with a recording have tended to throw up their hands and say "I can't say a thing until I've written it down"— until I've "transcribed" it.

Transcription is widely discussed in the general literature of ethnomusicology, as in a comprehensive survey by Doris Stockmann (1979) and a brilliant history and critique by Ter Ellingson (1992b), which appropriately treat transcription as a complex concept that overlaps with others such as description and analysis of music. But most immediately it is interpreted to mean simply the reduction of recorded sound to standard Western music notation. Looking at the matter more broadly, transcription should include other notation systems, such as those developed for a variety of purposes in Asian societies (see Kaufmann 1967; Ellingson 1992a; Malm 1959: 261–75) and certain ones invented especially for ethnomusicological study (e.g., Koetting 1970). Beyond this, transcription includes graphs and other ways of presenting data provided by automatic devices. All of these systems tell us, on the one hand, how a musical performance we're hearing changes from one moment to the next but, on the other, what the characteristics are that endure throughout a piece or a song, such as a tone system, a way of using the voice, and so on. Thus the concept of transcription might well also include general characterizations of singing style or descriptions of the musical vocabulary on which the composer of a piece draws.

Only with difficulty can transcription be separated from description and analysis of music, techniques that normally both precede and follow it. It is often regarded as the central and most difficult task of an ethnomusicologist, who is distinguished from other kinds of scholars by this competence. In transcription, the ethnomusicologist presents himself or herself as a kind of superperson, able to control and make sense of a plethora of previously inexplicable sound with a set of extremely demanding techniques. Thus Kunst: "The transcription of exotic phonograms is one of the most difficult and intricate tasks which ethnomusicological research has ever put before its devotees" (1959: 37). Bartók: "We should never tire of improving and changing our methods of work in order to accomplish this task as well as is humanly possible" (Bartók and Lord 1951: 20). Merriam: It is assumed that the ethnomusicologist "has available to him accurate methods of transcribing music sound to paper, but this is a question that is far from resolved" (1964: 57). Hood, in whose general book on ethnomusicology transcription is one of the fundamental concerns, also dwells on the need for accuracy: "The process must begin with the most specific and detailed transcription possible" (1971: 320). Ellingson (1992b: 146): "The best transcription, which conveys the most essential features of the music, may be the most difficult to read."

All agree: Transcription is enormously difficult, and one should strive continually to prove oneself competent and to improve competence. It is not only difficult, but some seem to consider it hopeless. Sachs: "Even the most painstaking method will not give us ultimate satisfaction. No musical script can ever be a faithful mirror of music" (1962: 30–31). Estreicher, as summarized by McCollester: "The ideal goal of a musical transcription then cannot be realized because it seeks to find a visual equivalent to an oral phenomenon" (1960: 132). Charles Seeger: "A hazard of writing music lies in an assumption that the full auditory parameter of music is or can be represented by a partial visual parameter" (1958: 184). But these somewhat hand-wringing caveats in the general discussions of ethnomusicology contrast with the typical study of a specific culture or repertory that includes transcriptions, wrought with difficulty and imperfect, and that provides matter-of-fact explanations of the procedures used. It's hard, but one does the best one can.

Until well into the 1950s, the ability to transcribe was viewed as the basic and perhaps even the diagnostic skill of the ethnomusicologist, and even in 2000 many still regard this ability as essential. My own training in fact began thus: I approached my teacher, George Herzog, about specializing in what was then still called comparative musicology, and, after a sentence or two of congratulation (or condolence?), he told me that I must first learn to transcribe, asked me to come to his office to get some material (then available on acetate discs, in the pre-tape era), and put me to work. And for a year or so I did little else. Hood (1971: 50–55) relates a similar experience in his initial studies with Jaap Kunst. Like the student of unwritten languages in the 1920s, whose major activity was the collection of phonetic transcriptions of texts, and like the scholar of Renaissance music, whose transcribing of earlier into modern notation was the daily bread, the ethnomusicologist for a long time was in the first instance a transcriber of music. The first task of the discipline as a whole was thought by some to be the transcription of all available recordings.

Here's a history of transcribing in a nutshell (but see Ellingson 1992b: 110–44 for a more detailed account): In the nineteenth century it was the idea of preserving disappearing musics that dominated. The first decades of the twentieth century saw concentration on establishing standard methods of objectively stating on paper what happens in sound, for the purpose of providing a way to describe and analyze (see Abraham and Hornbostel 1909–10). Toward the middle of the twentieth century there appeared attempts to increase this objectivity by drawing on acoustic and electronic machinery to do the work of humans. After 1955 there was increasing diversification of methods of transcription, of ways in which transcription was used as a part of a larger research design. In the 1970s the art is characterized by a tendency to use transcription for the purpose of solving specific problems, each tending to generate a particular kind of notation. The 1970s and 1980s have also seen interest in the theory and methodology of transcribing. Publications of the period since around 1990 have fewer transcriptions than the earlier, and these have decreased in complexity, functioning for the reader as an accompaniment to available recordings rather than having the function of substituting for the recording.

Several issues dominate this history: (1) the contrast between prescriptive and descriptive notation; (2) the nature of the unit of musical thought, song, or piece that is being transcribed; (3) the relationship of transcription, as the outsider's interpretation, to notation as the way a society expresses its own understanding of its music; (4) the roles of humans and machines; and (5) transcription as a unified technique for the field, as against the development of specialized techniques for providing special insights. A bit more on these five issues follows.

Seeger's Dyad

In one of the most influential pieces of writing on the subject, Charles Seeger (1958) identified two purposes of musical notation: One provides a blueprint for the performer, and the other records in writing what has actually occurred in sound. How do they differ? Ludolf Parisius (see Weber-Kellermann 1957: 1–23), an exemplary collector of the mid–nineteenth century, wrote down hundreds of song texts and some 200 melodies from the Altmark, his native area in central Germany, mainly in order to preserve a repertory that was quickly going out of existence. "Whoever wishes to collect from the mouth of the folk ought to hurry; folk songs are disappearing one after the other," he wrote in 1857 (Weber-Kellermann 1957: 7); and that he did. But he produced collections whose purpose, like that of others of his time, is actually a bit unclear. Following the trends of the time, Parisius wished somehow to make his collection part of the intellectual mainstream, and he was therefore mainly interested in the songs as artifacts, and less in the results of the process of oral tradition in the folk community. He corrected and improved some of the texts and combined versions into archetypes, and he notated the tunes quickly as they were being sung, unable thus to give attention to singing style, ornamentation, metric irregularities. What was to be done with these songs? Presumably they could be read and even sung by those who wished directly to experience the folk culture of Altmark. There was little doubt in the minds of the collectors of the time that this kind of notation would give the reader a realistic idea of textual and musical style, and if one could sing the song from Parisius's written version, one could also understand it. The notations in this collection are both prescriptive and descriptive.

In the middle of the nineteenth century, when close analysis of music had not yet become a practice, the issue of the prescriptive/descriptive distinction had not arisen. After all, in dealing with the folk music of his own culture, Parisius (like many nineteenth-century collectors) was transcribing material in a style known to him before his field experience, and presumably also known to the typical reader. Actually, one of the fundamental truths that confront us today in the use of transcription may already have been clear to him: Whether intended for performance or analysis, a transcription gives readers an accurate idea of the specific sound of a song only if they already know in general the kind of sound to be expected, if they are already acquainted with the style. Otherwise, it serves only as a vehicle for abstract perception of style characteristics. Depending, of course, on their context, many transcriptions equally serve prescriptive and descriptive purposes.

On the surface, an ethnomusicologist simply sits down with a CD—at one time it was with a disc, harder to use but adequate, or a cylinder, or a spool of wire, a reel-to-reel tape, an audio cassette; earlier yet, with an informant and possibly with only the memory of a piece once heard—and writes down what he or she hears or remembers. But, in fact, attitude and conception determine much of what is done. Two different transcriptions of the same piece do not simply indicate varying competence but also differences in the purpose of the task at hand, in the conception of what constitutes a piece of music. The distinction between prescriptive and descriptive notation was Seeger's terminology for music for performance versus analysis. But there is an obvious correlate. Typically, outsiders, trying to be "descriptive," start by writing everything they hear, which turns out to be impossible. Some have tried, like Bartók in his incredibly detailed transcriptions of eastern European folk songs (e.g., Bartók 1935; Bartók and Lord 1951), but of course even this master with the infallible ear didn't have symbols for many aspects of singing style. Even so, it is hard to make head or tail of his notations because of their immense detail. On the other hand, the writer of a prescriptive notation normally includes only what is needed by a native who knows the style. Ordinarily, it's the cultural "insiders" (however defined) who write music to be performed. In order to learn a new mazurka by Chopin, a pianist reads his or her notes with an aural knowledge of how Chopin is supposed to sound. Some of the notation systems of Asian nations tell only what the musician needs to know about a piece; they have no intention of describing its style. But a descriptive notation tries in fact to provide a thorough and objective accounting of what happens in a particular performance of a piece, presumably without making (or accepting) judgments as to the relative significance of events and units. It's similar to the method of a phonetician's first attempt at describing the details of an unknown language. Seeger might also have named his two kinds of notation "emic" and "etic"—terms that began to be used soon after his article was published—or perhaps "cultural" and "analytical"; but the parallels aren't really precise.

Some years after Charles Seeger (1958), Mantle Hood (1971: 90) proposed three solutions to the general problems of transcription. One depends on the notation systems of non-Western societies, a second on the mechanical or electronic melograph, and a third includes dance and movement notation with the notation of sound. The first appears to be in essence prescriptive, and the other two descriptive. The first is the notation of the culture's insider, the others are or can be the work of outsiders. For Hood, the three approaches appeared to be different solutions of the same problem, but I would suggest also that they also result from different aims.

Transcription has ordinarily meant notation that distinguishes temporal segments in a piece, one phrase from another, one note from the next. But the need to characterize, to transcribe, as it were, those elements of a performance found throughout the entire piece has always been recognized as well. Thus even some of the earliest transcribers typically included verbal remarks about tempo, dynamics, and singing style, but these are usually regarded not as aspects of transcription but of analysis or description. The transcriber is thought to divide music into style elements, which are described, and musical content (see chapter 5), which is *transcribed*. The content of pieces has been recognized as increasingly complex as recording devices have become more sophisticated, and at the same time the number of musical traits generally present in a repertory or throughout a performance piece has also increased. Thus the method of rating musical traits developed by Alan Lomax in his cantometrics project (Lomax 1968, 1976), thirteen of whose thirty-seven parameters could be considered elements of singing style, is most readily regarded as an analytical tool (illustrated in Lomax 1968: 86; also reproduced in Blum 1992: 191). The "profiles" that gives the ratings for each parameter (e.g., high rasp, medium nasality) of individual pieces are also a kind of transcription. A person trained in cantometric analysis could look at such a profile and get a sense of the sound of the music, just as one can from a perusal of a conventional notation. Cantometrics was intended to be descriptive, but potentially it's also prescriptive. A singer with the simplest notation, if trained to read a cantometrics profile, should theoretically be able to render it in the right singing style. The difference between descriptive and prescriptive notation, insightful as it appears, is not always as clear as Seeger suggests, and history presents various alternatives that are points of interaction between the two.

The Piece and the Performance

In nineteenth-century transcription practice, European folk music dominated, but notation of music from cultures foreign to the transcriber's experience was carried out as well, though in much smaller quantity, with the main purpose less preservation or performance and more the provision of some hard evidence that this was, indeed, music. Before the days of recording, any scholarly writing about music was hardly complete without notation. The transcription proved that the music existed, and that the transcriber had really heard it. But the notation was not of great help to readers of the accompanying commentary because it didn't really tell how the music sounded. Taking recording for granted, it is hard for us today to step into the shoes of a scholar of those days.

You can get the feel of these shoes from one of the early classics of ethnomusicology, Carl Stumpf's article about Bella Coola Indian songs (1886). Having heard a group of touring Bella Coola singers and dancers in Halle, Germany, he arranged to spend several days with one of them. Describing his experience of transcribing from live performance, he tells that he very quickly concluded that the work was difficult and that many earlier transcriptions had perhaps been done hurriedly and unreliably. Lacking recordings that could simply be repeated, he asked his consultant to sing each song many times while he notated. He first listened all the way through and got a sense of the total structure, then notated only the main pitches, transposing the song to C, and then began to fill in other pitches and the rhythm (406–7). He included considerations of tempo and dynamics, and noted major departures from the standard Western tempered scale. And he understood that performances especially elicited might differ from those in a proper cultural context (425).

Stumpf's transcriptions are explicitly descriptive, and on the surface they look very much like later ones done with recordings, such as those of Frances Densmore or George Herzog. But in substance they are different, for as much as his informant may have tried to repeat each song precisely, each one is a combination of several renditions, a kind of archetype. Densmore and Herzog, and most others later, provided notations of individual recorded renditions. Stumpf claims to represent the song as a unified concept, while scholars using recorders usually present what happened on a particular occasion. We're tempted simply to patronize Stumpf as working under handicaps, but it's not so simple.

There are at least three kinds of descriptive transcription: One gives us the events of one performance, and another attempts to give the essence of a song or piece; perhaps a third provides what the culture might consider an ideal performance. A case can be made for each. Stumpf (I cite him mainly as an example of transcription before the advent of recording) gives us not the singer's certified conception of the essence of the piece but the closest thing to it, a kind of average of several performances, a statement of what happens most frequently in a group of closely related variants of a song. In making an interpretation of "the" song as a concept in a culture, or in the total musical experience of a singer, Stumpf's approach may actually go beyond that of the transcriber of a recorded version.

After Stumpf, the idea of providing a notation that gives an "average" version based on many performances was abandoned, most intensively after 1950, by the champions of mechanical means. With the exception of some transcribers of folk music of their own culture, most scholars of the twentieth century used increasingly sophisticated descriptive notations. But they also felt a growing need to view each music from the inside, in its own terms, and it is perhaps strange that this need was not in part met by making transcriptions that claimed to give "the piece" or "the song" as a unit of musical thought in a particular culture, rather than as a statement of an individual performance. Even so, notation whose purpose is clearly not prescriptive but which builds on Stumpf's approach, not of necessity but from conviction, continued alongside the increased emphasis on the individual performance. "The musical transcriptions represent the generalized norms of the children's songs," says Blacking in his classic book on Venda children's songs (1967: 35). "No excuse need be made for the omission of these details, as this is a study of the children's *songs,* and not of the numerous *ways* [emphases mine] in which Venda children sing the same songs." To Blacking there was a difference between the song and its many renditions, and he insisted that the distinction was relevant to making transcriptions even from recordings.

Balance of Thoroughness and Elegance

Possibly the main issue in the history of transcription is the balance between thoroughness and elegance. One of the factors contributing to the prescriptive-descriptive and performance-piece dichotomies is the need, in a truly satisfying description of a performance, to provide a great deal (and by the standards of some, enormous amounts) of detail. The prescription, on the other hand, need provide only what informed performers or their scholarly surrogates require to distinguish one piece from another; there is much that can be taken for granted. Given that standard Western notation is essentially prescriptive, its use in description ordinarily requires accommodations such as the addition of symbols for types of events not found in Western music, and also for the kinds of details that need not be stated in the prescription for a piece in a style you already know. It's a distinction sometimes compared to that of phonetics and phonemics in linguistics (Anttila 1972: 207–8; Bloomfield 1951: 127–38). Phonetics deals with the actual sounds produced, phonemics organizes them into a system with a limited number of significantly distinctive units, from which, for example, an alphabetic orthography might be derived. A descriptive musical notation ideally gives all musical sounds and all distinctions; a "phonemic" transcription would group the random or predictable variants so as to provide a list of significant units. These might comprise, for example, a limited number of pitches or note lengths that allow a performer to render a piece, or a scholar to understand its character and structure at a glance. (Or do we ethnomusicologists, looking at transcriptions, inevitably hum under our breaths?) But the phonetic-phonemic analogy has limitations. For one thing, linguists seem to have begun with phonetics and to have moved in the direction of increasingly sophisticated ways of stating phonemic systems. Ethnomusicological transcription has moved from something like a phonemic beginning ("prescriptive") in a phonetic ("descriptive") direction.

The first significant attempt to establish a general method and set of techniques for transcribing was made by Abraham and Hornbostel (1909–10), described by Ellingson (1992b: 125–31) as "Hornbostel's Paradigm," and included a set of special symbols for aspects of sound not normally notated in Western music. Hornbostel was, after all, the first to try to transcribe large amounts of music from many cultures. But after him, in the period 1930–50, before automatic devices had been developed, a number of scholars, among them Bela Bartók, George Herzog, and Frances Densmore, greatly influenced the development of detailed, descriptive transcription, much of it, though, more culture-specific in approach.

A look at the transcriptions of all three quickly indicates greater degree of detail and less rhythmic and performance-practice regularity, in comparison with the nineteenth-century work of the likes of Parisius and Stumpf. Bartók in particular abounds with grace notes, with small notes symbolic of sounds barely intoned, along with the larger notes written normally (see Bartók 1935). He gives variants departing from the main notation appearing in the various stanzas of the song by bracketed numbers. Herzog (e.g., 1936a) is more interested in rhythm and structure, using bar lines to divide phrases, shortened bar lines for rhythmic subdivision, his notation indicating an awareness of the close interaction of rhythm and form. Where no metric superstructure can be discerned, formal devices such as repetition of rhythmic motifs, rests, or contours may give a sense of rhythmic structure, and Herzog's transcriptions show that he did a good deal of analytical listening before proceeding to write. It seems likely that these two scholars differed in their approaches in part because they dealt with music to which they had different kinds of relationship. Bartók, steeped in the styles of Balkan folk song, wanted to preserve, but to pre-serve everything he heard, moving doggedly through the song from the first note to the last, measure by measure. Herzog, using transcription as a way of discovering music unknown to him, followed a technique of getting a general sense of the structure, then putting down the pitches, gradually getting to the rhythm.

Frances Densmore (e.g., 1913, 1918), who transcribed more Native American melodies than anyone else, followed yet a different approach. If Bartók and Herzog used the transcription process as a way of avoiding the constraints of Western musical thought (as with the use of special modificatory signs), she seems rather to have used it as a way of bringing Native American music closer to the Western conception of musical sound. Thus, instead of eliminating the concept of Western-style meter as irrelevant in American Indian music and using formal devices to shed light on rhythmic phenomena, she shows the complexity of Native rhythms by frequent changes of meter in her transcriptions.

One of the most instructive publications on transcription resulted from a symposium on the subject held by the Society for Ethnomusicology in 1963. Four scholars, Robert Garfias, George List, Willard Rhodes, and Mieczyslaw Kolinski, were asked to transcribe the same piece and then to compare the results (Symposium 1964; also reproduced in Ellingson 1992b: 136). It may seem curious that such a comparative project was not undertaken until some seven decades after the first transcriptions based on recordings had been made. But I think the art of transcription had always been regarded as a very personal one; to many scholars, the emotional impact of publishing transcriptions seems almost to have been like that of composition. And yet, one has normally assumed that transcriptions, once published, are "correct" or "right." To accuse someone of incorrect transcription is still tantamount to denying competence in ethnomusicology as a whole. Possibly it's for this reason that examination of transcriptions in publications or reviews has usually been avoided. The 1963 symposium was intended to shed light, not to produce a competition. The recording used by the four, a Hukwe Bushman song with musical bow recorded by Nicholas England, shows the transcriptions to have occasional mistakes, modest and easily forgiven, and in any case not damaging to the general understanding that the transcription provides. But while the four transcriptions don't differ greatly in their approaches from the notations of Bartók, Herzog, and Densmore made some thirty years earlier, or greatly from each other, the differences they do exhibit illustrate approaches to the process, and the interaction of "phonetic" and "phonemic" components.

The sound of the musical bow is comprised of two simultaneous pitches, a fundamental and an overtone produced by manipulation of the resonator. The fundamental produces one or more overtones, but what it is can itself be predicted from the overtone. Kolinski and Rhodes faithfully produced both fundamental and overtone, giving the reader accustomed to Western notation an idea of the total sound; it's a descriptive notation, but one that rather gives the impression given by standard Western notation, which is usually prescriptive. But List and Garfias reproduced only the overtones, which is really a kind of "phonemic" device, since the readers can fill in the fundamental. The basic metric scheme is stated differently by Rhodes and List. List also provides two forms of the vocal line, with different rhythmic interpretations, one correlating the melody with that of the musical bow accompaniment, the other based on the dynamics and phrasing of the vocal line itself. Garfias avoids a Western bias in establishing the tone system by using the five lines of the staff to represent adjacent notes in a scale of the song rather than nodes along the diatonic template. Attacking the sanctity of the "note," he uses a horizontal line instead.

From the beginning, aural transcription—done by "ear"—has used Western notation because of its breakdown of musical structure into often abstract units represented by notes. Graph notations and automatic, "melographic" devices readily dispel this assumption, as a graph, once drawn, cannot easily be retranscribed into notes. The concept of the articulated note works well for certain musics, especially instrumental, and Garfias successfully used notes to represent the repeated strokes of the musical bow. In other kinds of music, perhaps singing most of all, notes are useful prescriptive devices, but they are not particularly descriptive. Lines may be preferable, providing opportunities to show glides and other ornaments. In fact, there may be in certain cultures segments of sound more significant than those that we label as the "notes." Aural transcription need not depend exclusively on Western notation, nor need scales or intervals be shown exclusively on the Western staff. If we recognize notes as abstractions, the door is open for using other and often more appropriate abstractions as well. If the four scholars in the transcription symposium had set out to make phonetic, strictly descriptive transcriptions, these might well have been more alike than they in fact turned out to be. The issue for them was what, of the universe of what they heard, should be of greatest use to readers to give them a sense of what happens in this music. It was in the interpretive components of transcription that they differed most.

If four scholars at the same convention provided four rather different transcriptions of one song, the many, many people who have transcribed Native American songs over some three centuries turn out to have followed a large number of principles, methods, and techniques. The anthology edited and annotated by Victoria Levine (2002) offers the most important history of transcription so far done for a single culture group, providing over 100 examples of what has been done, by ethnomusicologists, amateurs, missionaries, composers, non-Natives and Natives, and for many purposes. This work provides an excellent accompaniment to Ellingson's broader but less specific survey and helps the reader to judge just how effectively the various approaches to transcription realized their purposes.

Humans versus Machines

A major ingredient of the history of transcription in ethnomusicology is a struggle on the part of proponents of mechanical devices to establish them, and to replace a lot of transcribing done by humans listening to music. They have—so far—never quite made it. By the twenty-first century, ethnomusicologists were doing far less transcribing than before; they could after all give their audience recordings, and one no longer had to prove by transcribing that the strange sounds were proper music. The human component continues with unabated strength. The comprehensive accounts of Doris Stockmann (1979) and Ter Ellingson (1992b) concentrate on it as if it were bound to remain dominant. Charles Seeger, one of the most powerful proponents of automatic devices, in his closing comments on the 1963 transcription symposium, admitted the continued usefulness of Western notation and transcription by ear: "Best for the present and for the foreseeable future must be, I think, a combination of the two techniques" (Symposium 1964: 277).

The classic beginning date of automatic and mechanical transcription is 1928, when Milton Metfessel, using a stroboscope, photographing its oscillations, and superimposing a graph against the photograph, produced a publication with graph notations (Metfessel 1928). As a matter of fact, using a broader interpretation, one may claim that recording itself, mechanical instruments, and piano rolls all provided something related to transcription even earlier. Metfessel actually had few serious followers until the 1940s, when melographic devices began to be developed in various nations, and at that point one suddenly senses great enthusiasm on the part of many scholars for what they hope will be a permanent solution of sorts for the problems of the ethnomusicologist's central activity. Thus Seeger, in reviewing Dahlback's study of Norwegian folk song (1958), the first to present large quantities of melographic transcriptions, heralds a new age: "From now on, field collection and study of musics of whatever era . . . and of whatever idiom . . . cannot afford to ignore the means and methods of the . . . present work. Thus a new era of ethnomusicology has been entered" (C. Seeger 1960: 42).

Some of the new devices made no attempts to provide complete transcriptions of performances, remaining limited to one or several elements. Thus Bose (1952) tried to show differences in singing style between black and white American singers, Obata and Kobayashi (1937) concentrated on a device for recording pitch, and Jones (1954, 1959) produced a transcription device for the complex percussion rhythms in West Africa. List (1963b) carried out spectrographic analysis to distinguish speech from song and other intermediate categories of sound-making, while Födermayr (1971) and Graf (1966, 1972) used sonographic analysis to distinguish various kinds of singing style and other sounds in and associated with music. The most significant methods for transcription of entire pieces were developed at the University of California, Los Angeles (UCLA), by Seeger (1953b), in Norway by Gurvin and Dahlback (Dahlback 1958), and in Israel (Cohen and Katz 1968).

For a long time it was surprising to observers like myself that these various devices were not rapidly supplanting human efforts, as was the case in other spheres of life. Aside from being labor-saving and more precise and efficient than the ear, they were generally conceded to exhibit less Western bias and thus be more conducive to both the elimination of ethnocentrism and the development of comparative method. Eventually it became clear that widespread use of melographic devices—and various kinds of graph notations—were simply not going to become, for the time being, part of the standard arsenal. Ethnomusicologists as a whole continue to remain untrained in reading them and unable to derive from them directly some sense of musical sound and structure. There have been relatively few publications based on melographic transcriptions, and there has actually been widespread resistance. Thus Kunst: "It is possible, by applying a mechanical-visual method of sound-registration . . . to carry the exactitude of the transcription to a point where one cannot see the wood for the trees" (1959: 39). Herzog: "The profusion of detailed visual data . . . will have to be re-translated into musical reality and musical sense" (1957: 73). The International Folk Music Council: "Notation tending to mathematical exactitude must necessarily . . . entail the use of signs intelligible only to the specialists" (1952). List: "The inescapable conclusion is that the capability of the human ear should not be underestimated" (1974: 375–76). And Jairazbhoy, though accepting mechanical devices as useful for many things: "There is, and perhaps always will be, a large gap between what an automatic transcriber would 'hear' and what an experienced listener of a particular musical idiom might 'hear'" (1977: 269).

But why should we have been resisting something that appears to any right-minded individual an incredibly useful device, one that would drive away human error and cultural bias and save labor to boot? Briefly: (1) We have an excessive association of music and notation, equating conventional Western notation with musical sense and musical reality. We can't quite remove ourselves from this hallmark of urban Western academic music culture. (2) Ethnomusicologists, most of us believe, must be able to *hear* music, not merely to analyze, and reliance on automatic devices deprives them of a way of giving evidence of their competence. List (1963c, 1974), in assessing the reliability of aural transcription, emphasized the value of teaching this skill to students. (3) A good many ethnomusicologists are emotionally tied to the sound of music and get much pleasure in their work from transcribing; and having made a transcription gives them a certain sense of direct ownership and control over the music that they have laboriously reduced to notation. (4) Although transcription is supposed to be descriptive notation, it nevertheless, in the corner of the scholar's mind, is potentially prescriptive. At the very least, someone can look at the notation and, humming under one's breath, get out of it a general sense of how the music sounds.

To the Western ethnomusicologist, Western notation makes the music seem like "real music." (5) Just as Western notation may omit significant distinctions in the music, automatic transcription cannot distinguish what is significant from what is not, what is physiologically heard from what the member of a society chooses to hear or ignore. It does not provide the possibility of interpreting the sound as a particular culture would interpret it.

These may not be good arguments, and their proponents may be accused to be Luddites of a sort, and yet even Hood, who did much to further automatic transcription, admitted the widespread service rendered by Western notation. But in the long run, he felt, transcription by ear will have to go. "The fact that some of us are determined to solve the problem . . . will one day result in the abandonment of this ethnocentric crutch" (1971: 90). But thirty years after that was written, automatic transcription had not provided anything like the volumes of songs and pieces that have always been produced by Western notation. Even so, melographs have taught us to view music in a new light. For example, the heuristic value of the Israel melograph discussed by Cohen and Katz (1968: 164) taught the authors that "even the measurement of all the intervals occurring in the performance of a particular song can be misleading if the concept of interval is that of a fixed size." It is a device that would "give a picture of the stylistic elements which take place "between the notes." To be sure, the ear can hear attack and decay of tones, vibrati, glissandos, and interval differences, but Cohen and Katz suggest that the melograph, in questioning the basic assumption of the note as a unit of music, points out what the constraints of Western notation have kept away from us. As suggested already by Herzog (1936a: 286), tones are convenient but sometimes misleading abstractions.

An important contribution of the melograph, then, is to help us to hear objectively. Having had certain things pointed out by inspection of a melographic notation, the scholar can then go on to trust the ear. It almost seems that ethnomusicologists are the victims of an analogue of the Whorfian hypothesis, according to which thought is regulated by the structure of language; musical hearing and cognition on the part of musicologists may be profoundly affected by the characteristics of Western notation. It may be a major role of the melograph to liberate us from this constraint.

A Plethora of Techniques

After about 1960, the role of transcription as a method of providing the principal permanent record of music came to be abandoned, as recordings of various sorts—LPs, discs, tape, CDs, and various computer-assisted devices assumed that role. And melographic transcriptions had shown just how incredibly complex a group of musical sounds can be. But transcription has neither been abandoned nor unified under the aegis of technology; rather, ethnomusicologists have developed a plethora of techniques. While the typical ethnomusicologist of the 1930s would have said, "Let's get this piece down in notation, then we will see what it is like," the scholar of the 1960s was more likely to say, "Now we've listened to this piece (and to many like it) carefully and know in general what they are like, so let's transcribe some of them in order to get better insight into [for example] ornamentation." Transcription is used to solve specialized problems, and for this many kinds of techniques, mechanical and manual, have been developed, including notation based on a culture's own notation system, or simplifications such as solmization, or various sorts of graph arrangements. The point is that a transcription or notation system may be developed to solve a particular problem in the music of a specific culture.

One issue is the analysis of nonmetric music, in which rhythm and duration cannot adequately be represented by traditional note values. A possible approach is the presentation of notation in a time-space continuum, each line of music, for example, representing ten seconds (Nettl and Foltin 1972), or each inch one second of performance (Tsuge 1974). Touma (1968) provided two transcriptions of the same Arabic nonmetric material, a second-by-second notation using Western note values as approximations, and lines indicating length of notes within a framework of spaces representing seconds. The study of metrically precise materials may require other approaches. Koetting (1970), dealing with West African drumming, used a kind of graph notation that avoids reference to pitch but distinguishes types of strokes and sounds, and amounts of elapsed time between strokes, in what he calls a "time unit box system." A variety of graphs-notations appear in Reck's survey of world music (Reck 1977). Transcriptions that combine sound and video showing the relationship of performance and audience reaction have been presented by Qureshi (1986). These are just a few examples of the many devices for solving special problems outside the framework of Western notation; many more are listed in Ellingson (1992b: 142–44).

Melographic analysis, as well, has been used for the solution of special problems. One issue of the *UCLA Selected Reports* (vol. 2, no. 1, 1974), devoted entirely to melographic research, includes "Vibrato as Function of Modal Practice in Qur'an Chant," "Vocal Tones in Traditional Thai Music," and similar studies, each based on a small amount of music, as little as a few seconds, and in most cases the purpose is to analyze rather minute differences within or among pieces. The kinds of findings one may expect in this type of study are illustrated by those of Caton, on "The Vocal Ornament *Takiyah* in Persian Music" (1974: 46), which is "distinctly simpler in tone quality than the melody notes." Its loudness is determined by the accentuation of its syllable. It is more distinct from its melodic environment in folk music than in classical music and religious chant.

Although the value of such findings may depend, in the end, on the degree to which they are significant in the culture, one of the issues may be whether the kinds of distinctions that Caton draws can be heard by the human ear. There is the typical dilemma: If the distinctions can be made by the ear, why does one need the melograph? And if not, are we justified in assigning significance to them? Perhaps the melograph serves to draw our aural attention to certain musical events, or its contribution may be more in the realm of psychology, psycho-acoustics, and physiology than in the study of music in culture. This is not to cast doubt on the validity of the conclusions; rather, we have not always made clear to ourselves just what the role of melographic transcriptions may be.

Predicting in 1960 the ethnomusicology of 2000, one would perhaps have expected to find a much larger proportion of automatic transcription, acceptance of the push toward more detailed and more comprehensive transcriptional statements with the use of highly sophisticated techniques, and the relegation of aural transcription to an essentially educational role. This has not turned out to be the configuration of events. The value of aural transcription continues to be emphasized, while automatic transcription, along with various electronic measuring devices, has a more specialized niche. But new approaches to ethnomusicological fieldwork, particularly the emphasis on participant-observer methods involving performance, give human transcribers greater hope that they can provide transcriptions that reflect the insider's perception of the music, by depending on their firsthand authority as participants in the musical culture. But also, Western notation is being adopted by musical cultures throughout the world, modified to account for diversity, and it has become (e.g., in Iran) a reasonably adequate prescriptive system, and this is leading to a kind of vindication of Western notation for purposes of transcription.

And so, we are likely to see the continued use of Western notation and of the human transcriber, aided, but not replaced, by special techniques and technologies extending from variable speed controls and loop repeaters (Jairazbhoy and Balyoz 1977) to methods resulting from the development of computer technology (e.g., Fales 2002; A Schneider 2001). The concept of transcription has expanded in its combination with various analytical methods. Thus we will be faced on the one hand with transcriptions that give us only part of the musical picture, such as ornamentation, singing style, or melodic contour, but give it in enormous detail; we may, on the other extreme, having admitted that the Western concept of the note is equally an abstraction, now come to view abstractions such as formal schemes as particular kinds of transcription as well.

After about 1960, after a period of emphasis on the development of automatic transcription, scholars again began debating the value of aural transcription. Jairazbhoy (1977: 270), who worked hard in the 1970s to revive the UCLA melograph as a device of practical value, maintained, that for certain purposes "aural transcription by a trained ethnomusicologist . . . may be far more meaningful." The amount of transcribing and the role of transcription in the career of the typical ethnomusicologist have decreased, and now, with the coming of the digital age, the concept of transcription itself is in question. But still—at least this is my own perception—we need to maintain the skill of transcribing in the old-fashioned way, by ear, less maybe for formal research than to show ourselves that we comprehend recorded music. And for better or worse, as we continue significantly to deal with music in its visual form, transcription remains one of the few diagnostic techniques of the ethnomusicologist.

8

In the Speech Mode: Contemplating Repertories

In the Analysis Class

You have returned from the "field," and two months later (or after a few days, in the jet age) arrives a trunk full of audio tapes, or video tapes, or DVDs. Or maybe it came with you, but you let it sit while you reentered. You had been spending your time asking questions, recording performances day by day, maybe becoming an annoyance to your consultants and teachers. And now you're finally unpacking the central product of your work. You survey a rather vast pile of little boxes, make a quick count, and find that you have some 120 hours of music, some 750 separate songs and pieces and units of performance of some sort, and it dawns on you dramatically, perhaps for the first time, that one of your jobs will be to say in words and with symbols just what this music is like. You may feel that you have to transcribe it, but maybe that you must first work out a description for yourself; or you may say to yourself, "I'll just doggedly transcribe five pieces a day, and be done in five months." But eventually you will come face to face with one of our salient issues, how to analyze and finally describe, in words, synthetically, a large body of music.

It's a problem that has been faced, more or less in the way just described, by hundreds of scholars and graduate students, and in a more general sense by most musicologists. It would be presumptuous of me to propose a specific, generally applicable solution to these problems, and my purpose is not to survey and discuss all of the vast literature that speaks to them from an ethnomusicological perspective, something done comprehensively by Stephen

Blum (1992). My purpose here will be to select for comment a few of the major intellectual issues, referring selectively to a small portion of an immense body of literature.

We begin with reference to some familiar scenes—the interface between universal and culture-specific, between insider's and outsider's perspectives, between a comprehensive methodology and techniques that speak to special problems. Questions pop out at us from all directions. Can one establish a way of talking about music that will work for all imaginable musics? What is the difference between analysis and description? Should there be a single procedure for analyzing music, a sort of paradigm of ethnomusicology, or can one safely rely on the characteristics of each music to guide one, or on the way in which a society conceives of its own musical structure? Again, should ethnomusicologists be like scientists, able to produce replicable statements, or should analysis be much more a matter of personal interpretation? Can one scholar, in a reasonable amount of time, make a comprehensive yet synthetic description of a music, concisely stating everything worth saying? Or are we obliged to concentrate on those aspects of music that help us to answer a particular question? And is all this even necessary, or can't music speak for itself?

These are questions for scholars working with music—musical sound—alone, but they will be back, slightly modified, when we turn to the study of music in culture. They all in the end boil down to an issue identified long ago by Charles Seeger, repeatedly discussed by him, and again clarified in one of his last works (1977: 16–30). It is the problem of using language, or, as Seeger would put it, the "speech mode of communication," for discourse about music, seeing speech and music as related but distinct forms of communication. It's hard to imagine practical alternatives, but there is no doubt that the first and most general difficulty of analysis and description of music results from our need to integrate them with a way of thinking that is substantially conditioned by the characteristics of language and its particular way of using time.

Most teachers, and certainly most students, take all this for granted, and so while keeping Seeger's caution in mind, it's best to move to more everyday matters. Perhaps one can get some insight into the special nature of ethnomusicological analysis by studying its relationship to the way in which it was taught, and to the way in which the analysis of Western music was approached. Let me for a moment look back to 1950, my days of undergraduate study, when things were, as the cliché instructs us, very different. I'll reconstruct a day. I attended a class in fourth-semester music theory. We spent our time distinguishing German, French, and Italian sixth chords, and as I look back at the earlier semesters of theory classes, I realize that almost all of the time had been spent on chords, very little on melody and rhythm. Certainly this represents much of the training that American and European scholars experienced for another couple of decades. I then went to a class in "Analysis of Form," where we looked at broad outlines, finding highly abstracted general principles—the names of Heinrich Schenker and Paul Hindemith are prominent here—that could be shown to govern the genesis and development of a piece lasting twenty minutes.

Later I went to a class called (logically, for the terminology current in 1950) "Folk and Primitive Music," taught by Dr. Herzog, and listened to a Native American song. Our teacher took it apart, beginning with something called "scale," on which he spent much time; going on to something called "rhythm," with which we all had a hard time; then saying a few words about the (curious) way the singers used their voices; and finally attempting to divide the song into phrases and assigning to each a letter in order to show similarities and differences.

How very different were the approaches to Western and to Native American music in these classes! I ask myself whether they were due to differences among the musical systems, or whether they suggest that a society looks at its own and another music in fundamentally different ways. The concepts of analysis and description then most widely used in ethnomusicology would have appeared laughable if applied to Western art music, not because they were intrinsically inapplicable but because the purposes and the traditions of scholarship differed. It's hard, actually, to distinguish description and analysis in the context of this discussion, and the two terms often appear together. But conventionally, description should give an incontrovertible accounting of the object or event, while analysis provides interpretation of relationships that may not be obvious and may be quite specific to the analyst's approach. Speaking very broadly, music scholars dealing with music strange to them are more inclined to be descriptive, and those working in their own culture, analytical. In comparative study, however, one would expect the description and analysis of a concept called music to be based on a set of assumptions applicable to all music. But the approaches to analysis for Western and non-Western music actually have quite separate though interrelated histories. Quite beyond this, as Blum (1975b, and again 1992) has pointed out in detail, musicological analysis is itself a product of a particular social context and a special, culturally determined, set of values. A history of analytical thought in ethnomusicology can't possibly be attempted here, or by myself, but a few samples, milestones as it were, might provide a taste of this history.

Hornbostel's Paradigm and Herzog's Synthesis

The idea of establishing a single, universally applicable system was actually in the mainstream of ethnomusicological research throughout much of its history, but it declined in importance in the 1970s, and in the recent literature it exists only in vestige. The earliest history explains a lot about the issues with which we have lately been concerned.

In selecting for discussion the work of a few scholars who have made major contributions to this tradition, the logical figure with whom to begin is Erich M. von Hornbostel (sometimes publishing jointly with Otto Abraham) and some of his immediate followers. Through a long series of publications Hornbostel tried to deal with a large number of musical repertories, each sampled rather modestly (see, e.g., Abraham and Hornbostel 1903, 1906; Hornbostel 1906). Not having done the fieldwork and having little beyond a few cylinder recordings at his disposal, he perhaps perforce developed a way of dealing with all musics in essentially the same way, and this characteristic as well as the more specific traits of his method are evident in the work of some of his students and further even of their academic progeny.

Hornbostel has for decades been considered the "father" of ethnomusicology, but not until the 1980s, some fifty years after his death in 1936, did one see much in the way of analysis of and commentary on his work. By the early twenty-first century, however, a lot had been published (see Christensen in Nettl and Bohlman 1991; Klotz 1998), and his methods of analysis of music have been deconstructed (Blum 1992). To attempt a brief synthesis: What may strike the reader first is Hornbostel's great emphasis on the melodic aspects of the music, particularly on what he calls scales. Enumeration of tones, and the relationship of the tones to a not always thoroughly defined tonic, and, beyond that, the specific intervallic distances, are what he speaks to most frequently and immediately. Throughout his work there is evidence of a feeling of urgency to uncover a theoretical framework that, while often unarticulated, must surely exist in each culture for the creation of melodic material. Thus Abraham and Hornbostel's study of songs of the Thompson River Indians (1906) has a detailed accounting of numbers of pentatonic, tetratonic, and tritonic scales, an attempt to indicate frequency of intervals calculated to quarter tones, and indications of relative emphasis on different tones in order to establish a hierarchically defined tonality. The same is true in the study of Tunisian melodies (1906), while the short article on the music of "Neu-Mecklenburg" by Hornbostel (1907) is devoted almost entirely to scalar matters. The distinction between *Materialleiter* (vocabulary of tones and intervals on which a composer may draw) and *Gebrauchsleiter* (the tones used in a particular piece) illustrates his theoretical thinking (Hornbostel 1912).

While the scale of each song is calculated and weighted, and statistical methods are brought in for comparative purposes, other aspects of the melodic process are characterized more briefly and generalized. The same is true of rhythm, which is handled largely as a function of meter (although general statements about the relationship of components such as the vocal and drum rhythm are found); and of vocal style, which is briefly and informally characterized; and of form, which, too, is the subject of generalization, although Hornbostel occasionally divided musical material into sections whose interrelationship is schematically indicated.

This characterization of Hornbostel's technique of analysis may not be quite fair, for in individual cases he often went a good deal further. He was typically working in terra incognita and no doubt casting about for adequate ways of establishing a generally applicable method, and his publications are usually uncommonly insightful. Yet there remains the curious emphasis on the difficult scalar characteristics, outweighing all else, while rhythm (easier to perceive, I admit, though hard to describe) and overall formal organization would be perhaps the elements easiest to understand. A likely reason for this emphasis is the way in which the educated Western listener who focuses on the classical tradition thinks—thought—of music. The Western musician from the late nineteenth century into the middle of the twentieth was simply more interested in melody, in intervals, than in form and rhythm. Theory books and music dictionaries tilt heavily in that direction. The classic seminal publication of ethnomusicology, A. J. Ellis's relativistic statement about the coexistence of many musical scales (1885), established the primacy of melodic considerations in the early history of the field. Western classical musical thinking places harmony, melody, and scale first. My fellow-students and I, around 1950, were always first struck by the strangeness or similarity of non-Western tone systems in relation to our own. So Hornbostel's emphasis on scale probably came about through his own cultural background. This particular aspect of his approach—the tendency to deal statistically with scales and more generally with other components of music—became for a long time a paradigm of analysis. Hornbostel's own students refined but followed it, and those not directly associated with him, from Frances Densmore to Alan Merriam, were obviously heavily influenced by it. And the emphasis on scale continued into later time, as seen in McLean's (1971) analysis of 651 Maori scales, and continued into the work of theorists such as Jay Rahn (1983).

Hornbostel led the way in contemplating music as sound in many ways, but perhaps most important, he tried to apply his approach—which changed with the size of the corpus and the progressive stages in his thinking—to a variety of musics so large that one might well regard it as a sampling of world music.

George Herzog modified Hornbostel's standardized method, adding to it elements from Bartók's approach to form and bringing to bear his anthropological field experience, synthesizing several streams. Clearly his work grows out of Hornbostel's, but certain subtle shifts are evident. While recognizing the variety of the world's music, Herzog, like his teacher, tried to approach a number of musical styles—Native American, Oceanian, European folk music—in essentially the same way. But he made it evident to me that he regarded this standardized approach—the limited sample being almost a necessary evil—as something to do in the absence of a larger corpus, a native theory, a field method with which one could develop something more sophisticated. He saw the method that he taught and often used as an initial foray.

In his study of the music of the Yuman tribes (1928) Herzog followed Hornbostel in analyzing each song individually, more systematically and thoroughly in fact, but devoting himself mainly to scale and overall form. In his general analytical discussion he devotes equal space to "manner of singing," interestingly placed first in his order; to tonality and melody; to rhythm, accompaniment, and form. The discussion of melody is generalized, less dependent on a statistical approach to scale than is Hornbostel's. The detailed discussion of the formal principles, particularly the description of the "rise" form of the Yuman peoples in its various manifestations, heralds a gradually increasing emphasis on the ways composers work, as they move from phrase to phrase. While Hornbostel had worked mainly toward establishing the composer's basic musical vocabulary, he showed how this vocabulary was handled over a span of musical time.

Herzog's dissertation (1936a) comparing Pueblo and Pima music follows the same approach but also establishes song "types" within a repertory, subsystems of the total musical language. One thus no longer spoke only of "Pima music" or "Jabo music" but of the different kinds of music a society maintained for itself. He did not overtly theorize about a typical repertory structure, as suggested in chapter 6, but he was aware that such a structure exists.

Herzog did less than Hornbostel with statistics, perhaps a result of his broad field experience (which Hornbostel lacked), which showed musical culture to be more fluid than rigorously quantified statements suggest. Correspondingly, his treatment of the Ghost Dance songs in another major study, a landmark in ethnohistorical research (1935a), with material recorded by others and with a closed corpus—the Ghost Dance songs having been largely abandoned by the time he came to study them—is more statistically oriented.

Herzog's technique of presentation—an individual analysis of each song or piece together with a statistical survey—became something of a standard. Alan Merriam, in his thorough account of Flathead music (1967a) used tabular form and gave more detail in doing essentially what Herzog had also done. In one of the exemplary studies of European folk song, Jan Philip Schinhan (1957), editing Anglo-American songs, gave information about the tonality and structure of each song and, in an appendix, a statement of each scale with precise frequency of tones, in addition to tabular information on many aspects of style for the repertory as a whole and for subdivisions.

Grand Schemes for Comparison: Kolinksi, Lomax, Herndon

Herzog's approach contrasts interestingly with that of Mieczyslaw Kolinski, a fellow-student of his under Hornbostel. Kolinski tried to be considerably more rigorous and established frameworks for the classification of the musics of the world. In his work the issues of analysis and comparison overlap greatly. Hornbostel and Herzog were faced with musics, one at a time, that would be described in similar terms; for Kolinski, the job became to establish a classificatory system of analysis, or rather a network of systems, providing niches into which songs and then musics would be placed. In retrospect, this was a valiant attempt at developing a universally usable methodology, which, however, found few takers.

In 1978, after having published many articles that together comprise his system, Kolinski wrote that "only when recognizing both the extent of the sociocultural diversification and the nature of the psycho-physically rooted constraint, and only when utilizing methods of analysis developed through a cognition of these two vital factors, will one be able to approach objectively, comprehensively, and meaningfully the structure of the music of the world's peoples" (1978: 242). This statement reconciles Kolinski's understanding of musical diversity with his insistence that it can nevertheless be subjected to comparison through a single classificatory system, a system reflecting and determined by the outer limits of and range of possibilities within the mentioned constraints. And it also exhibits his interest in the *comprehensive* approach to the world's music. The article from which it is taken follows his publication of a number of articles dealing with the analysis of various components of music: melodic movement (1956, 1965a and b), tempo (1959), harmony (1962), scale (1961), and rhythm (1973). In most of these publications Kolinski states possibilities or options of which musicians and entire musical cultures may take advantage, and gives examples of how these options may have actually been used. Together they constitute a grand scheme for describing and comparing musics of the world.

In his "Classification of Tonal Structures" Kolinski established a series of 348 types of scalar and modal arrangements in accordance with number of tones and their interrelationships (1961: 39–41). The scheme has some problems, not accounting for intervals that are incompatible with the chromatic scale, but it is a highly comprehensive system for such classification. To show its usefulness for comparative study, Kolinski tabulated the presence or absence but not the frequency of each of the 348 types among five repertories—Teton Sioux, Papago, Suriname, Dahomey, and English-Appalachian. Similarly, a number of melody types become a system within which one can plot the distribution of materials in actual repertories (Kolinski 1956).

Kolinski's principal area of concern, the "translatability" of cultures, is particularly evident in his scheme for comparing tempos (1959), criticized by Christensen (1960), which he defines as the average number of notes per minute, without regard to the concept of beats or culturally perceived speed. His most ambitious scheme involves the analysis of melodic movement. In the final version of his study of this musical element (Kolinski 1965b) he provides a complex classification of melodic structures using a number of criteria: degree of recurrence of a motif; dominant, initial, and final direction of movement; and concepts taken from visual representation such as "standing, hanging, tangential, overlapping, distant, and including." Kolinski's approaches were not widely followed and his methods rarely developed further, but in the area of melodic movement he had a successor, Charles Adams (1976), who provided a yet more intricate system.

It is interesting to see that, like Hornbostel and Herzog, and like typical Western music theorists, Kolinski is much more tentative when dealing with rhythm than with melodic phenomena. In his major publication on this subject (1973) he develops broad categories—isometric and heterometric, that is, with tendency to have measures of equal or unequal length; superimposed on this are the concepts of "commetric" and "contrametric," which involve the degree to which audible accents support or contradict a preconceived metric structure.

Incidentally, early ethnomusicologists took good care of melody and of systems of pitches, but their work—and this includes Hornbostel and Herzog—with the configurations, in space and time, of pitches heard simultaneously was less systematic. Harmony is the hallmark of Western music to both Westerners and others, but ethnomusicologists have often been cavalier in their treatment of this musical element, sometimes going no further than using the term "polyphony" to indicate any music in which one hears more than one pitch at a time, and using as subdivisions such concepts as harmony (emphasis on the relationship of simultaneous pitches), counterpoint (emphasis on the melodic progress of the voices or instruments performing together), and heterophony (simultaneous variations of the same melody). Among the early authors who tried to develop a universal framework for analysis, Kolinski (1962) proposed a system for dealing with consonance and dissonance; M. Schneider (1934) compared musics in accordance with the degree to which the various voices use the same tonality; and Malm (1972) suggested adopting the concepts of homophony, heterophony, and disphony to indicate various kinds of relationship among voices. But a more or less generally accepted set of concepts analogous to those in the realm of scale, about which one can at least argue, has not appeared for this element of music—an element for which I can't even find a proper term!

Kolinski's work shows a belief that the possibilities of musical creation are limited and can be divided into classes, and that one way of describing the world's musics is to find for each the appropriate classificatory niche, not necessarily related to a class as perceived by the owners of the music. He was surely aware of the importance of studying each culture on its own terms, but found it necessary to short-circuit this approach in the interest of comparison, doing so on the basis of evidence from perceptual and Gestalt psychology (1978: 230, 235–39).

A second grand scheme, as controversial as Kolinski's but more influential, is the method established by Alan Lomax broadly known as cantometrics—although it consists of a number of separable subsystems. By its nature it would appear almost to be an outgrowth of certain aspects of Kolinski's work, but as a matter of fact Lomax makes little mention of Kolinski in his publications (see Lomax 1959, 1962, 1968, 1976). His agenda was to show that musical style correlated with culture type, but it is possible to separate out, as a distinct contribution, his system of musical analysis, developed for defining musical styles and their boundaries. The purpose of cantometrics is simply "to provide descriptive techniques for the speedy characterization and classification" of musical style (Lomax 1968: 8). Lomax provided a diagram that can be produced on a single page and on which the characterization, or profile, of a music is given, the result, of course, of a complex procedure. With musical sound divided into thirty-seven parameters, any musical piece can be rated as to the presence, strength, or force of each of these parameters. Averages of the pieces in a repertory can then be established, giving a characterization for each music.

Cantometrics has for decades been severely taken to task for many shortcomings. The parameters are unevenly distributed; some are clearly single components that are readily measured, but others are really groups of components not easily distinguished. "Range," the distance between highest and lowest tone, and "register" or tessitura are in the former category. "Rasp," an extraneous noise that obscures the clear articulation of pitch, or "basic musical organization of the voice part" are harder to define. Recordings are not equally applicable to the method. For example, the analyst is expected to determine how loudly a singer is singing, which cannot be determined from a record and which a singer is likely to vary with the presence or absence of a microphone. Criticisms of this sort could be applied to a good many of the parameters.

In order to carry out cantometric analysis, one must undergo special training. But despite an elaborate set of training tapes that Lomax published in order to allow students outside his own staff to learn the method (1976), I have found it difficult to achieve agreement on the ratings from a homogeneous group of fairly experienced students. Beyond this, Lomax's implied belief that a folk culture normally produces a homogeneous musical style that can be deduced from a small sample turns out to be untenable (Henry 1976).

But the cantometrics system deserves credit for having moved vigorously in a direction previously uncharted: the description of singing style and of the nature of musical sound in general, things in the realm of what is usually called "performance practice"—vocal width or tension, glissando, glottal shake, tremulo, rasp, volume, pitch level, vocal blend, degree of accentuation of stressed tones. Lomax's work has not been carried further by many scholars, but attention to singing style has grown since the invention of several melographic devices, carried forward particularly by scholars working in Vienna (see Födermayr 1971) and at UCLA (see the special issue of *Selected Reports in Ethnomusicology*, vol. 2, no. 1, 1974). It continues to play a role as advanced technology provides greater sophistication (see bibliography in Fales 2002).

The approaches I have briefly described are a kind of mainstream of the history of ethnomusicology, but by no means are they the only ones that have been followed. They are, as it were, music-specific, deriving from Western thinking about music, from the history of Western music theory, and they claim to apply equally to all musics. But there are also some systems of analysis that approach music—and all music is again implied—from the viewpoint of other disciplines, particularly semiotics and linguistics, touched on in chapter 22 (see, e.g., Boiles 1967, 1973b; Chenoweth and Bee 1971; Nattiez 1971, 1975; Turino 1999). And of course there are the culture-specific approaches, based on the theories and perceptions of the individual societies.

Given that there are many different approaches to analysis, do they really tell us different things? Marcia Herndon, in a significant article entitled "Analysis: The Herding of Sacred Cows," tried to find out. As an introduction to the presentation of a new method of her own, Herndon (1974) analyzed and/or described one piece of music, a song from Madagascar, providing eight separate renditions, each based on the method given in a major text or study (some mentioned above). Herndon may have misinterpreted and in some cases parodied the approaches taken by various earlier scholars. But she provided the first attempt to compare analytical models by applying each to the same piece of music. The analyses compared by Herndon look different on the surface, but they didn't really tell different things about the song. The kinds of things that we still continue to find significant about most of the world's music from methods supporting comparative study are the insights that we can, more or less, establish rather quickly through listening. Trying out the procedures that the likes of Hornbostel, Herzog, Kolinski, and Lomax have developed often seems to confirm what is already evident from hearing.

It is all rather frustrating. We can trace our problems to the antithesis between attempts to provide universally applicable analytical models and the longstanding realization that music is not a universal language but a group of related or unrelated systems. The obvious alternative to universal systems is to analyze and describe each music in terms that are applicable to it alone. There seem to be three distinct avenues. (1) Most obviously: We derive an analysis of a music from the discourse—informal discussion, formal theory—of its own society, from the way a people appears to perceive, classify, and conceptualize its music. In many cases, the society has a standardized way of analyzing its own music. I'll look at this in the next section. (2) Our analysis could also concentrate on those features of the music that appear to the analyst to be particularly significant or interesting; thus the analysis satisfies the criterion that it should give the analysts and their readers fresh insights. (3) We establish a method especially for the solution of a specific problem derived from historical, anthropological, or psychological inquiry. These three approaches are not unrelated to those described in chapter 7 on transcription.

But after all this discussion, we ought to be asking, at least rhetorically, why we should describe and analyze music in the first place. Presumably in order to be able to talk and write about it. But here is the crux of the issue about which Charles Seeger so frequently regaled and even harangued his colleagues. We continue asking whether one can really talk about music, whether one must find a meta-language to do so, and whether in the end it is all not related to our tendency to want visual representation—notation, description, play-by-play accounting—of music (and of everything else that is not already speech). It is interesting, therefore, that Seeger himself, despite misgivings about dealing with music in the "speech mode," was also one of the first to write comprehensively on the methodology of describing a music (1953a).

Listen to the Insider

If we lay aside the comparative perspective that allows us to look at all musics the same way but try instead to follow the way the society that produced the music analyzes or presents it, it stands to reason that we are likely to come closer to perceiving how members of that society hear their music. It's a view that was strongly articulated in the early 1970s by such scholars as Blacking (e.g., 1970) and Danielou (1966), who insisted that such an approach is the only one that makes sense, and some thirty years later, it has become the norm. By the 1990s, determining the discourse—how people talked and maybe debated about their music—had become one of the primary tasks of ethnomusicologists in the field. For cultures with a detailed, articulated theory such as India or Japan, this is an obvious strategy, but for others such as the Native American culture it may help to find formulations of a music theory from texts of some sort (see Haefer 1981). But while it was once believed that the musical cultures of indigenous or nonliterate peoples were characterized by the absence of articulated music theory (but may have had what Browner 2000: 10 terms "unconscious theory"), it has become increasingly evident that this assumption was actually quite off the mark. Among the earlier landmark publications that show this are Zemp's (1979) analysis of the music terminology and typology of the 'Are'are of the Solomon Islands and William Powers's (1980) study of Oglala musical terminology. More recent studies that try to present an indigenous theory for analyzing music include those of Charry (2000) for the West African Mande and Browner (2000) for the northern Plains powwow style.

Since 1980, ethnomusicologists have usually explained a musical system in the terms in which it was presented to them by their teachers in the field. Not a simple matter either. Given that each culture has a kind of music theory, a way of thinking about the technicalities of music, in most societies people do not talk much in those terms. And when analytical statements are made, there is not always much of a consensus. For example, when asking various musicians in Iran to analyze one performance on record, I found divergence on not only the details ("Is he now playing this, or is it still that?") but also on the approaches ("Should one be looking for these components of music, or should we rather talk about those?"). This will be no news to the American and European music theorist; it might in fact always make more sense to describe a musical culture in terms of what people in it argue about than on what there is agreement. But let's look first for agreement.

We could be content simply to report, to describe music precisely as the culture does, or would; alternatively, we could use the culture's own approach to go further, establishing a new system of description that is nevertheless derived from and continues to be compatible with what would be done by the native experts. The second is riskier but may contribute more. Let me explain what I mean by giving a somewhat simple-minded example from my own time in Iran. Iranian musicians taught the *radif,* the body of music that is memorized and then used as the basis for improvisation and composition (see Zonis 1973: 69–92, During, Miradelbaghi, and Safvat 1991, and Nettl 1978b or 1992 for detailed description). They labeled its sections (*dastgahs*) and their subdivisions (*gushehs*) clearly, although there was some disagreement on terminology and in determining which *gushehs* properly belong in a particular *dastgah,* and although there was much overlapping in this complex set of materials. Musicians then were willing to analyze certain performances, dividing them into sections, and stating upon which section of the *radif* each of them, in the improvised performance, is based. An ethnomusicologist who has studied with Iranian musicians can analyze such sectioned performances in this way but can't be sure, on account of the lack of complete consensus, that the analysis will be accepted by every Persian master. This is the kind of analysis in which the ethnomusicologist does what the musicians of the culture do.

But one could also go further. There are, for example, performances or sections that masters of the *radif* are not willing to analyze in this fashion, giving their equivalent of "he's just improvising here." They may say about such a performance that the musician does not know the *radif*; he is purposely and expertly mixing materials from several sources; he is simply playing *avaz* (nonmetric improvisation) in a *dastgah* in general, not taking account of the differences among the subdivisions of the dastgah that the *radif* provides. The first approach mentioned here would simply report these anomalies, and perhaps point out the difference between the carefully sectioned and the other performances and refer to the fact that it seems to be readily recognized by Iranians. The second approach would take these unsectioned performances and, with the use of motivic analysis, determine almost moment by moment on which part of the *radif* each short bit of performance is based. Instead of just accepting the statement that a particular five-minute segment is simply "*avaz* of the *dastgah* of *Shur*," one could show that it is comprised of materials from three *gushehs* (e.g., *salmak, golriz,* and *shahnaz*) and makes fleeting reference to three other *gushehs*. Now, certain Persian musicians, when confronted with analysis of this sort, pronounced it correct but found the information only mildly interesting, and not really particularly relevant. It seemed that I had tried to take their way of looking at their own music further, and had managed to avoid violating their way of approaching the analysis, but I had gone beyond where they were inclined to go, had divided their concepts into units smaller than those they were willing to use. I had gained some insights into how the music is put together; on the other hand, I could no longer claim simply to be presenting the system as it presents itself.

Blacking's study of Venda children's songs (1967) likewise used a society's own musical perception to construct a description that goes beyond the culture's own way of describing itself, showing the materials within the adult repertory upon which the children's songs are based, something the Venda know but were not inclined to articulate. He dealt with the music on the Venda's own terms but does things the Venda themselves would not do, but that are compatible with Venda ways of thinking, and that he would not do in the same way if he had been dealing with another repertory and another culture. T. Viswanathan (1977), a famous performer of Carnatic music who also worked as a Western-trained ethnomusicologist, made a detailed study of ways in which Indian musicians performed one raga, asking each to perform improvised raga alapana especially for him. His analysis of the individual performances used the concepts and terms of Carnatic music, but the idea of eliciting performances and the statistical way of making comparisons came from his ethnomusicological arsenal of methods.

We can find similarities in the history of analysis in the Western music tradition. Thus, the highly influential Schenkerian system is essentially based on classical and early nineteenth-century German and Austrian music and does not work as well, at least without considerable modification, for other kinds. It uses the general conceptual framework of the musicians of that period and the way it is interpreted by later musicians who regard themselves as part of this tradition. But it also goes further, showing within this framework what its practitioners—the nineteenth-century composers—might accept but would not do on their own, and would likely consider only mildly interesting or even irrelevant.

Combining Three Perspectives: Maqam Nahawand and the Songs of Ishi

The professor of analysis asked, "What is it that strikes you about this piece?" For Wagner, it would have to be the harmony. For Ives, maybe the way familiar tunes were buried in the dissonance. For Béla Bartók (1931), one thing that was significant in Hungarian folk music was the configuration of cadential tones, the ending tones of the (often four) lines of a song, in relation to a tonic. By contrast to Bartók, the transcriptions of Anglo-American folk ballads published by Sharp (1932), Bronson (1959–72), and Schinhan (1957) were accompanied by descriptions, for each song, of scale and mode. Bartók also had interest in the relationship of lines ("form" or "structure"), but the students of Anglo-American folk song cited paid little attention to this, or for that matter to rhythm, which Bartók studied mainly in relation to the rhythmic patterns of the poems. The literature of ethnomusicology is full of discussions of music that focus on what somehow seems salient or significant or interesting to the author. Why analyze Hungarian and English folk songs so differently? Both are European, monophonic, largely pentatonic, have a lot in common. It must have something to do with the analyst's agenda.

Now, we can hardly debate whether there is something inherently interesting about Anglo-American modes and uninteresting in the overall form of these songs. But there is probably a reason, beyond the general Western preoccupation with pitch, for Sharp's, Bronson's, and Schinhan's attention to scales and modes. The search for a connection between folk music and medieval music, particularly chant, was long a major focus of folk song scholarship—maybe on the assumption that, once established, the relationship would help to legitimize folk song research, and to document the age of folk music. What was known about medieval music in Sharp's time was substantially in the domain of the melodic, and the medieval classification system of rhythm also began with the concept of "modes." It would have seemed appropriate to do the same with folk music.

Bartók's interest was less the relationship to medieval Western liturgical or art music and more to establish a group of types or strata that could then be placed in a hypothetical historical sequence, for reconstructing history, including the comparison of Hungarian folk music with that of other Finno-Ugric peoples to which it may be historically tied, and to other folk musics in southeastern Europe; and finally also to find a way of placing various melodies in some kind of musically logical order in a large collection. And Bartók was evidently struck by the usefulness of certain parameters—form, cadential tone configurations, rhythmic types—for accomplishing this. Walter Wiora too, in a limited illustrative anthology (1953) of European folk songs aiming at a demonstration of the unity of European folk music, emphasized melodic contours that, to him, suggested the ultimate genetic relationship of tunes found in various parts of Europe.

In each of these cases it seems that the scholars whose work I have used as examples were struck and attracted by a particular feature of the music with which they were concerned. Their analytical statements made no attempts to say everything about their musics, or to find a way of looking at the music that would also necessarily be applicable to other musics. Their approaches, therefore, are a combination of personal predilections and of the characteristics of the music in relation to their own musical and musicological backgrounds. This method, which seems to place excessive emphasis on the personal reactions of an individual scholar, is not one specifically and systematically espoused in the ethnomusicological literature, yet it is present in a lot of publications. It is one corner of a triangle: a personal approach, based on the culture's perception, the analyst's agenda, and the distinctive characteristics of the music.

The most recent publications in ethnomusicology in which analysis of musical style is emphasized actually show the expansion of this triangle. Universal systems such as those of Kolinski and Lomax may have occasional uses applied to broad problems, but they are going out of use. Instead, it has been necessary (for our field as a whole) to devote considerable energy to each of a group of problems, culture-specific and specialized, and to find, for each, an analytical procedure that satisfies the need. For example, most of what we have learned about the classical music of India is based on the ways in which Indian musicians and traditional music scholars lay out the musical system. The notion that each music is a stylistically compact system has turned out to be dangerous. For example, the supposition that Indonesian gamelan tunings are standardized because they are arrived at with great precision was refuted by Kunst, who found that of forty-six measured slendro scales, none were identical, but that Javanese musicians recognized many kinds of slendro scales (Ellingson 1992b: 138).

The history of ethnomusicological analysis has moved in gingerly fashion and very gradually from universalist or "etic" to "emic," and to problem-specific approaches, and, as suggested in the discussion of the Iranian project above, it has also moved to combinations of the three. Let me illustrate with two personal experiences: In each case, I'll try to explain what was done, although at the time the nature of the methodology wasn't really clear to me. For the first (Nettl and Riddle 1974), the corpus of material to be analyzed was a group of sixteen recordings of Arab music, all improvisatory *taqsims* in the *maqam Nahawand*. (*Taqsim* is a major genre of Arabic solo music, largely nonmetric and consisting of several sections.) These were played in especially elicited performances on the bouzouq and nei by the distinguished Lebanese American musician Jihad Racy in 1970. The purpose was to determine in what respects these sixteen improvisations were similar and how they differed; and to ascertain the range of options and differences, finding out what is typical or exceptional, what is rare or evidently forbidden, or what is ubiquitous or required. Riddle and I drew no conclusion about the same musician's performance of other maqams, or at other times in his life, or about other Arabic musicians. Transcribing and then using a general comparative approach in analysis, we found that Racy did more or less the same thing in his treatment of ornamentation and rhythm in all of the *taqsims*. Because of their ubiquity, these parameters to a large degree determine the style and should, for other purposes, be dealt with in great detail, but not for my particular purpose, which was to find the extent and distribution of elements whereby the performances differ.

It then seemed logical to divide the pieces into sections marked by pauses, a decision supported by the fact that *taqsim* means something like "division." And indeed, the way in which the performances were most readily distinguished was by length, number, and temporal relationships of the sections. Along these lines, it was possible to distinguish three types of structure: (1) The *taqsim* consists of a number of minuscule or short sections followed by a single long one. (2) It is comprised of more or less regular alternation of a short section with one of medium or great length. (3) After an initial long section, it consists of a small group of short sections followed by one of medium length, and this sequence is repeated. This finding is the result of following the "What is it that strikes you?" approach.

We also asked Jihad Racy to analyze and comment on the performances, following the "What is it that the culture—that is, the performer—regards as significant for solving your problem?" approach. What Racy stressed most verbally turned out to be the practice of modulating within a *taqsim*, from the basic *maqam* to secondary ones, and to return, periodically and at the end, to the original. But how was this practice of modulation consistent or variable? There were patterns but no clear typology, and a rather common kind of distribution: one taqsim modulated to no secondary maqam, two each modulated to only one, or to five; five performances modulated to two secondary maqams, and three each to three and four—something like a bell-shaped curve. A similar distribution was found for the total length of the performances and for the number of sections. This was, then, not a comprehensive description of a corpus of music. Rather, it was in accordance with the desire to solve a specific problem that we analyzed certain parameters with care and neglected others. (See Racy 2003 for further elaboration of these issues.)

My second illustration, following a somewhat similar approach, concerns the structure of the repertory of Ishi, a man once referred to in newspapers as the "last wild Indian," and in fact the last living member of the Yahi, a tribe that had been totally eliminated in the nineteenth century in the course of its attempts to cope with the incursions of white ranchers and settlers. Discovered in California in 1911 (T. Kroeber 1961), Ishi did what he could to show anthropologists A. L. Kroeber and T. T. Waterman the details of his culture, and this included singing all of the songs he could recall. Studying the recordings fifty years later (Nettl 1965), I had the help of no living consultant. My job was to identify the general character of the repertory and of its mainstream, its relationship to other Native American repertories, and to determine what general principles of composition could be specified. It was impossible to learn about the culture's own way of looking at musical structure, except to note that Ishi identified songs (as do many Native American peoples) by their overt use or context, labeling them as gambling songs, doctor's songs, sweat house songs, and so on, and to determine that there was evidently some considerable correlation of songs defined by function or use with types established through my outsider's analysis.

The typical first reaction to these songs is that they seem incredibly simple and alike; but closer examination shows a complex interrelationship of various parameters of music and give us a rather complex picture of this very limited body of material. It turns out that even the world's simplest musics are really complicated and ingeniously structured organisms. But leaving aside now the many interesting things one should say about Ishi and his songs, let me try to explain retrospectively how my procedure fits into the confluence of the three approaches. First, using techniques derived from the work of Hornbostel and Herzog, came a generalized description of each song (i.e. scale, form, general rhythmic structure, singing style). The singing style was hardest to pin down because of the age and quality of the recordings, but we can say at least that it appeared to be the same throughout the recordings. The rhythmic system in terms of beats, tempo, and meter was hard to categorize and not susceptible to dividing into classes or types, but however hard to define, is more or less the same throughout the repertory. A system of scales could be more easily derived. The tone material of the individual songs varied from two to five tones, with intervals extending from major thirds to minor seconds. Three tones seem to be the scalar norm for a song. There is a variety of forms, but songs are extremely short and consist of from two to four sections. These are the *kinds* of statements that would have been made by Herzog (1928, 1936a), for a broad comparative perspective, though of course he went further.

But once this general description is done, we would proceed to a second approach, finding a special method to shed light on a particular problem, which is, for my purposes here, the identification of musical types: a mainstream and minor styles. It turns out that scales and forms, which vary considerably but lend themselves to grouping and typology of their identities as well as their interrelationships, are the most useful for establishing mainstream-sidestream distribution, as well as characterizing Yahi music in relationship to other indigenous styles. It is here that the problem determined the analytical method. Having found that form, in some way, is significant for solution of the problem, we had to decide what parameters to use to describe the form of the various songs, and the formal system as a whole. On first blush, there are only short stanzas (four to seven seconds), repeated many times. Dividing one stanza into its major subdivisions, we usually find two halves (some of unequal size); proceeding further, we find a total of four or five subdivisions, which in turn can frequently be grouped into two. It is the interrelationship of the smallest subdivisions that determines the general relationship of the halves, and examining this, we realize that the main structural principle of most of Ishi's songs is the statement of a musical idea that is repeated once, with some kind of variation. Interestingly, the second, varied phrase may relate to the first in a number of ways, including expansion, contraction, inversion, extension, internal repetition, substitution of one pitch for another in cadential position, and so on. Now, this dominant form type correlates roughly with the tritonic, and this is the mainstream style. Then there are a few other "minority" form types that correlate somewhat with the scales of more than three tones, and that are based upon formal principles also found in other Native American cultures. But attempts to match these correlations with rhythmic and other parameters do not yield what appears to be significant results or insights. It is interesting to see that Ishi's major form type makes use, in a kind of microcosm, of the general principle that also dominates the forms of Indian songs in other areas of North America, particularly the Plains and the eastern Pueblos, a form type in which a group of phrases is partially (and often with variation) repeated: for example, AABCD BCD, although what this may mean is not clear and not actually at issue for the moment.

We come to the third branch of our attempt at a synthetic method, Ishi's own analytical view. From what we know of other peoples with extremely short songs, we might guess that Ishi's people would also not have articulated a theory or given verbal information on these forms. In any case, we can do no more than to cite his classing of songs by use. But taking a comparative perspective can be suggestive. In my experience, some Blackfoot singers don't regard their songs as being basically in two unequal sections but describe the form as consisting of two pairs of sections, the above-cited arrangement then interpreted as A A BCD BCD. Similarly, Hatton (1988: 80) suggests that for Gros Ventre culture, describing the song form as consisting of announcement, thought, and closure is appropriate. Comparing these repertories on the basis of the cultures' own approaches would not by itself have yielded insight into the relationship of the form types, though it would tell us something about the way societies relate their music theory to the specifics of their cultural values. On the other hand, adhering to a single universal method such as Kolinski's or Lomax's, without elaboration, would not have gone far enough to solve the particular problem of the relationship of the mainstream of Ishi's songs to Plains and Pueblo styles. To have followed the traditional approach of "what strikes the listener" as giving general insight into the music would probably have led one to attempts to measure the sizes of intervals, or in any of a number of other directions, but perhaps only by chance to the detailed examination of forms. From a combination of the three approaches, however, a way of attacking one particular problem posed by this repertory emerged.

There is not much agreement among ethnomusicologists on standardized methods for describing musical styles, and the result is largely recourse to each culture's own cognitive system—probably best for most purposes in any case. The increased interest on the part of theorists (e.g., Agawu 1995a;

Rahn 1996; Temperley 2000; Tenzer 2000) suggests, however, that what the likes of Kolinski and Lomax tried to do before 1970 may be revived in more modern guise. The desire to avoid ethnocentrism, always a feature of ethnomusicology, has been intensified and sharpened. The tensions between universal, culture-specific, and problem-specific analysis may be resolved by the development of a synthetic method drawing on all three. In this way we may yet succeed in getting true insight into music in the speech mode.

9

The Most Indefatigable Tourists of the World: Tunes and Their Relationships

The "Top of Old Smoky" Effect

It may seem pretty obvious, but it's worth pointing out: In the world of music, one ordinarily does not just sing, or play an instrument; in order for musical behavior to result in what may properly be considered music. One must ordinarily be singing or playing something, some unit of musical conceptualization that is somehow identified, but may change when it moves in space and time. We usually call such units "songs" or "pieces." Some of them behave as if they had lives of their own, moving across national boundaries, rivers, mountain ranges, oceans, across language and culture areas, stimulating one of their earliest observers, Wilhelm Tappert (1890: 5), to nominate them as "the most indefatigable tourists of the earth." As they move, they usually change, but not beyond recognition, retaining their integrity, and this justifies their existence as units in musicological conceptualization, however their culture may interpret them. The nature of this unit of musical thought, the "something" that is performed, and just how it is distinguished from its fellows, is a kind of counterpart to the study of music; and like other major issues, it concerns the interface between general and culture-specific, between the cultural outsider's and insider's perceptions.

In identifying a culture's units of musical thought, ethnomusicologists and music historians face different problems. To music historians and the Western academic musicians, there is little controversy upon what constitutes a unit of music in the Western classical system; it is something we call "the piece," and it usually has a name (distinctive, as in *Parsifal,* or more general, as in "Symphony no. 7 in A major, Opus 92") that is further associated with a composer. There's agreement even when a piece (such as *Don Giovanni*) can actually be regarded as a group of units, because all concerned—composer, performers, scholars, the audience—regard these short, separate pieces as belonging together. The practice of using opus numbers, practically but also literally dividing the music of a composer into distinct works, supports the interpretation. In popular music, too, the repertory is organized along such lines, with names of pieces based on the verbal text and the work associated not so much with a composer but more often with a performer or group. The system of copyright and the philosophy of intellectual property—you can copyright a song, even a theme, but not a sequence of three chords—is based on this concept of units.

Lacking a single model, we try, for any society, to use the local system. But in contemplating songs or pieces that cross cultural boundaries, we often resort to practices and paradigms developed in the study of European folk music, to whose special significance in the evolution of ethnomusicological method this chapter pays homage. The most standard conceptualization of folk music as music in oral tradition is derived in large measure from a different idea than the "opus 17" model of what constitutes a piece. A "song" is actually the group of tunes derived from one original that, like the opus of classical music, theoretically represents a single, if complex, creative act. In the simplest illustration, a person composes a song and teaches it to others who go on to change it, and eventually it is altered by innumerable singers, all possibly singing (or believing that they are singing) the same song in different ways. They create what is known as versions and variants, all of which, taken together, at least in the abstract, may be designated as a single, isolated tune family. In a certain sense the variants are all simply performances of the same song, just as all of the performances of Beethoven's *Waldstein* Sonata, however different in interpretation and conception, are versions of the same piece. The difference among all the tunes in a folk tune family is greater than that found among the Beethoven performances, but perhaps this difference is one only of degree, and in any case, we need at some point to take into account the way a society classifies its tune material, whether it recognizes these relationships, and if so, what kinds.

But let's agree that in European folk music, *the* piece is something that is created once, plus all of the different ways in which it is performed. The model is ideal but only rarely real. Tunes that are strikingly similar may be related in several ways, and only if we could observe the live process could we determine the kind of relationship. Thus, for example, the person who creates a new tune may be just imitating one he or she already knows, and it's hard, coming along after the fact, to distinguish something created as a variant from something that is the result of imitation. Variants may come into existence as the result of forgetfulness or creative embellishment. Cecil Sharp (1932) collected over a dozen variants or versions of "Barbara Allen" in the southern Appalachians; the differences among them seem most likely to have come about in an almost random fashion, though it is known that folk singers a hundred years ago had their interests in maintaining personal versions. Later, in the course of the Anglo-American folk song revival (see Cantwell 1996; Rosenberg 1993), the individuality of song variants and their association with individual singers played a much greater role. The field of popular music, related to folk music on account of its broad appeal but different because of its dependence on mass media, shares in the significance of variants, but these are typically associated in the first instance with the performer, who is thought to have—to be permitted to sing—her or his particular version of a song.

But variants do not come about only in the vacuum of a tune family, they also develop under the influence of outside forces such as musical styles newly introduced, or a foreign stylistic environment—as maybe when a tune crosses an ethnic, linguistic, or national boundary, to say nothing of influences of popular and vernacular church music. Further, a variant of a tune may take some of its content from another tune family, perhaps one line from an unrelated song. The historical sequence in folk song transmission can even cause a complete turnover of musical content, to the extent that no folk taxonomy could be expected to account for it.

Considering configurations of variants that arguably constitute families, we ask in what ways they may differ. Bayard (1954), who did much to develop the "tune family" concept, presented two tune families that he thought represented two processes of development. In the case of the life of one tune, "Brave Donelly" (that name wasn't used by all singers of course—it's Bayard's), he suggests that when one line or phrase or motif is originally followed by a contrasting one, a second singer may sometimes replace it by a simple repetition of the first, or by some monotonous "noodling around." Any two versions of a folk song known to the reader will probably differ in this simple way. In a more radical kind of variant-building, a song may lose a significant portion; this seems to have happened to one tune of a British-American broadside ballad "The Pretty Mohea," whose first half was dropped, and whose second half, with few changes, and sung twice, appears as the country-and-western song "On Top of Old Smoky" (see Cox 1939:

31–33). The relationship of the two seems clear, but we don't know whether the two songs were considered, in the Appalachian folk community that sings (or sang) both, to be somehow related. But this truncating of the first half of a song seems to be fairly common in Anglo-American and also in German and Czech (and no doubt other) folk traditions, and so we'll give it a nickname: "The 'Top of Old Smoky' Effect." In "Little Mohea," the tune with the form AABA seems to have changed to BABA. But Bayard (1954: 19–23) reconstructed this kind of song history more dramatically, in the tune family he called "The Job of Journeywork." Here the structure ABCD seems to have spawned a version consisting only of CD, which, in time, added new material from an extraneous source, and so became CDEF. Very likely, if this process occurred in many songs, CDEF may in one case or another been reduced to EFEF. If we know for sure what happened, we would easily identify a clear genetic relationship between the two forms of the song, ABCD and EFEF. But they have no material in common, and we, coming on to the scene later, as is normal, would have no way of spotting the two as relatives if the intermediate versions weren't available. And yet even these two are in a sense manifestations of the same piece.

If we take these tune families to be the equivalents of the sonatas and lieder of classical music, the variants of one comparable to the individual interpretations of the other, their number, and their scope are very different. Bayard in various publications (e.g., 1953) suggested that the Anglo-American folk music repertory is comprised of forty or fifty such families, each of them a group of essentially similar tunes. The difficulty lies, of course, in equating similarity with genetic relationship, for there are other ways of accounting for great similarity between tunes in even a large culture. List (1979a) examined a group of tunes, including "Twinkle, Twinkle Little Star," and the "Hatiqva" from a number of European folk repertories, showing that they together have the kind of similarity the tunes in families identified by Bronson (1959) exhibit, or the group of tunes of "Barbara Allen" studied by Charles Seeger (1966). George List also argued that this represents the diffusion not of a tune (1979a: 50) but rather of a "style," that it was the way of putting a song together rather than a song itself that was taught and learned. Tune family studies did not maintain their importance into the last decades of the twentieth century, but a couple of studies are worthy of note—Boiles (1973a) tried to reconstruct the original tune from which a group of related tunes may have been derived, and Cowdery (1990) explored three types of tune family development. If the tune family concept and Bayard's suggestion of the limited number of families makes sense, then European cultures clearly differ greatly. Jardanyi (1962) gives many dozens of Hungarian folk music types, each clearly equivalent to the Anglo-American tune families. The more recent and more comprehensive accounting of the Hungarian Academy of Sciences (1992) has more, showing the component variants of each related in a number of complex ways.

I Play It the Same Way Every Time

If a musical system can be comprised of a small number of units of creation, such as forty in Anglo-American folk music, this has nothing to do with a culture's degree of creativity. We can also usefully look at much more complex music with this tune family approach. Having already mentioned the way in which performances of one sonata is analogous to variants in a tune family, I found the same issue played out a bit differently in my experience of Persian classical music. I was surprised to find that one musician, asked to play two performances of one *dastgah* for me on two different occasions, wondered why I should wish to have these, and when I pointed out that I was interested in the differences between the two, he said pointedly, "No, I play it the same way every time." In the end, he acknowledged that he played "from the heart" and that each performance depended on his mood, but he wanted me to understand what was really important, that those things that were essential to the dastgah were present in each performance. It was a bit like saying, "Of course each time it is really 'Barbara Allen,'" or "When I play the *Waldstein* Sonata I always play the same notes."

The songs and pieces I have been talking about have this in common: They may be performed separately and individually. Their performance by themselves, outside a context, sometimes under protest, can normally be elicited by a fieldworker without (we would hope) total violation of the indigenous musical values. A singer in Appalachia would be willing to sing a song by itself, even in a recording studio; Blackfoot singers were normally prepared to perform a song once (even though they may say that it should be sung four times), in isolation from the other songs to which it was normally attached in a ceremony, even in recordings made in 1897. An aria can be lifted out of an opera. A unit marked off in this way has its own history, not necessarily shared with others from the same context.

The same may not be true of shorter units of musical thought. Musicians making field recordings are less willing and sometimes unable to perform individual phrases, motifs, or lines in isolation. In that sense, these do not properly constitute music. But they too sometimes have a degree of independence, as musicians move them from song to song, piece to piece, quoting, parodying, inserting—creatively or as a result of misremembering or random error. In analysis they, too, may be treated individually as units of musical thought that have variants, individual origins, and their own life stories. Historians of Western music have been concerned with motifs that pass from composer to composer, usually inferring knowledge and conscious quotation from the relationship. Stating categorically and enthusiastically that "the melodies wander," Tappert (1890: 5) listed and gave the distribution of a number of motifs, certain ones used by many composers and in the folk music of a substantial part of central and western Europe. Yet the compositions from which the motifs are taken may in other ways be only slightly or not at all related to each other. The similarity or identity resides in the motifs. Evidently they do or did travel and sometimes, as Tappert enthusiastically asserted, frequently "cross violent rivers, traverse the Alps, cross oceans and nomadically pass through deserts."

In Czech and German folk songs, and in much American popular music before 1950, the third line in an AABA form is often interchanged. Similarly, certain musical and textual lines in North American Peyote song repertory appear in variant form in several songs, confirming the way in which some composers of Peyote songs describe one process of composition, when they say that one can create a new song by singing to oneself songs one already knows, combining parts of several to make a new song. There are units of music that cannot be performed alone but nevertheless have some independence and a life of their own.

Relatives, Friends, and Compatriots

As a way of explaining the similarity of tunes and their history, the model of a tune family is attractive. We never have the complete genealogy, but instead, a group of tunes from one country or a related group of countries, and a theory of variant development. They have some similarity, and we would like to think that they are related in some way. But are they relatives, or just friends, or perhaps merely compatriots? Which of the three it is depends on a number of factors, and, importantly, this is one of the major issues of musicology and ethnomusicology, the measurement of similarity and difference. The difficulty of the situation was long ago illustrated by the judgment of an Arapaho friend and informant. In comparing two pairs of practically identical songs, he maintained that one was a set of variants, and the other independent though similar songs. I was obviously not aware of the musical criteria he used, and supposed that very intimate knowledge of the music is necessary in order to make such judgment. Yet it is not just musical criteria that are involved, as when two songs of the Blackfoot Indians are clearly almost identical, fill the same function, are recognized by their singers as identical in sound, but are accorded separate status because they appeared—were created—in two separate visions.

A number of Czech songs, with humorous or light verbal content and probably of eighteenth- or nineteenth-century origin, usually sung by or for children, have the same general structure and very similar contours and configurations of the main notes. They are readily distinguished by the content of the words. Let me reconstruct the genesis of such songs in a fictitious parable. We imagine that we were there when they came into existence, entering at a time when the repertory includes one song with the specified style and structure. A lighthearted farmer who spent his evenings in the tavern and his Sunday afternoons with his children took it upon himself to make up some new songs for the kids so that they could spend an hour singing together, and to amuse them he made up some silly texts. First he took a song he already knew and fitted it with new words, changing the tune slightly to accommodate his longer lines. This pleased the children, but as he continued the practice, they became bored with the same tune. He decided to make up some new tunes, but, not being very imaginative, he came up with tunes that were hardly distinguishable from the first. He tried to change some old songs but kept ending up with tunes that differed only very slightly from the original one he knew, when he was simply revising it to make room for additional syllables. But of an evening at the tavern he heard songs from the city that were quite different, and one day he tried his hand at making up some words for children to one of the more sophisticated (and perhaps bawdy) tavern ballads. Unfortunately, it was too hard for one of the children, and for another somehow uncomfortable because it went too high. They begged their dad for songs like those they already knew, and he learned in no uncertain terms that if he was to introduce new songs for the children, they had to be acceptable in terms of what they already knew. The children had rather specific and quite limited ideas of how children's songs should sound, and so he continued his practice of making up new songs that sounded like the old ones, learning to be careful not to step outside certain limits. They wouldn't accept songs with five lines, preferring four; they won't take minor or Dorian, only major; the four lines must be alike, except for the third, which, comprised of two similar sections, must in some way do the same thing twice. This imaginary but perhaps realistically conceived folk composer has now created variants, has also composed songs imitating the old, and has found that the stylistic limits within which the new songs can be composed are narrow and dictate to what extent he may innovate. Years later, when his repertory of children's songs is collected by a folklorist from Prague, the differences among the songs are minor, all sound like variants of the original, and the old man, his children now grown, no longer remembers how each one came about. He may say, "Yes, they are really all the same song," or more likely, "Well, they are all simply children's songs," and detailed perusal by a scholar from the university who knows hundreds of Czech folk songs indicates that they are all equally similar to each other. All of the Czech tunes in this little tale are in various ways derived from a single original, but the kinds of relationship differ. And they are not closely related in the sense that a group of successive generations think they are singing the same song and simply making changes in it.

To illustrate further this intriguing matter of the unit of musical creativity, we should confront a set of tunes from different countries but with considerable similarity. Take one of the tune groups brought together in Wiora's (1953: 70–71) anthology (also reproduced in Blum 1992: 192–93). They sound rather alike, these tunes under Wiora's group number 70—they have four lines and an arc-shaped contour and similar but not identical scale configurations, and they coincide in the identity and location of structurally significant tones. In the relationships of their lines, however, there is diversity, from the progressive ABCD (number 70g, Polish), to the reverting ABBA (number 70f, Ukrainian), to the almost iterative AA(5)A(5)B (number 70i, English), where the second line is simply a fifth upward transposition of the first. Comparing rhythms, we get even more variety. The Finnish song has quintuple meter, the Hungarian a parlando style, the Irish has lilting dotted progressions, and the Ukrainian alternation of two eighths and a quarter. The notations tell us nothing about the singing style, but we can imagine that there were different ways of using the voice. We ask ourselves why these tunes seem so similar, and why upon a closer look they have such great differences. They have something in common, but we have trouble putting our finger on just what it is. We perceive differences, noting that the English tune shares characteristics of other English tunes that we know; the same is true of the Spanish, Hungarian, Rumanian. We may, for the time being, have to be satisfied with the conclusion that we can perceive the likelihood of identity in content but cannot specifically define it and, thus dissatisfied, might be tempted to accept List's implication that it all amounts only to identity of style, that it was somehow the way of composing songs that united and distinguished them.

Assuming, however, that these songs have the same musical *content* but differ in *style,* we ask how they got distributed around Europe, and whether we can go beyond Tappert's generalized embrace of musical tourism. Musical content moves from one culture to another; we know this well even from non-Western cultures, from the diffusion of Peyote songs among dozens of North American Indian peoples in the last hundred years, and of the Ghost Dance songs among Plains Indian peoples in a short decade after 1880, from the statements of Blackfoot singers to the effect that this song came from the Cree, that one from the Cheyenne. Specific rhythms, with names, have been diffused among peoples of Nigeria and Ghana. It's likely that units of musical thought of a much broader sort, such as the modal units known as Indian ragas, sometimes came into the Indian classical system from Iran, the Arabic world, and Southeast Asia, even though they don't share—any longer in any event—their musical content, the identity of the specific melodies on whose backs, as it were, these modes traveled.

It may seem strange to the reader that an essay about the study of the individual piece of music within its repertory should be so concerned with the history, diffusion, and geographic distribution of songs. But for studying a "piece," we must determine what it is, and I have noted the many ways in which different cultures divide their world of music into units of musical thought. One way to isolate such units and to separate them from their accompanying stylistic superstructure is to trace them through their travels in space and time, something that requires attention to the relationship between content and style.

A Note-for-Note Steal

Musical universals, the world of music as a series of musics, comparative study, and of the identity of repertories, and contemplating individual pieces, have all led to an underlying and frequently frustrating issue. Most of the research to which I have referred depends in one way or another on assessment or even measurement of degrees of similarity between musics and among their components. Actually, a vast proportion of musicology consists of statements that implicitly measure difference. The issue appears in the comparison of composers, of periods in a composer's life, of schools; it is basic to decisions about periodization in history and for establishing order on the musical map of the world. It appears even to be basic to the work of the music critics surveying their contemporary scene. In Western academic musical culture generally, someone evaluating a musical work or placing it in a musical context or style must understand and state the degree to which it is new and different from what came before.

Given the importance of measuring similarity and difference, it should be surprising that musicologists have not developed some kind of a unit, perhaps nicknamed the "sim" (a term coined by my colleague Lawrence Gushee) to express degrees of difference. It would be delightful to be able to say that the difference between Blackfoot and Arapaho Indian music is one sim, and between Arapaho and Menominee, three; between West African and Native American generally, six sims, but between the African and the European, only four; or that Bach and Handel are separated by three, but Handel and Haydn, by four-point-five. Actually, statements of this general sort, lacking the numerical component, have often been made. The few studies attempting measurement and its expression are rather outside the mainstream.

Musicians may have intuitive ability to discern degrees of difference, but their opinions on any one case often differ widely. Oscar Levant (1940: 71) tells of an incident in which the composer Erich Korngold, hearing Gershwin's "The Man I Love," declared that it was "a note-for-note steal" from "Tea for Two." Levant couldn't see the slightest resemblance between the two songs, and neither can I, but there is common tone material. Korngold's motive may have been to show that Gershwin had little originality as a composer, and in any case, while the two were obviously not drinking the same musical tea, this anecdote shows that the value critics accord to matters of difference and similarity may determine their judgment.

Similar though less amusing events seem to have occurred in the history of ethnomusicology. One involves the hearing, decades ago, of a group of American Indian songs from the North Pacific Coast by someone unacquainted with Indian music but knowledgeable about certain Buddhist chants of East Asia. This listener maintained that "an Indian song seems similar to a Buddhist chant for funeral services, used among the nomads of Mongolia" (Barbeau 1934: 110); Barbeau accepted this remark as evidence for the Asian origin of contemporary Native American music. Ethnomusicologists, smiling, assure each other that today such a bald generalization would be inconceivable. The songs could not have been alike, they would say; and the listener must have simply regarded the Indian music as incredibly exotic and uncritically joined it to his knowledge of other exotica; or they were alike in being very different from Western music; or the listener misremembered the Mongolian song, heard years before the incident. And so on. Of course, it's quite possible for two musics with certain surface similarities to create, by chance, two similar pieces. To link two musical systems because of the similarity of two items is surely unjustified, but the strong desire to do this reflects the typical tendency of ethnomusicologists, when comparing musics, to seek out similarities and attach significance to them (see a critique of this tendency in Agawu 2003).

But if there is no standard technique for establishing degrees of similarity, there are certainly methods that, at least as a byproduct, suggest ways in which one could proceed further. Each of these methods has an agenda and uses some kind of measurement of similarity as a technique. Here are three: One is the study of genetic relationships, that is, tune families and types, as established by students of Anglo-American and Hungarian folk musics. A second is the comparative study of repertories with methods such as the paradigms of Hornbostel, Kolinski, and Lomax. I've discussed these and will briefly touch on them again, but let's begin here with the third approach, the classification of tunes in a repertory.

The Best Method . . .

The nineteenth century saw widespread collecting of European folk songs and the beginning of the publication of large, even vast collections intending to encompass total repertories of folk communities and nations. Collectors and publishers were faced with the problem of putting the songs in some kind of rational order. While some were content to group songs by overt use and cultural context or by content of the works, others wished to go further, finding typologies that would make it possible to locate tunes by their musical characteristics, or that would unite those tunes with genetic relationship. There ensued a broad literature dealing with the classification of folk tunes. The first milestone is a pair of publications that, among other things, may hold the record for length of title. The first, by Oswald Koller (1902–3), is titled (in English translation) "The Best Method for the Lexical Ordering of Folk and Folklike Songs," and classified 300 German tunes by assigning to each tone a number that indicated its distance in semitones from the tonic, using Arabic numerals for those above, Roman for those below. This is an adequate finding list if you know a tune precisely, but it will not necessarily locate a tune if you know even a close variant of it. For that reason Ilmari Krohn (1902–3) replied with an even longer title ("What [in fact] Is the Best Method for the

Lexical Ordering of Folk and Folklike Melodies According to Their Musical, Not Textual, Characteristics?"). He suggested a system that reduced each phrase of each song to a "Stich-Motif," a motivic three-note abstraction, and subdividing the tunes first according to the initial note and its distance from the tonic, then the final, and then the "midpoint of melodic expression."

With these two publications began two strands of the history of folk tune classification, one seeking to establish a simple finding list, and the other a way of identifying truly musical or perhaps even genetic relationships can be identified. Krohn evidently came to regard his method as too subjective and thus not reliable for placing together the tunes that struck him, intuitively, as being related, and he went on to recommend a configuration of cadence notes of the four lines of his tunes as a more reliable diagnostic feature. As happened in this case, a more mechanical approach frequently either follows or is tested against the firsthand knowledge of the scholar, as was true of Bartók (1931), who used a number of criteria of descending importance to order Hungarian folk songs: number of syllables per line in the text, configuration of cadence tones, and overall form. This curious order of criteria, which does assemble tunes that appear to be similar, could probably only be devised by someone who already knew which tunes were similar and could, ex post facto, identify the criteria that had led him to make the identification in the first place. The same configuration wouldn't work for other repertories, for example, English or German folk songs, for which different features, such as melodic contour, may be more relevant (Poladian 1942). Bartók's work in classification resulted, after his death in 1945, in a large body of scholarship (see Elschekova 1966; Erdely 1965; Hungarian Academy of Sciences 1992; Jardanyi 1962).

Working in another direction, the American folk song scholar Bertrand H. Bronson pioneered the use of computers (in an incunabular incarnation; 1949, 1950, 1951), deciding that aspects of melody—mode and contour—rather than rhythm, form, or for that matter singing style, were the criteria that would enable him to put similar materials together. In other words, he sought to assemble tunes that exhibited similarity in certain parameters, believing (correctly for his Anglo-American repertory) that these remained more constant in the life of a song and its variants. Like his predecessors, he does not state specific degrees of similarity, but he implies clearly that there is at least a vague line separating similarity from difference, or sufficient from insufficient similarity, to enable him to make judgments regarding relationships. In most of the classification schemes there is the implication that tunes falling close together by examination of particular criteria are more likely to be related than those farther apart in the list. There is perhaps even the unspoken belief that adjacent tunes represent the smallest available degree of differentiation and thus maybe something like a standard unit for measuring degrees. This approach could conceivably be the foundation for a way of measuring that is culture-specific, providing for each culture an emic statement of the minimal unit of difference necessary to set apart discernible variants of a tune.

In the history of classification of tunes, further work with computers has moved us to more complex statements made with more precision, but still specific measurement of degree of difference is normally implied rather than stated. Classification has continued to gain in importance among scholars of European folk music but has not found a very receptive climate in research dealing with other areas of the world. The conclusion of the latest literature is that each repertory must determine its own system, based on criteria specific to it (Elschek 1977; Elschek and Stockmann 1969; Hungarian Academy of Sciences 1992; Stockmann and Steszewski 1973). The history of folk song classification is discussed in detail by Bohlman (1988: 33–51). Curiously, computer applications since 1980 haven't played all that much of a role in classification projects in folk and non-Western music. In historical musicology, they have been more significant, for example, in the large-scale study of English and Anglo-American hymn tunes headed by Nicholas Temperley (1998), and in comparison of the sketches of Ludwig van Beethoven for the purpose of determining aspects of his creative process by William Kinderman (1987, 2003).

A Question of Boundaries

Although classifying a repertory and establishing genetic relationships among its components would seem to be different kinds of work with different aims, we have seen that the two are closely associated. Only a few specific studies exist, and we return again briefly to Bayard's (1954) classic description of two families and Wiora's presentation of groups of similar tunes from a variety of European cultures (Wiora 1953). While both have brought together tunes with certain similarities from a broader yet stylistically limited repertory, it is important to note that to do so they have weighted their criteria, concentrating on aspects of melody, especially contour and the correspondence of main tones. Bayard's grouping is done by informal measurement of similarity, taking into account only certain features. Meter and mode are not criteria; the members of his tune family share a wide variety of metric schemes and modal configurations with the rest of the repertory. Nor are the broadest outlines of melodic contour critèria but, rather, the details of melodic movement; all of the related tunes have several distinctive phrases, motifs, or measures in common. The overall forms, shared with the repertory, are used as criteria on some level, but only in the formal relationships of a few short bits does this group of tunes show itself to be unique. Wiora's study gives us two groups of tunes (1953: 48–49, 50–51). The first seems pretty homogeneous, the second less so. But if the two groups were intermingled, in some respects they might easily just form one group. Measuring contour gives us one grouping, and measuring form another. Indeed, Walter Salmen (1954) looked more critically at the issue of similarity and relationship in that group of songs.

In following one of the fundamental assumptions of our field, the view of the world as a group of discrete musics, we confront the same question when trying to identify them and drawing boundaries—the degrees of difference and similarity. These are at the base of some of the most fundamental thinking of historical musicology and ethnomusicology; they constitute the basic paradigm of mapping the world's music in time and space, of stating most broadly what goes with what. In historical musicology the issue looms behind some of the basic facts students for decades have been asked to learn in music history courses. The concern with style, the division of history into periods, the attempts to establish "central" and "peripheral" styles in eras such as the Renaissance and the nineteenth century (Einstein 1947a; Reese 1954), and the division of a composer's work, like the early, middle, and late periods of Beethoven, all depend on the seldom articulated assumption that one can take such things as three pieces of music or three repertories and show that two are similar and, in turn, different from the third. For example, Renaissance and Baroque are usually presented as highly differentiated periods. In his classic book on the Baroque era, Manfred Bukofzer (1947: 1617) draws distinctions between their styles on the basis of eleven major criteria, these revolving mainly around relationships between instrumental and vocal music, harmony, general characterizations of rhythm, counterpoint, and melody. Though this is a large complement of parameters in the context of music-historical literature, many other elements such as singing style, sound, ornamentation, and vast numbers of detail in melody, rhythm, and orchestration are not mentioned. If the two periods were to turn out to be indistinguishable according to these unused criteria, one might argue that they should not really be separated. Bukofzer goes on to distinguish three phases of the

Baroque period, pointing out the great differences between the early and late Baroque, between Monteverdi and Bach, Peri and Handel. There seems little doubt that the music of Monteverdi is really more similar to that of the late Renaissance than to Bach's, and that his place in the Baroque era has to be based on minor distinctions from late Renaissance, distinctions derived from a small number of heavily weighted criteria. In part the distinction is an "emic" one, followed by scholars working "etically." Around 1600, a number of musical thinkers insisted that something radically new was taking place, and this lead was subsequently followed by historians. If this example is characteristic, judgments of musical similarity have often been made by historians selecting certain criteria for special attention; they have worked a bit like the students of tune families. The substantial agreement of music historians (never mind the modest differences among Lorenz 1928, Clark 1956, and Einstein 1947b) on periodization of Western music, as exhibited in major compendia from Adler (1930) to the multivolume *Handbuch der Musikwissenschaft* (Dahlhaus 1980–92), is noteworthy, though the subtle shift from Adler's grouping (medieval, Renaissance, 1700–1880, the latest) contrasts interestingly with the view in Dahlhaus to the effect that grouping by centuries is justified because anyway the clarity of boundaries recedes as knowledge increases. The same kind of insight might inform the drawing of musical maps, establishing major world musical areas, a practice discussed in chapter 23; one of our principal ways of presenting basic data has always been to tell what happens where. But large-scale interpretive drawing of maps has met the fate of music-history periodization; the more we know, the less clear the boundaries.

How Similar or Different? Biting the Bullet

Well, the literature is full of measurements by approximation and implication, that this music is like that, and that piece unlike this one, but not many have bitten the bullet of trying to come up with some kind of precise measurement. A few scholars, usually as byproducts of other quests, have presented something approximating inches and feet. Let's look at a few of examples, all the while wondering why they haven't often been emulated.

An early landmark is Melville Herskovits's (1945) rating of Africanisms in the music and other cultural domains of various Negro populations in the New World. There are five degrees of similarity, described only as "very, quite, somewhat, a little," and "absent" or with a trace. One notes from Herskovits's table (14) that music is generally more African than other domains. Indeed,

Herskovits assigns the "very African" rating to the musics of Guiana, Haiti, most of African-derived Brazilian cultures, and parts of Trinidad and Jamaica; the rest, including even the northern United States, is "quite African." The musical distinctions are thus limited to two categories, and one wonders about Herskovits's unwillingness to separate, say, Cuba from the United States. But it is interesting to see that in all of these cultures music is the most African domain, that folklore and magic follow, that religion is less African, and technology and economic life least. Herskovits may have missed an opportunity afforded by the fact that the music lends itself readily to being divided into elements and is capable of being quantified, but he was surely a pioneer in making comparative statements among musical repertories of an area, and among domains of culture, using a generalized African model as a base. He went well beyond the completely general and often sentimentalized way of putting it that dominated earlier writing.

Unsurprisingly, some other pioneering attempts came, so to speak, out of Herskovits's shop. One of the most formidable, in its later effect on studies of music under cultural change (though I think the author had no thought of being formidable), was Richard Waterman's comparison of African, African American, and European musics (1952; critiqued by C. Waterman in Nettl and Bohlman 1991), made for the purpose of showing why an African-derived music would flourish in a Western cultural context. Waterman simply said that African and Western musics have a number of common features, leaving to implication their mutually greater difference from other large bodies of music. Merriam (1956), student of both Herskovits and Waterman, took the matter a step further, bringing in Native American music, which, he asserts, is more distant from and less similar to either African or European than they are to each other. The large number of recent studies of syncretic musics in the Caribbean (e.g., Averill 1997; Guilbault 1993; Moore 1997) considered these kinds of stylistic measurements to be helpful to their interpretations.

A major landmark in the enterprise of measuring similarities among such large bodies of music was continued by Alan Lomax in his often-mentioned cantometrics project (1968: 80–105). His measurements may be questioned and criticized, though they frequently confirmed what was widely assumed anyway, despite his weighting of the criteria in favor of those involving performance practice and singing style. Some of his conclusions surprised: For instance, Oceania is internally less homogeneous than Africa, which turns out to be highly unified but lacks the perfect homogeneity of Europe—a bit curious, since Lomax elsewhere (1959) made sharp distinctions among some European areas. Some conclusions resulting from his musical analysis are difficult to accept, as are, even more emphatically, many of the conclusions about the relationships of musical style and culture type.

Some earlier, less sophisticated and comprehensive statistical studies can again be traced to Herskovits's influence. Although studies by Densmore (1929b) and Kolinski (1936) are worthy precursors, Freeman's and Merriam's (1956) work stands out as a rigorously controlled early evaluation of the interval frequencies of two African American repertories, songs of the Ketu cult of Brazil and the Rada cult of Trinidad. The "discriminant function" technique was used to state differences and to determine the degree to which a newly analyzed song has a chance of being in one or the other repertory. The authors went to great lengths to show how different or similar these song groups are to each other, grasping firmly the nettle of this particular issue. Formal statistics was also used by Keil (1966), a sometime student of Merriam, in dealing with a completely different problem, the degree to which a number of musics are perceived as being different from each other by a group of American students. Using the semantic differential technique of psychology, this study compared four Indian ragas and selections of jazz and Bach. The results reflected not an interpretation of broad stylistic differences but perception along several specified continua, for example, flexible to rigid, warm to cool. I mention this study here because it, too, is an early attempt to measure comparatively the difference among musics, at least as perceived by a specific group of listeners.

One would expect that studies of tune families such as those of Bayard would go in for statements of degrees of similarity, but these are at best present by implication. Moreover, the question of simple similarity and difference is sometimes obscured by the question of genetic relationship. Further, the analyst's assessment of similarity may well differ from that of the informant. In a study that tries to take into account similarity, relationship, and the folk evaluation, Goertzen (1979) attempted to measure similarity among versions and variants of the North American fiddle tune "Billy in the Low Ground," according to criteria that are revealed and weighted within the performance of fiddle tunes. The nature of repetitions of each strain makes clear what sorts of difference are considered significant by the performers. For instance, rhythms are varied at will while overall contour is varied only slightly, and diagnostic tones not at all. Replicating Bayard's findings, Goertzen showed that if two tunes differ drastically in the rhythms employed but are otherwise much alike, they are regarded by "insiders" to be more similar than two tunes identical only in rhythm.

The question of measuring degrees of musical similarity and difference and associating this to genetic relationship has always been one of the most vexing in musicology and ethnomusicology. Although often not made explicit, it seems always to be with us, but those who have bitten the bullet and gone on record with some kind of even very rudimentary technique have not been widely followed. In the real world of music, however, in the age of globalization and of domination of technology, the measuring of works by degrees of similarity, determining whether there is chance similarity or a "note-for-note steal," has become a major issue in the negotiation of intellectual property, and some ethnomusicologists have been expert witnesses and have been called upon to establish method and theory. Making such measurements might also play a role in ethnomusicologists' interest in protecting the musics and musicians whose work they study (see Frith 1993 and the bibliography in Mc-Cann 2001).

But within the immediate concerns of ethnomusicology, formal attempts at determining kinds and degrees of relationships in both style and content have not fared well in the period since 1985, a period in which personal interpretation, informed by consciousness of reflexivity and the belief that the position of the observer plays a major role in the quality of observations. In the first edition of this chapter, I wrote that "if we could increase the sophistication and precision of measuring similarity, and if we could also distinguish simple similarity from genetic relationship, many of the outstanding problems of analysis, description, and comparison would no doubt fade away." Twenty years later, while the social analogues of true "tune family" and mere "type"—nature and nurture—continue to be the subjects of raging debates, the interests of students of music seem to have moved in other directions.

PART 2

In the Field

10

Come Back and See Me Next Tuesday: Essentials of Fieldwork

Arrival

I have arrived in the "field." It's a little town in the northern Plains of the United States, on the surface hardly different from many other crossroads I've just driven through. When I stop at a filling station, a bit of a chill crawls up my neck: The attendant is a Native American, one of the people with whom I now wish to spend some months, whose music and musical culture I wish to study and describe. He is an old man with a tattered shirt, speaking English with a tiny bit of an accent. I've arrived, I would like to say to him, I'm here because I want to learn what you know, because you have something to offer that is different from all I've learned before, because you live and think differently. This is a great moment for me: I have finally made it to the "field," and fate somehow selected you to be the one to introduce me. I am wondering how to put these thoughts into more informal words, can't quite get up the nerve, and he just says, "Three dollars, please; don't look like you need any oil," and starts attending to another customer. I drive on into the tiny town, park at a sandwich shop. Several people sitting at the counter, white, Indian, maybe some others, some in between? The server looks Native but gives me my hamburger like any midwestern waitress. All these people—there must be one with whom I could strike up a conversation! But if this is a great occasion for me, my coming into that restaurant means nothing to them.

I turn to my neighbor, a man dressed like a road worker. "Nice day," he says. "Goin' to the mountains?" I clear my throat, getting ready my prepared speech about wanting to learn about Native American music, but before my thoughts collect sufficiently he has gone. I pay my check, begin a walk through the dreary streets. Stop in a store or two, in a bar, at a bench where several old men are passing the time of day. Long ago I had determined that this would some day be my town, and now I'm surrounded by "my" people, but they don't know it, and I don't know how to begin. Each time I reach a point at which I think I have found someone who will listen, to whom I can somehow make known my lofty wishes, needs, desires, I'm defeated, and I begin to fear that I'll never have the courage to reveal myself. When I do, they will laugh at me, probably a city dweller who should know better than lowering himself to learn something so useless as old Indian songs, or maybe a white man who aspires to study things an Indian had to spend a lifetime learning, surely one of the exploiters, or possibly someone who could provide badly needed help if only he weren't involved with a frivolous subject like music. I begin to fear that I'll end up a hermit in this town, never meeting anyone with whom I can talk. Fear and anxiety. Several hours have passed, and I have made no progress. I'm on the verge of turning around, giving up on these people. I have come to them, my "field," ready to give them energy and heart; they see me as just another white tourist, or perhaps they don't see me at all.

Where does one go in a strange town, lonely and despondent? The public library? A bar? I enter a barbershop; one can always use a haircut. The barber is Native. "Just passing through?" he asks, and I blurt out, no, I would stay the summer. "Here?" he says, astonished. "Nobody spends a summer here if he don't have to." I'm doing research, I tell him self-consciously. "Research? Are you one of them anthropologists?" A bit of distaste evident in his voice. Well, not really, but I'm interested in learning about Indian songs. "Oh, you ought to talk to one of them singers. There's one lives just two houses away, usually sits on the stoop. Joe F., an old timer, knows a lot about the old days." Heart skips a beat: my chance, has it come after all? I pay, tip heavily, walk down the street. Just as the barber said: a ramshackle hut, probably just one room, old man sitting in front staring into space. I greet. "Got any cigarettes?" came the answer. I didn't. "Got a dollar so I can buy some?" Sure. "I hear you know a lot of the old songs of your people." "Naw, I don't know nothing. My brother, he knows a lot, lives fifty miles away, he'll be coming to see me in a week or some time." "Sure, I'd like to meet him. But I was told you know more than anybody else in this town." "You want me to sing some songs on your tape recorder?" He seemed to know something about ethnomusicologists. "That's Indian work; I'll have to charge you a lot." I have some money, not much. "Well, you've got a car," he says. "Come back and see me next Tuesday, and bring your machine." He took a swig from a bottle of cheap bourbon. Dismissed.

Through this one conversation I felt that I had made my entry, had suddenly become a fieldworker, graduating from my first role as tourist passing through town. By the next Tuesday I had actually met several men whom I could ask to work with me. Some were willing on the spot, others made it clear they wished to have nothing to do with me, most of them temporized and postponed. I told them that I had met Joe F., who had promised to help me, and some were impressed by that.

Tuesday I presented myself at Joe's little house. "I have to go to G. [a town forty miles east]," he said. Fortunately I knew my proper place in this relationship, and so I spent that day taking Joe in my car, with four other members of his family, all of whom treated me rather like a chauffeur to whom one gave directions but otherwise didn't speak, attending to various bits of personal business. At the end I asked about recording some songs. "I don't have time today, but come back in a few days," I was told.

To make this long story from the 1960s short, it was another week before Joe consented to be interviewed more or less formally and to sing a few songs, in a weak voice, with a poor memory, for my recorder. I learned less clumsy techniques, and after a few weeks Joe had become a friend with whom one could converse easily about many things. I joined his family on picnics, moved from outsider to observer to something approaching participant-observer. Why had he made me wait, come back twice? Some of my consultants didn't but were ready at once, said they had time, which Joe in fact also had but wouldn't admit. Was it to teach me some respect for his way of doing things, to tell me that I couldn't just rush in, or to test whether I had more than a casual interest? I have since heard variants of "come back and see me next Tuesday" in other countries. Getting started in the field is actually a time of stress, the moment of entry sometimes one of great tension, self-searching, requiring courage, patience, wit. A number of ethnomusicologists have described or commented on their more recent experiences in a volume edited by Barz and Cooley (1997), showing that the same problems may still be around—plus some others. This chapter presents some thoughts on the general nature of ethnomusicological fieldwork.

A Very Private Matter

Others in my situation, of course, would have handled the matter more efficiently and given absolutely different explanations, reactions, feelings from those I've just described. In contemplating the concept of fieldwork, the first question to which we should attend asks whether there is, or should be, a unified field methodology, or whether each scholar develops an individual approach. Ethnomusicological literature, throughout its history, has had a good bit to say about fieldwork as part of research design, ways of dealing with recording and filming machinery and video, general principles of intercultural relations. But it had much less to say—at least until the period after around 1990—about the day-to-day personal relationships that are the heart of this kind of research. All subsequent analysis and interpretation of data depends so heavily on fieldwork, but it is also the most personal part of the job, the part that cannot really be taught, that all of us have had to learn on our own, finding ways of mediating between our own personalities with their strengths and weaknesses and the individuals whose shared beliefs we will learn and interpret, using confidence and mastering timidity. In considering fieldwork, Helen Myers (1992: 21) wrote: "We unveil the human face of ethnomusicology." Since fieldwork principally involves interaction with other humans, it is the most personal side of the profession, a very private matter, and only with difficulty do we let others in on what we said and heard, and how we felt.

The professions of anthropology and folklore are the principal mentors of the ethnomusicological fieldworker. They claim fieldwork as theirs par excellence, though they, too, like ethnomusicologists, until recently, have rarely told in detail what happened in the field. In the earlier parts of the twentieth century, one did not often find straightforward accounts of daily life and feelings in an exotic environment, such as the posthumously published diary of Malinowski (1967), a scholar often cited for his prowess as a fieldworker. Very occasionally were transcriptions of interviews or field notes provided (Merriam 1969a; Slotkin 1952). But like the foregoing little parable on my experience, most publications dealing with fieldwork focus on the role of the consultant and culture-bearer, the person through whom the ethnographer learns a culture, and whose moods, empathy, attitude toward a visitor, idiosyncratic ideas, genius for discovering the instructive, and interest in looking at life in a structured fashion all determined the quality of understanding that ensued. An anthropologist may begin by seeing informants as faceless representatives of a homogeneous mass, but that fallacy quickly becomes apparent and—as illustrated already a half-century ago by the many warm and emotional essays in Casagrande's (1960) collection of portraits of "favorite" informants by outstanding scholars—special kinds of human relationship develop. A major change in attitude was exhibited in the development of the so-called new ethnography of the 1960s (see, e.g., Tyler 1969) explicitly displaying the contrast between insider and outsider views, to be elaborated in chapter 11.

It is in the importance of fieldwork that anthropology and ethnomusicology are closest: It is the "hallmark" of both fields, something like a union card. Members of both professions are expected to have some fieldwork under their belts. Early on, theoretical statements on the strengths and limitations of fieldwork were made, though usually buried in ethnographies. Thus Malinowski (1935: 317) gave general impressions and advice: The anthropologist must not only observe but constantly interpret, structure, relating isolated bits of data to each other; be highly self-critical, realizing that many approaches inevitably lead to false conclusions and dead ends; and be ready to start over. He found that byproducts of his main work often provided the most valuable insights and suggested that one subordinate but also impose one's self on the "field." Malinowski insisted that the culture concept plays a major role in the nature of the fieldwork, which "consists only and exclusively in the interpretation of the chaotic social reality, in subordinating it to general rule" (1954: 238).

Much earlier, Malinowski (1935) recommended three kinds of data to be gathered. I'll paraphrase: (1) texts—he meant things like tales, myths, proverbs in nonliterate cultures, and presumably all kinds of writings elsewhere, but for us this importantly includes songs and pieces of music; (2) structures, by which he meant things people say that permit the fieldworker to abstract principles of behavior, such as rules about social organization, property, power-relations, and that for us might include rules and contexts for performances, such as the structure of concerts; and (3) the "imponderabilia of everyday life." It is in the third that the genius of anthropological perspectives comes into play, as it includes noticing what might not be noted by just any observer—who speaks with whom in a society, what body language is used in various relationships, the many details that people everywhere take for granted but that are essential to acceptable behavior, the quality of their discourse. Malinowski's may be as good a statement of the general nature of fieldwork as has been developed, and it shows that while in its interpretive aspects, and in its technology, anthropology has changed enormously through the twentieth century, there are important respects in which it has remained constant.

Within this standard, though, the variety of field techniques and methods in cultural anthropology is immense, comprising everything from biographical approaches to parallel interviews on the same subject with many informants, the collection of texts, questionnaires, outright participation, teamwork, and much more. Interdisciplinary teamwork, from conventional associations (e.g., teams of social, linguistic, and archeological anthropologists) extending to the imaginative description of an African society from the perspective of an anthropologist and a novelist (Gottlieb and Graham 1993) has been significant, but the personal nature of fieldwork that I have been emphasizing has prevented anthropology from becoming team-centered as have many of the "hard" sciences. If there is an overriding issue characterizing anthropological fieldwork through its history, it may be the interface between data gathering in a scientific, replicable way and the significance of the personal relationships developed in the field (see, e.g., Turner and Bruner 1986). The concept of restudy, to assess change but also to test replicability (see Mead 1928 and Freeman 1983; Redfield 1930 and Lewis 1951), has some fascinating insights. But in general, interpretation and the recognition that the stance of the observer is of paramount significance characterizes anthropology at the end of the twentieth century.

A body of theoretical and instructional writing about fieldwork has emerged in anthropology, but major works from such classics as Harris's history of the field (1968) and Ingold's (1994) encyclopedic treatment eschew the coverage of fieldwork as a specific subject and activity. An extended essay by Morris Freilich (1970) illustrates attempts to circumscribe the field. He divides fieldwork activities into fourteen areas, beginning with such mundane things as preparing a research proposal and finding funds, but concentrating on problems faced in the field. Informants see their culture in a special way, play particular roles in their societies, and have peculiar views of their roles in the quests of fieldworkers. Freilich divides them into three groups—traditionalist, operator, and speculator—and subdivides them further, in accordance with the ways in which they are willing to tackle problems of their culture as expressed in the fieldworker's questions (1970: 572–73). He classifies kinds of information that may be gathered—public, confidential, secret, and private (549)—weighs social and economic risks faced by both partners, and so proposes a formal theory of fieldwork.

Freilich's approach can be a valuable guide to the prospective fieldworker, and it can give the nonanthropologist a sense of the complexity of relationships that are involved. Most textbooks and guides do not so much tell you what to do as provide case studies as examples (see, e.g., Freilich 1977; Georges and Jones 1980; Wax 1971). Hortense Powdermaker (1967), in one of the first books devoted specifically to the nature of fieldwork, suggested such fundamental steps as making a census, providing a sketch of the society to be studied before proceeding to more specialized tasks, ascertaining matters of tabu and etiquette. That all this can be a difficult, frustrating, slow process is obvious; but realistic accounts of what was actually done in a particular situation have finally become significant in anthropological literature (see, e.g.,

Dumont 1978; Farrer 1991; Foster and Kemper 1974; Spindler 1970; and the humorous but realistic Barley 1983).

Fieldwork in the History of Ethnomusicology

In ethnomusicology, by contrast, fieldwork as a theoretical concept does not often appear as a subject to be discussed out of a broader context of research design. Ethnomusicologists and folklorists seem to need more practical information than anthropologists about techniques of recording, filming, videotaping, special problems of text-gathering. Thus, the earlier publications that concern fieldwork involve mainly the practicalities. Karpeles (1958) provided an early attempt at suggesting standardization of techniques. Goldstein (1964) gave a detailed volume of advice, and there are many guides to making recordings, among the most thorough and thoughtful being Hood's book *The Ethnomusicologist* (1971). In all of this literature the stress is on techniques suited to a particular situation. Occasionally there are also suggestions of generally applicable procedures. Hood's book and Herndon and McLeod's text (1980) are exceptions, each devoting two insightful chapters to the problem, discussing concepts as well as giving specific advice. Hood, despite his attention to other matters and interesting accounts of personal experience, does seem to be mainly concerned with the gathering of recorded material. A chapter in Myers (1992: 50–87) provides a comprehensive account of recording and other data-gathering procedures.

Before about 1950, fieldwork and "research" were often separated. Ethnomusicologists such as Hornbostel were obliged to work with the results of the field research of others, and the voluminous correspondence of George Herzog with dozens of anthropologists gave them advice on making recordings that, he assumed, would be turned over to ethnomusicologists for transcription and analysis. Hence the earlier emphasis on techniques over theory. Fieldwork and desk work could be seen as separable processes. In the second half of the twentieth century it became more or less axiomatic that researchers do their own fieldwork, and Merriam (1964), reflecting the view that separation is not really thinkable, discussed it as an aspect of research design and general theory. In this book he does not tell specifically what to do in the field and, for that matter, like most authors, avoids giving in detail what he himself did. In later works (1969a, 1977b) he comes closer to giving such an account; indeed, self-revelation may be becoming a trend, as indicated by the appearance of musical ethnographies with great attention to the activities and experiences of the fieldworker (e.g., Berliner 1978, 1994; Keil 1979; Myers 1998; Sugarman 1997; among many others). Also important in the last four decades is the growing concern with the ethical aspects of researchers' interrelationships with their informants and teachers (see chapter 15; for critical appraisal of the issue, see Gourlay 1978; Slobin 1992a).

As the main interest of ethnomusicology is in total musical systems, the question of sampling, to which chapter 13 also speaks, is crucial, and the selection and evaluation of consultants and teachers are a major component of the way in which we sample a culture. With this in mind, it seems appropriate to try to identify several approaches to ethnomusicological fieldwork, presenting them in a more or less chronological arrangement, providing a bare outline of their history. If these are stages, they certainly overlap. Each represents only part of a mainstream and omits the work of scholars who did not conform to prevailing trends, were ahead or behind, dealt with problems outside the field's main thrust. But in a sense the history of ethnomusicology is the history of changing approaches to fieldwork.

In the period between 1890 and 1930, research most characteristically concentrated on artifacts, that is, songs or pieces, collected with some attention to cultural context and in small samples. The recordings were often made by missionaries or ethnographers who would not ultimately do the analytical and interpretive work. For example, studies made by Hornbostel, Stumpf, and their contemporaries are based on a dozen songs or two, on the assumption that a small sample of songs would give one something approaching the musical universe of the culture, or at least its major characteristics. Emphasis was on "collecting," in the sense of plucking the pieces out of the culture for analysis and preservation elsewhere, something that sounds a bit like colonial exploitation. To be sure, at this time and earlier, some Asian musical cultures were studied by individuals who had the opportunity of extended residence and a large accumulation of more or less random musical experience. Among these were the missionaries, travelers, and colonial administrators who produced some of the early classics—Fox-Strangways (1914) for India, Amiot (1779) for China, Villoteau (1809) for Egypt.

More or less simultaneous but extending further into the twentieth century is a type of fieldwork that, like the first, involved collection of artifacts, but with the intention of preserving and recording a total musical corpus. The word "preserve" is used advisedly; the scholars in this group tended to regard preservation to be a major function of their work. Large collections of European folk music came into existence. In the twentieth century the work of Béla Bartók, who collected songs from many eastern European cultures in enormous quantity, is surely an outstanding exemplar. But the approach was also followed in some work with non-Western cultures, for Frances Densmore's early publications on Chippewa and Sioux music must be considered as attempts to record the total repertories of these peoples. At the same time, more recent collecting projects with the same purpose are not uncommon, as for example the large collection of Cheremis songs published by the Hungarian scholars Vikar and Bereczki (1971).

There followed a more diversified approach characterized by (1) continued concentration on the recording of musical artifacts, (2) extended residence in one community, (3) greater sensitivity to the cultural context and study of music in culture, and (4) attempts to comprehend an entire musical system, usually emanating from a small community with little or no musical or verbal literacy, a tribal or folk culture. This type of work seems to have been most common from 1920 to about 1960, and the various field trips taken to parts of the southwestern United States by George Herzog may be illustrative of its early period. In 1927 Herzog spent several months with the Pima in Arizona. By later standards this stay of some eight weeks is brief, but close to 200 songs were recorded, and much information regarding uses of music and its role in society was gathered, appended to the songs in Herzog's major publication on the subject (1936a) and presented elsewhere as well (1938). More extensive fieldwork, spread over several visits or residence of one or more years, characterizes the later portion of this stage. Hood came to regard a year as minimal. There are David McAllester's repeated visits to the Navajo, resulting in and inspiring a series of publications by himself and some of his students that display the entire musical culture in pieces, present and describe the music itself, and speak to general problems of music in culture (see Frisbie 1967, 1980; McAllester 1954; Mitchell 1978; etc.).

All of these approaches cast the fieldworkers in the role of observers, although they may at times have been occasional participants. Emphasis on actual participation is characteristic of the fourth type of field venture. The fieldworker appears as a student of performance, even including the sensitive areas of improvisation and composition, more or less on the same terms as the native music student. Dating from the early 1950s and still very much in evidence, this development coincides with several other important events. Following World War II, it came at a time of increased opportunity for travel and thus of increased exposure of Westerners to the ancient and high civilizations of Asia. These cultures had developed systematic ways of teaching their music, sometimes in the process separating it from its cultural context. I do not suggest that other societies, such as Native Americans or Australian aboriginals, lacked ways of teaching their music. But very commonly these were not distinct or formalized activities and could not as readily be separated from the ceremonial, religious, social, or enculturative functions of the music. Thus the entry of an American or European into the musical system as a student would probably depend more heavily upon the person's ability to enter the entire cultural system. In the case of India, Iran, Japan, and Java, music teaching was at least somewhat separable. One could go to India, study with an Indian vocalist, live in the Westernized section of society, and yet not be obliged to become thoroughly a participant in Indian culture (although indeed some such participation would be a desirable result).

Another factor was the rather sudden expansion of interest on the part of Western musicians in the Asian classical musics, an interest that had heretofore been nurtured only by a few, usually with a historical orientation. The study of Asian and African performance techniques and practices was carried out not only by ethnomusicologists but also by others who had no interest in research but wished simply to learn to play or sing. This cannot properly be called "ethnomusicology" any more than studying the cello can itself be called historical musicology. There is certainly no reason to discourage such learning. But in the 1950s and 1960s, the contrast between participant and observer in fieldwork was a major source of conflict in ethnomusicology, the one side being blamed for neglect of scholarly objectives and the other for lack of truly musical interest. Direct study of performance became, however, extremely useful for understanding a musical system. Like that of our third stage, this kind of fieldwork involves extended residence in one community, and in a certain way it too is an attempt to comprehend the entire system, at least as seen, perceived, and taught by one full-fledged member of the musical culture. Typical of the approach in its earlier stages was the work of those who studied in the UCLA program in ethnomusicology (see Hood 1957 and 1960 and, for analysis of a personal experience, Koning 1980). Also illustrative would be the work of Ella Zonis (1973) and Gen'ichi Tsuge (1974), who for years at different times studied primarily at one institution in Tehran, the Conservatory of National Music, along with Iranian students.

A fifth stage differs from the rest in that there is no attempt to be comprehensive but, rather, to carry out a strictly limited project whose task it is to make a specialized contribution. It is nevertheless difficult to separate from the others, for even its characteristic project is usually in practice accompanied or preceded by a good deal of general ethnographic work and recording. As many of the world's musical cultures have become reasonably well known and broadly covered in the literature, the need for solving specialized problems has emerged as a further stage of research.

An early example of this type of study is work by A. Jihad Racy in Egypt (1976), whose subject was the history of the record industry in Cairo and its impact on classical music early in the twentieth century. Much of this research was conventionally historical, with printed and archival sources. But he also engaged in fieldwork, with a group of informants who were not musicians but rather collectors of old records, and with elderly individuals who could give firsthand accounts of musical life in the period involved. Somewhat more characteristic are the many studies dealing with specific cultural problems, such as Daniel Neuman's work (1980) concentrating on the background and social structure of classical music in Delhi. Musicians had to be interviewed primarily on matters not dealing with music per se. For other examples, making selective recordings such as performances of one piece by many, or improvisation on one model by one person at different times, provides a slice but not all of a musical system and yet solves problems of performance practice or improvisation. The vast number of attempts to study (and for that matter to record or film) one ritual, context, person also fall into this broad category. The study of special institutions within a society, such as the "early music" scene in Boston by Shelemay (2001) or of recording studios in South Africa by Meintjes (2003) and in Canadian First Nations cultures by Scales (2004), require different approaches to fieldwork and particularly to the issue of relating such institutions to the culture at large.

In the 1980s, a more unified approach to fieldwork seems to have been established, at least in the North American tradition, as the concepts of anthropological participant-observer methodology and the practice of studying music as insider and with insiders became the norm. The typical fieldworker still carries out specialized projects to solve particular problems, but he or she approaches the work from the perspective of someone well versed in anthropological and perhaps social theory, but also as a musician learning a musical system as it teaches itself. The compendium of essays edited by Barz and Cooley (1997) provides examples of the variety of approaches, in studies carried out in several continents, and with musics extending from tribal India and traditional African cultures to modern Europe and North America.

Informants, Consultants, and Teachers

Some disciplines in which fieldwork has a role—sociology, political science, economics—tend to depend for their data substantially on written sources such as constitutions, statistical abstracts, voting records, and surveys such as questionnaires directed to large numbers of people. Their research has sometimes been characterized as typically quantitative. By contrast, anthropologists, folklorists, and, perhaps even more, ethnomusicologists, are typically distinguished by their belief that a (musical) culture can best be understood through intensive work with a relatively small number of its representatives. In the world of social science research, their method of data gathering is sometimes labeled as qualitative, the implication being that one goes into a subject in greater depth than the fields that collect their data more broadly. Of course, ethnomusicologists also have an interest in quantifying data and statistics (see chapter 9), and in such procedures as comparing hundreds of songs in a repertory, they may do their share of numbers-crunching.

But most ethnomusicological fieldwork involves learning things from individuals, perhaps from a very few individuals. Known traditionally as informants, they should be, and have gradually been, more typically called consultants, and then teachers, for that is precisely what they are. Since ethnomusicologists do not usually deal with many individuals, they are involved in a more delicate sampling procedure than those scholars who attain statistical validity with larger samplings. The selection of teachers, informants, consultants is therefore a major issue, but I cannot presume to tell someone how to do it. Consultants often select themselves; they appear in the fieldworker's life fortuitously, and while they may not necessarily be the most representative, one may have little choice. Even so, one must consider what is happening.

In working with Blackfoot people, I was introduced to a man who was described as a singer. I did not ask further; he had been so designated in contrast to dozens of others who were not. I didn't care whether he was considered the best or the worst, as I was grateful for anyone's help, and I assumed that he would be somehow representative of that part of the population who were titled "singers." I had it in mind to study the musical culture as it existed, was interested in the mainstream of musical experience, not in what was exceptionally good or, for that matter, bad. I valued most the contact with someone who would speak articulately, give me lots of information. I hoped he would in some way be typical, and thought I would later be able to put my hope to the test.

All of this hinged on the ethnomusicological interest in learning what actually happens in society and not what the society would wish to happen, as it were, if each member had control over his or her experience. Although I needed to know what the ideal was, I did not mainly want to study it. Unlike some of the early scholars, I no longer assumed that all informants in an indigenous society would tell me the same thing; I had discarded the idea of essential homogeneity. But I did believe, rightly or not, that among the fifty or so "singers" whom the community turned out to have, perhaps half a dozen would be considered outstanding, another few barely adequate, and the majority simply good, in a sort of bell-shaped curve. This last group most interested me. The members of the society seemed to find my approach compatible, didn't feel that I should be concentrating only on the best. The degree to which what I learned is actually authentic or representative of Blackfoot culture depends on the way in which my teacher was able to articulate (verbally and musically) the norms of Blackfoot musical culture.

Working later in Iran, I had the good fortune to find myself under the wing of a man who was highly distinguished as a musician though a bit controversial among his colleagues. He became my principal teacher, and I learned the system through his presentation of it. Subsequently I spoke to lots of musicians, many of whom agreed that he represented the best their culture had to offer, while some considered him overrated and recommended other authorities, including themselves. In any event, each Iranian musician, like American twentieth-century composers, would probably have an idiosyncratic way of representing the musical system. Interestingly, after my teacher died in 1978 and after another decade during which classical music in Tehran did not thrive had passed, several younger musicians became prominent, and as it happened, they were largely students of my teacher, whose reputation as a perhaps singular authority increased greatly after his death. So did my reputation, as someone who had studied with the greatest of masters.

Iranians wanted to be sure that I should study with the greatest authority. The Blackfoot people thought there were a good many who "had it right," and thought I could learn their musical culture properly with any of them. In each case I was lucky to have stumbled on a way of operating that fitted the society's values. In each, one might have taken an opposite approach, created friction, conceivably learning equally valuable though different things. There is not one right way; it's just that one must know what one is doing and, later, has done. We need to discern between ordinary experience and ideal, but the "ideal" musician may also know and do things completely outside the ken of the rest. My teacher in Iran was able to explain things about Persian music that might have been beyond the comprehension of others. Learning them was itself worthwhile, but I should also have found out whether they are things shared by only a few, the ordinary musician being unaware of them. The question is worthy of Malinowski's admonition to create structure out of chaos: Were these things that I learned uniquely from my teacher properly part of the culture?

There are other ramifications of the process of selecting teachers. For example, if it is important to you as fieldworker to be accepted in a community, and if this acceptance is enhanced by having a prestigious local sponsor, you must decide whether such a person, regardless of other qualities, should become a key informant or teacher. You have to decide to what extent one should depend on those who know things about older traditions but cannot participate, or how important it is to have a main consultant who is an active participant in musical culture, depth of knowledge aside. We must deal with the self-selection tendencies of informants, realizing that those who do this may have ulterior motives, and while they provide the advantage of being readily available, they might not be otherwise representative. To what extent should one talk to consultants about each other, ascertain their reputation in the community? There is no end to the questions of selection and relationship.

A former professor of mine, experienced for decades in linguistic field research among American Indians, put it this way: "Your relationship to your informants is a uniquely satisfying one. He is one of the few people in your life whom you don't contradict, with whom you never disagree." You have to be able to trust your informants; or you lack intellectual security. Purposely, or from ignorance, they may give what their compatriots might think is misinformation, but even the selection of this misinformation on their part may tell us something about the culture. Of course fieldworkers often do argue with their informants, about facts, money, roles. And yet the relationship is surely unique. They are our teachers, but unlike those from whom we learn our own culture, they usually may have no real stake in the students' successes and need not regard them as potential competitors. Or, in some cases, they might, as ethnomusicologists increasingly perform the music they have studied, and as our consultants increasingly want to write their own books.

Ideal ethnomusicological fieldworkers are formidable individuals indeed. According to various writers on the subject (e.g., Jacobs in Freilich 1970; Hood 1971), they should control several disciplines—anthropology, history, art, religious studies, biology, psychology—besides their musical training. They must be talented musicians so that they can quickly learn a strange system. They must know the languages of peoples they are studying. They should excel as recording engineers and cinematographers. They must be able to stay in the field for long periods but not lose themselves in it, have prodigious energy in order to comprehend without much help materials of great complexity under difficult physical conditions. They must have outgoing personalities. By the year 2000, they hoped for preliminary work in the home community, and study with an informant-teacher from the goal country who is teaching at the home institution. There's no end to the requirements, and little in the way of generally applicable instruction materials (but see, e.g., Herndon and McLeod 1983; Myers 1992: 50–87).

To do the job right, all say emphatically, one cannot just go somewhere and turn on a tape recorder. Teamwork is recommended, as there is just too much to do to prepare really well, to make really complete use of the field opportunities. Yet almost all that has been accomplished has been the work of individuals. Nevertheless, significant team efforts deserve to be mentioned; Diamond, Cronk, and von Rosen (1994), on instruments in Eastern First Nation cultures, and Lassiter (1998), working with a Kiowa teacher in a collaborative ethnography, are recent examples. But how can one be confident in the face of the insuperable demands both of one's own scholarly community and of the culture and its material that is waiting to be interpreted?

Well, things may not be all that bad. I'll pat the prospective fieldworker who is reading these paragraphs on the shoulder. There are lots of difficulties, social political, medical (see Myers 1992: 41–42 for a discussion of "health in the field"), intellectual. But not many graduate students and older fieldworkers arrive, become frustrated, and flee; the vast majority stick it out, try do what they set out to do, maybe revise their plans and change scope and direction, but in any event learn something that is significant and useful to them and to the field as a whole. They return with horror stories, but, like Nigel Barley (1983: 190), who, six months after returning home from a year of unimaginable frustration, boredom, and sickness, heads out to the field again, they have become hooked.

Fieldwork is a kind of sampling. But ethnomusicologists are themselves also samples. Just as one cannot study the whole musical culture but must experience it in samples, one cannot satisfy all desired approaches but must depend on one's own capacities. Rarely in a position to be part of a team that provides expertise in language, performance ability, technology, anthropological theory, and so on, one must be willing to live with one's limitations. If one is expert in one or two of these respects and at least aware of the basic problems of the others, one will have a chance of succeeding in providing some reliable information and a credible interpretation. One can view one's self as a sample of ethnomusicological method and technique.

The purpose of making this point is to contradict those who say that if someone has visited a society and made recordings, its musical culture has been "researched." There is no single way to go about a task, and each contribution is at best partial. It's a mistake to feel that a particular culture or music has "been done" because someone has worked with its people in the field. The idiosyncratic nature of fieldwork assures the value of each serious attempt, and the more any one society is studied, the more of interest emerges to be done.

Direct inspection at the source, that's field work: The closest thing to science, it turns out to be more an art. Still, in one important sense we exact a standard from ourselves when we do fieldwork. We expect fieldworkers to show respect for their material and for the people with whom they work, and the informants, the teachers, know very well whether this respect is there. They test the fieldworker to determine if he or she is serious and takes them seriously. It is mainly for that reason, I think, that they so often start out by saying, "Come back and see me next Tuesday."

11

You Will Never Understand This Music: Insiders and Outsiders

The Ugly Ethnomusicologist

I was about to leave my lesson of Persian music in the spacious old house in south Tehran when my teacher suddenly fixed me with his forefinger: "You will never understand this music. There are things that every Persian on the street understands instinctively which you will never understand, no matter how hard you try." Startled, but realizing that he meant "understanding" in a particular way, I blurted out, "I don't really expect to understand it that way, I am just trying to figure out how it is put together." "Oh, well, that is something you can probably learn, but it's not really very important." My teacher was telling me that a member of a society may understand a culture quite differently from even an informed outsider. End of lesson.

Years later, in an American classroom, I was confronted by a young man from Nigeria. "With what rationale do you study the music of other cultures?" The tone implied that this was a most unnatural thing to do, he seemed hostile, and a lot of discussion could not satisfy him that I was doing something legitimate.

My teacher didn't think there was anything wrong with my trying to understand Persian music in the way Iranians understood it but only thought it was futile. The Nigerian questioned the morality of even trying. The distinction has come to play an important role in ethnomusicological thinking and discussion. The difference between my Iranian teacher's understanding and mine was recognized but given a more positive spin by Mantle

Hood in a conclusive statement in his book *The Ethnomusicologist* (1971: 374): "The American or French or British ethnomusicologist because of *who* he is—that is to say, what he has succeeded in becoming through years of training—is capable of insights and evaluations, as a transmitter of a non-Western music, which no Javanese, even with training abroad in Western methods, could ever duplicate." The converse is true of the Javanese scholar. Recognizing the difference between the insider's and the outsider's perspectives, Hood asserted that each makes a contribution.

But others—and not exclusively outsiders to Western society—question the validity of cross-cultural approaches on intellectual and moral grounds. Many, from Danielou (1973: 34–35) to Ravi Shankar (1999) and Agawu (2003), indict the profession of ethnomusicology for dealing with non-European music in a condescending way, treating it as something quaint or exotic, failing (for instance) to make the kinds of distinction between fine art and folk genres conventionally made among strata and degrees of learning in Western culture. In this chapter I am primarily concerned with the intellectual problems that face outsiders *because* of who they are and only secondarily with the morality of dealing with the music of another culture or the ethical questions confronting the fieldworker, which I'll save for chapter 15. But it is difficult to separate these issues.

The young Nigerian's question might not have been able to put his finger on the reasons for his anger, but certainly there is good reason to question the activities of ethnomusicologists who come, after all, in many guises, have many roles. In all cases there is an imbalance. They come as students, but they quickly pretend to become masters. They theorize that intercultural study is a reciprocal affair, but they proceed to study non-Western music on their own terms, and then they also expect foreign scholars to come and study Western music on Western terms. They usually live well in the "field" and go on to exploit what they have learned and collected. What they learn is the most valuable of cultural and intellectual properties, but they treat it like artifacts and commodities. At least it has often been thus, and surely it's how fieldworkers are frequently perceived.

Some ethnomusicologists define themselves as any persons, from any cultural background, who, as outsiders, study the musical cultures of the world's societies. But, in fact, the overwhelming majority have been simply members of Western society who study non-Western music, or members of affluent nations who study the music of the poor, or maybe city folk who visit the backward villages in their hinterland. The imbalance might not have arisen if there had been, from the beginning, a network of intercultural scholarship consisting of individuals from many societies who studied each other's musics from many perspectives, more or less evenly distributed. This is in the realm of the "it might have been," but we can get glimpses of the kinds of insights of which we have been deprived by the one-sided history of our field.

A new graduate student from Ghana appeared in my class. He had studied Western music in Europe, but as a villager in his youth had also mastered the percussion ensemble music of his native tradition. My course dealt with Native American music, a field that (other) Americans have been inclined to study primarily in terms of its melodic aspects. As students of Western music, we had learned how to deal with and to perceive melodic material reasonably well, felt confident that we could also do this for Indian songs, but were rather at a loss to treat rhythm in a very sophisticated way. Yet from the beginning, the Ghanaian student turned to the complex relationships between the rhythmic structures of drum and voice, able to comprehend them readily. Throughout the semester he enriched the class with insights that came from the African drummer's thorough grounding in the perception of rhythmic phenomena. If Western ethnomusicology, because of Western preoccupation with melody in its classical system, has usually been better at dealing with the pitch-derived aspects of music, it is conceivable that an "African" ethnomusicology, more qualified to deal with rhythm, would have given us a different "outsider's" picture of American Indian music, had there been scholars encouraged to carry out such work (see Cachia 1973 and Tsuge 1974 for parallel cases). Such unrealized possibilities boggle the imagination. So, in the real world, why indeed shouldn't one be asking, "With what rationale do you study the music of other cultures?"

Let's hear some more of the frequently uttered objections to ethnomusicological outsiders. They represent a kind of musical colonialism, manipulating the societies they visit, keeping them from controlling their own musical destiny. They may encourage the retention of old materials or segments of a repertory, and they take away music—at the same time leaving it behind, to be sure, but perhaps polluted by having been removed, recorded, its secrecy violated—for their own benefit and that of their society. They take advantage of their membership in a wealthier society, with economic and military power, to cause musical turmoil and dissent, giving allegiance to a few sycophants who may then artificially become an elite because of the association. Walking with heavy tread, they leave footprints after their departure. As pointed out variously in works on Africa—a classic article by Meintjes (1990), and books by Turino (2000) and Erlmann (1999)—and Australia (the essays in Neuenfeld 1997), they are in cahoots with the American- and

European-dominated music industry in appropriating traditional material and incorporating it in the "world music" universe.

We aren't all like that, some ethnomusicologists may say; sometimes the natives even love us. One certainly needn't swallow such an apocalyptic version of the ethnomusicologist's evil effect whole hog. Yet already Alan Merriam, an observer who participated in his host culture to only a small extent, found upon his return to a village in Zaire, in which he had worked fourteen years before, that his earlier visit was the most significant event in remembered music history (Merriam 1977b). Since then it has become clear to all of us, in the wake of intellectual currents emphasizing ethics as a major guide to behavior in our field (see Slobin 1992a for a summary, and Nicole Beaudry in Barz and Cooley 1997: 77–83 for a sensitive analysis), and the recognition that the role and position of observer plays a key part, encapsulated in the term "reflexivity," that ethnomusicologist outsiders very much affect the "field." Their very presence can even get in the way of their own research.

But if we claim that no actual harm comes from the visit of an ethnomusicologist, one is often asked just what good such a study does the people whose music is investigated, and increasingly this question has come from those people. I'll leave aspects of this issue for chapter 15, which looks more at political contexts. The major *intellectual* objection (with its own political overtones—as brilliantly presented by Said 1978) to fieldwork by an outsider is based on the belief that musical systems are essentially untranslatable. There are field situations in which the ethnomusicologist is viewed as a threat because of the comparative approach, sometimes explicitly presented in speaking of "Eastern," "Oriental," "African," "Western" styles, all concepts that assume comparison of musics. The adverse reaction results from three beliefs typically held in the host cultures, as follows.

1. Ethnomusicologists come to compare non-Western musics or other "other" traditions to their own, not to study them because they are interesting or significant, and do not respect them for their own sake. The purpose is, so it is thought, to make comparisons in order to show that the outsider's own music is superior, and that the host music is merely a stage in the development of the perfect music. Needless to say, no ethnomusicologist actually does that any more, but this kind of primitivism and orientalism is distasteful to thoughtful members of host societies.

2. Ethnomusicologists want to use their own approaches to non-Western music, but these will not work and without doubt result in misunderstandings. Non-Western scholars, especially if trained also in Western methods (e.g., J. H. Nketia, Kofi Agawu, Nazir A. Jairazbhoy) tend to see European and Amer-

ican publications full of errors. What is really significant cannot be learned, as my teacher said, at least not with an essentially comparative approach. As we have seen (in chapter 5), it's a belief shared by some Western scholars.

3. They come with the assumption that there is such a thing as African or Asian or American Indian music, disregarding boundaries obvious to the host, ready to lump and generalize in ways they would never tolerate in contemplation of their own musics. Members of all societies regard their own music as something special, and the ethnomusicologist is accused of underrating its musical diversity. Many Asian and African intellectuals think that this is the way it has been done.

One may argue that things have not always been so bad, that ethnomusicologists do better by a music than do the other Western musicians, the composers, arrangers, members of the recording industry, who come into contact with the third world—that ethnomusicologists help tradition-minded musicians maintain the independence of their art and aid in the revival of native musics about to disappear. They admit that they are aware of the limitations of their approaches, are doing the best they can, and accomplish at least something to help international understanding. They often take political stances in opposition to their own nations' colonialist foreign policies. In the face of this, though, the message sometimes seems to be "Never mind, we'd rather take care of things ourselves" and even "Go home, stupid white person." It is a personal and disciplinary dilemma.

But we come to yet another objection, given already by implication in Mantle Hood's statement (above). The culture's "insider" and "outsider" provide different interpretations, both valid. Reasoned thought accords primacy to the former view; it is clearly the more important. It is the insider who provides the perspective that the culture has of itself. The outsider, with an essentially comparative and universalist approach, merely adds something less significant. If we as Western scholars believed that Indian and Chinese scholars had something to tell us about Western music, which they could study as outsiders free of our biases and special emotional attachment to our art, we'd nevertheless reject the relegation of our own findings and interpretations to a background status and would expect the Indian and Chinese insights to remain supplementary. Conversely, non-Western scholars resent being put in the role of minor contributors to the understanding of their own music. Indeed, as Blum (1991: 5–9) makes clear, there have been a lot more significant and published scholars from non-European cultures in the history of ethnomusicology than we (Americans) usually like to remember.

As my teacher said, it may be that I will never understand his music the way his compatriots do, and that the best I can expect is to be able to point out some interesting things they hadn't noticed.

Who's an Insider?

One of the major events in ethnomusicology since 1950 has been the emergence of scholars in non-Western nations who study, if not the music of their personal tradition, then that of their nation or region (for early examples and comment, see Mapoma 1969 and Euba 1971, and for later ones, Chou 2002 and Chan 1991). The relative roles of Western and non-Western scholars in ethnomusicology have been debated in international gatherings, where it has sometimes been shown how many modern nation-states in the third world exist in violation of culture boundaries otherwise determined, such as tribal and language groups, urban and rural cultures. It's taken for granted that a Briton doing research in Nigeria is an outsider but that a Nigerian of Yoruba background is an insider in relationship to his or her Hausa compatriot. But only by coincidence did British colonization throw these peoples, as it were, into the same nation. The same is true of the Javanese studying in Sumatra, though he or she may have politically and intellectually greater claims to insidership. So does the Bostonian in the Louisiana bayous, but you might not know it from talking to Cajuns. It is interesting, however, to see that scholars in the more industrialized African and Asian nations are beginning to admit that they, like European and American fieldworkers, are also outsiders to the rural societies with which they deal. They admit this as a liability to their scholarship, but they may also insist that their political right to be "insiders" remains unimpaired. On that front, there is even a tendency for insider identity to be accorded to residence on a continent. Asian music should be studied by Asians, African music by Africans, one sometimes hears.

The concepts of continent, nation, ethnic group or enclave, and many other culture groups (as described for music cultures as "micromusics" by Slobin 1992b) play parallel, different, alternating roles. Development of the world as the "global village" may make everyone potentially an insider to all societies as musical homogenization grows. The question of the outsider's intellectually meaningful and valid contribution has been muddied by political issues, by the guilt the industrialized nations have to bear for colonizing the others and whites for enslaving other populations, and by the hegemony of the industrial North over the postcolonial "third world."

Two experiences of my own in 1988 illustrate the dilemma. Some eighteen months before the fall of the Berlin wall, in the days of *glasnost* and *perestroika*, I was invited to a small conference of ethnomusicologists from the United States and the Soviet Union. We Americans hoped to introduce our Soviet colleagues, from a number of different Soviet republics, to our "advanced" methodologies. But our gracious hosts scolded us gently because, instead of studying our own backyard, we were being colonialists. They thought it was better scholarship and better ethics to work at home, to look at the "other" in one's own neck of the woods. But in the same year, at a conference on the history of ethnomusicology in Urbana, Illinois, one of the distinguished guests, Oskar Elschek, made a point of telling us that although he had done most of his fieldwork in his native Slovakia, he always saw himself as an outsider and was thus seen by the villagers whose music he, the urban professor, had come to study.

It can come as a surprise to fieldworkers that the people with whom they work and from whom they learn want to know what good this work will do them, what they will get out of it. The days of glass beads as the colonialist's universal answer are long gone, but beyond being paid in some way for their time, informants want to know what of real value they will receive in return for having provided a unique service, for having taught what no one in the fieldworker's own culture can teach, what cannot be found in books, what even few in their own society can command. In somewhat the same way the officials in the ministry of culture may want to know how the cultural life of the nation will benefit. What is given has value and can in a sense be marketed. Will the nation benefit if its music is recorded, if works are published about it, if its records are disseminated by European scholars, institutions, companies? Or is it better to wait until the nation's own facilities and personnel are up to the task? Many other questions flow from this.

Exposure involves risk. Informants risk the disapproval of their fellows, ridicule if the visiting foreigner later misinterprets what has been learned or takes unfair advantage. They expose the vital organs of their culture, bound to include a component of secrecy. I am not referring only to those societies in which the recording of ritual music would automatically invalidate the ritual. Every society wants to keep aspects of its culture to itself. The way it lives provides social integration; all peoples wish to exclude others from certain of their ways. To teach an outsider your culture is a kind of sharing, sharing of yourself with people who will not remain but will discard you once they have what they want (see Umesh Pandey, quoted in Myers 1992: 42–43). You ask yourself to what extent you should share your culture for pay or prestige or just out of the goodness of your heart, and when it will no longer be worth the money—and at what point your fellow villagers will think you have gone too far and thus make *you* something of an outsider.

So That People Will Understand

Looking at a few of my experiences in the field, I ask myself what it was that my teachers and informants wanted out of their exchange with me. For sure, they wished the world to have respect for their music, and in time they could be convinced that sharing with me might work to that end. Some wanted adequate pay for their time. They wanted to be treated like human beings— like friends, teachers, associates, surrogate family members, not like robot-informants or clerks in a department store. Beyond this, they wanted their material to be used in accordance with their own ideas. Native American singers wanted to be sure that records would not be issued, since they were on the verge of issuing their own. They wanted to be sure that, in teaching, I would treat their music as something integral to their culture. They wished to avoid misinterpretation, and they wanted to know that I applied to their music those standards that I normally applied to my own. If as a music teacher I were careful to teach what I considered the best music of my culture, they wanted this attitude taken also with theirs, given, of course, different criteria. They did not want much of what they said to be widely publicized, did not wish individuals to be mentioned or singled out for attention. And they expected help with their problems, felt it would be churlish for me not to be concerned, even if I had no legal or official obligation to do so. In Iran it was similar, except that my teacher insisted that if he spent his time with me, what I learned must be imparted to the world. "When you return to America, you will write a book about what I have taught you?" "Well, I didn't really have that in mind; maybe I'll never know enough." "But you must, you must write such a book, so that people in America will understand . . ."

As a matter of fact, it is not clear that a host society necessarily prefers the "participant" approach. If the fieldworker wishes to change from outsider to something approaching insider identity, participation seems the most logical route. It is also often the most comfortable for the local musicians, who like teaching foreigners as they teach their own students and are uncomfortable in the face of unexpected questions or when asked to play into a microphone for taping (well, that's actually hardly a problem any more). But there are also cases in which members of a society don't want participation, but are willing to be observed.

Fieldworkers involved in the classical musics of India know that one is hardly taken seriously as a music scholar if one is not studying ragas and practicing every day. In the classical music world of Iran, too, participation to a degree was, in my experience, essential. My teacher was willing to have me play the role of observer, but he was not impressed; only when I indicated a desire to learn like his local students did I achieve some credibility. Even then, my observer-like insistence on recording particular things that I requested from a large group of musicians remained an enigma to him. But had I, visiting the villages and small towns of Iran, tried to learn the trade of a *motreb*, a minstrel, this would surely have been seen as an intolerable violation of many rules. I was from the wrong place, in the wrong social class, from the wrong family, wrong religion. Even if I learned the material correctly (an unlikely prospect), I simply wasn't the kind of person who could become a *motreb*. Similarly, American Indians of the northern Plains may be a bit ambivalent (though in the end usually agreeable) toward a white person who tries to sing Native social dance songs, but negative about one who tries to intrude in ceremonies. Some Native peoples of the Southwest would take a harsher view. If ethnomusicologists want to be welcome in a foreign society, they have to behave as much as they can in accordance with its standards.

One day I tried out one of my hare-brained theories about the interrelationships of *gushehs* in the Persian *radif* on my teacher. "My goodness, I never thought of that; of course you're right, and what you said underscores what I've been telling you about the magnificence of our *radif*," he exclaimed. Maybe an outsider could be of some use after all, as he or she could, because of who he or she is, as Hood says, make a significant contribution even to the insider's understanding. But the matter has to be approached carefully, under the right conditions. A foreign student submitting to the same discipline (well, close to the same) as the Iranian students gained the privilege of making her own discoveries, making use of her special outsider role; but that's quite different from the Western scholar who draws conclusions from distant observation.

And so, noting or discovering things that are meaningful to a society but not part of its ordinary musical thought can have the effect of mitigating political and intellectual objections to the ethnomusicologist's presence. He or she may determine such odd bits of information as the number of songs or pieces comprising the total repertory of a musician, or play records of strange musics, Western and other, in order to elicit commentary to approach the principles of an aesthetic. These are things non-Western musicians might not think of trying—or, for that matter, Western musicians either, as these approaches are a bit strange, really—but in most cases they do not really violate the rules of music-making and social relationships.

The idea of joint research by an "insider" and an "outsider" has been mentioned as a way of bridging chasms. In the strictest sense it hasn't often occurred, and there are so far few articles and books with the names of Western and Indian, Japanese, or African scholars as coauthors. But fieldwork is in all respects a cooperative enterprise, and the major informants and teachers should properly be the coauthors of most studies. The inclusion of a scholar native to the nation whose musical culture is being investigated may be of great value, and as better communication develops between Western and other ethnomusicologists, one may expect to see more such publications. But don't assume that the cooperation of an Indian, Nigerian, or Ecuadorian ethnomusicologist will necessarily satisfy the insider-outsider dilemma. Villagers may regard the scholar from the capital as much of an outsider as the American, and with the suspicion in which they hold bureaucrats of all sorts. There may be resentment of intrusions by an urban, government-connected person, whose intranational colonialism is as distasteful to the villagers as the international colonialism foisted upon them from the outside. Tension between urban and rural, government official and peasant, rich and poor, majority and minorities within third-world nations is a fact of everyday life. The inclusion of native scholars may provide needed musical and cultural expertise, and it may also please the academic community and the ministries in the capital, but such scholars are not necessarily "insiders."

If third-world scholars begin in large numbers to engage in ethnomusicological research, one may ask whether this will greatly change the intellectual stance of the field. Perhaps so—and a good thing, I think. For example, there is a longstanding tradition of musical scholarship in India, and Indian scholars publish widely. While it is difficult to characterize, their work has a unique flavor and character. A book resulting from a conference on Asian music attended only by Asian scholars and musicians (Koizumi, Tokumaru, and Yamaguchi 1977: 11) emphasizes the need of developing the concept of "ethnomethodology," derived from but not precisely parallel to the concept thus named by Garfinkel (1967), approaching research by going deeply into a society's own way of organizing its thinking and actions. The authors of this book, largely Japanese, are critical of ethnocentrism and perceive much research by Europeans and Americans to be thus flawed. But they are also keenly aware of ethnocentrism in an Asian context. "A close observation . . . will soon reveal a conspicuous attitude, i.e., comparing Japanese music with other Asian musics. One may call it 'Japan-centrism.' However, it is not meant so.

Rather, it is meant that such a perspective is only one among many that deserve attempting. Other perspectives must be fully explored in the future by ethnomusicologists of various nationalities" (viii).

A wise statement, for it avoids simply replacing Western objectivism or universalism (which is often a mask for Western ethnocentrism) with the generalization that Asians are one and automatically "have it right," an attitude sometimes heard among other non-Westerners, or yet by a mindless anticomparativism. Rather, Koizumi espoused the concept that one can only study from one's own viewpoint, but that a comparison of viewpoints may give the broadest possible insight; in any case, comparative study is "the principal means by which the quest for knowledge is pursued" (Koizumi 1977: 5). Armed with such wisdom, scholars of the future, among them many from Asian and African and other nations, can proceed with confidence. Anthropologists have also for a long time suggested the same thing but observed it, it seems, mainly in the breach (Hsu 1973). Firth spoke long ago of the need for "expert anthropologists coming from a great range of countries . . . not only to study the problems of their communities but also to give that useful comparative analysis of each other's problems" (1944: 22).

Ethnomusicologists are often contrasted to historians of European music; the former are said to work outside their culture but the latter within it. But there is reason to ask whether there is ever a true "insider" even in historical work. The American student of German music of 1830 is thoroughly removed from the culture that produced this music. The newly developed field of reception history in musicology takes this paradox into account. By chance, music from 1830 is still performed, and thus its sound constitutes a part of the musical culture of 2003. But no doubt the modern student understands the music of Schumann and Mendelssohn quite differently from the way in which it was perceived in their day, and actually, in a way contemporary students of Indian and Japanese music are at an advantage because they can at least observe at first hand and study with living teachers. If Schumann could speak to Americans of today, he might also say, "You will never understand this music," and yet our ability to understand it is taken almost for granted. It is hardly necessary to go further, to the Middle Ages and Renaissance, to make the point.

Some historians believe, indeed, that an "insider" cannot write history, that one needs the perspective of distance, of elapsed time. At one time ethnomusicologists took the analogue for granted as well, realizing that they provided a particular perspective. More recently, the division of roles has been muddied. But I believe that the best approach is to reconcile one's self to being an outsider, providing a limited if unique view. In the end, this is our proper role, whether it is as a European or American working in Turkey, a university-educated Nigerian or Indian working in a village, a woman from the countryside who has been trained to look at her culture in special ways not shared by her fellows, or an American trying to find rhyme and reason in the musical life of his or her own urban community.

Once more: What is it that our consultants and teachers want from us? Most significantly, they demand recognition of their art and their culture. Helen Myers (1992: 16) characterized ethnomusicologists as the "great egalitarians of musicology," though admitting that each quickly springs to the defense of "his" or "her" music. But to our teachers abroad, for us simply to be egalitarians may not go far enough. It may be a cultural universal, the belief that one's own music is special—not only to one's own society, but maybe globally. The German music historian Eggebrecht (Dahlhaus and Eggebrecht 1985: 191–92) tells us that the essence of Western music resides in its "primacy among the arts; it is incomparable in its nature and its ambivalence, reflection of the cosmos, creator and destroyer of the good and the evil." It's a strong statement of the uniqueness of Western culture, but as a lover of Mozart, Beethoven, and Schubert, in my heart I can't contradict. Elsewhere too, however, one hears of the uniqueness of cultures. A musician in Madras insisted to me that the world needed only two things to exist in peace: English literature—principally Shakespeare—and Carnatic music, which can express everything that humans wish musically to express. Carnatic music, he said, was the most essential music of humanity. And then, my Blackfoot teacher: "The right way to do something is to sing the right song with it." He corrected himself: "The right *Blackfoot* way to do something is to sing the right song with it." Wasn't this true in other societies, I asked? Could he imagine this? He didn't know, but he believed not, because this was a way in which the Blackfoot were distinct from other nations. And finally there was my teacher in Iran, who often spoke with me about various musics he had heard or heard about. Persian music, with its twelve modes, *dastgahs,* is the richest, as it has a universal expressiveness; it could reflect everything about Persian life and culture. European music has only two modes compared to the twelve. Music as a "reflection of the cosmos, creator and destroyer of good and evil," as Eggebrecht gave it; this was how my three cited consultants—and maybe many other musicians throughout the world—would have gladly characterized their own musical system. It's possible that my teacher in Iran, telling me that I would "never understand this music," meant that I would never appreciate its unique grandeur in a world context.

12

Hanging on for Dear Life:
Archives and Preservation

Archives of the World, Unite!

Of the many definitions of ethnomusicology, none explicitly or implicitly includes the concept of preservation as a major purpose or component. Yet the preservation of music in various forms has all along been one of the major activities. This urge, characteristic especially of the early history of our field, continues with us in the present. At the 1950 meetings of folklorists and ethnomusicologists in Bloomington, Indiana (reproduced in Thompson 1950 and also described in Thompson 1996: 259–71), major sessions were devoted to the subject, and in 1963, at the sixteenth annual conference of the International Folk Music Council in Jerusalem, a full session was held on "preservation and renewal of folk and traditional music." Alan Lomax devoted much of his life trying to defend against the "cultural grey-out" that would result from the disappearance of separable traditions, and indeed, among his many activities, the recording, preservation, and archiving of American and European folk musics were a major component of his career. As a matter of fact, many musicologists of all stripes have been motivated throughout their history by the belief that the interesting music of the world is disappearing, and that our field as a whole must hang on for dear life, recording and notating and storing as against some kind of musical famine. It's a warning that has been promulgated for almost 150 years, and while it must be admitted that music—songs, pieces, performance practices   is as interesting as ever, it is a warning well taken. Through the twentieth century, ethnomusicologists have sometimes worked hand in hand with, but sometimes also in opposition to, a lot of educational, commercial, artistic, and governmental (as well as antigovernmental) institutions that have devoted themselves to preservation of local and national traditions, often selectively and with ulterior motives, sometimes reviving (see Rosenberg 1993), occasionally just inventing.

Obviously, one must collect and preserve materials in order to study them. But collecting and preserving have sometimes become ends in themselves. In the nineteenth century particularly, but also later, many scholars were devoted more or less exclusively to preservation. They made recordings, sometimes in enormous quantity, and proceeded to store them in archives, perhaps transcribing them into notation, eventually preserving them in print as well; and often went no further. Scholars of Western folk music in particular built vast collections, and they were followed by students of Native American music and to a smaller extent by those of African and Asian musics. In the period before 1950 a few major archives, storehouses of recorded collections, were founded, beginning with the Phonogrammarchiv in Berlin, started by Stumpf and Hornbostel in 1900 (see Reinhard 1961, Katz 2003, and two publications surveying and documenting with recordings the first 100 years of its history: Simon 2000; Simon and Wegner 2000)—which was actually preceded slightly by the less prominent Vienna effort (1899). Also among the most eminent were the German Folk Song Archives in Freiburg (founded in 1914, at first consisting only of manuscripts), the Archive of Folk Song in the Library of Congress (in 1928), and the Archives of Traditional Music at Indiana University (in 1948). Major figures in the history of ethnomusicology have been in managerial positions in these archives—including, for example, Marius Schneider and Robert Lachmann in Berlin, John and Alan Lomax, Joseph Hickerson, and Alan Jabbour at the Library of Congress, and George List, Frank Gillis, and Anthony Seeger at Indiana (see Porterfield 1996; Spear 1978, 1991). Since 1950, many universities as well as libraries, state historical institutions, formally constituted tribal organizations, and other kinds of units have built their own archives of (or including) traditional music. National archives in old and new nations have been developed throughout the world, among the most prominent recent ones being the Archives and Research Center for Ethnomusicology in New Delhi. Ethnomusicologists at universities wished in the first instance to house materials collected by themselves and their students, eventually in order to provide large collections for teaching, study, and research. National archives, including some in new nations established since the 1950s, attempt to make comprehensive collections of national heritage. Some archives are incredibly large; the number of songs and pieces at Indiana University amounts to hundreds of thousands. Even the archive at the University of Illinois, known to be very modest in scope, includes over 400 collections comprising some 10,000 songs and pieces. A few archives, such as those at Indiana University and at UCLA, attempt to be comprehensive, providing research materials for all. Some are simply working collections for local products and needs. Others again try to be comprehensive for a special area; the Phonoteque in the Jewish Music Research Center in Jerusalem collects what may by some criterion be considered Jewish music and materials of all types found in Israel. The Archive of Folk Song of the Library of Congress, now associated with the American Folklife Center but also the Smithsonian Folkways project (whose job is not just preservation of musics but preserving a particular facet of the history of preservation itself), has concentrated on the musics found in the United States.

Clearly, one of the initial purposes of our field, stated early on by Hornbostel (1905), was simple preservation, using the then difficult techniques of recording on cylinders. Gradually, as recording became more convenient and efficient, and as the world's peoples began to produce their own recordings, the attitudes toward preservation became more sophisticated and critical. The history of music preservation includes a lot beyond archiving—publishing, performance, and more—but the development and use of archives has been a major preoccupation of ethnomusicologists and is thus the principal subject of this chapter.

Why archive, why try to save everything? For academics, the question might be considered a "no-brainer." Preservation, obviously, is necessary for historical research, for restudy, for comparison. But archives also play an important role in what has come to be called applied ethnomusicology—the use of ethnomusicological ideas and data to help outside the academy. This includes the production of text and instructional materials for schools, the support of ethnic festivals, the rebuilding of cultures, all of them dependent on sound and visual records of activities and performances no longer practiced.

One of the major problems of an archive is organization and cataloguing, given the many different ways in which the world's cultures classify and identify their musical works, and the problem is exacerbated by the tendency of many recordists to provide insufficient information to place a recording in its proper cultural context. The idiosyncratic tendencies of fieldworkers in organizing and identifying materials certainly didn't help. Library cataloguing systems provide imperfect models. Beyond this, the archives of the world, despite energetic efforts (e.g., the International Association of Sound Archives) have not found a way to cooperate fully in exchanging and combining information. It is, for example, extremely difficult to locate all of the field recordings that have been made in one culture or of one repertory, however small and localized, or all archival versions of one song. An early attempt to list all collections in American archives was published by Herzog (1936b), but this surprisingly large account was made at a time when the making of recordings was difficult and still fairly rare. After the introduction of magnetic tape, archives increased in size and number. In 1958, Indiana University began the publication of a small periodical whose job it was to exchange information, *The Folklore and Folk Music Archivist,* eventually replaced by a periodical titled *Resound,* and there have been other, larger initiatives to establish communication. They have gradually, increased the degree to which they have begun if not to unite and standardize their methods then to cooperate. Briegleb (1970) listed and briefly described 124 archives in the United States and Canada. Chaudhuri (1992) provides a succinct summary of the history and problems of archiving. Increasingly, archivists have found ways to pool their information and resources, but the amount of material going to archives grows exponentially, and so do private collections. Finding a way to fight entropy of disks and tapes and providing efficient compact permanent storage and retrieval is one of the great challenges of the early twenty-first century.

Most of these archives are of greatest use to individuals who are more or less permanently at their institutions, but they are gradually living up to greater potentials. Many of the recordings they contain are restricted by the collectors and may thus be heard but not fully utilized for research. It may amaze the reader that few recordings (with significant exceptions) are fully used by anyone other than the collectors. While the archives continue to grow, most scholars in their research rely upon their own recordings. But it is my distinct impression that the period since 1980 has seen a revival of interest in archives and increasing use. Some of this may be due to the tendency of small communities—for example, Native American nations, or provinces, states, and towns—to develop individual archives of their musical traditions. While this development is encouraging—and is itself a subject for ethnomusicological research—it doesn't necessarily improve the prospects for centralized discographic or bibliographic control.

Oldies Are Goodies

We talk about sound recordings as the norm of the preservation side of ethnomusicology, but of course films and videos and DVDs now accompany and may begin to replace them; and recordings are also accompanied—and were preceded by—still photographs. But preservation was first accomplished by the production of transcriptions published in large numbers in grand collections. There are hundreds of relevant publications, but as almost random examples, let me mention only the monuments of German folk music (Erk 1893–94, Deutsches Volksliedarchiv 1935–74); the many volumes of Hungarian and other eastern European folk song produced as a result of the collecting activities of Bela Bartók and Zoltan Kodály (e.g., Bartók 1959; Corpus 1953; Hungarian Academy of Sciences 1992); the collections of English folk songs found in the various states of the United States and in part stimulated in the 1930s by the Works Progress Administration (see, e.g., Cox 1939; for discussion, Canon 1963; Library of Congress 1942: 2–3; Wilgus 1959: 186–87), and the multivolume collection of Norwegian violin and Hardanger fiddle music (Gurvin 1958–67). The two forms of preservation, recording and notation, differ fundamentally in various ways. For one thing, collections of transcriptions undergo far more filtering; they are in effect collections of recordings processed, organized, and actually preserved selectively in the way transcription is selective in what is chosen for representation. Also, record archives might include materials recorded by amateurs who had no scholarly intent, and by anthropologists whose interests were not specifically musical, while the printed collections required musicianship for transcribing and making decisions on classification and order. The students of folk music were certainly interested in preserving a heritage they felt was slipping away, and this feeling of imminent loss was a powerful stimulus for more specifically ethnomusicological inquiry. The point is that these collectors often sought what was specifically old, partly because it was disappearing but partly, one feels, also because what was old was in a sense good. If today's disc jockeys defensively announce "oldies but goodies," many folk music collectors insisted that the oldies were ipso facto the goodies. Certain scholars who made truly enormous contributions with their insight into musical and cultural processes, such as Bartók and Sharp, were intent upon extracting from modernizing and urbanizing villages and small towns that which was ancient. To be sure, this attitude was not limited to printed collections but includes initiatives such as the resurrections of older recordings in catalog form (e.g., the listing of old field recordings at Indiana University by A. Seeger and Spear 1987), reissues of older recordings (Hornbostel's *Demonstration Collection* of the 1920s) and energetic recording projects (as in Feld 2001). Some collectors even went out of their way to prove that what they collected was indeed old.

Preservation characterized the early history of our field, but it continued as an important facet even while the value of contemplating the present came more to the fore, and in the late twentieth century, it came back to claim a greater role again. The publication of comprehensive collections of national folk music came to be characteristic of musical scholarship in eastern Europe after 1950. In the study of non-Western music, the idea of comprehensive collecting never attained the same importance—with notable exceptions, such as the hundreds of North American Indian songs published by Frances Densmore—and to some, at least, the idea of holding fast to early materials was not so much a consideration as was the very discovery of what was then a new phenomenon. Students of Western folk music, on the other hand, were no doubt affected by the movement in historical musicology to publish series of "monuments" of national music history. Beginning with the German *Denkmäler deutscher Tonkunst* (1892) and the more prestigious Austrian *Denkmäler der Tonkunst in Österreich* (1894), various national series were begun—the most recent, *Music of the U.S.A. (MUSA)*, being published under the aegis of the American Musicological Society—and much of the energy of music historians in the first half of the twentieth century was directed to the publication, in authentic form, of hundreds of often obscure but "historically" important works. In the end, one would in a sense "have" the materials of art music of a given country. Surely the tendency to publish large folk music collections with attention to their authenticity and to the inclusion of good and perhaps especially old versions and variants was similarly motivated. Folk music scholars and folklorists were interested in the preservation of the most important stories, songs, melodies of the rural societies of Europe and eventually the Americas. I am not sure whether much thought was given to the eventual use of such collections. As in the case of the classical *monumenta,* performance was at least sometimes considered. It was assumed, one suspects, that large-scale, artifact-oriented, multipurpose collections would satisfy a number of future needs, historical, ethnographic, and practical. It doesn't always seem to have worked out so.

While the collections grew, the scholars who after about 1960 were concerned with increasingly specialized problems in ethnomusicology tended to decrease concern with comprehensive collecting, and there seemed to develop something of a split between them and those we might label professional collectors. Having recognized that music in oral tradition is subject to constant change, that songs, styles, repertories are in a state of flux, we may wonder why so many individuals devoted themselves to collecting largely for the purpose of preserving what was in a sense a piece of ephemera.

Early in the twentieth century there developed an approach to preserving that one might include among the activities of "applied" ethnomusicology. Practical publications to be used for teaching, the development of records for promulgating what could be of interest to the amateur, the idea of urging people in various communities to continue the older practices of music and dance, finding government support for encouraging them and indeed in some ways improving their practice, all these seem to involve preservation in a different sense, holding materials for practical use by peoples thought to be in danger of losing their heritage. This kind of preservation is not a practice always resulting in unmitigated benefit. Much of it, especially in the 1930s, was to take on political and in some cases stridently nationalistic overtones: It also meant that the collector would intrude, trying to persuade people not to change their ways, insisting that it was incumbent on them to retain preindustrial practices. One senses resentment on the part of societies wanting social change and believing that it must be accompanied by musical change. As seen in my discussion of the roles of insider and outsider, the ethnomusicologist's lesson about the place of music in culture is one that indigenous societies have learned very well. There are interesting examples of conflict. Australian aborigines living in the countryside who did not wish their material to be preserved because the tape recorder would invalidate rituals were opposed by other aboriginals living in cities who felt that they had been deprived of their tribal heritage by their removal to a different setting, and wanted to have these recordings.

In the 1950s there developed a movement within the field of anthropology appropriately labeled "urgent anthropology," involving the recognition of the imminent destruction of societies, cultures, and artifacts by modernization. It emphasized the need for concentrating anthropological resources upon their preservation. In the case of archeology, this might involve the exploration of areas shortly to become inaccessible by the building of dams or roads; in social anthropology, it might be addressed to the forced movement of peoples and the dispersal of once homogeneous populations. For the historian, such preservation was obviously of paramount importance. For the social anthropologist, who studies change as it occurs, it did not outweigh the study of kinds of change constantly occurring; extinction of cultures was, so to speak, an everyday event. So it turned out that the thrust of "urgent anthropology" was mainly the study of the out-of-the-way, with the purpose of gaining insight into human exceptions.

Ethnomusicologists, coming out of a long tradition of looking for the exceptional while often virtually ignoring the readily available, might sympathize with this approach. Some, such as Wolfgang Laade (1969, 1971a), participated in the "urgent anthropology" movement in publications and letters noting cultures and musics in danger of extinction. But while we may be bemused by those who wish to exclude all but the exceptional, it is of course true that during the past few centuries many musical cultures, belonging to the weak end of power distribution, have in effect gone out of existence. This is relevant to scholars working in the Americas or Australia, areas of gradual social change, but even more in nations where culture change has been dramatic, such as Israel or parts of Central Asia and western China, for here, obviously, once highly heterogeneous populations appear to be on the way to thorough homogeneity. No doubt, then, much ethnomusicology has been motivated by a sense of urgency.

Recognizing that the principal owners of any music ought to be the people who created and performed it—or their descendants and relatives—ethnomusicologists began, in the 1970s, to encourage the development of music (and other cultural) archives in such institutions as local museums, or on Native American reservations, and in places relevant to the societies involved. The 1980s saw the growth of a process sometimes called "repatriation," which is, mainly, the development of archives in and for the cultures that produced the music, and particularly, then, the "return" of early recordings and artifacts such as instruments. It began, according to Frisbie (2001: 492) around 1960, and in the United States it was closely associated with the legal expansion of Native American rights to grave sites and human remains as well as intellectual property. A number of institutional and personal initiatives undertook to distribute material from large archives to ethnic and tribal repositories. Most notable is the Federal Cylinder Project (1984; see also Frisbie 2001: 495), which copied and disseminated the earliest collections of Native American music. The archives of Native American and First Nations communities, often very comprehensive, often contain material that may be used for the reconstruction of ceremonies and rituals whose content has been lost. The Smithsonian Institution and the American Folklife Center have deposited collections, sometimes with considerable ceremony, on Native American reservations.

One of the scholars who most emphasized the central role of ethnomusicologists as helpers in the preservation process was the Australian Catherine Ellis. The "Aboriginal Music Centre" that she helped to establish in Adelaide contained a large collection of tapes that aboriginal people living in the city, who claimed to have lost all traditional knowledge, could consult for a variety of purposes, including the reconstitution of older ceremonies or their adaptation to urban life. Meeting with a group of aboriginal users of this archive who told me that in their quest for some knowledge of their musical traditions they were having to start from a position of total ignorance, I found that they considered their visits to it important aspects of their lives, and that they welcomed the help of white ethnomusicologists. But small indigenous societies are not the only ones benefiting from the use of archival resources in their quest for reconstitution of their musical cultures. The large archives of folk music, such as those at Indiana University and the Library of Congress, were important resources for the musicians who led the twentieth-century revivals of Anglo-American folk song.

What's Worth Preserving?

What should we preserve? "Everything?" Impossible! There has to be some kind of a process of sampling. Just as fieldwork involves, in a variety of ways, the sampling of a culture, so archives try to work in ways that will assure adequate sampling of the world's musics. The point is that we must make clear our values, decide what we are seeking. We can start by asking whether we should preserve what we deem to be of high quality, or what is typical, or what a culture considers ideal. The fieldworker needs to grapple with some fundamental issues of ethnomusicological method before simply turning on the video camera. There is the question of authenticity, the problem of what is in some way representative of a culture. The point is that before going to work one must face the theoretical issues of sampling, plan one's collecting activities, understand what one is doing. This would be greatly preferable to recording everything within earshot and ending up with a collection with which one can do very little. We should design research carefully and then go after the material we need to carry it out, rather than preserving first and studying later.

Preservation and research may conflict. Sometimes the field methods we impose on the society we wish to study distort what is really going on. Let me refer to a personal experience, my project in Iran in which I tried to study certain principles of improvisation. I tried to use a single mode, a *dastgah*, as a sample, and to record as many improvisations in that mode as I could, and I believe I was reasonably successful. However, I am sure I did not arrive at something that is truly representative. All of the performances I recorded, I feel, would be acceptable to the Iranian listener and to the informed Iranian musician. Individually, they are part and parcel of the musical culture. However, since I was there with my tape recorder, requesting and commissioning performances and available for formal events, I no doubt failed to record certain kinds of musical phenomena that would appear only in other less structured and less formal situations. What I recorded was a group of performances each of which was probably acceptable as proper Persian music, but I wonder whether they as a group constitute a representative sample, or whether my particular recording procedure caused certain things to be done more, or less, than in real musical life. I may have found out important things about the way certain things are done in Iranian performance practice, but probably I did not adequately preserve a slice of Iranian musical culture. This kind of conclusion might have to be made in many studies, but particularly in those dealing with improvisation of folk music, where variation from a norm is a major point of observation. In our zeal to preserve, we should be careful to preserve what actually happens in society, or if we can't, at least be aware of the ways our work distorts it.

If we view ethnomusicology as a science of music history that emphasizes patterns and regularities, preservation pure and simple will play a minor role. But the gathering of data in systematic and controlled forms is important to scholars who need to deal with it in something approaching a scientific way. The result of such gathering is in the end also a form of preservation for the future. At the other end of the spectrum, we ask ourselves whether we should continue encouraging people to keep up their old practices, asking them to do what they perhaps would not wish to do, just for the sake of the rest of the world. I have no answer. But there is no doubt that ethnomusicologists, simply by their interest in certain kinds of musical phenomena, have stimulated the societies they study to keep up, develop, and sometimes isolate and preserve these phenomena in culturally traditional or in more artificial fashion. The role of collectors, with their technology and prestige, has in various places been enormous; we have heard of Asian and African performers who won't perform without the presence of "their" ethnomusicologist.

So what is our role, in the preservation game? One alternative is to study what actually happens, swallowing hard when we find that societies change all the time and allowing precious gems of creation to fall by the wayside. People must retain the freedom to do as they wish (something of an article of faith with me) or are forced by circumstances to do, and then observing what actually happens, because this makes better scholarship than mixing observation with the imposition of one's ideas. Or we may instead take it as a basic assumption the idea that preservation on our part and on the part of the cultures of the world is itself a supreme good and must be encouraged at the expense of other factors. An unresolved question for the individual as well as the profession.

Ethnomusicologists in recent years have concentrated on the study of change, and they need somehow to record and preserve change. How one goes about this, creating a record of change, a basic phenomenon of culture that isn't compatible with the concept of culture as a group of "things," may be beyond present-day practicality. But I would suggest that one theoretical direction in which we could move is to add to the musical artifact—the piece, song, individual situation as the focus of study—ways in which the fact and process of change itself can somehow be used as the main focus of attention. There is reason to believe that of the various components of musical culture, using Merriam's model, the musical sound itself changes least rapidly; behavior changes more quickly, and the conception of music most quickly. The sound of Blackfoot music today is much closer to what it was in the nineteenth century than is their system of ideas about music. If we are indeed to preserve something about music, we must find ways also of preserving and recording the concept part of the model; this seems to me to be in fact more urgent ethnomusicology than the continuing preservation of the musical artifact alone. If I am justified in being generally critical of the role of preservation in the ethnomusicology of the past, it is because it has often failed to recognize that there is much more to music than the piece. As the archives of the world continue to grow, those practicing preservation will increasingly need to expand and refine their approaches to the systematic sampling of the infinite musical universe.

And finally, the act and practice of recording by the societies that we're trying to understand has become, itself, a significant area of research, and one that requires increased attention and sophistication. Christopher Scales (2004: 346), suggesting that ethnomusicologists have recently been confronted with a division of loyalty between attending to their own recording and preservation and contemplating preservation itself as a field of research, sees their field "becoming increasingly intertwined with recording technologies and mass mediation (as both topics of and tools for study)."

13

I Am the Greatest:
Ordinary and Exceptional Musicians

Celebrating the Heroes

There is a curious disparity. While ethnomusicologists experience a great deal of face-to-face contact with individual informants or teachers in the field and specialize in concentrating on a particular person, the older literature of the field, particularly, provides surprisingly little information about the individual in music. Historians of Western music seem (at least on the surface) to be occupied principally with the work of individual musicians, their roles and contributions as persons, while ethnomusicologists have tended, though with a few notable exceptions, to be drawn to the anonymous. Given the kinds of data available, one expects to find such tendencies, but not such an outright split. Some possible explanations: The intrinsic value of non-Western music and folk music has, despite recent thrusts to the contrary, always been questioned in Western musical society, and the attention given to them defended with arguments to the effect that they are, if not great music, at least the music with which large groups of people identify themselves and only for that reason worthy of study. The long-held belief that rural communities, indigenous nations, and tribal groups are homogeneous in their musical and other experience has contributed to the neglect of the individual, as has the long-held assumption that music in non-Western and folk cultures is stable and unchanging until polluted by the West.

To reconcile this interest of ethnomusicology in the music of large population groups with the need to include an understanding of individual character and diversity, it has been reasonable for ethnomusicologists to focus in some of their research on representative musicians, some perhaps outstanding, others more likely average or acceptable, and, further, on the ordinary member of society who participates in musical life but cannot by whatever criteria the culture uses be called truly a musician. In a humanistic field this may seem to be an odd purpose. We don't wish to explore the mediocre for the mere purpose of giving mediocrity its just representation. But a musical culture contains such variation, and so, besides the excellent, the outstanding, who represents the musical ideal in composition or performance, we need understanding of the ordinary but musically acceptable person: the composer who barely makes it in a minor United States campus music department and gets performed occasionally, the kamancheh player who scrounges out a modest living playing at weddings in northern Iran, the person who buys a few CDs or can't do housework or study without the radio, the seventh-desk orchestra violist, and the member of a Drum (singing group) at an Indian competition powwow that never even wins third place. It is such people who comprise the real mainstream of musical life in the world, make music a cultural and human universal, constitute the acceptable everyday musical experience of a culture. But of course we also want to know whether a society distinguishes sharply, gradually, or perhaps not at all between the great and the typical. In order to explore the study of the individual in ethnomusicological fieldwork, this chapter considers three selected approaches: biography, personal repertory, and personal performance practice.

The tradition of scholarly biography in the literature of non-Western societies isn't a new thing, but it has recently begun to burgeon. The classical traditions of Asia have produced accounts of the lives of their "great" men who play heroic roles, usually of the past. Indian musical scholarship has accumulated a lot of information about the lives of some of the great composers of the eighteenth and nineteenth centuries, as illustrated best, perhaps, by the large amount of literature about and veneration for the "trinity" of great composers already mentioned in chapter 3, much of it from oral tradition.

For scholars who explicitly identify themselves as ethnomusicologists, by contrast, the use of biography—essentially autobiography, gathered through interviews that must be corroborated and edited—is a major thrust in anthropological field method. The practice goes back, interestingly, to the linguistically oriented method of text gathering of the late nineteenth century, as verbal material could be conveniently accumulated by asking an informant to tell the story of his or her life. A thorough biography of an individual who constitutes a sample of a society should provide some information about the role of music in the subject's life. Here and there this actually happens, as in Radin's (auto)biography of a Winnebago Indian (1963: 52–57), first published in 1920, which tells about the subject's learning of Peyote songs and the interaction of singing with other aspects of the Peyote experience. In midcentury, studies of individual composers and singers in the realm of folk music were more common, and were written with the kinds of perspective also used by historians of classical music (see, e.g., Glassie, Ives, and Szwed 1970; Ives 1964). After 1980, with greater fine-tuning of studies in the variegation found within musical cultures, studies of individual musicians came to play a significant role, as perhaps most prominently exemplified by Danielson's (1997) biography of Umm Kulthum, arguably the most prominent figure in twentieth-century Arabic music history, and Veit Erlmann's (1996) study of South African Isicathamiya music with focus on the life and career of—and participation by—its principal protagonist, Joseph Shabalala. There are, of course, many ways in which individuals can be sketched so as to shed light on their culture; biography is only one. But it's the way in which such biographies relate individual musicians to their culture and help provide an understanding of musical culture as a whole that distinguishes them as ethnomusicology. But not just musicians: To ethnomusicology, the range of musical phenomena experienced by one person in a single day or throughout a lifetime is of great interest.

Careers

About composers in a society, ethnomusicologists would ask such questions as: What kinds of composers are there? Are they all alike in background, training, and purpose? Are there types? What are their typical careers? How is the music they produce distributed through their lifetimes? Questions of interest for any culture, including that of Western classical music. The range of a composer's stylistic framework in any culture may be idiosyncratic, but it is also determined by the guiding principles of the culture, by the general attitude toward such concepts as art, innovation, the musician as creator or craftsperson, and by such details as the system of patronage, performance practice, and the state of musical and distributional technology. In certain respects this avenue would parallel one of the main approaches of historical musicology, whose literature is full of studies of the total opus of a composer, stressing what within it is typical, giving its distribution over a lifetime and the boundaries of creativity. The interest to ethnomusicology derives from the fact that the concentration on the study of specific composers provides the opportunity of identifying types and their range in any one culture.

It is tempting to look at typical careers of European composers with the kind of perspective one would wish to use in a comprehensive description of a foreign musical culture. Considering the vast amount of literature in the annals of musicology dealing with individual composers, it seems ridiculous to try to generalize about them. But even an unserious attempt may be instructive. And music historians have done some generalizing themselves. An early example is the work of Gustav Becking (1928), who classified composers by personality as expressed in their music, using a rhythmic typology, with Mozart, Beethoven, and Bach as exemplars, but a typology supposedly valid for all European music. Whether this rhythmic typology makes any sense or not, it is instructive, as it replicates what seems to me to be the fundamental myth of Western art music culture in the twentieth century, the opposition of Mozart (the divinely inspired) and Beethoven (the hard-working and very human). The overarching, sweeping generalizations that we often make about non-Western musics seem incredibly naive when translated into the European context. But for a moment, let me take an ethnomusicologist's bird's-eye view of the course of the compositional lives of some composers in the history of Western art music.

We're back in the realm of measuring degrees of similarity, and so we take a deep breath. What about diversity and changeability of style, as opposed to consistency of musical style? We might decide that Joseph Haydn, Ludwig von Beethoven, and Richard Wagner changed considerably in the course of their careers. Their approximate contemporaries, Mozart, Schubert, and Brahms did so to a lesser degree; and maybe in the case of Schubert and Mozart, this is related to their shorter life span. The diversity of work in the oeuvre of most of these composers seems to exceed substantially that of certain others, who are thus regarded as lesser artists. With the exception of Wagner and Verdi, a high degree of specialization doesn't get you "great master" status, and the biggies of the art music world all tried their hand at opera, song, symphony, chamber, and keyboard music. Indeed, such diversity is part of the pattern of a proper composer's career from the late eighteenth century on.

Two other patterns: Some composers had careers that lend themselves to division into contrasting stylistic periods. Beethoven's early, middle, and late works are readily distinguished. The same is not true of Mozart, whose musical persona didn't include such relatively sudden breaks. But in both cases, changes in musical style are present, and indeed they are expected in the work of European composers, so-called early works being judged in different terms from the mature ones. Obvious, you will say; but it must be noted, for such behavior might not be tolerated in another society. Furthermore, there is a tendency on the part of many Western composers to go back, near the endings of their careers, to musical principles of the past, related perhaps to their early years of study or to predecessors with whom they wish somehow to identify themselves. Thus Brahms's Fourth Symphony contains a passacaglia, a form widespread in the seventeenth and eighteenth centuries, not in imitation of this early period but as a way of reconciling his own approach to music with the past; both Beethoven and Mozart in their later years moved to a more contrapuntal style in certain ways reminiscent of the Baroque period.

I don't know whether the reader versed in music history can forgive such a quick glance at Western composers in the style of ethnomusicology, but it might help us to draw some conclusions about the way composers are seen by their society. Thus, music lovers of Europe and the Americas expect their composers to change musical style; they regard certain works of one composer as clearly superior; they express satisfaction at innovation (the more, the better) but also at the tendency to exhibit earlier influences near the end of life. They perceive that the output is divided into periods, tend to find that abrupt changes in style coincide with changes in residence or position, underscoring the view that the musician composes in part under the influence of particular social and political surroundings. They expect musicians to exhibit the lessons they learn from their teachers but also to depart from these. The expectation of change, of development, and a tension between unidirectional progression and circularity are evident. And so is the expectation that a composer may move from emotional to more intellectual focus. I provide this smattering of remarks about some of my favorite composers not as data or conclusions but only to suggest that looking at the patterns of their musical lives in the aggregate, and at the ways they are interpreted later—today—could provide important insight into the "concept" sector of our musical culture. Whether this is truly descriptive of the culture or not, it is the way many Western musicians and music lovers seem to see the role of the composer in their own classical system.

A typical musician's life? There's not the same profusion of biographical data and interpretation for non-Western cultures, but ethnomusicological literature provides some material on the basis of which one can tentatively generalize. In any one culture and in at least certain groups of non-Western cultures that share values, ecology, and technology, there are certain typical patterns of biography and perception. The individual is the agent and recipient of change. Richard Waterman (1956) found that music was used by the people of Yirkalla as a way in which to learn their own culture. The repertory of sacred music was learned gradually, and certain pieces were learned only by elderly men and women, who were also those who knew the most. Here we are dealing, presumably, not with a population of composers, as Western culture would understand the term, but of performers and consumers. For a similar example we can look at change in the life of the individual person of Blackfoot culture. He moved through a series of age-grade societies whose activities included ceremonies and music (Ewers 1958: 104–5; Lowie 1916). As an individual grew older, he or she was successively initiated into new societies, learning their songs and dances. Again, the oldest men would know the largest amount of music, learned gradually, more or less at four-year intervals. The vision quest of the Plains Indians and of tribes surrounding the Plains exhibited a similarly gradual learning of songs. A so-called medicine man or woman would have a succession of visions of his or her guardian spirit, each time learning more in the way of dealing with the supernatural, which included songs.

This is the traditional picture. For recent times, the tendency to gradual learning of new material is a pattern both supported and altered in the career of one Blackfoot singer with whom I worked. Born about 1915, this man was first exposed to Western music through his reservation school, learning French horn, but he also—sometimes secretly—learned a few traditional songs. As a young adult he took up the modern, intertribal repertory of the powwow culture, which consisted largely of social dance songs without words. In later life he gradually became interested as well in the ancient traditional music, learning it from older persons who knew but rarely performed the songs. This sequence has idiosyncratic causes; the third stage coincided with the death of the singer's stepfather, an esteemed tribal leader. But the pattern may also be typical, at least insofar as the most sacred music had long been the province of tribal elders. In this respect, my informant, although he was exposed to musics not known in earlier times, such as the so-called intertribal songs and powwows and the music of the whites, seems to have followed a traditional pattern. But in the sense that he withdrew from interest in one musical repertory as he learned a new one, he probably did not reflect the gradual and cumulative learning of a cohesive musical system. In any event, the concept of pattern in musical life can be found among the ordinary singers of a small tribe as well as the master composers of Western music.

The Importance of Being a Star

The biographical approach gives us a special kind of understanding of change in the life of a person. As a field technique for oral history, it is probably superior to simply asking one's teacher in general how things used to be, which might provide interesting but often unstructured observation. Musicians may be much better at providing views of their own lives, and while they may indeed wish to cast themselves in a special kind of light, they probably have more factual data available about themselves in memory than they have about the culture of their people as it may have changed over a series of decades. But beyond this, the study of individuals also tells us how they see themselves in their own culture, and how they represent themselves.

In 1969, I was visiting Stephen Blum, who was doing fieldwork in Mashhad, Iran, a large religious center that was not considered a hub of musical activity. Indeed, the sacredness of the shrine inhibited the development of a classical music culture. Through a musicians' agent, we chanced to meet and make recordings with a player of the tar, a type of lute widely used in Persian classical, folk, and popular music. Before playing, he said, "I am the best tar player." We must have looked incredulous, because we had lived in Iran long enough to know names, attend formal concerts, take lessons with musicians supported by the government because of their excellence, hear records and radio. "I am the greatest," he reiterated, reminding us of a great American. Then, softening his line a bit, he said, "me and Shahnazi," citing the name of a truly renowned tar player in Tehran. I remembered my American teacher's warning—"Don't argue with your informants"—and thus we proceeded to elicited performances. Disappointing: The man was definitely not an expert; indeed, one would have to assume that he would hardly make a living in Tehran, was perhaps not even in great demand in Mashhad. Clearly he was a long way, to put it mildly, from being a great tar player; he had little technique and seemed to know little repertory. Even so, other Iranians present at our session had not smiled or contradicted him.

This experience was the most extreme among a number in Iran in which there seemed to be a need for musicians to describe themselves as experts, as "the best," in contrast to their otherwise deferential manner, modesty, and ceremonial politeness. Without going into further detail, let me move to a possible interpretation. In Islamic Shi'ite societies, musicians have not been highly respected, and instrumental music in particular is undesirable, associated with sloth, indebtedness, adultery, prostitution, debauchery. It seems that the only way in which musicians could hold their heads up in society was to be stars. Ali Jihad Racy, too, had once told me that in his native Lebanon, "either you're a star or you're nobody." Now, in Iranian society, it was usually rather easy to persuade individuals who love music to rank musicians, especially on a particular instrument; they readily single out the stars, immediately associating an instrument with its best performer: "You want to hear setar? The setar of

Ebadi, of course. Or the nai? You mean, certainly, the nai of Kasai." Thus it seems important for musicians to label themselves as stars in order to maintain self-respect. Our moderately competent tar player in Mashhad was not, I believe, trying to fool us. By describing himself as the greatest tar player, he was merely telling us that he was worthy of our attention.

Now, this information did not come from detailed biographical study. But if we had not paid attention to the individual, taken an analytical view of his or her statements, but had simply assumed that he or she was lying, or a fool, or making outrageous claims, this interpretation would have eluded us. In some respects, our tar player acted like a typical Iranian; in some others, he exhibited the special character of his role as a musician (see also Sakata 1976). The idea of the male musician as a deviant in society, as one who is scorned for abnormal behavior and yet considered indispensable, is analyzed by Merriam (1964: 135–37, 1979), with particular attention to the Basongye of Zaire: "Being a musician is the only way a male [Basongye] can escape the dominant male role with its heavy load of 'normalcy' and still be tolerated as a useful member of society" (1979: 22).

Biographical information has also been of interest to students of the music of India who wish to see the role of the musicians within the context of their gharana, or school of musicianship, as described in the work of Neuman (1980), Silver (1976), and Kippen (1988). Brian Silver, for example, examined the lives of six musicians of one North Indian gharana, concentrating on their achieving the role of an ustad, or master musician, "through the perfection of required musical skills, the assimilation of certain cultural attributes, and the assumption of various postures characteristic of the ustad as a social type" (1976: 29). From his study it is clear that political changes in India during the twentieth century affected the way in which one becomes an ustad. Of three brothers, the older two fulfilled some of the traditional requirements, while the youngest, who grew up during the transitional stage of Indian independence, had to develop his role in other ways, influenced by the growing modernization of the musical system.

On Nour-Ali Khan

To provide here a brief example of ethnomusicological biography, a sketch of the career of my principal teacher in Iran, whom I have frequently mentioned in these pages, illustrates further the interface between musical personality and culture. He was Dr. Nour-Ali Boroumand, called Nour-Ali Khan by his friends, and he was highly regarded by many Iranians and foreigners engaged in the study of Persian music. There were also others who maintained a more critical view. To what extent was he unusual, in what ways did he reflect ideals of Persian musicianship, and what did he have that was ordinary? His musical biography falls rather conveniently into a number of stages: (1) in childhood, first exposure to classical Persian music and some study of the *radif;* (2) secondary school and medical studies in Germany, and the learning of Western classical music; (3) the onset of blindness, return to Iran, and continuation of study of the *radifs* of several teachers; (4) consolidation of the learned *radifs* into his own version; (5) teaching of his *radif* to a few selected private students; (6) the making available of his *radif* to a wide audience of students at two institutions, and to the general public; 7) late in life, a willingness to record his *radif* for the Ministry of Fine Arts, for posterity. In some respects, the history is idiosyncratic. Study in Europe and acquaintance with Western music and the teaching of the *radif* only late in life are not part of the tradition. The fact that he rarely performed in public reflects the Iranian distrust of music and the resulting idealization of the authoritative great amateur, seldom realized in recent decades at any rate. His social and musical conservatism may account for the fact that his contact with Western music does not appear to have influenced his view of Persian music, at least in the direction of Western music, but on the contrary reinforced the view that each culture has and must retain its own music. His study of Western music gave him, however—or so he believed—a greater sense of educational discipline. Studying several *radifs,* by several teachers, in stages from simple to complex, and developing from this his personal *radif*—all this appears to be at least to some degree part of an established tradition. It was the ideal of music study, not possible for many but held to be the best way of establishing oneself squarely in the tradition and at the same time as an individual.

From Boroumand's musical biography one can receive insights into various aspects of Persian musical culture. Some of these emerge only from such biographical study; others simply underscore what one can observe to be in practice. His emphatic and defensive view of himself as an authority underscores tensions between two extremes in Iranian views of classical Persian music: respect for authority and desire for change. Those musicians interested in authoritative preservation of the tradition tended to agree that he knew it better than anyone else; those wishing for change and modernization scorned his insistence that the old material must be kept pure and memorized by ear rather than learned from notation, and described him as a man who had done nothing more than memorize a lot of old music and in whom there was no creativeness. No one considered him run-of-the-mill; to some he was the greatest, to others scarcely worthy of attention, reflecting the way in which musicians in general are seen by traditional Iranian society. Boroumand's secretiveness about his knowledge and his gradual willingness to share parallel patterns in Iranian culture. The fact that he himself viewed his musical life as consisting of well-defined periods underscores the knowledge that we have of the Iranian intellectual's desire to organize life in relatively discrete units. Modernization and Westernization, processes well known in study in Iran, can be seen as they affect the individual in the course of his or her life.

Boroumand always maintained that he was the most authoritative Persian musician, not as a performer but as the one who knew the authentic material best. Some of his contemporaries agreed, but others thought he greatly exaggerated, or that he was a conservative old fogy. Interestingly, some twenty years after his death, he developed a reputation as the principal link between the late nineteenth-century creators of the *radif* and the virtuosos of the 1990s, and also as the teacher of some of the most prominent musicians of the present. During his life, under the Pahlavis, he had to struggle for the recognition of authenticity against modernizers and syncretizers; later, in the era of the Islamic Republic, when Persian classical music came to be encouraged in what was considered authentic and older versions because of its link to earlier times and their values, Boroumand's approach became the standard, and his name appears far more frequently, as inspiration, on recordings and publications.

In thirty years, the attitude toward Boroumand of the mainstream of classical musicians in Iran seems to have changed from one of respect tempered with criticism to one of veneration. He was greatly respected in his day, but after his death in 1978 he became the subject of an elaborate mythology, somewhat as did Mozart and Beethoven in Europe. I can't maintain that the contrastive myths of Mozart and Beethoven, which explain much about the role of art music in Western thought, has its analogues in Asia. But the mythology around Boroumand makes him into a Beethoven-like figure—he labored mightily, overcoming the handicap of his blindness, emphasized the intellectual, was demanding of his students and critical of his people of Iran, whom he nevertheless exalted, changed his attitude several times through his lifetime. Such analogies are hardly more than casual amusement, however. The point is to examine, in each culture, the great individual musicians and the roles they play in their society's musical thinking in their own time, and later.

Looking for the Songprint

Beyond biography and autobiography, ethnomusicologists are also interested in charting the total musical activity of one person. It's surprising that this has not frequently been the focus of research, for, after all, many studies in ethnomusicology are essentially based upon the performances and statements of individuals speaking alone for their culture. But while enormous effort has been expended to discover all the musical activities of a Bach or a Mahler, we hardly know what may be the total musical experience, creative and passive, of the person in the street. Do you, dear reader, know very much about your own musical knowledge, how many songs you can sing or have learned, how much music you have heard to the degree of knowing it, recognizing it? Ethnomusicologists should undertake to find out, especially in what we may call the "passive" repertory of music known and recognized. Attempts at ascertaining the total active repertory of individuals have been made, such as Schiørring's (1956) collection of the total repertory of a singer, Selma Nielsen. No doubt many collecting projects in fact though not explicitly produced such data. Let me mention one personal experience.

"Sing for me all of the songs you know," I asked one Blackfoot singer. The question was an unexpected one for him, but he agreed to try. His reaction was to sing, first, some twenty songs, one after the other, in no special order. He labeled each by function or use, and often indicated whether he liked the song, where he had learned it, and whether it was a song particularly loved by "the Blackfoot people," as he put it. I don't know what it was that led him from one song to another, but the order was not systematic, not determined by uses, associated ceremonies, or dances. After these twenty he had to pause, and to think of new ones gradually; after groping for some time, he asked to be excused in order to think, and to continue the next day. Indeed, the next occasion yielded a shorter string of songs quickly produced, followed again by a period of groping for new material. Some repetitions occurred, and he acknowledged them. After some five days of this, I had recorded about sixty songs, and he decided that he had sung just about all he knew at that time. But he admitted having forgotten songs known earlier in life, and expected to learn new ones from time to time.

Now, it makes sense to ask whether other members of the Blackfoot tribe have repertories of this size, similarly recalled. I have no direct information, but much earlier, and without the same purpose, I had made a similar though less direct attempt to collect all known songs from an Arapaho singer, a man regarded as highly knowledgeable in his tribe but not an acknowledged musical specialist. While this singer had musical knowledge of a completely different scope, concentrating substantially on Peyote songs, the total number was in the same vicinity of sixty. Curiously, this number also coincides with the repertory of Ishi, the last Yahi, who also presumably sang all the songs he remembered for A. L. Kroeber and T. T. Waterman (Nettl 1965), and to some extent—no doubt it's a coincidence—even with the repertories of Shoshone women, as described and studied in great detail by Judith Vander (1988), who also coined the term "songprint" to indicate the total repertory or musical experience of an individual, reminding us that each one is unique.

Vander's *Songprints* provides biographies and detailed accounts of the repertories (though there is no pretense that they are "complete") of five Shoshone women, indicating for each song whether it was sung, or whether it is known but not sung, and provides comparisons. This unusual study tells us a great deal about the relationship between the repertory of individual Shoshone women and of the Shoshone people as a whole. It is true that by the year 2002, studies of outstanding musicians such as Umm Kulthum, Nusrat Fateh-Ali Khan, Ah Bing, and many others had been made by ethnomusicologists. But as suggested earlier, the musical life and experience of the ordinary musician or average person is less well known. The reader can imagine the potential value of this kind of information when imagining two fictitious small societies, each with a total repertory of 500 songs. In one, all adults know and can sing all of the songs, while in the other, no person knows more than twenty-five; or in one, all adults share a repertory, while in the other, repertories of men and women are rigidly separate. Understanding the musical involvement of the individual, and learning how much alike and how different are the musical lives in any one society, is a significant challenge for ethnomusicology.

14

You Call That Fieldwork? Redefining the "Field"

Ethnomusicology "At Home"

In my student days, an ethnomusicological fieldworker was represented as someone working in an isolated village, living in conditions of considerable privation, having to make do with a monotonous diet shared with the villagers, living without running water, to say nothing of indoor plumbing, communicating for the longest time with sign language, perhaps the first outsider to confront the community. We knew this was usually an exaggeration, and that even in the most isolated places, missionaries had always been there first, for better or worse, and would lend a hand. But to be the first to pay attention to music, that we thought was our likely role, and we heard with fascination about George Herzog witnessing a small tribal war in Liberia, Bartók having to lug heavy equipment with cylinder machine and disk cutter into villages without electricity, Cecil Sharp transcribing songs as they were sung in Appalachian huts, Arnold Bake going from village to village on dirt roads in India in an old heap to record and film rural music. Actually, these people didn't suffer the exposure to otherness in quite the same degree as Bronislaw Malinowski or Hortense Powdermaker. And to be sure, a lot of the distinguished fieldwork of our early times was done in fairly comfortable circumstances: Carl Stumpf collected Bella Coola songs sung by singers in their rooming house in Halle, Germany. The supposedly primordial songs of Ishi were recorded by A. L. Kroeber and T. T. Waterman in the anthropological museum in Berkeley. Songs of ethnic groups from the far-flung Russian empire were recorded on cylinders by Robert Lach in Austrian prisoner-of-war camps near his Vienna home during World War I. But the tough side of fieldwork continued, as we hear from Anthony Seeger (1988) about his life in the 1970s with the Amazonian Suyá, living from the produce of his garden like his consultants, with emergency help available several days' paddling downstream; from Philip Bohlman (1996) about several days' walks on pilgrimages; about life in the camp of a BaAka extended family in the Central African Republic from Michelle Kisliuk (1997: 27–32).

Is this a panorama of what life is like in the field? Well, things have become more muddled. There are many kinds of venues, and thus also many kinds of relationships between scholars and musicians, guests and hosts, insiders and outsiders. And thus, a number of kinds of experience that diverge considerably even from this image of diversity I've just given. They include different physical venues and different relationships to teachers, as the concept of fieldwork has expanded from the model suggested above by my examples. This chapter briefly draws attention to the ways ethnomusicologists have redefined the "field" concept, contemplating their own home community and their personal musical culture, bringing the "other" into their home ground, and engaging in such traditional activities as pilgrimages and such modern phenomena as tourism.

In the middle 1950s I found myself in Detroit, accompanying one of my students to his Polish grandmother's home, where I recorded a couple of songs she sang and had some good afternoon cake and coffee. I reported to one of my anthropological colleagues. "You call that fieldwork?" he said with some indignation, feeling that if I was actually getting credit for this kind of an excursion, I was getting away with murder. Exception it was, to be sure, but as the twentieth century wound it way onward, and as the world's population became more urban, and as urban culture increasingly penetrated the rural venues, the proportion of fieldwork done in villages and nomadic camps decreased, and research in urban venues rose. And increasingly, that venue might be a city in one's own culture. There developed, somewhat in tandem with the growth of "urban anthropology," a field that might be called—though the name never seriously took hold—urban ethnomusicology. It was based on the understanding that the musical culture of cities was—is—very different from that of village and indigenous societies, with its social, economic, and musical strata, professionalism, ethnic diversity, government patronage, mass media, and so on and on. Urban ethnomusicology as such never developed a separate body of theory or a textbook—so much of the work of early ethnomusicologists was the collecting of urban music without attention to its urban-ness—but a few studies concentrated on the special characteristics of this music (see, e.g., Nettl 1978a and some of the essays in Kartomi and Blum 1994 and in Baumann 1991).

Although the notion of doing ethnomusicology "at home" is not necessarily related to that of urban ethnomusicology, I suggest that the tendency, in the period after 1985, for ethnomusicologists to look increasingly at their own musical culture has to do with the study of urban culture. Working in your own rural hinterland, that's an old custom, as already described; but the fieldworker, even though a compatriot, is usually an outsider. The notion of "at home" suggests looking literally in one's own backyard, investigating, as an ethnomusicologist, one's own culture.

It's a complex concept, because the first question has to be, what actually qualifies as your backyard? The idea that the world consists of a lot of easily distinguished societies, each with its distinct culture, and that you can tell easily which one you belong to and are an insider of, while being an outsider to all others—a model that, though unrealistic, was helpful in establishing our scholarly identity—has had to be abandoned. In modern American society, in any case, it is more realistic (as described by Slobin 1992b) to consider each person as possessing numerous identities, and thus having, as it were, numerous musics. You are, for example, an American, a midwesterner, an urban resident, an Italian American (and thus maybe also an "Italian"), a teenager, a female, a member of a factory-worker family, and more. And if you are an ethnomusicologist to boot, one asks to what musical cultures you qualify as an insider—whether as a "Westerner" you are an insider to all Western music, whether as a resident of Prague you are an insider to the Czech village twenty miles away, whether as a Navajo scholar you are an insider to all Native American culture, or as a woman an insider to all women's music. Bringing to this the fluidity of the concept of "music and musics," and the difficulty of identifying fieldwork as a separate methodology, and the idea of distinguishing research at home from away-from-home takes on considerable complexity. It seems that studying almost anything in culture and nature requires one to make it in some respects into an "other."

Nevertheless, ethnomusicologists have usefully made the distinction, looking alternately at insiders' and outsiders' perspectives, and moving from being exclusively the students of musics with which they initially do not identify to stepping back and taking outsiders' roles in examining musical cultures that are in some sense their own. The difference may often be one of attitude toward the field situation. In our earlier history, the emphasis was almost inevitably placed on the strangeness of the host culture, while more recently, the ethnomusicologists who have been working "at home" emphasize the points of identity.

One wonders what all of this does to our conception of fieldwork, whether the term still has meaning, whether we can now always be distinguished from tourists, journalists, sociologists. I would argue that we can, because we insist on being guided by our concept of the "complex whole," but our field techniques and our conceptions of cultural and personal identity have widened. The concepts of insider and outsider and their relationships have become even more complex. Let me comment on several quite different things one might mean by "ethnomusicology at home"—the study of urban popular music, the contemplation of institutions in Western art music culture, the study of foreign music through performance at home, the teaching of ethnomusicology through ethnographic exercises, and the role of tourism.

Popular Music

Let's look for a moment at issues of identity in the study of popular music in the period after 1950. I'm referring to the mass-mediated music that constitutes, eponymically, the kind of music loved or liked and known throughout the world. Of course it's not one music but many (with significant commonalities), everything from rock music and blues to rap, from Indian *bhangra* to Moroccan *rai*. First, there is a tendency for each culture, or subculture, to develop a distinct popular music; second, we've been experiencing musical globalization and the development of "world music" or "world beat," which combine and unite rhythms, vocal techniques, instruments from a variety of places; and third, many different kinds of popular music become accessible to much of the world through modern methods of distribution. But in ethnomusicology, popular music was long treated as an exception, neglected by most scholars because—in my opinion—its cultural and ethnic identity was always difficult to determine, and it was thus thought to lack authenticity. It was neglected also because of its supposed aesthetic inferiority and its essentially commercial quality. But in the period since around 1980, many kinds—repertories, genres, nationalities, manifestations—of popular music have been studied by ethnomusicologists who came to this research from having been its performers, or who in some sense identified themselves with it initially. Many of them knew their popular music well, before they faced it with an ethnomusicological perspective, and they may be considered to be working "at home."

Actually, the study of popular music in ethnomusicology has been around for a long time, and its early appearances include analyses of the American scene such as Charles Keil's *Urban Blues* (1966), Gerard Behague's presentation of the bossa nova (1973) from a social perspective, and the authoritative early study of South African urban black music by David Coplan, *In Township Tonight* (1985). But these were dots in the landscape until the appearance of Peter Manuel's survey, *Popular Music in the Non-Western World* (1988), which was followed by a flood of studies in the 1990s. Since 2000, research on popular music (admittedly in the broad sense of the word) has arguably become the mainstream. The concept continues to be difficult to circumscribe cross-culturally, and the studies to which I refer don't usually grapple with boundaries. Some music once classified as "classical," or "folk"—the music by the Iranian ensembles Kamkar and Dastan and a good deal of the music heard in Irish pubs come to mind—seems to have moved into, or closer to, the mass-mediated, often culturally hybrid entertainment that is literally widely "popular."

Ethnomusicology has been importantly affected by other disciplines that have taken up the cudgels in behalf of popular music. Authors in the field known as cultural studies or "critical theory" have taken an interpretive perspective of musical life and popular music, and the relationship of music and politics, in developing critiques of modern society (see, e.g., Frith 1988, 1989). Closely related, a distinct field of popular music studies has emerged (represented by the International Association for the Study of Popular Music with its journal; for a basic text, see Middleton 1990). It is often difficult (and probably unnecessary), from the reading of authors on popular music, to identify their disciplinary home.

After around 1990, popular music in its ethnomusicological impact spread out in several ways. There was just a lot more of it. More important, it came to occupy a central place in the development of ethnomusicological theory, as some major studies of the decade, such as Virginia Danielson's (1997) analysis of the Egyptian singer Umm Kulthum's life, music, and reception and the dialogs of Keil and Feld (*Music Grooves,* 1994), dealing with fundamental issues in the understanding of musical culture largely via popular music, saw this as the norm of musical life and not marginal in the panorama of musical cultures. But also, ethnomusicologists began to pay more attention to the popular music of their own cultures. At first this may have reflected the concept of popular music as distinctly "other," the ultimate cultural "inside" being Western classical music and its study. Keep in mind that a very special otherness was conferred on popular music by the teachers of the first half of the twentieth century, who admonished us to stay away from this mixed, inferior, and commercial phenomenon. By the time of this writing, the otherness of popular music seems to have receded, and some of us have become concerned with music with which, or by people with which, we are closely associated as individuals—as examples from the many, I'll mention Cheryl Keyes's (1996) study of rap music and Mark Slobin's (2000) survey of klezmer music. And ethnomusicologists began, as did Slobin (1992b) in seeing Western music as a network of "micromusics," to integrate popular music into the totality of musical culture.

I'm not sure whether I've interpreted history correctly, but it seems to me that this may have been the sequence: Contemplating the popular music of the "other," non-Western cultures led to seeing one's own popular music, also an "other," as appropriate subject matter. But as its otherness receded, looking ethnomusicologically at one's own music came to be a norm, and this led, gradually, to our acceptance of the ultimate "inside," the culture of Western classical music, as appropriate subject matter. Probably without knowing it, we followed anthropology, a field once determinedly devoted to the "other" but today increasingly analytical and critical of Western or international culture—following, however, an early work by Franz Boas (1928), writing late in his life about his modern environment. We see ethnomusicology beginning to ask itself whether the study of the 'other' taught us something about ourselves as members of Western musical academia. Shall we try our usual questions on our own culture, society, music?

The Names on the Building

A curious question kept coming up at university committee meetings on which I interacted with colleagues from many departments. "Why does the School of Music behave so differently from other departments?" I ended up replying that it's because the music school's social model is the symphony orchestra—a replication of a factory or a plantation—with its dictatorial arm-waving director, the hierarchical structure of its sections, its rigid class structure that doesn't permit promotion of the first violist to conductor, with the mediation of the concert master (overseer), who presents the orchestra to the conductor (owner). Music schools are usually run more autocratically than other departments, they almost always get their deans from the outside, and a dean who "steps down" rarely just goes back into the teaching faculty of his or her own school. Administrators, like conductors, try to find ways of distinguishing themselves from the faculty—something not true of anthropology or history department chairs. My colleagues were a bit puzzled but satisfied with my answer. It began to seem natural for me to see how my experiences in Montana, in Tehran and Chennai, might help me to figure out and interpret the musical culture that had all my life been closest to me.

I wasn't the only one. In the 1980s, Henry Kingsbury had earlier undertaken fieldwork in a large Eastern conservatory of music and published an account (1988) in which he built the investigation around the central concept of "talent" that distinguishes the music schools of the modern international classical music culture. Kingsbury carried out fieldwork in a relatively conventional sense, although as an accomplished pianist, piano teacher, and administrator, he had reason to feel an insider. But he carried out formal interviews, attended lessons, classes, and rehearsals and wrote each one up in his notes, and gave out questionnaires. Somewhat in contrast, I studied two music schools that I already knew very well and others I knew less well, combining them into a generalized "Heartland U." I did some interviewing but even more in the way of informal observation and conversation, and I used my years of experience as data. Kingsbury, then, appears as a student of a culture that he knows well, but he treated it as if he were an outsider, whereas in my project I acted and felt, mostly, an insider. "Is that fieldwork?" one is tempted to ask, and I'm not sure I have a good answer, because in the shifting relationship between ethnomusicological investigators and their subjects, the specialness of the fieldwork experience has gradually receded. We don't any longer feel that we *must* work without plumbing, *must* make recordings, *must* learn to play an instrument—though we may—but we include studying the work being done in an African recording studio, the procedures of a string quartet rehearsal, the meeting of a Bulgarian folk music orchestra's board of directors, the music criticism in a Chennai newspaper, all as field data. Instead of the uniqueness of investigative technique, we may claim that it is our interpretations, coming from a perspective of the world of musics and of the anthropologist's "complex whole," that characterize our field.

So the solution I came up with for interpreting the schools of music at this composite Heartland U. was to present myself in three voices: the traditional ethnomusicologist, the "native informant," and an imaginary figure whom I named the "ethnomusicologist from Mars," for the purpose of trying to imagine what an ultimate outsider who came to our music building with absolutely no knowledge would think, would be struck by. This last figure gave me the best insights. My four approaches looked at the school as (1) a religious system ruled by the great composers worshiped and interpreted by a priesthood; (2) a society of musicians who divide themselves into various kinds of conflicting groups for different purposes; (3) a meeting-place for many musics that interact according to the dictates of the central musics; and (4) a central repertory, Western art music, seen as a kind of society of genres, pieces, and styles that interact as if they were human. My study was interpretive and suggestive, and sometimes, by implication, critical. The dominant impression I had, and wish to convey, is that this was a religious and social system ruled by the personalities, compositions, and principles (as we imagine them) of a few great composers, whose names are on the buildings—Mozart, Beethoven, Bach, maybe also Schubert and the more controversial Wagner (who sometimes has the role of villain in this imaginary society).

There are others who have looked at Western art music from an ethnomusicological perspective. Christopher Small (1987, 1998) analyzed Western canonic music institutions. Finnegan (1989), surveying the musical life of a British town, celebrated the way in which art music is made into a vernacular by institutions such as town bands and choruses. Here it was again, the central question: What determines the musical style and character that a society chooses for itself? Surely it must be something about the way people relate to each other. But why are these hierarchical and authoritarian forms, such as opera and concerto, the ones most admired by the art music audience? Do they reflect the kind of society we want to have? I had to leave the question open. Shelemay (2001) also approached a branch of Western art music, the "early music" movement in Boston in the 1990s. This study perhaps is more typically ethnomusicological, as it involved a distinct musical society within the whole, a society devoted to a kind of musical "other" not generally understood by the mainstream population. Judith Becker (1986), mediating between the egalitarianism of the ethnomusicologist and the mainstream academic culture, which automatically puts forward the European classical tradition, judges wisely (or maybe throws up her hands?) in concluding that Western art music and others are not commensurate.

But to write about the institutions I loved in ways that might imply criticism had its difficulties for me. This was my own musical culture, but it represented things—such as the dictatorship and rigid class structure implied by the orchestra, and by the fact that in any two things happening at the same time, one was always clearly superior—that had implications I didn't like, and I didn't know how to deal with it. Kingsbury seemed to be quite open in his judgment, presenting that conservatory in some respects as a mean place that provided musical education as a series of hoops to jump through.

From Rose Bowl to Gamelan

It feels different—this doing fieldwork at home—from being abroad. I know I made a fool of myself in Montana, but I stopped worrying about it when I left the reservation; but making a fool of myself in Urbana, surrounded by students and colleagues, stays with me. My Blackfoot friends, a few of them, had admired me for having an interest in what they did. My Illinois colleagues, though, seemed to wonder why Urbana musical life should be interesting. Grin and bear it. But the concept of doing fieldwork at home as a way of learning something about fieldwork techniques and their problems has become fairly standard technique in seminars, on the heels of sending students home to collect songs from their grandparents. A group of my students (see Livingston et al., 1993) investigated local institutions and events such as background music in restaurants, rehearsals of the university symphony and the Russian folk orchestra, the social organization of a Korean drumming ensemble and a Korean church choir, and lots more.

Most interesting were two investigations carried out in different years at a popular Urbana bar known as the Rose Bowl, home of a country-and-western group famous for its large repertory. One of the investigators was an American graduate student, and the other a Brazilian ethnomusicologist, and they undertook similar approaches: attended on a number of evenings, and kept track of the repertory, the number and kinds of people present and in what kinds of groups, and the "imponderabilia," such as who spoke or danced with whom. They interviewed owner, employees, musicians, and a sampling of patrons, inquiring about their backgrounds, involvements with music, appraisal of the bar, the band, the songs. Although the bar did not cater to what would be called an "inclusive" clientele, the Brazilian found himself more welcome, but drew conclusions that placed the institution at the focus of political divisions and currents, while the American (his version was published: Hill 1993) saw it as a representation of community. Both lived within a mile or two of the institution, and each was seen, they said, as both insider and outsider.

A contrastive kind of "fieldwork at home" is the participation in noncanonic ensembles sponsored by academic institutions, a practice begun in the United States in the 1950s and widely adopted in Canada and western Europe as part of the educational system. Although ensembles representing many cultures and culture areas—at Illinois we had, in the late 1990s, ensembles of Zimbabwean mbiras, Andean panpipes, a multitude of Balkan and Middle Eastern instruments with chorus, and more, while other institutions maintained everything from Chinese orchestras and Japanese Gagaku and kabuki ensembles to West African drumming groups and Highlife bands; the emblematic ensemble is the Javanese gamelan—or rather, one of the many types of gamelan known in Java. These ensembles have played a major role in introducing Western students to other musics, preparing a certain few for field research, presenting Asian, African, and Latin American traditions to a wider academic public and local community. In certain respects, too, they function as loci for fieldwork, as they bring up to the participant some of the important issues, important cultural principles perhaps honored in the breach. Thus the participant looking at a gamelan rehearsal from the perspective of a fieldworker may be obliged to note questions such as the authenticity of the repertory and the learning process. (For example: Does the gamelan teacher use the techniques he would use at home when instructing Americans? Do the students observe the traditional social organization, personally and musically, of a Javanese gamelan?) Study, rehearsal, and performance in musics of the "other" at home can be seen as a certain type of fieldwork. But it's a complicated matter: Is one learning about, say, Javanese musical culture, or about the American musical culture of one's home institution?

Tourists and Pilgrims

Centuries ago, we imagine, songs moved by creeping, through one-on-one learning, from village to village—though it's true that traveling musicians were known in ancient Europe and West Asia—and so Wilhelm Tappert accorded the label "indefatigable tourists" to melodies whose movement tended very gradually to alter a musical landscape. In the late twentieth century, it's tourism by humans that has become a major source of musical experience, of change in musics as systems of sound and behavior, and change in the musical culture of the individual. Many people have molded their musical lives through experience of musical events while traveling; more important, many cultures have seen the way in which they have been represented to tourists—the ways they could select and develop for representing themselves to tourists with music and dance—as an important aspect of their intercultural relations. They have developed particular ways of representing themselves through music and dance to tourist audiences, and sometimes they have reintroduced aspects of these presentations back into their own cultural experience. To be sure, they have found that the entertainment of tourists could be a significant factor in their economies. Tourism has emerged as one of the principal ways in which culture contact is now made, and this is particularly true of the arts. Developing new forms of traditional arts, forms and genres that will provide good entertainment for tourists, is an important part of the work of artists, as well as government officials concerned with cultural politics. Tourism has helped musicians, dancers, and artists to preserve older forms and also to develop syncretic styles and genres.

Art tourism—and its opposite, touring by artists—is not as new as all that. According to Feldman (2002: 107), tourists from Europe to the Ottoman Empire in the eighteenth century typically visited Sufi shrines to see the performances of dancing dervishes. In the 1760s, Charles Burney had toured Europe to hear music and speak to musicians, in order to report his findings (e.g., Burney 1776–89). Native American singers and dancers toured in Europe in the late nineteenth century; and such a visit by a Northwest Coast troupe resulted in Carl Stumpf's 1886 Bella Coola study. The development of world's fairs, such as the 1893 Columbian Exposition in Chicago, brought musicians from various cultures and tourists from America and Europe together. But of course the development of jet travel made tourism and touring into an industry. The observation of music in a tourist context provides yet another way in which the concept of the "field" is being redefined, in an approach to fieldwork more related to "ethnomusicology at home" than to the observation of isolated communities.

Anthropologists in the late 1980s began to take an interest in tourism and similar exchanges. Most significant is the work of James Clifford (1997) and Barbara Kirshenblatt-Gimblett (1998) and also of Edward E. Bruner (e.g., 1996, 2005), whose investigations of tourism extend from Indonesia (Sumatra) to Ghana (mainly by African American tourists seeking the source of the slave trade), East Africa (European tourists seeking cultural entertainment in connection with safaris), Native American powwows (for Native and white tourists and white dance hobbyists), and the Abraham Lincoln shrine in Springfield, Illinois. In their consumption of music, tourists usually hope for something authentic, old, explicitly non-Western or noncanonic; but also they want to be entertained by something they can tolerate in the context of their Western musical tastes. The cultural politics establishments and the touring and hotel managements try to satisfy these desires, but they also wish to foster respect for the artistic abilities of their people and to present art in the context of multiethnic nationhood. The purposes of applied anthropology or ethnomusicology may also come to play a role. For example, Norman Whitten, an anthropologist at the University of Illinois and longtime student of Shuar and Canelos Quichua cultures in Ecuador, established a foundation to import art objects of these peoples into the United States, with the profits going to the support of a medical clinic. The trade became so lucrative to the Native artists that they expanded their styles and took up different genres and subjects of art, providing an example of the field worker affecting the "field's" culture. Similar, perhaps less dramatic examples are cited by a number of recent authors such as Tenzer (2000), Bakan (1999), and Sarkissian (2000). But it was not until around 1990 that tourism began to be taken seriously as an ethnomusicological subject; before that, although we were aware of it, we tended to look at it with disdain and, seeing it perhaps as the result of undesirable intercultural relationships, tried to pretend that it didn't exist.

How to carry out fieldwork investigating an essentially intercultural process and relationship—that's a question still open for contemporary investigators. The essays in Barz and Cooley (1997) mention it in passing. The index volume of Garland (1997–2002) has almost 100 entries under tourism but no synthetic discussion. It seems that attention is beginning to be paid. But I'm afraid that there are plenty of scholars who, seeing careful studies of tourists and culture bearers and their relationships by scholars who also hold the role of tourists might be tempted to wonder just how this fits into the concept of fieldwork.

Going back at least to the *Canterbury Tales,* there is a long tradition of narratives about pilgrimages that show them to be very special events in the lives of pilgrims and their societies, and that they are particularly significant as occasions for the interchange of culture, especially art and music. The experiences of pilgrims may not be unlike those of tourists, but a pilgrimage is itself a social event in which participants significantly interact. It has taken ethnomusicologists a long time to begin paying attention to pilgrimages, although there are some whose purpose is specifically the celebration of music. They are many kinds. I have in mind events such as the annual Tyagaraja aradhana in Tiruvayaru, which attracts hundreds of Carnatic musicians to celebrate the great composer and—by exception in full-voiced unison—to sing many of his songs. Or certain festivals, those celebrating Mozart in Salzburg or the season of performances of Wagner in his city of Bayreuth. Or for that matter, the so-called music season in Madras (Chennai), from around December 15 to January 8, at which Carnatic and some other musicians give dozens of concerts, as many as twenty in one day. In all cases, people from different communities, ethnicities, and nations come together, and performers who would not ordinarily be found in the same venue make music together. Some of these pilgrimages concentrate on the object—a shrine, a festival; others, perhaps the more interesting, focus on the trek, from the place of assembly to the final goal, and on the things people say to each other, the songs they sing together, or for each other, the music provided at way stations. One of the few studies of pilgrimages in ethnomusicology is by Bohlman (1996), who describes different types of pilgrimages he experienced in central and eastern Europe, and argues the special significance in musical processes of their international character. Are particular field methods needed? Possibly not, because the people on a pilgrimage are a community, to be studied perhaps like other music communities—multimusical communities perhaps—such as the inhabitant of a village or the denizens of an educational institution. But it is a community that has temporary existence, that brings together people from different cultures or segments of one society who might not ordinarily associate, and this temporary togetherness provides an exceptional venue for studying cultural, social, and musical interrelationships.

15

What Do You Think You're Doing?
The Host's Perspective

Who Owns This Music?

After the talk, anthropology students gathered in the back of the room for some coffee and discussion. Most students were deferential, but a young man with a Spanish accent scowled silently for a while, then chimed in, sounding resentful, concerned: "What do you think you're doing? How do you get away with studying other people's music?" A strange question in a department in which everyone was into somebody else's culture. Explanations came, but he wasn't buying. Since about 1960 such questions have been arising more and more frequently, and in the most recent years ethnomusicologists have had to address their many implications. Like these: Is our study of a foreign culture's music a kind of exploitation, bound to have an adverse affect on the people and their traditions, or an effect they didn't want? Are we taking economic advantage of the musicians? Can outsiders "get it right" anyway, and shouldn't people have control over the way they are represented? And shouldn't the ethnomusicologists in any one society have dibs on investigating their own music, and so shouldn't we (in North America and western Europe) be helping every culture to develop ethnomusicology? And in allowing us to study their culture, don't people have a right to expect that it will in some way do them some good?

These questions involve a lot of diverse issues, and they include power relations between peoples, ethnic groups, even individuals; the concept of intellectual property; the question of cultural and musical boundaries—is it music or musics?—and just plain personal and intellectual honesty. Ethnomusicologists have increasingly been concerned with this complex of questions, which may boil down to the ownership of and the right to music and to information about it. They have even compartmentalized the aspect of their work that concerns such matters, conveniently, if not always with precision, labeling it "ethics."

If scholars have only recently decided that music is not a universal language, this has all along been obvious to the people who constitute the "field." People everywhere readily speak of "our" music and "theirs," associating themselves with particular musics and caring what outsiders do with them. An ethnomusicologist is not always readily tolerated in the field. "Hey, boy, what you doing around here anyway?" was the rhetorical question scornfully asked by the Blackfoot man passing me in the alley. He knew perfectly well and made it clear that he didn't like it, or me, and didn't want to hear explanations. Elsewhere, fieldworkers may be viewed with more specific suspicion—as spies, exploiters, purveyors of invidious comparisons. Or they may be tolerated as necessary evils, aiding in the maintenance of cultural integrity.

The question of "ethics" actually pervades our work. It focuses on the relationship between fieldworker and informant—consultant, teacher—but has larger ramifications, extending to the relationship of one profession, ethnomusicology, to another, musicianship; and of the industrialized to the developing world; of rich to poor; of nation to tribe. It encompasses questions of attitude and of practicality, the respect of scholar for teacher, the etiquette of payment. It includes the degree to which judgments about the greater if unperceived good of a society in which they are strangers are the privilege of scholars, and involves the juxtaposition of generally valid and culturally restricted values. The fundamental question is who owns the music, and what may someone who does not own it do with it. The oral tradition of ethnomusicology has its repertory of horror stories: of musicians furious because they were recorded without their knowledge or consent, upset because performances given for study suddenly appear on commercial records, angry at a compatriot who divulged secrets; of Asian scholars worried about their inability to get their hands on recordings made on their own territory but now secluded in European archives; of Australian aboriginals disturbed because no one bothered to record their music while it was still widely known; of African professors annoyed because they must work with poor equipment while their American colleagues come in with the best and the latest. And so on and on, all the direct or indirect result of the economic and political exploitation of most of the world's peoples by urban Europeans and North Americans (and some others too), and of the divergent views that the world's peoples have about the nature and ownership, the function, and the power of music.

The annals of ethnomusicology actually include little about this broadly important and relevant topic. Formal and informal discussion has frequently been held at meetings, particularly since 1970 in the United States, when the international relationships implied here were transferred to international venues. The Society for Ethnomusicology (SEM; see reports beginning in 1974, 1975, and 1977) has had for over thirty years a standing committee on ethics, and the International Council for Traditional Music has dealt formally with the question in its policy-making organs. But besides the horror stories, there is little conceptualization of the problem or agreement on specific guidelines for the emerging scholar. In a thoughtful summary of the issues, Slobin (1992a) illustrates with seven cases: discovery of a rare musical instrument, making a documentary film, distributing record royalties, receiving permission for investigation from only a part of a community, problems in taking a teacher on tour in the United States, record liner notes, and reflexivity in publishing one's findings. My paragraphs below look at the problem from three perspectives: the relationship of fieldworker with individual teacher or consultant, the attitude of the scholars vis-à-vis the communities in which they work, and the relationship among modern nation-states.

Don't Tell Him, It's Our Secret

In the earlier history of ethnomusicology, most publications strove to present the impression of a homogeneous culture. We are often not told who sang a transcribed song, with the implication that any member of a tribe or village would have sung or said the same. There are notable exceptions: Stumpf, in his landmark study of the Bella Coola (1886), prominently mentioned and described the sessions with his singer, Nutsiluska. Densmore, in her many publications, consistently gave the names of singers below her transcriptions, quoting culture bearers at length. But very frequently it was not so. In earlier anthropological literature, too, despite a few notable exceptions of a biographical nature, the identity of informants and their particular standing in their communities was usually left unstated. Setting forth the informant was something underscored as exceptional: "Let it be admitted, too, that the successful outcome of field research depends not only on the anthropologist's own skills, but also on the capabilities and interest of those who teach him their ways," said Casagrande (1960: x) in a book published to counter this cult of impersonality. Incidentally, however, perhaps as a result of their concentration on work essentially within their own culture, folklorists—in contrast to anthropologists—have for longer had a tradition of dealing with informants as people in their publications.

It may seem monstrous that members of other societies should be treated so impersonally, almost as if they were specimens of flora and fauna. Yet this wasn't usually result of evil intention. Inevitably, fieldworkers made friends with singers and players, became attached, helped them as they could, and paid them, but rather than feeling guilty about the inadequacy of these small gestures in the direction of equal treatment for all humans, they tended instead to worry because they were getting involved with trees and ignoring the forest. In the years since 1960, informants and some of their political representatives have fought back, and guilt has been shifted to the callous attitude of the industrial nations and the wealthy classes and corporations.

I believe that most earlier ethnomusicologists did not simply ignore the human factor. In the interest of properly scientific inquiry in a field dealing specifically with the music of *groups* of people, they felt that an individual must be regarded primarily as representative of a society. His or her individual talent or accomplishment should be held apart. And thus it came about, I think, that such clearly humane persons as George Herzog (1936a) and John Blacking (1967), surely close to their informants and teachers, avoided mentioning names except in broad and general acknowledgments, while Frances Densmore, who was less interested in being scientific than in showing the accomplishments of Native American singers, gave personal ascriptions.

There are other causes of the widespread avoidance of naming and acknowledging informants. In 1971 the American Anthropological Society (*SEM Newsletter,* January–February 1974) adopted a "Statement of Principles" that speaks to the need and right of informants to remain anonymous in order to safeguard their welfare in their communities and nations. And indeed, in my experience, informants and teachers have been as frequently concerned lest their names and attitudes be divulged as that they be given proper credit. By the 1990s, at least in ethnomusicology, the issue of anonymity had largely receded, and the world's musicians now rather uniformly expect to be treated as individuals and to get credit for their contributions to our literature. They are much better acquainted with the Western/global musical world than before, and many of them expect to be included in its activities and reap its benefits.

Ethnomusicologists began to change their attitude toward informants and teachers after about 1965, as many began to concentrate on the study of Asian classical music, and in the wake of changing concerns in anthropology. The role of famed teachers and internationally recognized artists in their research motivated scholars to approach them as representatives of their culture, yes, but also as great artists in their own right. By the 1970s this attitude had spilled over into the study of other continents as well. Berliner (1978) described many individual Shona mbira players and devoted an introductory chapter to a famed player who had to be convinced, over a period of six years, of Berliner's genuine interest before a central piece of information was given to him. The artist finally concluded, and announced to his village, "Well, it seems to me that this young man is serious after all. I suppose I can tell him the truth [about the nomenclature of the keys of the mbira] now." Even then, villagers called to the old man, "No, don't tell him; it's our secret" (1978: 7). They felt that it was privileged information, that it belonged to the community and that they had the right to decide whether to share it or not. By the 1990s, as ana-lyzed by Coplan (1994: 244–47) and Turino (2000, esp. 4–12), attention to the individual musicians and their specialness within their culture had be-come a major component of the study of all kinds of music; it had helped to move the mass-mediated popular musics into the ethnomusicological world.

Here a village shared in a musical secret. Elsewhere, music may be owned by individuals, clans, tribes, nations, the world. The way in which ethno-musicologists approach their study depends in large measure on a society's ideas of who owns the music. Again the Blackfoot provide an interesting ex-ample. At least at the beginning of the twentieth century, they appear to have classed songs in three groups, in accordance with ownership (Wissler 1912: 27) by tribe or individual, restricted or transferable. By the 1960s actual obser-vance of this system had been abandoned or had little significance. In the 1980s, it had begun to reassert itself, though unevenly, among Blackfoot peo-ple. Perhaps it had always been more theoretical than practical, but the fun-damental idea that certain songs belonged to particular individuals was still there in 1970. Thus singers contributing to my collection would say, "This is my song, because I made it," or "This song was given to me by my mother." Conversation yielded the impression that while no official strictures or sanc-tions were available, and the matter was not taken all too seriously, a singer/ owner would feel a bit uncomfortable if another sang his or her song. For the Venda, Blacking (1965: 36–45) indicated that various levels of chieftain-ship controlled the performance of many kinds of music, and that certain pieces should not be performed without sponsorship of the proper political echelon. In Iran the teacher of classical music spoke not of teaching but of "giving" material to the student, implying that his *radif* is something that he "has" and is thus free to impart or not. Copyright law in the United States and the world provides a considerable measure of control over a piece of music by its creator, and the special problems of ownership of traditional music within such a copyright system has been, since the mid–nineteenth century, a worry for publishers and authors and the subject of a set of special guidelines proposed by the International Folk Music Council. In the period since 1990, global distribution of music and reproduction of recordings through computer technology have exacerbated the concern of musicians and music business with the question of ownership and control, and ethnomusicologists have tried to keep up, trying to protect the musicians with whom they work from exploitation (see Meintjes 1990), playing a role, as has been done by Ronald Riddle and Fredric Lieberman, for example, in the world of musical litigation, attempting to provide a theoretical template for dealing with both scholarly and intellectual problems (A. Seeger 1992b).

But ethical behavior in the field is often a matter of common sense. We assume that ethnomusicologists in the Western world should in the first instance be governed by the ordinary standards of ethical behavior in their own culture. It ought not to be necessary to tell one's students that they should not lie to informants about their intentions of using recordings and information, that one does not record singing without the knowledge and permission of the singer, that one pays what is, by some kind of standard, a reasonable sum or reciprocates somehow for services rendered. This is all obvious. After all, in Western culture we know that we should not lie. We are up in arms about having offices or bedrooms "bugged" by police, telephone conversations recorded. We may bargain with people about what we pay for services, but not if they are, for example, children unable to bargain effectively. The government provides minimum wage laws to protect those who cannot easily stand up for themselves. We should know enough not to issue records with performances by people who have asked us to refrain from doing so; and so on. It is part of our culture's conception of being a decent human being, and in the field we should adhere to our own standards. Certainly this is also what counts most in fieldwork done in some sense within our own culture area.

But beyond this, the particular question of music ownership in another culture becomes relevant. For example, fieldworkers may be befriended by individuals who live in one way or another on the fringes of their own society— partially Westernized persons in a village that is otherwise traditional perhaps, or outcasts and malcontents. Among them are those who would gladly, for appropriate return or out of sheer dissatisfaction, sing the songs belonging to another or record material not intended for general use. A man in need may succumb to the opportunity of acquiring what seems to him a fortune—little enough for a grant-supported European or American—and divulge secrets of his society. A fieldworker following through on such opportunities might well do considerable damage to a social (and musical) system and also hurt future opportunities for fieldwork by others. It thus behooves the ethnomusicologist to become sensitive to a society's ideas of who owns music or controls it, and to work within the constraints of the culture.

It is also obvious but sometimes forgotten that teachers and informants have a primary allegiance to their own societies. Paul Berliner's teacher, who waited for six years, had the right to present his system of mbira nomenclature when he was satisfied that Berliner was a serious student. He was an authority, but he allowed the village to assemble and give its assent before proceeding. It was *his* music, but he evidently wanted to be sure that he was following the desires of his society. On the other hand, I knew a distinguished Iranian performer who, finding that he had been recorded without his knowledge and that a performance he did not regard as worthy of his culture's musicianship standards had been issued on a record, remained suspicious of European and American collectors for years and avoided them. He felt that he had been made ridiculous in the eyes of his colleagues; it was his relationship to his own society that was at issue.

Great Offense Can Be Caused

The chairman of the tribal council gave me a piercing look. "What good will it do us if you go around collecting old songs from those old-timers?" I explained honestly that it probably would do little good, but that I would pay singers for their efforts, and might write something that would help white Americans understand Indian culture. "Well, go ahead, I guess it won't do much harm." He shrugged his shoulders and continued to take a dim view of me as I worked along, but didn't interfere. I wondered for a while about his hostility.

I had been concerned that I deal fairly and honestly with the individual informants and singers. Probably in the early years of exposure to ethnomusicologists, members of host communities regarded this kind of relationship as the paramount issue. As they grew in their experience with fieldworkers—and this was particularly true of North American Indians, who were often swamped (see the well-known joke about the typical Indian family including a father, a mother, three children, and an anthropologist)—they also began to display concern for issues that involved the community and its future. Thus, if one role of the fieldworker was to preserve the culture on film, tape, print, they wished to be sure that the data was "correct," that the truth would be recorded as they perceived it. And they worried about the appropriateness of divulging privileged information against the threat of culture loss. Communities tiny and global constantly debate the nature and direction of their own culture, but such debates are exacerbated in times of rapid change. Community leaders might well be inclined to direct fieldworkers, tell them how to operate, and gradually to be frustrated by their inability to keep them in line. Even more disturbing must be certain obvious interpretations: an offhand statement blown up into a major insight; total neglect of a major component of a musical repertory; and of course a group of songs and statements, down to earth, transformed into incomprehensible structuralist or post-modernist explanations. All of this can make people suspicious of what may be done with information they give, with what they teach. Since there is also the fear that a fieldworker's findings will be used, inevitably, to support some preconceived and probably pejorative notion of the value of a society, a suspicion sometimes justified even where nothing pejorative is intended, the attitude of my council chairman was surely understandable.

Leaders of a community trying delicately to direct their people's survival in a modem cultural ecology may fear that some of the activities of even a mere ethnomusicologist can cause things to be thrown into an uproar. Some ethnomusicologists, sensitive to this problem and torn between the needs of protecting the integrity of the community and communicating findings to their colleagues, may resort to secrecy, trying to guard against upsetting the people when they see themselves photographed in ceremonies and their statements quoted in books. Catherine Ellis, an Australian scholar particularly concerned with her relations to aboriginal people, wrote dramatically: "Attention fieldworkers: Great offence can be caused if this material is shown to [aboriginal] . . . people," says one publication that lays out in detail some secret ceremonial material (C. Ellis 1970: 207). But I wonder whether this is in the end an effective approach. Members of non-Western and folk societies are no longer so isolated from research libraries; they often find out what has been written about them, requesting and expecting to receive copies of what has been produced. Bookstores in Native American communities stock the works of Alice Fletcher, Charlotte Frisbie, William Powers. The members of urban American society have become callous to what is written about it in surveys, there are so many of them, and so few turn out to be conclusive. But elsewhere, people may believe that they cannot afford this luxury, knowing that what one isolated scholar writes may for a long time determine the outsiders' attitude, and they are much concerned that they be properly and, in their view, accurately represented, and that their values be respected.

But more important, beyond his skepticism about my ability to get things right, the council chairman looking askance at my activities was concerned that what I did should be of some benefit to his people. They were (like most whose music is studied by ethnomusicologists) poor and needed help, and he wanted to be sure that time and energy they spent in my service would help to improve their lot. There was just too much to be done to permit frivolities. He was aware that I would not become wealthy from publishing books or records, but he knew that I would nevertheless benefit, was building a career with what his people taught me, and he felt that they should also derive benefit. And that what they were giving me should not be inadvertently denigrated, relegated to footnotes, or played as background music at academic parties.

Just how to act properly in such a context has posed dilemmas of various sorts. If the fieldworker strives to preserve what is old and traditional, this may satisfy a certain kind of scholarship, but it can also arouse fear lest the community be viewed as incredibly backward and isolated. Community leaders are not always happy about the encouragement of old musical practices because they readily perceive that these may be symbolic of traditional and no longer competitive ways of dealing with problems of modern economics and technology. Should the collectors do anything beyond simply recording what they find? As far back as 1916, Cecil Sharp, entranced by the old English songs found in the Appalachians, wrote about what he regarded as the detrimental role of missionaries and their schools. "I don't think any of them [missionaries] realize that the people they are here to improve are in many respects more cultivated than their would-be instructors. . . . Take music, for example. Their own is pure and lovely. The hymns that these missionaries teach them are musical and literary garbage" (Karpeles 1967: 153). Thirty-five years later, the issue was still around, presented to the public in the film *The Songcatcher*. The same statement might have been made about any of hundreds of other societies.

On the other hand, these mountain folk could hardly have survived without some elements of standard education, and so Sharp's applauding of a girl who around 1915 had dropped out of school seems at best romantic. Had my council chairman, fifty years later, suspected me of urging his Indian people to avoid taking up country-and-western music, he might have demurred, for to him this was the kind of music that goes with the development of a modern rural lifestyle, the adoption of which may be necessary to the survival of his Indian nation as a people. Native American leaders know perhaps better than ethnomusicologists the close association of music and the rest of culture. The ethnomusicologist's role in bringing Western music to non-Western societies poses another dilemma. The people and their governments may want it, while the scholar wishes to preserve the world's musical variety. There is no simple solution, but the problem was already understood by the early masters of our field. Hornbostel: "In Africa, the introduction of harmony would check the natural development of polyphonic forms from antiphony. This is . . . regrettable" (1928: 42). In the course of the 1950s there developed a concept and a subdiscipline, applied anthropology, whose task it was to use anthropological insight to help solve social problems, particularly those occasioned by rapid culture change in the wake of modernization and Westernization. Anthropologists wanted to help but frequently ended up offending the local population and doing what was perceived as harmful. As a result, in the late 1960s and early 1970s they were widely attacked for doing work of no relevance to social problems, of mixing in local politics, of spying (Pelto 1973: 282). Ethnomusicologists shared in this criticism. But the picture is not entirely negative. Some societies are happy to have outsiders come and appreciate outsiders' efforts (283), their respect for the traditions, and their help in restoring vigor to rapidly disappearing musics (Jairazbhoy 1978: 61). Persian and Indian music masters are proud to have Western scholars as students, for it raises their prestige locally and legitimizes their traditional art in the face of modernizing doubters. Even so, there is often the feeling that members of the society itself, given the right training, equipment, and time, could do it all better. They sometimes asserted that they would benefit if the fieldworker shared with them not only what is collected and recorded (in the United States and elsewhere tribal archives have been emerging) but also the research methods. This attitude, along with the belief that the emic viewpoint must be given greater weight than before, has led some ethnomusicologists to espouse fieldwork in which informants become collaborators, the members of a community being studied in effect becoming coinvestigators. But in summary, the general principles in dealing with communities must be that local consensus of what is fair, proper, and true must be respected, and that the sense of the community—not just of the individual informant—must be taken into account.

Amid the Politics of the Modern World

It will be no surprise that political events of the world since 1945 have had an enormous impact on ethnomusicology, and particularly on fieldwork, as

Charles Seeger (1961) was one of the first to recognize. From an attitude widely held by musicians in the West, that the virtue—and a certain sacredness—of music was its distance from the rough-and-tumble of politics, we have come to look at music as a major weapon in politics and conflict, and we have seen research performed as substantially a political act. Significant among the critiques of ethnomusicology from this perspective is the work of Gourlay (e.g., 1978). The "third world" emerged as a group of nation-states whose boundaries were in many cases those that had arbitrarily been established by colonizing powers in the centuries before, and that often had little to do with the boundaries of traditional cultural or political units. India, Nigeria, and Indonesia are obvious examples. The breakup of the Warsaw Pact and then of the Soviet Union around 1990 caused widespread changes that have had significant effects on musical studies (see the essays in Slobin 1996). It goes without saying that eventually all these nations, and also the longer-established ones of Latin America, asserted their rights to political and cultural independence, and this included, eventually, the right of determining what kinds of research may be carried out within their borders, and finally of giving their own citizens priority in such research. After the 1960s and 1970s it became increasingly difficult for a North American or European simply and without question to set up shop and to study music or engage in anthropological fieldwork in most of the world, and indeed, in Native American territories at home.

A certain amount of distress was registered; it was pointed out that scholars from, say, India and Nigeria were welcome, after all, to study American and European culture in situ. Hardly a fair comparison, for Asian and African scholars beyond the age of graduate study had always come, and would continue to come, in only tiny numbers, and they carried out their studies in the humanities and social sciences largely under the tutelage and direction of Americans and Europeans. Until larger numbers of Asian and African scholars developed their careers, fieldworkers from abroad would outnumber native scholars, have superior equipment, decide what and how to study. Just as members of musically small societies had often felt that their heritage was effectively being removed by becoming known and published in the West, so the new nations came to be justifiably jealous of their national heritages. In this, they sometimes maintained attitudes once held by small and organically longer-established culture units such as tribes. They wanted to be sure that the heritage was preserved and studied correctly, that the nation derived benefit from the study. And they wanted a chance do it themselves.

It was a new ball game. The basic assumption of my chief of the tribal council had been that the members of the tribe would themselves best understand how their culture should be studied and presented. While such a view may not be easily accepted by the comparativists, it is easily justified if one accepts the longstanding integrity of the tribe as a social unit. However, to extend this view to the new nation-state seems less reasonable. It must be admitted that Japanese scholars have greater legal justification than non-Japanese for studying the music of the Ainu, who live in Japan, yet the Ainu may feel themselves not much more closely related to the Japanese than to Americans. The Blackfoot people in Montana probably couldn't care less whether a fieldworker is a U.S. or Canadian citizen or, for that matter, French, even though they themselves are United States citizens. And so, at a recent conference at which the familiar question was raised, it fell to Indonesian scholars from Java to point out that they were truly outsiders of a sort when working in Sumatra or Sulawesi and could themselves be blamed for the old problems of colonialism. The university-trained Hausa resident of Lagos may well, for all intents and purposes, be an outsider when working in a Hausa village. The question, as we have used it before, is, of course, what makes an "insider," and whether a true insider can do fieldwork at all. But beyond this, the identity of culture units is greatly complicated by the vagaries of politics.

I don't need to detail how the peoples of the new nation-states have been exploited by the industrial powers of the northern hemisphere. In general, ethnomusicologists have been among those who have objected. In contrast to the typical missionary, military administrator, or businessperson, though sometimes clumsily, they have tried to show that the peoples with whom they work have a worthwhile culture, should be treated as equals, should be encouraged to maintain their traditions and become known in the world for their accomplishments. Contrary to the views of some (e.g., Danielou 1973: 34–39), ethnomusicologists have not simply pointed their fingers at the quaintness of the exotic, chuckled at backwardness, or tried to prove that they were dealing with archaic phenomena. So it is curious that so many of them feel guilty about what they have done when confronted with the desire of Asians, Africans, and Latin Americans to share in their work. No point in feeling guilty, I think; but share they must and should. In any event, the new nation-states are here to stay. Just as England was once forged into a unified culture from several Germanic tribes, Celtic foundations, and Norman-French invaders, India, Indonesia, and Nigeria have become nations, however internally diverse, with distinct cultures. Intellectually and politically, ethnomusicologists have had to learn to deal with nations on their terms.

In nations under all kinds of government, it has been a basic assumption that music is a commodity. Governments believe that they own the music that is created and performed and disseminated within their borders and have the right to control it. In my experience in Iran before 1978, the Iranian state radio and the Ministry of Fine Arts had no qualms about recording and broadcasting the singing of diverse ethnic minorities, but government agencies had definite ideas about who else, citizen or foreigner, should be allowed to collect it, and how. It's an experience that would surely have been replicated, more intensely, after the 1978 revolution. It was the *national* government that assumed responsibility (not always well, to be sure) for the welfare of minorities. And so, while some of the world's new nations have readily admitted fieldworkers while others have not, all maintain the right of control. What, then, do they want, what moral obligations does the fieldworker assume toward them, their musicians, and scholars, and what should be done to assure their long-term hospitality and cooperation? What can the ethnomusicologist offer them? Let me mention just two possibilities.

A nation has the right of access to cultural artifacts collected within its borders. For us, this means recordings and supporting data. Depositing copies in national archives or in leading institutions is a convenient and automatic way to satisfy this desire. While this may almost seem like carrying coals to Newcastle, in many nations it is believed that the national heritage is in the process of disappearing. While modern ethnomusicologists may have little interest in it, it is through simple preservation that they seem best able to serve the people with whom they work. A related service is helping local libraries to build the holdings of literature and published records of their national music traditions. Much may have been published in North America and Europe without even the knowledge of local officials and scholars, and they are eager to find out what has been said about them, even if they frequently don't like what they eventually read.

Furthering the training of local individuals as ethnomusicologists, in the field or abroad, is another way in which non-Western research capacity can be aided; related to this is joint research by outsider and local scholars, on an equal and shared basis (Hood 1971: 371–75). Actively fostering respect in a third-world government for local musicians follows along the same lines. There is more, but these illustrations serve to make the point. It seems that common sense, the belief that at bottom all humans are equal and their values equally worthy of respect, and some understanding of the subtle concept of music ownership on the part of informant, tribe, village, or nation provide the best guidelines.

A World of Ethnomusicologies

The beliefs that each culture has a right to determine how, in the first instance, it is represented and that each society (read "nation") has primary control over its musical products have converged to direct ethnomusicologists in Europe and North America to greater recognition of—and support for—ethnomusicology in the rest of the world. In the first instance, this might mean helping institutions in nations as diverse as India, Iran, Nigeria, and Zimbabwe to train ethnomusicologists—or perhaps local musicians and teachers—in ways that would make them competitive in the West. To a degree, this has been accomplished; it is easy to cite prominent figures—Tran Van Khe, Fumio Koizumi, J. H. Nketia, Nazir Jairazbhoy, Jose Maceda, Hormoz Farhat, with apologies to the many not mentioned; and there is a multitude of accomplished though less internationally known individuals. The degree to which these scholars see themselves as "Ghanaian" or "Japanese" ethnomusicologists, or simply as ethnomusicologists who happen to be Indian or Peruvian, will vary. A question for our general understanding of disciplinary history is, however, the extent to which they see themselves part of their home musical culture, and how much the principles of their own musical experience shape the methods and conclusions of their scholarship.

The issue affects us all in several ways. For one thing, it is necessary to broaden our conception of the history of ethnomusicology from the narrow band leading from Hornbostel to Herzog, Merriam, Blacking. Blum (1991: 4–9) undertook to list scholars in the history of ethnomusicology born before 1905 by nation and area of origin, showing a very widespread ancestry of this field, in which individuals from Russia, China, Central Asia, and Latin America were engaging in essentially ethnomusicological activities. Recognizing that the traditions of musical scholarship are parts of the musical cultures, to be investigated, as has been done, for example, by Rowell (1992) and Shiloah (1995), is "a natural," but this attitude goes only so far, in that it objectifies these scholarly traditions and imposes "our" ethnomusicological analysis upon them.

A second effect is the recognition of modern Western ethnomusicology as only one among many possibly "ethnomusicologies." It's not a concept acceptable to all, and scholars who are concerned with comparative analysis of artifacts in laboratories (e.g., A. Schneider 2001, esp. p. 490) are particularly desirous of distinguishing between scientific fact and social scientific interpretation. But increasingly we have come to accept the importance of basic assumptions and cultural principles and values in the ethnomusicological enterprise. And so, just as a culture has its own ethnobotany and ethnohistory—its own interpretation of the incontrovertible findings about plants and events—it makes sense to talk about ethnomusicologies, which are based equally on the generally accepted definitions of ethnomusicology and the guiding principles of a particular culture. With articulate emphasis, Regula Qureshi (1999, 2000) makes a case for thinking about musicologies. But if we began talking about an Indian, a Chinese, and Arabic musicology, we soon came to add such concepts as gender-oriented women's musicology and gay musicology (represented by essays in Moisala and Diamond 2000 and Solie 1993). Recognizing these varied perspectives makes perfect sense to me, but there may be a danger in splitting the ethnomusicological world into too many subdivisions, to the point at which we have moved from a recognition that we (researchers) cannot keep ourselves out of the picture to a condition in which the interpretive component has become so powerful that we cannot communicate with each other.

If there's an "Indian ethnomusicology," a "Chinese," and an "African," is there then in fact a "Western" ethnomusicology? Well, it's probably true that we all know about a central body of literature, that which I've called "mainstream." But the fundamental or typical attitudes of North American, British, French, Italian ethnomusicologists are not identical. Indeed, the Society for Ethnomusicology, which has always considered itself in the first instance a society of individuals, no matter who they are, and only in the second tied to its North American base, has lately been confronted with competition from the European Seminar in Ethnomusicology, which provided a bit of a counterweight to SEM, and then, in the 1990s, from individual British and French societies, with the Iberian and Brazilian societies, and with other regional and national organizations. I'm not sure whether it's reasonable to generalize. And, wisely, SEM has avoided promulgating a formal definition to which it adheres officially. Still, the non–North American organizations concentrate more on studies in their parts of the world; some permit closer relationship between historical and ethnomusicological studies, and some are more concerned with folk music in the traditional sense. For some, preservation is of special importance, and for others, the understanding of contemporary urban musical culture. Their attitude toward the length, intensity, and methods of fieldwork differ. The differences are probably better perceived as distinct flavors. To a substantial degree, non–North American ethnomusicologists are better acquainted with American and Canadian authors than the opposite, and they generously respect the German, and then the Anglophone, literature that dominated in the twentieth century. But most of them don't consider the American approach, its emphasis on attacking the most obscure (with maybe the greatest naiveté), its colonialist flavor, its dual emphasis on anthropology and learning to play, to be the one they wish to follow.

I had the honor and good fortune of being invited to attend the founding meeting of the Brazilian Society for Ethnomusicology, in Recife, in 2002. I drew for my Brazilian colleagues the contrast between the modest and circumspect founding of SEM, in 1953, with 24 people present, and the Recife event, with some 150 enthusiastic scholars and students, many of whom had come at considerable trouble and expense from as far as 2,000 miles away. Quite a contrast with the tentative beginning of SEM. To me it became quite clear that national movements of ethnomusicology are at the point of thriving, and that the world of ethnomusicology will indeed come to be seen as a world of ethnomusicologies. Let's all try, though, to keep in touch.

PART 3

In Human Culture

16

Music and "That Complex Whole": Music in Culture

Ode to Tylor

Alan Merriam began his innovative ethnography of Flathead music thus: "All people, in no matter what culture, must be able to place their music firmly in the context of the totality of their beliefs, experiences, and activities, for without such ties, music cannot exist" (1967a: 3). Charles Seeger (1977: 217) wrote in 1946 that the ultimate purposes of musicology are "the advancement of knowledge of and about music [and] of the place and function of music in human culture." John Blacking ended his most influential book thus: "In a world such as ours . . . it is necessary to understand why a madrigal by Gesualdo or a Bach Passion, a sitar melody from India or a song from Africa . . . a Cantonese opera, or a symphony by Mozart, Beethoven or Mahler, may be profoundly necessary for human survival" (1973: 116). Three different but equally emphatic ways of expressing the same principle: for understanding music, the significance of its relationship to the rest of culture is paramount. The three authors are giants in the history of ethnomusicology: the first an anthropologist who started out as a composer and jazz clarinetist, the second a man who always referred to himself as a musicologist but began his a career conducting and composing, and the third an anthropologist who continued to maintain a career as a competent pianist. It became customary, in the 1950s, to divide ethnomusicologists into two groups, the "musical" and the "cultural," but actually, I think this distinction is in many ways spurious. Like Merriam, Seeger, and Blacking—and whatever their official disciplinary designation—the majority have a foot in each camp.

Nevertheless, in reading the literature of ethnomusicology in the period from 1950 to about 1990, one should be aware that a number of its authors were scholars who accused their counterparts either of having no interest in or knowledge of culture (in the anthropological sense of the word) or of not properly understanding the essence and technicalities of music. But the quotations by Merriam, Seeger, and Blacking don't reveal parochial attitudes, and the notion of two "sides" probably reflected personal rivalries, academic politics, and, at best, slight differences in career emphasis, more than schools of thought.

All ethnomusicologists, I would assert, consider the study of music in human life essential. The simple division between "anthropological" and "musicological" ethnomusicologists is too facile. There are differences in emphasis and primacy, differences in how one conceives the relation of music and culture (more properly, "music and the rest of culture"), and differences in one's perspective of the concept of culture, and of music. Before looking further at the alternative ways of relating music and culture, we should consider briefly the concept of culture, whose nature and very existence has for decades been a major issue in socio-cultural anthropology. There are hundreds of definitions and circumscriptions, and this is not the place to present them. However, the basic chord was struck early in the history of anthropology, in a formulation by Edward B. Tylor (1871: 1:1): Culture is "that complex whole which includes knowledge, belief, art, morals, law, custom, and any other capacities or habits acquired by man as a member of society." Few still read Tylor, but his place in history is secure as the first scholar to use the term "anthropology" systematically and to define culture in a way that is still quotable. Well, more than quotable; I have found his formulation a valuable point of departure for discussing music—better than later ones with more specialized focus, and given the fact that the concept of culture, as used by anthropologists, is in some quarters going out of use. Indeed, I developed a certain love for Tylor's definition. Let's look at its details. "That complex whole"—it's something that can be considered as a unit, complex because it has lots of components, but still unified, as its domains constantly affect each other; I like to think of it as a kind of glass ball with variously colored components, which one can hold and look at from various perspectives. One sees all of the subdivisions, but, depending on the angle at which it is held, one sees different configurations of color. The domains of social organization, economics, politics, religion, the arts, technology, all interact, and the view we have of this interrelationship, or our interpretation of it, depends on where we are coming from. Going on now: "which consists of knowledge, belief, art"—these are ways humans have developed of interpreting the world. "Morals, law, custom"—these are ways humans have developed for expressing rules for proper behavior in relationship to each other. "Any other habits or capacities acquired by man"—well, politically correct he wasn't yet, but culture consists of things learned by humans, not biologically inherited; and it consists of things that are learned by a person "as a member of society"—that is, things accepted and agreed on by society (however it might be defined) as a whole, and not, for example, just idiosyncrasies taught by a guru to a small band of disciples. It's a logical definition, stated elegantly and majestically. While differing enormously in their ways of studying and perceiving culture, anthropologists have not, it seems to me, departed so very much from this formulation.

Alan Merriam argued that ethnomusicology is the study of "music *in* culture," and later suggested that this definition did not go far enough, that it is the study of music *as* culture (1977a: 202, 204). This is rather different, at least in flavor and emphasis, from the concept of ethnomusicology as the study of music, "not only in terms of itself but also in relation to its cultural context," as Mantle Hood put it (Hood, in Apel 1969: 298). The differences among these three levels of relationship are blurred, but let me try to illustrate them for the novice. The approach most widely used in the period before 1975, best labeled "music in its cultural context," might include fieldworkers who studied tabla in Delhi, spending most of their time taking lessons and practicing but also learning as much as they can about Indian culture, trying to approach their work in a manner sensitive to Indian cultural values. It would also include those who collected rural folk music, recording it in the field, trying to learn for each song where it is normally performed and why, the singer's opinion of it, and so on, but nevertheless focusing on the song. The concept of studying music in culture implies a holistic view of culture as an organic unit, descriptively assigning to music a unitary role, ascertained in field research. The approach labeled "music *as* culture" moves further in that direction, suggesting that one takes up a theory of the nature of culture and applies it to music. Each approach has its disciplinary home base. If "music in cultural context" is standard musicology, the study of music in culture may be carried on with conventional methods of history and ethnography, while Merriam's study of music as culture, a term later taken up by others (Herndon and McLeod 1980), is an anthropological specialty. The study of music as culture would require the integration of music and its concepts and its attendant behavior and indeed, all musical life, into this kind of a model of culture. Anthony Seeger (1988) made a distinction between anthropology of music and musical anthropology, the latter integrating music even more thoroughly into the complex of culture. "Anthropology of music" suggests that the cultural complex includes, and the other domains strongly affect, the domain of music. "Musical anthropology" looks at the culture complex, too, but adds the belief that music is a force influencing and directing culture as a whole as much as do other domains.

Let me illustrate a bit further these three ways of going at the music/culture relationship, using from my field experience in Iran odds and ends of the kind of information and interpretation that typically would have appeared in an initial foray into musical life in Tehran of around 1968. No doubt, to be sure, things have changed mightily since that time. But what would an adherent of each of these three approaches have been likely to say?

First, conclusions drawn from the "study of music in its cultural context" approach might provide the following kind of information: Classical music is performed in concerts, at garden parties, and at small men's gatherings. Musicians have low status and are sometimes members of minorities. Folk music (the Persian term, *musiqi-ye mahalli*, actually means "regional music") in rural Iran is performed by specialists, each devoted mainly to one repertory and one kind of social occasion such as weddings. The "cultural context" alternative would give names of instruments, how they are made, who owns them. We would learn that the modes of Persian music are accorded certain characteristics such as aggression, affection, contemplation. We would hear something of how people learn music. This approach would show the production, performance, and experience of music.

The study of music in culture would have a different emphasis, going into greater depth with a view differently flavored. It might tell us that among various activities in which Iranians engage, music is one whose hearing occupies a good deal of time, but that people feel somewhat guilty about this attitude and deny it. It might compare the feelings toward music on the part of traditional and Westernized Iranians, or the techniques of music teaching with the teaching of other skills. Finally, the study of music as culture would make an attempt to seize the general nature of Iranian culture (my glass ball) and show how music accommodates its structure and its general character. It might identify certain central values of Iranian society such as hierarchy or individualism and show how these are reflected (or perhaps violated) in musical conceptualization, behavior, and sound. And it might show how the generally ambivalent attitude toward music affects ceremonies and social life.

Anthropologists and Musicologists

The successive appearance of these three approaches ("context," "in," and "as") in the history of ethnomusicology is an indication of the way in which ethnomusicology often follows anthropological theory, sometimes lagging behind by a number of years. They are successive in another way, as the second approach usually depends on data generated by the first, and the third on the information derived in the second. In a comprehensive field study, ethnomusicologists actually have to carry out elements of all three. Their borders are not easily distinguished, their overlapping is obvious, and perhaps they exhibit only a continuum. They are also basic to the historic, though in my opinion rather spurious, conflict between the "music" and "culture" orientations within our field. Anthropologically identified ethnomusicologists, feeling perhaps that anthropologists somehow own the concept of culture, argue that beginning in the mid–twentieth century they put culture back into the study of music. General musicologists, historians, and humanists may maintain that they have always been students of music in culture, but to them music is primary and culture a less explicitly defined concept. A similar conflict, incidentally, has been present as well within the music profession. Musicology is the study of people who are involved with music, so music theorists or performing academic musicians have been known to say, while they themselves study the music directly (and think themselves at times better persons for it). Beyond this, socio-musicologists, psycho-musicologists, sociologists of music all have different ideas of whose task it is—or better, who may be permitted—to study music in culture and how it should be done.

The issue, then, is not whether there is a cultural concern in ethnomusicology, but what should be the role of the concept of culture. Taking a very broad definition of culture—human knowledge agreed upon by some definable group of people—it is unfair to maintain that music historians have not paid attention to it as a context and receptacle for music. Particularly since the development of a methodology known as "new musicology," culture has been very much in evidence. Music historians have not been very technical or systematic in their treatment of culture, but ignored it they have not. A brief look at the works of a few prominent historians from the early history of musicology, and a couple of recent figures, as a sample may illustrate.

The earliest histories of Western music, works that predate the formal establishment of musicology, are hardly histories of music as such. Burney (1776–89), probably the most prominent before 1900, reads rather like social history with emphasis on music. A century later the more scholarly and academic work by Ambros (1862), the first person to hold a university chair specifically in musicology, could well be read as cultural history, or history of ideas, arts, philosophy, with special attention given to music. Toward the end of the nineteenth century the field of musicology began to develop as an independent discipline. The leading figure of that time was Guido Adler, whom we have already met as the author of a highly influential formulation of the field and its subdivisions (Adler 1885). His emphasis was on the direct study of music and musical style, often referred to as "style criticism," probably motivated by his desire to see the discipline recognized as a separate entity, but he seems also to have taken the study of music in culture for granted as a component of the discipline. His outline of musicology as a discipline with various subdivisions is replete with references to *Hilfswissenschaften* deriving from other, more established humanistic areas, particularly history. To be sure, anthropology and sociology are not among them for obvious historical reasons, although a subfield called *Musikologie,* devoted to the study of non-Western music, has the purpose of serving ethnological ends. This 1885 article is the first in the initial volume of the first professional periodical devoted to musicology and edited by himself, and it may be an indication of Adler's interest that the second article is a lengthy piece on Indian Vedic chant, a critique of the work of the pioneer Sanskritist Sir William Jones, by the Handel scholar Friedrich Chrysander (1885), much of it devoted to the cultural context of music.

It is true that after the turn of the century, many if not most musicologists turned to the study of the musical artifact, more or less separated from its cultural context, although it may be debated whether this was a matter of ideology or convenience. But some of the outstanding scholars in the field nevertheless continued to devote much of their attention to context. Thus Alfred Einstein's book on nineteenth-century music (1947a) has six initial chapters on the place of music in nineteenth-century culture. Walter Wiora (1965), in his attempt to show the history of world music as encompassing mainly four periods, depends on cultural typology for his framework. Knepler (1961) devotes most of his book on nineteenth-century music to the interpretation of musical events, including the broadly Western, the national, and the personal, in the light of a Marxist view of culture and history.

The philological and musical aspects of music history did indeed dominate the literature between 1960 and 1980, as some of the leading scholars, such as Carl Dahlhaus and Hans Heinrich Eggebrecht (1985; see also Dahlhaus 1989), attached music to its cultural context but usually went no further. Joseph Kerman (1985) examined "cultural musicology" but generally concluded that it does not contribute significantly to the ultimate aims of his discipline. Attempts to integrate music and the rest of culture, to show how musical values derive from cultural values, dominate a good deal of the innovative literature of the late twentieth century. Thus, Tomlinson (1993) examines associations between music, cosmology, and magic in sixteenth-century Italy, and McClary

(1991) looks at many aspects of the role and representation of women in European culture as expressed in classical music.

Whether the students of culture, anthropologists, have given consideration to music as a domain of culture is an instructive if not totally relevant question. The typical American anthropologist has been much more inclined to deal with visual and verbal art than with music. As a small sample, the large general though introductory works on anthropology by Harris (1971), Hoebel (1949), and A. L. Kroeber (1948) barely mention music but devote some substantial attention to visual art. Similarly, the major histories of anthropological scholarship (e.g., Harris 1968; Honigmann 1976; Lowie 1937; Manners and Kaplan 1968; Naroll and Cohen 1973; Voget 1975; the many works of George W. Stocking Jr., from 1968 on) almost unanimously avoid any mention of music. The existence of ethnomusicology seems to be passively accepted by American anthropologists, but on the whole they are unwilling to include it actively in their purview. It remained to scholars interested primarily in music to point out that musical studies can make important contributions to anthropological theory (Merriam 1955b) and to present the significant role of music research in the development of particular methodologies of anthropology, such as that of the German diffusionist school of the early twentieth century (A. Schneider 1976). Music in Western culture is broadly regarded as a symbol of happiness, but I am not inclined simply to write off this curious omission of music to unhappiness of the members of the anthropological profession. Rather, it may illustrate something else about the way Western urban society conceives of music. It is an art treated rather like science; only the professional can understand it properly. The fruits of music, like science, are enjoyed daily by practically all of the population, but the academic musical establishment has made the lay public feel that without understanding the technicalities of musical construction, without knowledge of notation and theory, one cannot properly comprehend or deal with music. This perhaps accounts for the anthropologists' habitual shyness (for further discussion, see Nettl 2002: 62–70).

Approaches to the Anthropology of Music

Back now once more to our three alternative approaches—"context," "in," and "as"—to the study of music as a part of culture. I'd like to give a few examples of approaches that have been taken, in the context of theoretical problems that involve the concepts of culture and music. The "study of music in its cultural context" approach seems not to pose major theoretical issues, although one should not make light of the problems of data gathering, sampling, and interpretation. The study of music in or as culture, on the other hand, requires a conception (going now beyond definition) of culture, and a conception of music for juxtaposition; so it is with these two segments of our tripartite continuum that this chapter is concerned.

Since about 1950 the various conceptions of culture seem to have moved from something static and subject occasionally to change to something in which change is the norm. The words *culture change* appear with increasing frequency in literature up to around 1985, after which the changeability of culture seems to be so taken for granted that one need hardly point it out. But how do we actually grasp culture so we can describe it, write about it? Well, as a start, nature is incapable of repeating itself precisely, and therefore constant change is a given in culture. But one may also argue that an observer is incapable of perceiving a complex phenomenon except in its static form, change being a rapid succession of stable states, and that therefore if culture is something constantly changing, one can deal with it only as an abstraction. Having begun with a model of music that is static, at least for the purposes of analysis, ethnomusicologists have followed anthropologists in gradually increasing their interest in musical change. Most approaches to the study of music in culture have actually used a static conception of culture. Music in or as culture implies a relationship, and what ethnomusicologists are about is the examination of views of this relationship. In all cases there is at least the implication of influence of one on the other, normally of culture on music, or of a time sequence, normally of music following culture. Here now are several approaches that have been followed by ethnomusicologists.

1. A large number of ethnomusicological publications, largely before around 1980, followed an enumerative approach to showing the relationship. This approach is based on the proposition that culture consists of a large number of separate components, interrelated to be sure, but a group of more or less separable domains. They include politics, religion, economy, each of which can be further broken down into components such as, say, public and private religion; rituals associated with birth, marriage, puberty, death; scriptures, prayers, interpretations, sermons; and so on. The essence of this approach, used in anthropology by Boas (Lowie 1937: 152) and some of his followers, is the desire to study each culture and each of the components individually, with no prior overall model or hypothesis about its workings. The emphasis is on the diversity of the cultures and the variety of their histories.

One can look at the music/culture relationship that way, too, the proposition then being that each aspect of culture has its own special relationship to music, and that the appropriate picture of music is one in which the roles and functions of individual items of musical concept, behavior, and sound are enumerated and explained separately. An enumerative approach to the musical culture of the contemporary Blackfoot Indians might tell us that there are many events at which music is heard: powwows, a major intertribal celebration in the summer, performances for tourists on and off the reservation, gambling games, small dances sponsored by local businesses, a pageant, reconstructions of older religious and social rituals. It would indicate that musical interests coincide with the division of the population into full-blooded and mixed ancestry. It would state that there are (or were, around 1985) some 100 men known as "singers" who perform most and who are loosely organized into some two dozen or so singing groups, or "Drums," but that there are another dozen men who know old ceremonial songs no longer sung. It would indicate that an average singer knows between 100 and 200 songs. It might well present this information in outline form, tying it, ad hoc, to other domains of the culture, but eschew the formulation of a theory of music in culture that depends on a single intellectual thrust.

Such a bare-bones description would have once been called "ethnography of music," to be followed by the more interpretive "ethnology." More recently, "ethnography" has been applied to a much larger circle of approaches and studies involving the culture concept. But even with an older view, it would usually not have been enough to enumerate details in a study of the way in which music can be viewed as an aspect of culture. One of the main problems of the ethnographer of musical life is to find a way of organizing a vast body of diverse bits of information. The establishment of typologies that can serve as templates for comparative description is a major task of ethnomusicology.

In the 1980s considerable attention was focused on the musical event as the main node of musical life. Thus, in an early attempt, Kaemmer (1980) proposed a set of relationships among the various roles involved in the realization of a musical event, listing five types of "music-complexes": individualistic, communal, contractual, sponsored, and commercial. As he indicated for the Shona people of Zimbabwe, any or all of these complex-types may be found in one society. Examples of later works moving more comprehensively into analysis of musical events are works by Ruth Stone (1982) and Anthony Seeger (1988). This sort of enumerative account is the outgrowth of simpler and more generally accepted typologies, such as the folk-popular-art music continuum and the distinctions between sacred and secular, public and private, professional and amateur, and more recently, presentational and participatory (see Livingston 1999; Turino 2000: 52–59).

2. Another way of looking at the music/culture relationship is to inquire what music does, what it contributes to the complex whole of culture. (Well, we're again talking about music as if it had a life of its own rather than being the result of human decisions, but that may come naturally if you accept Tylor's concept of the "complex whole.") Several approaches to the study of music in culture derive from the functionalist or structural-functionalist perspectives spearheaded by Malinowski and Radcliffe-Brown. In a fairly simple version, Radcliffe-Brown suggested (1952: 195; see also Harris 1968: 527) that culture is like a human or animal organism, with parts or organs interrelating and contributing something to the whole. The interrelationships and interdependencies of the organs are paralleled by the same kinds of relationships among the domains of culture. Music is one of these, and (like perhaps the liver?) makes a single main contribution and others of a less crucial nature. With this view, we could argue that music, in all societies, fills the same particular role, or assert, instead, that it has, in each society, a particular function not shared with other societies (the liver of social organisms everywhere; or perhaps liver here, stomach there, nose elsewhere?).

Aside from its role as one of several fundamental approaches to the study of music and culture (which is why it's in this chapter), the concept of functions of music is so important in the history of ethnomusicology that I also devote chapter 18 to its various implications. But for a couple of brief examples of what we are about here, let me cite Alan Merriam, who suggested a number of basic functions of music in general and everywhere (1964: 219–27), a kind of universalist approach to the issue of musical function; and William Kay Archer (1964a), who, one of many to try their hands at a variety of derivative approaches, used the principles of ecology to analyze the relationship of music to other domains. Although there are plenty of other universalist theories of musical function (e.g., integration of society, communication with the outside, expression of social organization), the idea that in each society music has a particular and distinct major function (or group of functions) has been more attractive to ethnomusicologists. In Western culture, the main function has to be entertainment in some sense. Among the traditional Blackfoot it seems to have been validation of ritual behavior (Nettl 1967c: 153); among the people of Yirkalla, enculturation (R. Waterman 1956: 41). In upper-caste Hindu society it may be a way of making the connection between religious values and everyday life, and for the Havasupai, of warding off dangers of the dark and maintaining what is of value in society (Hinton, personal communication 1967–68). If the culture-specific functional approach has been preferred to the universalistic, maybe that's because the diversity of human behavior is easier to understand and analyze than its unity.

3. A second kind of functionalist approach involves the hypothesis that there is for each culture a core or center, a basic idea or set of ideas, whose nature determines the character of the other domains, including music. The types of this core include broad characterizations, such as those suggested by Ruth Benedict (1934) in her influential book *Patterns of Culture*—the Apollonian Zuni Pueblo Indians, the Dionysian Plains peoples, the paranoid Dobu Islanders—and range from control of energy by Leslie White (R. Adams 1975: 11; Kaplan and Manners 1972: 45) and technology (Harris 1968: 662) to social structure (Radcliffe-Brown 1952) and a set of values or ideology (Kaplan and Manners 1972: 112–15). Logically, it would seem that the types of centers would proceed causally from control of energy to technology and on to social structure and values. It is difficult to disagree with White that control of energy is basic, and that from it flows technology, and hard to disagree with Harris that technology evokes social structure. A musicologist might ask, however, whether one should designate the "core" of culture as simply the kind and degree of control of energy that a people have developed, or whether more insight is gained, for example, by expanding this core concept to include technology or, further, the resultant social structure and the values to which it gives rise.

The point is that one can say little about the way in which control of energy is inevitably and directly accompanied by a kind of musical culture. Adding technology would enable us, for example, to speak to the differential development of musical instruments. The existence of stone tools alone allows the development of bone flutes and musical bows, the invention of pottery adds kettledrums and clay percussion instruments, and the development of metalwork makes possible the construction of brass gongs. Modern industrial technology provides the opportunity for highly standardized instruments. Beyond instruments, development of complex architecture gives us theaters and concert halls, electronics, the possibility of precise reproduction and unchanged repetition of performances. And so on to hundreds of other examples.

The specifics of musical culture, to be seen as culture and to be explained in terms of their intercultural differences, require a broader culture center. For example, social structure determines such things as the division of labor, providing opportunity for musical specialization. Even so, the mere existence of specialized musicians does not tell us much about the kind of music they produce. The general social organization of a people may also tell us much about the kind of interrelationship among musicians, in and outside of performance, and perhaps also, further, speak to such matters as the equal or hierarchical arrangement of parts in an ensemble, the blending or individual articulation of voices, the kinds of vocal and instrumental timbre preferred. But in order to establish a clear framework for the study of music in culture, the culture center as core might well be expanded further to include certain fundamental values or an ideology, for these might provide the most fruitful opportunity for studying in great detail the relationship between the nature of culture and society and the nature of musical style, concepts, and behavior.

The extraction of values from the conglomeration of statements and forms of behavior that a culture provides is no small matter. Characterizations of cultures, brief, distilled, and abstracted, are not numerous, and when they appear, they are often sharply criticized by those who regard the whole thing as too complex and who question the mutual translatability of culture systems into broad frameworks. Nevertheless, to the ethnomusicologist who needs a succinct characterization in order to tie to it the complex of musical systems, these few statements are attractive and insightful. Widely cited, because it was early on used in the interpretation of musical values, was Clyde Kluckhohn's formula for formalism as a central value of the Navajo approach to life, its function being "to maintain orderliness in those sectors of life which are little subject to human control" (McAllester 1954: 88). The now classic characterizations by Ruth Benedict mentioned above suggest ways in which musical behavior and musical style can be tied to a culture core.

Let me again give, in a bit more detail, an example from the culture of Persian classical music. As a basic cultural characterization, urban Iranian society maintains and balances significant values or guiding principles, and these can be traced in musical sound and behavior. Thus the conflict between equality, a basic Islamic tenet, and hierarchy, a principle of actual social and political structure, is reflected in the structure of the system of Persian classical music, based on a group of pieces collectively called the *radif*. These pieces (*gusheh*) are initially presented (to students, for example) as equal, equally capable of being the basis of improvisation and composition, but under the surface there emerges a carefully structured hierarchy of musical units whose relative importance is determined by various criteria. A countervailing value, individualism, significant in various aspects of social behavior, is reflected in music by the centrality of musical improvisation and the prestige of music that departs from norms. The related value of surprise is reflected in the centrality and prestige of musically surprising elements, from modulatory devices in the modes to the rhythmic unpredictability of nonmetric improvisations. The importance of precedence in socially informal situations, and of introductory behavior and personnel in more formal situations, is reflected in the differential positions of the important portions in learning materials and in formal concerts (Nettl 1978b).

This is all personal interpretation, supported, to be sure, by some agreement from Persian musicians, but what ethnomusicologists need is a way of determining what are central values or guiding principles of cultures, expressed in such a way that their distinctiveness becomes clear, but also so that comparisons among cultures are possible.

4. A fourth model, subsumed in part under the foregoing three yet worthy of special mention, envisions a line of relationships leading from a central or dominant cultural principle to music. Using Merriam's tripartite model of music (Merriam 1964: 33), it lays aside Merriam's further assertion that these three parts—concept, behavior, and sound—all interrelate equally, proposing instead that the part of the model closest to principles central to a culture is the "concept" sector of music. Thus the line moves from culture core to music concept, on to musical behavior, finally to music sound, clearly related but hard to pin down. Let me give an unelaborated example: Islamic culture places relatively low value on music, sometimes in theory forbidding it, or at least defining it narrowly. Thus one conception of music in the major Islamic cultures is that it is something low in the scale of values. The behavioral result is low status of the professional musician and higher status of the informed amateur, and associated ideas of freedom of the latter. This leads to improvisation as the form of musical behavior of greatest prestige and cultural centrality. The musical style or sound, then, is the result of musical choices made within an essentially improvisatory system.

5. Other models are less static, seeing culture as something constantly changing and characterized by shifting relationships, ubiquitously divisible and divided. Here we look at music and musical life as a result of—and maybe a reflection of—the relationships of components such as genders, majorities and minorities, classes, which always result in unequal distributions of political and economic and perhaps spiritual power. Music is seen as performing these unequal power relationships. Thus, the hegemony of Anglo-American society was able to force the elimination of various Native American repertories. Male-dominated Western society diverted attention from female composers. In certain Asian societies, music, as a desired but polluting part of culture, was relegated to subcultures with low status and prestige,

who might then in turn be blamed for having become involved with music. Much of the recent literature contributing to the anthropology of music takes this kind of perspective (see essays in Askew 2002; Radano and Bohlman 2000; Turino 2000 as significant examples).

Some Points of Debate

If ethnomusicologists agree that understanding music in or as culture is central to their pursuits, then what are the themes that underlie their discussions? Some of the subsequent chapters examine certain of them in detail, and a number of new perspectives have come to the fore in the wake of changes in both scholarly perspectives and the life of music in the world—see particularly chapter 30, which looks at the 1990s. Here, however, in line with my purpose of attempting a wide and historically oriented perspective of the music/culture relationship, let me mention just three of these themes, each of them explicitly the subject of debates, or at least in the background of debates in our literature. Actually, they have already put in their appearances: (1) the insider-outsider, or as it was called, the "emic-etic" interface, (2) determinist versus functionalist interpretations, and (3) the comparativist/particularist controversy.

Emic-Etic Interface

By now it's a truism: One may look at culture, at music, at music-as-culture from the perspective of a member of the society being studied or from the viewpoint of the analyst. This is probably the most basic of all ethnomusicological issues, and there is a lot to it, and we've already encountered it in my discussions of transcription, analysis, and fieldwork. The shorthand designation, "emic-etic," was widely used in the 1970s and has receded, but the issue is still very much with us. In the study of music and culture it takes on a slightly different slant. The crucial interface between investigator and informant is summarized thus by Harris (1968: 575): "Etic statements are verified when independent observers using similar operations agree that a given event has occurred." On the other hand (571), "emic statements refer to systems whose . . . things are built up out of contrast and discriminations significant, meaningful, real, accurate [to] the actors themselves."

So how might this work in everyday terms? The Flathead people (Merriam 1967a: 3–24) "emically" regarded music as something that comes about by dreaming, from supernatural visions, from other tribes. The American ethnomusicologist "etically" makes bold to say that it's the dreamers who compose. Again, the Blackfoot maintain that two songs have in a sense been created if two people have visions in which they learn songs, even if those songs sound identical. The etic view would instead identify the two products as one and the same song. In the 1950s, the emic view, if different from the etic, might have been given short shrift by a fieldworker, seen mainly as an exotic curiosity. In the 1980s, it would be accorded primacy in the researcher's interpretation, and indeed, one might have been attacked for bringing up the "etic" perception at all.

No need to belabor. If we are to construct a detailed but broad picture of the music of a society as culture, we must decide which route we are taking at any one time, but eventually we will probably find it necessary to follow both and to discover a way of reconciling them. If the routes are distinct, we will come to realize that informants can make both emic and etic statements. Thus, faced with the assertion (backed by hearing the recordings) that two songs he had sung sounded identical, my Arapaho friend William Shakespear said, "Yes, they do sound alike, but they are two songs." The point is, of course, to discover what it is about the way a culture works, in its core, that causes its practitioners to make certain kinds of conceptual, behavioral, and acoustic distinctions in their music. What does Bill Shakespear's interpretation tell us about Arapaho culture, musical ideas and discrimination, and cosmology?

Determinism versus Functionalism

I have touched on the way in which the character of a culture, as a whole, affects or determines musical ideas, behavior, and sound. An essentially historic process, it can be analyzed in (at least) two ways. A strictly functionalist view would propose that while a central core of culture is responsible for the shape and nature of what could be called the outer organs (the biological model) or the definitely less important superstructure (the Marxist model), the interaction is constant. The effect of the core of values on musical behavior is more or less immediate. A determinist view would lengthen the time span. A society might, for instance, develop a certain way of harnessing energy, then gradually develop a system of technology that takes advantage of it. Eventually there would emerge changes in the social structure that in turn would impose certain values most clearly evident in religion, philosophy, and law. These values would eventually come to affect the arts and other aspects of lifestyle. The time from the first stage to the last could be a matter of centuries. The difference between the functionalist and the determinist conception can be interpreted as a difference between the immediate and the gradual.

Now, of course, these are theoretical constructs that at best suggest ways of looking at music as culture. One is hard put to find examples that illustrate or totally negate either view. But let's consider briefly the function of the so-called new music in Western society in the 1970s, the period of greatest harmonic dissonance, and the kind of music stemming from the work of such composers as Webern, Cage, Stockhausen. Assessing it functionally, and holding it up against the template of culture, one might perceive the following characteristics of contemporary Western society: (1) highly developed technology, particularly in electronics; (2) fragmentation of society into many groups, determined by wealth, ethnic descent, age; (3) standardization of work habits and of products but a decline of interest in the standardization of ethical and moral systems agreed upon by all; (4) emphasis on personal ownership of products and their quantity. The "new music" depends on sophisticated electronic technology and is composed of a large number of styles that can hardly be subsumed under a single system of comprehension, drawing on other musics in and outside the society. It is a music that expects at times precise repetition from performance to performance, giving the most exacting directions to players and using instruments like tape recorders in live performance. But it may also give unprecedented latitude—to the point of aleatory or indeterminancy—to the performer, and yet the individuality of the composer and the association between a composer and his or her pieces are stressed. One might argue that this music system is a direct function of the culture that produces it, as it contributes to the general character of the culture; or so one might argue.

In the alternative interpretation, the perfection of electronics after World War II and continuing into the twenty-first century, resulting from a particularly efficient way of using and transforming energy, makes necessary a vast array of professional specializations. This development reinforces the emphasis on personal property, already present, and results in the development of a fragmented social structure, accompanied by the ready possibility of instant communication through the mass media. Such a culture, one could assert, is bound to give rise to the kind of music that was called "new" in the 1960s and 1970s. It is interesting for me to recall a lecture that I gave at the University of Isfahan in 1969, in which I was asked to illustrate Western music.

Playing some electronic work, I was asked why this music sounded so "ugly" or "broken" (*kharab* in Persian). I asked the students what they thought, and some of them concluded that Western culture must be very *kharab* if it produced such music.

Comparativist/Particularist Controversy

Finally, a word on comparative study, which in this case would seek a typology of music/culture relationships of the world's societies that one could map. Differences in theoretical perspective often reflect differences in research and personal experience. The typical ethnomusicologists' statements about the relationship of music and culture are based on the way in which the major cultures they have studied work and can be explained. The issue then becomes: Can we develop theories that explain music in culture everywhere, or does each society have its own way of living the relationship?

Among the theories to help explain music as culture in a way that would be valid for all societies, Lomax's (1968) cantometrics tries to provide a typology of correlations of the principal musical and social traits of entire societies, and Feld (1984), proposing a generally valid methodology for encapsulating the conclusions of a "sociomusicology" concentrating more on the insider's perspectives, shows the relationship to be much more sophisticated and variegated in even small indigenous societies. Unfortunately, the various systems that could enable us to make broad, intercultural comparisons have failed to attract a following. The most successful classic work in the music-in-culture sphere, by ethnomusicological fieldworkers such as Merriam, McAllester, and Blacking, has been in the presentation of specific cultures as exemplars, and the many musical ethnographies of the last twenty years, such as those discussed in chapter 17, have been valuable principally in showing the individuality and uniqueness of the cultures they have studied, and in presenting personal perspectives and methodologies. Comparative study has been more successful in the "sound" part of the musical spectrum than in contemplation of musical concepts and ideas, to say nothing of shedding light on the way different societies integrate music into the totality of culture.

17

The Meat-and-Potatoes Book:
Musical Ethnography

Doing Ethnography, Writing Ethnography

You're in the "field," doing ethnomusicology. My guess is that you are work-ing on two tracks. One is the solution of the particular problem you have set yourself—maybe the life history of a famous singer, or the way a particular genre of song has changed in a village, or how people teach a traditional in-strument, or how members of a folk dance club in Chicago construct their conception of their own ethnicity. But you are also (and maybe I should have put this first) trying to get a picture, as much of a panoramic picture as you can, of the culture of the society in which you're a guest, and about the way music interacts with the rest of that culture. That's what I'd call "doing" mu-sical ethnography.

The word *ethnography* has come to mean something different around 2000 from what it meant, say, in 1937, when Robert H. Lowie wrote that "ethnog-raphy is the science that deals with the 'cultures' of human groups. By culture we understand the sum total of what an individual acquires from his society" (1937: 3). Dictionaries define ethnography simply as the description of cul-ture. In either case, the implication is one of comprehensiveness. To describe a "culture" is to write about or take into account all of Tylor's "complex whole." In the 1990s, scholars and students in anthropology, but also in fields involved in cultural studies and interpretive theory, began to use the term more casually, often associating it with thorough, detailed description of an event, saying, for example, "I'm doing an ethnography of this concert" or "of this committee meeting." I wish here to follow more closely on the original meaning. Some of the more limited projects certainly qualify as "ethnography," significantly if and as they show what the event has to do with the rest of culture; some, in my opinion, may not. In any event, describing the "complex whole"—even if transferred to the microcosm of musical culture—is not an easy task, to put it mildly, and no one really accomplishes it completely, but the concept of ethnography grew out of the insistence that all of the domains of a culture are interrelated, and so when you are in the "field" doing the "ethnography" part of your task, you are hopefully working within this broad perspective, even when you are listening to one song or just taking a flute lesson.

There was a time when ethnography was downgraded because it was thought to be "mere" description, contrasting with the interpretive and thus loftier "ethnology" to which it led. Now it is "ethnography" that has the interpretive character (while "ethnology" is hardly used). Still, it's good to bear in mind that Harold Conklin's serious and by now classic admonition continues to have relevance: "The data of cultural anthropology derive ultimately from the direct observation of customary behavior in particular societies. Making, reporting, and evaluating such observations are the task of ethnography" (1968: 172).

"Doing" ethnography in the field is one part of the challenge; the second is "writing" ethnography, and that's what this chapter is principally about. The point is that while you may have learned a culture comprehensively— maybe you've been there for a decade and have countless notebooks, computer disks, audiotapes of data, and a lot more just in your head—your task now is to interpret all this material, possibly but not necessarily in accordance with theoretical basic assumptions, but in ways that on the one hand do not violate the culture's own perspective and on the other still communicate something meaningful to the society that is your audience. For musical ethnography, one of the great challenges has been the discovery of a systematic way of comprehending the enormous number of ideas, activities, and events that comprise the musical life of a society in their relationship to the totality of a people's culture. Examining the literature of ethnomusicology shows us that each author has a distinct way, and that there is much less consistency in these works than there is in the description of musical sound.

Many ethnomusicologists—I think I'm right in making this guess—would like, perhaps for their dissertations, to produce musical ethnographies, accounts that are comprehensive of musical cultures, circumscribed and limited by repertory or population or geographic area. Each would like to write *the* book about the musical life of a village or a nation or an ethnic group.

There was a time when we thought that folk or indigenous cultures were so homogeneous that one could learn all there was to be learned in a year. But it turns out that even in a society of a couple of hundred people, the musical culture is an extraordinarily complex—shall we put it this way?—organism, a small version of the grand "complex whole" of culture. But for some decades, the fundamental work that ethnomusicologists have aspired to is what I'll call the book-length "musical ethnography." It is the meat-and-potatoes book of our field.

I suggest that the literature of many disciplines, particularly the humanities, revolves around a kind of "meat-and-potatoes" book. In historical musicology, it is probably the life-and-works account of a composer; in literature, more likely the critical and historical evaluation of a major novel or set of poems; in history, a biography or a book about a war; in social anthropology, a book about a society; or in folklore, the folk tales or songs of an ethnic group of community or tribe. Well, in ethnomusicology it has been "the music of the . . . " I have a feeling that this is what most ethnomusicologists usually want to do, once in their lives. Their problem, though, has been the writing of ethnography, at least as much as the "doing" of ethnography.

Classics

Let's see how some scholars from the earlier period of our history solved this problem. Consider five approaches, illustrated by works that qualify as classics, from the period before 1975.

One elementary approach to making an inventory of a musical culture is to take all of the concepts and categories that a society uses in its musical culture as the basic material, deriving this from the terminology. We might use a dictionary of musical terms. Might this work for Western music? Well, we'd have to take into account the differential emphases that Western academic culture accords to various musics. The *Harvard Dictionary of Music* wouldn't show the overwhelming significance of popular music, for example. But what if the account of the terminology resulted from disinterested field research?

Ames and King (1971) provide what purports to be simply a glossary of terms and expressions used by the Hausa of northern Nigeria in talking about music and musical culture. It qualifies as a description of musical culture, using the vocabulary and thus generally the categories that the Hausa themselves use, therefore providing essentially an emic picture of the niche music occupies in the culture. It is a classified glossary. The authors first divided the subject into five broad areas, using their own taxonomy: instruments, professional performers, patrons of music, occasions on which music is performed, and music performance. Within each category some subdivisions, as that of instruments into the traditional categories of Hornbostel and Sachs (1914—idiophones, membranophones, chordophones, aerophones), were imposed from outside, while others, such as the division of vocal performance into categories distinguished by social context as well as musical style, were the Hausa's own: proclamation, ululation, challenges, acclamation. The authors' way of taking musical concepts and fitting them, as it were, into the culture, was to examine each term that is used somehow in connection with music. It turns out that in Hausa culture the degree of integration is great; very few words are specific to music, and the vast majority are terms normally used in nonmusical contexts but also applicable to music. This situation of widespread but not universal. The academic language of classical music in English was at one time much more music-specific, using loan words from Italian (allegro, andante), or words whose meaning is primarily musical (concert), and others with a specific musical meaning quite separate from their denotation in other domains (note, beat). This in itself may tell us something about the differences in the place of music in the two societies. In the case of Ames and King, there is an overarching taxonomy imposed for comparative purposes, but within it there appears clearly the taxonomy of Hausa culture and its principles. One way to study music in culture, clearly, is to use language as a mediator.

Reaching five decades back from Ames and King in the history of ethnomusicology, Frances Densmore's book on the songs of the Teton Sioux (1918) is the most comprehensive of the many collections of songs of Native American nations she published over half a century. It is basically a collection of songs, many dozens of them, arranged by social context and function, with comments about their genesis and use. Although it does not set out to give an account of musical culture, it accomplishes this more than other works of the time, simply because she put into it everything she was told by her informants. There are many weaknesses, unnecessary to discuss here; the book should be viewed in its own historical context. But if the book-length musical ethnography is our meat-and-potatoes work at the end of the twentieth century, the main course of the menu early in the century was the (usually article-length) collection of transcriptions, with musical analyses, such as those of Hornbostel and Stumpf. Densmore (1918) is like them, but it really tells a lot more about musical life.

McAllester's *Enemy Way Music* (1954), a landmark of a different sort—a classic study because it is among the first to deal explicitly with musical and cultural values in a non-Western society—examines the musical content of a Navajo Indian ceremony. Devoting only some twenty pages to the discussion, he manages to describe and comment upon a group of central values of Navajo culture, focusing on the perception of danger that comes through misuse of anything, including music, and further dividing values into aesthetic, existential, and normative. Examples are self-expression, quiet, humor, provincialism, formalism, and individualism. The differential treatment of these values—it is difficult to distinguish the degree to which each is aesthetic, normative, or existential—may be debated. But of special interest is McAllester's implied conclusion that while cultural values are reflected in music, this reflection appears in musical behavior and in attitudes toward music, and only secondarily if at all in the structure of the music. If I may venture to interpret his words, to McAllester it is concept and behavior that reflect culture, and if one is to study music as culture, one does so primarily through these components of music and much less through sound.

While the studies just described are by scholars with a substantial interest in anthropology, William Malm's (1959) general book on Japanese music makes no pretense of being a contribution to that field or indeed to concentrate on music as or in culture. More than the other works discussed here, it purports to be about music, but Malm makes it clear that an understanding of the music must rest on at least some understanding of Japanese culture, past and present. For example, in his section on koto music, he first gives a detailed cultural and historical context of this instrument and its music. There follows an account of the history of the instrument, not purely organological but also mentioning persons, events and occasions, places, literary sources, myths, characterizations of the Japanese historiography, schools of musicians and the basis on which they are formed, and relationships to social classes, repertories, and other instruments. He goes on to a discussion of teaching techniques and their relationship to musical and social structure, and finally moves on to the contemporary instrument and its music, again laying stress on the social context. By now an "old classic" superseded by more recent work, it is an unusually good illustration of the "music in its cultural context" type of study. The distance between the ethnomusicologists who come from anthropology and those who come from a background of a more strictly musical nature is hardly as great as it is sometimes made out to be.

Even earlier, some of the historical accounts of small cities in Germany and Austria by music historians of the first half of the twentieth century, who tried to exhaust all data and also worked at establishing a rational organization, might be considered forerunners of musical ethnographies; for example, Arnold Schering's *Musikgeschichte Leipzigs* (the second volume, covering 1650–1723, published in 1926). And in quite a different way, Constantin Brailoiu's small book *Vie musicale d'un village* (1960—but researched in the 1930s) showed the distribution of songs and song types and functions among the various components—age groups, classes—of the population of a Romanian village. Another study of a village, carried out in 1940 but not published for six decades (!) is Vargyas's (2000) work, *The Musical World of a Hungarian Village—Aj, 1940,* which does in over 1,000 pages what the title promises.

The works I've mentioned so far are intellectual precursors to the musical ethnographies that populate the 1980s and 1990s publishers' catalogues. In my view, the grandmother of comprehensive musical ethnographies is Merriam's study of the Flathead (1967a), not because he succeeded in being comprehensive but because he set out—even in his title—to write systematically about all aspects of Flathead musical culture and their interrelationships. Following in some measure his tripartite model of music, he divided the first part, whose main thrust is the presentation of music in culture, into chapters that deal mainly with concepts (those on sources and ideas of music) and others that discuss behavior (on instruments and uses of music, subdivided into some categories recognized by the Flathead). The second part of the book is comprised of transcriptions and analyses—the "sound" part of Merriam's model. While a brief glossary of terms is appended, there is no attempt here to use the Flathead language as the point of departure. Rather, observations combined with the recording of statements by Merriam's own and earlier informants, elicited through questions about music from discussion presumably in English, are the main source. The overall organization is Merriam's to a much greater extent than it is that of Flathead culture.

Surprisingly, what is less clear in Merriam than in the less interpretive Ames and King (1971) is the way in which music functions within, or is a part of, Flathead culture. The concepts of music and the ways in which people behave "musically" are described in exemplary detail. But other questions, such as the reflection of Flathead values in musical ideas, or how music relates to other domains of culture, are not frequently touched upon. It is interesting to see that even one of the most outstanding publications coming from the "anthropology of music" approach to ethnomusicology concentrates on the music, broadly conceived, and deals with music holistically, but less than Merriam might later have wished with music as culture.

Organizing "That Complex Whole" of Music

Although there were predecessors, some of them described above, the late 1960s marked a kind of threshold into a period in which ethnomusicology was characterized by the appearance of many extensive studies, most of them book-length, each of them in some way making a comprehensive statement about *a* musical culture. They were increasingly described as ethnographies, and I feel that most of their authors had in mind a holistic view of musical culture. They faced significant problems, one of which was organization. The number of things to be learned about a musical culture is, well, infinite, and even if one is pretty selective, as was Merriam in his Flathead study, the job is to find a reasonable and logical organization that reflects what the culture would, as it were, say about itself and also enhances the author's communicative intent. The second problem, maybe more interesting, involves two considerations. One, which speaks to the process of analyses, if the "complex whole" culture concept of Tylor (or concepts related to it) has utility—and the domain of music is a proper microcosm—then it should be possible to learn from every part or sector of the musical culture something that is significant about the musical culture as a whole. And second—this is more important in the actual writing of musical ethnography—if it's impossible to really give a comprehensive account (Merriam tried, but would have been the first to admit that it's a "first attempt," spotty and sometimes superficial), an alternative is to find a small piece, sector, or aspect of the musical culture that functions as a kind of point of entry into the larger whole, from which you can derive these more general insights.

Many of the musical ethnographies of the 1980s and 1990s seem to me to accept these basic assumptions. They rarely say so outright. But typically they deal with some aspect of the culture in great detail, their insights radiating outward to the rest of musical life. The points of entry may be a genre, a musician, an instrument, a process, a song—none of them, in most cases, of sufficient exceptionality to merit great attention, were it not for the ethnographer's ability to use them to demonstrate important insights about the culture as a whole. Let me mention a few important examples.

One of the earliest works in this genre is Steven Feld's *Sound and Sentiment: Birds, Weeping, Poetics, and Song in Kaluli Expression* (1982). Aside from many other contributions of this book, and also problems that it raised, one thing that struck me as important was the way Feld approached the comprehension of music in Kaluli culture—first by placing music in the Kaluli taxonomy of sounds (speech, weeping, singing, birdsong, and more), and then, in a way related to the thinking of Claude Lévi-Strauss (1969)—who believed that a central myth provided the key to a society's mental processes—by identifying a myth that, so he thought, explained the Kaluli world of sound. It was a myth about a boy who became a bird. Feld later told a story about the time he tried to tell the Kaluki people what he had written about them, and they asked him, "Why did you choose that particular story?" Well, clearly, ethnography is substantially an interpretive enterprise, but the question led to Feld's concept of dialogic editing, giving voice in the interpretation to the music's own society.

About the time of Feld's publication, there also appeared books by Daniel Neuman, Paul Berliner, and Lorraine Sakata, each using a different element to gain entry to the musical culture as a whole. Like many of the books that were to make up the standard literature of the end of the century, each of them was based on the author's dissertation and on fieldwork of well over a year. In a work that has since become a classic, *The Life of Music in Northern India* (1980), and a related article (1977) Neuman explained central elements of Indian musical structure through the ways in which Hindustani classical music was transmitted from teacher to student and the ways in which musicians were socially organized in relation to Hindu and Muslim social structures in India. Sakata, in *Music in the Mind* (1983), looked at the way basic concepts and assumptions about music in Afghanistan provided insight into the ways musical sound and musicians interact. In Berliner's book *The Soul of Mbira* (1978), an instrument, the mbira in Shona society, was a center from which ideas radiate into the domains of musical culture.

Neuman's (1977) study of hereditary musical specialists in North India illustrates an examination of the relationship of a social and a musical system. For example, Neuman compared the hierarchical structure of performance, divided into various levels of soloist's and accompanist's roles, with the hierarchical social organization, supporting the parallel with the finding that soloists and accompanists are drawn from separate social lineages. He relates the desire, probably of recent origin, of North Indian accompanists to become soloists to the coming of greater social mobility. Musicians become soloists by affecting the social appurtenances of the system within which the soloists normally live, such as officially recognized "gharanas," or schools of musicianship, which are also real or imagined genetic lineages. Neuman thus concluded that "the two phenomena are crucially interlinked" and "both affect and are affected by the changing character of the soloist-accompanist relationship" (1977: 233).

Neuman did not try to state the central value system of North Indian society but concentrated on one social value in the lives of groups of people who are particularly concerned with music, the groups from which musicians are drawn; nor did he try to establish the totality of musical values. His ethnography concentrated on an aspect of Indian musical culture whose understanding would have to precede a more detailed accounting of the technicalities of music.

Points of Entry

Let me cite some further examples of ethnographies whose authors have chosen a wide variety of points of entry to their cultures. Examining the life and work of the individual person as a way of sampling musical culture became an important method of ethnography in the late 1980s, but it had forerunners in anthropology, such as Paul Radin's presentation of the life of a Winnebago (Ho-Chunk) man, *Crashing Thunder* (1963), originally carried out in the 1920s. I want to mention three major works in this category. *Blessingway Singer,* the autobiography of the distinguished Navajo leader and religionist Frank Mitchell, edited by David McAllester and Charlotte Frisbie (Mitchell 1978), is unique in its comprehensiveness because it presents the singer's own story along with the informed analysis of the editors. More recently, Virginia Danielson's study of Umm Kulthum, the great Egyptian singer, *The Voice of Egypt* (1997), tells about many aspects of twentieth-century Egyptian musical culture from the perspective of a musician considered by many as the ideal. It would be a bit like portraying the musical culture of early nineteenth-century Vienna by concentrating on Beethoven, an approach that has its weaknesses because of Beethoven's uniqueness. (And yet in other respects, what other figure could be more representative of that musical culture?)

Following in certain respects in the footsteps of Brailoiu (1960) but also parallel to Danielson in its emphasis on the experience of individuals, Judith Vander's *Songprints* (1988) tells insightfully about the musical culture of the Shoshone though the life histories of five women. To me, the most significant concept here is the "songprint," the total repertory—music sung, known, recognized—by an individual person, because it provides insight into the musical counterpart of a longstanding problem in anthropology: the interface of personality and culture, of what is individual and what is shared.

In ethnomusicology we don't have the citation indexes that are used by scientists to identify the most influential authors, but Anthony Seeger's book on the Suyá (*Why Suyá Sing*), published in 1988, has in the 1990s been cited perhaps more than any other work from this literature of book-length musical ethnographies, in large measure because he made a felicitous distinction between Merriam's "anthropology of music" and the concept of "musical anthropology," which suggests an even greater degree of integration, insisting that music not only results from the guiding principles of a culture but is itself one of the forces that determine the character of a culture. One would think that the musical life of a society of some 150 people would be easy to describe and organize, but the Suyás' musical culture is a very complicated organism, and Seeger uses a central ritual, the Mouse Ceremony, as a kind of leitmotif to which he continues to return.

Other sectors of the musical domain have also served as points of departure for the kind of comprehensive insight one would wish to see in a book that could be called "The Ethnomusicology of . . ." Thomas Turino's *Moving Away from Silence* (1993) focuses on the way music plays a central role, and undergoes change as cultural environment changes, in the course of the migrations of Aymara people in Peru from the village to the town of Colima and then to Lima. Philip Bohlman's book *The Land Where Two Streams Flow* (1989) is fundamentally a musical ethnography of Israelis of German, Austrian, and Czech origins whose central music is that of Mozart, Beethoven, and Schubert. The main kind of event analyzed, musically and socially, is the house concert, a type of event that usually took place in people's homes on afternoons. One or a small group of musicians would play classical or Romantic sonatas or chamber music, people would speak German, and refreshments duplicated, as well as possible, the offerings of Viennese *Konditoreien*.

Jane Sugarman's book (1997) on the music of Prespa Albanians living in Macedonia and North America, largely women, gives important insights into Albanian musical culture, and into the culture of emigrants. Kay Kaufman Shelemay (1998) examines the musical culture of Syrian Jews in New York from the perspective of one major (not easily circumscribed) genre, the *pizmonim*. Timothy Rice's book *May It Fill Your Soul* (1994), about Bulgarian folk music culture, takes as its main point of departure the teaching of bagpipe music. Helen Myers's work on Hindu musical culture in Trinidad (1998) focuses on the part of the repertory that can be hopefully traced directly to the origins of the community in India, and concentrates on the ethnography of one village. Donna Buchanan's *Performing Democracy* (2004) uses a major instrumental folk ensemble in Sofia to shed light on the changing and changed musical culture of Bulgaria since the disintegration of the Warsaw

Pact. Theodore Levin's (1996) point of entry to Uzbek and other Central Asian musical culture is a kind of travelogue, a thoughtful account of a journey through the area whose music he describes.

Naturally, I tried my hand at this too, using, for Blackfoot culture (1989a) the system of ideas about music—Merriam's "concept" sector—as the foot in the door, and trying to organize it into four categories: fundamental concepts, music as it moves through time from its origins to recent change, music and societies of people (Blackfoot and others) and supernatural beings, and the technicalities of music. I suggested looking at music in Western academic culture as four different kinds of society. Attracted to the significance of myths to provide broad insights, I tried to make a case for a central Blackfoot myth that explained their ideas about music. For the Blackfoot, it was the myth of the supernatural beaverman who had an affair with a human woman and compensated her husband by giving him his powerful songs, singing each one once in exchange for the dressed skins of all of the fauna in the Blackfoot environment. And later, trying a similar technique for Western art music in midwestern schools of music, I nominated the familiar Mozart/Beethoven dyad.

This quick survey of the literature of musical ethnography is hardly exhaustive; there are many more books that might have been mentioned. And there are also others that could qualify, easily, as musical ethnography but concentrate on processes, on recent change, on political issues. Even in recent times we have seen significant attempts to do what Merriam tried, the really comprehensive study of the musical culture of a society. An example is Eric Charry's *Mande Music* (2000), which covers an astonishing number of aspects of the culture, from history to important older and modern genres, instruments, musical terminology, and the interface between tradition and change. Ellen Koskoff's (2001) account of the musical culture of the Lubavitcher Hasidim has the quality of comprehensiveness, looking at history and present, and devoting its most insightful chapters to the relationship of music to the past, the modern, gender, and social lineage.

Giving cultural insiders a voice has been an aspect of our methodological canon (more in theory than practice) since the 1960s, but the concepts of dialogic editing, as so labeled by Steven Feld (1987), and "collaborative ethnography," a newly coined term used by Luke Lassiter (1998), increase the significance of that voice, and the interface between insider and outsider, in the writing of ethnography.

Finally, ethnomusicologists have of course written about the concept of ethnography—trying to find ways of conceptualizing musical culture, organizing, providing an interface between insider and outsider, between fact and interpretation. One of the most comprehensive surveys of the issues and the literature is the essay by Anthony Seeger (1992a). Martin Stokes's introductory essay to a compendium (1994: 1–28) goes through a large number of the issues of concern to ethnography—performance and place, ethnicity, identity, nationalism, class, gender. Timothy Rice has long grappled with the need to provide an elegant statement of the fundamentals of ethnomusicology, stating (1987) in one sentence what ethnomusicologists are after, and (2003) charting new directions for ethnography from the description of a static norm to emphasis on what changes, given the revised concepts of "culture" and "society" required by recent history. Making ethnography less of a snapshot of a moment and more accountable for culture as constantly changing, Rice (174) looks to the future of the ethnographic enterprise in music: "Musical ethnographies that trace the movement of subjects in location, metaphorical understanding, and time, and the differing experiences such movements entail, take on a fundamentally dynamic character responsive to the new or newly understood complexities of the modern world."

18

Music Hath Charms:
Uses and Functions

Bend a Knotted Oak

Much of the literature on the study of music in culture involves the ways in which humans use music, which is therefore said to "carry out" certain functions in human society. It may be reasonable to believe that people everywhere have used music to do certain things, and at the same time that they thought that music, acting on its own, as it were, was capable of doing something to them. The early literature of ethnomusicology often dwells on the presumption that in prehistoric, folk, or indigenous cultures people used music principally to accomplish certain essential things for them, and that therefore this music is *functional*. Herzog (1950: 1034) cautiously said that "folk song is often said to be more functional in its use or application than cultivated poetry or music." This statement implies that the songs used to accompany turning points in a person's life and in the course of the year are more "functional" than those pieces used for performance in concerts, that a work song is more functional than Billy Joel's "Piano Man" or Handel's *Messiah*. The focus on this special characteristic of the music of folk and tribal societies is no doubt related to the earlier ethnomusicologist's felt need to justify the concern with simple, unsophisticated, and—in the academic musician's athletically judgmental view of music—inferior products.

But when Congreve said, "Music hath charms to soothe the savage breast, to soften rocks, or bend a knotted oak," he probably did not mean folk or indigenous music. If modern American academic tradition (depending on misspelling as a major creative force) often finds music soothing the savage beast instead, this recalls the various settings of the Orpheus myth and *The Magic Flute*, all hardly folk music. It depends how one defines use and functionality; and ethnomusicology, gradually discarding the distinction between "folk" and "art," has come to admit that the concept of function is applicable to all music in the analysis of the "complex whole."

It stands to reason. If most of the songs of the Blackfoot were used as parts of religious ceremonies, to accompany social dances, and to keep gamblers from revealing the location of a hidden object, religious services in eighteenth-century Leipzig or twentieth-century New York were and are hardly conceivable without music, social events such as dances and parties in modern America are inevitably musical events of a sort, a proper football game includes a marching band at half time, and a major league baseball game at least a hugely amplified electric organ swelling to glorify the Mudville team's home run. One may reply that this is true, but the complex cultures also have events such as concerts, whose purpose is to exhibit their "best" music. Yet, whether a Bach cantata or a Blackfoot Sun Dance song is religious or entertainment depends on the identity of the listener (at a powwow or a church service). By contrast, many American concertgoers conceive of concerts as social events or secular rituals, as their typical program structures, their obligatory forms of dress, their standard length, the ever-present intermission, printed programs, and so on all show us. We in academia often accord to art music an edifying, educational role, believing that important things of value can be learned from hearing Bach and Mozart. But it has also been said (R. Waterman 1956) that the function of music among the people of Yirkalla is essentially educational, and that they, like the North American Plains Indians, learned their culture gradually, accompanying each step with appropriate music. Thus, when we teach our children to go to concerts in order to learn important values in their own culture, we are doing essentially what the technologically simpler people of Yirkalla and the Plains also did with their music.

These are just a few examples to illustrate the usefulness of leaving human cultures undivided when it comes to looking at the functions of music. Ethnomusicologists agree that people everywhere use music to accomplish something. The old issue, whether music in certain types of cultures was used more for certain kinds of things, has been submerged by a concern for ways of looking at these uses. Ethnomusicologists have been concerned, rather, with the difference between what they called uses and functions, and the difference between the function of music in human society at large as opposed to individual societies, and beyond that, the specific function of individual segments of repertories, styles, genres, of change in function and context.

Response to Alan P. Merriam

The early literature of ethnomusicology deals with the concepts of use and function as if they were more or less the same. Later, in a very direct statement on the subject, Alan P. Merriam (1964: 209–28) definitively separated them: "When we speak of the uses of music, we are referring to the ways in which music is employed in human society, to the habitual practice or customary exercise of music either as a thing in itself or in conjunction with other activities" (210). But: "Music is *used* in certain situations and becomes a part of them, but it may or may not also have a deeper function" (210). Using the work of Siegfried Nadel and following widely accepted definitions suggested by Ralph Linton, Merriam took *function* to mean the "specific effectiveness of [music] whereby it fulfills the requirement of the situation, that is, answers a purpose objectively defined; this is the equation of function with purpose" (218). Merriam went on to list ten major and overall functions, as opposed to uses, of music (219): emotional expression, aesthetic enjoyment, entertainment, communication, symbolic representation, physical response, enforcing conformity to social norms, validation of social institutions and religious rituals, contribution to the continuity and stability of culture, and contribution to the integration of society.

A formidable list. "To soothe the savage breast" is perhaps hidden in it. Without being able to do better, I confess to a bit of uneasiness. The line between uses and functions is clear when we observe that a particular Native American song is used to accompany a Grass Dance, but it also has the function of contributing to the integration of society. But in the case of music for entertainment, use and function may instead be identical. Then, too, Merriam's list, intended to characterize music, is not specific to music but could apply to all of the arts, admittedly to different degrees, and possibly to other activities not normally classed as arts (although they might well be), such as religious ritual and speech.

But music, I would assert, is functionally different from the other arts. More than any, it is a product of human ingenuity alone. It is the most distant from nature, not normally speaking directly of or reproducing visually what the artist sees. It is likewise the most distant from the rest of culture. Unlike the other arts, it rarely depicts or deals directly with what humans do or think. Of the many domains of culture, music would perhaps seem to be one of the least necessary; yet we know of no culture that does not have it. Should one therefore not be able to articulate for it a unique function?

As a matter of fact, the distinguishing of function from use has not really been a major issue in ethnomusicological literature for some time. In the early stages of ethnomusicology it somehow seemed necessary to make a special point of saying that one's main purpose was to learn how music was used. The idea of identifying use/function was almost tantamount to the idea of studying music in its cultural context. At one point in the 1970s, ethnomusicologists divided themselves informally into "musicians" and "functionalists" or "contextualists," but except for matters of emphasis and approach this issue has long been settled, as we had all confessed, by the 1980s, to an interest in what the music was like, and what humans used it to do for them, and what it could accomplish for humans.

In contrast to Merriam, several authors who shared a broad acquaintance with a number of musical cultures converged in their belief that music has one principal function. Blacking (1973) continually stressed the belief that "there ought to be a relationship between patterns of human organization and the patterns of sound produced as a result of human interaction" (26). Lomax maintained that the principal discovery of his analysis of world music is "that a culture's favorite song style reflects and reinforces the kind of behavior essential to its main subsistence effort and to its central and controlling social institutions" (1968: 133). Christopher Small looks at it a bit more narrowly; music is a kind of weapon to defend the central expressive interests of a society. Thus, "a symphony concert is a celebration of the 'sacred history' of the Western middle classes, and an affirmation of their values as the abiding stuff of life" (Small 1987: 19). Those who have recently returned to contemplation of the origins of music as a source of insight (e.g., in Wallin, Merker, and Brown 2000) also focus on a single and thus fundamental function of music. Increasingly, in the history of ethnomusicology after around 1970, the issue of identity—or should I say "identity," it can mean so many things—takes on significance as the main function of music. To be sure, the interest in looking at a multiplicity of functions continued, and one reads of it also in literature on other performing arts, as wrote Anya Royce (1977: 83–84): "A multiplicity of functions tends to be the rule rather than the exception. Functions may be regarded as either overt or covert and either manifest or latent . . . any dance event, moreover, may have multiple functions at both levels." But, if pushed to the wall, we can perhaps still go no further than to say that "music hath charms," that it does the inexplicable, but that, as Merriam concludes, it "is clearly indispensable to the proper promulgation of the activities that constitute a society" (1964: 227).

The Coin and the Pyramid

For some time, ethnomusicology deemphasized its interest in functions and uses, at least stated overtly. It was sometimes there under the surface, where John Baily, for example (in Stokes 1994: 46–48), seemed obliged to tease functionalist viewpoints from publications concerned with identity, ethnicity, and musical change. More typically (after 1990), the relationship of music to the significant social and political trends and events of the postcolonial era pushed scholars to look at function again more seriously. Various models speaking to the heterogeneity of perspectives (see, e.g., Killick 2003; Rice 2003; Slobin 1992b) have been promulgated, but I take the liberty of suggesting that two models, proposed a quarter century ago, labeled "the coin" and "the pyramid" for convenience, juxtaposing the diversity of "insider" and "outsider" viewpoints and the contrast between functions and uses, may still be helpful for analysis of individual cultures or communities. Maybe unnecessarily, I remind the reader that all of this involves more the comparison of theoretical constructs than the establishment of verifiable fact. Borrowing from Burling's (1964) early insight into the need for the gingerly handling of theory, it often threatens to be more "hocus-pocus" than "God's truth."

The pyramid model has layers: a base, a tip, and something in between, moving gradually from uses to functions. The base is comprised of the overt uses of music, the activities that music accompanies, the many things that informants will tell you are associated with music, what they tell you music does, what they use music to do, or the things one sees music doing on the surface. In any one society, there are literally hundreds of these: entertainment, accompaniment of ritual, dance, concerts, military marching, and so on. In the middle there is increased abstraction of these uses. Here perhaps one might place Merriam's ten functions. Eventually, near the top, there is a statement of single, overriding, major function for any one society. One might here include statements such as McAllester's to the effect that in Navajo culture "many of the usual functions of music . . . are subordinated to an all-important function of supernatural control" (1954: 88), or Merriam's that among the Flathead Indians music functions "as a means for expressing the fact that they remain Flathead no matter what changes in their ways of life have occurred" (1967a: 158). At the top of the pyramid there is a single, overriding function of music for all humanity under which all others are subsumed. The top and the bottom are ideals. We may look for a way to articulate with extreme precision unique functions of music, but it is probably beyond us; and we will never get all uses of music onto one list.

But let's concentrate for the moment on the "coin" model, which importantly takes into account the differences between insider and outsider views, perhaps more aptly called the people's and the anthropologist's analyses, and subsumed under the proverbial "two sides of a coin." The situation is more complicated, and we have questioned the concepts of "insider" and "outsider" as well as the role of reflexivity, and still, I would maintain that the contrast between these two views continues to impinge on all ethnomusicological problems related to field research. Merriam (1964: 209–10) spoke to it, appearing to believe that an accounting of the uses of music strikes more closely to the culture's own expression of itself. "Music may be used in a given society in a certain way, and this may be expressed directly as a part of folk evaluation. The function, however, may be something quite different as assessed through analytical evaluations stemming from the folk evaluation." The extremes of these stances seem out of reach. Ethnomusicologists, claiming to be empirical scholars, always use the culture's own analysis or evaluation, at least to a degree. Nor can they eliminate their own cultural background completely.

Which side of the coin is up? One is tempted to associate the uses-functions dyad with the emic-etic distinction, but correlations end up being unclear. Merriam's view lends itself to extrapolation of uses as emic, functions as etic. But this contradicts some of the other implications of the emic-etic contrast. Etic is also the down-to-earth, the detailed description of specific events observed; emic is the generalization and structuring of the etic. Referring to the linguistic roots of these terms, in one sense, phonetics involves actual sounds made by people speaking, and phonemics structures them in abstract units that indicate functions used, identified, though not always easily stated by the speakers. On the other hand, it is phonemic distinctions that native speakers use to teach foreigners their language, create alphabets, keep linguistic categories separate, while phonetics is a highly complex characterization of sounds and their physical bases, and "native speakers" may not really know what to do with this kind of knowledge.

Emics and etics are related to the insider-outsider continuum, but the categories are not congruent, and the partial abandonment of emic-etic in anthropology has to do with this problem. In field research it is obvious that consultants are quite capable of making etic statements, that is, of describing their own culture "objectively" and comparing their description with the

culture's primary evaluations. Thus, if the theory (i.e., emics) of Persian classical music is that improvisors do not repeat themselves, Persian musicians
are nevertheless quite aware of the fact that repetition does occur. The emic
statement may be an expression of the ideal, and the real is presented by the
culture itself in subordinate, etic statements.

Despite the weaknesses of emic-etic analysis, it seems useful to present a
model along these lines, but in order to avoid confusion, it seems advisable to
speak simply of the culture's and the analyst's statements. If I may subject you,
dear reader, once more to a brief, very compressed comparative exercise intended to illustrate approaches rather than to present definitive data and interpretations, let me try the coin and the pyramid using my own cultural mi-
lieu: first the coin, applied to urban Western society, as viewed through the eyes
of the academic profession. These are some of the *kinds* of statements subsumed under each of the categories. Whether the model works, helps to give
insight, is a question left to the reader.

ANALYST'S STATEMENT OF USES   Music is associated with a plethora of
activities. Mostly it is used for listening, with the audience passive and the
degree to which it pays attention varying greatly. Rituals of all sorts are accompanied by music, which is also used as background sound for many types
of activity. Here we might present a list of all the activities that involve music,
from concert, church, parade, football game to obligatory background (in
the case of teenagers, foreground, at least in terms of volume) at parties, in
supermarkets, on elevators, for traveling in cars.

ANALYST'S STATEMENT OF FUNCTIONS   From the items on Merriam's list,
entertainment seems most prominent. Emotional expression and group or
subgroup integration are also factors.

CULTURE'S STATEMENT OF USES   Music must be available for listening
most of the time. It is something one must hear daily. Almost no activity can
properly be pursued without the presence of music. It is an indispensable
flavoring that makes other activities or inactivity tolerable.

CULTURE'S STATEMENT OF FUNCTIONS   Music does something to a person, something not done by anything else; nothing can be substituted for
it. As McAllester (1971: 380) suggests, and as Gilbert Rouget (1985) brilliantly
illustrates, music transforms experience, a major function of Western music.
We (modern members of Western society) do not consider music to have a

single main function except that, being music, it has powers in the realm of the abstract and emotional, though not in the concrete world, and we feel we cannot live without it. To my culture group, indeed, "music hath charms"—to soothe the savage breast but not to bend a knotted oak.

In contrast to the coin model, the pyramid avoids directly confronting the difference between analyst's and culture's interpretations. The analyst's interpretation, which in the coin model is justified as a device for comparative study, is replaced in the pyramid by the overarching view that music is an expression or reflection or direct result of a central cultural core. Uses and functions are presented not as contrasting halves of a dichotomy but, rather, as the opposite ends of a continuum that moves from the absolutely down-to-earth and factual to the most vitally interpretive and thus perhaps unprovable. Let me continue the exercise, using data from the city of Tehran.

We must take a large number of musical styles, types, and genres into account: the most traditional Iranian, including some folk music of rural origin as well as the classical music originating in the courts, as well as religious and ceremonial material, and popular music distributed mainly through mass media, using styles that mix traditional, Western, and other non-Iranian elements in various ways. This list is a combination of Iranian and Western taxonomies of the music, historical categories, and geographical venues, from a large and complex community. We ought to add to the complexity by including Western music also heard in Tehran, but for the purposes of this exercise, I deal only with categories accepted by Tehranis as Iranian music. The "present" is around 1970.

OVERT USES   Most music is used for listening and entertainment. There are relatively few concerts but many musical occasions in night clubs and music halls, whose patrons listen and watch but rarely, as a matter of fact, dance. Radio listening is common, more among adults and less among children than is the case in the United States. Records are readily available, and some listening takes place in lightly ritualized formats: parties, concerts, music halls each patronized by members of one occupation group. The records have a use beyond simple entertainment, contributing to solidarity of special groups and allegiance to a particular view of Iranian culture. Beyond this there is religious chanting, which is not regarded as belonging properly to the sphere of music. Music is used to accompany traditional gymnastic exercises, dance performances as well as social dancing, military activity, public ceremonial events such as parades of labor guilds, and as background for poetry readings. Needless to say, it is impossible to list all, but they correspond moderately well to those of Western urban culture and not well to those of the Flathead. In Herzog's terms, Iranian music would have to be regarded as not highly functional. Most activities can be carried out without music, and people do not seem to feel that music must be heard daily, frequently, constantly, as do many in the United States. That one could even consider the "outlawing of music" in 1979 is a case in point.

ABSTRACTED USES   If we apply Merriam's list of ten general functions, we find all of them relevant to Tehran but would have to emphasize particularly those of entertainment and symbolic representation (both by presence and absence of music), as well as contributions to religious ritual, continuity and stability of culture, and integration of society. But since many kinds of music are involved, diversity in religious observance, change as well as continuity of culture, and integration of a number of subcultures are the first-line functions of music. Different repertories within the culture can be interpreted as having specific functions. The religious music, chanting the Koran, calls to prayer, are in this case not ways of communicating with God but, rather, devices to remind humans of their religious duty. The music accompanying "lascivious" dancing in traditional night clubs has as its use the facilitation of dance. But beyond that, it functions as a force mediating between the human observer and the forbidden; it throws a cloak of formality over an otherwise unacceptable situation, a function of music noted as well for African cultures by Rhodes (1962) and for American folk culture by Greenway (1953) and others. The modernized and partially Westernized popular music had a function of symbolizing the process of Westernization; years later, when Westernization came under a special sort of fire, it was this kind of music that was first and foremost singled out for proscription.

Let me digress and point to a contrasting situation in South America. Anthony Seeger provides a parallel illustration of abstracted musical uses or overt functions among the Suya of Brazil (1979). Examining two genres of song very different in style and use, he concluded that the function of *akia* involves "the intention of the singer to be heard as an individual by certain female relatives," while the *ngere* functions as a way "of expressing the existence and unity of name-based ceremonial groups" (391). But the overt use of the music is ritualistic, and these functions do not emerge until uses are analyzed and interpreted. From a further analysis of this level of functionality there might emerge a single, more culture-specific function of music. Seeger gives more than a hint: Musical events actually create aspects of the social organization, in this case, dualism (392). If generalized, this would be a far cry from Tehran, where one can hardly claim that music has a dominant effect over other aspects of culture. Perhaps this has to do with the value of music, ambiguous in Tehran and high, Seeger maintains, among the Suya.

TOP OF THE PYRAMID   Time to show my colors. The fundamental function of music in human society, what music ultimately does, is twofold: to control humanity's relationship to the supernatural, mediating between human and other beings, and to support the integrity of individual social groups. It does this by expressing the relevant central values of culture in abstracted form. If we accept this, we find a kind of interdependence between the highest two layers of the pyramid model that does not exist among the other layers. In each culture music will function to express a particular set of values in a particular way.

As Alan Lomax famously argued (1968: 155–59), and as Blacking continued to suggest (1987: 133), music can abstract and distill the relatively unclear and obscure character of culture. Its ability to abstract values helps us in returning to 1970s Tehran, where we ask how the music of its society functions to mediate between humans and the supernatural, and to help integrate society. As in the vast majority of religious systems, music in Islam is a ceremonial device, a way of formalizing a religious statement. We must take into account that much of this "music" is not classed as music, which in its extreme (most "musical") form has low esteem in the society. Much has been published about the Muslim attitude toward music, so let me add yet another hypothesis. Islam is characterized by its insistence that humans may pray, speak directly, to God, without mediation. Understanding the importance of music as a mediator in other religious systems, particularly those that have priestly intercessors, adherents of Islam give it a role of low importance because, for them, this kind of mediation is not needed. It's there, but technically it's not recognized as music.

The role of music in integrating as complex a society as that of Tehran is significant in a number of ways. On the one hand, its classical system served in the 1960s as a unifying device for the nation, bringing together its diverse elements and setting it off from its Arabic and Turkish neighbors. Musicians and the cultural politics establishment emphasized a classical system that was intended to be perfect, to which nothing need or may be added, a symbol of the perfect society that was being claimed by the elite of Tehran. At the same time various rural traditions, symbolizing the nation's diversity, were brought together in the mass media, as was a repertory of Westernized vernacular music to suggest the desired ties to the outside, and to the modern world. A number of interrelated but separate musical systems flourished, some of them distinguished by their degree of Westernization. Many social groups identified themselves with a particular music. But for the nation at large, I suggest that the classical tradition in particular expresses some specific shared social values.

The main thing about the "pyramid" is that the insider-outsider dyad is played down. But still, the top of the pyramid turns out again to contrast observer and observed. I think I saw, in the 1970s, what it was that music did for Tehran society, but musicians, as well as others in Iran, did not find much to which they could respond in my direct questioning. They were, for instance, more concerned with liking or disliking music and its various subtypes. They sometimes exhibited a certain guilty tendency to defend their liking of music, and as individuals or as members of particular groups of the population—Sufis, the Westernized elite, members of minorities such as Armenians and Jews—they used their identification with music as a way of underscoring individualism or specialness. When asked what it is that music does, Iranians would surely not have said directly that it reflected their social and cultural values, although educated consultants declared that the classical music was particularly Persian, tied to the culture and the soil, while the popular music was there partly to show how Iranians could and did interact with other cultures, taking from them what they needed to become modern. To Iranians, the statement "Music hath charms" would mean something quite different from what it means to Americans or Europeans. But in the end, even they might agree with some of its implications.

Various Identities

"Things are very different now." That's what a Blackfoot friend said when I visited Browning in 2002 after having stayed away for years. But who in the world wouldn't have been tempted to say this, after the fall of the Berlin wall, the political realignments of the world in the 1990s, the growing contrast between the living standards of rich and poor nations, the dominance of global corporations, the revolutions in gender relations and sexual orientation, the growth of international religious fundamentalism, and the developments in the world of communication, the Internet, and digitalization. In the world of music, geography still matters, but we are getting used to a situation in which what you hear or see, and with whom you communicate, has little to do with where you are. The notion—not on very solid ground even in 1950—

that the world contains a lot of isolated villages and indigenous societies with a participatory musical life of agricultural and ritual music is now totally unrealistic. Most people in the world experience music largely in broadcast or recorded form. Most people also have access to a vast variety of musical sounds and styles, which, since so many people from different continents who came out of different musical milieus share in experiencing them, begin increasingly to resemble each other. Musicians of all kinds around the world are more into providing entertainment, performing on stage and in clubs and recording studios, and they speak increasingly to a world audience. To music mainly directed to the community and to the deities has been added the concept of music as expressing and communicating messages to—well, maybe all humans.

Ethnomusicologists around 1950 weren't very good at developing a realistic perspective. We were visiting Native American reservations, wishing that the tribal and cultural integrity of their peoples were still valid, looking nostalgically to an imagined past, and describing music and culture in those terms. Fifty years later, ethnomusicologists have become more up to date, promptly paying attention to many of the musical developments of the recent past and the present. As the world—and musical culture—have changed, so has the typical ethnomusicological literature. The books of the nineties and later increasingly emphasize various kinds of relationships among groups of people—gender issues, power relations, interaction of socio-economic classes, music in political movements, all perhaps related to the matter of identity— national, ethnic, class, gender, personal. So we ask whether the primary function of music has changed, and whether humankind has turned a totally unprecedented corner. Maybe; I won't deny that the good old days are gone forever, or argue that their return is just around the (next) corner; or that the old interpretations of, say, Merriam still work if we just adapt them, and instead admit that maybe they were way off the mark in the first place. But I suggest that a very significant group of functions of music—whether they have always done so or not—revolve around the concept of identity. At least that is what much of our recent literature suggests, and how it looks to me in Blackfoot country.

National identity was a matter of concern to European musicians and scholars in the nineteenth and early twentieth centuries, when small nations worked hard to free themselves from political empires and the German-Austrian-dominated "musical empire." In a way, and maybe significantly, the rise of ethnomusicology went hand in hand with that move. But the purpose in politics was to establish culturally and linguistically homogeneous nation-states, in the end with compromised results, such as Czechoslovakia, Yugoslavia, Poland. In the mid–nineteenth century, the development of national opera in Prague, the inclusion of nationalistic tropes from musical motifs to folk dance genres, as well as the beginning of large-scale collecting of folk songs in the Czech lands had been major factors in the national culture wars of that people. In the second, postcolonial wave of nationalism, following the political liberations in the wake of World War II from the late 1940s to the 1970s, one of the issues was the integration of culturally and linguistically independent ethnic groups that had been artificially shoehorned into colonial borders mainly in the mid- and late-nineteenth century by European colonial powers. In the large literature on political and cultural nationalism, the works of Benedict Anderson (1991) and Chatterjee (1986) have had a particular influence on ethnomusicological thought.

The creation of explicitly "national" musics was a factor in the political nationalism in nineteenth-century Europe, but it was mainly art music that functioned as a kind of weapon in the international culture wars. Over 100 years later, the expression of nationalism could be considered an important function of music in the postcolonial era, but we are now talking mainly about music in the realm of popular culture. The issues are helpfully discussed and carefully explained in the introductory essay in Stokes (1994: 1–27), while examples of highly contrastive national situations are provided for Zimbabwe by Turino (2000) and for Finland by Ramnarine (2003). The usefulness of the concept of ethnicity—discussed, with its difficulties analyzed, by Stokes (6)—seems to have the function of allowing a group of people to erect boundaries of language, custom, art; but an ethnic group is harder to define and identify than a nation. The function of music as expression of ethnicity is, however, an older subject in ethnomusicology than is nationalism, as it began to play a role when the significance of culturally heterogeneous societies such as modern cities began to arouse interest. The function of music as expression of class—criteria might be reading music and understanding certain technicalities for upper classes, knowledge of the political significance of popular genres by economically lower classes—has been discussed by ethnomusicologists, with considerable attention to the work of Pierre Bourdieu (e.g., 1984), for example by Chopyak (1987) and Capwell (1991).

If music expresses personal or group identity, it plays a role in negotiating relationships between unequals, as a way for a dominant group to reinforce its hegemony, or for a subordinate population to fight back at some level. The domination of Western culture everywhere is expressed, for example, by the international adoption of some version of functional harmony.

The counterpart is the tendency for colonized peoples such as Native Americans to use music and dance as a principal way of continuing to assert their identity. The role of national anthems in identity, which drew upon national and ethnic concepts with the purpose of social integration, has been examined after 1985 by several ethnomusicologists—for example, Capwell (1986), Guy (2002), and Daughtry (2003)—in the context of establishing the national identity of a society.

The idea that one makes or listens to music to show who one is, in national, ethnic, class, personal contexts, has been around for a long time, but identity hasn't been recognized until the last two decades as a major function of music. Is musical life also all that different, as Blackfoot people told me? It certainly is easy to interpret Blackfoot musical activities as major expressions of various kinds of identity. The major midsummer powwow, North American Indian Days, is a kind of event that would not have been conceivable in earlier Blackfoot history and even in the first part of the twentieth century. It is polysemic, overtly and subtly expressing (1) Blackfoot national identity— the M.C. says so, and occasionally speaks Blackfoot; (2) Native American ethnic identity (or is Blackfoot the ethnic group, and are Native Americans the nation?)—again, the M.C. tells us, the Drums, the singing groups, come from many reservations in the United States and Canada, and the dancers perform a widely intertribal repertory; (3) U.S. national identity—much is made of the presentation of the colors by military veterans; (4) age identity—there are dance contests for different age groups; (5) personal identity—there's the incredible variety of costumes. There is plenty of "white" music going on in town at the time of the powwow; country music and rock at dances for older and younger folks, respectively; U.S. patriotic song recordings at an "Indian" rodeo. But at North American Indian Days, while all kinds of appurtenances from "white" culture are in evidence, from flags to tape recorders, the music is totally "Indian." Even for the presentation of the military guard. The association of music with identity is very strong here.

Musical life otherwise is also dominated by Blackfoot traditions. Shops patronized by Native Americans have tapes and CDs by Blackfoot and other singers. Teenagers whiz by in their pickup trucks, Native American songs wafting out the window from their tape decks. Sometimes, though, it is country music, rock, or rap. There are lots of levels of identity, but it's possible to interpret all of these as ways for individuals to show that they are Blackfoot—Blackfoot as members of wider North American society, of Native American society at large, of the Blackfoot nation; and to show that there is a Blackfoot way to be a member of your age group and to have your own identity. Conversations support these interpretations—people in 2002 talked more about their "Blackfootness" than their other group associations. Musical life is indeed very different in 2002 from 1966, but have the functions of music changed all that much? In 1967, speaking of the Flathead just across the continental divide from Blackfoot territory, Alan Merriam (1967a: 158) wrote: "In music and dance, especially on occasions of [the large intertribal powwow] kind, but in individual expression as well, the people reaffirm that they are, indeed, Flathead."

19

In the Beginning: On the Origins of Music

"Mythology Is Wrong"

Thus the learned Curt Sachs startled his reader in the first sentence of a music history survey (1948: 1): "Music is not the merciful gift of benevolent gods or heroes. . . . And wrong, so far, are all the many theories presented on a more or less scientific basis. . . . Were they true, some of the most primitive survivors of early mankind would have preserved a warbling style of love songs, or signal-like melodies, or rhythmical teamwork with rhythmical work songs. Which they hardly have." In a brief paragraph, the venerable Sachs dismissed a large body of mainly speculative literature and, by implication, research by biologists and psychologists, and asserted that ethnomusicologists, because of their knowledge of the world's extant musics, were in the best position to establish how music came about and what it was first like.

Sachs certainly wasn't the first. Two of the earliest books dealing generally with the musics of indigenous societies had the word *beginnings* in their titles, and even they dealt mainly not with the origin of music itself but, rather, with what the authors presumed to be the earliest music. The actual question of origins was more typically the subject of other kinds of authors, earlier, a group less acquainted with the musics of the world. Towering figures in their fields, they included the pioneering social scientist Herbert Spencer, the composer Richard Wagner, and the economist Carl Buecher. But Sachs did not take their theories seriously, applauding instead those who would study the world's least complex contemporary musical cultures in order to ascertain the earliest stage of music history.

It is somehow anomalous to find that ethnomusicologists often present themselves as students of the present and yet are almost automatically the recipients of questions about the most distant past. They develop special techniques for observing change as it occurs, for describing musical systems and cultures that they can experience directly, and they have sometimes identified themselves as the synchronic counterparts to the diachronic historians. But if American cocktail parties begin with questions about the music of contemporary Native Americans or Japanese, they typically turn to ultimate origins. In the view of the general public, ethnomusicologists are also the prehistorians of music.

The literature on the so-called origins of music tends often to confuse issues that are actually separable, failing to distinguish the point of origin and what follows immediately, or music from nonmusic. The question of defining music is particularly, again, at issue. Hockett (as cited in Anttila 1972: 26) gives a group of characteristics of animal communication, pointing out that only certain ones of them are also specific to human speech. It has long been obvious that animals (including anthropoids) communicate, sometimes with the use of sound, but human sound communication can be separated from the rest and defined in a way that applies to all human languages. Universal features emanating from this definition are used in the literature on the origin of language (Anttila 1972: 26–28; P. Lieberman 1975, 1994; Stam 1976). Language, it is accepted, has an underlying "deep structure" that is related to the genetically established ability of all humans to learn it.

Defining the universals of music is harder than establishing those of language. But musicologists, if they can agree on what constitutes music, if not articulate a definition, may be a bit better off than linguists when it comes to finding a bridge between origins and the present. All languages are more or less equally complex, and also about equally removed from the origins of language, a subject linguists tend now to approach by reference to psychology, primatology, paleontology, physiology—all involving study of the brain—rather than by attempting historical reconstruction. All musics, as well, have a certain minimum degree of complexity, but the differences in complexity among recent and contemporary musics is much greater, and contemplating them may help us in speculating about the distant past.

In doing so, we should distinguish three questions: (1) Why did music originate? (2) What was the actual process by which music was first put into existence? (3) What was the nature of the original or first or earliest musical products? The issue was similarly divided by Hornbostel (1973; published some fifty years after it was written), who distinguished between "birth" and "early childhood" of music. The consideration of origins shows the ethno-musicologists at their most speculative, and many of them, feeling hopeless, have lost interest in the question for precisely that reason and have been inclined to throw in the towel, turning their energy to more easily soluble problems. I would argue that it continues to be a significant question simply because it is there. It's something people want to know, or at least to hear educated guesses about.

According to Barnett, in his anthropological classic on innovation, "when innovation takes place, there is an intimate linkage or fusion of two or more elements that have not been previously joined in just this fashion" (1953: 181). Humans, he implies, cannot create culture from scratch; they use building blocks already present, combining and recombining them. If we imagine a point at which music was something new, we would do well to view it as a unique fusion of elements that were already present in human culture. Most origin theories of music argue along these lines. Music, the classic writers on the subject assert, grew out of materials already present: animal cries, speech, rhythmic activity. By the same token, if we are to imagine that music came into existence by becoming a system of organized sound, it must have done so with the use of sounds already known and recognized by humans.

Following along these lines, we may imagine that there was probably at some point in human or prehuman history a kind of communication that embodied certain characteristics of what we now regard as music. But in the view of the society that used it, it was not "music," and probably it would not normally be regarded as such today. Perhaps it did not sound like what we think is music, not sharing the traits that the musics of today's vastly divergent world nevertheless share. Possibly it was also not distinguished from something else that was or became language. At any rate, somehow music was brought into existence.

Actually, many of the world's societies today have some ideas on how or why music came about, ideas significant in their mythology and cosmology. The genesis myth of the Blackfoot gives a "why," though not a "how": music was given to humans by the culture hero in order to help them with their problems (see, e.g., Grinnell 1920). Or again, according to one South American Indian people, music was given by supernatural beings in order to establish an orderly society (Smith 1971). Mythology (as Sachs said), even that of Indians, may be wrong, and the study of culture history via archeology doesn't go back far enough to tell us why music may have been invented. Although biologists concerned with the evolution of the brain and animal communications specialists have important contributions to make, the main thing to be contributed by ethnomusicologists is the study of musical universals, indicating whether there is anything that all humans do with their music, something so ubiquitous among the far-flung peoples that it makes sense for us to believe that they have always done so. The literature of ethnomusicology provides several statements of this sort.

There are theories relating the origins of music to vocal communication, deriving it from various special forms of speech. Among the more generally credible hypotheses is that of Carl Stumpf, to the effect that humans somehow developed music in order to increase the efficiency of vocal communication over long distances. Stumpf recognized the tendency for sustained pitches to carry farther than the ordinary speaking voice (1911; see Nadel 1930: 537), and perhaps indeed the need on the part of humans to call to each other over long distances led to the occasional use of a kind of vocal sound that has sustained pitch in common with music. Sustained pitches, held long enough so that they can be reproduced rather precisely by the hearer and even give rise to performances in unison, are a major characteristic of practically all known musics. Stumpf's guess tells us why humans may have developed a kind of communication that may sound like music, but he didn't show how it came to be music. To provide a credible bridge, something about the function of music as it now exists would have to be included. Following Stumpf, we would have to believe that vocal long-distance communication led to such paramusical phenomena as drum and horn signaling of tone languages, a practice widespread in Africa and elsewhere but nowhere claimed to be primordial, or to precede music. The fact that vocal music is so universally associated with words, and that everywhere humans sing what they also might speak, suggests that maybe speech and song were at one time even more closely related than today.

Stumpf's hypothesis is probably more attractive than the one suggested by Carl Buecher (1902; see esp. p. 364): that humans discovered the efficiency of rhythmic labor and developed music in order to facilitate it. As it happens, rhythmic work by groups to the sound of work songs or percussive accompaniment is actually not geographically widespread. But the close association of dance with music everywhere makes the idea of rhythm and physical movement as generative forces of music tentatively credible.

Confining ourselves to the "why" and leaving out entirely the "how," we are drawn to a suggestion of Nadel. Noting the close association in all cultures between music and religion, as well as the tendency to render the most serious and formal aspects of rituals musically, he hypothesized the beginnings of music as a result of a need for establishing a particular way of communicating with the supernatural, a way of sharing certain major characteristics of speech—the ordinary human communication—that is nonetheless readily distinct from it (1930: 538–44). How it was that someone hit upon vocal music as a way to satisfy this need is a question we can hardly touch. Presumably something from which music could be built must have already been available—conceivably the mating calls thought by Darwin to be the first music, the use of calls for long-distance communication, the recognition that heightened or emotional speech sounded different from ordinary talk. This speculation leads to the belief that the ability to learn singing may not have been far removed. The specific and reasonably sharp distinction between speaking and singing must at some point have occurred, and, following Nadel's suggestion, it may have been made in order to distinguish human and supernatural ways of communicating.

Of course we'll never know. But it is intriguing to note the many instances in mythology that ascribe the origin of music to the need for communicating with or within the supernatural. Leanne Hinton reported (1967–68) for Havasupai mythology that before there were humans, the supernatural beings communicated by singing. For the Blackfoot, a main supernatural presence is singing on the part of the nonhuman guardian spirits who appear in visions. In myths of various cultures (see Laade 1975 for examples) music is the language of the supernatural, but the spirits give music to humans as a way of approaching the unearthly. Such myths serve to explain the world of the society that tells them, but they may recapitulate symbolically what humans actually did and why they invented music. Mythology might not be all wrong.

To Frighten a Rival or Terrorize the Enemy Hordes?

After a period (ca. 1960–95) in which very few ethnomusicologists took an interest in trying to uncover the origins of music, the subject began to regain some attention at the very end of the twentieth century. The motivation comes from three directions; but in my chronology—what led to music; the moment of origination; earliest music—the recent literature speaks most to the first, the need for music.

One source of attention is the increased interest among biologists and psychologists in studying communication systems of other species. It is a subject of great fascination, but I have to confess to a bit of hesitation. The animals of greatest attraction to these scientists are songbirds, humpbacked

whales, and gibbon monkeys. And the sound of all of these species can easily be related to, compared to human music. But just because they sound to
us like music doesn't mean, in any way, that they function as music does in
human societies. Wouldn't we be equally justified in comparing these animals' sounds to human language? If that's how they communicate with each
other, isn't that more like what humans do when they speak? Even so, some
of the aforementioned species distinguish two kinds of sound communication, and these could conceivably be the analogues of language and music.
The scientists who examine animal communication usually don't try to
claim that what they've got is some kind of evolutionary predecessor of
human music. But conceivably the functions of the special, exceptional kinds
of sounds made in animal societies—if scientists can decipher them—could
suggest to us something about the original function of human music.

A second motivation comes from studies of music that derive from psychology and linguistics, involve studies of the brain and its evolution, and go
into the deep structure of music, somewhat as Chomskian linguistics proposes a commonality of language that is tied to the biological characteristics
of the brain. Just as the capacity for language and speech is "hard-wired" into
the human physiology, so music, too, is a universally human and thus biological characteristic. According to this way of thinking, music has always
been a part of humanity.

That's an idea musicians and music-lovers can accept—the notion that
music is fundamental to being human. Unfortunately, however, the third motivation I want to mention is something they may not find as easy to take. Earlier on, music was thought to come about because of a need for humans to
do something together in a peaceful fashion—call to a mate, speak with the
gods, communicate over long distances, work together effectively. Now, having learned a lot from students of animal communication, some have come
to think that music was a function of human individual and group compet-
itiveness. Gibbon monkeys and birds, and, who knows, maybe even whales,
seem to make their "music" in order to attract mates and protect territory.
Like them, early humans might also attract mates by showing—through
sounds with complex structure that require muscular effort, inventiveness,
memory, and stamina—that they have more energy, flexibility, imagination,
innovativeness, to be able to feed and protect the young, and to pass on the
DNA needed to compete successfully for survival. It was, the biologist Geoffrey Miller has argued (Miller 2000a: 349–56; see also Miller 2000b), first of
all an adaptive mechanism showing fitness to mate, maybe frightening a rival.
And then, if groups such as flocks, herds, clans, and bands can symbolically

show power by musicking (or premusicking) together—shout, sing, yodel, growl, beat drums and rattles—to scare neighboring bands or enemy hordes, that would be a plausible beginning of music. But rather than associating music with peacemaking, we have here the source of music associated with war and conflict.

I have to say that this idea of musical origins makes sense to me. Music is always something that stirs you, it's always there when competition and conflict are ritualized. In 1999 at a unique conference on the origins of music sponsored by the Swedish Institute for Biomusicology (for the papers see Wallin, Merker, and Brown 2000) the hypotheses of animal communication and of the evolution of the brain as the keys to answering our question were strongly put forward. The few ethnomusicologists who attended kept saying, "Wait a minute, we don't even have an interculturally accepted conceptualization of music," but the scientists who associated themselves with the newly established field of biomusicology were confident of being on safe ground.

But contrary to the "competition" theory, it's also possible that music originated in several different ways. After all, in modern human societies, the things that we in the Anglophone world call "music" are often divided into separate classes, and it's certainly conceivable that in early human society, musics to show fitness to mate, or to scare off unfriendly neighbors, or to speak with the supernatural, or to unify and integrate a society—the ancestors of Schumann's *Träumerei*, the "Horst Wessel" song, Gregorian chant, and folk singing at a teach-in—all came from different sources. In 2000 we may be farther along in reconstructing the reasons for the "invention" of music than in 1980.

The Moment of Invention

These may be some reasonably credible suggestions of why music came into existence. But if we can suggest reasons for the invention of music and its conceptualization as something distinctive, we certainly have hardly any idea as to the process by which it was created. We have the same problem dealing with invention at large: We are at a loss to describe process. Confronted with the creation of something new, a technology, a work of art, we can often see why it came about, see needs and contexts that made it possible or necessary. We can also identify its early stages, describe a primitive steam engine, the sketches of a painting, or the notebooks of Beethoven. But how one moves from conditions that make creation possible to the stage at which the product exists, albeit in preliminary, primitive form, is perhaps the most difficult thing on which to put one's finger.

We can use the traditional method of looking at change through a series of successive, static frames. If we don't know how music changes, we can perhaps describe the way stations of change. A simple, brief example: We can ascertain that at one moment a folk song exists in form A; in the next frame an interval of the scale has been filled in at the beginning of the song, resulting in form B; next the cadence of the song also adds a new filler tone for form C. At that point, change has taken place, and we see something about its working. Now let's imagine such frames in the prehistory of music, referring to an origin theory suggesting that humans at one time had a form of communication that shared elements of language and music. Sounds were made, but the distinctive features of vowels and consonants, now regarded as a hallmark of language, were not used. Pitch, length, and stress were present, but the technique of sustaining pitch, now universally essential to the concept of music, appeared only coincidentally. We can postulate a point at which one group of sounds appeared in two variants, another point at which two contrastive vowels were heard, remembered, and repeated, and another at which two contrastive pitches were similarly held, imagining that this kind of event was in fact (no doubt repeated and varied many, many times) the point of origin of music. But I dare go no further than to make this speculative suggestion.

Most of the literature concerned with the origins problem comes from relatively early times in the history of ethnomusicology. But in the 1970s the anthropological study of universals, some of it concerned with the origins of language (see, e.g., P. Lieberman 1975; Stam 1976), as well as research in the psychology of music and other forms of communication on an intercultural basis (e.g., Osgood, May, and Miron 1975), brought it back. Blacking (1973: 55, 58) spoke to the issue, wishing to avoid what he called evolutionist approaches, which reconstruct historical sequences: "The origins of music that concern me are those which are to be found in the psychology and in the cultural and social environment of its creators, in the assembly of processes that generate the pattern of sound" (58). Blacking proposed one of two processes. Each separate act of musical creation is a kind of origination, and one can find out things of general validity about the origin of music as expressed in each such act, extrapolating from these findings some general principles that help to illuminate the earlier, ultimate origins. And also, human behavior is sufficiently unified and historically stable that psychological insights themselves can tell us about early humanity.

In either case Blacking seemed to suggest substituting one kind of speculation for another (1973: 56). What justly seems to bother him most about the older theories of the origin of music is statements made in a vacuum about the reactions of early humans to their environment, reactions that are presumed to have led to the development of music. He also decries the tendency to try to reconstruct stages in a "world history of music" (55). Whether we agree with Blacking or try despite all problems to gain insight from extrapolation, it has to remain clear that what we are doing is indeed just speculating. It is supremely unwise to transform these speculations, willy-nilly, into established fact.

There is no doubt, as Blacking says, that "each style has its own history, and its present state represents only one stage in its own development" (1973: 56). But it is hard to believe that music was invented, if you will, many, many times, each "style" going back in an unbroken line to an act of invention, in a vast number of separate processes. It seems to me to make more sense to believe that music—definitional caveats aside—was invented, originated, created once or a few times, and that all present musical styles ultimately, each through its own separate stages, derived from one of these points of origin. Parenthetically, the older origin theories are not completely unilineal. Although he does not go as far as Blacking, or claim to provide an origin theory per se, Sachs proposes two ways that music has come about, from speech and from emotion, calling the resulting styles logogenic and pathogenic (1943: 41) and later referring to tumbling strains and one-step melodies as two strands of the oldest music (1962: 49–59). Sachs's suggestion may be predecessor to the argument that music originated in two distinct ways: (1) the "fitness to mate" adaptation suggested by Geoffrey Miller (2000a, 2000b)—the ancestor of virtuosity, of the "presentational" (as described by Turino 2000: 46–58); and (2) the participatory function for integrating and uniting a community for confronting outside forces, including the supernatural, and human enemies.

There need be no conflict. Once invented, music must have quickly or gradually become differentiated, each group of people developing it in order to satisfy their social, psychological, and aesthetic needs, in accordance with their technology, and as a result of contact with other human groups. Each music has its own history, and in the sense that all go back to, and are in time equally removed from, the point of music's origin, all have a history equally long. They took different courses, some changing more quickly than others. Blacking is, of course, right; we cannot simply class musics in accordance with certain stages through which all must pass. Yet history is always somewhat speculative; one can establish facts, but assessment of their relationships and their significance is always in part a matter of interpretation. The study of the origins of music is a legitimate part of ethnomusicological inquiry.

Real Old-Time Music

But what was the oldest music like? The issue is the documentation of age. If all music had been written down, then the oldest source would obviously be the oldest piece. In the context of increased interest in the origins of music, it's interesting to see the development of greater interest in archeological study of musical cultures, and of a subfield known as archeo-musicology (see, e.g., Hickmann and Hughes 1988). To a large degree this field is concerned with instruments, whose role in these speculations about origins is ambiguous. I don't think anyone doubts that something like singing preceded instrumental music, but who knows how early humans classified these various sounds? There certainly are instruments older than songs, the oldest, so far, being—arguably—a segment of a Neanderthal bone flute around 40,000 years old discovered in the mid-1990s in Slovenia (see Kunej 1997). Even granted that it is a flute, and that the three finger holes indicate intervals compatible with the diatonic scale, we get no sense of the kind of music that it might have produced.

Recent research has uncovered what seems to be the oldest extant musical notation, a Babylonian (more specifically, Hurrian) clay tablet from around 1400 B.C. (see, e.g., Stauder 1967; Wulstan 1971) that gives in cuneiform writing the notation and the text of a love song, as well as several lines indicating how the music is to be read. An attempt to realize a modern notational transcription into sound, made by Richard Crocker in 1975 and broadcast over national television, indicated that it was a rather extended, complex song. While this may actually be the oldest known piece, it is almost surely not the oldest kind of music extant. Oral tradition, with all of its vagaries, has probably preserved older styles, though perhaps not older songs. Ethnomusicologists also deny that the Hurrian song represents the oldest music on the basis of the assumption that the earliest music must have been simple, and with the belief that some of those things that are ubiquitous in the world's music today were present as characteristics of the oldest music. While there is much criticism of such hypotheses as immutable laws, there is considerable agreement, if not on what the first music was like, then upon which extant music is closest to that archaic stage. A number of scholars (e.g., Sachs 1943,

1962; Stumpf 1911; Wiora 1956, 1965) have concerned themselves in various ways with identifying the world's earliest music, and collectively they agree that there is an extractable oldest stratum present in the music of the twentieth century.

This stratum, thought to precede even the ubiquitous and presumably archaic pentatonic system (see Tran Van Khe 1977), has the following characteristics. (1) It is a style of music that comprises most of the repertory of certain technologically simple and relatively isolated tribal societies, but it is also found as a minority repertory in the music of many, if not most, other societies. (2) Where it comprises a minority of a repertory, it is characteristically associated with particular social contexts, including the songs of children, of games (including those of adults), of old and often abandoned rituals still present in vestige; it may also include songs told in stories. (3) The song forms of this music are short, usually consisting of one or two phrases that are repeated many times with or without variation. (4) Its scales are comprised of two to four tones, usually separated by major seconds and minor thirds. (5) It is prevailingly vocal.

The indigenous cultures whose repertories are largely or entirely in this simplest style include, for example, the Vedda of Sri Lanka, whose music was described by the psychologist Wertheimer (1909–10), peoples of Micronesia (Herzog 1936c), and certain North and South American Indian peoples, including the Yahi, the people of Ishi. But let's be clear: The "simplicity" resides in certain parameters of music; but in many respects these musical cultures are quite complex. As already mentioned, many other cultures also have *some* songs in this style, and it is further to be noted that some of the characteristics of these simplest musics are among the features of music acquired earliest in children. One might expect the latter fact to be corroborative evidence for a prehistory of world music, but musical development in infancy is scarcely understood, and the fact that there are data only for children in Western culture weakens this line of argument.

Speculative reconstruction gives the following, perhaps credible, picture. A once universal, simple musical style was expanded in most of the world's societies—three-tone scales extended or filled in, brief songs replaced by others with four or more musical lines, repetition replaced by systematic variation. In most societies some of the archaic songs continued to be sung, and new songs in their mold were composed, but they were pushed into a remote corner of the repertory for noncentral uses. There is a parallel phenomenon among instruments. The world's simplest—for example, rattles, the bullroarer, flutes without finger holes—were central in the ritual life of certain indigenous societies; in some, where the instrumentarium grew and developed, these simple instruments remained in existence but were relegated to less significant areas of life, becoming toys, or accompanied rituals whose function came to be merely antiquarian.

It seems a reasonable hypothesis. But aside from the sparsity of concrete evidence, it can be criticized on a number of bases. For example, those societies whose music is entirely in this archaic style, so far as scales and forms are concerned, seem otherwise to have little in common musically. The tritonic songs of Polynesia, with their sharply marked rhythms repeating the central tone, are rhythmically very different from the more evenly sung ritual songs of the Vedda. Singing styles may differ greatly. Only scalar content, general structure, and vocal monophony are common features. And so, more than describing the earliest human music, the hypothesis may tell us something important about ethnomusicology. A field that grew out of nineteenth-century Western classical music practices, it started out sophisticated in melodic and formal considerations, and relatively naive in theoretical thought about rhythm. While musicologists who engage in studies of comparative complexity at least come close to agreeing that the number of tones in a scale and the number of units in a musical form have something to do with relative simplicity and complexity of scales and structures, they have no hypothesis for a similar calibration of the rhythmic component of music. They don't know whether a strong, repetitive metric structure is to be regarded as close to an early stage of evolution or as the crowning achievement of a long development, whether they should count note values and regard the apparent lack of organization of a structure that has many sixteenths, eighths, fourths, dots, and fermatas to be simple or, instead, accord the label of simplicity to an endless repetition of quarter notes. Consideration of singing style would yield similar dilemmas.

While we're engaged in these speculations, we should consider one more. If we accept the possibility that those indigenous societies—of the Vedda, the Yahi, some Micronesian islanders—who still in recent times participated exclusively in the "simplest styles" have somehow maintained a musical sound that is close to the earliest music of humans, we ought also to guess at reasons for this curious state of affairs. These "indigenous" cultures are not greatly different from others; they are not "primitive" except in the technical sense of nonliteracy, something they have shared with many other peoples who have much more complex music. Their languages, social organizations, and religious systems are structurally as complex as the world's average. Can it really be that they got stuck in an early stage of musical development and were unable to go beyond it? Hard to accept; also hard to dismiss outright. Level of musical ability, musical "talent"—the notion that these peoples were "unmusical"—can't be seriously considered.

One possible explanation is a society's decision, for reasons unknown, to refrain from making changes in music, an extreme kind of musical conservatism. This is difficult to believe in the face of greater change in other domains of culture over long or short periods of time. One would expect the forces that impel a culture to change its political, religious, and social system also to affect its music. Yet, because of the close association of music with religion and its tendency to be used as an emblem of social and cultural identity and integrity, we ought to admit at least the possibility that some peoples singled out music for this special kind of conservative treatment.

The origin of music is so obscure that many ethnomusicologists have read it out of the purview of their field. But, psychology and biology aside, the most reliable guide to the origins of human music is still the plethora of contemporary and recent and older musics known to us, what they have in common and how they diverge. In my opinion, the issue is too important to be left exclusively to others.

20

The Continuity of Change:
On People Changing Their Music

Perspectives on History and Change

In the mid–twentieth century, believing that one could easily separate the two concepts, many authors widely used the expression "continuity and change . . ." in titles of books and articles. By the end of the twentieth century, it had become clear that it is change that is really continuous. A cliché about musical scholarship once divided historical musicologists, for whom music changes, from ethnomusicologists, whose emphasis is on what remains constant. The historians, it was thought, compare musical cultures at various points in their history, trace origins and antecedents and temporal relationships among repertories, pieces, composers, schools of musicians. Ethnomusicologists, seeing music as something that does not change, or in which change is an incidental, disturbing, exceptional, polluting factor, make synchronic comparisons. All this despite the widespread belief in ethnomusicology as a field that holds on to disappearing traditions and may in the end tell us the origins of music. But nothing is really further from a true characterization of ethnomusicology. Well, almost nothing. There is the occasional scholar who works on a musical or socio-cultural problem analytically with no thought to how things got the way they are. There have even been those who believed in the almost absolute stability of the musical cultures of non-Western societies, stability only occasionally disturbed by devastating and sweeping changes brought about by conquests and colonization. But this attitude has long been abandoned.

A very great proportion of ethnomusicological literature is concerned somehow with the fact that things do happen and that, in one way or another, happening implies process and change. I'm not sure whether one can distinguish music historians and ethnomusicologists in their attitude toward change, but here is a possibility: Historical musicologists wish to know what actually happened, and their interpretations may draw on parallels within the same culture; ethnomusicologists, confronted with events of the past or changes of the present, wish to interpret these in terms of comparisons across cultures or in the context of the several domains of culture, seeking regularities or norms, and developing theories of "what happened" or what may happen or in certain circumstances what (typically or normally) "happens." Although divided by a set of conceptual and methodological issues (see Dahlhaus 1977), historians in essence discover particular events and their relationships.

There is, however, among people who call themselves ethnomusicologists, also a tradition of straight-out historical research, particularly of the fine-art traditions of Asian music with their written records and notations going back for many centuries (e.g., Harich-Schneider 1973; Malm 1959; Provine 1988; Rowell 1992; and surveyed by Widdess 1992). Following trends in the field of general history and making use of a combination of oral transmission and documentation, this standard traditional approach to history has also become a major factor in research in African music (see, e.g., Wachsmann 1971a). The inclusion of such works—admirable and excellent as they are—in the purview of ethnomusicology is sometimes questioned, by social science–oriented ethnomusicologists as well as by music historians who may themselves be, say, Japanese, Chinese, or Indian. Should research on their music, the latter ask, be relegated to ethnomusicology rather than musicology proper, and does this mean that it is not of interest for itself but only in the development of cross-cultural comparison and theories of change? Well, I would think that historical studies, to qualify as proper ethnomusicology, should relate somehow to the central tenets of ethnomusicological definition—relationship to other cultural domains and a view of music as a world of musics. I would guess, then, that Harich-Schneider's (1973) book should count as true music history (the author would probably have agreed), and the same is true of the history of South Indian music by Ayyangar (1972), an Indian scholar. On the other hand, Bonnie Wade's book on music in Mughal art (1998) relates music, art, and culture, and thus is an example of work definitely within ethnomusicology. But these judgments are difficult to make, and in the end probably not worth making, as long as one avoids presenting a view that anything said about a music outside the Western canon is ipso facto ethnomusicology. For the most part, the approaches of ethnomusicologists to history, largely because of the lack of data but also because of the nomothetic theoretical tendencies of the social sciences, concern the processes of change more than the content of change.

But of course there have always been historians of Western music who were and are also deeply concerned with process. The past views of history and the various ways of interpreting change are important issues in the literature of historical musicology (see, e.g., Allen 1939 and Dahlhaus 1977 for earlier and more recent examples). In the period since around 1985, a good many works in the so-called new musicology movement have concentrated on developing theoretical interpretations (for discussion of these issues see, e.g., the essays in Solie 1993 and Bergeron and Bohlman 1992). And there have been major compendia that tried to combine the approaches to history. They include a large project titled *Music in Human Life,* spearheaded by Barry S. Brook in the 1980s, never in fact completed, but with the principle that the history of each culture should be written by an "insider," to which volumes of comparative study would be added; and the *Garland Encyclopedia of World Music* (1997–2002), which concludes essays of history and ethnography, with both "insider" and "outsider" voices. The number of ethnomusicologists doing work of an explicitly historical sort has increased to the degree that the term "historical ethnomusicology" has begun to appear in programs of conferences and in publications.

It might be advantageous to discard disciplinary labels and simply admit that all of us want to learn about the past, and its connection with the present and the future. It seems to me that in order for the course of human music to be understood, music scholars will have to engage in several activities, seriatim or simultaneously: (1) development of some kind of theoretical perspective and framework regarding the nature of the search, the relative significance of various kinds of data, the relationship of a source (manuscript or conquering neighbor) to the artwork, the artist, a repertory of works, a "style," a society; (2) gathering of data and development of specific conclusions on individual cultures, periods, and so on; (3) generalization of the conclusions to culture-wide and then universal processes; and (4) prediction (or do we need this one?). Historians and ethnomusicologists both have addressed themselves to the first, though often just by implication, and with a large variety of conclusions. Historical musicologists have perfected approaches to the second and rather made a specialty of it, although in limited venues of activity; ethnomusicologists have also engaged in it. The third of my series seems so far to have been carried out mainly by those who call themselves ethnomusicologists and, to a smaller degree, sociologists of music dealing with Western musical cultures. The fourth is left to the future.

A glance at a classic collection of essays on the state of musicology, edited by Brook, Downes, and Van Solkema (1972), illustrates the de facto division of labor. Essays by Blume, Lesure, Lowinsky, and Landon, a distinguished group of historians, concentrate on the specific problems of particular repertories and source types. Those of Nketia, Hood, Chase, and Harrison (all in this case explicitly espousing an ethnomusicological viewpoint) speak to the question of generalizing about the structure and significance of events. And yet the distinction is not a sharp line. In an essay that looks at musicology with exceptional breadth, Vincent Duckles (39) gives seven generating forces that in the eighteenth and nineteenth centuries led in one way or another to the study of music history. Along with some giving a traditionally historical impetus, as chant reform and the custodial role of collectors, librarians, and bibliographers, he also lists forces pointing toward ethnomusicology, such as "the discovery of world music" and "the discovery of national song." Coming from the same nineteenth-century roots, it seems that the two groups of scholars in the twentieth have simply jumped into the stream at different points. Some thirty years later, in a compendium titled *Rethinking Music* (Cook and Everist 1999) a number of authors, drawing on more recent theoretical models and terminology, covered similar topics and also showed that all musicology is still "on the same page."

We have seen a good deal of ethnomusicological work that tries to ignore change and to preserve traditions, attending to what appears to have changed least or not at all. But the most sophisticated thinkers have all along been aware that ethnomusicologists must take change into account because it is always there, and that they have a special stake in the understanding of history. Indeed, if there is anything really stable in the musics of the world, it is the constant existence of change.

To a considerable degree, the differences between the ethnomusicologist's approach to change and that of the typical music historian result from the former's association with the social sciences. Theoretical thinking about history and change in ethnomusicology is found most frequently in the writings of those who are most aware of anthropological thought. The early works by figures such as Curt Sachs and E. M. von Hornbostel were mightily influenced by the German diffusionist school of anthropology (A. Schneider 1976), and later scholars critical of that school, such as Merriam (1964: 307–8) and Blacking (1978), continued to emphasize the need for a study of musical change in the context of anthropological thought.

In the larger academy, history and anthropology have drawn closer since 1980, in a rapprochement discussed by Clifford Geertz (in many works; but see Geertz 2000: 118–23). Following this leadership, ethnomusicology and historical musicology should recognize that they share a major thrust. In both cases, emphasis is upon change of an entire system of interconnected units and materials—in the case of one, something called "culture," the descendant of Tylor's "complex whole," and in the other, "musical style," a term denoting a musical system, using it as a concept symbolic of all the things that go into a music or a musical culture.

Still, it would be a mistake to deemphasize the differences between history and anthropology in contemplating change. Throughout its history, cultural anthropology saw culture as a unit that one can view holistically, leaving aside the differences among its domains, worrying as little as possible about irregularities. Thus, in theoretically discussing culture change, anthropologists may sometimes brush aside details such as that in a given society religion changes more slowly than technology, or that a particular individual was "way ahead of his time," or for that matter that different cultures in their individual components change in completely different ways—because of their interest in the unity of culture and in the insights one may gain from this broad view. Murdock (1956) generalized about culture change, identifying innovation, social acceptance, selective elimination, and integration as a universal sequence. Speaking of regularities, he was surely aware of the Procrustean bed that would have to be created were one to apply this to each instance of change within a culture. Julian Steward, even in denying that all societies go through the same changes (1955: 14) and proposing a system of "multilinear evolution" as a way of explaining culture change in a comparative context, dealt only with those limited parallels of form, function, and sequence that have validity for cultures as a whole, ignoring local variation. Sahlins (1960) contrasted "general evolution," the tendency for cultural evolution to yield progressively higher levels of organization and complexity, with "specific evolution," the tendency for each culture type to adapt to its specific total environment. The variety of these examples illustrates the ways in which anthropologists tended to approach culture change as a unit.

Historians of Western music usually engage in studies dealing with the particular, but the implications often direct the reader to wider generalization about the history of musical style. Historians are clearly aware of the fact that a form type such as the sonata, or a practice such as that of modulation, or indeed the way in which a piece is performed may change. But there is the implication that each finding of this sort contributes to the understanding of change in style, by which is meant the aggregate of generally accepted ways of composing music and perhaps of performing it. In some of the most respected writings dealing broadly with musical change (e.g., Meyer 1967: 104–33, "Varieties of Style Change"; Szabolcsi 1965; and farther back, Bukofzer 1947), there is continual emphasis on the idea of a musical system that moves, changes, regardless of the individual diversity of its parts. Music historians normally define music by practices, not, say, by the use of specific pieces of musical content such as melodies. If one discovered that a melody such as "Dies Irae" or a folk song such as "Malbrough s'en va-t-en guerre" had been used widely in one decade and not in the next, that would be at best a minor point of consideration, but if one found that most works in one century are composed for a small ensemble, and in the next for large orchestra, that would be of greater import. Again, the fact that in one century the typical composer wrote many pieces and in the next far fewer is not a major consideration, but the resulting increase in complexity or diversity might well be. So, for the music historian the holistic notion of "style" as both essence and major symbol of a music (and thus the definition of musical change as change in style) seems to me a kind of analogue of the anthropologist's interest in culture change as a whole. In a certain sense the concept of culture (the particular way in which societies take care of their needs) is analogous to the concept of musical style (the particular way in which societies solve their musical problems).

Kinds and Degrees of Change

Typically, ethnomusicology studies the musical culture of a society through observation of the present. In a world that is constantly changing, the problem is to get a sense of organization from the bits and pieces in a musical system that undergo change. We can continue to use the concepts of content and style. Thus: A piece of music such as a song or a tune family may change. So may the normal construction of a type of piece, as in the way in which the procedure of varying a theme in a set of variations changed from the time of Bach to that of Elgar. Quite separately, this can occur in the distribution of style elements. Thus one can imagine the total repertory of an indigenous society having prevailingly scale type A, with scale type B in a minority, and then the positions of prominence reversed in a later period—all this without necessarily changing the inventory of the songs. But also there are changes in musical conceptualization and behavior, in the uses and functions of music, usually but not necessarily accompanied by changes in musical sound. The point is that musical change, viewed broadly, is a highly complex phenomenon. In order to organize this complicated picture a bit, let's consider several types or perhaps levels of change, all of them assuming that there will be continuity in some element of musical culture against which change in others can be gauged. (See also Blacking 1978; Bose 1966; Nettl 1958a; Sachs 1962; and Merriam 1964 and Wachsmann 1971a for examples of older approaches to the classification of musical change.)

First, for the case of the most complete kind of change, a population that shares and maintains one musical system abandons it for another. For this, I can't find examples of the most extreme manifestation, for even those societies that have moved from a traditional to a totally Western form of music have kept some small vestige of the earlier practice. Certain groups of Australian aborigines may have experienced something close to this kind of musical change—may have been forced, upon moving from tribal lands to cities, to abandon the older tradition and experience the complete substitution of another, Western-based system of music. The descendants of these peoples—and similar groups, such as certain Native American populations in North America and West Slavic minorities in eastern Germany—have tried with some success to recover and reinstate their older traditions, which, it turned out, had not been totally expunged. But in this most extreme form of "change," theoretically there is change but no continuity.

Second, radical change in a system of music whose new form can definitively still be traced in some way to the old is more easily illustrated. There is not only a constant population but also at least some stable element of the music to establish the continuity. In Europe the change from the essentially tonal music of Strauss and Mahler to the tonally quite different music of Schoenberg and Webern might be an example. There are plenty of elements with continuity—the orchestra, the chromatic tempered scale, and others—but the difference between old and new is easily perceived by even lay members of Western musical society. Parallel illustrations from other cultures might include the change from traditional West African to Hispanic-influenced Caribbean music among black populations in the New World, or the change from traditional Great Basin styles to the Plains style among the Shoshone in the nineteenth century.

Third, while the juxtaposition of "continuity" and change" is still around, it is clear that any musical system is likely to contain, or require, a certain amount of change as part of its essential character. Most societies expect of their artists a minimum of innovation, and some demand a great deal. In contemporary urban Western society, composers are valued if they depart from the norm very considerably, staying, of course, within certain—though often very liberal—limits that define the music system, or departing from these only in very exceptional cases. Doing something considered new is in itself good, and in Western academic music culture, doing something that has been done before is bad, though it be done well. But even in societies that do not value innovation as greatly, a certain amount of change is required. In European folk traditions, a singer might be expected to change her rendition of a folk song throughout her life. An absolutely static musical culture is actually inconceivable, and so it seems safe to hypothesize that every musical system has inherent in it a certain amount of constant change as one of its core elements, required simply to hold the system intact and to keep it from becoming an artificially preserved museum (but see Meyer 1967: 134–232 for detailed discussion of this issue). Change is the norm, more than continuity. Blacking agreed, calling attention, however, to the occasional presence of "non-change and repetition of carefully rehearsed passages of music" as a "characteristically human feature of music" (Blacking 1978: 7).

Fourth, for musical artifacts such as songs, or in song types, groups, repertories, a certain amount of allowable individual variation may not even be perceived as change. A folk song may be sung differently by a singer on various occasions, each performance representing a change from the past, but the artifact remains an unchanged unit of musical thought. I distinguish this fourth type of change from the third type by its lack of direction. This may be accepted by its society as part of its music system; or it may be regarded as permissible (or impermissible) error.

To summarize: We distinguish the substitution of one system of music for another; radical change of a system; gradual, normal change; and allowable variation. All societies may experience all four types of change, but probably to varying degrees. And we distinguish change of repertory, style, individual work or piece—to say nothing of the many components of musical culture outside the realm of sound. Blacking (1978), incidentally, presents a similar scheme, but accepts only what I've called "radical change" as proper musical change. But radical change is rare, and change that occurs within a system is the norm for ethnomusicological investigation. A musical system itself typically embodies change, but a population rarely totally replaces one music with another.

We are tempted to ask why music changes at all, but if change is the norm in culture and in music, we should rather ask the opposite question, that is, taking all of the mentioned possibilities into account, whether there are cultures or social conditions in which music does not change or in which radical and even gradual change is greatly inhibited. If we try to answer by looking at the world's musics from a comparative perspective, we're obliged to neglect the individual cultures' insiders, who may have quite different ideas of how much their music has changed. This approach certainly merits separate consideration. But asking as (hopefully objective) outsiders, we ask what would conceivably cause such exceptions to the norm. The literature of ethnomusicology does not generalize about this question very much, but here are some possibilities: (1) Musical change is (was) absent or exceedingly slow in societies with a minimum of technology. Some technology and maybe some division of labor is needed for the making of instruments, for the establishment of social contexts that foster musical events. It has been widely assumed, in many cases probably correctly, that the technologically simplest tribal and folk cultures experience little musical change. (2) Musical change may be slow in those societies in which the musical system has, through previous change, been adapted to the social system with a certain degree of perfection and thus need not adapt further, assuming musical change as adaptive strategy to a relatively unchanging cultural context. Examples? The unity of sub-Saharan music (admittedly not as unified as is often represented) in the face of great cultural differences might conceivably be a case in point. (3) It is likely that musical systems experience a certain ebb and flow in the degree to which they change. Accepting a cyclic interpretation of history, we may find a music to be temporarily in a state of stability, waiting for the rather convulsive changes that must come as the cycles progress. European music history has been interpreted in such cycles of 150 years. (4) A music may resist change if it is associated mainly or exclusively with a particular domain of culture that changes less readily than do most other activities. Religion is the most obvious example, and religious music seems in many societies to change less readily than the secular. Now, dear reader, please consider these thoughts and examples as merely rudimentary beginnings of a hopefully more sophisticated body of data and interpretation.

But let's also look at the other extreme, seeking instances in which music changes very quickly and dramatically. The most obvious example is the twentieth century, throughout the world. We may here have a special, exceptional situation, and it comes up in chapter 30. But the cultivated and popular musics of Western culture have changed in the twentieth century in many ways: (1) The "musical language" itself was changed; perhaps more properly, beginning shortly after 1900 a new language was added, one with different central features, such as a new type of harmony moving alongside the so-called functional system. (2) New technology of all sorts, from amplification to the generation of music through electronic means, and new ways of recording and transmitting music have been introduced. (3) Types of sounds, such as electronically generated products, white noise, incredibly small intervals, and industrial and animal noises, have all been introduced and accepted into the musical system. (4) Social contexts, audiences, and groups of participants have changed greatly, especially the replacement of live performance by recorded reproduction. Music historians from Walter Wiora (1965) to Jacques Attali (1985) have ascribed a special character to the twentieth century in Western and indeed in world culture.

Excursions into Conjectural History

Most ethnomusicologists consider the changes in world music brought about by the domination of Western industrialized culture and colonialism to be of a special order, and make a point of studying its causes and directions. They consider musical change in the world's cultures to be unrelated to Westernization of a different order. Our understanding of change in the past in indigenous and folk societies is extremely limited. But as an example, trying a bit of reconstruction and conjecture, let us see what can be known and conjectured of the Plains Indians before about 1800 A.D., noting conditions parallel to some of those characterizing the modern world. It is difficult to know when things happened in the history of the Plains Indians, but we know at least that certain things did happen. At some point, probably in the period between 1000 and 1500, a number of peoples from diverse areas collected in the western Plains. The diverse origin is attested by the diversity of languages: Siouan in the case of the Dakota and Crow; Algonquian in that of the Arapaho, Blackfoot, and Cheyenne; Kiowa (a language family of its own) and Uto-Aztecan for the Comanche. In the course of the eighteenth century a number of significant and related changes took place. A relatively unified buffalo hunt–oriented culture developed after horses had been introduced (indirectly, from the West). The Sun Dance, the large public ceremony probably radiating from the peoples of the central Plains (possibly the Arapaho), seems to have developed in response to the need for tribes to separate into bands for the winter but to unite in the summer. Partial dependence on agriculture was given up, and a sign language was developed for intertribal communication as travel began to be widespread, related to the nomadic lifestyle adopted in part because of the horse. (Among the many items of literature supporting these statements, see, e.g., Ewers 1958; Driver 1961.) Relatively dramatic changes thus seem to have taken place, and we have in a microcosm evidence of some of the characteristics of twentieth-century world culture: (1)

technology, suddenly improved by the introduction of the horse and other indirect acquisitions from the whites; (2) increased intertribal communication; (3) a unified religious system overlaying more individual tribal traditions; (4) no nation-states, but a unified culture that led to tribal allegiances and intertribal languages, such as the sign language and the widespread use of Lakota and, eventually, of English.

The evidence is extremely scanty, but there is a bit of an indication that rapid musical change accompanied or immediately followed this development. The geographic distribution of the so-called Plains musical style indicates rather recent origin, at least in the "classical" Plains culture, where this style developed its extreme characteristics. Distribution also suggests a diffusion to outlying areas—the eastern woodlands, the prairie tribes, and certain Salish and Great Basin peoples such as the Flathead and the Shoshone. Merriam particularly notes the Plains-like character of Flathead music and culture, despite the Salish background (1967b: 155). The overlay of Plains music in the Flathead repertory, contrary to the homogeneous style of the coast Salish, appears to be recent, as does the introduction of the Plains style in the previously simpler and homogeneous Basin repertory.

Again, it seems likely that rapid or at least substantial change in music and its surrounding social events occurred with, or perhaps followed, the development of technology, communication, and widespread standardization along with knowledge and tolerance of diversity. But of course this highly generalized and speculative discussion is intended to do nothing more than to suggest to the reader the possibility that certain kinds of cultural situations seem to be accompanied by large-scale change, and others by virtual absence of change.

Does music have its own laws? Historians of Western music often seem to believe that musical change is first and foremost to be explained in terms of the behavior of music itself (again, anthropomorphizing) and its tendency, because of its special character, to develop in certain directions. It's a view not often espoused by ethnomusicologists, but it is an undeniable fact that music sometimes changes in ways that cannot be explained by parallels to cultural or social change. Music sometimes seems to follow its own laws, changing while other domains remain stable, or conservative in the face of cultural change. I can deal with this broad topic only by way of a brief foray, suggesting one way in which music occupies a special place among the domains of culture.

A role for music as opposing the broad sweep of a culture has been proposed by various authors, particularly for Africa (e.g., Blacking 1978: 22; Coplan in

Nettl 1978a: 108–9; Merriam 1954; Tracey 1954: 237). One may say in song what one is not permitted to say in speech. In prerevolutionary Iran as well, criticism of the government and the secret police was sometimes voiced in song, a tradition with precedents in the Iranian revolutionary movements of the first decades of this century (Caton 1979). There are related phenomena. Minorities kept in national seclusion may be permitted musical prominence. A hierarchical political system may be reflected in the hierarchy of a musical ensemble, but unhappiness with the system may be expressed in singing style (see Lomax 1962: 442–43) and, as in the Middle East, the widespread ascription of sadness as the dominant emotion of music. Stated very simply, music may do for society what other domains of a culture fail to do—provide relief from everyday sameness, a way of communicating with the supernatural when other forms of communication are directed to humans, a kind of luxury among necessities. It stands to reason, then, that if musical change is normally to be seen within a context of culture change, it may also occur outside this general scope. Music may be an antidote, an expression of anticulture.

A particular role of music, as I have said, may be to symbolize in distilled and abstract form the character and values of a culture. As an object specifically treated as a symbol, it would have to remain in essence static, except for periods of rapid and radical change, like a flag, claiming to symbolize political unity, remaining unchanged despite governmental and political unrest, until an especially drastic event forces its replacement by another flag. If indeed music changes in ways contrastive to the other ways in which culture changes, this may also result from its generally close association with religion, tending to give conservation a special value. Music as a form of communication with the unchanging supernatural, as compared with the ever-changing human, may require stability, in contrast, for example, to a system of commerce or of warfare.

If there is a special dynamic of specifically musical change, perhaps the most plausible reason involves the systemic nature of music. A musical system may seek a kind of equilibrium in which the close interrelationship of the components plays a major role. Change in one parameter is likely to require or encourage changes in others. Thus addition of Western harmony in Middle Eastern music appears to strengthen the prominence of those modes that lend themselves to harmonization in major or minor, even when they are performed by a traditional ensemble. The change from solo to group performance may require adjustments in intonational or improvisational patterns and values. The various components of music must work together, and humans who make music try to find structures in which they are compatible. Having found such a way, people are not quick to accept change in the nature of the system, instead substituting constant internal change. And the better a musical system accommodates the need for the elements to interrelate, the more it will remain stable, and perhaps the more it will also permit and require changes *within* the system. Indeed, thinking of Western, Asian Indian, and African musics as examples, we may hypothesize that some of the most successful musical systems in terms of widespread acceptance, respect accorded in their own societies, overall stability, and demands made upon and fulfilled by musicians may be the ones in which the elements interact most perfectly.

Turning a Corner

Ethnomusicologists were slow to take an interest in the study of musical change, starting out as the students of "peoples without history," moving to theories of how musics may change and why, and accepting only slowly the view that in following a synchronic approach to music one comes face to face with the issue of change. But in the period after 1980, it seems that ethnomusicologists have turned a sharp corner, becoming, in a virtual sea change, almost a profession of scholars of musical change, interested most in music that has undergone or is undergoing change in some sense. In the course of this shift, they have drawn closer, but not much closer, to music historians. Their approach to history and change is really largely quite different, and their contributions distinct. Fulfilling the imperative to study all of a culture's music, they concentrate on popular musics more than other genres. They have a larger amount of historical data than before, but most of it is recorded material, and thus different from the typical music historian's source. They begin with the political movements of the mid–twentieth century—colonialism, nationalism, globalization—and trace their effects on music, and the way they may be affected by music and musicians. They follow intercultural and international movements. And they emphasize societies, classes, and groups that have been neglected by scholars.

Three areas of study stand out. The first is what I have already called "historical ethnomusicology," and this comes about because of the greater availability of historical sources of all sorts. Verbal and notated sources, though they have been around for decades, play more of a role in ethnomusicological consciousness, and many have been published in accessible form, as, for example, collections of Korean source readings (Song 1980) and historical transcriptions (Levine 2002). Much of the research on Chinese music has been a combination of historical and ethnographic interpretation (as described by Isabel Wong 1991). Accordingly, also, the development of music research in China, Japan, and Korea has avoided sharp distinctions between historical musicology and ethnomusicology (to illustrate, see Tokumaru et al. 1991). In Europe, too (more than in North America), the 1990s saw various attempts at rapprochement between ethnomusicology and music history, as indicated in various conferences bringing the two groups together (e.g., Mahling and Münch 1997). The greatly increased interest in the history of research has stimulated scholars also to see that changes in the attitudes of researchers often go hand in hand with changes in the musical cultures they study.

A second development that has motivated many ethnomusicologists to look increasingly at change as the main object of their concern is a group of events of worldwide magnitude and distribution subsumed under terms such as *nationalism, cosmopolitanism,* and *globalization.* Basically, they involve the rapid musical interactions among ethnic groups, nations, classes, and world areas, and among musical strata (folk, classical, popular) once seen as distinct. They are processes that seem to be, at least in their magnitude, without precedent in world history. Ethnomusicologists trying to contemplate the musical results of these major cultural processes, now readily documented in audio, visual, and print media, have been confronted with situations that can only be interpreted as dynamic. Much of the literature after 1990 speaks to these processes.

Let me mention, to illustrate the kind of work that has been done, three important studies. Thomas Turino (2000), in writing about the recent music history of Zimbabwe, gives the history of a musical style used by the distinguished musician Thomas Mapfumo. Music in the traditional mbira repertory combined with modern popular African American styles to form a genre that came to symbolize Zimbabwean nationalism in the wars of liberation. After independence, taking on characteristics of various African-derived New World cultures, this genre came to be associated with the newly established middle class. Peter Manuel's (1993) study of popular music in India analyzed the development of the audio cassette industry as a medium for reviving the musics of local subcultures, but also as a vehicle for regionalist, nationalist, and South/West Asian religious movements of significance also to the great number of Indians dwelling overseas. In a number of works, Veit Erlmann (1991, 1999) analyzed ways in which traditional musics of South Africa moved from ethnic to national symbols, were influenced by and in turn influenced African American music, and became part of a global popular music repertory. In *Music, Modernity, and the Global Imagination* (1999), he analyzed and compared the international effects of two events almost a century apart: a tour of South African choirs to England and North America around 1890, and the tours and recordings of the choir Ladysmith Black Mambazo in the 1980s, after they had burst on the world musical scene through participation in Paul Simon's LP record *Graceland* (see Meintjes 1990).

A motivation for ethnomusicologists to privilege the study of change was the development of urban ethnomusicology, the study of musical life of cities because of their heterogeneous nature. Urban studies in ethnomusicology, in contrast to more traditional, community or tribe-centered research, usually concentrate on relationships among musics, the musics of neighboring ethnic groups, the musics of a diasporic group and its homeland. (See Bohlman 1989; Nettl 1978a; Reyes Schramm 1982; Turino and Lee 2004 for a sampling of studies.) At first, the concept of urban studies seemed strange and had to be justified, but by 1990 the great majority of ethnomusicological research was being carried out in urban venues, and as urban culture became the world's norm—even small towns and villages came to participate in mass-mediated "urban culture" because of the revolution in communication—the special character of cities began to be taken for granted as an object of study or sometimes as an obstacle to more traditional sorts of research.

A Variety of Patterns, Directions, and Regularities

I will have occasion to deal with various aspects of musical change in other chapters. Having made some idiosyncratic suggestions, I feel it necessary to see whether there is much that most ethnomusicologists have come to believe about change in general. There are no results of polls or official statements of position, but on the basis of some prominent publications, going back to early in the twentieth century, let me try to give a summary.

While I have been speaking of music as if it were an independent organism, it is important to be clear that I am talking about changes in behavior and practice of humans. Blacking reminds us that we are dealing with "decisions made by individuals about music-making and music on the basis of their experiences of music and attitudes to it in different social contexts" (1978: 12). Merriam pointed out, in discussing change, that "no two people behave in exactly the same way in any given situation and thus there always exists an almost infinite series of deviations from the norms of society" (1964: 308). Such statements would almost parallel those of the most particularist historians, refusing to recognize patterns outside the individual.

But ethnomusicologists (including Merriam and Blacking) are interested in regularities. It is their understanding of the important role of individuals, as well as the complexity of music and the sheer quantity of data, that has kept them from adopting a single theory of change, and from a specifically nomothetic approach. One way of seeing these regularities is to recognize the distinction between change brought about by a society from its own internal resources, and that which comes about as a result of intercultural contact. We hardly know of cultures that have not been exposed to others, and most research deals with "external" change. Merriam distinguishes the two, asserting that ethnomusicology "needs a theory of change that will apply to both internal and to external factors" (1964: 307; see also Nettl 1958a). Such a general theory might view the phenomenon of musical change as the result of a balance, suggested earlier, between stability and continuity (the latter being "change" of the "internal" sort) and disturbances brought about by outside contact. Internal change may normally follow certain patterns established in a society and thus be in some measure predictable on the basis of its own conception of music, of change, the culture's technology and social structure. The results of outside contact would be subject to more variables but perhaps predictable in part from types of intercultural relationships.

Curt Sachs's statement about musical change in his last book (1962) paralleled Merriam's distinction between internal and external. He identified three fundamental types, "culture graft," "progress," and "simple change." Interpreting and expanding his brief statement, I suggest that progress is change in the direction of an objective or final goal, and this definition is Sachs's way of pointing out that there are regularities of change in any music. "Simple change" seems to be his way of identifying allowable variation, while "culture graft" distinguishes what results from intercultural contact. In these and other authors' statements, there is often the implication that a society, left alone, will develop music in a particular way, in a direction. Several have been suggested.

The most common belief is that music increases in complexity, adding tones to scales, sections to forms, notes to chords. Certainly some societies have followed this direction, if not constantly then generally; the precise way in which the increased complexity is manifest varies, and thus suggests the usefulness of an approach such as Steward's "multilinear evolution." Ethnomusicologists are inclined to believe this, I think, but they are disturbed by the lack of clear-cut evidence. So many musics have been affected by external contact to a really significant degree that one can hardly find examples of undisturbed "internal" change. But there may be a core of data sufficient to allow us to believe that while increased complexity is one of several things that frequently occur, we cannot tolerate this process as an immutable law of human musical behavior.

Related to this concept is a more difficult one that takes into account the broad differences between major groups of cultures. Max Weber (1958) and his follower Kurt Blaukopf (1951, 1970) distinguish Western music (which in the past few centuries changed greatly) from most non-Western (which they regard as more static) with the argument that Western culture, and its musics, proceeded in the direction of certain "ideals." Weber's work, an incomplete fragment, is today mainly of historical interest. But Weber's theory that music changes in directions determined by social and economic developments, and, in the case of Western culture, in the direction of increased rationalization, particularly of the organization of pitch, is surely relevant to ethnomusicology. It was his belief that Western society, because it ceased to accord mainly "practical" uses to music, increasingly "rationalized" or intellectualized its system by strengthening its theoretical basis (Blaukopf 1970: 162–63). One may question the special kind of uniqueness that Weber accords to Western music, but ethnomusicologists have generally tended to distinguish complex societies, with their art music and their professional musicians and theorists, in which music changes at least with deliberate speed, from the very simplest, in which musical change is thought to have been exceedingly slow.

In an earlier work, Sachs (1946) proposed that change is frequently a function of the tendency of societies to react against the past, that people are driven, after a given amount of time, to reverse the direction of what they have been doing, creating something contrastive. Sachs here followed the work of Lorenz (1928), who suggested a rather precise periodization of European art music in terms of thirty-year segments. Sachs points out that counterpoint dominates in the late Middle Ages, is replaced by more emphasis on melody and harmonic integration, but then reasserts itself in the late Baroque and again in the late nineteenth century. Classical is followed by Romantic, cerebral by emotional, lyrical by dramatic, even complex by somewhat simpler. The literature contains suggestions of other regularities. Oral tradition may produce simplification of a piece. Culture change is followed inevitably by musical change. Periods move from primitive beginnings to classicism to decadence. Musical concepts and behavior change more readily than music sound. In a related thought, Blacking (1978: 21–23) suggests patterns based on biological processes.

Most studies of musical change in ethnomusicology have, however, involved intercultural contact. While some specific instances are discussed in other chapters, I should say in summary that the determinants of change are thought to include the following: (1) the quality of the relationship—political, economic, demographic—between the societies affected; (2) the degree of compatibility between the cultures in contact and between the musical systems; and (3) a perhaps untestable aesthetic criterion, the degree to which a musical system is integrated, that is, constitutes a successful combination of interlocking components.

From all of this, we can see that there have been many attempts to generalize about change but no generally accepted theory. The recent literature about the concept of change shows a good deal of dissatisfaction. Blacking (1978) has suggested an approach to a "comprehensive and definitive study of musical change," including synchronic, diachronic, and biological approaches. But the best one may expect at this point, it seems to me, is a theory that would be enumerative, pointing out a group of regularities and patterns stemming from a variety of circumstances and contexts. We know there are components that change, that there are reasons for change, typical directions, internal and external factors. It would seem that one possibility is to view the process of change as depending on equilibrium among various factors. Let me try to state it as a hypothesis.

In the life of a music, some components always change while others do not. When style changes, content tends to remain, and vice versa. Where pieces themselves change, they are not often abandoned to be replaced by others, while rapid turnover in a repertory accompanies the avoidance of change of the individual pieces. Improvisation over a model, each performance signifying change of some sort, causes the model itself to remain constant. Where performance practice does not permit much change in a given piece, new pieces are more frequently created than where a performance style requires departure from a norm. Innovation and variation balance each other. Radical change and the kind of gradual, allowable, intrasystemic change that is always with us each claims its due, to different but balanced degrees. The hypothesis remains to be tested.

So far, ethnomusicologists have concentrated on their own perception of musical change, learning little and not having much to say about the perception of musical continuity and change in the various societies of the world. Over the years, doing fieldwork, I would ask my principal teachers how music had changed in the last few decades, and how much, and what they thought of it.

My Blackfoot Indian consultant: "Oh yes. Every year about a hundred new songs come to the reservation." Did they sound different from the old songs?

"No, they are new songs and we add them and that way we get more and more songs." The Blackfoot regarded change as basically a good thing. A South Indian music scholar: "No room for innovation in Carnatic music!" Change was basically undesirable, and should be confined to certain restricted components of music, and absorbed. My teacher of Persian music: "Yes," he said, "unfortunately we are having to change many things, otherwise our music may not survive. But we have always been doing that." Change was seen as a kind of defensive strategy. Change was neither good nor bad, but necessary. But what about amount and velocity of change? I asked him how long a particular practice had been extant. "We have always done that," he replied. "Always?" I asked, "You mean, for the last two hundred years, for example?" "Of course not," he replied; "nobody knows what was going on two hundred years ago." I had not penetrated his sense of change and of history.

21

Recorded, Printed, Written, Oral: Traditions

The Significance of Transmission

For a long time in the history of ethnomusicology, the differences between oral and written transmission loomed as a major definitional paradigm. Some authors, such as George List (1979b), actually labeled ethnomusicology as the study of music in oral tradition, and folk music, one of its diagnostic repertories, was often broadly defined as the music that was handed down by word of mouth (Herzog 1950: 1032), and a sharp line drawn between the two kinds of tradition. And early on, already, some of the most prominent figures in the field pointed out that the matter was not so simple, noting the importance of understanding the processes of memory, that "aural" (from "hearing") was a better term than "oral," and that there were various types of transmission. I'll follow that advice here.

In an article actually titled "Oral Tradition in Music," Charles Seeger (1950) suggested that what was interesting about aural tradition was not so much that it was radically different as a way of teaching and learning from the written, but the relationship between the two. Thus, at a time when a dichotomy between them seemed widespread in scholarly thought, this uncommonly insightful article showed the two to be inextricably connected. At a time when the typical student of art music had barely become aware of the impact of aural tradition on the creation of a folk song whose existence was a mass of variants, Seeger delineated the basic difference between the historian's and the ethnomusicologist's conception of a "piece." At a moment when we began to rejoice at the prospect that the proliferation of sound recordings would help us in the understanding of aural traditions, he already foresaw the impact that the development and dissemination of recordings would have on the very existence of aural traditions. About the same time, Curt Sachs (1948: 378) suggested that in regard to the essentials of transmission, there are four kinds of musical culture, dominated by aural, written, printed, and recorded forms. These could even represent a chronological order (see Blaukopf 1979: 80), valid for Western civilization, but it is also a continuum of relationships, from close to distant, among composer, performer, and listener.

To all kinds of music scholars, one of the most important things about a musical culture is how it, as it were, transmits itself. Considering this, ethnomusicologists have contributed modestly on the general nature of these different forms of transmission. The literature has concerned itself most with two areas, the reliability of "oral" traditions as sources for history, and the way in which that reliability leads to the shape of a repertory, something I have looked at in chapter 9. The role of recording in transmission received some attention in the mid–twentieth century (see, e.g., Gronow 1963), and as the ascendancy of recorded forms as the principal nodes of transmitting music developed and was increasingly taken for granted, studies about how it works from different perspectives began to be carried out. Thus, Berliner (1994) analyzed the ways jazz musicians use oral, recorded, and written sources in developing styles and techniques. Meintjes (2003) looks in great detail at the workings of a South African recording studio. But the field has not developed much by way of generalized theory.

The concept of transmission, though, should lead us to look comparatively at the different kinds of data that music and contextual information provide. Aural transmission has come to play an important role in the field of history, where it first became prominent in African studies (see, e.g., Vansina 1965). Historians have seen spoken accounts as a way of supplementing or sometimes replacing written or printed sources, particularly in cultures with unwritten languages, but also in materials coming from sources of so-called oral history. They are concerned about the degree to which it can provide reliable data and facts. This concern has sometimes been shared by ethnomusicologists. Mantle Hood (1959), in a study of Javanese music, discussed the maintenance of certain principles in an aural tradition that are necessary to hold a musical system intact. Music historians concerned with the role of aural transmission in medieval music have used the concept critically in their analyses (see Jeffery 1992; Treitler 1974, 1975, 1986). The nature of transmission and its effects on many aspects of music was the subject of a major conference and subsequent publication (Tokumaru and Yamaguti 1986).

But most students of folk music have been more interested in what might be called the unreliability of aural tradition, seeing it as a force for change. In studying the way in which a piece develops variants, they have marveled not at the consistency of tradition but at the differences and, in fact, suspected the presence of written versions when confronted with standardization. Like students of folklore generally, they saw in the very unreliability of orality the creative force of the community, developing for its tendency to proliferate within a strict set of guidelines the label "communal re-creation" (Barry 1933), a term derived from an earlier belief in the creation of songs and tales by the folk community at large, called "communal creation."

In the long history of folk music research, there is a close relationship between the definition of folklore as aurally transmitted and of folk song as anonymously composed. There is a difference, both in the process and as a subject for research, between a song composed and written down by an individual and then passed on orally and another composed without the availability of writing. But in both cases, one of the early questions for scholars has been whether folk songs (and, by implication, other music in "oral" tradition) are created by individuals or by the "folk" (see Barry 1914).

The most naive version of the concept of communal creation, of a primordial group of villagers somehow composing in concert, was never taken very seriously. An American pioneer of folk song research, Phillips Barry (1933), points out that German thinkers associated with it, such as the brothers Grimm and Ludwig Uhland, did not hold this belief. Yet the conception of creation by *the* people, encapsulated in the heraldic declaration "das Volk dichtet," is not totally without significance. Oral/aural tradition operates as a constraining, limiting, directing force much more than the written. So, too, in rather different ways, does the recorded.

It's important to see aural tradition in the context of the many types of transmission available in various cultures and periods—a complicated picture. In Sachs's model, written tradition is closer to the oral than is printed tradition. Where writing alone is available, it may develop variant forms through the vagaries of scribes, their creativity, errors, forgetfulness, laziness even, more readily than one that has printing. Learning aurally from a series of live performances is different from the repeated hearing of a recording. As usual, the world's cultures exhibit wide variety in the differences of aural learning. Here insistence on precise learning inhibits creation of variants; elsewhere one is almost required to make changes in a performance. Similar pieces may be regarded as variants here, identities there, imitations in a third culture, and easily separable units in a fourth. Aural traditions have had modifiers, beginning long ago to be supplemented with Western notation in

Iran, a unique musical shorthand in India, the cassette recorder among Native Americans, and by the end of the twentieth century, it was perhaps substantially supplanted by various forms of the "recorded" form of transmission.

The general literature on oral transmission is actually based on a small number of repertories. For example, Lord's (1965) highly influential book deals with Yugoslav epic poetry; Cutter (1976), Treitler (1974, 1975), and Jeffery (1992) wrote about Christian liturgical chant; Hood about Java. Barry, Bayard, and Bronson have developed the concept as it works in Anglo-American folk music, Wiora in German song and Europe generally. The conventional wisdom is based mainly on knowledge of European and American folk music (see Bohlman 1988: 14–32). But the world of music, and the world of musicology, are now far from the early figures, from Herder, Erk, Bartok, Barry, and Bayard, the scholars who tried to establish the validity of studying music that is aurally transmitted, who tried even just to gain its acceptance as "music." Today, we readily accept that existence of aural tradition earlier in our history, but we wonder whether it still exists anywhere in isolated and unadulterated form.

Some Fundamental Questions

Admitting that they should perhaps be phrased in the past tense, let's look at some general questions about aural transmission. What is it that changes in aural transmission, and what remains the same? We deal with a large variety of phenomena and a broad range of behavior. Returning to my distinction between "content" and "style," in order for a piece to be transmitted intact, its content must remain while its style may change. Bearing in mind the special definitions of these terms, some musics have a great deal of content and little that can be called style. The Samaritans of Israel, around 1970, we are told (by Avigdor Herzog, who did extensive fieldwork in their community), were extremely anxious to keep their liturgical tradition intact, permitting no changes—a statement also true of the Navajo (McAllester 1954: 64–65). Such cultures provide little opportunity for stylistic variation or change; everything in their music is essential content. By contrast, the classical music of Iran, consisting of memorized pieces used as the basis of improvisation, permits enormous variation in performance but insists on a small but significant core of stability, symbolized by the statement that one does not improvise upon a mode but "performs" it (Nettl and Foltin 1972: 11–13). The content of English folk music seems to reside substantially in its melodic contour (see, e.g., Poladian 1942), and of Hungarian, perhaps in configurations of cadential tones (Bartók 1931: 6–8). But however defined, when a piece is transmitted, style changes, content remains.

What is it that is actually transmitted? On the surface, we think of discrete compositions, songs, pieces, and no doubt these are the major units. But there are alternative approaches. One may think of a repertory as consisting of a vocabulary of units, perhaps melodic or rhythmic motifs, lines of music accompanying lines of poetry, cadential formulas, chords or chord sequences. We could study the process of transmission by noting how a repertory keeps these units intact, and how they are combined and recombined into larger units that are acceptable to the culture as performances. The smallest units of content may be the principal units of transmission (see Lord 1965, chaps. 3 and 4; Treitler 1975).

At the other end of the spectrum: While a culture creates, forgets, creates anew, and internally changes a repertory of musical content such as songs, with some turnover, it also transmits to itself (and perhaps very slowly changes) the stylistic superstructure. For example, the northern Plains Indians have probably for centuries acquired songs, composing them in dreams or learning them from other tribes, new ones replacing forgotten ones. We can also observe, by taking a broad overview of their music, that features of performance practice such as singing style, intonation, style of drumming, and range of melodies, have been handed down more or less intact yet have undergone changes in certain directions.

There is, furthermore, more to the question of transmission than the teaching and learning of music as a function of interpersonal relations. Transmission of a sort occurs also within the experience of one human being. The way in which a musician—concert pianist or indigenous singer—changes and perhaps develops a conception and therefore a performance of a piece in the course of his or her life is surely a type of transmission and, in just about all cases (classical, popular, folk), specifically aural transmission. James Porter (1976), in describing the stages of a song in one folk singer's experience, shows that the history of such a song can be interpreted as contributing to the way in which a tune family develops in aural tradition, as otherwise represented by a chain of singers each with his or her variant.

What do we know about changes in form that take place when a music moves from aural to written tradition? We have few cases where this, simply and precisely, has happened, and in such instances, we must cope also with other changes: for example, the Westernization of musical life, the introduction of Western music, the changing importance of mass media. Let me again illustrate from the classical music of Iran, into which notation began to be introduced before 1900, but which in 1970 was still prevailingly aural. The basic *radif* has now been notated and is frequently learned from written versions. In earlier times, we are told, each teacher developed his own version of the *radif*. This is still to some extent the case, but three major versions that have been published—by Abolhassan Saba, in a fashion that incorporates non-*radif* material as well, in pure but extended fashion by Musa Ma'aroufi (Barkechli 1963), and less extensively by Mahmoud Karimi (Massoudieh 1978)—dominated instruction in the 1970s, and the Ma'aroufi *radif* as transmitted by Nour-Ali Boroumand had ascendancy in the 1990s. We can only guess at the effects, but older musicians and old recordings suggest an increase in standardization that, given many other kinds of changes in musical culture, is difficult to relate to notation alone.

The introduction of notation may have allowed Persian music to survive, and the fact that it could actually be notated made it possible for its practitioners to hold their heads up in the face of encroaching Western musical culture. But gone is the reverence with which a student had formerly held his master's *radif*, which he had learned a bit at a time because contemplation of its miniature details was deemed essential, and for which he depended on the not-always-forthcoming good will of the teacher. After all, a musician can now learn the material quickly, looking up forgotten passages and controlling the pace of learning. Musicians sometimes feel free to depart from what is, after all, only another written musical artifact, not something to be revered and treasured above other music. On the other hand, in conjunction with other appurtenances of Western musical culture, notation has on the whole permitted Persian music to develop a broader scope and style, but at the center of its practice is a core comprising possibly the majority of performances, which are similar to each other and thus represent a narrowing of the tradition. The shape of the repertory has both broadened and narrowed. But we can assess the role of the introduction of notation only in the context of the introduction of other aspects of Western academic musical culture.

Do oral and aural transmission and oral creation affect the forms of pieces and repertories? No doubt they must, but we have no theory to explain just how. As a start, let me distinguish between the *creation* of pieces without notation and the *transmission* of pieces that may or may not have been composed with notation. We can't take for granted that all pieces that have been notated by their composers were actually created specifically with the use of notation. There is music composed aurally, in the mind of the musician (a Mozart or a Schubert?) but then handed down entirely through written tradition. So we are faced with several possible processes along with intermediate forms: Pieces composed without notation and also transmitted aurally probably account for the majority of musical artifacts in the world. In dramatic contrast, there are pieces composed with the use of notation and then performed only with the most exact use of the notes, by musicians who wish to follow the composer's instructions precisely and may indeed have little idea in advance of what sounds will emerge. But there is also music written by a composer and then passed on orally, something obviously true of much popular music. To it we should add music in which the writing of words is partially a musically mnemonic device. In the case of certain jazz traditions, we have music whose content is written but whose style is transmitted through recordings.

It may be that certain structural limitations are necessary if a piece is to be transmitted aurally. Dividing music into elements, I suggest that some of these must retain a degree of simplicity, repetitiveness, and stability, so that others may vary. There is probably some point beyond which it is impossible for any sizable population of musicians to remember songs and pieces, and if these mentioned limitations are not observed in the original composition, they will, in an aural-transmission culture, be instituted through the process of communal re-creation. Recurring events or signposts, such as motifs or rhythmic patterns, conciseness of form, brevity, or systematic variation, may, as it were, hold an aurally transmitted piece intact. Even in the complex pieces of South Indian classical music, such as the *kritis,* lasting as long as ten minutes, a function of their repetitive, variational, and cumulative elements of form, I would venture to guess, is to make aural transmission possible.

There is a widely accepted assumption that a piece transmitted orally changes slowly but constantly, supported only in part by a small number of studies. A study by Porter (1976), who examines the successive versions of a song performed by one singer over a period of years, some attempts to rerecord older Native American songs after decades (see Witmer 1991), and the retrospective studies of European folk music by Bayard and Wiora all indicate that we may be on the right track. No doubt, however, the particular view that a society has of change and the nature of music plays a greater role than any general law of human behavior.

Kinds and Types of History

To what extent does the way in which music is transmitted determine the overall shape of a repertory? Or, conversely, can one examine the structure of a repertory, the interrelationships among its units of content and style, and get some insights into the way it transmits itself, as a unit and as a group of separable units? Let me suggest a typology applicable to both pieces and repertories, in the belief that this could be a starting point for a comparative study of transmission.

Beginning with the microcosm, the piece and its history, let me propose that there are types of histories, a theoretical abstraction of four kinds of things that a piece, once composed, may experience. In type 1 it may be carried on without change, more or less intact. In type 2 it may be transmitted and changed, but only in a single version or one direction, so that it continues differently from its original but without the proliferation of variants. In type 3 it may experience the kind of transmission that produces many variants, some of them eventually abandoned and forgotten, others becoming stable once differentiated, others again changing constantly. In all three of these types, the history of the composition is essentially self-contained, all forms derived specifically from the original creation. A fourth type is similar to type 3, developing within the family principle but borrowing materials from other, unrelated compositions. Type 1 looks like a straight line; type 2 like a single bent line; type 3 like the diagram of a genealogical tree; and type 4 like a tree whose roots and limbs are attacked by shoots from elsewhere.

It is important to bear in mind that this typology is speculative and hypothetical, a model that sets forth extreme cases. The literature shows amply that the family type, type 3, really does exist, and we have seen evidence of the existence of type 4 in the wandering lines of Czech folk songs and Native American Peyote songs, the "bridge" in the third line of many popular songs and hymns (see also Olsvai 1963 for Hungarian examples). In its extreme form, type 1 may be totally absent, but something close to it occurs in the written, printed, and recorded traditions of modern urban culture, where pieces in particularly prominent performance versions may set something close to an absolute standard. Societies such as the Navajo or the western Pueblos may come close to this model in aural tradition. Type 2 must for the moment remain entirely hypothetical, but conceivably the liturgy of the Samaritans, known to have changed and yet the subject of laborious standardization, could serve as an illustration. The first two types may not exist in pure form; just because we find a tune without known relatives does not mean that we have a solid example. Translated into generalized tendencies, however, these four types of history may have credibility.

The other side of the coin, however, is also always there. For example, in what appears to us to be a family of type 3, with all variants directly derived from the parent, it is conceivable that the performers do not recognize derivation at all, ascribing each variant to separate creation. An example from the Blackfoot, who compose songs by learning them in visions: Each who had a vision was likely to receive songs from his guardian spirit. Many of the songs thus learned by different individuals, albeit perhaps from the same guardian spirit, may to the objective outsider be quite identical. It seems possible that the very act of separate creation that the two songs undergo may be enough to give them status as separate units of musical thought, quite in opposition to our observation, shared incidentally by the Blackfoot who hears recordings, that they are almost identical. This is quite different from the Iranian example cited earlier, in which a performer claimed to play a piece identically each time, despite the fact that to any outside observer the performances would sound completely different, having in common only certain motifs and scalar patterns. Javanese Matjapat songs may be an even more extreme example (Kartomi 1973: 159–60). The two sides of the coin may be very much opposite sides.

Having set forth four hypothetical kinds of history that a composition may experience, we next move to see whether entire traditions or repertories can also be thus classified. There is no doubt that a typical repertory—maybe every repertory—actually consists of a mixture of at least some of the types of compositional history, but it might be possible to find, for each one, a dominant type. But first let me introduce another variable, again a theoretical abstraction: the density of a repertory and the associated dynamics of change.

By *density*, I mean the degree to which separate units of a repertory are similar, whether or not genetically related. Or, putting it another way, how close or how far apart, musically, the units, pieces, songs, may be from each other. For both the outsider and the insider. To illustrate the concept, let us imagine two tune families whose internal relationship has been proved by observation of the process, beginning with the composition of the parent tune. One family develops variants, versions, and forms that in the aggregate are very different from each other, and there may be considerable difference between one variant and its closest neighbor. This family would be lacking in density and could be called, for lack of a better term, *sparse*. Ultimately, the classification of a family as sparse would depend on the classifier's having a complete knowledge of all of its members, and this is, of course, only theoretically or experimentally possible. The other, *dense,* tune family has variants that are very similar to each other, and its closest neighbor-variants are almost identical.

This leads to other considerations. It's possible for a family to be dense, that is, to have a vast number of variants covering a great many points that are musically far apart in terms of any of a large number of components. But it would also be possible to find a sparse family that, because of the small number of its constituent variants, still covers, musically speaking, the same ground. A tune family may also be broad or narrow, depending on the specifically musical distance between the variants exhibiting the greatest difference—never mind for the moment why these differences may come about, and how they may be differentially perceived in various societies.

Now, the same kind of thinking may be extended to an entire repertory, which may be dense or sparse and also broad or narrow, the two coordinates not necessarily correlating. Impressionistically speaking, with examples for which I have no more evidence than some firsthand acquaintance, I would say that twentieth-century Western art music is a broad repertory, and eighteenth-century Italian music less broad but quite dense. Blackfoot Indian music of the nineteenth century, from what we now know of it, was probably broad and dense, at least compared to Blackfoot music of the more recent past, which is much less broad but equally dense. The English and Czech folk song repertories are probably more or less equally broad, but the English repertory seems to me to be denser and perhaps also larger. This mode of thought should some day lead to a way of comparing musics in accordance with the criteria I have mentioned; at any rate, it seems useful to consider a repertory from this point of view, realizing that the internal interrelationships tell us something about the way in which it comes about and grows.

An analogous concept about which one could theorize is historical density, that is, the rate at which a piece or a repertory changes. We can simply call this component the dynamics of the tradition, but here, even more, the lack of documentation stands in the way. Still, following the findings of classifiers and tune-family proponents, we can imagine that one song may change very quickly, while a second might undergo the same changes but with the process requiring much more time. The dynamic distinction is relevant to my model types 2, 3, and 4. Type 1, of course, doesn't change at all.

Let me return for a moment to the relative dynamics of oral/aural and written tradition. Looking at the literature of ethnomusicology at large, one finds two contrasting implications: Written traditions change slowly because they are able to hold on to their artifacts in a way not possible for aural ones, for these are thought to change almost involuntarily, as a result of faulty memory, the aforementioned limitations, and the like. On the other hand, some believe that aural traditions change slowly because the simplicity of their cultural context makes them inert, while written traditions, because

of the very sophistication of their apparatus and even because there is a notation system, move quickly (see Herzog 1950: 1033; Hood 1959: 201). Within
the history of a written tradition, the speed varies—as in Western art music,
in which the rate of change seems gradually to have accelerated. And the interaction among live performance, notation, and recording probably provides a template for a large group of tradition types.

Ethnomusicologists, concerned with the musics of peoples, the total repertories of societies, should work toward finding ways of comparing them as
wholes. One important criterion in comparison ought to be the way in which
the music is distributed within its repertory and how its units (songs, pieces,
modes, etc.) interrelate. An understanding of a music from this perspective
is based in large measure on the way in which these units are transmitted,
and in what respects they change, and what remains unchanged. It is indicative of the state of musicological thought that written tradition has been
widely accepted as the normal form of transmission, if not of world music,
then of that music that may conveniently and effectively be studied—those
aspects of the music that are readily notated. Given the available sources, this
is an understandable thrust. Yet the approaches developed in ethnomusicology can underscore something not always understood among the Western music intelligentsia, that aural transmission is the world's norm, that
music everywhere—even when notated—is actually learned more through
hearing than through reading, and that aural transmission really dominates
the musical life of even a literate society, and typically also the life of a piece
of music.

22

The Basic Unit of All Culture and Civilization: Signs and Symbols

The Third Rasoumovsky

Anthropology defines itself as "the study of humans," but when a new student in anthropology told me that she had come "to study symbols," I shouldn't have been surprised, as the distinguished anthropologist Leslie White had written, in 1949, that "the symbol is the basic unit of all human behavior and civilization" (1949: 22). When he wrote that, not many paid attention, but it is now widely believed that if humans are, as White said, distinguished by the fact that they use symbols, it is symbolism in the broadest sense that anthropology must be about. For the same reason, there are now scholars who believe that music, like other human works, can best be examined as a symbol and as a system of signs or symbols, and an area of music research known as musical semiotics has developed. Narrowly construed, it involves the study of music as a system of signs and involves three principal approaches: one whose origins are associated principally with Ferdinand de Saussure, a pioneer in the field of linguistics whose work led to approaches labeled as structuralist, analyzing individual cultural domains such as language, or, conceivably, music; a second based on the work of Charles Sanders Peirce, which seeks to "understand how people are connected to, and experience, the world" (Turino 1999: 222); and a third, which takes its cues from philology and aesthetics.

But construed broadly, musical semiotics affects an immense field, the meaning of music. Our task here is only to see how it relates specifically to the aims of ethnomusicologists, but this nevertheless involves the whole question of musical meaning: of music as universal, culture-specific, confined to an individual; of the meaning of styles and genres, of modes, rhythms, chords, or pieces and songs; and of how something that a musicians means to convey is actually interpreted. It's a vast area, and I can only make a couple of limited illustrative forays.

Musical semiotics as a field of analysis is thought to have taken root in the 1970s, but its elements go back much farther, to times when the representation of nonmusical objects, events, and ideas were issues for composers such as J. S. Bach, for aestheticians such as Eduard Hanslick, and, farther back, for Arabic (see Shiloah 1979) and Indian theorists (Rowell 1992: 327–36) who argued about the nonmusical meanings of maqam and raga. Surely people have always speculated about what music means. Several publications coming roughly in the middle of the twentieth century, from quite contrastive directions, seem to me to provide landmarks for the backgrounds of more systematic approaches of the 1970s and later. I'll mention three of these landmarks (but there could be many more).

In the 1940s my father, a music historian, brought to the attention of the family a curious book, written by Arnold Schering, a scholar who had made major contributions to several branches of music history but in his advanced years threw his lot in with the 1930s Nazi movement. It was an interpretation of many works by Beethoven as literal representations of classic works of literature. Titled *Beethoven und die Dichtung* (1936), it interprets the Seventh Symphony as based on scenes from Goethe's *Wilhelm Meisters Lehrjahre,* the Kreutzer Sonata as based on Tasso's *Gerusalleme Liberata,* and the third Rasoumovsky Quartet, Op. 59, no. 3, as based on *Don Quixote.* The interpretations proceed in play-by-play fashion; motifs are assigned specific meanings, and instrumental melodies are interpreted as settings of words. Aside from the master's well-known interest in literature, Schering gives only internal evidence that Beethoven used these works as models, and the book was never taken very seriously by most Beethoven scholars, and today it's just a curiosum. Why is this interesting to ethnomusicologists? For one thing, it tells us things about the culture of classical music, as the desire to see in music something beyond itself has long been a significant strand of thought among lovers of Western classical music, especially of the last 200 years, and it was rather with sorrow that scholars had to conclude that the association was Schering's alone, and probably not Beethoven's. This misguided foray can lead us to contemplate one approach to musical meaning in twentieth-century Western art music culture. Did Beethoven have to have consciously set out to write works based on specific literature in order for there to be a valid association? The composer's intention is important for an understanding of his life and work. But for an ethnomusicological view of a culture, there might be further considerations. If the association of Beethoven and Cervantes is not to be found in Beethoven's life, it might nevertheless become a valid association in the mind of the believing listener, and in other ways it could conceivably provide a guide for understanding the musical work. The notion of music as narrative, with motifs and melodies symbolizing specific events in a story, is a major feature of Western musical thought. The fact that literary and musical works are perceived to have similar structural characteristics is indicative of some aspects of the role that the arts play in Western culture. An ethnomusicologist also wonders what it is about a musical culture that would make a scholar look at Beethoven in this way, and why his findings were accepted, at least by some, and given up with reluctance. And the study of meaning in Beethoven's works has of course been continued, often critically, by many, recently including Robert Hatten (1994) and Lewis Lockwood (2003).

The second, much more fruitful landmark is the work of Leonard Meyer, particularly his groundbreaking book *Emotion and Meaning in Music* (1956), which became very influential, mainly because of its call for attention to the relationship of structure and meaning in music at large, and in individual musical "languages"—styles, cultures. Although asserting that "meaning and communication cannot be separated from the cultural context in which they arise" (ix), Meyer believed that there is a "general nature of musical meaning and its communication" that is valid cross-culturally, a musical universal. There are some things that music everywhere "does," and—I'm interpreting, not quoting, Professor Meyer—they have the commonality of a system of meaning and thus produce emotional effects that are in some sense universal.

The third landmark came out of the ethnomusicological research of David P. McAllester, whose 1954 work *Enemy Way Music*, is arguably the first major study that tries to investigate meaning and values of music in their cultural context. In another foray, J. S. Slotkin (1952) collected information about the Peyote songs and ceremonies of the Menominee people for McAllester. In the interviews, Slotkin continued to ask consultants about "meaning," for example, "What does that song mean?" "What do you mean when you sing?" "What do these special Peyote words like *heyowicinayo* or *heneyowe* mean?" What becomes clear in these interesting interviews with people who were quite at home in English is that "meaning" to them referred to the meaning of the words of the song, that a number of consultants would give quite different answers to the same question, but that they were willing to discuss meaning as it applied to the whole repertory of Peyote song more than in individual songs. One learned that interviews don't work particularly well for this kind of investigation, that meaning might be a very individual matter even in a small traditional society, and that meaning was to be found at a number of levels. Each of these three strands had its followers.

Legacies of Saussure and Peirce

Ethnomusicologists have approached the study of symbolism in a gingerly fashion, taking bites of the pie from different sides. As one might expect, they have been affected by music historians and by anthropologists, and have mixed the influences. The anthropological literature dealing with culture as a set of symbols, large and impressive, seems to me to have peaked in the 1970s. Most of it is derived from perspectives broadly labeled as structuralist, but one may separate those that derive mainly from linguistics from those that deal mainly with symbols in culture. Some of the representative publications are by Clifford Geertz (1971, 1973), Victor Turner (1974), Dan Sperber (1975), Mary Douglas (1966, 1970), Raymond Firth (1973), and particularly Claude Lévi-Strauss (1963, 1969, 1971, etc.). The work of linguists, philosophers, and structuralists dealing with literary art has also played a major role (see Barthes 1974; Sebeok 1994; Sturrock 1979). Levi-Strauss regards culture as "essentially a symbolic system or a configuration of symbolic systems" (Kaplan and Manners 1972: 171), and to him it is the symbolic nature of human behavior, perceived in its structure, that makes it "culture" as distinguished from nature. But anthropologists are also involved in the recognition of symbols, in the broad sense of the term (and of various related phenomena such as signs, similes, metaphors, master symbols, natural symbols, icons, indexes, etc.—described, e.g., by Firth 1973: 57–71), and despite the widespread acceptance of the symbol as the basis of culture, a group calling themselves "symbolic" anthropologists dealt with symbols as a special phenomenon within culture. Thus Firth (1973) separates certain areas of life as special carriers of symbolism: food, hair, flags, giving and getting.

An alternative to a behavioral approach to identifying symbols from a culture is to use language, the central symbolic code of humans, as a point of departure. I am speaking of a line of scholars known as "structural linguists" (in contrast to "structuralists" such as Lévi-Strauss), beginning, as I mentioned, with Saussure, going on through Roman Jakobson and Zellig Harris, to Noam Chomsky, and eventually to Thomas A. Sebeok, whose work led in part to that of the structuralists of a more general sort. The characteristic of the "structural" approach, it seems to me, is to study language, culture, or domains within culture as systems with structural principles that can be uncovered without reference to specific symbols or their objects, or to meaning, but with the underlying principle that human behavior is symbolic behavior. Thus, according to Sperber (Sturrock 1979: 28), what Lévi-Strauss did was neither "to decipher symbols nor to describe the symbolic code." He was interested in "systems of relationships" (30) that show how the human mind works. The connection with language may at times seem thin. But it may help to point out that the relationship between the structure or sound of a word and what it means is usually arbitrary, and that language is best analyzed through study of its internal interrelationships. This is what structuralists also say of culture, and it may be significant that anthropologists interested in symbolic studies have sometimes turned to music. Lévi-Strauss, especially, refers to music in many publications and is particularly noted for his use of musical forms as metaphoric titles of the sections in *The Raw and the Cooked* (1969), and for his analysis of Ravel's *Bolero* (1971; see also the analysis of his work in Hopkins 1977).

The most comprehensive system for the contemplation and understanding of signs, and the inventor of the field of semiotics as a discipline, was the American philosopher and scientist Charles Sanders Peirce (see Merrell 1997). His work, produced largely in the nineteenth century, was rather neglected by many students of symbols and signs, but came to be recognized more widely near the end of the twentieth century. Peirce, working primarily as a logician, established a highly complex system of signs, types of interpretants (kinds of reactions to signs), and processes described by Turino (1999); but the fundamental concepts are three primary types of signs: "icon," which signifies by being like what it stands for; "index," tied to its object by some kind of causal relationship; and "symbol," which is an arbitrary but agreed-on sign such as a word.

While some music scholars have followed structuralist and Peircian approaches, others have approached symbolism quite differently. For much of their history, following Hanslick's aesthetic and contradicting widely held and accepted concepts of the lay population, most of them have tended to avoid the subject. Recently they have become more sympathetic, sometimes basing their work on philosophers such as Cassirer (1944) and Langer (1942, 1953), who broadly interpret music as symbolic. Scholars such as Meyer (1956, 1967) and Cooke (1959) have argued the general relevance of symbolic studies for music. But mostly, historical musicology has dealt with one aspect of the symbolic universe, the attempts on the part of composers to signify specific, non-musical facts, events, or artifacts through music, and the degree to which these can be discovered in a particular cultural, historic, or personal context. Some have looked for particular musical styles and repertories in which symbolism rises to the surface and dominates, such as the literature of the so-called *Affektenlehre* of the late seventeenth and early eighteenth centuries (Bukofzer 1947: 388), and as suggested for the Renaissance by Lowinsky (1946; see also Brown 1976: 80, 130). Studies of individual composers (e.g., Hatten 1994, who tackled the oeuvre of Beethoven) and individual works (Samuels 1995, on Mahler's Sixth Symphony) characterize the literature of the 1990s.

Anthropology and historical musicology, in their approaches to symbolism, can perhaps be thus contrasted in their main thrusts: Anthropologists try to find ways in which culture as a whole and at large can be viewed as a system of symbols. The existence of such systems is taken for granted, and the issue is how to use the concept of symbolism as a window to the special character of human culture. The music historian, however, seeks evidence of specific symbolic systems in particular repertories and is less concerned with generalized theory. The musical semioticians who come from the field of music theory seem to me to occupy a middle ground.

As Though It Did Have a Life of Its Own

In ethnomusicology the symbol has a curious history. The concept draws together a number of otherwise separable ideas and methods. It is actually a short history, whose earliest theoretical statements come from the universalist aspects of German diffusionism (Danckert 1956; M. Schneider 1951). Nketia (1962) presents an early statement of the contrast of insider and outsider interpretation. Merriam (1964) included a chapter on "music as symbolic behavior" but found himself able to draw on only a small amount of literature, devoting himself to relatively general studies of symbolism in philosophy, questioning whether the "theory of signs and symbols is truly applicable to music," and concluding that music does "function as a symbolic part of life, at least in the sense that it does represent other things" (1964: 234). He proposed four ways in which this relationship is "manifest in human experience": (1) Art is symbolic in its conveyance of direct meanings. (2) Music reflects emotion and meaning. (3) Music reflects other cultural behavior, organization, and values. (4) In a very general sense, music may (Merriam phrases it as a question) symbolize human behavior in general. Since Merriam's work of 1964, the literature of symbolic anthropology has grown enormously, and thus the term "symbol" and its relatives and derivatives have become commonplace in ethnomusicological literature. In the 1970s, there seemed to be several areas in which the concept has been used: (1) Repertories, genres, types of music may within any given society have specific symbolic value. (2) Specific pieces of music, sections of pieces, devices, motifs, notes, tone colors, and so on, may also have specific symbolic value within a given society. (3) Music, mainly symbolic or not, can best be understood if examined in the way in which other systems acknowledged to be symbolic, such as language, are examined. Repertories or groups of pieces in the first, units of musical thought in the second, and minimal components of the musical vocabulary in the third would be units to be studied or to form the bases of opposition for structural analysis.

To put it another way: Some work in ethnomusicology looks for symbols in music, and some at music as a set of symbols. These two currents in the literature, widely separated at their beginnings, have come to approach each other, in parallel to anthropology and linguistics. The scholar seeking symbols in music deals with the issue in a culture-specific way, deriving particular systems such as ragas or program music from the nature of their culture. The school of musicological analysis that derives models and methods from linguistics conceives of the relationship of symbol and symbolized as less important than the structure of the system, and usually does not deal with the particular nature of the music analyzed and its relationship to the culture that produced it. From these currents, once only incidentally related, has come a closer union, clustered around concepts from semiotics—the science of signs—and from linguistics. The most ambitious statement of its position, a book by Nattiez (1971; see also 1972, 1973, 1975), deals with both the structural analysis and the cultural context of symbols. His 1971 work, translated and revised (Nattiez 1990), remains one of the major statements in the field of musical semiotics.

Charles Sanders Peirce's work has played a substantial role in musicological work of the period after 1970, appealing particularly to theorists and systematic musicologists (e.g., Karbusicky 1986; Lidov 1975). In ethnomusicology, specifically, it played a modest role (see, e.g., Feld 1987, 1994: 80–85), until the appearance of a significant contribution by Thomas Turino (1999), who proposed a comprehensive theory for the analysis of music in culture, using the Peircian principles and concepts, and providing illustrations from the cultures of American popular music, Zimbabwe, and Peru; his work on nationalism and identity in Zimbabwe (Turino 2000) is importantly based on Peircian principles.

If all music is a system of symbols, one ought to be able to analyze it in a way similar to or derived from the accepted analysis of the intellectual grandfather of symbol systems, human language. Reasons for doing so present themselves: in order to integrate music among the various symbol systems in culture; to take advantage of the precise and rigorous methods of analysis developed by linguists and their elegant way of stating findings; to establish a comprehensive method of analysis valid for all musics; to explore a significant aspect of the music/culture relationship; to show how much music is like language; and to help in understanding the relationship between music and words in song.

The results so far are mixed. Linguistic and semiological approaches to music have stated ambitious goals and sometimes given the impression that they will save analysis of the musical artifact as well as the study of music in culture from the many pitfalls of the past. In fact, the publications in this realm have largely been devoted to case studies showing the usefulness of linguistic methods for the analysis of the specific musical piece. Leaning on the suggestions of major figures in linguistics (Saussure and Jakobson), music scholars have gingerly and sporadically attempted to make some sample studies in the pretransformational period, with the phonemic procedures of the Prague school serving as models for stating distribution of musical segments. In a seminal article, Bright (1963) suggested a number of ways in which linguistics could help musicology. Later on, transformational and generative grammar exerted great influence on a number of disciplines, and a series of musicological publications ensued. Among the early ones the most influential was Boiles's (1967) study of a ritual of the Tepehua people of Veracruz, treating motifs in songs (without words) as elements in a generative grammar, where specific meanings appear to be assigned to the motifs, and the culture verbalizes the symbolic system. Related studies include Blacking's (1972) attempt to deal with "deep" and "surface" structures in Venda music in a somewhat idiosyncratic way, using concepts developed by Chomsky, and Cooper (1977), who proposed a grammatical system through which the scales of Indian ragas can be derived.

Feld (1974, 1994), Kneif (1974), and H. Powers (1980) are among the most significant critics of this path. Feld, speaking perhaps for others, seems to be asking, "Has it all been worthwhile?" The thoroughgoing revolution into semiotic analysis foreseen by some in the 1970s has not taken place. But even if no great leap forward has been achieved, there have been contributions with substance and valuable byproducts. In his critique Powers points out that the use of linguistic models adapted to music is only a stage in a long history of scholarship making use of comparisons between language and music, a history that includes early medieval music theorists and scholars of the German Renaissance and Baroque concerned with the relationship of music and rhetoric. In Europe, as well as other cultures, musicians and theorists have long used language as a model for explaining music and for teaching aspects of composition. Going far beyond modern linguistics and semiotics, Powers concludes that "language models for musical analysis used circumspectly can contribute fundamentally and not superficially to the musical disciplines, as they have more than once over the past millennium or so" (55).

And the musical-semiotic literature has made its contribution to some of the familiar issues of ethnomusicology, in slightly disguised form. The typical member of this group hopes to build a universally valid procedure, but the greatest successes have been achieved in certain instances particularly susceptible to linguistics-derived analysis. Powers (1980: 37–38) insists on the "close resemblance between the way Indian classical music works and the way languages work" and adds that "few musics are as much like language as Indian music is." The universalist-particularist dichotomy shows up again, with a special twist. Music may be like language, and Powers stresses the "real insight available to musicology" (not just ethnomusicology) "from a knowledge of the study of languages." Culture is symbols, and language may be a key, but a key that works better for some musics than others. In some cultures, Powers implies, music has been constructed in a way similar to the structure of language; in others it has been constructed rather differently, more influenced, one might guess, by dance, ritual, emotion—an interpretation that may be a residue of Curt Sachs's division of music into logogenic and pathogenic, word-born and emotion-born.

One of Steven Feld's main criticisms of linguistics-based analytical systems (1974) sounded a familiar trumpet: Such analysis does not take into account the culture from which the music comes. Powers (1980: 8) gently corrected: "Some music may sometimes be more efficiently interpreted by discussing it as though it did have a life of its own." Here perhaps is the old conflict of anthropology versus musicology again, but, if so, it is interesting to see that most of those ethnomusicologists who try their hand at this game would incline to throw in their lot with the anthropologists. Perhaps here, too, semiotics et cetera has given us a healthy mix, producing strange bedfellows but also a new kind of integration; the different camps are communicating, if not better, then more frequently.

But the publications to date, and the critiques of Feld and Powers, make it clear that uncritical attempts to use methods from linguistics at random on music often fail; the similarities between music and language are important, but the two differ in essence and at many levels. The players of the game have had to bend the system, and perhaps they did not bend it enough to provide musically useful results. The desire to cleave to linguistics, to approximate its exemplary rigor, may have overshadowed the musicological needs. But taking what is helpful—perhaps the concepts of phonemes and morphemes, transformation and generation, emic and etic—and leaving what is not seems more hopeful than the insistence on analogy. In particular, specific and direct knowledge of musics and their underlying theory can temper the dangers of excessive linguistic enthusiasm (Powers 1980: 55). Feld also points out the degree to which structural linguistics outside a context of cultural study falls short of the aim of many linguists (1974: 207).

Some ethnomusicologists—for example, Nattiez, much of whose work deals with Inuit musical cultures, Turino, and Feld—have participated in the general furthering of semiotic analysis in the discipline of music. But what is different about semiotics and the study of symbols, particularly for ethnomusicologists? I would think that the answer involves the (my) definition of ethnomusicology, as the study of music in culture and from an intercultural perspective. In drawing conclusions about a society's system of signs, we take into account all of its music, and we gather our data in the field and not from speculation. And in our own interpretations, we need to work at the interface of insider and outsider observations. The contributions of a specifically ethnomusicological nature have involved the study of non-Western cultures, and the different ways in which music functions as a system of signs, reflecting many things about culture. Much of this kind of work has been done without reference to semiotics or its terminology, but much—most—of the research that results in demonstrations of the relationship of musical culture to the rest of culture, in both structure and meaning, contributes to our understanding of music and each of its components as a "basic unit of culture and civilization."

Song of the Nightingale

The stately theme near the end of "The Moldau" by Smetana clearly represents the river flowing past the ancient Bohemian castle, Vyšehrad. The marching band in the parade sends shivers up some patriots' spines. The sound of jazz at one time used to remind people that they could break their routine, do the (at least slightly) illicit. Three kinds of musical symbol. But is it really the music that creates these effects, capable of meaning something other than itself? How, and to whom? Must the creator mean what the listener perceives? On the whole, ethnomusicology has eschewed the philosophical issues, but it has sometimes been concerned with defining symbol and symbolized, when a society does not articulate such a definition or provides no consensus.

Bach may or may not have cared whether melodic movement that accompanies certain concepts, such as sharply rising melody for references to sky, came to the awareness of his audience. One will ask whether the audience at any level understood the relationship, whether this kind of elaborate symbolism was lost on them, and what the significance of such a system was. The music historian is likely to treat the matter as a special accomplishment of Bach, regardless of its role in Bach's society, and its significance would not be diminished if it were found to be absolutely idiosyncratic to Bach. Ethnomusicologists might admire Bach's genius, but their main interest would be in the degree to which this way of composing was shared and understood.

If we wish, therefore, to look at Persian classical music with a view to learning something about symbolism, we should study the way in which it is perceived as a sign or symbol (in detail and as a whole) by the Iranian listener, and even by the Iranian who barely knows its sound and hardly ever listens to it. We begin by pointing out that around 1970 this music existed largely in the city of Tehran, was performed at most by a couple of hundred musicians and had an audience of only a few thousand but nevertheless was a symbol of something to many more. It was only one of many kinds of music to be heard in Tehran; there were many other styles and genres, Persian and foreign, and most people listened to, or consumed, several of these kinds of music and had opinions about others as well. One way of approaching this structure of styles in a symbolic context is to identify for each type of music a specific symbolic role. This is a view provided by the outsider-analyst, who may say that Western music in Iran is symbolic of the Westernized and industrialized sector of society, and of those aspects and values of the broadly shared culture that in the early 1970s were rapidly changing to a completely Western character—jet travel, Paris fashions, skyscrapers. Certain popular music, using orchestras of Western and of Middle Eastern origin—violins, santours, cellos, dombaks—may be symbolic of the mixture of Western and traditional elements in a vast number of everyday matters. Iranian classical music may appear as a symbol of the traditional and unchanging values of society, just as this particular music is thought to be unchanging. Well, such an outsider's classificatory approach may be a useful initial orientation, but we next ask whether this kind of symbolism is in fact perceived by Iranians. The question begs for a very detailed exposition, but there is really very little data that can be provided to shed light on this complex problem. Outright interviewing of informants regarding questions of symbolism did not in my experience seem to be productive, and I must therefore depend on observations of musical behavior and on analysis of statements about music that were made for other purposes. The following considerations seem to support the contentions listed above.

In a survey of attitudes about Persian classical music made among Tehranians in 1969, more or less at random, it turned out that many individuals who did not know or listen to classical music had strong opinions about it, regarding it as a great art or as an obsolete artifact no longer consonant with the culture, something frivolous or something ponderous. But there was agreement on its peculiar Persian-ness, and its actually close relationship to Arabic and Turkish music was played down. Classical music was considered something above the regional limitations of folk music (seen as the music of smaller population groups), a kind of music representing the nation. It was also regarded as something old, tying the Islamic present to the pre-Islamic past. As already pointed out, detailed analysis of the *radif* shows that important cultural values or principles are reflected in its structure. To go into somewhat greater detail, the importance of a hierarchical structure in society, balanced by the need for direct contact with a source of power and guidance (once the shah and later Khomeini, or the father of the extended family, or the university president), can be shown as a dominating principle in the *radif*, which itself holds the position of central figure in relationship to performances derived from it. During a period of study with a master, the various portions of the *radif* were first presented as equal in importance, all equally capable of producing music, but gradually a hierarchy among the sections was unveiled, some parts emerging as more important than others. Importance correlates with position (what comes first is more important than what comes later), with exceptionality (those parts of a unit that depart from its typical scalar, melodic, or rhythmic structure are important), with size (longer sections are more important), and with the element of surprise (unexpected deviations from a scale are singled out for attention, and nonmetric sections, rhythmically unpredictable, have priority over more or even completely metric materials).

Similarly, individualism, another central cultural value, is reflected in the importance of the exceptional, as just mentioned; in the centrality of improvised music, as compared to the composed; and in the theoretical absence of precise repetition. Another value, surprise, is reflected in similar ways. The position of what is important in social intercourse, the important coming first in informal situations but being preceded by introductory behavior or personnel in the more formal, is reflected in the precedence of what is important in the *radif;* something studied with one teacher and practiced in solitude, as compared to formal performance, where the material most closely based on the *radif* appears late and occupies less time.

Clearly, this is a personal interpretation, and its validity can only be established by analysis and logical argument. Nevertheless, it is interesting to see that other kinds of music in Iran do not share these values and characteristics to the same degree. In folk and popular music improvisation does not play the same central role; nor does the concept of hierarchy. Individualism of the sort exhibited by the accompanying system, the soloist a couple of notes ahead, is rarely evident. Ensembles playing in unison, absent in the central parts of classical performance, dominate the popular music, where surprising tones are rare and metric structure gives rhythmic predictability.

The extraction of cultural values from a plethora of behavior patterns, particularly in a complex society, is a risky business. But those mentioned are evidently among the ones that seem to have been present in Iranian culture for a long time and, judging from changes that have taken place during the last thirty years, they seem to be consistent and shared by the traditional and modernized segments of society. Others, perhaps involving reactions to change, come and go. Of course the classical music is relatively constant while styles of popular music change rapidly.

The structure of the classical music system gives clues to the way it may reflect culture and act as a symbol of aspects of culture, but equally important is the Iranian musician's perception of this structure and his or her theories about it. These are not always realistic, but nevertheless may inform us about the society's perception of the relationship of music and culture. For example, there is the belief that the *radif* is perfect, contains all that can be included in a musical system, is all-encompassing of emotion and meaning, and cannot be changed; and that it is larger in its scope than Indian and Arabic music, systems objectively at least roughly equal in scope, something Iranian musicians know but do not accept. The integrity of the *radif* reflects the often stated belief in the wholeness of Iranian culture. The idea that it does not change reflects the abiding importance of certain cultural values, and the documentable fact that the *radif* is actually a recent restructuring of older materials that has changed a good deal since 1900 is typically ignored. In 1968 one said about classical music those things that one wished to be able to say about the culture of Iran.

Iranians themselves have a symbol for the classical music that shows its association with what is good, Iranian, and traditional. It is the nightingale, thought by Persians to be particularly common in their nation, a bird that sings better than all others, and that—very important—is thought not to repeat itself in song, a symbol of the ancient cultural treasures of Iran, such as the poetry of the great literary figures of the late Middle Ages, or of Shiraz, a great cultural center, "city of roses and nightingales." It is a symbol in a particular sense, for it reflects idea and ideal. The theory that neither nightingales nor Iranian musicians repeat themselves ties music to central cultural values. Like the bird, the music is symbolic of the whole nation and all of its past.

Most of the world's societies find themselves in the twentieth century participating in two or more musics that can be rather easily distinguished, and the idea that each music functions as a symbol of particular aspects of a culture is a convenient approach to the study of one aspect of musical symbolism. In the culture of the Blackfoot during the 1960s, three kinds of music were distinguished by insiders and outsiders: older, traditional, tribal music; modernized intertribal or "pan-Indian" music; and Western music. The three had different values, the first as a symbol of the tribal past, to be remembered but placed in a kind of museum context; the second, of the need of Indian cultures to combine in order to assure people's cultural survival as Indians; and the third, of the modern facts of Indian life. Integration as a tribe, as an Indian people, and into the mainstream American environment are symbolized. The relationships seem obvious to an outsider, but they are also articulated by the culture's own interpretation of itself (Witmer 1973: 86–90).

McFee (1972: 92–102), looking at modern Blackfoot society, followed a similar line of thought, dividing the Blackfoot population and its values into white- and Indian-oriented groups. For Indian culture he lists individualism, bravery, skill, wisdom, and generosity; for white orientation, self-dependence, acquisition, and work. The two groups overlap, but one can find some of the Indian-oriented values in traditional music and musical behavior. Individualism is evident in the need for people, ideally, to learn their own songs in visions, and to develop personal repertories of songs, perhaps also in the tendency for traditional music to be soloistic or, when performed by groups, to avoid a high degree of vocal blend. Bravery can conceivably be related to the practice of singing before a group, sometimes with improvised texts, in a ceremony replicating courage in physical conflict. Generosity is exhibited in the system of giving songs, the willingness to borrow from and give to other tribes. The three "white" values given by McFee can be associated with "white" music and with the modern Indian music used by the Blackfoot. The use of notation and the ownership of complex instruments such as pianos and electric guitars can in various ways be associated with all three. Composition (in contrast to acquisition of songs through visions) is related to self-dependence. The importance of size of repertory in the modern genres and the idea of rapid learning with the use of tape recorders are relevant to the value of acquisition. The practice of rehearsing and the conscious development of complex performance styles in the modern Indian music can be related to the value of work.

He Rides an Elephant among the Hills and Valleys

There is no intrinsic relationship between ascending melodic contour and going to heaven, but if this is the way a group of people agree to represent the Ascension, then a symbol has been created. Among the issues for ethnomusicology is the identification of general or specific symbol systems that might be interculturally valid, and I have explored one possible symbolic universal, the association of styles or repertories with major divisions of a culture, and perhaps can go no further in that direction. Let's turn instead to some of the many cultures in which explicitly symbolic systems exist within restricted repertories.

Probably the most widely known scheme is found in Indian classical music, in which ragas were frequently assigned nonmusical character. Associations range from season and time of day to attributes such as love, devotion, and aggression, to specific natural events such as fire and rain, and on to highly specialized images (also represented in paintings—see Capwell 2002), for example: "A youth, wearing a red cloth . . . he rides an elephant among the hills and valleys, at night, singing heavenly songs" (Deva 1974: 21), for raga *Deepak*. The existence of the system is well documented. Among the questions not thoroughly understood is the degree to which listeners in general are or were aware of and affected by the association. One should discover how essential the symbolic system is to an understanding of the music, whether it is thoroughly believed by musicians or simply used as an explanatory device for laypersons, much as teachers of music appreciation have sometimes explained the strictly musical difference between major and minor by associating it with the concepts of "happy" and "sad."

While the association of ragas with nonmusical things seems to have been well established in India at one time (though gradually lost on both audiences and musician—Deva 1974: 21), similar systems less widely accepted in their own cultures and less standardized exist or existed in the Middle East. The supposed extramusical character of the ancient Greek modes has been widely discussed and their traits—inspiration of enthusiasm for the Phrygian, sadness for the Mixolydian, and so on—attributed to interval sequences, range of scale, a particular type of music cast in a given tonality. We have little idea whether in Greece the Mixolydian music caused listeners to be sad and, if so, whether because of the characteristics of the mode; or whether other things about that music, cast by chance in the Mixolydian mode, associated it with sadness; or for that matter whether it simply made listeners aware that a quality of sadness was present, without in fact changing their mood. It's an issue that goes beyond symbolism, involving even music therapy, a subject only occasionally touched upon by ethnomusicologists (see Densmore 1927b; Robertson 1974), and yet it is an example of the direct practical use of a symbolic system.

Caron and Safvate (1966: 59–98) gave nonmusical characteristics of the *dastgahs,* the units analogous to modes, in Persian music. Thus the *dastgah* of *Shur* expresses tenderness, love, and pity, and incites sadness but also consoles. *Segah* represents sadness, chagrin, abandonment of hope, but *Chahargah,* which shares melodic motifs and many other details with *Segah,* though not the scalar interval sequence, gives the impression of strength. *Mahour* represents dignity and majesty. In my experience, Iranian musicians, asked to identify such nonmusical traits, tend to agree, but with moderate enthusiasm, typically suggesting that these considerations are not important in their everyday thinking about music. They may also disagree with Caron and Safvate, and among themselves, about the specific nonmusical traits of the modes. Thus *Chahargah* is said by some to be profoundly moving but by others to be warlike. Some ascribe to *Dashti* a plaintive, moving quality; others maintain that it is happy. But there are further ramifications. Rather specific characterizations can be found: One musician described *Shur* as an old man looking back at his life, finding much sadness but philosophically accepting it. When asked for the reasons for this association, he connected *Shur's* meditative, poetic, somber character with his perception of the Iranian personality and the nature of Iranian history, varied but prevailingly sad. And with this special Persian-ness also was associated the great significance of *Shur,* the most important *dastgah,* known indeed, because others are derived from it, as the "mother of dastgahs." The *dastgah* of *Chahargah* is warlike because outside the classical system it is thought to be used for chanting heroic epic poetry; indeed, a good deal of the chanting of the text of the *Shah-Nameh* by

Ferdowsi, while not truly in *Chahargah*, coincides or is compatible with its scale. The components of the symbolic system feed into each other in a chicken-and-egg situation.

A complex thing to comprehend. Do the *dastgahs* or ragas symbolize characteristics that can be abstracted in adjectives, or ideas about the aspect of culture with which they are associated, or are they simply related to uses and words of particular genres? We wish to know who in the consuming public shares in this system, and how much agreement there must be for us, as ethnomusicologists, to accept it as truly a part of the culture. Like music historians, ethnomusicologists seem to jump at the chance to find associations of such a qualitative sort between music and culture, and the tendency to accept them without taking these points into consideration may tell more about the cultural background of ethnomusicologists than about that of the music.

The concept of "program music" was developed in Western culture, and we are hardly in a position to say that other cultures also have it. Even the apparently related phenomena vary enormously. The parallels between *dastgahs* and the tone poems of Richard Strauss are modest at best. Australian aboriginals in Yirkalla use a different scale for ceremonial songs of each lineage, which, according to Richard Waterman (1956: 46), permits them to be identified at a distance even when the words are indistinct. The association seems to be arbitrary, the relationship somewhat like that of the sound of a word to the content it symbolizes.

But in a way close to that of nineteenth-century Europe, Chinese classical music, also in the nineteenth century, featured a genre of solo instrumental piece thought to represent images, scenes, objects, or even battles (F. Lieberman 1969; Malm 1977: 159, 1969), with titles such as "High Mountain, Flowing Stream," "Great Wave Washes the Sand," or "An Embroidered Purse." With a little effort, the Western listener can empathize, but whether there are aspects of a piece that are definitive symbols of water, ornamental art, or mountains does not seem to be stated in Chinese literature. Yet the association does not seem arbitrary—it has iconic as well as symbolic aspects.

At the other end of the continuum are some love songs of the northern Plains Indians, which may also be played on the flute. Singers often end such songs with two short, high cries or calls, using indefinite pitches related to the scale of the rest of the melody. When played on flutes, these songs end up with short "cries" on the instrument, in this case of definite pitch, but using tones outside the scale already established. The vocal cries are symbolized—not merely imitated—on the flute because of their relationship to the scalar structure.

In learning about music of the Shona people of Zimbabwe, I came upon an interesting conundrum parallel to Schering's idiosyncratic interpretation of Beethoven. Abraham Dumisani Maraire (1971), a well-known Shona musician and educator, explained the structure of a group of pieces, which he played on the *nyunga-nyunga mbira* or *karimba* and sang, by referring to the life of the human body. Beginning and ending on a basic pattern, for which the concept of a skeleton is used as metaphor, the musician, going through several required steps, adds to it thematic material, which is varied in many ways, fleshing it out, as it were, developing a more complex texture, then gradually dropping the elaboration and returning to the simple basic pattern. Maraire presented this music as a symbol of life and perhaps also of death, as only the skeleton is left at the end. The interpretation fitted perfectly, it seems to me, but I was interested to find that distinguished scholars of Shona music doubted its authenticity to the culture, maintaining that it was not something on which Shona musicians agreed, but idiosyncratic to Maraire. He "simply made it up," and it's not part of Shona culture, I was told. They were right; but can one simply leave it at that, or should we consider that Maraire's interpretation is an idiosyncratic but definitely a Shona interpretation that has some ethnographic validity? Was it something that Maraire created, as he was one of the first Shona musicians to perform abroad, to help him interpret Shona music to outsiders? If he had presented this interpretation to colleagues in Zimbabwe, might they have said, "Yes, that makes sense to us, but we never thought of our music that way?" Is there *a* Shona interpretation of that form? Complicated.

These are a few examples, and I have not even mentioned symbolism of instruments, musicians, musical occasions and rituals. With or without the use of formal methods of semiotics, structuralist or culture-oriented, it seems that there is almost no end to the number of ways in which we could illustrate the kinds of symbolic associations between music and something else in culture, the ways music functions as various types of sign, the number of ways in which music can have meaning—and no end to the different ways in which musical symbolism can be contemplated, explored, and interpreted.

23

Location, Location, Location!
Interpreting Geographic Distribution

Areas, Circles, Clusters

Through most of the history of ethnomusicology, the most important factor in providing information has been "location, location, location." Just as
in real estate. The first thing one has been told about an instrument, a musical style, or a genre has been "where" it is found on the map. Making a musical atlas of the world—sometimes with actual maps, more often in prose
form (e.g., *Garland Encyclopedia of World Music* 1997–2002) has been one of
our principal long-term ambitions. And once location was established, we
searched for reasons for the geographic distribution of a phenomenon, and
went on to speculate about what this might tell us about its history. Through
much of the twentieth century, these kinds of questions dominated ethnomusicological discourse. In the late twentieth century, they continue to play
a substantial role, but they are modified by two factors. One concerns the increased interest in processes compared to products, which means that we are
also more interested in how styles, genres, instruments move around the
world, and we have come to recognize that they did (and even more, now do)
move a lot more than they stay put. And with the enormously increased speed
in and opportunity for communication, culminating (so far) in the Internet
and cell phones, which means that communication is instantaneous and the
location of communicators or recipients of information may be known to
neither, talking about an abstract and ephemeral phenomenon such as music
in geographic terms loses much of its significance. This excursion into mu-

sical map-making is thus largely a foray into disciplinary history. Still, we haven't given up our cartographic proclivities entirely.

In drawing the singing map of the world, ethnomusicologists have mainly been inspired by three concepts developed early in the history of anthropology and folklore. The approach most clearly descriptive and found acceptable for the longest time is based on the so-called culture area concept, developed by American anthropologists and said by Driver (1961: 12) to be "a convenient way of describing the ways of life of hundreds of peoples covering a whole continent or a larger part of the earth's surface." First used in 1895 (Harris 1968: 374), it originated in the need to map and classify the large number of tribal groups of the Americas and especially the objects in museums that related to them.

On the surface, the concept seems simple enough. A group of peoples living in contiguous distribution and having similar kinds of subsistence, use of energy, social organization, religion, arts, and so on, would belong to one culture area. On the map, the boundaries between culture areas appear rigid, but anthropologists recognized that they "are actually the approximate lines where two neighboring types of phenomena are present in equal amounts" (Driver 1961: 13).

Culture areas have always been useful as purely classificatory devices. But it was probably inevitable that certain features of culture, such as the method of food production, would be stressed over others and thus weight the distributional statement. Moreover, it was quickly found that a group of societies assigned to the same culture area did not share in its culture type with equal intensity. For example, the Plains Indians of North America, a group of peoples with diverse origins, as indicated by their linguistic diversity, shared in the Sun Dance as a major ceremonial occasion. But the Sun Dance was developed differentially, taking its most complex form from the Arapaho, in whose culture it was also most dominant. Thus, early on, anthropologists found themselves using the culture area concept as the basis for historical interpretation. Kroeber proposed the theory that a culture area has a center, or "climax," in which the characteristic culture of the area is most developed; from this again grew the speculation that the main features of the area diffused from the center to the outlying, more marginal regions and continued until they met and merged with the diffusion of contrastive traits from a neighboring culture center. The use of the culture area concept developed among anthropologists who were concerned with Native American cultures, and it worked best when applied there and to other areas comprised of many small nations. But the idea of the culture area as an automatic guide to history was widely questioned from the beginning (Harris 1968: 375–77).

The so-called German diffusionist school, known because of its strong interest in historical interpretations as the "kulturhistorische Schule" (see Lowie 1937: 171–95; Schmidt 1939), provided a second approach. Comprised of research by such scholars as Leo Frobenius, Fritz Graebner, and Wilhelm Schmidt, and to a large degree based on studies in Oceania and of physical artifacts, the concept developed in this school came to be known as "Kulturkreis," that is, culture circle. Like the culture area concept, a culture circle is a statement that a number of peoples share a group of culture traits. These peoples need not be geographically contiguous, and since one society may have a number of trait clusters each of which is shared with a different group of peoples, it may be a part of several "Kulturkreise." Since the diffusion of elements from various points to one culture must have occurred at different points in time, the various culture circles in which a society shares also represent strata in its history. The relatively dogmatic approach of this school of thinkers, and their insistence that all similarities of culture traits result from diffusion, eventually made their approach unacceptable to most anthropologists.

The distinction made earlier between content and musical style may be helpful here. The culture area and Kulturkreis concepts both involve the *style* of culture, perhaps drawing together societies that use the same way of organizing a pantheon while not requiring belief in specifically the same gods. They expect similarities in social organization but not in terminology, in the nature of story-telling events but not in the content of the stories. But the third of these early approaches, the so-called historical-geographic method in folklore, involves the geography of *content*. Its practitioners traced the versions, variants, and forms of a story, song, or riddle, and showed the clustering of their distribution, and then drew conclusions about its history. Thus a particular story with characters and significant actions would be plotted on the map, but function, length, the narrative style itself, were generally ignored. Developed by Scandinavian scholars who in turn influenced a number of Americans (see W. Roberts 1958; Thompson 1946), and applied mainly to tales but also occasionally to ballad stories (Kemppinen 1954), the method compared versions by degree of similarity and intensity of geographic distribution, developing archetypes of events and characters, and hoping to reconstruct the story's original form and the place it was created. For example, in his classic history of the "Star-Husband" tale, a story of the marriage of two girls to stars followed by their return to earth to bring important elements of culture, widespread among North American Indians, Stith Thompson (1953) showed that its origin was likely to have been in the Central Plains but that special characteristic forms developed later on the Northwest Coast, while fragmentary versions developed on the outskirts of this area of distribution.

Questions of Space and Time

Nobody, quite rightly I think, pays very much attention to the German diffusionists of the early twentieth century any longer, but for a long time they had a substantial impact on ethnomusicology and on some of its most distinguished founders. They seem to have had more of a role in ethnomusicology than in anthropology itself, where these "Kulturkreis" theorists had a checkered career. A powerful but rather isolated group of scholars, working in the firm belief that they were discovering laws of behavior, first aroused the curiosity of the large group of Americans led by Franz Boas, then repelled them with their dogmatic approach. One finds them also being rather ignored by the French sociologists and structuralists and by the British social anthropologists, their work the subject of conflicting critiques of their espousal of unilinear cultural evolution and their nomothetic views of culture history. Some of the members were eventually blamed for a religious bias and then for supporting racist and political excesses. After World War II, their approach was largely abandoned by anthropology but lasted longer in ethnomusicology and became the basis for several specific theories of history, though in the end, they were criticized as wild-eyed fantasy. Even some of the sharpest critics felt obliged to praise the broad knowledge and suggestiveness of the Kulturkreis school. Lowie (1937: 177) respected the seriousness of their approach, Merriam (1964: 289) believed that aspects of their method "remain to be well used in studying diffusion problems of more restricted scope" (than of the globe), and Wachsmann (1961: 143) asserted, in a discussion of Hornbostel and Sachs, that German diffusionism was useful, at least as a working hypothesis.

In his extremely detailed account of the relationship between the Kulturkreis school and musical studies, Albrecht Schneider pointed out that some of the prominence of the diffusionist anthropologists resulted from the participation of comparative musicology (1976: 66). Some of the earliest Kulturkreis work, for example, is based on the mentioned studies of instrument distributions by Ankermann (1902), Wieschoff (1933), and of course Sachs and Hornbostel. Other prominent figures in the history of ethnomusicology worked with Kulturkreis concepts—Marius Schneider, Werner Danckert,

Walter Wiora. Merriam (1964) was attracted by the school's contribution to an understanding of instrument distributions and their historical implications. Indeed, Albrecht Schneider (1976) found several quite diverse strands of the history of musicological thought to be also part of the history of this school. Here are a few examples of the kinds of thinking that I am talking about. In all of it, however, it is important to remember that the basic uninventiveness of humankind, and the resulting assumption that any phenomenon is likely to have been invented only once and then diffused from its place of origin, are the points of departure. In retrospect, it seems to me that what attracted music scholars to the Kulturkreis school was its comprehensive view of human history and its nomothetic quality. They constitute a very interesting chapter in the history of our field, but one consisting of grand schemes gone awry.

Early in his career, Curt Sachs proceeded to map the distribution of all musical instruments, a formidable task even for one with his comprehensive knowledge of the literature. In what was perhaps his most ambitious book (1929), he organized his findings in twenty-three areas, which he then placed in historical order on the basis of distributional criteria as well as technological level. For example, stratum 7 includes Polynesia and parts of South America, the whistling pot, double-row panpipes, and bone buzzers. Stratum 13 comprises Indonesia and East Africa and includes the "earliest metal instruments," various kinds of xylophones and board zithers. Stratum 18 extends from Indonesia to Madagascar, dates from about the first century C.E. and is characterized by the tube zither. Hornbostel (1933) used a similar approach to establish twelve instrument areas for Africa. Sachs later went on to simplify, combining most of his twenty-three strata into three groups (1940: 63–64), but began to have doubts about the kind of detailed historical speculation in which he had engaged: "The geographic method, too, may prove fallacious. . . . Nevertheless, geographic criteria are safer than any other criteria" (63). Few today pay much attention to this work of Sachs, but no one seems to have tried a better or more comprehensive statement.

The tunings of instruments have also been the subject of interpretations derived from the thinking of the Kulturkreis school (but see also chapters 4 and 19). Some of Hornbostel's most prominent works (1910, 1911, 1917) involve the belief that panpipes were tuned with the use of a circle of fifths produced by overblowing. Instead of "pure" fifths of 702 cents (with 100 cents to the tempered semitone), the "blown" fifths were thought to comprise only 678 cents. Scales presumably derived from this interval were found on instruments in Melanesia and South America, giving rise to speculation about prehistoric connections. The theory turned out to have weaknesses, especially in the accuracy of measurement, and was exploded by Bukofzer (1937), among others. A. M. Jones (1964) tried to show the tunings of Indonesian and African xylophones to be similar and, with other factors, to point to a common origin of aspects of music style of the two areas. Jones was harshly criticized (Hood 1966) for methodological weaknesses, but the common origin of the two xylophone groups remains a possibility.

One of the major tenets of the Kulturkreis school was a belief in a particular order of events in world history, linking subsistence and social structure (discussed in detail by Harris 1968: 384–85). Although several stages and circles give the appearance of a complex picture, in essence the belief is that gathering cultures preceded and changed to hunting cultures, which added herding and cultivating activities, from the combination of which sprang the high cultures. This order of events was used for musical extrapolations by various scholars. Marius Schneider (1957: 12–14), in considering tribal musics, correlated style with culture and adds chronology. Hunters have much shouting and little tonal definition; cultivators have an "arioso style . . . the style is tonally regulated and form is rounded off" (13). Pastoral cultures, said Schneider, occupy a middle position. Accepting the important role of women as cultivators (and following Schmidt's notion of the matriarchate as the dominant social structure when agriculture became the norm of food production), Schneider believed that where men are more influential, one finds predominance of meter and contrapuntal polyphony; where it is women, predominance of melody and harmony.

Schneider also used geographic areas in his major work (1934), a history of world polyphony. Stressing the tonal relationships among the voices, he found four areas, noncontiguous in the Kulturkreis mold: (1) The area of variant-heterophony is sporadically distributed worldwide. (2) In Southeast Asia, Melanesia, and Micronesia one finds various kinds of voice relationships, with each voice holding to a different and unique tonal organization. (3) Characterized by but not limited to Polynesia, the third area exhibits more varied relationship among the voices. (4) Much of Africa is characterized by the tendency to homophony. More data would have allowed Schneider to extend these areas, but here we have an example of musical distributions arrived at essentially in the way in which the German diffusionists dealt with other culture traits.

Relationships between the Balkans, the region around the Black Sea, and Indonesia, resulting from a presumed migration around 800 B.C., were taken up by Jaap Kunst (1954), who noted similarities in several musical instruments and thus established something like a musical Kulturkreis of a rather early date. It has the traits expected in a culture circle, but the similarities are so modest and their basis, the presumed migration of the Tocharians (A. Schneider 1976: 212–18), so hypothetical that little has been made of this finding. Werner Danckert, in his studies of European folk music, also made use of the Kulturkreis concept in the sense of noncontiguous distribution and the establishment of strata, dealing with styles as well as distribution of tunes and tune types, and also with aspects of musical culture such as symbolism, kinesics, and physical features of humans (A. Schneider 1979: 23–27).

Evidently German diffusionists had more lasting impact on ethnomusicological literature than did many other theoretical movements from cultural anthropology. They also influenced scholars who did not associate themselves directly with their theories. Thus Wiora, in one example, notes the common elements of the music of herding peoples in the Alps, Scandinavia, Mongolia, and Tibet (1975: 84), without, however, claiming that these regions are part of a culture circle. Herzog's explanation of the fact that American Indian game and story songs usually contrast with other songs in their repertories but share an intertribal style because they are part of an archaic layer underlying later strata (1935b: 33) sounds amazingly like a Kulturkreis statement, despite Herzog's personal disinclination to accept the school's axioms and methods. Indeed, if one removes the quality of dogma from Sachs's basic axioms but regards them as statements that express likelihood, tendency, regularity, one can hardly disagree with him when he writes: "The object or idea found in scattered regions of a certain district is older than an object found everywhere in the same area. [And] objects preserved only in remote valleys or islands are older than those used in the open Plains" (1940: 62). The fact that music and instruments are relatively complex phenomena in human culture compared to certain implements or perhaps folk stories makes the insistence on a single point of origin relatively credible.

Drawing the Map

So how do you put music on a map? It's more complicated than is the case for a lot of data in socio-cultural anthropology or archeology, where one can often just say that something is simply present or absent in a culture. Artifacts may of course be broken down into components. For a particular type of string instrument, one might map the number of strings, the material from which the instrument is made, its shape, and so on (this was done for

Swedish dulcimers known as *hummel* by Walin 1952). Dealing with musical styles may require more finesse, because one might need to identify relationships among forms that are not identical and similar under the surface, and reject as unrelated some that may on the surface seem alike. As noted already in my consideration of similarity and difference (chapter 9), questions that might arise could ask which of various similar tunes are actually variants of one basic type, or whether two slightly different pentatonic scales are really subtypes of one form.

There is, moreover, the problem of deciding on geographic units to be used as a basis for statements of distribution—should they be determined by political affiliation, language, or physical geography, or are we plotting the distribution of a trait among villages or perhaps even families? As in speech, each individual has his or her own musical idiolect (Vander's songprints) and so one person could even conceivably be considered as the minimal unit of cultural geography. But for practical purposes, the linguistic, cultural, natural, and political units encompassing homogeneous groups of people have had to serve. Several ways of making musical maps have been used.

The distribution of individual elements, components, or parameters of music, such as scale type or specific instrument, may be most easily treated. The literature provides many examples, among them Baumann's (1976) study of yodeling in Switzerland. Although geographic distribution was not his main purpose, he provided a map indicating yodeling types in a large number of Swiss locations, using towns and villages as the main units of reference. More elaborately but schematically, using charts instead of maps, Alan Lomax's cantometrics studies (e.g., 1968) give distributions of individual elements or parameters, using large culture areas as units. Charting presence or absence of a trait yields information to the effect that culture A has rhythmic types X and Y, and culture B types Y and Z, but of course we would wish also to indicate relative quantity. More recently, Dale Olsen (1986) provided a scheme for accounting comprehensively and geographically for the many musics of Peru, focusing on individual traits.

Music can be reduced to its stylistic features or elements. It therefore makes little sense not to go beyond the mere "presence-or-absence" statement of distribution. There are, after all, few characteristics of music not found in a vast number of cultures, but in some they are overwhelming and in others they play an insignificant role. Statements of proportion are needed. Thus, when Collaer (1958: 67), in one of the earliest publications dealing explicitly with the problem, proposed the desirability of mapping the distribution of the anhemitonic pentatonic scale (like the black keys), he must have had in mind some sort of quantitative approach, for compositions using such a scale are found in most cultures. A statement of the strength of this scale in each repertory, for example, would show that it is found in the vast majority of Cheremis songs, in about half of those of the Native American Plains, with some frequency in India, rather rarely in Iran. Looking much farther back, the by now fabled Neanderthal flute found in Slovenia may have two major seconds, but no one knows whether this was normal Neanderthal tuning, or one of many arrangements, or an off-the-wall experiment by one individual. Sampling is always a problem.

Since studies of the percentage of compositions in a repertory that contain a given trait are still not common, let me give a brief example, based on small samples of varying reliability, and not even close to definitive, to show how such a study might work in a bit of detail. It concerns a phenomenon in Native American music known in the literature as the "rise," identified and so designated by George Herzog (1928). In a song with nonstrophic structure, a short section is repeated at least twice, then followed by another bit of music at a slightly higher average pitch, followed, in turn, by the lower part. This alternation can continue for some time, but the lower section tends to appear more than once at a time, while the higher or "rise" section is less frequent.

Herzog's description and terminology apply to some of the Yuman-speaking peoples of the southwestern United States, but somewhat similar forms are also found elsewhere. The rise actually occurs in the music of a fairly large number of nations along both coasts of the United States, given their locations when first discovered and disturbed by whites, and from data published or recorded largely before 1960. It is strongest, occurring in over 50 percent of the songs, among several of the Yuman tribes of the Southwest, and among the Miwok, Pomo, Maidu, and Patwin of central California. In the repertories of the Northwest Coast Tsimshian and the southeastern Choctaw, it occurred in 20–30 percent of the songs; among the northeastern Penobscot and the northwestern Nootka, in 10–20 percent; and in the songs of the Kwakiutl as well as the southeastern Creek, Yuchi, and Tutelo, in less than 10 percent. Provided the sample is minimally reliable, the rise had a center of distribution in the southwestern United States and thinning-out strength across the southern part of the country and up both coasts. This information might be interpreted in various ways—and questioned because identical form may not indicate related meaning or function—but it is in any case more valuable than a simple statement that these musics "have" the rise.

While we could follow certain distinct musical features throughout the world and get one kind of picture or map, we might approach the entire problem of cartography from the point of individual compositions, pieces or songs. As already discussed in chapter 8, our first problem would be to determine the identity of such a unit of musical creativity. But data for the distribution of the variants of songs and pieces (and for configurations and clusters of pieces) are available in European folk music (e.g., Hungarian Academy of Sciences 1992). For the rest of the world, there is less, but one early and classic example by Willard Rhodes (1958) tracing the opening song of the Peyote ceremony among several Plains and southwestern United States tribes comes to mind. The discovery of similar or almost identical tunes in the folk music of Hungary and the Cheremis (Kodály 1956: 24–57)—and their absence among the Finns, who are linguistically close to the Cheremis—leads to questions about the behavior of music relative to other domains of culture. More detailed investigation of this kind would show whether a number of songs coincide in their geographic distribution and thus form areas, or whether each song has a unique distribution, and whether such areas coincide with those of style.

There have been some attempts to provide comprehensive geographical statements about musical cultures, including musical artifacts, instruments, and aspects of musical life. Among the most recent is an atlas of musical culture in western Rajasthan (Neuman, Chaudhuri, and Kothari 2002) that indicates, village by village, the presence and strength of genres, musician types, instruments, and much more. This very intensive presentation contrasts with two projects, Alan Lomax's "Universal Jukebox" and Daniel Neuman's "Musical Pilot," whose aim was largely educational, using elaborate computer programs to enable students to find the locations of various musical traits.

The Singing Globe

While trying to learn how to draw musical maps, a few ethnomusicologists have also tried to see how music is distributed through the whole world—or *was* distributed, before the eras of colonialism and globalization. They encountered old acquaintances—problems measuring similarity, the tribulations of comparative method, and the temptations of universals. The history of attempts to divide the globe into musical areas is interesting because of basic assumptions and method. Collaer and Lomax depended on one or a few heavily weighted criteria.

Collaer (1960: pl. 1), on the basis of a few societies, divided the world into several *zones musicales* based entirely on scalar structure, distinguishing "pre-pentatonic," "anhemitonic-pentatonic," "heptatonic," and others. Assuming the existence of a typical, central musical style for any large group of cultures, he ignored the obvious—that Europe has seven-tone and five-tone scales in great quantity, and that seven-tone scales are found in China—and assigned Europe into the seven-tone area and China into the pentatonic category.

Using far more criteria, more sophisticated statistically, and showing a willingness to subdivide the world more closely, Lomax (1968: 75–110) also required the problematic concept of centrality. A "favored song style" (133) is diagnostic of each of fifty-seven areas. He established a group of naturally or culturally determined areas and then described the musical style of each, testing its degree of internal homogeneity and its similarity to others. It is interesting to see that some of his areas are far more unified than others. Essentially, however, he describes the music of culture areas rather than providing musical areas.

In an earlier publication, however, Lomax (1959) divided the world into ten musical styles, largely on the basis of what is usually called performance practice. Separating styles that he labels American Indian, Pygmoid, African, Australian, Melanesian, Polynesian, Malayan, Eurasian, Old European, and Modern European, he grouped some styles in correlation with geographic or readily recognized culture areas. In others, however, he identified styles that do not so correlate, among them the Eurasian, Old European, and Modern European, three varieties of European folk song, to the first of which he also appended most of Asia. The distinctions among the European styles are insightful: The Eurasian is "high-pitched, often harsh and strident, delivered from a tight throat with great vocal tension" (1959: 936). Old European is "relaxed . . . facial expression lively and animated . . . unornamented" (936). The modern European style is hybrid, physically and musically, between the other two. In his attempt to deal with the world, it is obvious that Lomax had a lot of experience in European folk music, while his combination of most of Asia into a single area indicates less experience in this domain. But Lomax's ten major areas may actually be the least unsatisfactory grouping of the various musical globes.

Another theory of musical distribution appeared in an appendix to the history of melody by Bence Szabolcsi (1959), the Hungarian music historian, who dealt with the question of world musical geography more holistically than have most others. He did not confine himself to the presumably less volatile folk and tribal musics but considers classical systems as well. Relating musical styles to geographic factors such as river valleys and access to the sea, he saw the musical map as a combination of areas with boundaries and of a patchwork resulting from musical differences of locales with varying degrees of isolation. Generalizing about principles of musical distribution, he concluded: (1) Musical life is closely tied to the natural divisions of the earth. (2) Geographically "closed" areas preserve musical styles, while open ones favor change and exchange, providing a venue for the development of cultivated or classical systems. (3) The center standardizes and unifies materials developed throughout the area, while the margins develop and preserve diversity. (4) Diffusion of musical styles from the center is the typical process of music history; the longer a musical style exists, the further it becomes diffused. (5) The unity of archaic folk music styles is evidence of the most ancient intercultural contacts (313). Here is a set of fundamental hypotheses on which one can build a cultural geography of music.

Szabolcsi gave these as a set of preliminary conclusions. Developed on the basis of musical data alone, they lead to a concept somewhat like the American culture area, which coincides, according to Kroeber (1947), with a natural area. Unity is at the center, the source of diffusion, and there's variety at the edges. As a matter of fact, the idea of a musical area with a strong center and a more diffuse outer circle can also be found in other interpretations of the geographic-stylistic structure of European art music. Reese (1954) in his survey of Renaissance music described an area in which the "central musical language" of the Renaissance developed—France, Italy, the Low Countries—which was subsequently and gradually introduced to a peripheral area: Spain, Germany, England, and eastern Europe.

Szabolcsi's as well as Kroeber's conceptualizations are related to older theories to the effect that normal cultural distribution comprises a progressive center and marginal survivals. Once widely used by folklorists, it is generally associated with an old and obsolete definition of folklore as *gesunkenes Kulturgut*. Developed by German scholars of the nineteenth and early twentieth centuries such as Rochus von Liliencron and Hans Naumann (see Danckert 1939: 9–12; Naumann 1921: 4–6; Pulikowski 1933: 167–68), the concept suggests that folk songs, tales, riddles, and beliefs are remnants or imitations of practices developed at culture centers such as cities and courts, where they had been abandoned in favor of further developments and left to live as archaisms in the surrounding countryside. As a general theory of folklore, the concept was quickly abandoned, but it might apply in individual cases. For example, the hurdy-gurdy was once used at western European courts and in churches, but after the Middle Ages it became mainly a folk instrument. But the tendency for artifacts to be retained at the margins of an area when they are superseded in the center has been noted and explains some of the musical effects of emigration in diasporic situations.

Musical Areas

Given the generally geographic orientation of ethnomusicologists, it's surprising that studies of the distribution of musical styles, of clusters of traits, or of the total configuration of elements have not been carried out all that widely, given the rather basic quality of this information for other kinds of study. A number of publications have made general statements of distribution. Slobin (1976), for example, distinguished several subcultures in northern Afghanistan, stating their common characteristics as well as their differences. Merriam (1959: 76–80) divided Africa into seven musical areas coinciding more or less with the culture areas established by Herskovits. McLean (1979), in a statistically and geographically sophisticated study, established musical areas for Oceania, separating musical structure from instruments, though the distribution of each shows broad correlation with the conventionally recognized culture areas. Twenty years later, McLean (1999) provided a more comprehensive, also geographically oriented, synthesis of the musical cultures of Polynesia. In a collection of American folk songs, Lomax (1960) found areas largely on the basis of performance style but also by distribution of tunes and texts, specifying the North, the West, the southern mountains and backwoods, and the Negro South, and provided a map with quantification. A. M. Jones (1959: vol. 1) included a map of types of harmony in sub-Saharan Africa, using as a basis the most prominent intervals between the voices (unison, thirds, fourths, and fifths). But no indication is given of the amount of such harmonic music in the various repertories or of possible overlapping distributions. Distributions of archeological artifacts with maps are found in several studies in Hickmann and Hughes (1988). These examples illustrate some of the kinds of statements that have been made.

The most numerous musical area studies involve Native American cultures, probably because of the importance of native North America in the development of the culture area concept, with the number of easily separable culture units, and with the relatively good sampling of available music. It was quickly noted that each culture area does not simply have its own musical style; indeed, the maps are more interesting. Herzog (1928, 1930) was probably the first to suggest the existence of distinct areas and their usefulness for creating some order in the vast data, noting particularly that the singing and formal characteristics of the Yuman peoples of the Southwest differed from those of the rest of the continent. In a significant study, Helen Roberts (1936) described the distribution of instruments and vocal styles. In view of the role that instruments had played in the work of the German diffusionists, it was characteristic that she would devote more space to instruments than to the vocal styles, which, after all, accounted for most of the musical activity. Interestingly, Roberts's instrument distribution areas differ somewhat from those of the vocal styles. Her vocal style areas are substantially based on culture areas, not on musical groupings of smaller culture units. She lists Eskimo; the Northwest Coast and the Western Plateau; California; the Southwest, the Plains, and the Eastern Plateau; the East and Southeast; and Mexico. I later published a more statistically oriented approach, revising Roberts (Nettl 1954a), and dividing the area north of Mexico into six not always contiguous areas: Inuit–Northwest Coast; California and the Yuman style; the Plains and the Pueblos; the Athabascans; the Great Basin; and the East and Southeast. Methodological problems revolved about the lack of sufficient data and its unevenness, the different degrees of nineteenth- and twentieth-century change, the difficulty of separating musical style from instruments and social context, and the need to work statistically because Indian musics have much in common and can only be distinguished by relative frequency of traits. The main problem, again, was the difficulty of measuring degrees of similarity, and additional data now make this exercise more useful for its methodological lessons than for the substance of its conclusions.

On the whole, these musical areas were arrived at in a manner similar to that evidently used to establish culture areas by Wissler (1917), A. Kroeber (1947), and Driver (1961). A single, outstanding, striking trait that correlates roughly with a group of less concrete and perhaps more questionable isoglosses is the determining factor. In the culture areas the striking trait may be associated with contrasting aspects of life. Along the Northwest Coast it may be the Potlatch ceremony or a distinctive style in art; in the Plains, dependence on the buffalo. Similarly, the music areas were sometimes distinguished primarily by noncoordinate traits in music. Examples are the moderate complexity of drum rhythms for the Inuit and Northwest Coast cultures, and of antiphonal and responsorial singing in the East. A musical area may, on the other hand, be based on the prevalence of a trait that is also found elsewhere with much less frequency. This is true of the California-Yuman area, characterized in large measure by the frequency of the rise, which we also found extant but less prominent elsewhere. But although it was hoped that this study of geographical distribution would help us to understand history and the relationship of cultural domains, the musical area scheme did little more than provide an outline for initial orientation for scholars going into study of specific situations. Recognition of the rapid changes in musical style during the periods in which the studied repertories had developed—changes due to the forced movements of the Indian peoples, to intertribal contact, and to Westernization—all weakened the musical area concept. Attempts to revise these areas (Nettl 1969) to four main areas, and a more refined study by Erickson (1969) did not substantially change the outline.

The fact that the arrangement of Native American music areas has had to be successively critiqued and modified does not necessarily eliminate the value of the musical area concept as a classificatory device; it only proves that areas are hard to establish. This was also the experience of anthropologists, as may be noted in the gradual revision of the North American Indian culture areas by Wissler, Kroeber, and Driver. At one point it was thought that culture areas could be regarded as units with individual separable histories, but in the end they served mainly as ways of creating order out of the chaos of ethnographic data. The same may be true of musical areas. Like culture areas, they may have centers and marginal regions, and sometimes the relationship between the two can give insight into the past. But the thought of establishing a set of musical areas for the world in the belief that this rather specialized concept would provide a key to prehistory and its laws is no longer taken seriously.

Music on the Move

It may seem reasonable to put musical facts on a map, but in this context we have to take into account the strong tendency of music to be constantly on the move. I have noted that songs, "the most indefatigable tourists," move around the world, but mostly they move on the backs (or in the heads) of people who change their residence. Beginning in gingerly fashion around 1950, the study of people who have moved and populations that have spread around the world in many diasporas, and of their musical cultures and repertories, became a major thrust of the ethnomusicological endeavor. Studying the music of African-derived communities throughout the New World, of Indians living throughout the world, of Jewish populations descended from the original diaspora in the first century and leaving their homes again 2000 years later to immigrate to Israel—that kind of work has played a major role in ethnomusicology of the late twentieth century. It's not exactly cartography, but geography plays a major role.

Since the 1950s, the music of immigrant enclaves has become a major field of study. Although there are early models (e.g., Schünemann 1923, on eighteenth-century German immigrants to Russia), a major breakthrough came with the realization that North America could be a major source for the collection of old English folk songs (see Sharp 1932: xxi), and from a contrastive discovery: that historical processes could be extrapolated and explained from the comparative study of African and African American music (e.g., Herskovits 1945).

A large body of knowledge has been built up about the folk music and folklore of non-English-speaking immigrant groups in the United States and Canada, producing hypotheses of typical immigrant musical behavior that reinforce hypotheses about stability as related to marginal survival of archaic culture traits, about the development of syncretic styles, and about the gradual modernization, Westernization, and linguistic and cultural Anglicization of older European musical traditions, as well as issues of identity. Considerable work has also been done in Israel. (For samples of studies see, e.g., Katz 1968; Shiloah 1992, 1995; Shiloah and Cohen 1983; Gerson-Kiwi, 1963; Erdely 1964, 1979; the "Canadian" issue of *Ethnomusicology,* vol. 16, no. 3, 1972; Reyes 1999; Myers 1998; Lornell and Rasmussen 1999; and Turino and Lee 2004.) All of this literature is part of the body of research about musical change as an aspect of culture change (see chapters 20 and 30).

Taking one's music along in the course of emigration and immigration has been a major force in the world's music history. Certain major events, or waves of migration, stand out: the movement of Europeans to distant parts from the seventeenth century into the middle of the nineteenth: mainly to the New World, but also to Australia, South Africa, Russia; forced migration (that's the most restrained way to put it) of Africans as slaves to North and South America, and the Caribbean; a stupendous movement of east and south Europeans to North America between 1880 and 1920; large numbers of people fleeing Nazi, fascist, and communist oppression in the 1930s and 1940s; large-scale migrations within Asia and Africa in the second half of the twentieth century, as a result of oppressive governments and poverty; substantial migration of educated people from Asian and African nations to Europe and North America, for better opportunities. These are high points; there's lots more. There have been large numbers of musical results: preservation of old forms in new venues, but with changed functions; development of mixed, hybrid, syncretic forms of music; changed concepts of ethnic, national, and personal identity; and lots more. Many variables determine the musical and social outcome: relative size and selection of the diasporic population, the motivation for immigration, the amount of contact later maintained with the original traditional home, the degree of physical, cultural, and linguistic isolation and cohesion of immigrants in the host country; the cultural and musical differences and compatibilities of an immigrant culture in its relationship to the host culture; the attitudes of such a group toward diversity and change; the role and value of music in immigrant and host culture; and, most important, matters of hegemony, oppression, and power relations.

The term "diaspora," originally used only for the major event in Jewish history after 70 C.E., has begun to be used widely to describe populations who have for many reasons dispersed, and developed scattered communities that remain in touch with the original home and with each other. In the 1990s, studies of migrant groups from Asian and African nations, particularly from India and Vietnam, and of Jews fleeing or surviving the Holocaust, have played a major role in ethnomusicology. The development of new genres of Indian music in the Caribbean has been studied especially by Manuel (2000), and the retention of Hindu traditions in Trinidad by Myers (1998). The musical culture of Vietnamese refugees first in the Philippines and then in the United States has been intensively chronicled by Reyes. The musical culture of urban Jewish refugees from central and Western Europe who went to Israel and to the United States was studied by Bohlman (1989) and in several studies in *Driven into Paradise* (Brinkmann and Wolff 1999). The spread of klezmer music through eastern Europe and then to a new center in North America is traced in *Fiddler on the Move* by Slobin (2000).

In all of this, not only the reasons for and process of immigration need to be considered but also the sometimes changing identity of the immigrant in relation to home and host. Thus, a refugee may be someone who barely escaped with his or her life and, in the new country, is at the mercy of the hosts, not looking forward to any future. Eventually such refugees may become exiles, which I define as persons who see themselves as temporarily dwelling abroad but expecting to return home. They may, eventually, decide to stay and thus to become immigrants in the technical sense. There are many variations of this configuration, and the musical culture of group and individual may be substantially affected. Thus, Indians and Iranians in North America who are proper immigrants but wish to return home for visits are likely to take a greater interest in their home traditions of music than they did before leaving, but they have usually tried to keep it for themselves, not to make it an emblem of their ethnicity to the outside. European Jewish musicians escaping from the Nazis often brought their musical culture and tried to promulgate it in their new homes—North America, Britain, South Africa. Greek Americans have used their folk music as a way of associating themselves with members of other ethnic groups, providing music for Anglo, Italian, or Polish weddings.

The situation in Israel is particularly instructive, and I present it here as a major illustration because of the large amount of immigration there from many diverse places and the number of active local scholars. In a number of ways, the absorption of immigrant groups in Israel, allowing for their larger proportion and the greater speed, parallels the United States situation. Like American studies, most in Israel have concentrated on the ways in which the old traditions from eastern Europe and from Jewish groups in the Islamic world have been preserved. Israel has been referred to as a nation in which the heritages of many other nations are at least temporarily kept intact, and the studies of Moroccan, Kurdish, Syrian, Yemenite, Iraqi, and other Jewish groups have been undertaken as much in order to find out what the musical culture of the homeland was and has been as to assess musical behavior after arrival in Israel. A number of interesting if tentative conclusions have emerged.

Immigrants to Israel from Arabic-speaking countries brought with them the music of two streams of musical culture: one comprised the traditional Hebrew liturgical music and its semireligious and secular correlates, the folk music specifically of the Jewish minority, sung in vernacular languages— Ladino, Turkish, Arabic, sometimes also Hebrew; the second, since Jews in Muslim societies often occupied a major role as musicians for the Islamic community, consisted of the mainstream traditional music of the home country (see, e.g., Loeb 1972: 4–6). In regard to the first, some communities, which remained relatively intact though often impoverished in Israel, appear to have kept their heritage and even to have developed it further under the active stimulation of official Israeli cultural establishments. In respect to the latter music, which is actually Arabic or Persian, the absence of a cohesive and numerous audience or of a patronage system has contributed to a great decline in frequency of performance, thus perhaps also of expertise (see Cohen 1971 and Shiloah 1974: 83 for contrastive views). Despite official efforts to the contrary, Jewish musicians of Arabic and Persian music seem to have diminished in number. The folk music of Jewish immigrants from eastern Europe who came before World War II changed to a more general "Israeli" style with texts relevant to the contemporary resident of Israel. These songs abandoned the dominant subjects of eastern European rural life and adopted a musical style mixing east European and Balkan elements with certain characteristics of Middle Eastern music and with elements of modern western European popular music. More recent immigrants, largely urban and exposed to modern

Western popular and art music, have established close contact with Western musicians, participating in their tradition and its ongoing changes. It seems a reasonable hypothesis that traditional secular music has been kept alive more readily in communities that remained intact after immigration and in those that took up rural residence.

In working to find ways of mapping the world's music, ethnomusicologists have come to understand that the musical accompaniments and results of diasporas are significant components of the world's musical atlas.

24

The Whys of Musical Style: Determinants

The Central Question

Average American academics may not know much about the world's musical cultures, but after a leisurely dinner, some were quick to identify some of the most fundamental questions of my field, and they showed a variety of opinions about them. "You have certainly traveled a great deal"—I'm paraphrasing an elderly gentleman—"and you've observed how the peoples of the world play on different instruments, sing with different scales, make all sorts of strange sounds which we can't understand. Do you ever ask yourself what it is that has caused them to be so different?" "Oh, but it must be simply because there are such different races," broke in someone at his left. "I know it's not fashionable to say this today, but how could people who look as different as African Pygmies and Chinese not also do everything differently, including making music?" And the first: "But the musics you have heard aren't all that different, are they? After all, you yourself seem to enjoy them all and get something out of hearing them. Maybe they were once linked. Isn't it true that the chants of some South Seas islanders are very much like those of the ancient Greeks? And didn't I read somewhere that African music is rather like that of the Middle Ages in Europe? Don't all cultures inevitably move through the same stages?"

"Well, it's very complicated"—that's how I inevitably began to respond; but fortunately I was quickly interrupted by a young, scholarly looking lady. "Doesn't it just stand to reason that peoples who speak such different languages would develop very different kinds of singing? I've heard that in South

Africa, some native people use strange-sounding clicks as if they were consonants, and that the Chinese language is almost sung instead of spoken.
Wouldn't they then just have to sing their music in a very special way?" A
portly gentleman expressed another viewpoint: "It's not just that they speak
differently, they live differently. Can you imagine a small band of people who
used to have to spend all their time finding food for themselves developing
great music like that of Bach? Or, for that matter, like Ravi Shankar? And also,
I understand that there are indigenous people in which women have all the
power; their music must certainly be different from ours because it is the
women who determine how it will sound."

I was about to say, "I'm not so sure whether ultimately it is men or women
who determine music, but I'm afraid it's been a men's world almost everywhere, so far," but the subject at hand obviously fascinated the little group,
and so a sixth member felt compelled to chime in. "Can you imagine that
our concert music would have turned out as it has if it hadn't been for Beethoven? In this age of ethnic groups and social forces, we seem to have forgotten that our lives are really shaped by the actions of a few great men and
women."

I would have had to admit that it was really the great diversity of musics
and musical behavior that had turned me on to ethnomusicology, and that
indeed I had often wondered why different societies have different music,
and that a number of scholars had tried to find something, even some kind
of law of nature or behavior, from which one could predict what kind of
music a society would create for itself. Fortunately I was interrupted at that
point by somebody's elaborate farewells—saved by the bell, as it were, from
having to admit ignorance in what has long seemed to me to be the central
question of ethnomusicology. But you've just read, in this conversation, an
anthology of widely held (and in many cases rejected) answers, stated as conventional wisdom, to the general question of just what it is that determines
the nature of the musical style—and also of the system of musical ideas and
behavior—of a human society or ethnic group.

I am not sure whether ethnomusicologists will agree that there can be a
central question in their discipline. Some of them might well put forward
other questions, including the search for function or universals of music, or
Timothy Rice's (1987) comprehensive formulation, reduced to "How do humans make music?" But I feel that ultimately the determinants of music, a
question that ties music to other domains of culture and nature, are what
we have all in the long run been after. It's a question that brings together various leitmotifs of ethnomusicological thought: comparative study of musics;

the music of the world's peoples; the normally oral way of transmitting music; music as culture, because culture is what we share with all humans and with our group of humans. It sometimes even seems to have about it a certain sacredness that keeps us from engaging it directly. We seem to be afraid of what would happen if we definitively knew the whole truth (or afraid of people who think they know the whole truth), wishing but also not wishing to know, afraid that the answer might tell us things about humans we don't want to accept. And so we remain convinced that for this question we can arrive only at partial answers, that we will never be able to give a comprehensive, detailed picture of the actual causes of the particular and unbelievably complex pattern of ideas, behavior, and sound that constitutes the music of a people, and we tend to be suspicious of attempts to be definitive.

And so the ethnomusicological literature, dealing with issues such as music and technology, music and social organization, music as symbol, music and the diversity of intercultural contact, rarely speaks directly to the question of determination, focusing instead on relationships and typically avoiding a leap from relationship and correlation to causality. The few writings that comprehensively (if often just implicitly) bring up causality can be grouped in two categories, conveniently if simplistically labeled historical and synchronic. The historical orientation sees whatever music is to be examined mainly as a result of the past, arguing that an earlier music has been developed and changed to produce the later or present form. This orientation, too, has two strands. In one, music is determined by more or less fortuitous and in any case unique configurations of events—the idiosyncratic decisions of composers, perhaps. In the other, history follows a predetermined sequence, modified (but not in its essence) by the vagaries of fate. The synchronic orientation, on the other hand, extrapolates cause from relationships, seen as they exist at one time, to other domains of culture or nature.

Historians of European music have sometimes been very concerned with causality, but their conclusions have usually applied to particular situations. Even elementary texts are full of hypothetical statements involving relationship to what came before, musical and nonmusical. Thus, the music of Bach "grew out" of the music of his German predecessors, that of Schoenberg "out of a need" to provide something contrastive to the exhausted harmonic procedures of the late nineteenth century. The characteristics of the Baroque are the result of tendencies developed in the Renaissance but also of a desire to do things differently. On the other hand, the Venetian concerto style has been related to the peculiar architecture of the San Marco cathedral. Beethoven's unique role is in part a result of wide-ranging social and political changes of his time. Today's "new" music is traced to developments in electronic technology. Two implications emerge: On the one hand, musicians and their audiences experiment with what they have, moving in a new direction determined in large measure by the directions already established. On the other hand, changes in society, general and particular, determine changes in music. The characteristic stance of music historians argues that what happens musically can be traced to a balance of social, aesthetic, and personal forces.

This doesn't speak to broader and intercultural aspects of the question. If ethnomusicologists were given a multiple-choice test, many would probably opt for the answer that says: "The most important factor in determining musical style is in some sense the nature or character of a people's culture." I probably would. But some of us might do this with hesitation, and maybe, instead, check the "no opinion" box; and so, before turning to the relationship of music and culture as the obvious answer, I ought to look at ethnomusicological history and examine some factors outside the culture concept that have had a role in the literature involving this central question.

Genetics, Geniuses, Geography, and Speech

In a human population, are there biological factors that determine its musical style? Ethnomusicologists on the whole stay away from this question, fearing the undesirable connotations of racism but aware of the importance of biology and genetics to understanding humanity. Blacking courageously insisted on the role of biological considerations in ethnomusicology: "All musical behavior and action must be seen in the relation to their adaptive function in an evolutionary context, whether this is limited to their function within the adaptive mechanisms of different cultures, or extended to their function in biosocial evolution" (1978: 31). He was right in pointing out the biological basis of all human behavior, continuing to remind us (e.g., in his summary 1992) that culture is in the end part of nature, and he was prescient in that, by 2002, scientists agree that the two are difficult to separate and affect each other constantly and profoundly (for detailed commentary see Ridley 2002). But it is still possible and important to try to distinguish between genetic equipment and physical environment (nature) and the choices made by humans in dealing with these (culture).

The attitudes suggested in Blacking's statement are rare among ethnomusicologists (and the bibliography in his 1992 summary lists few items from our discipline). It's an area of greater concern to bio-musicologists and psycho-musicologists (see Wallin, Merker, and Brown 2000 and Sloboda 1985 for syntheses), but ethnomusicologists have largely taken this attitude: Humans are very much alike, and they all have music. Nineteenth-century social and political thinkers made much of the supposedly innate musicality of certain peoples, and no doubt a society's belief in its own special musicality would itself become part of its culture. In one small country, nineteenth-century Bohemia, this was a claim of all population groups—Czechs, Germans, Jews, and Roma. But stereotyping and denigrating by outsiders was more common; we have heard about African Americans who "have rhythm" and Jewish musicians who are "prone to melody"—neither, therefore, so the statement suggests, understanding the higher musical value of harmony.

To mainstream ethnomusicologists, physical differences among population groups have rarely been factors in musical style. It is accepted that a member of any racial group—better said "gene pool"?—can learn to do what a member of another group can do, although indeed this statement does not speak to the possibility of general proclivities of any population. That genetically related populations often constitute culture units makes it hard to separate physical and social factors, as does the fact that the physical elements we use in the social construction of race are themselves culturally determined. If a tall population has music different from its shorter neighbor nation, and we were somehow to decide that there are contrastive "tall" and "short" people's musics, would we still be unable to correlate this fact with a "tall person's" music associated with large individuals within a society? Extremely low singing, once thought to be a characteristic of the tall Russians and thus associated with "tallness," is, it turns out, also found in the musical culture of typically shorter Tibetans and Native Americans of the southwestern United States. No need to belabor: Ethnomusicologists generally don't believe that the genetic apparatus determines a people's musical style. One reads statements about this or that society being especially musical, but that's usually related to cultural factors of value and function; anyway, most fieldworkers insist that "their" people are particularly musical.

Still, Blacking's statement showed a renewed and sophisticated consideration of biology, in which ethnomusicologists are only beginning to take an interest in the twenty-first century. To be sure, he was interested in the biological aspects of music-making in the entire human species, not in how musical differences might reflect human differences. This renewed focus followed a hiatus no doubt connected with the end of the Nazi era, a period in the history of musicology in which racial matters received much attention. During that period, described in detail by Potter (1998), many books were written about "music and race," some purporting to show the—often undesirable—results of (a certain) heredity. It is hard to know whether authors of 1930–45 were taken very seriously, but the movement continued beyond 1945 in publications such as Moser's (1954), which discerns musical differences among the remnants of ancient German tribal groups; Fritz Bose's (1952) attempts to show racial differences between black and white Americans by examining their recordings of the same songs; or Marius Schneider's statement that "racial characteristics in music are easily detected when one actually hears a singer, but they cannot be described in words. Race shows itself by timbre, by the general rhythm of movement" (1957: 13). It is not clear whether Schneider wished to separate out biological factors or uses the term "race" in a broad sense simply to mean a population group with a unified culture. The implication seems to be that singing style and body movement are genetically determined, but whether the music is polyphonic or uses quarter tones is a matter of culture. The most benevolent criticism of this position must revolve about the difficulty of separating race and culture in the practical situation. Still, strands of thought rarely disappear without a trace, and so it was interesting in the 1990s to note Josef Jordania's (1997) attempts to associate polyphonic development with physical type for explaining the unique and spectacular development of polyphony in Caucasian Georgia.

There are no known racial differences in the human brain that might affect music, and the music-producing organs do not differ significantly. Such matters as talent and perception are not well enough known to be tested interculturally or outside a cultural context. In any case, we do not know what aspects of special ability, abstracted from musical activity, would show specific musical talent in an individual or a group, and whether it is aural or kinetic acuity, a work ethic, or the belief in the supernatural power of music that makes some peoples more "musical" than others. And certainly the criteria of musicianship differ among societies.

In his last book, Curt Sachs, contradicting Marius Schneider, took a definitive stand on the issue. "Most suspicious are we of the slippery and often criminally exploited concept of 'race.' . . . The word . . . has been so abused that it has become at once meaningless and too full of meaning" (1962: 47–48). Most ethnomusicologists have rightly followed Sachs in this respect, biding their time at least until the biological factors are more adequately separated from the cultural (see Graf 1968, 1972). But let me be clear: I am cautioning against the acceptance of *racial* criteria or, better said, criteria derived from the external appearance of homogeneous population groups, as factors in determining the musical direction of individual cultures, not the recognition of biological factors in the musicality of humans generally.

Moving to another cultural domain, the suggestion that topography or climate determine musical style may elicit a chuckle from humanists and social scientists. Is it conceivable that one could take seriously the correlation of monophonic and ornamented singing with the stark desert ecology of the Middle East, or the development of long ballads in northern Europe with the need to remain indoors during long winters? And yet there are aspects of geography that appear to play a direct though secondary or contributing role. Grame (1962), for example, suggested that in those parts of the world in which bamboo is found, there is a tendency to develop particular types of instruments. Somewhat more specific to musical style was Blacking's statement that the tempo of Venda music is related to the steady walking pace of the people, "thrust upon them by the mountainous environment" (1965: 47). Blacking also related the Venda's preference for circle dances to the mountains, which do not provide space for line dances. The neighboring Tsonga, he said, live in the flatlands, walk faster, and have music of more rapid tempo (47). From such examples, though, one could hardly claim that an entire musical style is determined by geographic factors.

Beyond this, climate, availability of water, the presence of seaports, types of raw material available for technology all play enormous roles in the formation of culture, and if music derives from the whole of culture, these too must in some sense be underlying factors. But could they determine, for instance, the presence or absence of quarter tones? Still, aspects of geographic determinism as a fundamental theory of culture, known already to the ancient Greeks, continues to be an explanation to be considered. Kroeber's (1947) delineation of North American Indian culture areas, let's remember, coincides remarkably with natural areas. As Szabolcsi (1965) suggested, the isolation of certain mountain dwellers may preserve musical styles, as may that of remote islands, while complex and stratified musics develop in accessible river valleys open to many influences and capable of supporting large populations. Yet in all of this, music is not affected by geographic features directly, but via the central core of culture.

The content of language is obviously related to culture, but it is hard to make the same case for linguistic structure. There is no evidence that a particular kind of grammar goes with a lifestyle, and the members of one language family may differ culturally as much from one another as do the Indo-European Bengalis and Swedes, or the Algonquian Penobscot and Arapaho. Features of language such as initial stress, the existence of tone, or proportion of vowels seem not to be related to culture type. On the other hand, styles of speech, by which I mean elements such as the amount of pitch variation, dynamic contrast, and various aspects of rhetoric, could clearly be relevant.

But given the close association of music and language, one would expect to find some general relationships between the structure of a language and the music of its people (beyond those of a specific piece of vocal music). Again, the relationships are there but as minor contributing factors. The typical patterns of linguistic tone sequence in some African languages seem to affect the patterns of composing melodies (Blacking 1967: 166–68; Nketia 1974: 77–88; H. Powers 1980; Waengler 1963). Thus, the Czechs and Hungarians have languages in which utterances begin with stressed syllables, and their folk songs typically begin with stressed beats. It's worth noting, in this context, a track in our intellectual history that associates the origin of music with language, and a side of this that proposes a kind of communication that has in common certain characteristics of music and speech (see, e.g., S. Brown 2000; Levman 1992). These publication suggest theoretically that not only language but languages affect the structure of musics. It is difficult to establish, in any of these cases, that music in its general style characteristics was molded to fit the characteristics of language, that the structure of language determined musical style.

Western society conceives of itself as being determined by the thought and action of highly influential men and women. And yet the idea that certain individuals influence and determine the main musical style of a society because of their personal character and what they do not share with their fellows somehow goes against the grain of ethnomusicological tradition. Those idiosyncratic geniuses who are of great interest to historical musicologists, but whose works were never accepted by any sizable portion of their society, are rarely the object of ethnomusicological study. This somewhat unjustified neglect of the individual can be traced to the characteristic belief in the musical homogeneity of most of the world's cultures, which would have each informant knowing the same repertory, and each person equally capable of producing new music. Well, this is at best an enormous oversimplification. Western culture was not the only one to have a Mozart or a Schoenberg, and there are studies of Asian art musics and of some indigenous societies that indicate the great effect of certain individuals in determining the course of music. Berliner (e.g., 1978: 3–7, 231–33) described the special role of great masters of the mbira among the Shona, and Merriam (1967a: 140) asserted that the greatest changes in Flathead Indian music in recent times were caused by the missionary zeal of a tribesman who returned after years of absence to revive aspects of supposedly traditional musical life. The role of nonmusicians, such as the Paiute prophet Wovoka, who brought the Ghost Dance to the Plains Indians and with it a new musical style, must also be considered.

But few ethnomusicologists would subscribe to a "genius" theory of history, believing that talented individuals who effected change that became widely accepted must have worked within a culturally valid system of values and rules. The world's cultures differ, of course, in their appraisal of the role of great men and women. Some Native American peoples, while ascribing the creation of songs to individuals, do not associate them with large-scale changes of style or determination of musical direction. But in some high cultures of Asia, musical innovators are remembered through document and oral tradition, their roles perhaps exaggerated.

The individual is part of his or her culture but, as recognized by anthropologists since the 1930s in their studies of "culture and personality," is also its prisoner, as illustrated by Jules Henry in *Culture against Man* (1963). The exceptional person in music may try to escape, and the history of music probably owes much to the conflict. The specific musical consequences are far beyond the scope of this foray. But there is something ironical in the picture of ethnomusicologists who study what population groups hold in common, but who often depend for the bulk of their data on the teachings of one person regarded as unusual in his or her society.

Biology, climate, geography, language, the talented individual—they all have a certain part in determining the nature of a music. But in the end, the overriding determinant must be the special character of a culture. The ways in which people live, relate to each other, see themselves in relation to their natural and human environment, control energy, and subsist determine the kind of music they have. Although I have suggested that most ethnomusicologists agree with this assertion, it is more than anything else an article of faith, and it certainly depends on one's conception of culture. Most ethnomusicologists are not yet ready to pinpoint that part of culture that provides the main clue. And so, instead of trying to generalize further, let me recapitulate briefly some musics I have used widely for illustration on these pages, in order to see what can conceivably have determined their particular character.

Why Is Blackfoot Music . . . ?

"Why is their singing so strange?" I was asked after a talk about their musical culture. But it's not, I defended. So, then, why do they sing as they do? (For a detailed description of the Blackfoot style and musical culture, I refer the reader to Nettl 1989a; and a record, *An Historical Album of Blackfoot Indian Music,* Folkways FE 34001; but many commercial CDs are readily available.) Let's go through our list: Physically, the Plains Indians, extending from the Blackfoot in the north to the Comanche in the south, are not particularly alike. Yet Blackfoot music is very similar to that of other Plains tribes, and so we rule out biological factors. There is a closer relationship between the distribution of the Plains musical style and the physical environment of the high Plains. But while it's difficult to separate culture from ecology, the Plains musical style is also found among peoples living in other areas (Merriam 1967: 328–30), and it has become a major component of the more recently developed intertribal powwow culture. Language also appears not to be a factor. While the minor musical differences among Blackfoot, Crow, and Comanche (members of three language families) might in part be related to differences in language and speech patterns, the main thrust of the musical style of these peoples is the same, even though the languages belong to four or more language families.

On to matters of culture. The Blackfoot in their recent "precontact" history were a hunting and gathering society in the western Plains, but there is evidence that they came from farther east and once enjoyed a different lifestyle, possibly including some horticulture (Driver 1961: 28; Ewers 1958: 6–7). Marius Schneider's description of the music of hunting cultures sort of fits them: It is "interspersed with much shouting, is formed from free speech-rhythms, and has little tonal definition" (1957: 13). But Schneider's correlation of hunting with polyphony and with metric predomination over melody (13) doesn't apply here at all. Here's my summary of traditional old-time Blackfoot culture, coming from standard ethnographies: Based on human and animal energy, it had little social stratification. The social organization was quite complex, revolving about the individual's association with nuclear family, with a band, with various societies, and with other individuals who share the same guardian spirit, and so on, all however within a rather informal framework. For all of these characteristics, we can easily identify close relationship to musical concepts, functions, behavior. But when it comes to musical style, we look far and wide for correlation. The variety of social relationships is paralleled by a number of musical genres with stylistic boundaries that are blurred, reflecting conceivably the informal approach to life's rules. The lack of complex technology is reflected in the predominantly vocal music. In a more speculative vein, we could associate the great difference between Blackfoot singing and speaking styles to the supernatural association of music. We can try to relate some of the central values of Blackfoot culture as stated by McFee (1972: 96–102)—individualism, bravery, generosity, wisdom—to aspects of music, but this works best when considering musical conceptualization. In the end, some of the most obvious musical traits cannot be related to a culture core, however defined, and are unable, say, to associate pentatonic scales with bravery, and heptatonic with cowardice.

As Alan Lomax (1968: 133) might have led us to expect, an aspect of culture that seems more likely to lend insight is the quality of interpersonal relationships, of which musical relationships may be illustrative. Let's see: In traditional Blackfoot culture (described in Wissler 1912 and Ewers 1958) there was a great difference in cultural role between men and women. In most respects, human relationships were informal and easy. A person was associated with several social groups. Political hierarchy was absent and authority temporary. People did cooperate and showed little hostility to each other, but most actions were carried out by individuals, while collaboration was not pervasive.

In Blackfoot music there are also substantial differences in men's and women's activities and repertories. The singing styles differ considerably. Informality is evident in many aspects of music, notably in the difference between theory and practice, between stated rules and execution. Thus songs are said to be repeated four times, but recordings show a lot of variation. The musical system is exhibited as a large body of separable songs, but in fact the difference between similar songs and sets of variants is not easily drawn. Songs have texts but may also be sung with newly created words or meaningless syllables. As a person is associated with several groups, a melody may be associated with several uses. Musical authority resides in part with song leaders, who, however, hold musical power temporarily and informally.

In a powwow singing group—a "Drum"—there is a male (or, recently, sometimes a female) leader whose tasks are mainly administrative. He also leads more song performances than others, but the leadership role in a song's structure is confined to the beginning, after which others, again informally determined, hold roles of prominence. Singing in groups is common, but in earlier times, solo singing predominated. In group singing, a loose kind of musical cooperation is necessary, and articulation of notes and drumbeats must be in good unison, but singers make little attempt to blend voices, and it is easy to hear the individual. Nonmembers of singing groups may be welcome to "sit in," and a singer may perform with several groups though being associated mainly with one. Those elements of style that are most readily drawn in, that can be best related to components of social relations and conceptions of life, are the ones, conventionally called "performance practice," present throughout a musical performance. But contemplating Blackfoot musical culture hasn't helped us to go far toward answering our central question.

Kaccheri and Concerto

In societies with greater populations and more musical diversity than Blackfoot culture, we might have more luck identifying determinants of style, though perhaps we could be accused of fudging in seeking those genres and ensembles that seem best to reflect a central cultural guiding principle. What we might be after, though, is music that is considered in some sense central by the society. In the culture of Carnatic music in Madras (Chennai), the term *kaccheri* is used for a large concert with an ensemble. Briefly, the ensemble consists of various levels of leadership and accompaniment: For example, a solo singer is the principal, a virtuoso in singing technique and improvisation, and a master of the complex musical system. He or she is accompanied by a violin, which follows along, repeating and recapitulating the singer's improvisations, and a mridangam (drum), which accompanies the metric passages. The violin, which occasionally gets to improvise, is accompanied by a second violin, which also follows, and assumes the main accompanying function when the first violin plays solo. The mridangam, too, gets a chance to solo and is accompanied by a second percussion instrument, a ghatam (actually a pot of fired clay). It's a complicated structure, but the principle is that there is always leadership and accompaniment, various levels of it, and that the leader (or temporary leader) gets to make musical decisions and must be followed by the accompanist. The tamboura, a large four-string lute, which plays a drone throughout, performs an essential function but is outside the system.

It's a kind of event that has always struck me as a reflection of the older Hindu social organization, the caste system, no longer legally operative but still in evidence. The ensemble reflects a variety of castes, and even the outcastes are represented by the tamboura. Parallels can be drawn at various additional points, but suffice it to say that structurally, the parallels are clear. But what do they mean? If asked why this is the favorite music of the learned Hindus of Madras, musicians provide technical and historical information, and don't really respond well to suggestions that it reflects the social system. And if they are opposed to the caste system, why do they continue to maintain this music? Well, I was told, this is a grand musical system developed by great masters, and it requires its structure to be as good as it is. But I doubt that it would have developed as it did were not the musicians members of this particular kind of society. A bit of corroborative evidence: Singers are usually high-caste Brahmins, while the main accompanists may also be members of lower castes, and the second-string accompanists even more so, while the tamboura player may be one of the soloist's foreign (and thus out-caste) students. At least it's that way some of the time.

If the kaccheri is the South Indian classical music buff's favored music, the piano concerto might play the same role in the life of the European culture vulture. A Beethoven concerto sounds totally different from a performance built around a Tyagaraja kriti, but the social organization of the music is not all that different. The orchestra, with its conductor, concertmaster, first chairs, and hierarchy within a section expressing ability, the whole ensemble in the service of accompanying a master solo pianist, and also the nature of the score, in which someone or something is always accompanying and subordinate to something else; and the accurate visual representation of these relationships in concert; all of this looks like a reflection of a rigidly hierarchical social system. Now, just what the relationship suggests depends in part on your assessment of this social system: We could say that our (contemporary Western) social structure is really very hierarchical, much as some might deny that, and the music proves it; or that it was like a caste-like class system in the eighteenth century, and the music is just a behind-the-times reflection; or this music, with its rigid social stratification, gives us egalitarian-minded folks a chance to take a deep breath and take a vacation from our norms. Different kinds of reflection—fine. But causality? It's harder to make a case, and yet we can't really imagine an egalitarian society such as that of the Khoi-San peoples of Botswana producing musical ensembles with the stratified social structure of a kaccheri or a symphony orchestra—never mind the problems of technology.

So, How Come in Iran . . . ?

In a survey of musics, the styles of Blackfoot singing, Carnatic concerts, and Persian classical music are worlds apart in style, even given some surface similarities such as monophony. The cultural differences are equally great. Are these differences the result of differences in other domains of culture?

In Iran, where outsiders and insiders distinguish classical, rural folk from urban popular musics (and recognize other divisions), let's take the following into account. Certain aspects of performance practice such as the use of the voice are essentially the same in all repertories and strata. These exhibit at least some of the traits—tension, ornamentation, tightness, nasality, high pitch—associated by Lomax with a despotic social order, sexual repression, and lack of concerted cooperation: culture traits arguably relevant at least to the past (Lomax 1959: 933; see Jacobs 1966; Ramazani 2002; Sullivan 2001 for illustrations). Some features of musical style are found in all three main musical categories but to varying degrees. A hierarchy of accompanying instruments in relationship to the leading solo—somewhat as in Carnatic music—is more pronounced in the classical genres, and less evident in rural music, which has fewer accompanying strata and in which the accompanying instruments are often in the hands of the soloists. In the popular music, which had much more of a presence in the 1970s than in the 1990s, it is only occasionally found, though replaced by other kinds of relationship of ensemble performance. Yet the hierarchical kind of accompanying structure is a close reflection of the social order at large.

Certain features of music are generally restricted to one of the repertories or strata. My discussion of symbolism included the role of hierarchy, individualism, surprise, and temporal precedence as characteristics of classical music and urban social behavior. By contrast, a characteristic of the popular music, also urban, is the acceptance and encouragement of variety and of outside influence, reflecting a heterogeneous, accepting kind of culture. Improvisation, largely absent in popular music, may be found in the rural music, but in the classical music it is set off from lower-prestige performance of precomposed materials, reflective of the importance of individualism and the avoidance, in social life, of long-range planning. It is aspects of performance practice and not the specific scalar or formal types that can be related to the characteristics of culture.

Looking for ways in which the character of a culture, using Tylor's "complex whole" as a model, may determine musical style requires us first to seek ways in which one reflects the other. Trying this gets us into a network of often insurmountable difficulties, but we can try a very tentative conclusion: Certain components in the music of a society, prominently including singing style and the relationship among performers in a group, seem often to be related rather directly to the society's culture. Others, including scales and forms, are the development of earlier forms in directions determined by cultural values such as attitudes toward change, but their specific character seems to have nothing to do with the central values and guiding principles of their society. Music may be affected by a culture's central values, but it might also help to establish them. Aspects of performance might help us to understand social organization; thus, one might contemplate societies by the relative significance and quantity of two major types of live performance recognized by Turino (2000: 47–49; see also A. Seeger 1988), "participatory" and "presentational." In any event, having found a credible relationship or a parallel between music and culture in a society does not permit us to automatically claim that we have discovered what has determined the kind of music this society has chosen for itself.

It would be fine if there were a laboratory in which culture, nature, language could all be manipulated to give us musical results. We have none. Peoples of similar origin living in diverse conditions—Africans and Europeans in the New World, Indians dwelling overseas, members of a variety of Native American cultures finding themselves together in the ecology of the Plains—have been contemplated as the closest thing to a natural laboratory. But there are too many variables. In the end, it seems to make sense to suggest that the style of each music is determined by a unique configuration of historical, geographic, and linguistic factors, and that the kind of culture of which the music is part is surely the major determining force. But why musics are as they are—that's something remaining very much a question.

PART 4

In All Varieties

25

I've Never Heard a Horse Sing:
Musical Taxonomies

The Importance of Being a Folk Song

We never seem to get away from the question: Is all music "one," or are there lots of musics? Maybe better stated: Is it more helpful to look at music as a single unified entity, or to think of it as a conglomeration of national, class, ethnic, personal repertories? In this chapter, I want to look at some of the ways societies divide their musics by these classes, categories, types.

A lot of musicians have been fighting for the "unified." "All music is folk music, I've never heard a horse sing" is the least colloquial version of a statement attributed to various American musicians, most famously Big Bill Broonzy and Louis Armstrong. "There are only two kinds of music, good music and bad music" has no doubt been said by many, but it's documented for Kurt Weill, and I've heard Ray Charles make the same remark on television. Both quotations seem to be scolding us: "For crying out loud, don't worry so much about the category to which a piece of music belongs. There's nothing greater about being a folk song than something else, and why should it be better for someone to compose operas than Broadway musicals?" They are voices in the wilderness, as most people in Western urban society seem to be convinced that there are more kinds of music than just good and bad, and they label music in accordance with its style and its social and cultural associations, constructing a hierarchy of musics. Music is part of a person's identity; individuals have their "own" musics. Maybe all cultures contain a bit of this kind of thinking; still, we always have to remind ourselves, the members of a society may not agree upon or share the same values.

It is part of the ethnomusicologist's credo that all musics, and all of the music in each society, should be investigated, are worthy of study. All music that is accepted by some community as its own has this minimal qualification by virtue of that fact. Yet ethnomusicologists have from the beginning been concerned with the stratification of music within a society, imposing models such as the folk music–art music dichotomy or the folk-popular-classical continuum, sometimes buying into Adorno's E and U (serious and entertainment) categories, and—sometimes unwisely using these templates—trying to determine the hierarchical taxonomies of other cultures. They have also been aware of the fact that the subdivisions of a society may identify themselves with particular repertories and styles of music, each regarded as in some way superior by its people. They have been drawn into the conflict and come close to establishing groups of scholars extolling the virtues, respectively, of folk, popular, and classical traditions. In the nineteenth and twentieth centuries, the concept of "folk music" played a special role in the musical life of Europe and the Americas, and this specialness had important effects on the development of ethnomusicology.

It was at the height of the 1950s folk song revival. A few stragglers stayed behind to ask questions after a talk titled "Folk Music." "Isn't 'On Top of Old Smoky' a folk song?" asked one. "And how about some of our great hymns, 'Onward, Christian Soldiers,' and such?" Well, I wasn't sure. The questioner hung his head in disappointment. And another: "Don't you think that jazz is the true folk music of America?" Well, I wasn't sure about that either. The first retorted more aggressively: "But these are great songs; how can you say that they are not folk songs?" I tried to talk about formal criteria, but no luck, I had obviously offended a lady simply by implying that her favorite songs weren't folk songs. "Why does a song have to be a folk song in order for it to be respectable to you?" The next day in my classroom I saw that one of my colleagues had left some definitions on the board: "A folk song is a song whose composer isn't known. An art song is a fine song composed by a great composer." Why does a song have to have a known composer in order to be a fine song? I was tempted to write Big Bill's bon mot on the board.

The term "folk song" has strong emotional connotations in Western society. In American culture of the last fifty years, it stands variously for class, political orientation, ethnicity, tradition, purity, social attitude, environmental consciousness, and contrasting views on education, as discussed in detail by Philip Bohlman (1988). It has signified heritage, cultural integrity, a symbol of better things to come, a way to keep an enclave group intact, a way for people from many groups to communicate. Since its inception before 1800, the term and the concept have meant different things to various constituencies, as already illustrated (for German culture alone) by Julian von Pulikowski (1933), who showed, in a large study of the term, how the concept was batted about by politicians of the left and right, by social reformers, nationalists, educators, antiquarians, musicians theoretical and practical, even already in nineteenth-century Germany. Its prevailingly oral tradition and its supposed association with entire ethnic groups have put it under the particular aegis of ethnomusicology. Various revivals have resulted in a variety of musics with different relationships to the older rural oral traditions from which they claim to be derived. Suffice it to say that the "revived" music of the 1840s in the Czech lands, the U.S. folk song revival of the likes of Woody Guthrie and Pete Seeger, and the music of Hungarian street bands of the 1980s all exhibit very different relationships to their more traditional antecedents. Finnish folk music, as described by Ramnarine, exists, for Finnish society, in distinct "old" and "new" categories, the latter being also a part of the category of popular music. (For a thoughtful summary of the relationship of folk music and folk revivals, see Ramnarine 2003: 3–23.)

Where does folk music fit among the musics? It's a question that leads us to the more general issue of musical taxonomies. But how does one gather data to draw conclusions? There is curiously little literature on that subject. Matters of taxonomy were taken up in regard to classical music by sociologists such as John Mueller (1951) and Paul Farnsworth (1958) but not developed significantly further. There is little that looks panoramically at the music of, say, North America or Europe, with the exception—as is often the case—of Charles Seeger (1977: 146–54), who lays out the world of creative practices in a holistic outline. In the 1960s I asked a lot of people (in a totally unstructured study), "What kinds of music are there?" and got a variety of answers, the mainstream of which suggested that there were folk, classical, popular, and jazz musics.

But looking at musical life in ways that go beyond a questionnaire, it seems that in late twentieth-century modern American urban society approaches the identification and classification of music in several ways; but, except for the small minority who insist only that they have never heard a horse sing, people consider music as comprising several types or repertories, often in a hierarchical arrangement. The criteria for taxonomy vary with class, education, or ethnicity of the classifier. Two of the most widespread criteria for musical stratification are social classes (with each of which one being identified mainly with a particular kind of music) and origin (of repertory or individual piece). The educational establishment, as exemplified by the terminology of library catalogues, considers "art" music to be the true and central music of the entire society, labeling it simply as "music," while other types have distinguishing adjectives. Some decades ago, all non-Western music (or more precisely for the Western classifier, all music from outside his or her own culture) would have been classed as "primitive." Folk music would have been the music of remote rural populations orally transmitted by nonprofessionals who create variants that must satisfy in order to remain extant. "Popular" music, difficult to distinguish from folk or art music, would have been that of the lower social and educational classes. Thus four classes of people—urban elite, urban mass, rural, and those totally outside the culture—were socially and musically distinguished by this taxonomy.

The other criterion, origin, tells us that what we once called "primitive"—and later "tribal," and more recently "indigenous"—music comes from "elsewhere" and, in the minds of many, a very remote era; folk music is associated with the anonymous mass, art music with specific composers, and popular music mainly with performers (more than with acknowledged composers). Beyond this, people distinguish music by the time of its creation. These are some of the ways in which North Americans divide music. I bring up the subject mainly to suggest its relevance and interest. But it continues to be clear that where you place a particular song can make an important statement about society and art, about your view of yourself and "others."

All the Things You Are

Besides asking individuals in my home town, I found it instructive also to look at the ways in which educational institutions and record stores classify musics, how they group all the things that music is. I've mentioned midwestern university schools of music as a fruitful venue before, and so I'll recapitulate. In the schools' official programs, here are all the things that music is: (1) the central music—Western classical, but essentially that composed between 1650 and 1950, the music everyone must study at least to an extent, and the music most protected against exigencies such as budget cuts; (2) a secondary stratum of classical music, mainly "early" and "new" music, respected like the first but less significant in curricular performance requirements, as it is also the music that uses nonstandard instruments; (3) jazz, somewhat lower on the continuum of value because of its improvisatory nature and its typical performance venues outside the concert circuit, and no doubt other social factors also help to give it this subordinate status; (4) marching and concert band music, associated substantially with the university's athletic program; (5) non-Western and folk musics, not musics in which one may major as a performer, performed by ensembles whose resources are restricted and that may be the first to go when funds are short; (6) popular musics such as rock, blues, rock-and-roll, Latin American genres, and so on—these appear only as the subject for ethnomusicological study, with emphasis on sociopolitical issues; (7) country and western music, treated like (6) but, to some, totally beyond the pale. There are other musics that I didn't include, because they don't appear as categories in the life of the school—for example, music for ballroom dancing and ordinary Protestant hymns.

These musics are differentiated also by the costumes usually worn at performances, by performers and audience—though this description applies less to the period after 1990, when increased informality encouraged homogenization. But typically, the central classical repertory is performed in formal (tuxedo and evening dress) outfits, early music in period costumes, "new" music in turtlenecks, jazz in uniform sports jackets—though its desire to count as "classical" is symbolized by the occasional use of tuxedos. Non-Western ensembles use national costumes, even though the same ensembles on their home ground may perform in Western street dress. Popular music genres have their traditions, replicated on the occasions when they appear in the school of music: outrageous nonconformity in rock groups, shirts reminiscent of farmers' outfits in country music. In any event, a classification related to the very general one outlined earlier but also specific to the educational institution is used, and tells us about the value structure of a segment of Western musical society.

Record stores must classify their material carefully so customers can find what they want, and they have to conform to the customers' own custom and the marketing approaches of the recording companies. So in one college-town shop, in 2000, I found categories such as "classical" and "opera" separated—opera lovers being something of a separable breed. There is jazz, there are several subdivisions of the classical sphere (rock, R & B, soul, rap), one finds "folk" as a subdivision of popular music because it is presented largely in arrangements that blend into popular styles. "Folk" includes only American materials, but "Native American" is separate, integrated with "new age" music. There is a category "international," which includes traditional music of Asia and Africa, as well as folk music of European cultures. Latin America, however, is a separate category.

This pattern, though not all of the specifics, was found in other shops in this community, and I present the findings only as suggestive. But years earlier, around 1970, I had found record stores a help in determining categories of musical thought in Tehran. One store, Safhe-Beethoven (Beethoven Records), carried only twelve-inch LPs of classical Western and Persian music. The Western music was arranged by composer, and the Persian by instrument and series, but in fact there were few LPs available, so taxonomy wasn't an issue. A few blocks away was Musik-e Houshang (Houshang's Music Store), which had only seven-inch 45–rpm disks. While the LPs were expensive by Iranian standards, with prices similar to American prices—the equivalent of $6 or $7—the 45s were very inexpensive, around 35 U.S. cents. Produced in Tehran by a large number of mainly smallish companies and studios, they varied greatly in quality. Here the categories were by language—one large section, arranged by singers, with two subdivisions, one for classical music (though in arrangements and form appropriate to the 45–rpm format and more readily acceptable to lovers of popular music) and one for folk music (*musiqi-ye mahalli*—regional music)—and by region, that is, provinces of the nation. Then there were sections for Turkish, Arabic (some of it by musicians from Arabic countries), Kurdish, and Armenian music. Finally, there was a section of records of Qur'an readings and prayers. Again, I think this grouping corresponds in part to the way many Tehranians thought of their music. We're pretty sure that all cultures have taxonomies of music, but how to get at them in ways that can be defended at applying to an entire culture—that's still beyond us.

On the matter of musical taxonomy, ethnomusicology appears to have gone through several indistinct and overlapping stages. At one time there was a tendency to recognize only two classes, Western art music in the one and everything else in the other (Adler 1885: 14). Soon, recognition of the fact that Asian cultures had a stratification of music not unlike that of Europe led to a tripartite model, "primitive, art, and folk" music. Those cultures with an art music, that is, a kind of music performed by professionals who were highly trained and had the technical and speculative conceptualization of music that we call music theory, were also said to have, in other strata of society or in a different tradition, a folk music. The cultures with no such art music were thought to be "primitive" and thus to have "primitive" music. A third stage is implied in Hood's statement (1963: 316) to the effect that art, folk, popular, and primitive music are the norm. But the ethnomusicological study of popular music was slow to be formally accepted (see, e.g., Vega 1966, who coined the term "mesomusic" as less loaded). Eventually, there also came the realization that each culture has its own way of classifying music, a taxonomy that may have several groupings or perhaps none, and that may exhibit a hierarchical arrangement, or may not. But I suggest that while most cultures do indeed have their own way of classifying music, so that the terms "folk," "art," and "popular" are at best culture-specific to the West, each culture tends to have some kind of hierarchy in its musical system, a continuum from some kind of elite to some kind of popular, related to the society's distribution of power. Just where the lines should be drawn has been the subject of discussion in each culture and for certain analytical purposes in our general literature (see Bose 1967; Elbourne 1976; Karpeles 1968; Wiora 1957).

A World Turned Upside Down

If we define folk music as the music known to all and performed by the entire community, while classical music is only for an elite, and if we believe that it's in Asian high cultures that we can find the closest approximation of the Western model, we may sometimes find the world turned upside down. Let's look at two familiar cultures. Blackfoot society is conventionally thought to lack socio-musical stratification, yet two approaches taken from what is admittedly fragmentary information provide alternate interpretations. Wissler's (1912: 263–70) three types of song ownership seem not to have been observed to the letter, but they are still evident, at least in vestige, today. Songs of general ownership, for example, were songs of social dances. Songs that were owned individually but were transferable included the vision songs associated with the medicine bundle ceremonies. Nontransferable songs were to be sung in moments of danger and impending death. There seem also to have been intermediate categories such as the songs of the various men's societies, which were sung only by members but passed on to new generations entering the societies every four years or so.

Now, in certain ways the individually owned songs correspond to the Western conception of art music. They belonged to an elite—religious if not musical, the men with great supernatural power—and were associated with individuals. As a group, they seem to have had a larger variety of style, at least of formal structure. They had greater prestige because of their supernatural power. The social dance songs, known to all, corresponded to folk music. Less emphasis was placed on their specific origins, and they had more standardized forms. Specific statements of value from these earlier times are lacking; they do appear in more recent times. They must be extrapolated from more general information, but they conform, interestingly, to ways in which the modern Americans mainstream tends to differentiate and evaluate portions of its own musical culture. Thus, in the 1960s one could distinguish older Blackfoot ceremonial music (i.e. medicine bundle songs) from modern social dance songs of the powwow tradition by their association with two different groups of people who knew and performed them. Older material was typically known by full-blooded Blackfoot (a cultural category, on the whole, comprising individuals who had little or no white ancestry, spoke little English, and were poor). Newer, social dance, and pan-Indian songs were known to the so-called mixed-blood people, typically younger and more Westernized. The older group was smaller and respected for knowledge of the old tribal traditions, and the younger prized because of its ability to sing. It is a bit like modern Western culture: Composers of art music were regarded as intellectually, artistically, and perhaps even morally superior, even when their music is not well understood and liked. Musicians in the popular music field are respected for their entertainment value but less venerated. The parallel has its limits, surely, but the two strata of Blackfoot music do, perhaps, have something in common with the art-popular or possibly the art-folk dichotomies. Elements of musical hierarchy do exist in Blackfoot culture. A few songs, labeled by the earlier literature and by some singers as "favorite" songs of the people, might be regarded as the classics or, on the other hand, maybe they are the "true" folk songs, beloved by all.

In some Asian societies, including that of India, the distinction between art and folk music seems to be relatively similar to that made in Western music. To a degree, it was so in the Iran of around 1970 as well, although the criteria for distinction are different, and the specialist-generalist opposition, widely used to distinguish art and folk music in the West, does not apply. Classical music, thus named by Iranians but also called "original," "noble," or "traditional," the music of the courts of the past, centers on improvised performances and includes an articulated body of music theory. The concept closest to folk music, mentioned as a category in record stores, has a name literally meaning regional or local music. According to Blum (1975a: 86), it is distinguished by performance by nonprofessionals, antiquity, cultivation in rural areas, and identification with particular regions. A body of popular music was also recognized and, typically, denigrated; it was of urban provenance and seen as a polluted form of classical music by learned musicians, and as sinful by the devout. But in contemporary Iran before the revolution, various kinds of Western music also existed and should be taken into account in an attempt to establish a folk taxonomy and an associated hierarchy.

That's the verbal taxonomy. Here now is an attempt to represent sketchily the whole of Tehranian musical life, around 1970, as a group of strata, based on my observation of behavior. Venues of performance, evaluations by individuals, cost of tickets, associations with social, economic, and educational classes, all suggest that in modern Tehran the art music of the West (some of it composed, and most of it performed, by Iranians) was at the top of the musical hierarchy. There followed, side by side, Western popular music and Persian classical music. Next was folk music, and finally the Iranian popular music (including that of films), its styles mixing indigenous, Western, and Asian elements. It is possible to separate the Western and Iranian strands, to see that each has its own classical, popular, and (at least to some extent) folk components, and to find two systems both corresponding reasonably well to those of the United States and Europe. However, a full perspective of Tehran culture gives a more complex picture, including, with those already mentioned, religious and other ceremonial music not regarded as truly music by devout Muslims and thus difficult to place in the hierarchy.

In comparing traditional Iran and the contemporary West, societies with similar kinds of strata, there are interesting contrasts. Most striking is the attitudes of folk musicians. The quintessential American folk singers (traditional, or in the "revival") are unwilling to admit that there are strata and are inclined to include within their purview, at least potentially, all music with which they come into contact. The musician of Iranian folk culture looked at music as a group of separate, specialized domains, placing them (even within the folk repertoire) in separate categories, with special terms for the repertories of practitioners of music for weddings, narrative songs of a secular nature, songs of religious import performed at teahouses, chants performed at traditional gymnasiums. The tendency is for both kinds of folk singers to avoid hierarchical thinking, the American tending to lump all music into one, the Iranian establishing several separate but equal categories. It may indeed be true that some kind of hierarchical classification of music is present in a great majority of cultures, but the terms "folk," "art," and "popular" no longer seem adequate for an instructive comparison.

How Musical Are Humans?

That's probably how Blacking would have titled his book (1973) had he written it twenty years later. He argued, rightly I think, for the essential and more or less equal musicality of all humans, and certainly all human societies, laying differences in musical talent and achievement at the door of the tendency for societies to create social classes. Most societies do distinguish, rank, and group musicians by ability, accomplishment, musical or social role, and other criteria, and find ways of showing differences of status. Thus, not only do most musical cultures have hierarchies of repertories, they also rank musicians, sometimes by their personal accomplishments but more frequently by their roles in musical and social life.

Merriam (1964: 129–30) describes five classes of musicians among the Basongye. The highest, a versatile individual, is truly a full-time professional. The others also have the status of musicians—it is a low status, since musicians are undesirable but indispensable—but are paid very little. Society ranks them, and their pay corresponds roughly to their rank. The basis of the ranking seems to be the importance of percussion instruments in Basongye culture, their status and musical role. The higher-ranking musicians play percussion instruments, the lowest are vocalists. Whether this could be regarded as ranking according to the intrinsic difficulty of the music I cannot say; it does not seem so.

Hood (1971: 244–45) described the relative pay, and thus the status, of musicians in Javanese gamelans. Two kinds of musical roles appeared to confer high status: responsibility for keeping the integrity of the gamelan intact, and responsibility for innovation, for departure from the basic melody in carrying out the paraphrasing function. If technical virtuosity itself was rewarded, it was incidental, a function of the other values. A musician must respect the musical authority, keep the integrity of the musical system intact.

In the Western symphony orchestra, pay and evaluation by the audience tend to go hand in hand. Conductors are highest in both respects, sectional first chairs (i.e. the first viola, or cello, or bass player) high, others lower. Conductors have responsibility for both integration and innovation, keeping time, keeping the orchestra together, giving a faithful interpretation of the score, but also imposing their own ideas on it by providing a personal reading. First chairs have only the integrative function; their job is to keep their sections playing together. The concertmaster's task is to maintain the integrity of the orchestra, but imaginative playing of solo passages is occasionally part of the job as well, so that he or she shares to an extent the dual responsibility of the conductor and is rewarded for it.

In the South Indian classical music culture of Madras, musicians are judged essentially as superb technicians and by aspects of spirituality. If they are soloists, they are required to adhere to the principles of the raga and tala, and in other respects, they must innovate imaginatively and personally, excel at improvisation. If they are accompanists, they must follow precisely. But certain traditional social principles color the evaluations (L'Armand 1983). There was an underlying assumption, for example, that Brahmins make better vocal soloists, that lower castes are more suited to accompanying, that men are better improvisors than women. Musicians today recognize that this is in fact not so, but the ways in which musical roles were assigned even early in this century, in part by caste and sex, still play a role in at least the initial expectations of the informed audience.

If one were to look for a ranking of musicians among modern Plains Indians, one could do it most conveniently by comparing ensembles of singers who habitually perform together, and by examining the social and musical structure of the individual ensemble. At the major Blackfoot powwow, "North American Indian Days," in the 1960s, several singing groups—Drums—alternated, each performing for an hour or two. The groups were associated with towns on and off the reservation—Browning, Heart Butte, Starr School, Cardston (Alberta), and so on. Members need not be residents, and membership was informal and floating; a singer from one group could occasionally sing in another. Each group had a leader who began many but by no means all of the songs and who assembled the singers. Each singer in a group could lead songs, for example, determine and begin, and there was no set order for the leading of songs. On the surface, at least, the situation was one of informality and equality. Most of the time little was made of distinctions among groups and singers. In the powwow sector of the culture, there is only one class of individuals who make up something of a musical hierarchy, the class of (mainly) men known as "singers." But the Blackfoot do distinguish quality and status of musicianship. The singing groups competed for prizes, and during my stay with the Blackfoot there was one that had the reputation of being the best, its superior quality attributed to the members' musicianship, with details unspecified. Individual singers were also singled out as being particularly excellent. The criteria included knowledge of a large repertory, as well as the ability to drum well (quality of actual singing was evidently a less important criterion), with emphasis on the ability to drum in a precise "off the beat" relationship to the vocal rhythm, and in perfect unison. Men who made songs were also (automatically) regarded as superior singers but not put into a separate class as composers. Since the 1960s, the culture and social organization of powwow singing groups—the Drums—has become much more formalized and commercialized, and related to professional musicians in American society as a whole, and become part of American mass-mediated musical culture (analyzed by Scales 2004).

The Folkness of Folk and Nonfolk Music

If each culture has its musical strata, from elite to mass, complex to simple, specialized to broadly accepted, cultivated to folk, each also has elements that hold the strata together. They may be stylistic—tonal, rhythmic, formal, harmonic characteristics present at all levels. For example, the singing style of Iranian folk and classical music is more or less the same, and the importance of the triad is readily evident in German classical, popular, and folk music. On the other hand, the common elements may comprise musical content. Alan Lomax put it in aesthetic terms: as he saw it, the "favored" song style is a particular reflection of the social and economic core of a culture, and his cantometrics project depended heavily on identifying this core (1968: 133). What Lomax had in mind, as a matter of fact, was folk music, at least when he dealt with European and American cultures. When his considerations moved to Africa and the Far East, he was prepared to include classical music, though I'm not sure why. In any event, we may accept the premise that if a music has several repertory components, each associated with one stratum or segment of society, there might nevertheless be one that holds the society musically together, and that symbolizes for it the unity of the entire culture.

But actually identifying the "favored" song style may often be a hopeless enterprise. In an age of nationalism and globalization, and a world of "micromusics," and of the individual's multiple musical identities, as theorized by Slobin (1992b), the concept may be useless. To scholars of the nineteenth and early twentieth centuries, folk music would occupy this role, for it was regarded, after all, as the unchanging, ancient heritage that preceded the creation of courts, cathedrals, cities, and the middle class. For the cultures of the twentieth century, the favored style is likely to be what we call the "popular" music disseminated through the mass media—but which popular music?

If a large society can claim a central or "favored" music, we may find it also by a stratum of music that ties together a large number of otherwise musically and culturally diverse segments of society, ethnic groups, and geographical areas, because in some way it reflects some of the central values of society. The classical music of today's Iran did not make a distinctive appearance on the stage of history until the late nineteenth century, when it emerged from a period of neglect accompanying the decline of Persian culture and political power under the Qajar dynasty (1797–1925). In recent years, however, there is no doubt that it became a proper classical system, in the sense that it was (incorrectly) considered to be very old as well as truly and distinctly Persian. It related to various currents of Iranian life, and it came to be regarded as the music of the whole nation, symbolizing its unity and its distinctiveness, in contrast to various folk and popular musics (which spoke to its diversity, regional, cultural, linguistic, religious) and Western music (which bespoke the submersion of distinctiveness in favor of amalgamation with the West). Its structure exhibited certain characteristics of folk musics but developed them further. As I have repeatedly shown, one could trace in it some of the major social values of traditional Iranian society. It drew on material from far-flung parts of Iran. It was associated with the elite population of Iran, the court, the aristocracy, and eventually the educated but traditional-minded middle class.

In a survey of attitudes, a cross-section of Tehranians gave a variety of opinions and evaluations of Persian classical music. Many (including those who hardly knew it) said they liked it, others didn't. Some regarded it as a symbol of an undesirable past, others of what is good, beautiful, truly Persian. To most, however, it was something special.

In India a similar picture emerges in intensified form, the two classical systems transcending the many linguistic and cultural diversities. In another way Western classical music fulfills the same function, for it is a kind of music that, despite regional and national diversity, musically unified Europe and European-derived culture, while national and regional folk musics symbolize this diversity. The popular music of the mass media fulfills this unifying function as well, but with less stability of style and—the popular music repertories of Italy, Germany, and the United States differing more than the repertories of their symphony orchestras and opera houses—uneven geographic distribution. In Western culture, too, only a small part of the population really knows the classical music. It can be accorded "favored" status mainly because of its role as a symbol of what is musically great, the respect it has even among those who do not particularly like it. In most ways it is musically exceptional, differing rather sharply from folk music, popular music, hymns, and marches, all of which have elements of form, brevity, and harmonic simplicity in common; it does not provide the stylistic unity of folk or popular music.

In the music of the Blackfoot, something that we could call a "classical" repertory can possibly also be distinguished. Informants give certain songs the status of being "favorite songs of the tribe" (Nettl 1967b: 148; see also McClintock 1910). Evidently there are social as well as musical criteria. The songs associated with the most traditional venerated activities may have this status; those that must be sung at certain points in public ceremonies—for example, while raising the pole of the Sun Dance lodge in preparation for this major tribal ceremony—seem to have been so designated. But the criteria may be musical as well. When a group of songs that have in various ways been labeled as favorite by the Blackfoot were compared, as a group, to the rest of the repertory, they showed a slight tendency to be exceptional. Some use more tones in their scales, others have unusual and sometimes more complex forms, or include less repetition. The difference is not great or obvious, but within the Blackfoot repertory, these exceptional and favorite songs play a role just a bit like that of classical musics in Europe and Asia.

We may have to find a "favored" song style in a culture by looking for what is common, or what is exceptional. Authenticity is a concept most frequently associated with the idea of folk music, but if it is to be used to identify the music most central to a society, it may just as frequently have to be applied to other kinds and strata of music. The question of a "favored song style" intersects with the definition of folk music, its relationship to other musics in its society, and its symbolic role. Two contrastive views emerge in the literature.

The first view, widely accepted in modern times, separates classes and suggests that each population group within a society has a primary musical allegiance. Thus, in rural Iran, the Kurdish, Turkish, and Persian villages, and in an Iranian town, the Armenians and Jews, as well as the Persian majority, all have their own musics. These may exhibit different musical status, but in any event they correspond to differences of social status. In India various castes and communities had their own musics—the Bauls, the Kota, the Pillai; in the classical music system, castes tend to have different roles in an ensemble, lower ones being more frequently the accompanists (Neuman 1980: 124–29).

The other view holds that all members of a society are united musically by a fundamental stratum, which may be labeled "folk music." Wiora (1957: 22) stated it clearly, in its complexity, in a way that reflects the thinking of his time. "Not all folkish music, [music which is] non-professional [and] easily understood, is to be called folk music in the true sense. Rather, this term is used only for that which is properly the culture of the folk. And by 'folk,' we mean not only the totality of the basic strata of society such as peasants, herdsmen, miners, folk musicians, etc., but also that which is truly and generally valid for an entire society" (my translation).

The point Wiora is making is that what can be called the folk music of a society must be music held in common by all its components and classes. In the revision of a paper titled "The Folkness of the Nonfolk and the Non-folkness of the Folk" (1977: 335–43), Charles Seeger argued that the people of the United States "are divided into two classes: a majority that does not know it is a folk; a minority, that thinks it isn't" (343). Clearly Seeger thought that the whole population had enough in common to constitute, in some sense, a "folk" that shared a folk music, if not as repertory then as conception, and he mourned the lack of awareness. Wiora's and Seeger's emphasis is on what the members of a society musically have in common. Certain individuals may go beyond this basic "folk" stratum to create such things as "art" music, but what ties them together continues to be the common folklore. It's this that has led, they suggest, to the revivals of folklore and folk music in various kinds of Western urban contexts.

Another version of this same theme holds that it is rather the classical tradition—the "great tradition," as it was put by Singer and Redfield (Singer 1972: 7–10)—that holds together people whose folk traditions are actually quite diverse. Various ethnic groups, castes, communities, and religions in India that have, for their everyday musical experience, a different repertory, nevertheless are united by their respect for, their allegiance to, a common classical repertory. To a smaller extent, this may also be said of Iran.

There are few, if any, studies of the role of rural folk music in the world's urban cultures, and of the symbolic value of various repertories in an urban society. Emphasis has been on the role of folk music as symbol of the separateness of ethnic groups. But it is not always so restricted. In central European cities of the first half of this century, a selected body of folk music was known, taught in schools, and brought to the attention of middle-class children by nannies from the countryside, and members of this middle class usually knew something they considered to be folk music. To them the folk repertory is a unifying factor because it is a fact of musical life. A "great tradition," functioning more as a symbol, may be a unifying factor in another respect. Many Indians and Iranians do not hear or know their classical traditions but respect them and regard them as symbols of cultural and national identity. It is also as symbol of national identity that the European folk song of the nineteenth and early twentieth centuries served. Following Seeger, we note that either a simple or a complex repertory may fulfill this unifying function. The common stratum may be high or low. Bill Broonzy may be wrong, and all music is not folk music. But all people may have a kind of music that fulfills Wiora's function of folk music, the integration of the larger society.

We Never Heard a Bad Tune

Ethnomusicologists sometimes appear to be hypocritical. They claim to wish to study all of the world's music, on its own terms, and to introduce only those values that are held by the culture investigated. But their writings frequently show their inability (or unwillingness) to avoid injecting certain of their own values. Thus Western ethnomusicologists deal with European folk music, African music, and Chinese music in ways that reflect their relationships to the values of Western culture, including those that attracted them to these musics in the first place (see Blum 1991). European folk music research has typically produced large printed collections, while the music of India has stimulated studies revering the wisdom of theorists and the complexity of musical design. African music has often been the vehicle for assessments of intercultural relationships, and South American Indian music of the complex functions of music in shamanism. Many folk music studies give off a feeling of intimacy; those of Tibetan music, an aura of archeological curiosity; of American Indians, a kind of defensiveness about the importance of presumably uninteresting music in the complex organism that is culture.

It has become accepted that we find out how a society evaluates its various musical products, and that we try to see how the fundamental values of a culture may be reflected in its music. I have discussed ethical and social values that determine the kind of person an ethnomusicologist is likely to be or become. But I wish now also to examine some of the values that have moved the profession in particular scholarly directions.

What, by an ethnomusicological standard, is good music? One may say that all music is worthy of equally thorough study, or reply by concentrating on that part of a music that a society itself regards as its most valued. Or one may, as an outsider, identify by one's own criteria the most valuable style for preservation and research. For determining cultural or musical quality or value, a number of criteria appear to have been used, but in all cases they determine music that conforms to an ideal, an ideal that may be the scholar's own.

The concept of the "authentic" for a long time dominated collecting activities, became mixed with "old" and "exotic" and synonymous with "good." Subsuming age and stability under the rubric of authenticity, Charles Seeger (1977: 51–53) accuses ethnomusicologists of practicing ethnocentrism in reverse and chides us for the application of preconceived ideas as to what is worthy of study, and thus missing out on much that should have been investigated. Indeed, until very recently, the music most often chosen as the object of ethnomusicological study was that which contrasted most, in any of a number of ways, with the scholar's own musical experience and background. Most typical of these objects was the supposedly pure, unpolluted style of the folk or tribal community. Nineteenth-century ideas of musical and cultural purity held on for decades in the understructure of a field that was striving to separate itself from practical society and politics. Curiously, the concept of a pure music as the mark of a pure and unpolluted society has continued into the late twentieth century. Even a look at our transcriptions and analytical procedures shows that they are conceived for homogeneous, unmixed repertories, and comments accompanying them suggest that what we are looking for is the music unmistakably belonging to a particular society.

Describing his work in the southern Appalachians in 1916, Cecil Sharp reveled in the purity of the folk song style of that isolated area: "When, by chance, the text of a modern street-song succeeds in penetrating into the mountains, it is at once mated to a traditional tune and sometimes still further purified by being moulded into the form of a traditional ballad" (1932: xxvi). His collaborator of many years, Maud Karpeles, describing the same field trip, exulted in the fact that "throughout our stay in the mountains we never heard a bad tune, except occasionally when we were staying at a missionary settlement" (1973: 97). The scholarship of Sharp and Karpeles was dominated by the belief that certain kinds of music were good, others bad, and the criteria are evident in these short statements (see also Karpeles 1951). But pollution is inevitable everywhere. "The country has been opened up, roads have been built, and the serpent in the guise of radio and records has penetrated into this Garden of Eden" (Karpeles 1973: 98). Never mind that the serpent in this case was the vanguard of Christian evangelism. Sharp evidently did not wish to collect all of the music extant in the Appalachian communities but had specific ideas of what music properly belonged, and it was music believed to be old, to have uniformity of style, and to be unique in comparison to other musics that might be around. These criteria determined purity and authenticity.

Scholars from non-Western musical cultures often share this approach, supplementing it with insights into the practical problems and issues confronting their societies. One of their most articulate, Habib Hassan Touma, has indicated in various published and oral statements the importance of identifying and studying as authentic that which is regarded as excellent in the culture. Critical of the mixing of Arabic and Western elements in modern Arabic music, he maintained that "the typical Arabic musician now practices a kind of music which is neither genuinely Arabic nor genuinely foreign, but which is greatly influenced by public taste and demand . . . thus the new developments are nothing but incredible deformation of the traditional music through the use of foreign elements from non-Arabic cultures" (1975: 129, my translation). While not explicitly denying the usefulness of understanding modern, mixed styles, he wished to see ethnomusicology support modernization by helping to produce a new music that—in contrast to what has been done—is a genuine continuation of the traditional art music (132). Having stated his cultural and musical values, he builds an approach to field-work upon them, using them as criteria to identify the best performers. If one is to understand properly the essence of a musical culture, Touma asserted, one must concentrate on the best musicians (1968: 22).

One can hardly fault a fieldworker for seeking what is in some respect the best. One would surely get a different picture of Western classical music if one studied it through the performances of Isaac Stern and Mstislav Rostropovich than if one learned from the playing of high school orchestras. Lest we use the latter as norm on account of their frequency, let's remember that high school orchestras would not exist were not the great virtuosos known and available as ideals. Guidance from informants often pushes one in the direction of looking for the best. Sometimes it is inconceivable to them that a scholar might have anything else in mind. My principal Iranian teacher did not understand why I should have an interest in making comparative studies of several performers. Finally it dawned on him: "You are doing this to show why I am a better musician than the others!" That I might wish to understand what was done by the average musician made no sense to him; after all, these people were trying but failing to quite accomplish what the great musicians succeeded in doing, and they knew it. Why study a culture through what it itself regards as imperfect? Historians of Western music sometimes take the same approach, but since they are not Renaissance or eighteenth-century musicians, they cannot speak with the authority of my teacher, who was, after all, an authentic informant for his culture. But my teacher would have fitted excellently into the framework of modern Western humanism.

In a presentation critical of values used in ethnomusicology, Eugene Helm states the humanist position strongly: "We seem to have forgotten about *quality*. I do not advise my graduate students in historical musicology to resurrect inferior composers of the past, and by the same token I am not ready to treat all non-Western musics as equally worthy of study" (1977: 201). Richard Franko Goldman, in an article, "In Support of Art" (1976), that was controversial when published, argued at length for the superiority of the Viennese classicists and Gothic cathedrals over music from Afghanistan and Inuit igloos.

One can easily find points of disagreement with these statements, based on the belief that one can use a kind of universal measuring device for quality, since it is not just the consensus or judgment of a society upon its own musical values with which they are concerned. Laying aside the obvious questions raised by reception history, the claims that some Western composers are better than others is not analogous to the suggestion that some musics are better than others. They are horses of different colors, and combining them sends shivers up the spines of many ethnomusicologists, each of whom would fear that *his* or *her* music could be withdrawn from accreditation. The music historian who studies seemingly insignificant, though perhaps in their day popular, composers might wish to join them, and the ethnomusicologists would ask whether it is not enough to say that each music, by its own standards, has its good and bad works. But even this generalization may go too far. What should we say about the Blackfoot tradition, in which there is good and bad singing but in which people feel uncomfortable saying that any song is "bad," since songs, in their belief-system, are all the gifts of the supernatural? Or about the Persian masters who are willing to single out important and significant parts of the *radif* but who would never suggest that parts of it are "bad"—and thus, that performance might be bad, but the music itself never?

Music historians have long had to deal with problems occasioned by the question of the relative worthiness of their subject matter. They often find it necessary to justify working with the opus of a particular composer by claiming that it is better on strictly musical grounds than had heretofore been supposed, or that it was historically significant because it exhibits influences and connections. Ethnomusicologists, asked why they work with this or that tribe, may give the equivalent of the mountain climber's answer, "Because it is there." But they, too, are often substantially affected by the belief that one should study what is in some universal (or perhaps Western) sense good or outstandingly important, and guidelines for writing grant proposals may require this kind of justification. There's a bit of hypocrisy in this line of thinking, but we often succumb to it even when no grant is involved. Titles such as "Diasporas and Preservation: English Dance Songs in Northern Ohio" or "Music in Warfare and Conflict: The Enermartin of the Ecuadorian Shuar" (I'm parodying the structure of some recent titles) seem to suggest that what is important is the theoretical conclusion; the musical or cultural material that leads to it is in itself of no value except to support the theory. I don't want to argue one side or the other here, but suggest that in contrast to the ethnomusicologist, a music historian who found a Mozart manuscript wouldn't use a title like "Methodological Advances in Manuscript Identification: Mozart's 42nd Symphony." The implication is that Mozart's music is valuable for itself but that Ohio songs or the music of Ecuadorian natives are worth studying, or at least presenting, only if they can be used to illustrate a general point. I hope we've gone beyond this perspective of the world's music. To say that there is just good music and bad music doesn't tell us enough.

26

The Creatures of Jubal: Instruments

A Musician? What Do You Play?

The study of instruments from various perspectives is essential in ethnomusicology. Most obviously, who plays what, and what that means, are questions that occupy us. We want to know why, in Carnatic music, women are largely singers; and why that used to be the case in American schools of music as well; or why until recently, brass instruments (and to a degree woodwinds as well) were male territory. But also, the subdiscipline of organology—the systematic study of instruments—has been an important part of our field, and it continues to have a presence because of the increasing importance of museums and because of the gradual establishment of the field of archeomusicology, in good part a subfield of ethnomusicology, which depends principally on the study of instruments as ancient artifacts. The proper role for the study of instruments in the academy has for decades been a subject of discussion. Should it be a separate field that partakes of the methods of historical, ethnomusicological, and systematic musicologies; should instruments be viewed principally in their social and historical contexts? Should they mainly just be played, in styles both traditional to them and innovative? Some surveys of ethnomusicology (e.g., Blacking 1973; Bose 1953; Czekanowska 1971; Merriam 1964) don't treat instrument study as a separable subdivision, while in others (such as Hood 1971; Kunst 1959; Myers 1992; Nettl 1964; Sachs 1962) individual chapters, sometimes of great length, are devoted to organology separately from discussion of the music they produce or the societies that use them. The debate is not about the intrinsic importance of instruments, but about where, disciplinarily, this study best belongs. So, with whichever camp they associate themselves, most ethnomusicologists actually devote quite a bit of their time to the study of instruments, from collecting specimens and integrating them in a classification system to semiotic analysis and on to learning how to play. And increasingly, teachers introducing the content and the ideas of ethnomusicology in higher education do it by encouraging students to concern themselves with instruments and playing them. This may include assigning students to invent and build simple instruments, to giving lessons in any of the world's traditions, to establishing ensembles.

One role of organology in the history of music research has been its tendency to draw various subdisciplines of musicology together. In Adler's 1885 conspectus, it is one of the major subdivisions of "systematic musicology," and some of those few institutions that maintain this field very much include the study of instruments—though sometimes as part of programs in psycho-acoustics or psycho-musicology. To historians of music concerned with performance practice, instruments are essential artifacts for learning how music sounded, and a lot more. For ethnomusicologists, they are part of the infrastructure that enables them to see music in society and culture. Instruments are the principal objects for the student of musical iconography. The archeologist of music is concerned with instruments more than with anything else. Students of tuning systems work most with instruments or at least need instruments to see how theory matches reality. Instruments seem to be a cultural universal. In Western culture and its Middle Eastern antecedents, music — sometimes a good, sometimes a bad thing—is very commonly seen as quintessentially instrumental. Genesis 4:21 describes Jubal as the "ancestor of all who handle the lyre and the pipe"; folk tradition often casts him as the inventor of music—although it seems certain that singing preceded playing. And so now, in modern North America, when told that someone is a musician, one automatically asks, "What does she play?"

The literature that claims to be specifically organological has a core of concerns: the classification of instruments in a system that is universally applicable, the representations of instruments in visual art, catalogues of the complete instrumentarium of a culture, and the building and maintenance of instrument collections. All of these relate to ethnomusicology, but ethnomusicologists also have further concerns in the study of instruments. In an exposition of ethnomusicology as a group of concepts and issues, we should ask what aspects of organology are the subject of argument and debate. Let's look at a few.

But Is It an Instrument?

That may actually be a complicated question, one that has at least two approaches: Is it an instrument by "our" (Western? scholarly? objective?) standards, and do the people who own or owned it consider it part of the musicking world? Two recent publications speak to that question, from insider and outsider perspectives. Emblematic of the increased interest in archeological work, articles in Hickmann, Kilmer, and Eichmann's collection (2002) present studies of recent archeological discoveries or continue debates about old ones, concentrating on their identities and the tone systems they might represent. *Visions of Sound* (Diamond, Cronk, and von Rosen 1994) studies instruments of Native (or First Nations) peoples of eastern North America; its principal aims concern symbolism of sound made by instruments, the ways in which instruments facilitate interaction and relationships, and the need to present the information from a variety of Native and outsider perspectives. Briefly, archeologists want to know whether that object is "really" a flute; ethnographers want to know what it means to say, "This is a flute."

During a recent conference of the Society for Ethnomusicology, while some 600 people devoted to that field had gathered in Toronto, the *New York Times* and the Toronto papers published an article about what is supposed to be the oldest musical instrument, that bone flute with at least two finger holes discovered in 1995 in a Neanderthal archeological site in Slovenia (Kunej 1997). Curiously, no one at this meeting, to my knowledge, publicly noted or mentioned this discovery, even though that artifact later on became the subject of argumentation in scholarly and journalistic literature. Some of the claims: It's obviously part of a bone flute with finger holes; the arrangement of the finger holes suggests the rudiments of a diatonic scale or scale segment; it tells us about the origins of music, or at least the earliest music. (I was about to write "human music," but the evolutionary status of the Neanderthals is still not clear to biological anthropologists.)

These claims lead to interesting questions: How can one be sure that this small segment of bone is an instrument? Perhaps it's just a random configuration of who knows what. The degree to which three finger holes can identify the scale of the whole instrument is questionable; one can't know whether this was an octave-based or a fourth-based instrument; worse yet, whether this represents one of several tunings that the Neanderthals used, or whether they "tuned" at all. Indeed, there is no way of knowing whether this was an instrument accepted by its society or something that one individual, an off-the-wall guy maybe, made for himself. And then, if the Neanderthals were a separate gene pool and even a different species from Homo sapiens, is this an instrument that belongs in the study of human music at all? Some conclusions that have been drawn result from our enormous desire to legitimize our Western musical practices by showing that they have ancient roots.

The issue is whether that "flute" is actually an instrument, capable of producing music, and second, whether it was accepted as a proper part of the culture by its society. It is 40,000 to 80,000 years old. But in the early twentieth century, the Blackfoot people appear to have had no flutes. I asked some of them; they knew that most Native peoples did have flutes. "Well, we think there were flutes here long ago, but we don't seem to have any." A careful search of museums yielded one artifact, a flute made of a gun barrel. Surely, even if there were Blackfoot flutes long ago, they were not made of gun barrels, so I had to ask myself whether that was a proper instrument, playable and accepted. But then, studying in Madras in 1981, I heard of two musicians who played Carnatic music on saxophones. The issue was not whether saxophones were instruments but whether they were properly instruments belonging to South Indian culture, or temporary interlopers. Today we know: They have been accepted, and there are more saxophonists of Carnatic music, but this raised the question of determining whether an instrument is actually part of a musical culture. And then, in a culture that distinguishes between musical and nonmusical sounds less with acoustic than with social criteria, one needs to ask whether an airplane motor (used in George Antheil's "Airplane Sonata") or a helium bomb (used in Salvatore Martirano's "L'sGA" to raise the narrator's voice) are subjects for organological investigation.

This fundamental question, whether an object is an instrument and considered so by its society, and thus appropriate to ethnomusicological study, leads us then to construct an inventory of the instruments that belong to a culture. Books with titles such as "The Musical Instruments of . . ." are probably the most common genre of organological publications, and a listing would occupy several pages. As major examples from history, let me mention just three landmarks. One of the earliest and also most comprehensive is Fernando Ortiz's (1952–55) five-volume study of Afro-Cuban instruments, which told everything that could be known about a geographically limited instrument culture—structure, social role, history, music, and more. Earlier, and the opposite of Ortiz in its breadth, is Izikowitz's (1935) work on South American Indian instruments, a study based largely on museum collections and early ethnographic literature, concentrating on instrument structure and geographic distribution. The sophisticated nature of this work is seen in its title;

Izikowitz understood that calling something a "musical instrument" required understanding a society's conception of music and its boundaries. As a third landmark, I propose the multivolume *Handbuch der europäischen Volksmusikinstrumente,* whose general editors, Doris Stockmann and Oskar Elschek, produced, through the 1970s and 1980s, a number of volumes surveying the instruments of each nation (e.g., Kunz 1974, for Czechoslovakia), taking into account structure, history, provenance, and to a degree, repertory.

In Society and Culture

These major works, and others like them, look at instruments as a somewhat separable aspect of musical culture. An important aspects of ethno-organology (dare one suggest this term?) is the role of instruments—beyond their musical role—in society and culture. We could examine instruments as aspects of other domains. Thus, a study of the technology of a society should include instrument-making, and those who carry it out quickly discover that in many societies, instruments were among the most advanced and sophisticated products. This may be true of the ancient Neanderthal flute, made perhaps by someone whose only other tools were sticks and clubs. And it is true of the pianoforte of the late eighteenth century, with its complex hammer and escape mechanisms, its pedal action, its highly developed arrangement of strings. Or is the Baroque pipe organ a better example?

Instruments are also properly a part of the study of household furnishings, their aesthetic and their role in society. Again the piano: surely a piece of furniture, just ask your furniture moving company; also an icon of middle-class Western society, found in households where its purpose is just to be there, even if never played, and a part of Asian and African households wishing to exhibit modernness (see, e.g., Kraus 1989). And an important component of the world of symbols; think of the role of the piano's keyboard arrangement, with its white and black keys, on birthday cards for musicians. Similarly, exhibiting Asian or African instruments in North American or western European households where there is no thought of playing them (or even hearing recordings of their music) symbolizes a broad-minded, relativistic attitude of the owner. In Western society, instruments are among the most important indices of other cultures: Note the importance of Indian sitar, African harp and drum, Australian didjeridu on travel posters and postage stamps.

Instruments are important in gender studies, and in other kinds of studies that examine the interaction of subdivisions of a society. In American middle-class culture of around 1940, women rarely played brass instruments and even less commonly percussion. Largely, they played piano, bowed strings, perhaps flute, and then there was their special domain, the harp— many symphony orchestras had just one woman, their harpist. In the realm of popular music, they rarely appeared as instrumentalists. It's a kind of stereotyping that persisted late in the twentieth century. Thus, even as late as the 1980s, students of trumpet, trombone, and tuba at one midwestern school of music were largely men, while the vocal divisions had disproportionate numbers of women, and of African Americans, suggesting that white males maybe thought (or had once thought) that they were the only ones qualified to handle complicated machinery. But certainly during World War II, when women (like "Rosie the Riveter" of song) had begun to enter into many kinds of work previously reserved for men, women also crossed the musical labor line, forming "all-girl bands" and replacing boys in the patriotic drum-and-bugle corps of small-town America.

In Iran of the 1960s, and Madras (Chennai) of the 1980s, instruments were important as markers of gender, and there, too, lines were being crossed. In Iran before the revolution, instruments were largely played by men, but the situation was complex and in the process of changing. In the popular music field, the musicians were men, except for vocalists. In classical music, there were also few women, and they were prevailingly singers as well; but a few were active as instrumentalists, though typically in private environments and rarely on the stage. Their instruments were the strings—the santour, the setar, and sometimes the violin. I don't remember observing female tar, 'ud, or nei players; but in the modernized classical music scene, there were some female pianists. The folk music culture, that aspect of it that involved public per-formance by specialists in narratives or devotional materials, was entirely male. Doubleday (1999) documents widespread special association of women with frame drums (dayereh, daff) throughout the Islamic Middle East. In Iran and Afghanistan, music-making, especially with instruments, was carried out only in rigidly segregated contexts. According to Doubleday (1999: 166–67), "women use the frame drum for informal musical entertainment in the pri-vacy of their all-women domestic space . . . they say it is 'bad' to play when men are at home."

In South India, singing in popular religious genres was accompanied by drums often played by women. In Carnatic music, however, women were mainly singers, and sometimes played violin or vina, but very rarely played flute, and never, I think, the oboe like nagaswaram. Percussion, too, was in the hands of men, but in the early 1980s a few women were beginning to enter this realm. One of the characteristics of South Indian classical music has been its tendency to absorb and adapt foreign, mainly Western instruments, incorporating them into the sound ideal of Carnatic music. I'm talking about the violin and the harmonium in the nineteenth century, and the saxophone, clarinet, guitar, and mandolin in the twentieth. In each case, the instrument was first played exclusively by men, although those instruments that have been established for some time—violin, harmonium—also have female performers. In both the Tehran of 1970 and the Madras (Chennai) of 1980, instruments were important objects in middle-class households, and it was customary for young women to learn to play them even when no professional career was envisioned. In Tehran, even in some households devoted to Persian music, a piano, not played, was present as an icon of modernity. But then, in the households of midwestern university towns, one may see sitars on exposed bookshelves, Chinese *chins* exhibited on the wall, African drums standing on the fireplace, Peruvian panpipes and Native American rattles exhibited around the living room. (Not usually all of these together, I'm sure.) Nobody plays them, their identity may not even be known to the owner, but they are iconic of the intercultural tolerance of the household, or they are trophies of the traveler (surely preferable to antlers or tiger skin rugs), and they function as instruments in quite a different sense of the word from the guitars the family teenager has in his room for use in his garage band, or the pianos in the music school's practice rooms.

In my friend's household, some instruments are so beautifully fashioned and decorated that the owner is considering donating them to a museum— not an ethnographic or organological museum, where they would be viewed principally as music-makers, but a museum of fine arts. If instruments were among the crowning achievements in the technology of many cultures, in some they were also considered objects of exceptional physical beauty, and they were and are often decorated with mosaic or painted, and special care is taken to provide felicitous shapes. I confess that I can't think of a culture whose instrumentarium I have seen in which special efforts had not been undertaken to make the instruments themselves beautiful, attractive, and often the carriers of many kinds of visual signs and symbols. I'm loath to suggest any general theory to explain this, because in one culture this may be the result of the tendency to decorate everything made by humans, in others it may add to the spiritual power of the instrument, and elsewhere again it may make an object associated with a despised art (music) acceptable because it contributes to a more respected (visual) art. But if pressed, I would be inclined to think that instruments, seen perhaps by early humans as perhaps the most powerful tools in establishing relationships to the supernatural and to strange humans, could be enhanced by acquiring additional "visual" power.

So, in an important sense, the role of organology in ethnomusicology includes the study of instruments in society to accomplish things that go far beyond the production of humanly organized sound.

The Legacy of Mahillon and Sachs

Of course it wasn't Victor-Charles Mahillon, the longtime curator of the instrument museum of the Brussels Royal Conservatory—a collection he built into one of the world's most prominent—who invented the idea of cataloging musical instruments. As Margaret Kartomi (1990) points out in great detail in her comprehensive history of instrument classification, many—maybe most?—cultures have developed classifications of instruments, usually of those of their own society. But Mahillon found himself in need of a way of putting the vast number of instruments he was accessioning into some kind of order, providing ways of showing similarities between instruments from distant places, making sense of a body of material, some of which—fieldworkers and tourists and amateurs were often very imprecise in their reporting—could not even be designated by the culture or location. Evidently inspired by a plan developed in India, he developed a system that provides categories for all known instruments, and even some for instruments not known but possibly yet to be discovered. This system (see Mahillon 1880–92), revised in its most widely used format by Erich von Hornbostel and Curt Sachs (1910) and also by André Schaeffner (1932), and becoming the basis of a more complex system by Hans-Heinz Draeger (1948) and further modified by a number of others, including Mantle Hood (1971), has become the mainstream of instrument classification in the musicological world. At the same time, the idea of classifying instruments has continued to fascinate scholars from many cultures. Kartomi (162–210) cites a large number of classifiers, showing particularly the expanding conception of what constitutes an instrument in Western culture.

Given my old bifurcated definition of ethnomusicology, what in particular do ethnomusicologists wish to do with instrument classifications? The concept of classification itself fits our field exceptionally well: They wish to have a system that makes possible intercultural comparisons, and they wish to study the classification of each society in order to see what it tells them about the relationship of fundamental guiding principles of the culture and musical values. Kartomi (1990) shows that many, probably most, of the world's societies give some thought to the grouping of instruments, and describes many systems, including those that classify according to sound production, material, manner of activating, social and ceremonial uses, and according to any number of musical functions. Any of these might conceivably have been expanded to have universal application, but in fact there are few, if any, schemes that have threatened the hegemony of the Mahillon-Sachs-Hornbostel system.

Interestingly, in important works in the organological literature of Japan, a nation where interest in and the nurturing of older traditions and emphasis on the uniqueness of culture play major roles, alongside the highly developed participation in Western-derived scholarship, instrument classification is heterogeneous. Thus the catalog of the instrument collection of the Tokyo National University of the Arts and Music (Koizumi Fumio Memorial Archives 1987) lists and illustrates around 650 instruments, a collection from many cultures (excluding Western classical traditions) according to the standard system—idiophones, membranophones, chordophones, aerophones, to which is added a category of electrophones, illustrated by a Japanese electric drone producer. The catalog of the comparably large collection of the Kunitachi College of Music in Tokyo (Kunitachi College of Music 1986) uses a revised, probably more logical, version of this system, dividing the instruments first by form of the vibrating body (4): massophones (the body is solid—e.g., a stone); cupophones (cup-shaped bodies, e.g., slit drums, rattles); clavophones (stick-shaped, e.g., claves, or the Brazilian cuica); tabulophones (board-shaped instruments that include cymbals but also "reed" instruments, and by extension all winds—i.e., lip-reeds); membranophones (drums) and chordophones (strings). Each category is subdivided by method of application—percussion, friction, plucking, air current, electronic oscillation. In Japanese tradition, however, musicians and the intelligentsia grouped instruments by social and ceremonial function. Kartomi analyzed several ways in which Javanese instruments are classified, including one scheme (1990: 92) by material—bronze, leather, wire, wood, and bamboo—and a number of systems based on musical function or social hierarchy.

There are lots of anomalies. Whether a society has a system of classifying instruments at all, and what kind of system was selected, depends on various factors. Probably the typical way of grouping instruments in the world's vernacular cultures is by musical or maybe social function. Whether a special system of classification based on other criteria has been developed may depend on the existence of instrument ensembles. Thus, the 'Are'are of the Solomon Islands, a numerically small society, has large panpipe ensembles and classifies elaborately on the basis of musical and social criteria (Zemp 1978), while most Native American peoples, with often larger populations but a prevailingly vocal musical culture, don't find this procedure necessary. The terminology of instruments in Blackfoot cultures derives from the ritual or social associations of instruments—for example, medicine drum, Crazy Dog Society drum, medicine pipe rattle—and there is no special system or terminology for the grouping of instruments.

In traditional Western classical music culture, and in junior high school music classes of the 1940s America, one learned that there were string, woodwind, brass, and percussion instruments, and that woodwinds included flute, single-reeds, and double-reeds. This comes from the typical grouping of instruments in the orchestration of Haydn, Mozart, and Beethoven, and it persists in the grouping of instrument departments in university schools of music. Nonorchestral instruments find their places in these departments with difficulty. Harps and guitars are string instruments, to be sure, but show me the string department whose chair is the professor of harp or guitar. Where does the piano go?—strings, yes, it has lots of them, but its keys are beaten. The Brazilian *berimbau*, a musical bow, technically a struck chordophone, takes its place among percussion instruments in North America. The conception of where musical instruments belong in relation to each other leads, as well, to the consideration of where they belong in relation to the humans who use them. Thus, in English, German, French, and most other European languages, the verb for making music on an instrument is "to play," relating it to the other meanings of that word. In Persian, instruments are "beaten" (*zadan*), and while this might seem logical for percussion instruments, for the hammered dulcimer (santour), and even for plucked strings, it is used for bowed and wind instruments as well. And then there is the area of instrument iconography, an area, according to Seebass (in Myers 1992: 238), as yet insufficiently developed, that looks at the depiction of instruments as imparting facts about musical life in different periods and cultures, but also the semiotics of instruments. Here too, various kinds of classification are appropriate.

Beyond classification, I wish to mention two other branches of organology, both involving history, that intersect with the fundamentals of ethnomusicology. Many scholars have devoted themselves to the history of instruments—I mean the history of instruments as a whole, not just of individual instruments or groups or cultures, for which the number of publications is legion, but all instruments. It makes sense to think of this Herculean kind of task only if it's a basic assumption that the instruments of the world, or the instrumentariums of all cultures, have some connection. Best known for this approach was Curt Sachs, mentioned earlier for his contribution to classification (and in earlier chapters to many aspects of the development of ethnomusicology) and the person who, it is often argued, knew more about instruments in the world than anyone before or since. The author of an early but amazingly comprehensive dictionary of instruments (1913), he undertook to write a world history of instruments, giving the entire field an evolutionist framework. There is much in it with which one would have to argue, but also a good deal of wisdom, and there are a lot of stimulating ideas. One thing Sachs does not say, though it flows from his thinking, is that the borders of the concept of "instrument" are vague, and vaguest perhaps in both early human history and the most recent times. There have always been objects that could be considered both instrument and something else, but Sachs suggested (1940: 25) that the earliest instrument was the human body, which might be slapped, or used to stamp the ground, in ways that led to the development of the earliest instruments. Instruments developed out of other things that were available. It's interesting to see that around 2000 c.e., we are again finding the boundary between instruments and noninstruments vague, as musicians fashion new sound tools for one-time use and sounds are produced by synthesizers and other electronic sources that are also used for a variety of communication. Is the concept of "musical instrument" as a consistent class in culture gradually fading from at least one major society?

In Museums

Curt Sachs, who knew so much about the instruments of the world, never did any extended fieldwork himself. His studies are based on private and museum collections, and the task of some ethnomusicologists is to fill, analyze, and care for many of these. They are found in a variety of museums: Some, like the aforementioned collections in Japan and Brussels, or the Horniman Museum in London, or the Stearns Collection at the University of Michigan (see Libin 1992 for an introduction to and listing of major collections), are freestanding collections assembled ad hoc or given as a unit by a donor and later expanded. A few are associated with art museums—most prominently, the large and distinguished collection in the Metropolitan Museum of Art, in New York City—and these present instruments as objects of visual art. In these institutions, an instrument must thus qualify as a work of visual art to be included, but, interestingly, some museum curators and many art lovers in Western culture consider instruments to be, ipso facto, works of visual art and design. The most important collections for ethnomusicological work, however, are in museums of anthropology, or museums named "natural history museums," on the rather absurd but once widely held assumption that the material products of certain cultures belong more to "nature," and of others more to "art." But never mind. The distinguished collections of the Musée de l'Homme in Paris, the collection in Berlin's Museum für Völkerkunde, the various parts of the Smithsonian complex in Washington, D.C., the Field Museum in Chicago, and similar ethnographic museums around the world all contribute importantly to the understanding of instruments in society and culture and history. Museum collections have increasingly become centers of proactive education. They provide information on the cultural context of objects, including instruments, and they often have sound and video recordings to illustrate use of these instruments. Many of them have become centers of applied ethnomusicology and disciplinary outreach.

But what are ethnomusicologists to make of the obvious fact that many of these instruments were collected under false pretenses, or bought for far less than they were worth, or maybe even stolen, and in any case that their acquisition may have contributed to the depletion of native material cultures and traditions? Should not these instruments be returned, as is being suggested for major art works—even the Elgin Marbles, taken in the nineteenth century from Greece to the British Museum? The "repatriation" of recordings such as the National Cylinder Project can serve as a model.

And which instruments should be considered for this kind of repatriation? Here, too, we run into the problem of boundaries, a problem that keeps returning to us in many of the issues discussed in these chapters. Then there is the question of authenticity. Should Native American instruments made by non-Natives be exhibited if the makers had a special relationship to the society in question? How can personal or national ownership be determined? Actually, the investigation of instrument collections as institutions itself is an interesting challenge for students of music in culture.

27

How Do You Get to Carnegie Hall? Teaching and Learning

Practice, Practice, Practice!

The Broadway barfly's smart reply to the tourist who asks how to get to the famous concert hall. But there are actually many ways in which one arrives at the Carnegie Halls of world music and, like practicing as a concept, "learning music" means many things. One may learn pieces, or a way of performing, or the abstract fundamental principles of a musical system. Perhaps one learns how to listen and appreciate music, perhaps exercises such as scales, or short and easy pieces composed for learning. Surely also a set of attitudes and kinds of social behavior. It all can be broken down to learning a musical system, consisting of many (and sometimes various types of) discrete units of many sorts that a musician—composer, performer, improvisor, even informed listener—learns to manipulate. In one way or another, the method of teaching breaks a system down into these basic units. In Western academic or classical music they may be pieces or compositions, or smaller ones such as chords, characteristic sequences of chords, or tones in a melody.

It took a long time for ethnomusicologists to take much interest in studying the way a music is taught, or, if you will, transmits itself. Music not notated was often simply said to be learned "by rote," with no concern for the variety of things that might mean. It has become clear, though, that this area of study is quite central to our concerns, helping us to understand the essentials of a musical system, its grammar and its syntax, by learning what within it is taught by its practitioners, discovering how, as it were, a musical culture, as manifested in individual and in group, lives in time. And on the practical side, we may find out how to learn a music foreign to us and incidentally how to interact with music educators and others who make practical use of ethnomusicological findings.

There is a bewildering number of ways in which the world's societies learn their own music, and how some of their members acquire professional excellence. In some, including in particular some of those of the South Seas, children and young people learn the important elements and values of their own culture through musical experience, and adults continue to undergo this process into old age (Ramseyer 1970: 28–31). Among the people of Yirkalla, South Australia, only old men knew the entire ceremonial musical repertory (R. Waterman 1956: 49), and the men in some North American Plains Indian nations moved over the years through a series of warrior societies, learning each time new ritual and cosmological materials, this education continuing well past middle age. Perhaps music has somewhat of this enculturative function everywhere, but if we have recognized its importance in the learning of culture, we have not paid much attention to the way in which people actually learn music, and surely not to the ways in which the elements and values of a culture affect the learning of music. A comprehensive understanding of the music of a culture includes the way it is learned and the materials that are used to teach it.

In modern Western culture, there's a lot to be contemplated about the way classical music is learned. It's an intricate system of music, and the concept of "learning," in itself, both for becoming good at music and simply for becoming good at learning, is quite important. Study and teaching at all levels come up in many American conversations about music. A large proportion of musicians make their living by teaching, and much of the population spends time and energy in the formal learning of music, though in most cases not with the aim of professional musicianship, and a lot of published music is didactic in nature. We care greatly with whom one takes lessons and in general how one goes about studying. If one could monitor all musical sound produced in this society, a large proportion would turn out to be for the purpose of learning, in some sense of that word. And obviously, practicing is not just for learning but also for maintenance.

There are also other important aspects of music learning with which ethnomusicologists are concerned. For one thing, we wish to know how the youngest children learn the essentials of music, and for this, an entire body of studies (surveyed by Minks 2002) has provided insight, suggesting an interaction between biological and cultural factors. Just how the youngest children learn their own music and to what extent it is "music" or "a music" has hardly been clarified yet, partly, in my view, because in much of this research, the concept of "music" has been taken entirely from its Western manifestation. The musical lives of young children who are learning their musical system have been ethnographically illustrated and analyzed by Campbell's (1998) case studies of children in Seattle.

Merriam (1964: 145–64) was one of the first to look at the problem as a whole, and since then, ethnomusicologists have become increasingly interested in the issue of how music is learned and taught, as part of standard musical ethnography, but also to get insight into the ways musical cultures, as it were, transmit themselves. It's an area in which music educators with a commitment to ethnomusicology have played an important role. The bibliography includes significant surveys, such as Campbell's *Lessons from the World* (1991), ethnographic accounts (Berliner 1994; Kingsbury 1988; Neuman 1980), edited and analyzed accounts by musicians of their learning experiences (e.g., Mitchell 1978), and works directed to both ethnomusicologists and music educators who try to include some aspects of a native system of transmission in materials intended for music teachers of all culture (e.g., Lundquist and Szego 1998; McCullough-Brabson and Help 2001).

There are lots of issues for us to contemplate in this large area. Here are just a few. Most fundamentally: When music is transmitted, what is actually learned? While there is a sense in which it is helpful to look at a musical system in written or oral tradition as being transmitted more or less as a unified whole, there are surely certain things that people learn about it that are most important, and that must be carefully imparted, while others are left more or less to being picked up by chance without special attention or instruction. Another issue is just how people practice, in what activities they actually engage when they are teaching themselves music, how and when they carry out the instructions of a teacher, mediating between the points of instruction and performance. And related to this is the use and nature of special materials whose purpose is to help people learn—exercises, etudes, texts on the principles of musicianship. Then there is the identity of teachers and their role in society and in music. And we should know, in an intercultural context, how people in infancy acquire music, and how a musical system, first heard by small children before they are in a position to reproduce it, is perceived by them. There are many other matters, but the general point that I am trying to make is that a musical system, its style, its main characteristics, its structure, are all very closely associated with the particular way in which it is taught, as a whole and in its individual components.

In the sense that a musician is primarily involved in one aspect of the "music delivery" process—composing, performing, teaching, producing, directing, and so on—Western culture of classical music is surely one of the most specialized. It stands out further in rather rigorously separating various kinds of musicians from each other. Singers in the United States are not even members of the musicians' union. Solo and chamber music violinists rarely play in orchestras. A pianist is either mainly a soloist, or an accompanist, or a jazz ensemble musician. Yet the course of musical education is much the same for all. The following may be typical. One begins with an instrument (even if one ends up as a singer), and almost everyone at some point learns to play piano. Piano lessons normally begin with exercises, and the terror of serious beginning students is the requirement that, before all else, they must master the scales in all of the keys and always begin practice sessions with them, with the knowledge that even if they become virtuosos, the need for practicing these scales will not abate. After becoming somewhat proficient on an instrument, one is likely to take up the study of music theory, a subject "theoretical" not in the general sense of the word but rather in that one learns material that does not apply directly to the making of musical sounds but is generalizable to all aspects of musical activity. Until recently, music theory concentrated almost exclusively on harmony and began with its basic units, the types of chords.

In both instrumental and theoretical instruction, one first learns things that do not normally constitute music but that must be manipulated and extended in order to be recognized as components of music. The musical system is presented in an abstracted and somewhat artificial format. Thus, few serious pieces merely use scales or chord sequences precisely in the way they are learned at the beginning of music theory classes. In Western academic music, then, what the teacher may first teach is largely theoretical concepts and gymnastic exercises rather than the units of a higher order, the actual compositions. But in characterizing this system of musical education, it is important to realize that teachers, too, are very specialized, and that for this reason a student going through a bachelor of arts in music education may have some fifteen to twenty teachers of various kinds of musical activity and knowledge over a four-year period.

In most of the world's cultures, compositions—the proper content of music—are imparted directly by the teacher to the student. Not so in Western academic music. Piano students usually do not learn Beethoven sonatas *from* their teacher, with the latter first playing the piece for them, asking them to interpret what they have heard. Rather, the teacher usually confines himself or herself more to general observations, to the instruction of technique and of the materials that make possible the learning of technique, and beyond that asks the students to imbibe Beethoven from the written page, learning, as it were, from the composer. I see our system of teaching as a combination of theoretical and practical materials, with the teacher playing a much larger role in the theoretical.

Learning the Building Blocks

In the classical music of South India, the situation is somewhat similar. While the Western musician learns the basic system through piano and theory classes, students of Carnatic music are likely to learn it by exposure to vocal music, even if they turn out to be instrumentalists. At the knee of the teacher, the student studies a long series of exercises that exhibit the characteristics of raga and tala, melody and rhythm, and juxtapose the two in various combinations. These exercises and some simple introductory pieces constitute or include fundamental units such as rhythmic and melodic motifs that are later used in learned compositions and, more important, in the improvisation that forms much of the core of musical performance. The emphasis is upon memorizing materials that will make it possible for one to improvise. Indian composers who, in contrast to improvising, create songs such as the extended South Indian kriti, whose structure has common features with improvisations, evidently undergo training similar to that of the performer. In the Western classical system, by contrast, performer and composer, in part at least, have rather different kinds of learning experiences.

Western and Indian musicianship have in common the concept of discipline, the need to practice the building blocks of music for many hours at a time, directing one's effort only indirectly to what will happen in a performance. A pianist spends much time on scales and exercises, even with a Chopin recital coming up. South Indian singers do not spend their time only trying out various combinations of material and improvising, as they will have to do in public, but also devote hours every day to exercises, from the simple to the very difficult. Indeed, Indian musicians are evaluated by each other only partly in accordance with their musicianship as exhibited in performance, or with their knowledge of repertory, but also in large measure by their reputation for disciplined practice and study, called *riaz* by North Indians (Neuman 1980: 32–43). "If a musician wants to celebrate the genius of another musician, he will do so . . . in terms of practice habits" (31).

To these two cultures, Persian classical music provides a contrast. The musician of Iran studies the *radif,* memorizing it precisely from his teacher's version, which may be similar but not identical to that of other teachers. The teacher is concerned only with the student's ability to reproduce what he or she sings or plays in lessons with utmost exactness. He does not explain the minutiae of the structure of the *radif,* although the student needs to learn these in order to engage in improvisation, the central activity in true performance. The student must deduce from the *radif,* with its many examples of variation, melodic sequence, extension and contraction of motifs, that its very structure is the guide to improvisatory procedure. Once the *radif* is memorized, the student is considered ready to perform without further instruction. He or she has learned a theoretical construct and must now suddenly move to improvisation. The Indian musician had to study building blocks of varying degrees of complexity, units that gradually become increasingly like real music. The Iranian musician leaps directly from study, detailed but at only one level of conceptualization, into true performance.

By contrast with these three high cultures, we have much less detailed information about teaching and learning from societies without musical literacy or written theory. Blackfoot people traditionally believed that humans could learn music in two interconnected ways, from supernatural powers such as guardian spirits in visions and from other humans. The ideal was the learning of songs from the supernatural, and the concepts of learning and creating music are therefore closely associated. The way in which songs were thought to be learned in visions, normally in a single hearing, has influenced the concepts that people have about learning music in an entirely human context. In the culture of the Blackfoot, once may presumably mean four times through, so the concept is there, but the idea that the guardian spirit teaches you a song simply by *singing* it to you is important, and human teachers instructed similarly. Thus a medicine bundle, with its attendant songs, was transferred from one person to another by a single performance of the ceremony, during which the new owner was expected to learn the songs. Today, when people learn songs from each other and recognize the process as such, they say that quick learning is desirable and certainly possible, though lately often violated by the ever-present cassette recorder. The standardization of form and the possibility of roughly predicting the course of a song from its initial phrase as teaching devices are also cases in point.

The varying emphases on various kinds of units and different aspects of the musical system given by a teacher help to identify the building blocks of the music. It is obvious that in northern Plains music, the head motifs that begin songs are the most important things, actually identifying the songs, which frequently do not have names. On the other hand, when I studied the *radif* with an Iranian musician, I was told that parts of it were important, and while these are stressed to some extent in the performances, the fact that they are singled out as important particularly in the teaching of the *radif* may well reflect ideas extremely important in the culture. Those parts of a *dastgah* that tended to depart from the norm were often stressed by my teacher as being important, and in other respects, in Iranian culture, events or actions that departed from a norm were sometimes particularly valued. By a similar token, the fact that the Western music student learns a theoretical system based largely on a particular part of his or her repertory, that of the period between 1720 and 1900, indicates rather forcefully what we consider most important in our musical experience, an attitude that contrasts interestingly with our tendency to prize innovation. While we are surely cognizant of the fact that melody and rhythm are of major importance to our own music-making, the fact that music theory has always stressed harmony indicates that perhaps of all the things that make our music properly an art, the system of harmony is one of the most important.

If I Skip a Day . . .

Not only what is taught but also the activities involved in learning can tell us what is valued in a music. Practicing seems to be almost a universal. One reads about the incredible energy of Indian, Persian, and European musicians who practice, throughout their lives, eight hours a day. The intricacies of practice routines in jazz occupy major portions of Berliner's (1994) definitive work on jazz. Western practitioners of art music have many techniques of practicing. Constant vigilance is required: Paderewski said, we are told, that if he skipped practice one day, he would know it; two days, and the critics know it; three days, and the audience knows. In practicing, the repetition of a great deal of didactic material—scales, exercises, and etudes—is standard. Many musicians are unwilling to practice "real" music without first going through theoretical material of the aforementioned sort. The function of these "theoretical" scales and exercises may not be quite clear, but surely the concept of warming up mentally or physically is rather important. In India, musicians have a similar approach to practicing, the daily repetition of exercises being an almost religious necessity, and their function as building blocks for improvisation is clearer. Elsewhere again, among the Shona people of Zimbabwe, according to Maraire's interpretation, the introductory section of a formal performance is also a kind of warming up. In Western classical music, there doesn't seem to be much agreement on the practicing component of music teaching. Some teachers rely on exercise books to guide practicing; others, as it were, practice with the student—lessons are mainly supervised practice sessions that serve as models—while others again leave it all to the student's idiosyncrasies.

In a second aspect of practicing, Western academic musicians try to memorize things that might not really have to be memorized, mainly in order to show the ability to absorb musical materials. One might have thought that the development of notation could lead to specifically the opposite. Third, the habit of singling out short bits of music in order to repeat them indicates the great stress on technical proficiency we have developed in Western music. Indeed, a Western concert is to a large extent an exercise in mental and dexterous ability. The idea of doing something very difficult, of music as a craft, is highly developed. Such a view is also found in India, but to a much smaller extent than in Iran, for the tradition of learning the Persian *radif* was that one had to learn it slowly because of the music's essentially philosophical and mystical significance. The introduction of Western notation into Iranian music has always been controversial, partly because it made possible the learning of the *radif* very efficiently and very quickly, violating the belief that the music was in itself something to be contemplated. Nour-Ali Khan, for example, wished to teach only a very small amount of it to me every week, saying that it was important for me to play it frequently, to look at it from all sides, listen to it, examine it, contemplate it. Perhaps contemplation acts as a stimulus for students to learn to understand the way the structure of the *radif* teaches the techniques and concepts of improvisation.

What do we know about the way in which traditional Native American singers practiced? Today, the rehearsal techniques of powwow Drums are comparable to those of mainstream popular music groups. But earlier on? There is evidence that those cultures in which the precise rendering of music for validation of religious ritual was very important also required systematic practicing and rehearsing and looked at it all competitively. We are told this about the Navajo and the north Pacific Coast peoples (Herzog 1938: 4, 1949: 106–7; McAllester 1954: 76–77; but see also Frisbie 1980 for discussion of various cultures of the Southwest). Rehearsing was essential, mistakes were punished, rituals in which mistakes were found would have to be repeated entirely or in part in order to be valid. Some northern Plains peoples took a less formalist attitude. Having been learned largely from visions for the use of one person, music was more closely associated with the individual and private rituals, and therefore the control of the community over musical performance was less highly developed. Evidently a man who learned a song in a vision would use his walk or ride back to camp as an opportunity to rehearse or work it out. No doubt, actual composition took place along this walk; the inspiration from the white heat of the vision would be rationally worked out. Practicing in effect took place at this point, and the song would be readied for presentation to the other members of the tribe. But since music was primarily a personal and individualistic activity and experience, practicing was not done systematically to any large extent, and not much heed was paid to the accuracy of performance. Just as composing and learning are related concepts, composing and practicing overlap.

The introduction of Western notation to many non-Western cultures accompanied and perhaps caused changes in practicing. The various types of notation long used in Asian societies (Kaufmann 1967) were hardly used for reading while performing, but they functioned as references and perhaps even more as aids to scholarly discussion of music (Hickmann 1970: 45–47). Along with Western music, mainly in the nineteenth and twentieth centuries, came the idea of learning music visually rather than aurally. In Iran and India, musicians critical of dependence on notation understood that it was more than a mechanical convenience, and that fundamental changes in the music system would result from its use.

Gurus and Spirits

One might expect notation to become so thoroughly developed that from it a student could learn an entire musical system without hearing it, and without human intervention. We haven't yet arrived at that point, and, indeed, the learning of music is almost everywhere an experience of intense relationship between student and teacher. The identity, social role, and approach of the music teacher is an important component of a socio-musical system, and ethnomusicologists have in recent times come to describe some instances very thoroughly. (See the following publications for examples: Bakan 1999; Berliner 1978, 1994; Danielou 1973; Nettl 1974a; Neuman 1980; Tracey 1948; and, in a very unusual way, Mitchell 1978.)

It is interesting that in many cultures, including those used to illustrate this chapter, there is a distinction between the practicing musician and the master teacher. To be sure, ordinary musicians do teach, but great teachers are often people who know material well but are not necessarily best at rendering it. The concept of the specialist music teacher actually exists in a large number of societies. In Western music we have, of course, a large group of professionals who do little beyond teaching. They are often people who are not highly respected and may be denigrated by performers and composers as people who have not made it in the practical field and are therefore relegated to teaching. Actually, society does not treat them all that badly. It is interesting to see that most performers are paid worse than are teachers, that teachers develop certain kinds of job security not shared by performers and composers; all of this may be related to the low evaluation of music and the somewhat higher value of the concept of education. Interpreting much more broadly, it may be that in our culture the handing on of the tradition is regarded as more important than its expansion.

In India as well, great teachers are not necessarily great performers, but they are renowned for their *riaz*. For a performer it is important, even more than elsewhere, to be associated with a highly qualified teacher. The genealogy of student-teacher relationships is often recited in introducing Indian concerts, and a performer is praised for carrying on the tradition of his teacher's *gharana*. It is therefore interesting to see that in the most recent period of Western culture, the Indian concept of guru has come to symbolize the idea of devoted study and teaching. In fact, two terms are widely used in India, "guru" (originally associated with Hinduism) and "ustad" (of Muslim origin). The two concepts are no longer limited to religious or ethnic groups and are more or less interchangeable in actual use. But they represent two approaches to the concept of teaching (Neuman 1980: 44–45), with both terms applied to the same person. The term "ustad," best translated as "master" or even "professor," symbolizes the technical expertise of the teacher, the musical ability and the knowledge. The term "guru" symbolizes the teacher's role in molding not only the student's musical learning but also the adoption of an appropriate lifestyle, the student's absorption of music as a part of culture.

In the classical tradition of India one was expected to become a particular kind of person in order to be recognized as a musician. As modern and Western approaches to music teaching came to be used in the twentieth century, there developed a bifurcation between those who studied in the traditional way, with guru/ustad, and those who went to music schools, spending three years in a conservatory atmosphere taking courses with various professors and emerging with a B.A. The latter might be given credit for excellent knowledge and technique, but they were accorded little respect by those more traditionally schooled. It would seem that they lacked the close personal association, comprising much more than simply music, with the figure of authority.

Normally, music teachers are human, but some, like certain figures in Indian music history, have become mythological figures, the subjects of stories of incredible accomplishment. Ustad Allauddin Khan, father of the modern development of North Indian classical music, is said to have mastered eighty instruments. Another musician was said to have practiced daily for sixteen hours without interruption. Of course, there are also many legends about the ability of master musicians to affect the course of nature and history through their control over ragas. Stories about the power of music are almost universal, and familiar from the figures of Orpheus and Tamino, but in India the powers of the great teacher seem to be particularly stressed. In yet other cultures we find the music teacher to be a directly supernatural figure. The Plains Indians, we have seen, learn their songs from beings who appear in dreams, and thus the concept of teaching songs, if not the process, appears prominently in folklore and mythology.

But in modern Blackfoot culture (as I experienced it in the 1960s), there is also a sharp distinction between individuals who, in guru-like fashion, know the older traditions but do not perform in public, and others who sing for social dances. A mixed system of supernatural and human teachers is described by Berliner (1978: 136–45) for mbira players of the Shona of Zimbabwe. Spirits are thought to encourage students and players in dreams, and also to teach the instrument and its repertory. The human teachers of the Shona use a number of ways of approaching their task. Some (140–41) break down the music into component phrases, teaching them one at a time. Others teach the part of each plucking thumb separately, then combine the two. Berliner stressed the looseness of a common method, which goes no further than an insistence that there be a proper approach (whatever that may be in the individual case), and on developing a good memory. This diversity of method must be related to the highly individualistic approach that Shona musicians have to their instruments and their repertory. Again, the musical system results from, but also determines, the way of teaching.

Multimusical Culture or Multicultural Music

Studying how the world's peoples teach and learn their musics leads to the question of what ethnomusicology may have to do with the way we (in mainstream American culture) teach our music, and this leads to a consideration of the concept of multiculturalism, and the way culture and particularly the arts are presented to children in our schools. There is a vast literature on the subject, and rather than attempt a summary, I wish to describe briefly two personal experiences that helped shed some light on the problems for me. The fundamental question is whether we—and our children—are divided into lots of social groups, each with its own music, a multicultural music, or whether we are better described as a society with a multimusical culture. It's our familiar theme: One musical world, or a world of discreet musics—which approach is more helpful and provides better insight?

A few years ago, I carried out an annual ritual that I have always found satisfying but always prepare with several days of stage fright. I visited the first-grade class of my daughter, an elementary school teacher, to teach for an hour and a half about Native American music. Of course it was fun for me to see my daughter, whom I still saw as a little girl, now the experienced educator very much in charge; and fun for the children to imagine their (they thought) middle-aged teacher having a dad who knew her when she was small. But why really was she asking me to do this? There were no Native American children in the class. There were, to be sure, members of other American minorities; did that provide justification? A unit on Native Americans was part of the syllabus, but she wasn't the music teacher, charged with directing proper musical attitudes (either "three Bs" or "world music"), so why music? Did it make sense for me, a non-Native, with no training in elementary school music teaching, to go into this at all? May it suffice to say that my reason for teaching about Native music is simply that it's there, and worthy of attention as much as anything else.

So, now, what to teach? A number of texts in music education provide material and sophisticated relevant discussion, but the purpose was for me to bring my own experience and background. I could play recordings, but the attention span wouldn't be long; I could teach the young students some songs, but in the end they wouldn't sound the least bit like Native American singing; I could try to explain some rudimentary things about musical style, but that's a lot to ask of first graders. We could imitate some activities, learn a gambling game or a Stomp Dance song, or have a miniature pow-wow. These activities would show something about the musical styles and a bit, too, about music as it contributed to culture.

Actually, I tried them all, none with great success, none total failures. Surprisingly to me (but broadly described by Campbell 1998), the children quickly picked up simple songs, and bits of typical dance steps, and at least some comprehended the difference between the cascading melodic contour of Plains music and the undulations of a Navajo melody. But I wondered whether they would, the next week, be able to recall anything—identify contours, tell what a Stomp Dance is like, know that songs are important in worship, say that drums and rattles and flutes are the principal instruments.

Probably not, my daughter thought, but rather, twelve years from now, in college, in a world music course, one or two of them might say to themselves, "Oh yes, I remember this from first grade." So, I'm not sure how worthwhile my attempt was, but throughout I kept wondering about my mission—not the cultural one, which was fairly clear, but the explicitly musical one. I wondered whether I should be trying to show that this music is really like "ours," whatever "ours" is, easy to understand and internalize. In that case, would these songs have been integrated more, given English words and piano accompaniment? Maybe it made more sense to stress that this music is really very "different," very "strange," show how we can't really make our voices sing it without a lot of practice, rather like a different language, if you will. Should I rather say to the kids, "this is really like the other kinds of music you know," and compare the Stomp Dance to some call-and-response games they knew, and the Peyote syllables to tra-la-la or e-i-e-i-o? Or should I keep pointing out how the songs always go with other activities—ritual, recreation. I wondered how to bring up, at a first-grade level, concepts such as ethnicity, questions such as "whose music is this" and the validity of comparison. Most important, how should I guard against the implication that this music is only interesting because it is associated with Native Americans, while the great music by Mr. Bach and Mr. Mozart—the kids had heard of them—is always interesting to everyone? Well, in the end, these energetic first-graders didn't think this music strange, didn't question whether it sounded like music, took for granted that this was indeed the music of Native Americans, different from their own, but one could listen to it and sing it; they made my worries irrelevant.

The questions raised in my experience are also the ones that I always faced as a college teacher of world music, who must decide whether the basic assumption in their courses is that all of the world's music is basically one system that can be comprehended by all of our students with modest effort, or that the world of music is a group of discrete musical languages each of which can be learned only with great effort and never completely, whose role in culture cannot be fully comprehended by outsiders. And the approach to my daughter's pupils that I should have followed, had I had time and expertise, results from the following assertion: In any society, the way in which music is taught and transmitted is an integral part of the musical culture. And so, in thinking of how to teach something essential to my first-grade friends, I should really have tried to do it in the way the Native Americans, whose music I was presenting, taught their children.

The Fifth-Grade Chorus and the Politics of Representation

That December was evidently my month for excursions in the public schools of my home town, because I also had the opportunity of hearing my grand-daughter's fifth-grade chorus perform a concert. An unmitigated success: the children were enthusiastic and had clearly worked hard to learn a good many songs, with a teacher who obviously was both slave driver and angel. Tech-nically, the children had achieved a lot. Intonation, rhythm, ensemble were good. With me they got high grades on "standards," on aspects of musician-ship. But the program was billed as "music from many lands," and of the twelve songs, one was described as South African, one as Israeli, one Carib-bean, one Old English, one Mexican. There was also a song titled "Hello from the World," with greetings in a number of languages worked in. The melodies were largely tunes composed especially for music teaching in schools. I asked myself in what ways this repertory was teaching world music, in what sense it was multicultural. The South African and Caribbean tunes departed a bit from American mainstream school melody patterns, but they were accom-panied by piano and one rarely even heard a minor triad. The words were, naturally, in English. The children weren't learning that different cultures have very different musical sounds. Mainly, it seems to me, one was learning that different cultures have their musics, and that all of this music deserves respect and, in fact, sounds pretty much the same. Social goals were being met, and musical goals, too, in the sense that the children were learning Western music and performing for their parents. But the world's musical diversity?

I don't know how typical such an event is in America, but I'm struck by a parallel to what we have recently been teaching in classes in "world music," in contrast to the courses of earlier times. Do we present world music as part of the contemporary world, or as an essentially historical phenomenon? Ethnomusicologists are accustomed to use the ("ethnographic") present in their rhetoric. Describing a ritual she observed two years back, my student says that "they do this," "they play this," not "I heard that." This leads to op-posing implications: (1) that we make no claims about the past, which can't be recovered, and (2) that the societies we study are static and consistent— or perhaps that in characterizing a culture we concentrate on those elements that are constant. We observe the present and analyze processes and changes as they occur. That would suggest that the repertory on which we should concentrate in presenting Native American music should be the popular music, the music of Carlos Nakai, Jim Pepper, Xit; and the intertribal repertory of powwow songs.

This all leads to a more fundamental issue, the question of how Native Americans wish to be represented. Some of them surely would stress the here-and-now. Others again may wish us outsiders to know this: There are large repertories of older music, some known only to a few, which ought to be preserved. But does preservation suggest knowledge by a privileged few, or a scattering in the American and maybe world population as a whole? Do we give our students the sense that the old ritual music is the "real" Native American music, and the recent popular music is only a subterfuge? Or again, should we suggest that Native Americans, earlier on, had simple, unharmonized vocal music but escaped from it as soon as they were exposed to the superior Western music, creating then their own version of Western music? Just what conception should we be encouraging? The International Society for Music Education has made valiant efforts to approach this and related questions, but we are not very far along. (See Lundquist and Szego 1998 for analysis and bibliography from intercultural and multicultural perspectives.)

The norm of Western music in our system of education is classical music. Yes, often, in our school curricula, in simplified versions and pieces, and sometimes with a nod in the direction of rock and jazz, but underneath, let's not kid ourselves, it's the classical repertory of the common practice period that is the center, and that we use to represent the ideal of Western culture to our students. We should ask what effect this structuring has on our presentation of world music.

When I conversed with musicians in Iran about how they would wish to be represented in American music education, there was no question: by the classical repertory and performance practice. Folk music of the villages— yes, but it is interesting largely because it nurtured the classical—a viewpoint similar to that of many European musicians a few decades ago. I don't know whether these ideas had come to Iran from Europe, but actually I doubt it. Rather, it was the way in which the classical music had come, actually as part of the cultural politics of the Pahlavi dynasty, to be regarded as an explicitly national product and emblem. The folk music, called "regional" music, characterized the various districts. It was the classical music that integrated and also distinguished Persian culture. But no one ever mentioned popular music; it was the music that least conformed to the Islamic traditions about music, that mixed the musics of the world with those of Iran in undesirable ways. Still, people clearly loved the popular music.

What a complicated situation we've come to! From elementary school teaching that was determinedly unimusical to conflicts on the nature of the world and of multiculturalism, and on to competition between multiculturalism and standards, K to 12. From world music as marginal in the college curriculum to a position of centrality. From notions such as the world of music as a group of musics, or as a universal language, to the concepts of micromusics and music as an emblem of personal identity. It has been a half century of trial and error, at all levels of musical education.

We have been trying to have it both ways, in elementary schools and in the universities. We want our students to be conscious of a multifarious world of music, to marvel at diversity, but we also want them to think "I can sing that African song with the musical equipment I have," or "I can learn to play on that gamelan in a couple of half-hour sessions." And also, with a bit more contemplating: "Long ago, when recordings were first made, much of the world's music sounded strange, but now most of the world's music has a familiar sound to us, uses something like our diatonic scale, slips into the mold of functional harmony and of accompanied melody." We are faced—in first grade and in the university—with the question of which end to emphasize.

The literature on the subject, summarized by Lundquist and Szego (1998) gives many perspectives on teaching non-Western music in Western or Western-oriented musical education systems. But for me, in the end, it has been the diversity, the degree of difference from familiar sound, from the social contexts and concepts I once considered to be normal, that have driven my interest in the world's musics. So, when I visited my daughter's first-graders, I felt more comfortable saying to them, "Wow, doesn't this sound different from anything you've heard? And isn't that interesting?" instead of saying "Here's a Native American song; you can sing it easily." We want our students, above all, at all levels, to be able to locate themselves in a wide cultural, historical, and musical space. To marvel at the incredible diversity of the world's ideas about music, and of the world's musical sounds, that, it seems to me, is a worthwhile attitude for teachers of children, and of the child in everyone.

28

I'm a Stranger Here Myself:
Women's Music, Women in Music

What Took Us So Long?

In Kurt Weill's "One Touch of Venus," a department-store mannequin who turns out to be the goddess of love complains about American men's inability to understand women, explaining it all to herself by the refrain "I'm a stranger here myself." It asks, by implication, whether men and women, or maybe also people from different places, can ever understand each other. Among the various paradigm shifts that ethnomusicology experienced in the last 100 years, two developments, both striking at estrangements previously unappreciated, seem to me to have been most instrumental in establishing the field's dominant directions as it entered the twenty-first century. One is the recognition that the understanding of gender as a factor in personal identity, and of gender relations in all aspects of society, is essential to the interpretation of musical cultures; and this is closely related to the second, the realization that virtually all relationships, and all developments in music, among societies, and of groups of people within a society, can be seen as a function and expression of power relationships. In the development of ethnomusicology, these recognitions seemed suddenly to become formidable in the 1970s and early 1980s, but of course they have an earlier history, and more recently they have become issues that constitute the leading edge of ethnomusicological discourse. I mention them together because the unequal distribution of power between men and women and the domination of women by men in a variety of ways and to different extents is recognized as a virtual universal in known societies. As a result of the development of these understandings, we (ethnomusicologists) know a lot more about the musicking of women, having earlier on taken for granted that only men's music-making was significant, or that musical activity was essentially gender-neutral. But also, these realizations have made us question an important basic assumption: the fundamental homogeneity of culture in whose beliefs and concepts all member of a society participate with some degree of equality.

This chapter looks briefly at the very broad topic of women in music and in musical life; and at music in women's lives. It's a topic framed by the "power relations" concept, and by the distinction between sex and gender— the one a biological "given," the other "socially constructed and maintained arrangements made between men and women based on culture-specific gender ideologies" (Koskoff 1987: 5). I ask whether there are, inevitably, differences between men and women in the way they perceive, create, interpret, and, as ethnomusicologists, study music; whether men and women are ever really part of the same culture or inevitably "strangers"; about the musical effects of the various arrangements made between genders in the societies of the world. They are fundamental questions in disciplines or fields of women's studies, gender studies, and feminist theory. For ethnomusicology, these fields address, interpret, and to a degree redress the marginalization of women as scholars and music-makers. It's not, however, just women who are or were marginalized, and these questions may be asked as well in a broader context including other distinct groups—children and homosexuals come to mind, but minorities of all sorts are relevant here too. But in this chapter, the focus is women in music and women in ethnomusicology, and on the interaction of discrimination, exclusion, and specialness.

Here are some of the very general questions with which we are concerned, questions that should be answered for individual societies and for "human society" at large: (1) What has been the role of women, and the contribution of women, in the world's musical cultures? (2) What is the musical life of women—everywhere—and are there interculturally any regularities? (3) In what way have women, as a distinct culture group, affected the development of all musical life in human societies? (4) In what ways does the quality of relationship of men and women in a society affect music? (5) How have women reacted musically to male domination? (6) How does music provide for interaction of genders? (7) Maybe too simple: Does women's music sound different from men's? But then, also, on another side of the spectrum: (8) Is there a characteristic women's way of doing ethnomusicology; that is, are women inclined, because of their particular kinds of training, background, and concerns, to favor particular problems, approaches, methods?

That question leads us to the double bind of trying to understand gender issues in societies in which we are strangers in the first place. And then, there is the relationship of study and advocacy: How can what we have learned help to improve the world?

Women surely make, arguably, half of the world's music, but ethnomusicologists (and music historians too) didn't take this into account for a long time. There are lots of reasons: for example, the ambiguous role of women in the canons of history, and even in the present, of Western musical culture—our point of departure for contemplating other music—and its effect on all kinds of understanding. There's been a disinclination, until recently, to deal with interactions of genders in musical life. It's also true, perhaps, as suggested by some, that the burgeoning literature on women's studies and gender analysis has led to some "separation from the mainstream of academic discourse" (Sarkissian in Myers 1992: 337). But it seems to most ethnomusicologists to make perfect sense that women's musicking and the interpretation of gender have come to play a major role in our field. Thus, contemplating the older body of our field's literature, almost a century of it, in which women's participation in music is given a very unfair shake, and looking at the world's musics with the perspective of the large number of recent studies that attempt to redress the situation, I'm inclined to ask, "What took us so long?"

A Complex of Interactions

One reason is clearly the matter of longstanding male domination. Another, though, derives from the great complexity of the ways gender roles and musical roles are constructed in a person's life, in a complicated set of interactions. The ethnomusicological literature describes many different kinds of musical relationships between men and women throughout the world, some of them reflecting totally different musical and social worlds inhabited by the genders, more of them, however, showing women's musical culture to be a kind of extension of that of men. I haven't discovered accounts of societies in which men and women participate in musical life with total equality. So, moving from the general to the specific, a short case study illustrating the complexities of gender interaction in music follows.

It took me a long time to realize that women in the culture in which I lived were the objects of discrimination in music and in musicology. In my childhood household, my mother was a pianist, my grandmother sang operetta tunes while she was cooking, and my nanny taught me Czech folksongs. My father, I perceived, spent most of his time reading or dictating to a secretary. Obviously, then, women were the authorities on music, music was a women's thing. Did this lower the status of music as "women's work" (for a discussion of which see Susan Cusick in Cook and Everist 1999: 472) or raise the status of women as the suppliers of one of life's delights? Or did it contribute to my perception of music as possessing a certain gentleness?

Later I learned about male composers such Bach and Mozart; but they weren't really "men," but rather, names that comprised collections of pieces, and in any case I couldn't meet them. But soon I was sent to take violin lessons, to a married couple of violinists, and the wife became my teacher, as she would be better for children than her more distinguished husband. Later I saw that my original perspective was incomplete, that musical life as I learned to observe it was really dominated by men. But wait a moment: My mother was praised by someone because she "played like a man." And then, a bit farther along in school, I found that a career of practicing violin after school was more easily tolerated, in the elementary school social scene, by (and for) girls than boys. But by seventh grade, it was boys who would aspire to independent musicianship practices such as ear-torturing dance bands trying to play Tommy Dorsey covers. And a decade later in music school, women sang, and played piano and strings (which men did too), but only men played brass and, significantly, studied composition; and the two female composition majors were eyed with some suspicion. Even so, I also heard that smaller men's colleges sometimes didn't even have music departments, as these were maintained by the women's colleges across town—music was "women's work."

I don't know whether I was a stranger in this culture, Western culture straddling the midcentury point, but if not, then my group of experiences shows an astonishing ambiguity in the assignment of musical roles to men and women. Obviously men and women don't (didn't) do the same things: thus, for children, music was a "girls' thing," but when it came to risk-taking, it was more a "boys' thing." One learned the basics of music from women. Men and women controlled different sounds, had different roles in performance and particularly in teaching. Even in this twentieth-century European culture in which men and women lived relatively similar lives (compared to many other societies), differences were obvious. An ethnomusicologist from a distant planet wishing to generalize might perhaps have concluded that music in that society was "made" by men and "taught" by women. But it might also see women simply more involved in music than men. In any event, music and musical culture were important ways in which I learned principles of my culture.

My experience reflects, very roughly, the conclusions of case studies presented by many ethnomusicologists. Societies use music to teach, symbolize, and reinforce gender relations; music is often the center of social relationships. Some prominent illustrations: In the culture of Prespa Albanians, Sugarman (1989) argues that singing styles, ways of using the voice, are of primary importance in enculturation of males and females, and shows (1997) that at wedding ceremonies, gender relations and, indeed, the organization of society are negotiated through singing and musical style. Anthony Seeger (1979) describes a system of musical and social exchange in Suyá culture, in which men may address their sisters and mothers, whom they cannot directly visit, only through certain song genres, sung in unison by groups of men, but in a way that permits their individual voices and vocal styles to be detected by their relatives.

The identity of field workers and recordists is a major factor. Here's a relevant example. Catherine Ellis described the beginning of her work with a specifically women's ceremony among Australian aboriginal people (1970: 101): "Initial contact with Andagarinja women's ceremonies was made in 1963, at the reserve in Port Augusta. The women were very shy, and hesitated to perform at all. It was not my suggestion that they sing, but rather their own husbands', who were themselves familiar with the idea of the collection of their songs, and who recognized the value of the preservation of the women's songs in this manner, by a woman collector. At first the women sang (their efforts interspersed with a great deal of giggling) and the men stood by and encouraged them, and offered explanations of the songs. After only one session, the women came to me independently and asked if I would go away from the camp with them, where they could sing their secret songs to me without fear of the men overhearing."

Among the Blackfoot in mid–twentieth century, the musical relationships seemed to be complicated. Women probably sang little in public (my consultants regarded it as evidence of immodesty). I was told they had some songs of their own (some of these songs could be given to men), but often they "helped" the men, and they seemed to know—though usually not to sing—many of the men's songs. But I was told (and read) that women were important as sponsors of music-bearing rituals, and in the mythology they are instrumental in bringing songs into existence. Since 1980, however, women have become very active in the powwow repertory, participating as a minority in many of the Drums, and forming a few "women-only" Drums. Early recordings show women's singing style to have been rather different from that of men. Thus, in the public dance repertory, the rhythmic pulsations that in men's singing consisted of sudden, momentary increases in amplitude or dynamics were rendered by women as slight changes in pitch. When participating in Drums, in recordings made after around 1980, women's singing style approximates that of men.

Looking Back

As mentioned earlier, significant research in the related fields of women in music, women's music, and gender studies in music began to spring powerfully onto the American and western European intellectual scene in the late 1970s. This history is sketched by Ellen Koskoff (in Moisala and Diamond 2000: x) as comprising three somewhat overlapping stages. She calls the first, beginning shortly before 1980, a stage of "women-centric" studies that principally took on the task of pointing out the neglect of women's contributions, mainly to Western art music, and the attitude that they were just filling gaps. Publications of this sort have continued to appear into the present, but in the later 1980s they were joined by a second wave of studies in which women's musicking is framed within a broader context, looking at the relationships of women's and men's musicking, going beyond women's music to the contemplation of gender relations. A third wave, coming in the early 1990s, broadens the subject again, in three ways: including a wider view of gender to include gay and lesbian roles in music; reaching out to methodologies from other fields, some of them newly developed, such as feminist theory, cultural theory, performance studies, and semiotics; and striving to understand the links between social and musical structures from gendered perspectives. Here, in particular, scholarship often goes hand in hand with social and political commitment to social and cultural change, as articulated by Diamond (in Moisala and Diamond 2000: 7), who, for example, proposes to use her position as a university teacher "to disrupt the presumed naturalness about who or what is important."

This period, in which gender studies came into its own, naturally has its antecedents, and there are earlier publications—but few before 1950—from which there is a lot of information to be gained about women's music and gender relations. There is a small handful of works broadly treating the subjects of women as musicians—in contrast to biographies of famous performers, patrons, and institutions—listed in the article "Women in Music" in the second edition of *The New Grove Dictionary of Music and Musicians* (2001). The first significant work bringing in issues of gender and social relations is Sophie

Drinker's classic *Music and Women* (1948, discussed in detail by Solie 1993). Drinker certainly touches on anthropological issues. But in ethnomusicology specifically, they didn't appear until later. To be sure, women as important singers, informants, consultants did appear in many early works, such as the collections of Cecil Sharp (1932—but with collections made before 1920) and Schiørring (1956, a collection of the repertory of Selma Nielsen). Bartók and Lord (1951: 247) presented the song repertory of Serbo-Croatians divided into "men's" and "women's" songs, the first comprising epics, and the second all kinds of lyrical songs that may be sung by women or men.

Generally speaking, though, ethnomusicologists before around 1975 had not frequently tried to contrast what women do musically with the activities of men, usually instead concentrating on the total repertory of a society or community, happy to get what they could from any musician, male or female, seeking informants as was possible, regardless of gender. On the surface, it appears that in many societies men engaged in more musical activity than did women; it's certainly the impression one gets from the bulk of field collections and publications. While this impression may be a result of the larger number of male field workers in ethnomusicology over the years, many collections by female scholars reflect more or less the same tendency. Whether men really are more active musically than women is difficult to determine; it may simply have appeared so because in many cultures men are the people who live a more or less public life and are thus responsible for dealing with the outside world—which includes ethnomusicologists. Fieldworkers may often have encountered difficulty in attracting female consultants.

Still, it is interesting to see that the issue of gender relations—then without label—was not neglected by some of the pioneers of our field. Ethnomusicologists had anthropological models to draw upon, beginning with classic works such as those of Bronislaw Malinowski and Margaret Mead, in asking how the quality of social relations between men and women is reflected in music. It's interesting to look at what some earlier scholars made of the role of gender in determining musical style. Some of the suggestions now strike us as downright weird, and others may be worthy of some careful scrutiny. If there is in some cultures such a thing as a separate women's music, as well as a variety of ways in which women participate in a generally known repertory, there is also the relationship of genders to be explored as a factor in the determination of the general musical style of a society. These relations have played a role in the history of ethnomusicological theory. Two of the most daring generalizers from earlier history qualify as precursors.

Curt Sachs (1943: 40) proposed a basic difference between men's and women's singing in tribal societies: "If singing is indeed an activity of all our being, sex, the strongest difference between human beings, must have a decisive influence on musical style." In dancing, he noted, men strive for strong motions forward and upward while women's motions are diminutive; they move "inwardly" and keep to the ground. "In the same way, the sexes also form opposite singing styles." He goes on to give examples: "Boat songs of the Eskimo rest on the third; when women row, they sing the same songs with infixes to avoid masculine stride." It remains to be seen whether these examples represent a chance distinction; they certainly are not part of a universal norm.

But the distinction of musical styles suggested by Sachs, between widely ranging melodies with large intervals and songs with narrow ambit and small intervals, may have another sort of sexual significance. There was once a long-held belief that certain societies are dominated by principles of male psychology and physiology and, indeed, dominated by men; in others, the same is true of the female. Associating agriculture with domination by women, Sachs wrote: "The more a people is marked by planter culture, the more closed is its dance; the more completely it is totemistic and patriarchal, the more it will make use of the leap" (1937: 33). Sachs found it possible to equate small steps in dance with small musical intervals and symmetrical forms, and leaps with large intervals and wildly irrational forms. Thus "the same contemplative, patient, imperturbable, introvert disposition which through ascendancy of female characteristics creates a predominately feminine culture . . . makes itself felt in dance and music through close movement and through an urge toward the static and the symmetrical. The alert, impatient, vivid, and impulsive extrovert disposition which leads to the dominance of the masculine qualities in a culture and to hunting and cattle-breeding, is reflected in dance and music through expanded movement and through the urge toward the dynamic and the asymmetrical" (203). Later Sachs suppressed the forcefulness of this view, though he did not entirely abandon it, still in his last book maintaining that "women seemed to prefer smaller steps, just as they do in dancing" (1962: 62).

The belief that some societies are dominated by men and others by women has for many decades ceased to have much credence in anthropology. "Matriarchy has never existed," says Harris without reservation (1971: 582), and in more detail: "Despite the persistent popular notion that the presence of matrilineal descent groups reflects the political or economic domination of men by women, it is the men in these societies no less than in patrilineal societies who control the corporate kin group's productive and reproductive resources" (328). Sachs's attempt to classify musics by sexual dominance may strike us today as downright weird, but nevertheless it shows that even in these earlier times of our discipline, it was suggested that musical style could relate to the quality of relationships between the sexes. Sachs begins, after all, with a hypothesis that men and women are prone to sing differently; observes that in some societies all people sing in a way that appears to him like that of men, and in others, women; and concludes that this is a function of type of relationship, that is, which sex dominates.

The thread was later picked up by Alan Lomax, who, after examination of a broad sample of world music, finds correlation between musical style and six aspects of culture, two of which are severity of sexual mores and balance of dominance between male and female (1968: 6). In several publications and many statements, he stresses his belief that relative equality of women and men produces well-blended ensemble singing and a relaxed, unembellished vocal technique, while suppression of women produces, in both men and women, a nasal, narrow, ornamented vocal technique. Lomax places the burden of musical style differences among cultures very heavily on the quality and type of relationship between the sexes. His findings are best taken with a grain of salt, for at the least, sampling is uneven, and other factors may not be given enough recognition. But it seems reasonable to believe that the great differences in musical style among the peoples of the world can in good measure be attributed to the way in which people relate to each other, and a major aspect of this relationship concerns gender.

A Few Landmarks

The recent bibliographies of publications surveying gender studies in music (Magrini 2003; Moisala and Diamond 2000; Sarkissian in Myers 1992) list large numbers of works dealing with this subject. In addition, many publications of a more general sort now pay considerable attention, where their predecessors did not. Let me try to list, as landmarks, some anthologies, monographs, and essays.

Two anthologies of studies, Bowers and Tick (1986), consisting of fifteen essays about women composers and performers, and women's institutions, and Koskoff (1987), also fifteen essays on all kinds of musics throughout the world (the Western art tradition included), constituted a kind of great leap forward. The essays in Bowers and Tick present their subjects in a traditional historical style; those of Koskoff's volume are more interpretive, and they were seen as first steps in locating gender studies as central to the understanding of music in culture. Together, they provided insight into women as primary preservers of tradition, into the special role of women as musical mourners, into gender relations as expressed in musical style and repertory, into culture change and its effect of women's participation in music, and much else. *Women in North American Indian Music* (Keeling 1989) presents six short, accessible essays that explore the role of women as singers and song-makers in six Native American societies, looking at such issues as gender complementarity in musical life, music in women's spiritual life, and the development of female singing styles in conditions of culture change.

Musicology and Difference, another anthology, edited by Ruth Solie (1993), includes both historical and ethnomusicological contributions. Its sixteen essays are more concerned with analysis of gender relations and ideologies from perspectives of postmodern cultural studies and critical theory, and include studies of gay and lesbian movements and of power relations. The fifth important anthology is the aforementioned work edited by Moisala and Diamond (2000). Its fifteen essays (the magic number?), consisting of studies of performing groups, biographies, "gendered musical sites in the redefnition of nations," and the role of technology, focus on the developments of the present. The essays, dealing with European folk and popular traditions more than with others, are actually very closely interwoven, framed by an introduction by the editors that represents a conversation among the authors, giving their various views of the role of musical gender studies in their lives and their careers. Finally, combining gender-oriented scholarship with the approaches of area studies, Magrini's (2003) edited anthology of essays explores music and gender along the Mediterranean, a culturally diverse region whose societies are drawn together by commonalities in gender relations.

Interestingly, the majority of the classic publications are the result of the kind of cooperation that leads to anthologies in edited volumes. Is this a development of a culture of scholarship in which women are more likely to cooperate than men? But, of course, there are significant monographic works. Let me mention a few. Judith Vander's *Songprints* (1988), discussed earlier, important because of its contribution of the concept of the fingerprint-like personal songprints, gives five biographies of women that together tell about the society and about individuals, the role of music in tradition, and about changes, for women and men, in musical values and practices as the culture of the Wind River Shoshone changed in the period after 1940. Jane Sugarman's *Engendering Song* (1997) studies women's music and gender relations in music, by presenting the culture of Prespa Albanians through their most significant ritual, a wedding, analyzing the activities of bride and bridegroom, their families, men and women generally, and the ways in which music both results from and guides social and cultural values. And, although it makes no pretense to be ethnomusicology, Susan McClary's *Feminine Endings* (1991) should be mentioned as a work that has influenced ethnomusicologists, and that attempts to show relationships between musical structure and socio-cultural values. Further, while it is not framed explicitly as an example of gender studies, Virginia Danielson's (1997) biography of Umm Kulthum, the great Egyptian singer, contextualizes her subject in the patterns and contradictions of gender relationships of Egyptian society.

Finally, three essays with important methodological implications should be noted among the landmarks. First, for historical perspective, Solie's (1992) account of the history of Sophie Drinker's *Music and Women* shows that the problems engendered by musicology, a field of scholarship that later came under sharp criticism because of its exclusively male-dominated perspective, were recognized already in the 1930s by a perceptive if not formally trained intellectual. Drinker (quoted in Solie 1992: 38) repeatedly confronts "one of the perplexities in men's scholarship and writing of history that baffles a sincere woman's mind." Second, for sophisticated views of fieldwork, I mention Babiracki's "What's the Difference? Reflections on Gender and Research in Village India" (1997), which gives a very direct account of her experience in gender relations in ethnomusicological fieldwork, in situations in which gender identity in music-making and dancing play a major role. And for a combination of history and advocacy, Cusick's essay (1999), "Gender, Musicology, and Feminism," is in part a survey and in part a prospectus for a more symmetrical future.

This list of landmark publications covers the so far rather short history of gender studies in ethnomusicology. The reader who sees them in the context of the history of ethnomusicology will note that the separation of ethnomusicology from historical musicology, evident in the earliest group, gradually recedes, and that ethnomusicologists increasingly show interest in historical data and interpretation, while music historians experience growing influence from anthropology. Unquestionably this body of literature has done much to make ethnomusicology more of a whole.

A Different Ethnomusicology?

It seems appropriate to examine the study of gender relations and issues in the world's musical cultures in the context of gender relations in the academy, among the scholars. Does it matter who does the research? We have looked at cultural "insider" and "outsider" (see chapter 14). How about men and women, straight and gay scholars? Well, obviously it makes a difference, as Babiracki (1997) made clear in describing her complex of fieldwork relationships as a woman, unmarried, outsider, student, collaborator. But the effect of gender relations between fieldworker and consultant can't be predicted. In the aforementioned Australian example by Ellis, women had, at least in part, a separate repertory, and the men of the society valued it and recognized its importance, but recording it was certainly facilitated by a female collector. Considering the constraints that power inequities between societies and genders inject into the fieldwork situation, it seems unsurprising to me that female fieldworkers are often exceptionally successful in learning from both male and female consultants. In Iran, where women even before the 1979 revolution were frequently shielded from any kind of public exposure and associated mainly with relatives, the earlier field recordings seem to reflect mainly men's performances. Nevertheless, much of the research was done by female scholars such as Edith Gerson-Kiwi, Ella Zonis, and Margaret Caton, and they too worked mainly with male musicians. But the existence of a rich separate women's repertory in the Middle East was later illustrated by many authors, including Danielson (1997), Naroditskaya (2000), and Doubleday (1999). By contrast, I had (I think) gender-associated problems in recording sessions among the Blackfoot people in the 1960s, as I found it difficult to persuade women to sing alone, although they sometimes sang along with men, helping them, as they put it, in a repertory that consisted of songs normally sung by men.

Actually, women, despite the fact that they suffered the same kinds of exclusion they also experienced in all academic disciplines, began early on to make significant contributions to ethnomusicology, and I believe that this helped significantly to shape the character of the discipline. For example, the five most significant scholars of Native American music before 1950 were the following four women (plus George Herzog). The major accomplishments of this group comprise the classics of that period: Alice C. Fletcher (1904) published the first detailed description of a ceremony, with complete transcriptions. Frances Densmore's oeuvre of publications still probably exceeds what has been published by anyone else, but her detailed musical and ethnographic collections of Chippewa and Teton Sioux musics (1910, 1918) are early exemplars of comprehensive accounts of musical culture. Natalie Curtis's main work, *The Indians' Book* (Curtis Burlin 1907) did much to bring Native American music and culture to the attention of the public. And Helen Roberts's imaginative analytical work on Native Californian and Northwest Coast music, and her study of geographic distribution (1936) of musical styles, providing the first continental synthesis, belong to the central literature of this area. After 1950, too, women scholars, including Gertrude Kurath, Charlotte Frisbie, Judith Vander, Victoria Levine, Beverley Diamond, and Tara Browner, continued to provide leadership. To an only slightly lesser degree, the same could be said for other world areas and repertories.

It's interesting to contemplate the cultural or personal roots of the special contributions of women scholars to Native American music studies. It may be suggested that women were motivated in this direction because their own unfavorable social position made them sensitive to oppressed peoples, and also because they found themselves directed to the margins—to marginal peoples, and to music, a marginal field in the Western academy, and in America, marginal even among the arts. No doubt a few early figures, who had arrived by chance and through personal interest and determination, such as Densmore and Fletcher, became models for others. Franz Boas encouraged women to enter anthropology in its early American years. Considerable female participation may generally have been characteristic of new and yet unestablished fields; ethnomusicology was not taken as seriously as ancient history and Latin philology, for example, thus permitting women easier access. The fact that American and English women are particularly well represented in this group may also be related to the common relegation of music in Anglophone cultures to women, and thus to the fact that music departments in North America were first introduced at women's colleges.

It's interesting to see that when music research became more acceptable in polite academic society, and scholarly organizations were founded, women didn't get the opportunity to participate as they had in research. The New York Musicological Society, founded in 1930, had no women, and the story about the explicit exclusion of Ruth Crawford by the main organizer, Charles Seeger (whom she later married) has been thoroughly analyzed (Cusick 1999: 471–72). From its founding in 1934 until the 1980s, the American Musicological Society was dominated—and determinedly so, in order to achieve respect among learned societies—by men, and the Society for Ethnomusicology did no better. Charlotte Frisbie (1991) describes the discrepancy between women's very considerable scholarly contributions and their quite subordinate role in the workings of SEM, as women made up, before 1965, only about 16 percent of the Society's governing executive board and Council. If the tradition in American society was to permit men to call the shots and provide intellectual leadership while women did the routine work, one is tempted to inquire whether the male leadership in ethnomusicology considered the running of their professional society to be a more significant task than the intellectual work of their field—the work to which women were devoting themselves—whether they saw fieldwork and data-gathering as merely the filling of gaps, something that could safely be left to women, while the political leadership of SEM had to be "men's work."

It was not until 1971 that Barbara Krader was elected the first female president of SEM. The situation has been enormously different in the period since around 1988, when the majority of presidents and board members have been women; indeed, in the 1990s and through 2003, the board of directors has typically consisted of six or seven women and one or two men. And (back to research), while the 1950s saw important contributions by female scholars—the names Gertrude Kurath, Barbara Krader, Johanna Spector, Maud Karpeles, Eta Harich-Schneider, Edith Gerson-Kiwi, Doris Stockmann, Rose Brandel come most quickly to mind (but there are lots more)—in the mid-1980s, the body of literature involving women, gender issues, and related subjects began to build, and by the 1990s the contributions of women were incomparably greater. Thus, of forty-three volumes in the Chicago Studies in Ethnomusicology series published between 1990 and 2003, eighteen were by female authors or editors. In the years 1999–2002, the editor of the journal *Ethnomusicology* accepted thirty-seven articles by men and twenty-nine by women. It almost seems that the roles were reversed; in the 1950s, men ran the Society while women contributed significantly to research; in the 1990s, women ran the Society while men continued to make about half of the scholarly contributions. Similar statements could be made about the British Forum for Ethnomusicology, the European Seminars in Ethnomusicology, and the Societé française d'ethnomusicologie.

Koskoff's three "waves"—studying women's music, looking at musical life as a function of gender relationship, and bringing methodologies from recently developed theoretical perspectives—have very broadly changed the orientation of ethnomusicological research, and changed, or are changing, the attitudes of most ethnomusicologists. The literature in question is often severely critical of what has been done in past scholarship, as it seeks to overturn biases that have been with us seemingly forever and introduce a more evenhanded approach to the study of musical life. The criticism of canons as bodies of music and thought constructed by male domination; the insistence that the fieldworker's and scholar's identity, sex, gender all play a determining role in research; the understanding that Western gender-based concepts such as homosexuality and heterosexuality may not be valid as categories in other cultures; and, perhaps most important, the reversal of a basic assumption assigning female cultural practices a role of deviancy or departure from the male-derived "norm"—these (and other) critiques, all based on the body of literature explaining social life as a function of power relations, have helped to make ethnomusicology since the 1990s into a different field.

Examining the gender-oriented literature from a broad and hopefully historical perspective, this particular stranger also asks about its stylistic specialness. Is it distinctive in relationship to other ethnomusicological studies of its time? First, the body of literature suggests a profession emphasizing cooperation and teamwork. Many landmark publications are collections of essays in which authors refer and defer to each other. Further, there is a tendency—in these landmarks, and in other prominent works on women in music (e.g., Danielson 1997; Vander 1988) to tell a story. It may strike the reader as a curious observation, but I feel that in much of the ethnomusicological work by women there is a focus on an individual musician and (frequently) her story, a tendency providing a needed corrective to the cultural generalizations common in the mainstream of literature. In this, despite its sophistication in dealing with theory and its concepts, as well in the insistence that gender is an issue in all considerations of culture, the body of ethnomusicological literature by women injects a needed note of realism into our perception of culture. And then, I am struck by a certain note of urgency, by a feeling that much needs to be done, and done quickly, for women as musicians in the world to be understood on equal terms, though not necessarily identically, with men, for women's contributions to musical life to receive proper recognition, and for the development of an understanding that gender construction and relations vary enormously from culture to culture.

Much has been accomplished. But, looking to the coming of a different ethnomusicology, Marcia Herndon, in her posthumously published afterword to Moisala and Diamond's (2000: 347) collection, asserted correctly that "the inclusion of gender as an essential aspect of all ethnomusicological research is far from becoming a reality."

29

Diversity and Difference: Some Minorities

Ethnomusicology and Difference

The word *difference* as defined in dictionaries is neutral enough. When it was drawn into everyday American social life in the 1990s, it acquired a negative aura, as children, for example, are taught that they shouldn't criticize those who are "different" (referring largely to difference in race, nationality, ability, appearance). We see the world as consisting of series of oppositions—most simply ours/not ours, but also north-south, east-west, men/women, maybe going back to a primordial (but recently rediscovered) good/evil. Authors in the field of critical theory have gone further in developing a specific theoretical use for the term, concluding that differences are used to structure worldviews and establish hierarchies. Binary oppositions, according to Derrida (1982: 129, interpreted by Korsyn 1999: 54), are used to create hierarchies and orders of subordination, where one side of the opposition dominates or controls the other. *Difference* thus also becomes a code word for a large number of relationships characterized by unequal power. It is gender boundaries, according to Stokes (1994: 22), that "articulate the most deeply entrenched forms of domination which provide basic metaphors for others." In other words, the ways in which dominant (white, male, Western) society characterizes the nature and behavior of women has been a model for the ways in which other gendered groups (homosexuals, transsexuals, hermaphroditic), racial, national, religious and other kinds of minorities, social and economic classes, occupations, and so on, have been characterized, judged, stereotyped. Ruth Solie asserts (1993: 8) that "few if any of the meaningful differences between groups of people are innate but, rather . . . constructed." This aspect of ethnomusicology—attention to "difference"—concerns the musical results of ways in which Western society and others classify the world into hierarchies by processes conveniently labeled as "othering" and "saming" (terms used by Naomi Schor, cited in Solie 1993: 2); and it critiques, also, how these processes are used by ethnomusicologists in their studies.

If "difference" has acquired a negative aura, the concept of "diversity" has become its positive counterpart. If children are taught to avoid "othering" groups of people, they are taught also to recognize, appreciate, and celebrate diversity. Ethnomusicologists have all along been students of groups of "others," and they have been the champions, in the academy, of diversity. They claim, however, to be students of music in culture—culture as what members of a society agree on. It's a paradox.

We are being tugged in different directions. We call music a cultural universal, and we look at the music of *cultures,* saying that culture is what people agree on, that what is important about it to us is its unity, its ability to speak to all in a society, a people, to speak for a whole nation. We—ethnomusicologists, that is—started out by making our statements representations about the music of peoples, nations, societies, such as Stumpf's Bella Coola, Hornbostel's Fuegians, Herzog's Yumans, and a hundred years later, we still (or again) find the investigation of music as a factor in building and maintaining the "imagined communities" a major interest—as in works by Askew (2002), Peter Wade (2000), Ramnarine (2003), and Turino (2000)—and we accept nationalism both as a fact of life and as an explanatory device.

And on the other hand, and just as much, we are the field that looks after the neglected, at repertories from out-of-the-way communities, music left out of the canon, sounds of peoples thought to be disappearing, songs hardly anyone knows any more, instruments played competently only by a nation's two or three "national treasures." And thus ethnomusicology is the field that inevitably looks after the music of minorities, studying the way a society divides itself into categories of race, class, gender, age, each of which has its "own" music. How to deal with minorities has been a special problem of twentieth-century nations, and in the United States, especially in the period since 1990, the importance of understanding, accepting, and celebrating the heterogeneity of society has become a matter of public policy under the code word *diversity,* leading to an increase in the public support for the work of ethnomusicologists and for some of the music with which they are concerned. Ethnomusicology has benefited in educational institutions because it promises to help understand, and celebrate, cultural diversity, to aid in the process of making minorities of all sorts, those who are "different," less marginalized, without at the same time absorbing them, in helping to establish a cultural mosaic, rather than forcing everyone into a melting pot. And so, altering the old slightly sexist punch line that replies, "Long may it live" to the assertion that there is little difference between men and women, and down-playing it, we now celebrate, in human cultures, the concept and fact of diversity.

That we deal with the music of minorities, of oppressed majorities, of all sorts has thus long been taken for granted. Some see us as the "musicologists" of the "ethnics," a definition against which we fight but which we admit is not totally off the mark. We accept that racial, cultural, linguistic minorities, the musics of Native Americans, Italian Americans, tribal peoples in India, Moroccan Jews in Israel are principally our responsibility. Certain concepts, such as diasporas, marginal preservation, power relations, have been helpful in explaining them. Some ethnomusicologists have examined other kinds of minorities and "others," most prominently women, but also homosexuals, children, the aged, and others yet, from intercultural perspectives. Chapter 28 provided a few glances at the many things that could be included in the term "women in music," and surveyed major publications on gender studies in music. This chapter continues on the same tack, making brief excursions to certain groups of people who may be found in every nation, and who usually constitute excluded minorities, and may be considered in some sense as "others."

Identities and Relationships

Ethnomusicology does not seem to have come up with a general theory of what a variety of gender-determined identities and relationships, such as homosexuality, bisexuality, or the transgendered, have to do with music. This is surely related to the difficulty of finding interculturally valid and acceptable terminologies and taxonomies of identities. As Marcia Herndon pointed out (2000: 347), it is ethnocentric to assume that categories such as heterosexual and homosexual translate neatly to other societies. But it is clear that in many societies, homosexuals and other gender-defined minorities make special contributions to musical life. The subject is often subsumed under gender studies, but studies that consider homosexuality most specifically have emerged from historical musicology, with leadership provided by the work of Philip Brett, Elizabeth Wood, and Gary C. Thomas (1994) and the aforementioned work by Solie (1993). The best survey of the field appears in an article by Philip Brett and Elizabeth Wood in the newest edition of *The New Grove Dictionary of Music and Musicians* (2001), and it provides literature and a summary of the issue in non-Western cultures.

In this area of study, ethnomusicologists are just at the beginning. As Carol Robertson asserts, "gay, lesbian, homosexual, bisexual, heterosexual . . . conjure but a limited glimpse of the variations on gender that are beginning to emerge from cross-cultural research" (quoted in Brett and Wood in *New Grove* 2001: 604). A rewarding area for ethnomusicologists, it also requires exceptional sensitivity in fieldwork and careful social analysis, but surely the musical roles of people who are homosexual or otherwise seen in some societies not to fit into the mainstream of gendered culture as they construct it is of great interest. A few examples follow.

In the twentieth-century American world of classical music, homosexual musicians have played leading roles and comprise a disproportionately large minority. At least this is the conventional wisdom, though I don't know of any reliable statistics, and if one looks for reasons, the "outsider" role of musicians generally, and the common historical association of music with women in the Puritan background of American society, are initially suggestive. In India, the supposedly hermaphroditic Hijras (actually people who, having birth defects of sexual organs, constitute a caste-like community) work as musicians and entertainers. In Native American northern Plains cultures, men known in English and French as *berdaches*—sometimes homosexual, sometimes simply attracted to a female lifestyle—were evidently musically particularly active. In Blackfoot culture, according to Lewis (1941), certain so-called manly-hearted women (of whom some were lesbian) assumed male roles in musical life.

Why there should be, in a number of societies, a special association between musicianship and homosexuality is a question that has hardly been examined. In the history of Western music, the fact that certain composers were known to be homosexual (Tchaikovsky, Britten, Copland, Cage, for example) has led to attempts to show that their musical style reflected this orientation. And the sexual identity of certain composers, such as Schubert and Handel, has been the subject of considerable speculation, sometimes in the hope of leading to explanation of their musical choices, and sometimes on the basis of perception and analysis of the music (see, e.g., Kramer 1993; McClary 1991, chaps. 1 and 3; Solomon 1989). But we (musicologists in Western cultures) know, really, so little about these composers as persons, how they felt and what they were willing to express; and far less about musicians in other cultures. It's an area of musical life still to be explored on an intercultural basis. As a start, it makes sense to look at minorities in the area of gender relations in the context of minorities generally. There's no doubt that in many cultures, mainstream society is so ambivalent about the enjoyment and the practice of music that minorities are particularly associated with it, and that a lot of music is, as it were, forced to make its primary home in the culture of social minorities, various kinds of "others" who are the object of discrimination.

In League with the Devil

In segments of Western society, particularly in the past, and in other societies, musicians were thought to be strange people, able to do things inexplicable to others, possessing skills that ordinary humans could explain only as the result of a Faustian bargain, but also with strange personal habits that would make you wish your daughter wouldn't marry one of them. Their virtuosity proves that they are somehow in league with the devil. And "strange people," foreigners, members of oppressed minorities, were often thought to be the primary owners and purveyors of music. The conceptual stereotyping sometimes led to fact in social organization. In American history, groups of foreigners were successively seen as the quintessential musicians—Germans, Irish, Italians in the nineteenth century, eventually African Americans and Jews, and maybe in certain fields we'll now have Asian Americans. In some countries of southern and central Europe, it was the Roma; in Iran, non-Muslim minorities; and in India, certain Muslim groups. Is this correlation coincidence, a tradition in a group of related cultures, the result of the character of music itself? Possibly that generalization won't hold up in the face of more thorough scrutiny. But also, if musicians are often members of minorities, we should look for a special role for music in minority cultures.

A huge subject—but allow me a brief idiosyncratic excursion. In a sense, music is a part of "anticulture," opposing the stream of culture, providing relief from requirements and norms. One sings instead of speaking, one invents sounds not found elsewhere in life, one appears masked—literally in theater and rite, personally on instruments, spiritually in religious ritual, socially in being a strange person. Everywhere (well, almost) people turn to music to get away from the ordinary. It's a side of life in which the forces governing other aspects of life are contradicted. It may be this character of music as it is constructed and practiced in society that associates music with people who are in some sense "strange." Merriam (1979) was among the first ethnomusicologists to note the special role and reputation of musicians as eccentrics or even social deviants, attesting to the powerful musical roles of nondominant segments of society. Merriam spoke of individual deviants, but in the interaction of the groups that together make up a society, the typical "deviant" groups are minorities of various sorts.

A vast proportion of ethnomusicological literature deals with minorities, but there is little in the way of generalization or theory about the musical behavior of these groups and about the special role of music in minority cultures (see for example Porter 1978, Diamond and Witmer 1994, and more recently, Turino and Lee [2004]). Let's skip over the technical definition and such obvious things as the fact that every person is in some way a member of one or several minorities. We are talking about population groups often called "ethnic" (but the two are not coterminous), numerically small, who share a language and a culture that contrasts substantially with those of the dominant population among whom, in some sense, they happen to live. In addition, I am concerned with population groups that are distinguished from the majority by descent, and sometimes only slightly, if at all, by culture or language. A number of types emerge. For example: (1) minorities that have been established as such within a dominant culture for a very long time, perhaps beyond the reach of ascertainable records, such as the Jewish populations of Iran before 1979; (2) those that became established through immigration but have retained minority status, such as the German-descended Amish of the Midwest; (3) those that have immigrated from one area to another, occupying the role of minority temporarily while completing a process of acculturation to the dominant culture, including many European ethnic groups in North America, such as Irish and Scandinavians; and (4) those who have become minorities by virtue of being surrounded and overwhelmed by a newly arrived majority, such as the North American Indians. In all of these cases the minority lives with or in a dominant majority. But there are also other kinds of situations: the caste or community in the culture of India, each a minority where there is no true majority, or the black people of South Africa, numerically not a minority but formerly dominated by another group.

While it might be difficult to show that musical style is directly affected by minority status, we should first ask just what is *the* music of a minority, a query related to the question: What indeed is the music of any culture group? An answer might include all of the music the group knows and in some way uses, or only that part of the total musical experience the group regards as uniquely its own and with which it identifies itself. In the case of certain majorities, these two ways of defining a culture's music may substantially overlap. Thus, members of a minority may participate in the music of the majority, which is in a way also their music, but they usually also identify themselves with a particular repertory that is not shared.

Native American peoples of the northern Plains readily distinguish between "Indian" music and "white" music, both of which they perform and hear. The two are symbolic of the cultures in which the Indians move. "White" social contexts, such as drinking in a bar or going to a Christian church, are accompanied by white music performed by Indians. The traditional contexts of Indian music may be largely gone, but when the people are engaged in activities in which they wish to stress their Indian identity, such as powwows, social dances, or gambling games, they use Indian music.

Similarly, Iranian Jews residing in Israel participate in the general, largely Western-derived musical culture of Israel. But in social contexts in which the Iranian heritage is stressed—and this extends from weddings to social gatherings to which only Iranians are invited, carried out in an unmistakably Iranian middle-class style—the music is Persian. We see this trend also among Greek Americans, Irish Americans, and so on. What is interesting in all of these cases is the great importance of music in the minority-specific social contexts. When the minority engages in activities whose role is to symbolize group identity, to strengthen the integration of the group, music is essential and almost ubiquitous.

But what of the specifically musical relationship between the minority and the dominant majority? One factor on which it depends is the degree of stylistic similarity between minority and majority musics. A people who have been thrown into a minority situation may react musically in various ways, but in many cases they are affected by the musical style of the majority. The folk music of Greek Americans has adopted western European urban instruments, functional harmony, ideas of ensemble playing. The people of the Andean Highlands, a cultural though not a numerical minority, have adapted their orchestras of panpipes and their melodic style to a Western harmonic base. But it is also well known that minorities sometimes react by maintaining their unique style and, indeed, exaggerating the difference between it and that of the majority.

A typical minority seems to wish to maintain, even in the face of massive contrary evidence, the belief that it has a unique music with a separate style. In a meeting with a group of urban aboriginal people in Australia, I heard complaints about the loss of their traditional culture, aboriginal language, ceremonies, songs, customs. Nevertheless, they keenly felt that they were a separate group from whites, who were of course treating them as a minority. I asked whether there was not some kind of music they thought was really their own, with which they identified themselves *as* aboriginals. The surprising answer, from a man with whom others were quick to agree: "The Old Rugged Cross." But this is a song also sung by white people, I insisted; and the reply was, "Yes, but we sing it differently," so they proceeded to gather around the piano to show me. I could find no difference between this performance and what I expected of white Australians and, unless more thorough analysis shows otherwise, suspect that the *idea* of having a unique *style*, if not a unique repertory, was important to them as a symbol of group identity.

In many societies minorities play a special musical role vis-à-vis the majority. One may ask whether there is a relationship between this fact and the tendency of many minorities to turn particularly to music as an integrative device. In the Middle East the general suspicion, especially of instrumental music, among devout Muslims evidently led to the partial turning over of musical activity to religious minorities who do not share the proscription. Chief among these are Jews, who, in Iran and Arabic countries, appear for a long time to have held a disproportionate number of musical positions. In early twentieth-century Iran they played roles as professional entertainers at weddings and other Muslim events, participating in and developing the Iranian musical systems, in towns and small cities such as Kerman and Yazd. More recently in Tehran they have played a role somewhat disproportionate to their numbers in the classical music but a still much larger one in the popular music, which was regarded as even less desirable by observant Muslims. As far as I can tell, other minorities did not stand out as much, but some of them also had special roles to play in music. Thus in the village culture in northeast Iran the Kurds, who typically lived in separate villages close to and associating with Persian-speaking ones, were thought in the folklore of the culture to be particularly great singers and also, for that matter, particularly great lovers. The Armenians, largely an urban minority in Iran, maintained a somewhat separate musical culture, but in Tehran they were also specialists in the making of instruments. Interestingly, they did not specialize in retail sale of instruments, which was more typically a Jewish trade, nor were they in disproportionate numbers performers. To be sure, the lines of these specialties in Tehran were not drawn tightly, and there were also Persian-speaking Muslims among musicians, instrument makers, and salesmen.

Special musical roles for minorities are of course found in the West as well. There is much speculation about the reasons for the large number of Jewish musicians; their minority status may itself be a contributing factor. Similarly, black Americans have interacted with whites more in the field of music than in many other aspects of life, in ways too numerous to mention, and other minorities, Irish, Italians, Germans, have at times played special musical roles within the Anglo-American context. Actually, the idea of the foreign musician, of music as something especially reserved for strangers, is a widespread phenomenon in European history. One could even suggest a distant relationship between the popularity of the gypsy musician in European villages and the tendency of American symphony orchestras to have foreign conductors (or at any rate hardly ever selecting one of their own members for the job). In a broad band of cultures from South Asia westward, music is viewed with some suspicion by ordinary folk: as entertainment, associated with acrobatics and sports in medieval Europe and modern America; something not for serious people; a difficult activity, properly learned only by strange individuals who may even be in league with the devil (Halpert 1943) in order to learn their uncanny skills. It is something reserved in many societies for people with low status who are nevertheless indispensable. As Merriam (1979) suggests, it is frequently the province of deviants—people who engage in unacceptable behavior—debtors, promiscuous persons, homosexuals, drunkards, drug addicts, keepers of odd hours, lazybones, temperamental figures—but then also of members of strange cultures and minorities, people who somehow behave differently from and in ways unacceptable to the majority. Maybe the best of them are really in league with the devil. How else could they stand doing all that practicing?

The Future Belongs to Them

In a recent article surveying the ethnomusicological study of children, Amanda Minks (2002) showed this to be potentially a very large field of study with a surprisingly modest literature. It should investigate how children acquire music in the first place, relating it to language acquisition; the musical repertories of children, which would include what they hear, what they sing without formal learning, what songs they learn at an early age, and what musical sounds they make with their hands; what the repertories of children throughout the world may have in common; how children's music differs from that of adults; children—preschool, elementary students, preteens, teenagers—as distinct culture groups or minorities. All of these questions are of interest to ethnomusicologists; some are principally the purview of other disciplines (music education, cognitive studies, even biology), but we would be most interested in the study of children's repertories throughout the world from a comparative perspective, in the study of music in the distinctive culture of children, and in children as minorities. Although a number of major figures in the twentieth-century history of ethnomusicology have contributed to this field (see Blacking 1967; Brailoiu 1954; Campbell 1998; Kartomi 1980, 1991), the study of children's music isn't far along, which may be the reason for the general American public's widespread acceptance in the late 1990s of ridiculously ethnocentric notions such as the "Mozart effect."

The children of the world participate in music-making in various ways, but societies differ in the degree to which they create a separate repertory for children or designate certain songs or pieces as children's music. Merriam's survey of children's music learning (1964: 147–50) suggested that their activities are largely directed to learning the music of adults. But children are also musically separate, the youngest minority. In Western cultures their songs are a separate category with a distinctive musical style that, according to Herzog (1935b: 10), is the same all over Europe, "no matter what the specific traits of the individual folk music styles in which they are carried along." As for other cultures, a brief look at some classic ethnomusicological literature will quickly convince us that there are special children's songs everywhere—in Chinese (Reinhard 1956: 170), Japanese (May 1963), Arabic (Simon 1972: 24), Nootka (Densmore 1939: 229–41), Sioux (Densmore 1918: 492–94), Ashanti (Nketia 1974: 36), Australian aboriginal (Kartomi 1980, 1991; R. Waterman 1956), Venda (Blacking 1967), Afghan (Baily and Doubleday 1990), and Yoruba (C. Waterman 1990) repertories, to name just a few. A cursory glance at, or hearing of, examples of this children's music indicates that much of it is quite different from that of adults. Some of it, to be sure, is just simpler, comprised of limited range and scale and of short, repetitive forms. But simplicity may not be the only diagnostic trait of distinction. Blacking: "I was also puzzled by the apparent lack of relationship between the styles of children's songs and other Venda music. This seemed illogical in a society in which there was no nursery culture, and in which children were frequently involved in adult activities, though as junior spectators. . . . Children's songs are not always easier than adult songs, and children do not necessarily learn the simple songs first" (1967: 28–29). Similarly, in writing about Australian aboriginal children, Kartomi (1980: 211) argues: "This difference in style between adult and childlike music exists . . . because the children perform, reproduce, and create according to their own sense of priorities as children."

If children are capable of learning music that in complexity equals that of adults, why does children's music frequently have a separate style? Do children "wish" to be musically (and presumably otherwise) separate, or do adults just wish to keep them, so to speak, in their place? I suggest that it's possible that our children, whom we love above all else, to whom—we say—the future belongs, are in certain respects an oppressed minority (never mind that some parents think they are oppressed by their demanding children). And like other minorities, their distinct status is represented by the distinctiveness of their music, and a certain special role in the musical life of the whole society.

Throughout the world, children's music has a number of uses. There are lullabies or other kinds of songs sung by adults to quiet and amuse children; songs associated with children's games and with play; and music, perhaps instrumental, that is itself play. There are songs intended to help children learn their own culture, with the words of proverbs or stories from which one may draw conclusions to guide behavior. And music intended to teach rudiments of musicianship. The cases of truly separate children's traditions, as suggested for Venda culture by Blacking (1967: 29), who believes that it is "conceivable that many of the songs were composed by children, and not handed down to them," may actually be relatively rare.

In most places, it's my guess, on the basis of the modest survey of cultures that the ethnomusicological literature provides, that it seems to be adults who decide how and what children should sing. They teach a separate, distinct style, but one they share for particular purposes. The simple style found in European and some other children's songs is also found in some adults' games (e.g., gambling songs of some Native Americans) and of outmoded rituals (e.g., vestiges of pre-Christian seasonal rites in Europe). In Europe, too, simple children's instruments such as rattles, the bullroarer, and flutes without finger holes are maintained in entertainments descended from ancient serious ceremonies no longer in use that were eventually attached to Christian feast days such as St. John's, Christmas, and Easter.

We may speculate why adults in some societies, including Western, should have chosen a particular kind of music to give to children, why they didn't get them started on adult music from the beginning. There may be everywhere the assumption that simple music—music simple by some agreed-on criteria—is appropriate because of children's presumed abilities and preferences. Beyond this, and perhaps more significant, is the need to symbolize for children their separate status in society, a status necessarily devoid of many adult responsibilities and privileges. But, as Campbell (1998: 168–94) details, children's musical culture is rich and varied, and for children, music accomplishes many things. But children's songs also play a role in adult culture. If in older, traditional societies they are related to earlier rituals, no longer functional or taken seriously, in modern society, in which the children's repertory is more consistent and less changeable than adult music, they perhaps become a heartwarming reminder of the cultural past, as children remind adults of their own past.

Children's songs in many cultures are not simply a kind of *gradus ad Parnassum* through which one learns, in stages, the music-making capacity of adults. Studying the separateness and heterogeneity of children's repertories has many-sided significance to ethnomusicology. Blacking concluded that it marks children as a separate social group, that the reason children do not perform adult music is that "each social group has its associated style of music, its audible badge of identity" (1967: 29). In contemporary American musical culture, too, children are treated as a minority, and they look upon themselves as such, continuing even to adolescence to represent their social separateness by insisting on adhering to their own music, often to the despair of parents desperately fighting the superior power of the amplifier. And, following M. M. Bakhtin and going back to the nineteenth-century work of William Wells Newell, Minks argues that children's music (and other) expression must be analyzed with attention to power relations and ideologies of value. Children, too, then, participate musically in the tendency for societies to divide the world into themselves and others. The music and musical life of national and ethnic minorities, of people who in other ways live outside the mainstream of society, and of young children are really very different kinds of phenomena; yet in the ways in which inequality of power is reflected in musical life and leads to distinctive musical existence, they have important things in common.

30

A New Era:
The 1990s and Beyond

Cultural Greyout?

No doubt it has been said many times. The world has changed, and our lives are no longer as they had once been: For people in Western countries, after the French Revolution, or maybe after the 1848 upheavals, and after World War I, and again after World War II, at the end of the Cold War, after September 11, 2001; in the United States, after 1865; in Native American culture, when it became clear that the whites couldn't be defeated; in parts of Africa, after the continent was divided among European powers in 1885. But this time, about 2000, to say that we are in a new era rings particularly true, in all aspects of our lives, as computer technology provides instant access to all parts of the world, everything can be electronically synthesized, and the cell phone permits one to call anyone without even knowing where he or she is. And the life of music, too, transmittable by computer networks, heard mostly in recorded form, and rarely performed live without sound technicians, has an unprecedentedly different existence. And we're tempted to think, as a result of this seeming technical unification of the world, that the fears of many music lovers and of the first generations of ethnomusicologists have been realized, as the principal elements of Western music—harmony, instrument hegemony, and simple meters—have penetrated the world's cultures and have been adapted by them into their own traditions, while the world's peoples have developed their individual versions of the popular musics that grew out of combinations of ultimately European and African elements, with input from the Middle East and South Asia. Has the "cultural greyout" foreseen by so many who loved the world's musical diversity actually come about?

Well, it depends on how you look at it. We can find commonalities all over the world, as for instance in the most recently composed music by Chinese, African, Latin American, European composers, and one could make a case that we're living in a single, globalized musical culture. Still, it makes sense to me to continue, as ethnomusicologists, to approach the world as comprised of many discrete musics, but now, as musics (always as sound, behavior, ideas) that relate to each other and influence each other in lots of ways, far more than may have been the case before the explosion of communications technology. Certainly the intensive interconnectedness of the world goes back farther. Although never on even remotely as large a scale, cultural (and musical) homogenization has occurred before, as in the expansion of Chinese culture in the fourteenth century, the Islamic wars of conquest, or perhaps even the course of Aztec or Inca expansion. Homogenization has always been there, but since the 1700s, and enormously accelerating in the twentieth century, throughout the world, processes deriving from the development of capitalism in Western culture have continually increased its intensity.

I'm talking in the first instance about colonialism, which forced the world's societies, or at least their elites, to adopt certain Western cultural values and many aspects of Western music; about nationalism, which threw the small societies of which the world once consisted into larger entities that maintained themselves through shared language and culture, although its members might be largely ignorant of each other and thus could coexist only as "imagined communities"; about cosmopolitanism, defined by Turino (2000: 7) as "objects, ideas, and cultural positions that are widely diffused throughout the world and yet are specific to only certain portions of the population [read "elites"] within given countries, a process often also called globalization." About a series of concepts—postcolonialism, postnationalism, diasporic networks, transnationalism, and lots more—developed in the social sciences to grapple with the many different kinds of interactions of groups of people. Or, better stated, this is about people who see themselves as members of various groups on the basis of their relationships to each other and to their own pasts (see Appadurai's *Modernity Writ Large*, 1996). In simple terms, I am talking also about two processes with opposite motivations, designated by terms no longer widely used, but still helpful—*Westernization* and *modernization*—which represent different ways in which non-Western societies have adapted Western culture, the one representing a kind of "buying into" Western ways, accepting the principles and values of the West, and the other using Western technology and techniques to permit maintenance of the indigenous traditions. And I am talking about the increased significance of relationships determined by inequality of power among the world's social groups of all sorts, which also is something hardly new, but is exacerbated by the increased possibility of contact and communication.

If this picture of a fundamentally changed world of intercultural relationships is a true one, then it must naturally be there in music; and indeed, the investigation of that aspect of musical culture has become, it seems to me, the principal preoccupation of ethnomusicologists since the late 1980s. Compare two issues of *Ethnomusicology*. In January 1982, we find eight articles, six of them describing and analyzing traditions as discovered by the author—trance and music in a Hausa culture, by Veit Erlmann; factors shaping a style of Qur'anic recitation, by Kristina Nelson; shape-note tune books and Primitive Baptism, by Brett Sutton; a source for the study of American instrumental folk music, by Chris Goertzen; Buddhist ritual music, by Jackson Hill; a method for cross-cultural comparison of musical structure, by Mieczyslaw Kolinski. Only two articles touch on current or recent cultural and musical change, and they do it gingerly at that—studies of song repertories of Shoshone women by Judith Vander, and of popular music in Ibadan by Christopher Waterman. Then look at fall 2002, twenty years later. Of six articles, five grapple with what has lately been happening to the musical world: Christian hymns in South African Native culture, by Carol Muller; Chinese minority musicians on tour in London; explorations of the cultural insider and outsider as fieldworker and musician, by Chou Chiener (for China) and Greg Downey (for Brazil); generational change in Berber women's songs, by Katherine Hoffman. These contents illustrate the changed picture of the musical world, and the accompanying changes in ethnomusicological emphases.

Things have changed so much, but in some respects we have also come full circle. Beginning with attempts to see the whole musical world in its diversity and its unity, we moved to a high degree of specialization, but now that the world has, as we often hear, shrunk to a "global village," we are again becoming interested in the course of human music in its entirety, particularly the most recent segment of its history. We see the world as a set of issues, valid everywhere, to be debated, and less as a group of repertories. Our conferences have sessions, for example, on music ownership and control in traditional North American Plains, Australian aboriginal, South African popular, and Los Angeles film music culture; in women's funeral singing in Ireland, Lebanon, and Polynesia.

Well, Not All That New

Naturally, this sea change in emphasis in ethnomusicology has its prehistory. Most of the literature concerns the ways in which the world's cultures have responded to the coming of Western culture and Western music—music in the sense of musical style, ideas about music, instruments—into their lives. One of few before 1950, an article by Frances Densmore (1934) attended to the issue. By then the practical effect on non-Western musicians and musical life had become a factor, resulting in a landmark conference in 1932 of Middle Eastern and European musicians and scholars in Cairo (see Racy 1991) and later of others, including one in 1961 in Tehran (see Archer 1964b). The parts of the world first subject to thorough study of the interaction of traditional and Western music were those in which Europe and sub-Saharan Africa were musically juxtaposed.

By the 1970s, Western influence had been shown to be powerful even in such genres as Javanese gamelan music, once thought to be relatively immune (Becker 1972). The study of the interaction of musics has more recently given rise to the subfield of urban ethnomusicology, whose studies are based on the characteristic of modern cities of being composed of a variety of ethnic groups, in varying degrees affected by modern Western musical culture. An early landmark in systematization of the ethnomusicological study of the twentieth-century world is Wiora's (1965: 147–97) description of the last of his four ages of music as "global industrial culture." Wiora sees the twentieth century rather pessimistically as a period of musical homogenization.

Sometimes affecting an uncaring attitude, many ethnomusicologists nevertheless sorrowed at the disappearance of musics, of styles, genres, instruments. It is difficult not to share this sorrow. But I would so far hardly agree that the widely feared greying-out of musical diversity is actually taking place. Whether the twentieth century is such a bad period for world music is arguable. But then, how does one evaluate a music, from the outside, as it were? It's hard to overstate the harm done to most of the world's peoples by colonialism, capitalism, and globalization, but difficult to make a case for a pejorative evaluation of the musical results. The musical experience of the average individual is much broader today than in the past. The hybrids and mixes resulting from intercultural contact could be interpreted as enrichment as easily as pollution, and old traditions as a class have not simply disappeared.

To contemplate the history of ethnomusicological research into the results of colonialism, nationalism, globalization, it seems best to view the musical world not so much as a group of musics but as a large network of musical interrelationships. In discussing ways in which musics affect each other, the earlier ethnomusicological literature revolved around two major concepts by which interacting cultures can be compared: relative complexity and degree of compatibility. These concepts overlap, and both involve us in difficulties of definition and interpretation. One reason generally accepted for the great influence of Western music upon all others is its presumably great complexity, and its accompanying technology and economic power. It's an assumption derived in part from Western views of world music but also from the nature of the particular Western music that has generally been the first to be presented to non-Western cultures—classical music to a small degree, popular music somewhat, but mostly, classically derived military and church music; and rural folk music only slightly. Using the idea essentially as a quantitative concept, the presumably great complexity of Japanese and Indian classical music and the relative simplicity of Native American, or South Asian tribal, or Australian aboriginal music have been considered as predictors of musical response. I've already said it: We have no precise measurements of musical complexity—and anyhow, complexity here is not a value but a descriptor—but the literature is full of statements that are intuitive, and based on anecdotal evidence, but not to be rejected out of hand. If we equate complexity in some way with quantity of components and of their interrelationships, we may be justified in making some working hypotheses. For example, a repertory in a purely oral tradition will normally be simpler than a partially written one; a tradition with music theory of an articulated sort more complex than one lacking it; and traditions with professional training of musicians more complex than others.

A second concept used for some decades as a predictor of musical history is the relative compatibility of musics; in somewhat simpler words, this may just mean degree of significant similarity. Discussion of this issue goes back to questions, raised in the late nineteenth century, about the ultimate source of Negro spirituals, the degree to which they came out of African or European traditions. Not a useful question, with answers that often came out of a racist arsenal. But why certain musics should readily combine, while others resisted—this question led to conclusions that the basis was something in the quality of music itself, not the intercultural relations of proximity and power of its human carriers. Thus, some classical studies (e.g., Merriam 1955b; J. Roberts 1972; R. Waterman 1952) tried to show that African and Western musics are more compatible than are Western and American Indian, bringing about certain musical effects. Musics were changed by the adoption of elements from more complex musics, and by the confluence of musics that possessed certain compatibilities. Complexity may not be too hard to identify, but compatibilities, obvious on the surface, may be no more than conclusions drawn after the fact. But let's look further at what has been happening.

We can probably agree: One of the most important events in the history of twentieth-century music is the coming of Western music in the lives of all cultures, and one of the most important processes is the ways in which the world's cultures adapted their musical cultures, changed them, in order to achieve some kind of survival. This understanding seems to me to characterize the ethnomusicological approach to being in a "new era" well into the 1980s. What kinds of survival are we talking about? Let's look at various imaginable results along a theoretical continuum. At one end is complete maintenance of the musical tradition, and at the other complete abandonment of the tradition and acceptance of Western music in toto. I haven't heard of a culture that can be described by either extreme; they are theoretical abstractions, though the people of Ishi might come close to the first, and those Australian aboriginals I met in Adelaide could illustrate the second. But the judgments I'm suggesting are based on an outsider's hearing of the music, not on musical behavior, contexts, concepts, and not on an insider's evaluation. Literature looking at the interaction of Western and traditional musics in the 1980s tended to try to identify different reactions or responses to Western music—more than one for any one culture, to be sure.

A quarter-century ago I tried to identify ways in which many of the world's musical systems reacted to the coming of Western music and musical ideas. These are not at all alike in their applicability to entire or partial repertories, they are overarching or class- or person-specific, but nevertheless they illustrate the enormous variety of things that happened in the world as a result of the cultural, political, and, in the end, musical upheaval. But all of them could be seen in the context of one continuum—whether the principal effort was to preserve the older musical tradition at any, or at great, cost, or whether the reaction was primarily to abandon cultural tradition and become part of the newly imported musical culture. It's probably accurate to say that the world's cultures found themselves at various points between these extremes, and the question is what techniques they used to achieve musical survival.

Adaptation, Change, Survival

Much in the way of twentieth-century musical change may thus be interpreted as strategy for survival, changing aspects of the old system in order to save its essence. Each culture has reacted differently, in ways dictated by the power relations with the colonialists, the functions and values of music in society, musical compatibilities, and more. Together they address the need to balance advantages of old and new. As a template for comparison, I tried also to introduce a very abstract concept called—using terminology compatible with 1970s thinking—"musical energy" (Nettl 1985: 20, 26). In each culture, I would hypothesize, a certain maximum amount of energy is available for musical creativity and activity; the term "energy" may have been fashionable, but others such as "capacity" or "limit" might also be applicable. By this I meant a society's total musical effort, suggesting that as Western music came into the lives of other of the world's peoples, they had to find ways of maintaining their older tradition with reduced energy, and this might mean a reduction in the number of people, or the amount of time, or the number of genres, styles, instruments henceforth devoted to it. The way in which a society distributed its musical energy between older and imported practices and styles might determine specific musical results.

A quick rundown follows, of things that have happened in various locations and societies, to illustrate the variety of phenomena. The type of response about which we have heard the most in the way of laments is total loss, *abandonment* of the musical tradition. As already stated, this seems rarely, if ever, to have happened quite as completely as the word suggests. It seems doubtful that there is a population that has remained biologically alive but whose musical experience has been completely replaced, without trace, by the Western counterpart; certainly this is rare. Certainly sectors of repertories have disappeared, and the coming of Western music (and there may be parallel cases of Middle Eastern–based music) has stamped musics, repertories, and styles. We can see how hegemonic forces from dominant cultures such as certain evangelical Christian missionaries and the Islamist Taliban managed to eliminate music traditions in Oceania and Afghanistan. But in an amazingly large proportion of cases, music traditions, as victims of asymmetries of power, seem rarely to disappear without trace. Rather, they may remain extant in vestige, as in the memories of a few people, in practices of secular rituals once sacred, in children's and game songs. They have changed, been recast for different uses, but it seems to me that some kind of presence is always maintained, maybe even subliminally, and occasionally powerfully resurrected.

This sounds rather like a value judgment, something from which I wish to refrain. Whether what has happened—in life, in music—is good or not must be judged by the people to whom it has happened. My statements here represent the outsider's perspective. There may be peoples who believe that their traditional music has disappeared, notwithstanding outsiders who still detect its presence in substance or vestige; and peoples who insist that their music is unique to them, despite formal analysis that shows it identical to another (e.g., Western) music. Some are glad it's gone, others don't know it was once there. Changes in instruments, disappearance of traditional religious uses of music, changes from three-quarter tones to semitones in a scale may make all the difference in the world to their owners. So, admittedly, the statement that non-Western musics continue to exist everywhere, like the majority of descriptions of the other responses below, stem from general, comparative, and, of course, Western-oriented views that try to take into consideration, but in the end cannot duplicate, the perspectives of all, or indeed any, non-Western cultures.

One sometimes used to hear this, perhaps from believers in the Western canonic tradition: It's terrible, what we did to indigenous peoples around the world; but at least we brought them some good music to replace that awful screeching. But even putting the kindest face on it, accepting the fundamental indivisibility of cultural domains that is fundamental to ethnomusicology, it's hard to see how the economic, political, social, and physical oppression of peoples by Western-based forces could bring with it musical results morally or aesthetically acceptable.

But to continue my account of responses to Western music: If there is no such thing as complete abandonment of traditional music, there certainly has been the abandonment of some of its components, and thus substantial *impoverishment* or *reduction*, resulting from shifts in musical energy. For example, some Native American Plains Indian cultures once had a vast quantity of religious music; today there is little of that but, instead, much more music for a small number of social dances mainly associated with powwows. The total traditional repertory of a typical Native American tribe seems now to be very much smaller, in number of songs or of song types, than in the past. The repertories in Japanese classical music have shrunk. Mervyn McLean (1965) similarly described the process and function of "song loss" among the Maori. Elsewhere instruments have been lost and replaced by Western counterparts; traditional technology has been forgotten and replaced. Standardization (as in the forms of the Plains Indian songs) and simplification (as in rhythmic patterns of African-derived percussion music, if you compare it with West African in the Caribbean) may release energy to be expended on the absorption of Western music. In certain musics—the Carnatic musical culture is a good example—a distinct musical sound, based at least in part on its older musical tradition, is maintained, but the musical behavior has often been abandoned in favor of Western counterparts, for example, concerts, paid musical professionalism, records and radio, sitting on chairs to perform, applause, newspaper criticism. The traditional concepts of music, how it comes about, what it is, how it is defined, its major role in life, what power it has— all of this may, curiously, be closest to being abandoned by the cultures of the world in favor of Western concepts of music, and maybe this can be interpreted as a sacrifice to permit the musical sound to remain intact.

Another response to Western music is the artificial or perhaps *isolated preservation* of the tradition in a restricted environment— relegation, as it were, to a museum (see Archer 1964b for a sample of approaches). The mainstream of functional musical life of a people changes to Western patterns, and in some cases to Western musical forms merely influenced by the native tradition. But the music that a people regard specifically as their own traditional heritage is preserved in isolated pockets of existence, often under the protection and patronage of government agencies. The population recognizes this music but regards it as something belonging to the past or as a musical ideal rarely experienced and reserved for special purposes, events, social classes. Musical organizations are created and tour the nation in order to exhibit its own musical past. In some countries, such as South Korea, distinguished older musicians are formally given special status as "national treasures." The desire is to preserve this older music without change, to give it a kind of stability that it in fact probably did not experience in the past, and to do this at the expense of permitting it to function as a major musical outlet for the population. Sometimes this sort of artificial separation and preservation has been used as a temporary expedient. In Iran, for example, classical music was for a time preserved under the aegis of the Ministry of Fine Arts; then, in the period after 1968, it again began to play more of a role in everyday life and thus began to undergo more change. This temporary preservation of music by artificial means, followed by reintroduction in new forms into the mainstream of musical life, seems also to be a characteristic of twentieth-century Western musical culture. We have preserved older European classical music, medieval, Renaissance, Baroque, and certain kinds of folk music in educational institutions and with government support, in a decidedly static and museum-like environment. Some of it has again moved into the mainstream.

We come to a group of phenomena more readily found in small segments of repertories and unlikely to be representative of the musical behavior of an entire society: *Diversification* of styles in unified contexts is the combination of diverse elements into a single musical or social context. Thus Iranian and

Indian films may include, in one musical number or in a single sequence of pieces, a number of different styles originating in various regions and exhibiting among themselves several different kinds of response to Western music. *Consolidation,* related to but also in a sense opposite to diversification, has occurred often as a function of the creation of nation-states from what once were groups of politically separate entities, tribes, chiefdoms, kingdoms, or of the change of a people from independence to colonized minority. The establishment of a reasonably compact and, in terms of musical energy, not very demanding North American Indian style to replace what was once a large variety of tribal repertories is an example. So also is, in another sense, the establishment of African repertories presented by especially trained troupes of musicians and dancers whose purpose is to consolidate a nationally recognized music from a number of once more distinct traditions.

An interesting although probably not widespread development of the nineteenth and twentieth centuries is the *reintroduction* of musical styles to their place of origin after a sojourn elsewhere, best illustrated by the role of African American and Caribbean musics in the development of twentieth-century central and southern African musics. *Exaggeration* of seemingly exotic elements is a phenomenon resulting from the Western listener's expectation of great exoticism in the sound of non-Western music. In some venues, music appears to have changed in order to conform to the European and the Westernized elite's conception of what the tradition should be, stressing the difference and emphasizing what is, from the European viewpoint, an exotic musical sound. Ruth Katz (1970) showed certain modern Arabic music to have exaggerated traits that Westerners would regard as particularly Arabic; modern Plains Indian songs seem also to have exaggerated their peculiarly Indian characteristics, possibly in deference to ideas originating with white Americans. Finally, worthy of a brief note is the *humorous juxtaposition* of Western and non-Western elements—humorous in the thinking of the Western, Westernized, and traditional listener. Music stimulating this reaction seems to have arisen in certain American Indian and African cultures, in some of the film music of India, and in the performance of Western classical pieces in popular style by Mexican mariachi bands.

Finally, a concept—or better, a process—that plays a role throughout the interactions I've been describing is *syncretism.* It was a term widely used in the 1960s and 1970s, and now largely abandoned but, in my view, still helpful to explain why societies make certain musical choices (see C. Waterman 1990: 9 for recent commentary). Defined by the *Encyclopedia Britannica* simply as "fusion of elements from diverse cultural sources" but used in anthropology more specifically to explain the growth of culturally mixed phenomena when the elements are similar or compatible (see Merriam 1964: 313–15), it was used in ethnomusicology most notably to explicate the broad spectrum of styles in African-derived cultures from the New World to Africa. It has also been touched upon as a contributing factor in the evolution of modern Middle Eastern, Indian, and African musics. The mixed or hybrid styles characteristic of the later twentieth-century world music may have developed most readily when the sources are similar, compatible, and share certain central traits.

New Perspectives on the "Other"

If, after 1950, we moved from looking at the world as a group of discrete musics to studying the musical results of their interactions, beginning in the 1980s we proceeded further, to greater emphasis on the ways in which the interactions of the world's societies themselves determined musical life. We began to look more at what we had been doing, noting critically the social, intellectual, and ethical consequences of seeing the world as consisting of "us" and "others." Significantly, this meant an expansion of interest in various kinds of thinking frequently combined under the rubric of "theory," and importantly including the directions of thought known as critical theory and cultural studies, that is, attempts to provide generalized explanations for individual phenomena or, more typically, regularities, from points of view that seek ultimately to find ways of redress. This body of theory, to which most publications try to contribute, makes use of a large group of concepts that mainly have in common their applicability to relationships among groups of people—nations, societies, races, classes, genders, ethnic groups—with emphasis on their inequality in terms of power relations and hegemony. If once we were most interested in finding out why certain musical styles developed, and drew on knowledge of social interrelationships for explanations, we now are more inclined to look at the social relationships first, and try to comprehend the musics to which they give rise. Martin Stokes (in *New Grove* 2001, 8:386–95) expertly lays out the area in which ethnomusicologists, finding themselves in a "new era" of music and musical life, are developing approaches for making a "new era" for themselves.

An area in which ethnomusicology has made strides in recent times is the concern for what good ethnomusicologists' work, their findings, might do for the people from whom they have learned, and for those who might hear and read what they have to offer. They have, accordingly, become increasingly interested in helping the world's oppressed and underprivileged peoples, and their musicians, to become known, to perform and produce recordings, and to gain recognition and respect. They have been involved in organizing festivals, bringing their teachers to universities, gaining a voice in the mass media. This suggests a gradual but very desirable shift in their perspective of "others."

Looking critically at the anthropological concept of culture as something that itself played a role in developments in world culture and music, Stokes presents a group of issues that are in the forefront of ethnomusicological study: the concept of musical community; ethnicity; nationalism; diasporas and globalization; race, gender; the concept of the "other" inside one's own culture; and more. Some of these categories subsume others worth special mention here, such as the increased emphasis on questions of ownership and control of music, the effects of communications technology, the importance of music in representation. And ethnomusicologists have applied themselves to the rapid changes in the world's political picture and their almost immediate effects on music, as, for example, the end of the "Cold War" and the development of musical nationalism in eastern Europe and the Middle East (e.g., Buchanan 2005; Slobin 1996; Stokes 1992); the musical results of social changes in the wake of nationalist movements (e.g., Erlmann 1999; Turino 2000); and more specifically ethnomusicological results, such as the examining and maybe erasing of boundaries in the canons and taxonomies of music (e.g., Bergeron and Bohlman 1992; Bohlman 2002; Keil and Feld 1994) and the increased recognition of the world not only as a group of musics but as a group of ethnomusicologies (see, e.g., Blum 1991; Diamond and Witmer 1994; Myers 1993; Qureshi 1999; Racy 2003; and for a critique, Agawu 2003).

In all of these areas of consideration, emphasis seems to have moved from primary focus on musical styles and sound to the other sectors of Merriam's model, to the ideas about music that motivate people to make certain musical choices and decisions, and to things for which people use music, and things that music does for them. We may be in a new era in the world, but probably people have always seen themselves in their place in history as experiencing something that would have been inconceivable to their parents and ancestors. But in ethnomusicology, with its much shorter history, we may perhaps justify saying that we are in a new era in many ways, all summarized by the explanation that when we started out, we learned how musics differed, showed their separateness, but now we concentrate on comprehending and interpreting their constant and ever-increasing interactions.

31

The Shape of the Story:
Remarks on History

Should Ethnomusicology Be Abolished?

We come to the end of this group of thirty-one chapters, each devoted to a principal issue or concept or question of ethnomusicology, typically looking at this field as a phenomenon of the twentieth century—the whole twentieth century—trying often to see continuities and changes, in most respects taking a historical perspective. What now has been the shape of our story? I'm trying four approaches—the history of our identity, the relationship to musicology, a periodization, and a list of questions we have been asking in the past and the present.

One of the central issues has been where in the academy ethnomusicology belongs. Vignettes from the 1970s: A friend accompanied me to a meeting of the Society for Ethnomusicology. "Good heavens, it certainly is colorful," was his comment upon seeing professional-looking types delivering papers in one room, a group of dashiki-clad Anglo-Americans playing enthusiastically in an ensemble of drums, bells, and rattles before an obviously empathic audience in the next, and some students in jeans looking at kits for making sitars at a table in the hall. Then, upon attending a panel discussion, he gave a different sort of comment: "They're wonderful people, but each of them knows something different, and there doesn't seem to be much that they all know." Not necessarily an exaggeration. At another meeting, I heard: "The development of ethnomusicology is the most significant thing that has happened in musicology since 1950." A statement made by a music historian. And at a third: "Should ethnomusicology be abolished?" Title of a panel (and a publication by Lieberman 1977). No one wanted physically to remove the ethno-musicologists. But wasn't it perhaps time to call them, again, just plain musicologists, or anthropologists, or whatever it was that they came from? On the other hand, panels at the 2002 meeting of the Society for Ethnomusicology were titled, "What Is Ethnomusicology Doing in a Music Department?"

And similar questions are raised elsewhere. It would be tempting to make an anthology of writings that question the existence of ethnomusicology, but let me mention only a sharp exchange in the German journal *Musikforschung* (particularly Greve 2002 and the main rejoinder, Brandl 2003), in which it is suggested that ethnomusicology has no future, that it has done what it can do, that it was all along perhaps something of an aberration.

There are a number of ways in which the continued desirability of our field could be discussed, but in much of the critical literature it's not clear whether: (1) what the people who have called themselves ethnomusicologists do shouldn't have been done in the first place, (2) because of recent culture change, their task is no longer available, (3) they have accomplished what they set out to do and should hang up their hats, (4) their field should have no standing as a specialized field, (5) their existence has been all along a political gesture no longer valid, (6) as suggested above, they don't have enough in common to deserve to have a name, and (7) they have all along been part of the political and economic oppressors and should stop, or stick to European research. And there are other related questions.

All together, though, we have to ask whether ethnomusicology has developed into a coherent field, and whether we know what that field is. The implication of the vignettes at the head of this chapter is that there sometimes appears to be little to hold ethnomusicology together and much to tie it to older, more established fields, and also to newly developing areas. It is a tempting suggestion. One might be able to separate those interested in serious scholarship from those seriously interested in hearing interesting music or learning to play and sing. There seem to be many people doing many different things, some of them intellectually more removed from each other than any one of them is from conventional historical musicology, music theory, anthropology, folklore. As for the ethno-scholars, their approaches and their substance can be of great service to these older and emerging disciplines, and they would in turn benefit from exchange. It is gratifying to realize that now, more than in the past few decades, the ideas that are the stock in trade of ethnomusicology have begun to have an impact on related fields.

If it is true that there's little that ethnomusicologists have in common, then surely the disciplinary identity of ethnomusicology, its own unity and its relationship to other fields, would be among of the major issues of debate, past and present. But I would assert that ethnomusicology does have a unified past and a tradition that is to a considerable degree its own. It has its distinct history of ideas, its culture heroes and heroines, its landmarks, its moments of glory and of pathos—a story with a distinctive shape.

It's a history closely tied, to be sure, at many points to that of other disciplines. Vincent Duckles (in Brook, Downes, and Van Solkema 1972: 39) suggested that in the nineteenth century and earlier, seven main motivations set the stage for musicological inquiry, including the music of the ancients, the discovery of world music, and the discovery of national song, all clearly leading to what later became ethnomusicology, along with more specifically historical drives such as chant reform and the arts of custodianship. The people who did most to found the discipline of musicology—the likes of Guido Adler and Charles Seeger—contributed as well to the development of ethnomusicology. On the other hand, anthropology has also been centrally involved; a large proportion of the intellectual leaders have come from training in anthropology, and the rest have read their share of anthropological literature. Major figures—Herzog, Merriam, Blacking come most immediately to mind, but there are dozens more among our leadership—considered themselves in the first instance to be anthropologists.

But the history of ethnomusicology is not simply that of a subdivision of another discipline—musicology and/or anthropology. Nor is it simply the sequence of events in the research of individual world areas. If it makes sense to view the history of our field as a unit, it is a unit because our story is shaped by events of general significance to all who identify themselves with it. Contributions to ethnomusicological insight go back to the Renaissance (see Harrison 1973). It was, however, in the period in which it developed as a distinct field, between 1880 and 1900, that a group of first paradigms was established. Most important among them was a consensus to the effect that in certain ways, at least, it was reasonable to consider all musical systems as equal. The implications of cultural evolutionism, leading through various stages to the rational tonal system of modern Europe, had been dominant in the nineteenth century and has, for that matter, continued its effect. But at some point there emerged the belief that all musical systems—as represented particularly by the parameter of scales and tone material—were equally natural or, if you will, equally unnatural. The influential publication that resulted in this acceptance was A. J. Ellis's study "On the Musical Scales of Various Nations" (1885), and from that time stems a general belief in relativism as at least the intellectual point of departure. The decade of the 1980s also saw the first attempts at broad synthesis (Baker 1882), specialized monograph (Stumpf 1886), and in 1890, field recording. And soon after—just a century ago—Hornbostel (1905) began his first, modestly couched article (actually a lecture) on the nature of the field, suggesting the establishment of new paradigms, with a bit of heraldry: "A new field within an established discipline is obliged to justify its right to existence." The ensuing history has been frequently touched upon on these pages and won't be rehearsed here, but it has continued to be dominated by certain abiding issues, such as the interface between cultural insider and outsider, the significance or the uselessness of conceptual boundaries of all kinds, music as the sphere of the individual or the community, the validity or falseness of universals, and a special methodology that includes fieldwork and transcription and other techniques—issues that give our field its special character among the many intellectual streams pursuing the comprehension of music.

Among the -Ologies

If the decades around 1900 are the period of the first paradigms, a second high point of our history came some fifty years later, after World War II. It is at this point that the issue of "where do we belong" came more prominently into the foreground. Let me start by giving a personal account. When I was a student at Indiana University in Bloomington, the name had been invented but wasn't yet very current, and my teacher, George Herzog, still called it "comparative musicology." In my last years of study, I took mostly anthropology. But my degree was in music, and there was never any doubt in my mind that I was a kind of musicologist—one who ought to know something about anthropology and folklore and linguistics, but certainly a kind of musicologist. This was true of some of my fellow students, but others, similarly outfitted, never questioned that they were anthropologists. This breadth of approach—should I call it ambivalence? or ambiguity? or is it a kind of ambidexterity? or in some ways, maybe ambition, or maybe even its very large ambit—has been the paradigm of ethnomusicology in its history in the United States.

Writing the title of this section, I think in my unconscious I was remembering a *Nova* television program around 1998 called "Cheetah among the Lions," depicting a rather sad situation in an African valley in which a small group of cheetahs were constantly being pursued and persecuted by a larger group of more powerful lions. They could only survive on account of their wits and their exceptional speed. The zoologist-narrator suggested that the

REMARKS ON HISTORY · 117

lions feared that allowing the cheetahs to multiply would cut dangerously into the food and water resources of the lions. A strange and unsympathetic association, I admit.

Well, there's no doubt that many anthropologists, and some anthropology departments, have been very welcoming to ethnomusicology, and sympathetic to ethnomusicological concerns, but I think it's reasonable to claim that the field that has accepted the ideas and concepts of ethnomusicologists and welcomed them as colleagues most—and also the field that has needed them most to round out its discipline—is the field of general musicology, populated largely by music historians. As a student in the school of music, in the early 1950s, I was readily accepted by the musicologists as one of them, and we musicologists all made common cause against the rest of the music students, who in turn looked down on us as mere scholars who could only get in the way of playing and singing.

But when it came to sharing resources, as in looking for a teaching job, it was another story. Interviewed by administrators, I was told that there are hardly any jobs in music history; but for this stuff I was doing, whatever you call it, there would never be any jobs! Indeed, at that time there were very few jobs, and later, when jobs did come along—for myself, and for some colleagues—the historical musicologists sometimes got worried. Do we really need someone to teach only courses on non-Western and folk traditions? Later on yet, if one spoke of the need for a second ethnomusicologist to balance the five music historians, one might hear a fearful "The ethnos are taking over." There was a time when the lions-and-cheetahs metaphor actually seemed to apply.

True maybe of the 1950s. But not in earlier times. The predecessors of ethnomusicology before and shortly after 1900 seemed actually to be central to the then developing field of musicology. Let's look for a moment at the history of musicology. The first two volumes of the *Vierteljahrschrift für Musikwissenschaft* (1885, 1886), the first serious and comprehensive journal in musicology, contain twenty-three articles, and of these, five could be considered old-time ethnomusicology. Anthropology was involved early on, too; figures such as Alice Fletcher, and Carl Stumpf, A. J. Ellis, Otto Abraham, and even Erich von Hornbostel had nonmusical disciplinary allegiances. But in the end, I am convinced, all of them saw themselves as contributing principally to the field of music. Later, in the 1930s, when the predecessor of the American Musicological Society, the New York Musicological Society, was formed, its principal actors were theorists such as Joseph Yasser and Joseph Schillinger, composers such as Henry Cowell, librarians such as Harold Spivacke and (then) Oliver Strunk, ethnomusicologists such as George Herzog and Helen Roberts, and only a couple of traditional historians, along with the great generalist Charles Seeger.

From a small field in which the traditional subdivisions were evenly distributed, musicology in the United States had, by the early 1950s, become a discipline consisting largely of historians of Western art music who were ambivalent about the contributions to their general enterprise that could be made by students of non-Western musics. How this change in American musicology came has to do with the immense diaspora of European humanistic scholars from Europe fleeing Nazism and fascism, the Holocaust, and war. After these refugee scholars had settled and begun to build American historical musicology into an intellectual powerhouse, after World War II, ethnomusicologists responded in several ways. One was to establish first the *Ethnomusicology Newsletter* in 1953, then SEM in 1955—an SEM that at first lived under the protective wing of the American Anthropological Association. Second, a school, if you will, of ethnomusicology developed with a major interest in the music of non-Western, largely Asian cultures from the perspective that they perceived was taken by historians of Western art music, and by music department in general. This was the school developed in the first instance by the programs at UCLA and secondarily at Wesleyan University, the University of Michigan, and the University of Washington, and it had two principal characteristics. One was the privileging of art or classical traditions, with an interest in showing that they excelled by standards similar to those used by historians of European traditions. And second, since music historians were always expected to exhibit a minimum of competence performing Western music, the idea of teaching non-Western traditions through performance by Americans was heavily promulgated. In the United States, through the 1960s and 1970s, two somewhat contrastive approaches, headed respectively by Alan Merriam and Mantle Hood, vied to induce students to become anthropological or musical ethnomusicologists.

But musicologists have always, since the earliest publication defining the field, in 1885, claimed to include in their formal self-definitions the kinds of things that ethnomusicologists do—study the world's musics from a comparative and relativistic perspective, and study music in or as culture, and include all of the different kinds of music in a society under their purview. Never mind that they don't always adhere to these criteria. And so it has happened that ethnomusicology has come to have a much greater effect on the field of music than on anthropology and other social sciences. It seems that by now, in many institutions, one can't be a "compleat musicologist" without knowing something about ethnomusicology. At the same time, anthropologists are glad to have ethnomusicology around and available, but most feel that they can, personally, live without it. Interestingly, music department people think of ethnomusicology as an anthropologically oriented field; to them, one of the benefits of having ethnomusicologists as colleagues is that it brings anthropological perspectives into their lives.

Where are we now? These two approaches had too much to give to each other to remain separated, and by the 1980s, a kind of mainstream had become established in practice, and even more in training. The typical student, by the 1980s, got involved in performance, at school and in the field, and also read a great deal of anthropology; and I guess by now, even though there are misgivings about the authenticity of gamelans and mbira ensembles at American and European schools, and about the usefulness of critical theory, and so on, a kind of mainstream type of ethnomusicologist developed. But I don't think any more that when members of SEM got together, there was hardly anything that you could reasonably expect all of them to know about. Now there is, I feel, a shared core of knowledge and commitment.

Of course the activities of the typical ethnomusicologist changed enormously. I can hardly enumerate the ways. Let me try a couple. Preserving the world's music: from field recording we've moved to an interest in the recordings, LPs, CDs, and videos produced by societies for their own use. From transcription we've gone on to a larger arsenal of techniques. From being the scientists confronting the interpretive music historians we've gone on to being—along with anthropologists—the principal interpreters. At one time, synchronic and diachronic were the distinctive labels; now, we ethnos are just as much concerned with history as those other historians. From eschewing popular and culturally mixed musics as inauthentic we've gone on to a focus on how musics and musical cultures affect each other.

And so I come back to my contention that ethnomusicology has had a lot of effect on musicology, and on music. Of course, music historians think of ethnomusicology as a "smaller" younger brother, though the label of youth is not particularly justified, considering that both areas tend to use 1885 as a kind of starting date. Ethnomusicologists think of the interests of most music historians as arcane, dealing with a corner of music that's definitely admirable but of interest to a small minority of the world's people. And those who are called systematic musicologists—working in the fields such as psychology of music, psycho-acoustics, cognitive studies—see themselves as the quintessential musicologists who are concerned with the most general questions of all. But these musicologies have tended to come together, in books, for example, such as *Rethinking Music* (Cook and Everist 1999), which undertook to assess in twenty-four essays the state of music scholarship, six essays by out-and-out ethnomusicologists, about eight by scholars well known as historians, and the rest by theorists, semioticians, students of popular culture. This compendium reflects developments in other major research tools. The revered *Grove,* once a haven for true believers in the exclusivity of the Western art music canon, was enormously enlarged in 1980, including, for the first time, long and authoritative articles on the musics of the world's cultures, and on vernacular traditions. In 2001 the next edition appeared, enlarged from twenty to twenty-nine volumes, with half of the enlargement devoted to longer and more thorough coverage of musics outside the canon.

Giving more space to ethnomusicology is fine. But is there really a substantive rapprochement? How is anthropological perspective brought to the humanistic historians? Are the two doing things that are more alike than they used to be? Let me mention two trends that suggest that the answer is affirmative:

In the 1980s, a movement developed in general musicology that began to call itself the "new musicology." Related to so-called postmodern movements in other humanistic fields, it began to move into new areas: busting the traditional canons of great music; getting into gender studies, gay and lesbian studies, critical theory, cultural criticism, and many kinds of interpretation— some in my view very insightful ad others totally off the wall. And maybe most important, there arose the understanding that music can be comprehended fully only if one takes into account the culture from which it comes, the culture in which it does its work, the culture that affects and constructs it. Where did they get these ideas? Well, they've never been quite absent among historians, and not many of them have told me that it was reading ethnomusicology that brought them to these interests. But the "new musicology" bears many relationships to the "old" ethnomusicology, and while some historians haven't liked to hear me say "But we've always known or believed that," this turn of events provides lots of common ground, common areas of interest. One of the dramatic moments in this rapprochement occurred at a 1993 meeting of the AMS at which a plenary panel, titled "Music Anthropologies and Music Histories," by five scholars, two ethnomusicologists, two historians, and a theorist, was attended by hundreds, and the subjects—Renaissance perceptions of ancient Mexico, Western ideas of African rhythm, jazz, eighteenth-century opera, and Indian music scholarship—were all analyzed with approaches of postmodern interpretation. There's no doubt that the emergence of the new, postmodern musicology has drawn music historians and ethnomusicologists together.

The other movement concerns a smaller number of scholars, but I feel that it's equally significant in cementing the interaction of musicology and ethnomusicology. Mentioned from other perspectives in chapter 14, it's what we sometimes call "ethnomusicology at home," and it concerns, as the term suggests, the study of what is in some sense our own culture. To the kind of local concern that involved taking a bus from Seattle to a Native American reservation thirty miles away, or traveling across town to ethnic enclaves, we add the critical study of the musical culture of academic institutions and the music with which they are most associated, and from which a large proportion of ethnomusicologists come. Ethnomusicologists study the values that govern their own society's educational institutions (Kingsbury 1988) and performing organizations (Shelemay 2001). In various other ways, "ethnomusicology at home" made rapprochements with historians of Western music, who, themselves, began to interpret what they found in ways related to the ethnographies written by ethnomusicologists. And of course they all were also influenced and inspired by the directions of other traditional and newly developed research foci such as folkloristics, performance and media studies, narratology, and critical theory.

A Grand March

Let me finally add to these comments, with their attempts to present identities and paradigms, the suggestion that the shape of our story comprises four periods overlapping but nevertheless distinct. The first is one of initial examination and discovery, and of generalization. It is characterized by the attitudes that non-Western and folk musics are worthy of study, that comparisons among them can be made and historical insights gained from them, and that a relativistic approach is best. It includes separation of field and laboratory work, and the insistence on the collection and preservation of authentic artifacts. We still have much from this early period with us. But soon (perhaps beginning by the 1930s) a second period, one of greater specialization, replaced it. The leadership of a Hornbostel, trying his hand at many cultures, was replaced by individual and idiosyncratic research by many scholars, each devoted perhaps throughout a career to one or two of the world's societies. This approach seems to have culminated m the 1950s and 1960s, but it too is very much with us still.

More recently, perhaps beginning in the middle 1960s, a third period emerged. It is one of consolidation of gains from the many specialized stud-

ies and of resumed and increased interest in generalized theory and methodology. Old problems are brought back and viewed with greater sophistication: the matter of origins of music, universals, comparative study. There
were attempts to be nomothetic about the way in which music is related to
culture. Analytical approaches from linguistics and semiotics began to play
a major role. Scholars were still interested in how a particular culture and
its musical system work, but this interest is tempered by a conviction that
their own approaches and procedures must be carefully honed to produce
credible findings and interpretations.

There's a fourth period, and maybe we're just getting into it (though there
may be some who wish we were already getting out of it), and it is difficult
to characterize accurately. First, it is dominated by the emphasis on theory, a
term perhaps better rendered as "intellectual positions from which intepre-
tations emerge," and the insistence on the interpretation of data—rather than
simply positivistic presentation of data—as the principal purpose. Compared
to music historians and music theorists concerned with analysis, ethnomusicologists have perhaps always emphasized "theory," have always taken
into account the fact that the observer's position determines the way data is
perceived and interpreted. Nevertheless, the insistence on interpretation on
the basis of stances derived from social theory whose purpose is both intellectual and practical is one important feature of contemporary scholarship.
Second, this fourth period is also characterized by the enormous changes—
the result of economic, political, and technological forces—that the world
of music has undergone in the last few decades, changes that require us to find
new ways of perceiving and interpreting the world of music.

If one way to look at our history is as a series of contrastive periods, another is to see it as a kind of grand march, consisting of a mainstream of paradigms articulated by a dominant group of scholars whose work is of abiding value. But this is a stream with great diversity of ideas and methods, and
yet it has considerable unity of purpose. It's a march that has been periodically slowed or speeded by intellectual revolutions. Looking back, I think we
have been concerned mainly with three very broad questions: (1) What is it
that causes different cultures to have differently sounding music, and different attitudes toward music? What, then, determines a culture's principal musical style? (2) What do the world's peoples use music for? What does music
do for them? And (3) How do the world's musics transmit themselves, maintaining continuity and also engaging in change? These questions were the ones
that dominated our thinking in the 1950s, and they were in the background

of the lectures we heard from our teachers in the period in the period of great expansion after 1950. And they are the questions that are still around.

But also, we have recently been facing questions that people were not asking fifty years ago, issues we were not debating in 1950, and these have come to the foreground in recent years. To them our field will increasingly turn for giving itself direction. Here are some of them, combined under the rubrics of ethics, technology, and education.

1. *The role of ethnomusicologists in relation to the people in their field of study, for which the word "ethics" has become a shorthand.* What are our obligations to the people, the musicians, whose music we have studied? What is our role in the protection and use of intellectual property? When I was a student, the question of performers' or informants' or consultants' rights played a very small part; we dealt with artifacts far more than people. What are the roles of cultural insiders and outsiders? Can we even make such a distinction? In the 1950s, this was not an issue widely recognized; in the 1970s, it began to play a role, but we continue, not too successfully, to grapple with the issue of participant-observation, the question of who speaks for a culture, the definition of culture—is it what people in a society agree on, or what people in a society argue about?

2. *The relationship of ethnomusicology to the technologized world.* I'm an old-timer and thus still struggling to understand this area, so let me just say that ethnomusicological study of recording, distribution, globalization, the role of the Internet, are essential for giving us an understanding of today's musical culture. A good many younger scholars have bitten off parts of this new puzzle, but obviously we're just at the beginning. As a basis, though, let me point out that on the one hand, the distinctions among musical cultures seems to be receding, and musical variegation is maybe declining. On the other hand, the typical individual in the world has access to a vastly greater variety of music than was the case fifty years ago. So we must be concerned with control and ownership, and with the effects of recording and computer technologies on the world's musical public and on ourselves.

3. *The role of ethnomusicology in education.* In the 1950s, the few of us beginning to teach were an academic luxury. When I first tried to persuade music department colleagues that we were the branch of musicology that was asking the most fundamental questions, I got curious stares. Now we're fulfilling requirements—for world music to music educationists, for foreign cultures in general education, for an essential branch of musicology for musicology majors. But we should address ourselves to the task of influencing our

neighboring disciplines and fields further. We should go further in persuading our music historian colleagues that approaches developed in ethnomusicology might be crucial in interpreting historical and recent events, and in issues such as the relation of performer and audience, the history of performance practice, and the reception of music. We should persuade psychologists and biologists who are interested, for example, in the origins of music and the relationship of animal sounds and human music that knowing something of the immense variety of the world's human musics, and the fact that each society has its own, unique configuration of the concept of music, would add to the sophistication of their theories. We should persuade anthropologists that they can learn easily to deal with music as a major aspect of culture, and that they must include it because music, as the anthropologist Paul Bohannon (1963: 193) famously said, "has been proved one of the most diagnostic traits of any culture."

Once the cheetahs of the academic valley, surrounded by the lion historical musicologists (and incidentally also by the tigers and foxes of anthropology, the bears of folklore, the elephants of the sciences), we've survived and thrived, made our place. It's widely accepted that with its group of distinctive problems and approaches, ethnomusicology has made and continues to make distinctive contributions. The lions and the other creatures have been unexpectedly kind, and we cheetahs might be in danger of turning into lions ourselves, acting like kings of the valley. It may be a comforting feeling, but intellectual perils may be lurking. So, actually, I believe that we in ethnomusicology need to continue being like the cheetahs, maintaining our intellectual swiftness and our disciplinary flexibility, and learning further from anthropology, musicology, folklore, cognitive studies, biology, and other disciplines and fields more recently developed, in order to be able to continue our claim that our field is the one that deals with the issues that are most fundamental for understanding the music in human life, and in the world.

References

Abbreviations

AA	*American Anthropologist*
AM	*Asian Music*
EM	*Ethnomusicology*
JAF	*Journal of American Folklore*
JAMS	*Journal of the American Musicological Society*
JIFMC	*Journal of the International Folk Music Council*
MQ	*Musical Quarterly*
WM	*The World of Music*
YIFMC	*Yearbook of the International Folk Music Council*
YTM	*Yearbook for Traditional Music*

Aarne, Antti A. 1961. *The Types of the Folktale.* Trans. and enl. by Stith Thompson. 2nd rev. ed. Helsinki: Suomalainen Tiedeaka temia.

Abraham, Otto, and E. M. von Hornbostel. 1903. "Tonsystem und Musik der Japaner." *Sammelbände der internationalen Musikgesellschaft* 4: 302–60.

———. 1906. "Phonographierte Indianermelodien aus Britisch-Columbia." In *Anthropological Papers, Written in Honor of Franz Boas,* 447–74. New York: Stechert.

———. 1909–10. "Vorschläge für die Transkription exotischer Melodien." *Sammelbände der internationalen Musikgesellschaft* 11: 1–25.

Adams, Charles R. 1976. "Melodic Contour Typology." *EM* 20: 179–215.

Adams, Richard N. 1975. *Energy and Structure: A Theory of Social Power.* Austin: University of Texas Press.

Adler, Guido. 1885. "Umfang, Methode und Ziel der Musikwissenschaft." *Vierteljahrschrift für Musikwissenschaft* 1: 5–20.

———, ed. 1930. *Handbuch der Musikgeschichte.* 2nd ed. Berlin: Keller.

Agawu, V. Kofi. 1995a. *African Rhythm.* Cambridge: Cambridge University Press.

———. 1995b. "The Invention of African Rhythm." *JAMS* 48: 380–95.

———. 2003. *Representing African Music: Postcolonial Notes, Queries, Positions.* New York: Routledge.

Allen, Warren Dwight. 1939. *Philosophies of Music History.* New York: American Book.

Ambros, August Wilhelm. 1862. *Geschichte der Musik.* Vol. 1. Breslau: Leuckart.

Ames, David W. 1973a. "Igbo and Hausa Musicians: A Comparative Examination." *EM* 17: 250–78.

———. 1973b. "A Socio-Cultural View of Hausa Musical Activity." In Warren L. d'Azevedo, ed., *The Traditional Artist in African Societies,* 128–61. Bloomington: Indiana University Press.

Ames, David W., and Anthony V. King. 1971. *Glossary of Hausa Music and Its Social Contexts.* Evanston, Ill.: Northwestern University Press.

Amiot, Père. 1779. *Mémoire sur la musique des chinois.* Paris: Chez Nyon l'aîné.

Anderson, Benedict. 1991. *Imagined Communities: Reflections on the Origin and Spread of Nationalism.* London: Verso.

Ankermann, Bernhard. 1902. "Die afrikanischen Musikinstrumente." Doctoral diss., University of Leipzig.

Anttila, Raimo. 1972. *An Introduction to Historical and Comparative Linguistics.* London: Macmillan.

Apel, Willi. 1969. *Harvard Dictionary of Music.* 2nd ed. Cambridge, Mass.: Harvard University Press.

Appadurai, Arjun. 1996. *Modernity Writ Large: Cultural Dimensions of Globalization.* Minneapolis: University of Minnesota Press.

Archer, William Kay. 1964a. "On the Ecology of Music." *EM* 8: 28–33.

———, ed. 1964b. *The Preservation of Traditional Forms of the Learned and Popular Music of the Orient and the Occident.* Urbana: University of Illinois Institute of Communications Research.

Askew, Kelly M. 2002. *Performing the Nation: Swahili Music and Cultural Politics in Tanzania.* Chicago: University of Chicago Press.

Attali, Jacques. 1985. *Noise: The Political Economy of Music.* Minneapolis: University of Minnesota Press.

Averill, Gage. 1997. *A Day for the Hunter, a Day for the Prey: Popular Music and Power in Haiti.* Chicago: University of Chicago Press.

Ayyangar, R. Rangaramanuja. 1972. *History of South Indian (Carnatic) Music.* Madras: Author.

Babiracki, Carol M. 1997 "What's the Difference: Reflections on Gender and Fieldwork in Village India." In Barz and Cooley 1997, 121–38.

Bailey, Derek. 1992. *Improvisation: Its Nature and Practice in Music.* New York: DaCapo.

Baily, John. 1976. "Recent Changes in the Dutar of Herat." *AM* 8/1: 29–64.

Baily, John, and Veronica Doubleday. 1990. "Patterns of Musical Enculturation in Afghanistan." In Frank Wilson and Franz Roehmann, eds., *Music and Child Development*, 88–99. Ann Arbor, Mich.: Book Crafters.

Bakan, Michael B. 1999. *Music of Death and New Creation: Experiences in the World of Balinese Gamelan Beleganjur*. Chicago: University of Chicago Press.

Baker, Theodore. 1882 (1976). *On the Music of the North American Indians*. Trans. Ann Buckley. Buren, Netherlands: Knuf.

Barbeau, Marius. 1934. "Asiatic Survivals in Indian Songs." *MQ* 20: 107–16.

———. 1962. "Buddhist Dirges of the North Pacific Coast." *JIFMC* 14: 16–21.

Barkechli, Mehdi. 1963. *La musique traditionelle de l'Iran*. Tehran: Secretariat d'état aux beaux-arts.

Barley, Nigel. 1983. *The Innocent Anthropologist: Notes from a Mud Hut*. New York: Holt.

Barnett, H. G. 1953. *Innovation: The Basis of Cultural Change*. New York: McGraw-Hill.

Barry, Phillips. 1910. "The Origin of Folk Melodies." *JAF* 23: 440–45.

———. 1914. "The Transmission of Folk-Song." *JAF* 27: 67–76.

———. 1933. "Communal Re-Creation." *Bulletin of the Folk-Song Society of the Northeast* 5: 4–6.

———. 1939. *Folk Music in America*. National Service Bureau Publication no. 80-S. New York: Works Progress Administration, Federal Theatre Project.

Barth, Frederick, ed. 1969. *Ethnic Groups and Boundaries*. Boston: Little, Brown.

Barthes, Roland. 1974. *S/Z*. New York: Hill and Wang.

Bartók, Béla. 1931. *Hungarian Folk Music*. London: Oxford University Press.

———. 1935. *Melodien der rumänischen Colinde (Weihnachtslieder)*. Vienna: Universal-Edition.

———. 1959. *Slovenske l'udove piesne*. Bratislava: Akademia Vied.

———. 1967. *Rumanian Folk Music*. Vol. 1. The Hague: Nijhoff.

Bartók, Béla, and Albert B. Lord. 1951. *Serbo-Croatian Folk Songs*. New York: Columbia University Press.

Barz, Gregory, and Timothy Cooley, eds. 1997. *Shadows in the Field: New Perspectives for Fieldwork in Ethnomusicology*. New York: Oxford University Press.

Baumann, Max Peter. 1976. *Musikfolklore und Musikfolklorismus*. Winterthur: Amadeus.

———. ed. 1991. *Music in the Dialogue of Cultures: Traditional Music and Cultural Policy*. Wilhelmshaven: Noetzel.

Bayard, Samuel P. 1942. "Ballad Tunes and the Hustvedt Indexing Method." *JAF* 65: 248–54.

———. 1950. "Prolegomena to a Study of the Principal Melodic Families of British-American Folk Song." *JAF* 63: 1–44.

———. 1953. "American Folksongs and Their Music." *Southern Folklore Quarterly* 17: 130–38.

———. 1954. "Two Representative Tune Families of British Tradition." *Midwest Folklore* 4: 13–34.

Becker, Judith. 1972. "Western Influence in Gamelan Music." *AM* 3/1: 3–9.

———. 1986. "Is Western Art Music Superior?" *MQ* 72: 341–59.

Becking, Gustav. 1928. *Der musikalische Rhythmus als Erkenntnisquelle*. Augsburg: Filser.

Behague, Gerard. 1973. "Bossa and Bossas." *EM* 17: 209–33.

Belzner, William. 1981. "Music, Modernization, and Westernization Among the Macuma Shuar." In Norman E. Whitten, ed., *Cultural Transformations and Ethnicity in Modern Ecuador*, 731–48. Urbana: University of Illinois Press.

Benedict, Ruth. 1934. *Patterns of Culture*. Boston: Houghton Mifflin.

Bergeron, Katherine, and Philip V. Bohlman, eds. 1992. *Disciplining Music: Musicology and Its Canons*. Chicago: University of Chicago Press.

Berliner, Paul. 1978. *The Soul of Mbira*. Berkeley: University of California Press.

———. 1994. *Thinking in Jazz: The Infinite Art of Improvisation*. Chicago: University of Chicago Press.

Bingham, W. V. 1914. "Five Years of Progress in Comparative Musical Science." *Psychological Bulletin* 11: 421–33.

Blacking, John. 1965. "The Role of Music in the Culture of the Venda of the Northern Transvaal." *Studies in Ethnomusicology* (New York) 2: 20–53.

———. 1966. Review of *The Anthropology of Music*, by Alan P. Merriam. *Current Anthropology* 7: 218.

———. 1967. *Venda Children's Songs: A Study in Ethnomusicological Analysis*. Johannesburg: Witwatersrand University Press.

———. 1970. "Tonal Organization in the Music of Two Venda Initiation Schools." *EM* 14: 1–56.

———. 1971. "The Value of Music in Human Experience." *YIFMC* 1: 33–71.

———. 1972. "Deep and Surface Structure in Venda Music." *YIFMC* 3: 91–108.

———. 1973. *How Musical Is Man?* Seattle: University of Washington Press.

———. 1977b. "Can Musical Universals Be Heard?" *WM* 19/1–2: 14–22.

———. 1978. "Some Problems of Theory and Method in the Study of Musical Change." *YIFMC* 9: 1–26.

———. 1987. *A Commonsense View of All Music*. Cambridge: Cambridge University Press.

———. 1989. "Challenging the Myth of Ethnic Music: First Performances of a New Song in an African Oral Tradition." YTM 21: 17–24.

———. 1992. "The Biology of Music-Making." In Myers 1992, 301–14.

———. 1995. *Music, Culture and Experience: Selected Papers*. Edited and with an introduction by Reginald Byron. Chicago: University of Chicago Press.

———, ed. 1977a. *Anthropology of the Body*. London: Academic Press.

Blaukopf, Kurt. 1951. *Musiksoziologie: Eine Einführung in die Grundbegriffe mit besonderer Berücksichtigung der Soziologie der Tonsysteme*. Vienna: Verkauf.

———. 1970. "Tonsysteme und ihre gesellschaftliche Geltung in Max Webers Musiksoziologie." *International Review of Music Aesthetics and Sociology* 1: 159–68.

————. 1979. "The Sociography of Musical Life in Industrialised Countries: A Research Task." *WM* 21/3: 78–81.

————. 1982. *Musik im Wandel der Gesellschaft.* Munich: Piper.

Bloomfield, Leonard. 1951. *Language.* Rev. ed. New York: Holt.

Blum, Stephen. 1972. "Musics in Contact: The Cultivation of Oral Repertories in Meshhed, Iran." Ph.D. diss., University of Illinois.

————. 1975a. "Persian Folksong in Meshhed (Iran), 1969." *YIFMC* 6: 68–114.

————. 1975b. "Towards a Social History of Musicological Technique." *EM* 19: 207–31.

————. 1987. "On the Disciplines and Arts of Music." *WM* 29/1: 19–29.

————. 1991. "European Musical Terminology and the Music of Africa." In Nettl and Bohlman 1991, 3–36.

————. 1992. "Analysis of Musical Style." In Myers 1992, 165–218.

————. 1998. "Recognizing Improvisation." In Nettl and Russell 1998, 27–46.

Blum, Stephen, Philip V. Bohlman, and Daniel M. Neuman, eds. 1991. *Ethnomusicology and Modern Music History.* Urbana: University of Illinois Press.

Blume, Friedrich, ed. 1949–79. *Die Musik in Geschichte und Gegenwart.* Kassel: Bärenreiter.

Boas, Franz. 1928. *Anthropology and Modern Life.* New York: Norton.

Bohannon, Paul. 1963. *Social Anthropology.* New York: Holt, Rinehart.

Bohlman, Philip V. 1988. *The Study of Folk Music in the Modern World.* Bloomington: Indiana University Press.

————. 1989. *The Land Where Two Streams Flow.* Urbana: University of Illinois Press.

————. 1996. "Pilgrimage, Politics, and the Musical Remapping of the New Europe." *EM* 40: 375–412.

————. 2002. *World Music: A Very Short Introduction.* Oxford: Oxford University Press.

Boiles, Charles. 1967. "Tepehua Thought-Song." *EM* 11: 267–92.

————. 1973a. "Reconstruction of Proto-Melody." *Yearbook for Inter-American Musical Research* 9: 45–63.

————. 1973b. "Semiotique de l'Ethnomusicologie." *Musique en jeu* 10: 34–41.

————. 1978. *Man, Magic, and Musical Occasions.* Columbus, Ohio: Collegiate.

Bose, Fritz. 1952. "Messbare Rassenunterschiede in der Musik." *Homo* 2/4: 1–5.

————. 1953. *Musikalische Völkerkunde.* Zurich: Atlantis.

————. 1959. "Western Influences in Modern Asian Music." *JIFMC* 11: 47–50.

————. 1966. "Musikgeschichtliche Aspekte der Musikethnologie." *Archiv für Musikwissenschaft* 24: 239–51.

————. 1967. "Volkslied-Schlager-Folklore." *Zeitschrift für Volkskunde* 63: 40–49.

Bourdieu, Pierre. 1984. *Distinction: A Social Critique of the Judgment of Taste.* Trans. Tichard Nice. Cambridge, Mass.: Harvard University Press.

Bowers, Jane, and Judith Tick, eds. 1986. *Women Making Music: The Western Art Tradition, 1150–1950.* Urbana: University of Illinois Press.

Brailoiu, Constantin. 1954. "Le Rhythm enfantin." Republished in translation in his *Problems in Ethnomusicology*, 206–38. Cambridge: Cambridge University Press, 1984. Originally published in 1954.

———. 1960. *Vie musicale d'un village: Recherches sur le repertoire de Dragus (Roumaine) 1929–1932*. Paris: Institut universitaire roumain Charles Ier.

———. 1973. *Problemes d'ethnomusicologie: Textes reunis et prefaces par Gilbert Rouget*. Geneva: Minkoff Reprint.

Brandl, Rudolf. 2003. "Si tacuisses Greve: Das notwendige Erhalten der Musikethnologie." *Musikforschung* 56: 166–71.

Brett, Philip, Elizabeth Wood, and Gary C. Thomas, eds. 1994. *Queering the Pitch: The New Gay and Lesbian Musicology*. New York: Routledge.

Briegleb, Ann. 1970. *Directory of Ethnomusicological Sound Recording Collections in the U.S. and Canada*. Ann Arbor, Mich.: Society for Ethnomusicology.

Bright, William. 1963. "Language and Music: Areas for Cooperation." *EM* 7: 26–32.

Brinkmann, Reinhold, and Christoph Wolff, eds. 1999. *Driven into Paradise*. Berkeley: University of California Press.

Bronson, Bertrand H. 1949. "Mechanical Help in the Study of Folk Song." *JAF* 62: 81–90.

———. 1950. "Some Observations about Melodic Variation in British-American Folk Tunes." *JAMS* 3: 120–34.

———. 1951. "Melodic Stability in Oral Tradition." *JIFMC* 3: 50–55.

———. 1959. "Toward the Comparative Analysis of British-American Folk Tunes." *JAF* 72: 165–91.

———. 1959–72. *The Traditional Tunes of the Child Ballads*. Princeton: Princeton University Press.

Brook, Barry S., Edward O. D. Downes, and Sherman Van Solkema, eds. 1972. *Perspectives in Musicology*. New York: Norton.

Brown, Howard M. 1976. *Music in the Renaissance*. Englewood Cliffs, N.J.: Prentice-Hall.

Brown, Steven. 2000. "The 'Musilanguage' Model of Music Evolution." In Wallin, Merker, and Brown 2000, 271–300.

Browner, Tara. 2000. *Heartbeat of the People: Music and Dance of the Northern Powwow*. Urbana: University of Illinois Press.

Bruner, Edward M. 1996. "Tourism in Ghana." *AA* 98: 290–304.

———. 2005. *Culture on Tour: Ethnographies of Travel*. Chicago: University of Chicago Press.

Buchanan, Donna. 2005. *Performing Democracy*. Chicago: University of Chicago Press.

Buecher, Carl. 1902. *Arbeit und Rhythmus*. 3rd ed. Leipzig: Teubner.

Bukofzer, Manfred. 1937. "Kann die Blasquintentheorie zur Erklärung exotischer Tonsysteme beitragen?" *Anthropos* 32: 402–18.

———. 1947. *Music in the Baroque Era*. New York: Norton.

Burling, Robbins. 1964. "Cognition and Componential Analysis: God's Truth or Hocus-Pocus?" *AA* 66: 20–28.

Burman-Hall, Linda C. 1975. "Southern American Folk Fiddle Styles." *EM* 19: 47–65.

Burney, Charles. 1776–89 (1935). *A General History of Music.* New York: Harcourt, Brace.

Burton, Frederick R. 1909. *American Primitive Music.* New York: Moffat, Yard.

Cachia, Pierre. 1973. "A Nineteenth-Century Arab's Observations on European Music." *EM* 17: 41–51.

Calhamer, Tatiana. 1993. "Shrine, Zoo, Museum, Archive, Lab: A Record Store in Campustown." In Livingston et al. 1993, 15–28.

Cameron, Catherine. 1996. *Dialectics in the Arts: The Rise of Experimentalism in American Music.* Westport, Conn.: Praeger.

Campbell, Patricia Shehan. 1991. *Lessons from the World.* New York: Schirmer Books.

———. 1998. *Songs in their Heads: Music and Its Meaning in Children's Lives.* Oxford: Oxford University Press.

Canon, Cornelius Baird. 1963. "The Federal Music Project of the Works Progress Administration: Music in a Democracy." Ph.D. diss., University of Minnesota.

Cantwell, Robert. 1996. *When We Were Good: The Folk Revival.* Cambridge: Cambridge University Press.

Capwell, Charles. 1986. "Sourindro Mohun Tagore and the National Anthem Project." *EM* 31: 401–29.

———. 1991. "Marginality and Musicology in Nineteenth-Century Calcutta: The Case of Sourindro Mohun Tagore." In Nettl and Bohlman 1991, 228–43.

———. 2002. "A Ragamala for the Empress." *EM* 46: 197–225.

Caron, Nelly, and Dariouche Safvate. 1966. *Iran (Les traditions musicales).* Paris: Buchet/Castel.

Casagrande, Joseph B., ed. 1960. *In the Company of Man.* New York: Harper and Row.

Cassirer, Ernst. 1944. *An Essay on Man.* New Haven: Yale University Press.

Caton, Margaret. 1974. "The Vocal Ornament *Takryah* in Persian Music." *UCLA Selected Reports in Ethnomusicology* 2/1: 42–53.

———. 1979. "Classical and Political Symbolism in the Tasnifs of Arefe Qazvini." Paper presented at the meeting of the Society for Ethnomusicology, October 13, 1979, Montreal.

Chan, Sau Y. 1991. *Improvisation in a Ritual Context: The Music of Cantonese Opera.* Hong Kong: Chinese University Press.

Charry, Eric. 2000. *Mande Music.* Chicago: University of Chicago Press.

Chase, Gilbert. 1958. "A Dialectical Approach to Music History." *EM* 2: 1–9.

Chatterjee, Partha. 1986. *Nationalist Thought and the Colonial World.* Minneapolis: University of Minnesota Press.

Chaudhuri, Shubha. 1992. "Preservation of the World's Music." In Myers 1992, 365–73.

Chenoweth, Vida, and Darlene Bee. 1971. "Comparative-Generative Models of a New Guinea Melodic Structure." *AA* 73: 773–82.

Chopyak, James D. 1987. "The Role of Music in Mass Media, Public Education and the Formation of a Malaysian National Culture." *EM* 31: 431–54.

Chou, Chiener. 2002. "Experience and Fieldwork: A Native Researcher's View." *EM* 46: 456–86.

Christensen, Dieter. 1960. "Inner Tempo and Melodic Tempo." *EM* 4: 9–13.

———. 1988. "The International Folk Music Council and 'the Americans': On the Effects of Stereotypes on the Institutionalization of Ethnomusicology." *YTM* 20: 11–18.

———. 1991. "Erich M. von Hornbostel, Carl Stumpf, and the Institutionalization of Ethnomusicology." In Nettl and Bohlman 1991, 201–9.

Chrysander, Friedrich. 1885. "Über die altindische Opfermusik." *Vierteljahrschrift für Musikwissenschaft* 1: 21–34.

Clark, Henry Leland. 1956. "Towards a Musical Periodization of Music." *JAMS* 9: 25–30.

Clifford, James. 1988. *The Predicament of Culture: Twentieth-Century Ethnography, Literature,and Art.* Cambridge, Mass.: Harvard University Press.

———. 1997. *Routes: Travel and Transformation in the Late Twentieth Century.* Cambridge, Mass.: Harvard University Press.

Clifford, James, and George E. Marcus, eds. 1986. *Writing Culture: The Poetics and Politics of Ethnography.* Berkeley: University of California Press.

Cohen, Dalia. 1971. "The Meaning of the Modal Framework in the Singing of Religious Hymns by Christian Arabs in Israel." *Yuval* 2: 23–57.

Cohen, Dalia, and Ruth Katz. 1968. "Remarks Concerning the Use of the Melograph in Ethnomusicological Studies." *Yuval* 1: 155–68.

Cole, Hugo. 1974. *Sounds and Signs: Aspects of Musical Notation.* New York: Oxford University Press.

Collaer, Paul. 1958. "Cartography and Ethnomusicology." *EM* 2: 66–68.

———. 1960. *Atlas historique de la musique.* Paris: Elsevier.

Conklin, Harold. 1968. "Ethnography." In David L. Sills, ed., *International Encyclopedia of the Social Sciences,* 5:172–78. New York: Macmillan.

Cook, Nicholas, and Mark Everist, eds. 1999. *Rethinking Music.* Oxford: Oxford University Press.

Cooke, Deryck. 1959. *The Language of Music.* London: Oxford University Press.

Cooper, Robin. 1977. "Abstract Structure and the Indian Raga System." *EM* 21: 1–32.

Coplan, David. 1985. *In Township Tonight: South Africa's Black City Music and Theater.* New York: Longmans.

———. 1994. *In the Time of Cannibals: The Word Music of South Africa's Basotho Migrants.* Chicago: University of Chicago Press.

Corpus musicae popularis hungaricae. 1953. Budapest: Akademiai Kiadó.

Cowdery, James R. 1990. *The Melodic Tradition of Ireland.* Kent, Ohio: Kent State University Press.

Cox, John Harrington. 1939. *Folk-Songs Mainly from West Virginia.* American Folk-

Song Publications no. 5. New York: National Service Bureau, Works Progress Administration.

Crafts, Susan D., Daniel Cavicchi, and Charles Keil. 1993. *My Music.* Hanover, N.H.: Wesleyan University Press.

Curtis-Burlin, Natalie. 1907. *The Indians' Book.* New York: Harper.

Cusick, Susan. 1999. "Gender, Musicology and Feminism." In Cook and Everist 1999, 471–98.

Cutter, Paul F. 1976. "Oral Transmission of the Old-Roman Responsories?" *MQ* 62: 182–94.

Czekanowska, Anna. 1971. *Etnografia muzyczna.* Warsaw: Panstwowe Wydawnictwo Naukowe.

Dahlback, Karl. 1958. *New Methods in Vocal Folk Music Research.* Oslo: Oslo University Press.

Dahlhaus, Carl. 1971. *Einführung in die systematische Musikwissenschaft.* Cologne: Hans Gerig.

———. 1977. *Grundlagen der Musikgeschichte.* Cologne: Hans Gerig.

———. 1989. *The Idea of Absolute Music.* Trans. Roger Lustig. Chicago: University of Chicago Press.

———, ed. 1980–92. *Handbuch der Musikwissenschaft.* Laaber: Laaber-Verlag.

Dahlhaus, Carl, and Hans Heinrich Eggebrecht. 1985. *Was ist Musik?* Wilhelmshaven: Heinrichshofen.

Danckert, Werner. 1939. *Das europäische Volkslied.* Berlin: Bard.

———. 1956. "Tonmalerei und Tonsymbolik in der Musik der Lappen." *Musikforschung* 9: 286–96.

Danielou, Alain. 1966. "The Use of the Indian Traditional Method in the Classification of Melodies." *JIFMC* 18: 51–56.

———. 1973. *Die Musik Asiens zwischen Misachtung und Wertschätzung.* Wilhelmshaven: Heinrichshofen.

Danielson, Virginia. 1997. *The Voice of Egypt: Umm Kulthum, Arabic Song, and Egyptian Society in the Twentieth Century.* Chicago: University of Chicago Press.

Daughtry, J. Martin. 2003. "Russia's New Anthem and the Negotiation of National Identity." *EM* 47: 42–67.

Densmore, Frances. 1910. *Chippewa Music.* Bull. 45 of the Bureau of American Ethnology. Washington, D.C.: Smithsonian Institution.

———. 1913. *Chippewa Music II.* Bull. 53 of the Bureau of American Ethnology. Washington, D.C.: Smithsonian Institution.

———. 1918. *Teton Sioux Music.* Bull. 61 of the Bureau of American Ethnology. Washington, D.C.: Smithsonian Institution.

———. 1927a. "The Study of Indian Music in the Nineteenth Century." *AA* 29: 77–86.

———. 1927b. "The Use of Music in the Treatment of the Sick by the American Indians." *MQ* 13: 555–65.

————. 1929a. *Papago Music.* Bull. 90 of the Bureau of American Ethnology. Washington, D.C.: Smithsonian Institution.

————. 1929b. *Pawnee Music.* Bull. 93 of the Bureau of American Ethnology. Washington, D.C.: Smithsonian Institution.

————. 1934. "The Songs of Indian Soldiers during the World War." *MQ* 20: 419–25.

————. 1939. *Nootka and Quileute Music.* Bull. 124 of the Bureau of American Ethnology. Washington, D.C.: Smithsonian Institution.

Derrida, Jacques. 1982. *Margins of Philosophy.* Chicago: University of Chicago Press.

Deutsches Volksliedarchiv. 1935–74. *Deutsche Volkslieder mit ihren Melodien.* Berlin: de Gruyter.

Deva, B. C. 1974. *Indian Music.* Delhi: Indian Council for Cultural Relations.

Diamond, Beverley, M. Sam Cronk, and Franziska von Rosen. 1994. *Visions of Sound: Musical Instruments of First Nations Communities in Northeastern North America.* Chicago: University of Chicago Press.

Diamond, Beverley, and Robert Witmer, eds. 1994. *Canadian Music: Issues of Hegemony and Identity.* Toronto: Canadian Scholars' Press.

Doubleday, Veronica. 1999. "The Frame Drum in the Middle East: Women, Musical Instruments, and Power." *EM* 43: 101–34.

Douglas, Mary. 1966. *Purity and Danger.* New York: Praeger.

————. 1970. *Natural Symbols.* New York: Pantheon.

Dournon, Geneviève. 1992. "Organology." In Myers 1992, 245–300.

Draeger, Hans-Heinz. 1948. *Prinzip einer Systematik der Musikinstrumente.* Kassel: Baerenreiter.

Driver, Harold E. 1961. *Indians of North America.* Chicago: University of Chicago Press.

Dumont, Jean-Paul. 1978. *The Headman and I.* Austin: University of Texas Press.

Durbin, Mridula A. 1971. "Transformational Models Applied to Musical Analysis: Theoretical Possibilities." *EM* 15: 353–62.

During, Jean, Zia Mirabdelbaghi, and Dariush Safvat. 1991. *The Art of Persian Music.* Washington, D.C.: Mage.

Einstein, Alfred. 1947a. *Music in the Romantic Era.* New York: Norton.

————. 1947b. *A Short History of Music.* New York: Knopf.

Elbourne, Roger P. 1976. "The Question of Definition." *YIFMC* 7: 9–29.

Ellingson, Ter. 1992a. "Notation." In Myers 1992, 153–64.

————. 1992b. "Transcription." In Myers 1992, 110–52.

Ellis, Alexander J. 1885. "On the Musical Scales of Various Nations." *Journal of the Royal Society of Arts* 33: 485–527.

Ellis, Catherine J. 1970. "The Role of the Ethnomusicologist in the Study of Andagarinja Women's Ceremonies." *Miscellanea Musicologica* (Adelaide) 5: 76–208.

Elschek, Oskar. 1977. "Zum gegenwärtigen Stand der Volksliedanalyse und Volksliedklassifikazion." *YIFMC* 8: 21–34.

————. 1991. "Ideas, Principles, Motivations, and Results in Eastern European Folk Music Research." In Nettl and Bohlman 1991, 91–111.

Elschek, Oskar, and Doris Stockmann, eds. 1969. *Methoden der Klassifikazion von Volksliedweisen*. Bratislava: Verlag der slowakischen Akademie der Wissenschaften.

Elscheková, Alica. 1966. "Methods of Classifying Folk Tunes." *JIFMC* 18: 56–76.

Elsner, Jürgen. 1975. "Zum Problem des Maqam." *Acta Musicologica* 47: 208–39.

Emsheimer, Ernst. 1991. *Studia Ethnomusicologica Eurasiatica*. Publications issued by the Royal Swedish Academy of Music, no. 62. Stockholm: Royal Swedish Academy of Music.

Engel, Hans. 1987. *Die Stellung des Musikers im arabisch-islamischen Bereich*. Bonn: Verlag für systematische Musikwissenschaft.

Erdely, Stephen. 1964. "Folksinging of the American Hungarians in Cleveland." *EM* 8: 14–27.

———. 1965. *Methods and Principles of Hungarian Ethnomusicology*. Bloomington: Indiana University Publications.

———. 1979. "Ethnic Music in America: An Overview." *YIFMC* 11: 114–37.

Erickson, Edwin Erich. 1969. "The Song Trace: Song Styles and the Ethnohistory of Aboriginal America." Ph.D. diss., Columbia University.

Erk, Ludwig. 1893–94. *Deutscher Liederhort . . . neubearbeitet und fortgesetzt von Franz M. Böhme*. Leipzig: Breitkopf und Härtel.

Erlmann, Veit. 1991. *African Stars*. Chicago: University of Chicago Press.

———. 1996. *Nightsong: Performance, Power, and Practice in South Africa*. Chicago: University of Chicago Press.

———. 1999. *Music, Modernity, and the Global Imagination: South Africa and the West*. New York: Oxford University Press.

Euba, Akin. 1971. "New Idioms of Music-Drama among the Yoruba: An Introductory Study." *YIFMC* 2: 92–107.

Ewers, John C. 1958. *The Blackfeet: Raiders on the Northwestern Plains*. Norman: University of Oklahoma Press.

Falcs, Cornelia. 2002. "The Paradox of Timbre." *EM* 46: 56–95.

Farhat, Hormoz. 1990. *The Dastgah Concept in Persian Music*. Cambridge: Cambridge University Press.

Farnsworth, Paul R. 1958. *The Social Psychology of Music*. New York: Dryden Press.

Farrer, Claire R. 1991. *Living Life's Circle: Mescalero Apache Cosmovision*. Albuquerque: University of New Mexico Press.

Al-Faruqi, Lois Ibsen. 1985–86. "Music, Musicians, and Muslim Law." *AM* 17/1: 3–36.

The Federal Cylinder Project. 1984. Vol. 1. Ed. Erika Brady, Dorothy Lee, and Thomas Vennum. Washington, D.C.: American Folklife Center.

Feld, Steven. 1974. "Linguistic Models in Ethnomusicology." *EM* 18: 197–217.

———. 1982. *Sound and Sentiment*. Philadelphia: University of Pennsylvania Press.

———. 1984. "Sound Structure as Social Structure." *EM* 28: 383–410.

———. 1987. "Dialogic Editing: Interpreting How Kaluli Read Sounds and Sentiment." *Cultural Anthropology* 2: 190–210.

————. 1994. "Communication, Music, and Speech about Music." In Keil and Feld 1994, 77–95.

————. 2001. *Bosavi: Rainforest Music from Papua New Guinea.* Washington, D.C.: Smithsonian Folkways. 3 CDs and book.

Feldman, Walter. 2002. "Music in Performance: Who Are the Whirling Dervishes?" In *Garland Encyclopedia of World Music*, 6:107–12. New York: Routledge.

Ferand, Ernst. 1938. *Die Improvisation in der Musik.* Zurich: Rhein-Verlag.

Fewkes, Jese Walter. 1890. "The Use of the Phonograph among the Zuni Indians." *American Naturalist* 24: 687–91.

Finnegan, Ruth. 1989. *The Hidden Musicians.* Cambridge: Cambridge University Press.

Firth, Raymond. 1944. "The Future of Social Anthropology." *Man* 44/8: 19–22.

————. 1973. *Symbols, Public and Private.* Ithaca, N.Y.: Cornell University Press.

Fletcher, Alice C. 1904. *The Hako: A Pawnee Ceremony.* Twenty-second Annual Report of the Bureau of American Ethnology, pt. 2. Washington, D.C.: Smithsonian Institution.

Födermayr, Franz. 1971. *Zur gesanglichen Stimmgebung in der aussereuropäischen Musik.* Vienna: Stiglmayr.

Foster, George M., and Robert V. Kemper, eds. 1974. *Anthropologists in Cities.* Boston: Little, Brown.

Fox-Strangways, A. H. 1914 (1965). *The Music of Hindostan.* Oxford: Clarendon Press.

Freeman, Derek. 1983. *Margaret Mead and Samoa: The Making and Unmaking of an Anthropological Myth.* Cambridge, Mass.: Harvard University Press.

Freeman, Linton C., and Alan P. Merriam. 1956. "Statistical Classification in Anthropology: An Application to Ethnomusicology." *AA* 58: 464–72.

Freilich, Morris, ed. 1970. *Marginal Natives: Anthropologists at Work.* New York: Harper and Row.

————. 1977. *Marginal Natives at Work: Anthropologists in the Field.* New York: Schenkman.

Frisbie, Charlotte Johnson. 1967. *Kinaalda: A Study of the Navaho Girls' Puberty Ceremony.* Middletown, Conn.: Wesleyan University Press.

————. 1991. "Women and the Society for Ethnomusicology." In Nettl and Bohlman 1991, 244–65.

————. 2001. "American Indian Musical Repatriation." In *Garland Encyclopedia of World Music*, 3:491–500. New York: Routledge.

————, ed. 1980. *Southwestern Indian Ritual Drama.* Albuquerque: University of New Mexico Press.

Frith, Simon. 1988. *Music for Pleasure: Essays on the Sociology of Pop.* New York: Routledge.

————. 1989. *World Music, Politics, and Social Change.* Manchester: Manchester University Press.

————, ed. 1993. *Music and Copyright.* Edinburgh: Edinburgh University Press.

Gardner, Howard. 1983. *Frames of Mind: The Theory of Multiple Intelligences*. New York: Basic Books.

Garfinkel, Harold. 1967. *Studies in Ethnomethodology*. Englewood Cliffs, NJ.: Prentice-Hall.

Garland Encyclopedia of World Music. 1997–2002. New York: Routledge.

Geertz, Clifford. 1973. *The Interpretation of Cultures*. New York: Basic Books.

———. 2000. *Available Light: Anthropological Reflections on Philosophical Topics*. Princeton: Princeton University Press.

———, ed. 1971. *Myth, Symbol, and Culture*. New York: Norton.

Georges, Robert A., and Michael O. Jones. 1980. *People Studying People: The Human Element in Fieldwork*. Berkeley: University of California Press.

Gerson-Kiwi, Edith. 1963. *The Persian Doctrine of Dastga Composition*. Tel Aviv: Israel Music Institute.

Gillis, Frank, and Alan P. Merriam. 1966. *Ethnomusicology and Folk Music: An International Bibliography of Dissertations and Theses*. Middletown, Conn.: Wesleyan University Press.

Glassie, Henry, Edward D. Ives, and John F. Szwed. 1970. *Folksongs and Their Makers*. Bowling Green, Ohio: Bowling Green University Popular Press.

Goertzen, Christopher. 1979. "'Billy in the Low Ground,' a Tune Family Study." Unpublished paper, University of Illinois.

Goldman, Richard Franko. 1976. "In Support of Art." *College Music Symposium* 16: 12–18.

Goldstein, Kenneth S. 1964. *A Guide for Field Workers in Folklore*. Hatboro, N.J.: Folklore Associates.

Gottlieb, Alma, and Philip Graham. 1993. *Parallel Worlds: An Anthropologist and a Writer Encounter Africa*. Chicago: University of Chicago Press.

Gourlay, Kenneth A. 1978. "Towards a Reassessment of the Ethnomusicologist's Role." *EM* 22: 1–36.

Graf, Walter. 1966. "Zur Verwendung von Geräuschen in der aussereuropäischen Musik." *Jahrbuch für musikalische Volks- und Völkerkunde* 2: 59–90.

———. 1968. "Das biologische Moment im Konzept der Vergleichenden Musikwissenschaft." *Studia Musicologica* 10: 91–113.

———. 1972. "Musikalische Klangforschung." *Acta Musicologica* 44: 31–78.

Grame, Theodore. 1962. "Bamboo and Music: A New Approach to Organology." *EM* 6: 8–14.

Gramsci, Antonio. 1971. *Selections from the Prison Notebooks*. New York: International.

Greenway, John. 1953. *American Folksongs of Protest*. Philadelphia: University of Pennsylvania Press.

Greve, Martin. 2002. "'Writing against Europe': Vom notwendigen Verschwinden der Musikethnologie." *Musikforschung* 55: 239–50.

Grinnell, George Bird. 1920. *Blackfoot Lodge Tales*. New York: Scribner.

Gronow, Pekka. 1963. "Phonograph Records as a Source for Musicological Research." *EM* 7: 225–28.

———. 1978. "The Significance of Ethnic Recordings." In Howard W. Marshall, ed., *Ethnic Recordings: A Neglected Heritage, 1–50*. Washington, D.C.: Library of Congress.

Grout, Donald Jay. 1960. *A History of Western Music*. New York: Norton.

Günther, Robert, ed. 1973. *Musikkulturen Asiens, Afrikas und Ozeaniens im 19. Jahrhundert*. Regensburg: Bosse.

Guilbault, Jocelyne. 1993. *Zouk: World Music in the West Indies*. Chicago: University of Chicago Press.

Gurvin, Olav, ed. 1958–67. *Norsk folkemusikk—Norwegian Folk Music*. Oslo: Universitetsforlaget.

Guy, Nancy. 2002. "'Republic of China National Anthem' on Taiwan." *EM* 46: 96–119.

Haas, Wilhelm. 1932. *Systematische Ordnung Beethovenscher Melodien*. Leipzig: Quelle and Meyer.

Haefer, J. Richard. 1981. "Papago Indian Musical Thought." Ph.D. diss., University of Illinois.

Halpert, Herbert. 1943. "The Devil and the Fiddle." *Hoosier Folklore Bulletin* 2: 39–43.

Hamm, Charles. 1995. *Putting Popular Music in Its Place*. Cambridge: Cambridge University Press.

Harich-Schneider, Eta. 1973. *A History of Japanese Music*. London: Oxford University Press.

Harris, Marvin. 1968. *The Rise of Anthropological Theory*. New York: Crowell.

———. 1971. *Culture, Man, and Nature*. New York: Crowell.

Harrison, Frank. 1973. *Time, Place, and Music*. Amsterdam: Knuf.

———. 1977. "Universals in Music: Towards a Methodology of Comparative Research." *WM* 19/1–2: 30–36.

Harrison, Frank, Mantle Hood, and Claude Palisca. 1963. *Musicology*. Englewood Cliffs, N.J.: Prentice-Hall.

Harwood, Dane L. 1976. "Universals in Music: A Perspective from Cognitive Psychology." *EM* 20: 521–33.

Hatten, Robert. 1994. *Musical Meaning in Beethoven*. Bloomington: Indiana University Press.

Hatton, Orin T. 1986. "In the Tradition: Grass Dance Musical Styles and Female Powwow Singers," *EM* 30: 197–219.

———. 1988. "We Caused Them to Cry: Power and Performance in Gros Ventre War Expedition Songs." M.A. thesis, Catholic University of America.

Heartz, Daniel. 2003. *Music in European Capitals: The Galant Style 1720–1780*. New York: Norton.

Helm, E. Eugene. 1977. Response to F. Lieberman, "Should Ethnomusicology Be Abolished?" *College Music Symposium* 17/2: 201–2.

Henry, Edward O. 1976. "The Variety of Music in a North Indian Village: Reassessing Cantometrics." *EM* 20: 49–66.

Henry, Jules. 1963. *Culture against Man*. New York: Random House.

Herndon, Marcia. 1974. "Analysis: The Herding of Sacred Cows?" *EM* 18: 219–62.

———. 2000. "The Place of Gender within Complex, Dynamic Musical Systems." In Moisala and Diamond 2000, 347–60.

Herndon, Marcia, and Norma McLeod. 1980. *Music as Culture.* Darby, Pa.: Norwood.

———. 1983. *Field Manual for Ethnomusicology.* Norwood, Pa.: Norwood.

Herskovits, Melville J. 1945. "Problem, Method, and Theory in Afroamerican Studies." *Afroamerica* 1: 5–24.

Herzog, George. 1928. "The Yuman Musical Style." *JAF* 41: 183–231.

———. 1930. "Musical Styles in North America." *Proceedings of the Twenty-third International Congress of Americanists,* 455–58. New York.

———. 1934. "Speech-Melody and Primitive Music." *MQ* 20: 452–66.

———. 1935a. "Plains Ghost Dance and Great Basin Music." *AA* 37: 403–19.

———. 1935b. "Special Song Types in North American Indian Music." *Zeitschrift für vergleichende Musikwissenschaft* 3/1–2: 1–11.

———. 1936a. "A Comparison of Pueblo and Pima Musical Styles." *JAF* 49: 283–417.

———. 1936b. "Die Musik der Karolinen-Inseln aus dem Phonogrammarchiv Berlin." In Anneliese Eilers, *Westkarolinen,* 263–351 Hamburg: de Gruyter.

———. 1936c. *Research in Primitive and Folk Music in the United States.* Bull. 24. Washington, D.C.: American Council of Learned Societies.

———. 1938. "Music in the Thinking of the American Indian." *Peabody Bulletin,* May, pp. 1–5.

———. 1939. "Music's Dialects: A Non-Universal Language." *Independent Journal of Columbia University* 6: 1–2.

———. 1945. "Drum Signalling in a West African Tribe." *Word* 1: 217–38.

———. 1949. "Salish Music." In Marian W. Smith, ed., *Indians of the Urban Northwest,* 93–109. New York: Columbia University Press.

———. 1950. "Song." In M. Leach, ed., *Funk and Wagnall's Standard Dictionary of Folklore, Mythology and Legend,* 2:1032–50. New York: Funk and Wagnall.

———. 1957. "Music at the Fifth International Congress of Anthropological and Ethnological Sciences." *JIFMC* 9: 71–73.

Hickmann, Ellen, and David W. Hughes, eds. 1988. *The Archaeology of Early Music Cultures.* Bonn: Verlag für systematische Musikwissenschaft.

Hickmann, Ellen, Anne Kilmer, and Ricardo Eichmann, eds. 2002. *Studien zur Musikarchäologie III.* Rahden: Marie Leidorf.

Hickmann, Hans. 1970. "Die Musik des arabisch-islamischen Bereichs." In *Handbuch der Orientalistik,* pt. 1., supp. vol. 4, 1–134. Leiden: Brill.

Hill, Stephen. 1993. "Country Music at the Rose Bowl." In Livingston et al. 1993, 41–52.

Hinton, Leanne. 1967–68. Personal communication and unpublished papers on Havasupai music, University of Illinois.

———. 1984. *Havasupai Songs, a Linguistic Perspective.* Tübingen: Gunter Narr Verlag.

Hoebel, E. Adamson. 1949. *Man in the Primitive World: An Introduction to Anthropology.* New York: McGraw-Hill.

Hohmann, Rupert Karl. 1959. "The Church Music of the Old Order Amish in the United States." Ph.D. diss., Northwestern University.

Honigmann, John J. 1976. *The Development of Anthropological Ideas.* Homewood, Ill.: Dorsey Press.

Hood, Mantle. 1957. "Training and Research Methods in Ethnomusicology." *Ethnomusicology Newsletter* 11: 2–8.

———. 1959. "The Reliability of Oral Tradition." *JAMS* 12: 201–9.

———. 1960. "The Challenge of Bi-Musicality." *EM* 4: 55–59.

———. 1963. "Music, the Unknown." In Harrison, Hood, and Palisca 1963, 265–375.

———. 1966. Review of *Africa and Indonesia,* by A. M. Jones. *EM* 10: 214–16.

———. 1971. *The Ethnomusicologist.* New York: McGraw-Hill.

———. 1977. "Universal Attributes of Music." *WM* 19/1–2: 63–69.

———. 2000. "Ethnomusicology's Bronze Age in Y2K." *EM* 44: 365–76.

Hopkins, Pandora. 1966. "The Purposes of Transcription." *EM* 10: 310–17.

———. 1977. "The Homology of Music and Myth: Views of Levi-Strauss on Musical Structure." *EM* 21: 247–61.

Hornbostel, Erich M. von. 1905. "Die Probleme der vergleichenden Musikwissenschaft." *Zeitschrift der internationalen Musikgesellschaft* 7: 85–97.

———. 1906. "Phonographierte tunesiche Melodien." *Sammelbände der internationalen Musikgesellschaft* 8: 1–43.

———. 1907. "Notiz über die Musik der Bewohner von Süd-Neu-Mecklenburg." In E. Stephan and F. Graebner, *Neu-Mecklenburg,* 131–37. Berlin: Reimer.

———. 1910. "Über einige Panpfeifen aus Nordwest-Brasilien." Final chapter in Theodor Koch-Gruenberg, *Zwei Jahre unter den Indianern,* 2:378–91. Berlin: Wasmuth.

———. 1911. "Über ein akustisches Kriterium für Kulturzusammenhange." *Zeitschrift für Ethnologie* 3: 601–15.

———. 1912. "Melodie und Skala." *Jahrbuch der Musikbibliothek Peters* 20: 11–23.

———. 1917. "Musikalische Tonsysteme." In Friedrich Trendelenburg, ed., *Handbuch der Physik,* 8:425–49. Berlin: Springer.

———. 1928. "African Negro Music." *Africa* 1: 30–62.

———. 1933. "The Ethnology of African Sound Instruments." *Africa* 6: 129–57, 277–311.

———. 1936. "Fuegian Songs." *AA* 38: 357–67.

———. 1973. "Geburt und erste Kindheit der Musik." *Jahrbuch für musikalische Volks- und Völkerkunde* 7: 9–17.

———. 1975–. *Hornbostel Opera Omnia.* Ed. Klaus Wachsmann, Dieter Christensen, and Hans-Peter Reinecke. The Hague: Nijhoff.

———. 1986. *Tonart und Ethos: Aufsätze zur Musikethnologie und Musikpsychologie.* Leipzig: Reclam.

Hornbostel, Erich M. von, and Otto Abraham. 1904. "Über die Bedeutung des Phonographen für die vergleichende Musikwissenschaft." *Zeitschrift für Ethnologie* 36: 222–33.

———. 1909. "Vorschläge zur Transkription exotischer Melodien." *Sammelbände der internationalen Musikgesellschaft* 11: 1–25.

Hornbostel, Erich M. von, and Curt Sachs. 1914. "Systematik der Musikinstrumente." *Zeitschrift für Ethnologie* 46: 553–90. English translation by Anthony Baines and K. P. Wachsmann, "Classification of Musical Instruments," *Galpin Society Journal* 14: 3–29, 1961.

Hsu, Francis L. K. 1973. "Prejudice and Its Intellectual Effect in American Anthropology." *AA* 75: 1–19.

Hungarian Academy of Sciences, Institute for Musicology. 1992. *Catalogue of Hungarian Folk Song Types Arranged According to Styles.* Vol. 1. [By László Dobszay and Janka Szendrei.] Budapest.

Hustvedt, Sigurd Bernhard. 1936. "A Melodic Index of Child's Ballad Tunes." *Publications of UCLA in Languages and Literature* 1/2: 51–78.

Ingold, Tim, ed. 1994. *Companion Encyclopedia of Anthropology.* London: Routledge.

International Folk Music Council. 1952. *Notation of Folk Music: Recommendations of the Committee of Experts.* Geneva.

Ives, Edward D. 1964. *Larry Gorman: The Man Who Made the Songs.* Bloomington: Indiana University Press.

Izikowitz, Karl Gustav. 1935. *Musical and Other Sound Instruments of the South American Indians.* Goteborg: Kungl. Vetenskaps-och Vitterhets-Samhülles Handlingar.

Jackson, George Pullen. 1943. *White and Negro Spirituals.* Locust Valley, N.Y.: J. J. Augustin.

Jacobs, Norman. 1966. *The Sociology of Development: Iran as an Asian Case Study.* New York: Praeger.

Jairazbhoy, Nazir A. 1971. *The Rags of North Indian Music.* London: Faber and Faber.

———. 1977. "The 'Objective' and Subjective View in Music Transcription." *EM* 21: 263–74.

———. 1978. "Music in Western Rajasthan: Continuity and Change." *YIFMC* 9: 50–66.

Jairazbhoy, Nazir A., and Hal Balyoz. 1977. "Electronic Aids to Aural Transcription." *EM* 21: 275–82.

Jairazbhoy, Mazir A., and Amy Catlin. 1990. *Bake Restudy 1984.* Video. Van Nuys, Calif.: Apsara Media.

Jakobson, Roman. 1941. *Kindersprache, Aphasie, und allgemeine Lautgesetze.* Uppsala: Almquist och Wiksell.

Jardanyi, Pal. 1962. "Die Ordnung der ungarischen Volkslieder." *Studia Musicologica* 2: 3–32.

Jeffery, Peter. 1992. *Re-Envisioning Past Musical Cultures.* Chicago: University of Chicago Press.

Jones, A. M. 1954. "African Rhythm." *Africa* 24: 26–47.

———. 1959. *Studies in African Music.* London: Oxford University Press.

———. 1964. *Africa and Indonesia: The Evidence of the Xylophone.* Leiden: Brill.

Jordania, Josef. 1997. "Perspectives of Interdisciplinary Research of Part-Singing Phe-nomenon." In Mahling and Münch 1997, 211–16.

Kaden, Christian. 1984. *Musiksoziologie.* Berlin: Verlag Neue Musik.

———. 1993. *Des Lebens wilder Kreis: Musik im Zivilisazionsprozess.* Kassel: Bären-reiter.

Kaemmer, John E. 1980. "Between the Event and the Tradition: A New Look at Music in Socio-Cultural Systems." *EM* 24: 61–74.

Kaplan, David, and Robert A. Manners. 1972. *Culture Theory.* Englewood Cliffs, N.J.: Prentice-Hall.

Karbusicky, Vladimir. 1986. *Grundriss der musikalischen Semantik.* Darmstadt: Wis-senschaftliche Buchgesellschaft.

Karpeles, Maud. 1951. "Concerning Authenticity." *JIFMC* 3: 10–14.

———. 1967. *Cecil Sharp, His Life and Work.* Chicago: University of Chicago Press.

———. 1968. "The Distinction between Folk Music and Popular Music." *JIFMC* 20: 9–12.

———. 1973. *An Introduction to English Folk Song.* London: Oxford University Press.

———, ed. 1958. *The Collecting of Folk Music and Other Ethnomusicological Mater-ial: A Manual for Field Workers.* London: International Folk Music Council.

Kartomi, Margaret J. 1973. *Matjapat Songs in Central and West Java.* Canberra: Aus-tralian National University Press.

———. 1980. "Childlikeness in Play Songs: A Case Study among the Pitjantjara at Yalata, South Australia." *Miscellanea Musicologica* (Adelaide) 2: 172–214.

———. 1981. "The Processes and Results of Musical Culture Contact: A Discussion of Terminology and Concepts." *EM* 25: 227–50.

———. 1990. *On Concept and Classifications of Musical Instruments.* Chicago: Uni-versity of Chicago Press.

———. 1991. "Musical Improvisations by Children at Play." *WM* 33/3: 53–65.

Kartomi, Margaret J., and Stephen Blum, eds. 1994. *Music-Cultures in Contact: Con-vergences and Collisions.* Basel: Gorden and Breach.

Katz, Ruth. 1968. "The Singing of Baqqashot by Aleppo Jews." *Acta Musicologica* 40: 65–85.

———. 1970. "Mannerism and Cultural Change: An Ethnomusicological Example." *Current Anthropology* 2/4–5: 465–75.

———. 1974. "The Reliability of Oral Transmission: The Case of Samaritan Music." *Yuval* 3: 109–35.

———. 2003. *The Lachmann Problem: An Unsung Chapter in Comparative Musi-cology.* Jerusalem: Hebrew University Magnes Press.

Kauffman, Robert. 1973. "Shona Urban Music and the Problem of Acculturation." *YIFMC* 4: 47–56.

————. 1980. "African Rhythm: A Reassessment." *EM* 24: 393–416.

Kaufmann, Walter. 1967. *Musical Notations of the Orient.* Bloomington: Indiana University Press.

Keeling, Richard, ed. 1989. *Women in North American Indian Music.* Society for Ethnomusicology Special Series no. 6. Bloomington, Ind.: Society for Ethnomusicology.

————. 1992. *Cry for Luck: Sacred Song and Speech among the Yurok, Hupa, and Karok Indians of Northwestern California.* Berkeley: University of California Press.

Keesing, Roger M. 1976. *Cultural Anthropology: A Contemporary Perspective.* New York: Holt, Rinehart and Winston.

Keil, Charles. 1966. *Urban Blues.* Chicago: University of Chicago Press.

————. 1979. *Tiv Song.* Chicago: University of Chicago Press.

Keil, Charles, and Steven Feld. 1994. *Music Grooves.* Chicago: University of Chicago Press.

Keil, Charles, and Angeliki Keil. 1966. "Musical Meaning: A Preliminary Report." *EM* 10: 153–73.

Kemppinen, Ivar. 1954. *The Ballad of Lady Isabel and the False Knight.* Helsinki: Kirja-Mono Oy.

Kerman, Joseph. 1985. *Contemplating Music.* Cambridge, Mass.: Harvard University Press.

Key, Mary. 1963. "Music of the Sirionó (Guaranian)." *EM* 7: 17–21.

Keyes, Cheryl. 1996. "At the Crossroads: Rap Music and Its African Nexus." *EM* 40: 223–48.

Kiesewetter, Raphael. 1842. *Die Musik der Araber.* Leipzig: Breitkopf und Härtel.

Killick, Andrew. 2003. "Road Test for a New Model: Koran Musical Narrative and Theater in Comparative Context." *EM* 47: 180–204.

Kinderman, William. 1987. *Beethoven's Diabelli Variations: Studies in Musical Genesis and Structure.* Oxford: Oxford University Press.

————. 2003. *Artaria 195.* Urbana: University of Illinois Press.

Kingsbury, Henry. 1988. *Music, Talent, and Performance.* Philadelphia: Temple University Press.

Kippen, James. 1988. *The Tabla of Lucknow.* Cambridge: Cambridge University Press.

Kirby, Percival. 1934. *The Musical Instruments of the Native Races of South Africa.* Johannesburg: Witwatersrand University Press.

Kirshenblatt-Gimblett, Barbara. 1998. *Destination Culture: Tourism, Museums, and Heritage.* Berkeley: University of California Press.

Kisliuk, Michelle. 1997. "Undoing Fieldwork: Sharing Songs, Sharing Lives." In Barz and Cooley 1997, 23–44.

Klotz, Sebastian, ed. 1998. *Vom Tönenden Wirbel menschlichen Tuns: Erich M. Von Hornbostel als Gestaltpsychologe, Archivar und Musikwissenschaftler.* Berlin: Schibri.

Kneif, Tibor. 1974. "Was ist Semiotik der Musik?" *Neue Zeitschrift für Musik* 135/6: 348–53.

Knepler, Georg. 1961. *Musikgeschichte des 19. Jahrhunderts.* Berlin: Henschelverlag.

Kodály, Zoltan. 1956. *Die ungarische Volksmusik.* Budapest: Corvina.

Koetting, James. 1970. "Analysis and Notation of West African Drum Ensemble Music." *UCLA Selected Reports* (Institute of Ethnomusicology) 1/3: 116–46.

Kohs, Ellis B. 1976. *Musical Form: Studies in Analysis and Synthesis.* Boston: Houghton Mifflin.

Koizumi, Fumio, Yoshihiko Tokumaru, and Osamu Yamaguchi, eds. 1977. *Asian Music in an Asian Perspective.* Tokyo: Japan Foundation.

Koizumi Fumio Memorial Archives. 1987. *Catalog of the Musical Instrument Collection.* Tokyo: Tokyo Geijutsu Daigaku.

Kolinski, Mieczyslaw. 1936. "Suriname Music." Supplementary chapter in M. Herskovits, *Suriname Folklore*, 491–716. New York: American Folklore Society.

———. 1956. "The Structure of Melodic Movement, a New Method of Analysis." In *Miscelanea de Estudios Dedicados al Dr. Fernando Ortiz*, 2: 879–918. Havana: Sociedad Economica de Amigos del Pais.

———. 1959. "The Evaluation of Tempo." *EM* 3: 45–57.

———. 1961. "Classification of Tonal Structures." *Studies in Ethnomusicology* (New York) 1: 38–76.

———. 1962. "Consonance and Dissonance." *EM* 6: 66–74.

———. 1965a. "The General Direction of Melodic Movement." *EM* 9: 240–64.

———. 1965b. "The Structure of Melodic Movement: A New Method of Analysis." *Studies in Ethnomusicology* (New York) 2: 95–120.

———. 1971. Review of *The Ethnomusicologist*, by Mantle Hood. *YIFMC* 3: 146–60.

———. 1973. "A Cross-Cultural Approach to Metro-Rhythmic Patterns." *EM* 17: 494–506.

———. 1978. "The Structure of Music: Diversification versus Constraint." *EM* 22: 229–44.

Koller, Oswald. 1902–3. "Die beste Methode, volks- und volksmässige Lieder nach ihrer melodischen Beschaffenheit lexikalisch zu ordnen." *Sammelbände der internationalen Musikgesellschaft* 4: 1–15.

Koning, Jos. 1980. "The Fieldworker as Performer." *EM* 24: 417–30.

Korsyn, Kevin. 1999. "Beyond Privileged Contexts: Intertextuality, Influence, and Dialogue." In Cook and Everist 1999, 55–72.

Koskoff, Ellen, ed. 1987. *Women and Music in Cross-Cultural Perspective.* New York: Greenwood Press.

———. 2001. *Music in Lubavitcher Life.* Urbana: University of Illinois Press.

Kramer, Lawrence, ed. 1993. "Music, Sexuality, and Culture." *Nineteenth-Century Music* 17/1, special issue.

Kraus, Richard Curt. 1989. *Pianos and Politics in China: Middle-Class Ambitions and the Struggle over Western Music.* New York: Oxford University Press.

Kroeber, Alfred Louis. 1947. *Cultural and Natural Areas of Native North America.* Berkeley: University of California Press.

————. 1948. *Anthropology.* New ed. New York: Harcourt, Brace.

Kroeber, Theodora. 1961. *Ishi in Two Worlds.* Berkeley: University of California Press.

Krohn, Ilmari. 1902–3. "Welche ist die beste Methode, um volks- und volksmässige Lieder nach ihrer melodischen (nicht textlichen) Beschaffenheit lexikalisch zu ordnen?" *Sammelbände der internationalen Musikgesellschaft* 4: 643–60.

Kunej, Drago. 1997. "Acoustic Finds on the Basis of Reconstruction of a Presumed Bone Flute." In I. Turk, ed., *Mousterian "Bone Flute" and Other Finds from Divje Babe I Cave Site in Slovenia,* 185–97. Ljubljana: Zalozba.

Kunitachi College of Music. 1986. *The Collection of Musical Instruments.* Ed. Kunitachi College of Music Research Institute. Tokyo: Kunitachi College of Music Research Institute.

Kunst, Jaap. 1950. *Musicologica.* Amsterdam: Royal Tropical Institute.

————. 1954. *Cultural Relations between the Balkans and Indonesia.* Amsterdam: Royal Tropical Institute.

————. 1959. *Ethnomusicology.* 3rd ed. The Hague: Nijhoff.

Kunz, Ludvik. 1974. *Die Volksmusikinstrumente der Tschechoslowakei.* Leipzig: Deutscher Verlag für Musik.

Kurath, Gertrude P. 1960. "Panorama of Dance Ethnology." *Current Anthropology* 1: 233–54.

Laade, Wolfgang. 1969. *Die Situation von Musikleben und Musikforschung in den Liändern Afrikas und Asiens und die neuen Aufgaben der Musikethnologie.* Tutzing: Hans Schneider.

————. 1971a. *Gegenwartsfragen der Musik in Afrika und Asien: Eine grundlegende Bibliographie.* Heidelberg: Laade.

————. 1971b. *Neue Musik in Afrika, Asien und Ozeanien.* Heidelberg: Laade.

————. 1975. *Musik der Götter, Geister und Menschen.* Baden-Baden: Valentin Koerner.

Labov, William. 1972 *Sociolinguistic Patterns.* Philadelphia: University of Pennsylvania Press.

Lach, Robert. 1924. *Die vergleichende Musikwissenschaft, ihre Methoden und Probleme.* Vienna: Akademie der Wissenschaften.

Lachmann, Robert. 1929. *Musik des Orients.* Breslau: Jedermanns Bücherei.

Langer, Susanne K. 1942. *Philosophy in a New Key.* New York: Mentor.

————. 1953. *Feeling and Form.* New York: Scribner.

L'Armand, Kathleen and Adrian. 1983. "One Hundred Years of Music in Madras." *EM* 27: 411–38.

Lassiter, Luke Eric. 1998. *The Power of Kiowa Song: A Collaborative Ethnography.* Tucson: University of Arizona Press.

Leach, Edmund. 1970. *Claude Lévi-Strauss.* New York: Viking Press.

Levant, Oscar. 1940. *A Smattering of Ignorance.* New York: Doubleday, Doran.

Levin, Theodore. 1996. *The Hundred Thousand Fools of God.* Bloomington: Indiana University Press.

Levine, Victoria Lindsay. 2002. *Writing American Indian Music: Historic Transcriptions, Notations, and Arrangements*. Music of the U.S.A., vol. 11. Middleton, Wisc.: A-R Editions.

Lévi-Strauss, Claude. 1963. *Structural Anthropology*. New York: Basic Books.

———. 1969. *The Raw and the Cooked: Introduction to the Science of Mythology*. Trans. John and Doreen Weightman. New York: Harper and Row.

———. 1971. *Mythologiques 4: L'homme nu*. Paris: Plon.

Levman, Bryan G. 1992. "The Genesis of Music and Language." *EM* 36: 147–70.

Lewis, Oscar. 1941. "Manly-Hearted Women among the North Piegan." *AA* 43: 173–87.

———. 1951. *Life in a Mexican Village: Tepotzlan Restudied*. Urbana: University of Illinois Press.

———. 1956. "Comparison in Cultural Anthropology." In W. L. Thomas, ed., *Current Anthropology, a Supplement to Anthropology Today*, 259–92. Chicago: University of Chicago Press.

Libin, Lawrence. 1992. "Major Instrument Collections." In Myers 1992, 423–43.

Library of Congress. 1942. *Check-List of Recorded Songs in the English Language in the Archive of American Folk Song to July, 1940*. Washington, D.C.: Library of Congress.

Lidov, David. 1975. *On Musical Phrase*. Montreal: Les Presses de l'Université de Montréal.

Lieberman, Fredric. 1969. *The Music of China*. Vol. 1. Notes to the record, Anthology AST-4000. New York: Anthology Record and Tape.

———. 1977. "Should Ethnomusicology Be Abolished?" *College Music Symposium* 17/2: 198–201.

Lieberman, Philip. 1975. *The Origins of Language*. New York: Macmillan.

———. 1994. "The Origins and Evolution of Language." In Tim Ingold, ed., *The Companion Encyclopedia of Anthropology*, 108–32. London: Routledge.

List, George. 1963a. "An Approach to the Indexing of Ballad Tunes." *Folklore and Folk Music Archivist* 6/1: 7–15.

———. 1963b. "The Boundaries of Speech and Song." *EM* 7: 1–16.

———. 1963c. "The Musical Significance of Transcription." *EM* 7: 193–97.

———. 1968. "The Hopi as Composer and Poet." *Proceedings of the Centennial Workshop in Ethnomusicology*, 42–53. Vancouver: Simon Fraser University Press.

———. 1974. "The Reliability of Transcription." *EM* 18: 353–77.

———. 1979a. "The Distribution of a Melodic Formula: Diffusion or Polygenesis?" *YIFMC* 10: 33–52.

———. 1979b. "Ethnomusicology: A Discipline Defined." *EM* 23: 1–6.

———. 1983. "A Secular Sermon for Those of the Ethnomusicological Faith." *EM* 27: 175–86.

Livingston, Tamara. 1999. "Music Revivals: Towards a General Theory." *EM* 43: 66–85.

Livingston, Tamara, Melinda Russell, Larry Ward, and Bruno Nettl, eds. 1993. *Community of Music: An Ethnographic Seminar in Champaign-Urbana*. Champaign, Ill.: Elephant and Cat.

Lockwood, Lewis. 2003. *Beethoven, the Music and the Life.* New York: Norton.

Loeb, Laurence D. 1972. "The Jewish Musician and the Music of Fars." *AM* 4/1: 3–14.

Lomax, Alan. 1959. "Folksong Style." *AA* 61: 927–54.

———. 1960. *The Folk Songs of North America in the English Language.* New York: Doubleday.

———. 1962. "Song Structure and Social Structure." *Ethnology* 1: 425–51.

———. 1968. *Folk Song Style and Culture.* Washington, D.C.: American Association for the Advancement of Science.

———. 1976. *Cantometrics.* Berkeley: University of California.

Lord, Albert B. 1965. *The Singer of Tales.* New York: Atheneum.

Lorenz, Alfred Ottokar. 1928. *Abendländische Musikgeschichte im Rhythmus der Generationen.* Berlin: Hesse.

Lornell, Kip, and Anne Rasmussen, eds. 1999. *Musics of Multicultural America.* New York: Oxford University Press.

Lortat-Jacob, Bernard. 1987. *L'improvisation dans les musiques de tradition orale.* Paris: Selaf.

Lowie, Robert H. 1916. "Plains Indian Age-Grade Societies: Historical and Comparative Summary." *Anthropological Papers of the American Museum of Natural History* 11, pt. 13: 877–1031.

———. 1937. *The History of Ethnological Theory.* New York: Rinehart.

Lowinsky, Edward. 1946. *Secret Chromatic Art in the Netherlands Motet.* New York: Columbia University Press.

Lundquist, Barbara, and C. K. Szego. 1998. *Music of the World's Cultures: A Sourcebook for Music Educators.* Reading, England: International Society for Music Education.

Lyons, John. 1977. *Noam Chomsky.* Rev. ed. New York: Penguin Books.

Magrini, Tullia, ed. 2003. *Music and Gender: Perspectives from the Mediterranean.* Chicago: University of Chicago Press.

Mahillon, Victor-Charles. 1880–92. *Catalogue descriptif et analytique du Musée instrumental du Conservatoire royal de musique de Bruxelles.* Ghent: Hoste.

Mahling, Christoph-Hellmut, and Stephan Münch, eds. 1997. *Ethnomusikologie und historische Musikwissenschaft—Gemeinsame Ziele, gleiche Methoden?* Tutzing: Hans Schneider.

Malinowski, Bronislaw. 1935. *Coral Gardens and Their Magic.* New York: American Book.

———. 1954. *Magic, Science, and Religion, and Other Essays.* New York: Doubleday.

———. 1967. *A Diary in the Strict Sense of the Term.* New York: Harcourt, Brace and World.

Malm, Krister. 1995. "Music on the Move: Traditions and Mass Media." *EM* 37: 339–52.

Malm, William P. 1959. *Japanese Music and Musical Instruments.* Tokyo: Tuttle.

———. 1969. "On the Nature and Function of Symbolism in Western and Oriental Music." *Philosophy East and West* (Honolulu) 19/3: 235–46.

———. 1972. "On the Meaning and Invention of the Term Disphony." *EM* 16: 247–49.

———. 1977. *Music Cultures of the Pacific, the Near East, and Asia.* 2nd ed. Englewood Cliffs, N.J.: Prentice-Hall.

Manners, Robert Alan, and David Kaplan, eds. 1968. *Theory in Anthropology: A Sourcebook.* Chicago: Aldine.

Manuel, Peter. 1988. *Popular Music of the Non-Western World: An Introductory Survey.* New York: Oxford University Press.

———. 1993. *Cassette Culture: Popular Music and Technology in India.* Chicago: University of Chicago Press.

———. 2000. *East Indian Music in the West Indies.* Philadelphia: Temple University Press.

Mapoma, Isaiah Mwesa. 1969. "The Use of Folk Music among Some Bemba Church Congregations in Zambia." *YIFMC* 1: 72–88.

Maraire, Abraham Dumisani. 1971. "Mbiras and Performance in Rhodesia." Notes to the record, *Mbira Music from Rhodesia,* UWP-1001. Seattle: University of Washington Press.

Marcel-Dubois, Claudie. 1972. *Pour une analyse de contenu musical.* Paris: Musée national des arts et traditions populaires.

Massoudieh, Mohammad T. 1968. *Awas-e-Šur.* Regensburg: Bosse.

———. 1978. *Radif vocal de la musique traditionelle de l'Iran.* Tehran: Ministry of Culture and Fine Arts.

May, Elizabeth. 1963. *The Influence of the Meiji Period on Japanese Children's Music.* Berkeley: University of California Press.

McAllester, David P. 1949. *Peyote Music.* Viking Fund Publications in Anthropology, no. 13. New York: Viking Fund.

———. 1954. *Enemy Way Music.* Peabody Museum Papers, vol. 41, no. 3. Cambridge, Mass.: Harvard University Peabody Museum.

———. 1971. "Some Thoughts on 'Universals' in World Music." *EM* 15: 379–80.

McCann, Anthony. 2001. "All That Is Not Given Is Lost: Irish Traditional Music, Copyright, and Common Property." *EM* 45: 89–106.

McClary, Susan. 1991. *Feminine Endings.* Minneapolis: University of Minnesota Press.

McClintock, Walter. 1910 (1968). *The Old North Trail.* Lincoln: University of Nebraska Press.

McCollester, Roxane. 1960. "A Transcription Technique Used by Zygmunt Estreicher." *EM* 4: 129–32.

McCullough-Brabson, Ellen, and Marilyn Help. 2001. *We'll Be in Your Mountains, We'll Be in Your Songs: A Navajo Woman Sings.* Albuquerque: University of New Mexico Press.

McFee, Malcolm. 1972. *Modern Blackfeet: Montanans on a Reservation.* New York: Holt, Rinehart and Winston.

McLean, Mervyn. 1965. "Song Loss and Social Context among the New Zealand Maori." *EM* 9: 296–304.

———. 1971. "An Analysis of 651 Maori Scales." *YIFMC* 1: 123–64.

———. 1979. "Towards the Differentiation of Music Areas in Oceania." *Anthropos* 74: 717–36.

———. 1999. *Weavers of Song: Polynesian Music and Dance.* Honolulu: University of Hawaii Press.

McLeod, Norma. 1964. "The Status of Musical Specialists in Madagascar." *EM* 8: 278–89.

———. 1966. "Some Techniques of Analysis for Non-Western Music." Ph.D. diss., Northwestern University.

Mead, Margaret. 1928. *Coming of Age in Samoa.* New York: Morrow.

———. 1973. "Changing Styles of Anthropological Work." *Annual Review of Anthropology* 2: 1–26.

Meintjes, Louise. 1990. "Paul Simon, *Graceland,* South Africa, and the Mediation of Musical Meaning." *EM* 34: 37–74.

———. 2003. *Sound of Africa! Making Music Zulu in a South African Studio.* Durham, N.C.: Duke University Press.

Merrell, Floyd. 1997. *Peirce, Signs, and Meaning.* Toronto: University of Toronto Press.

Merriam, Alan P. 1954. "Song Texts of the Bashi." *Zaire* 8: 27–43.

———. 1955a. "Music in American Culture." *AA* 57: 1173–81.

———. 1955b. "The Use of Music in the Study of a Problem of Acculturation." *AA* 57: 28–34.

———. 1959. "African Music." In William R. Bascom and Melville J. Herskovits, ed., *Continuity and Change in African Cultures,* 49–86. Chicago: University of Chicago Press.

———. 1960. "Ethnomusicology: Discussion and Definition of the Field." *EM* 4: 107–14.

———. 1964. *The Anthropology of Music.* Evanston, Ill.: Northwestern University Press.

———. 1967a. *Ethnomusicology of the Flathead Indians.* Chicago: Aldine Press.

———. 1967b. "Music and the Origin of the Flathead Indians." In George List, ed., *Music in the Americas,* 129–38. The Hague: Mouton.

———. 1969a. "The Ethnographic Experience: Drum-Making among the Bala (Basongye)." *EM* 13: 74–100.

———. 1969b. "Ethnomusicology Revisited." *EM* 13: 213–29.

———. 1973. "The Bala Musician." In Warren L. d'Azevedo, ed., *The Traditional Artist in African Societies,* 250–81. Bloomington: Indiana University Press.

———. 1975. "Ethnomusicology Today." *Current Musicology* 20: 50–66.

———. 1977a. "Definitions of 'Comparative Musicology' and 'Ethnomusicology': An Historical-Theoretical Perspective." *EM* 21: 189–204.

———. 1977b. "Music Change in a Basongye Village (Zaire)." *Anthropos* 72: 806–46.

———. 1979. "Basongye Musicians and Institutionalized Social Deviance." *YIFMC* 11: 1–26.

———. 1981. "African Musical Rhythm and Concepts of Time-Reckoning." In Thomas Noblitt, ed., *Music East and West: Essays in Honor of Walter Kaufmann,* 123–42. New York: Pendragon Press.

Metfessel, Milton E. 1928. *Phonophotography in Folk Music.* Chapel Hill: University of North Carolina Press.

Meyer, Leonard B. 1956. *Emotion and Meaning in Music.* Chicago: University of Chicago Press.

———. 1960. "Universalism and Relativism in the Study of Ethnic Music." *EM* 4: 49–54.

———. 1967. *Music, the Arts, and Ideas: Patterns and Predictions in Twentieth-Century Culture.* Chicago: University of Chicago Press.

Middleton, Richard. 1990. *Studying Popular Music.* Milton Keynes, England: Open University Press.

Miller, Geoffrey. 2000a. "Evolution of Human Music through Sexual Selection." In Wallin, Merker, and Brown 2000, 329–360.

———. 2000b. *How Sexual Choice Shaped the Evolution of Human Nature.* New York: Doubleday.

Minks, Amanda. 2002. "From Children's Song to Expressive Practices: Old and New Directions in the Ethnomusicological Study of Children." *EM* 46: 379–408.

Mitchell, Frank. 1978. *Navajo Blessingway Singer.* Ed. Charlotte Frisbie and David P. McAllester. Tucson: University of Arizona Press.

Moisala, Pirkko, and Beverley Diamond, eds. 2000. *Music and Gender.* Urbana: University of Illinois Press.

Monson, Ingrid. 1996. *Saying Something: Jazz Improvisation and Interaction.* Chicago: University of Chicago Press.

Moore, Robin. 1997. *Nationalizing Blackness: Afrocubanismno and Artistic Revolution in Havana 1920–1940.* Pittsburgh: University of Pittsburgh Press.

Moser, Hans Joachim. 1954. *Die Musik der deutschen Stämme.* Vienna: Wancura.

Mueller, John H. 1951. *The American Symphony Orchestra: A Social History of Musical Taste.* Bloomington: Indiana University Press.

Murdock, George Peter. 1934. *Our Primitive Contemporaries.* New York: Macmillan.

———. 1956. "How Culture Changes." In H. L. Shapiro, ed., *Man, Culture and Society,* 247–60. New York: Oxford University Press.

Myers, Helen. 1998. *Music of Hindu Trinidad: Songs from the Indian Diaspora.* Chicago: University of Chicago Press.

———. 1993. *Ethnomusicology: Historical and Regional Studies.* New York: Norton.

———, ed. 1992. *Ethnomusicology: An Introduction.* New York: Norton.

Nadel, Siegfried. 1930. "The Origins of Music." *MQ* 16: 531–46.

Naroditskaya, Inna. 2000. "Azerbaijanian Female Musicians: Women's Voices Defying and Defining the Culture." *EM* 44: 234–56.

Naroll, Raoul, and Ronald Cohen, eds. 1973. *A Handbook of Method in Cultural Anthropology.* New York: Columbia University Press.

Nattiez, Jean-Jacques. 1972. "Is a Descriptive Semiotics of Music Possible?" *Language Sciences* 23: 1–7.

———. 1973. "Linguistics: A New Approach for Musical Analysis." *International Review of the Aesthetics and Sociology of Music* 4/1: 51–68.

———. 1975. *Fondements d'une semiologie de La musique.* Paris: Union generale d'editions.

———. 1990. *Music and Discourse: Toward a Semiology of Music.* Trans. Carolyn Abbate. Princeton: Princeton University Press.

Nattiez, Jean-Jacques, ed. 1971. "Semiologie de la musique." *Musique en jeu* 5 (special issue).

Naumann, Hans. 1921. *Primitive Gemeinschaftskultur.* Jena: Diederichs.

Nettl, Bruno. 1954a. *North American Indian Musical Styles.* Philadelphia: American Folklore Society.

———. 1954b. "Text-Music Relations in Arapaho Songs." *Southwestern Journal of Anthropology* 10: 192–99.

———. 1958a. "Historical Aspects of Ethnomusicology." *AA* 60: 518–32.

———. 1958b. "Some Linguistic Approaches to Musical Analysis." *JIFMC* 10: 37–41.

———. 1961. "Polyphony in North American Indian Music." *MQ* 47: 354–62.

———. 1963. "A Technique of Ethnomusicology Applied to Western Culture." *EM* 7: 221–24.

———. 1964. *Theory and Method in Ethnomusicology.* New York: Free Press.

———. 1965. "The Songs of Ishi." *MQ* 51: 460–77.

———. 1967a. "Aspects of Folk Music in North American Cities." In George List, ed., *Music in the Americas,* 139–47. The Hague: Mouton.

———. 1967b. "Blackfoot Music in Browning, 1965: Functions and Analysis." In *Festschrift Walter Wiora,* 593–98. Kassel: Bärenreiter.

———. 1967c. "Studies in Blackfoot Indian Musical Culture." Pts. 1 and 2. *EM* 11: 141–60, 293–309.

———. 1968. "Studies in Blackfoot Indian Musical Culture." Pts. 3 and 4. *EM* 12: 11–48, 192–207.

———. 1969. "Musical Areas Reconsidered." In Robert Snow, ed., *Essays in Musicology in Honor of Dragan Plamenac,* 181–90. Pittsburgh: University of Pittsburgh Press.

———. 1974a. "Nour-Ali Boroumand, a Twentieth-Century Master of Persian Music." *Studia Instrumentorum Musicae Popularis* 3: 167–71.

———. 1974b. "Thoughts on Improvisation: A Comparative Approach." *MQ* 60: 1–19.

———. 1978b. "Musical Values and Social Values: Symbols in Iran." *Journal of the Steward Anthropological Society* 10/1: 1–23.

———. 1978c. "Some Aspects of the History of World Music in the Twentieth Century: Questions, Problems, Concepts." *EM* 22: 123–36.

———. 1984. "In Honor of Our Principal Teachers," *EM* 28: 173–85.

———. 1985. *The Western Impact on World Music.* New York: Schirmer Books.

————. 1989a. *Blackfoot Musical Thought.* Kent, Ohio: Kent State University Press.

————. 1989b. "Mozart and the Ethnomusicological Study of Western Culture," *YTM* 21: 1–16.

————. 1992. *The Radif of Persian Music: Studies in Structure and Social Context.* Rev. ed. Champaign, Ill.: Elephant and Cat.

————. 1995. *Heartland Excursions.* Urbana: University of Illinois Press.

————. 1998. "Arrows and Circles: An Anniversary Talk about Fifty Years of ICTM and the Study of Traditional Music." *YTM* 30: 1–11.

————. 1999. "The Institutionalization of Musicology." In Cook and Everist 1999, 287–310. New York: Oxford University Press.

————. 2001. "Mozart, Carnatic Music in Madras and Tanjore, and the Masters of the Persian Radif." In *Mozart and Asia 2001,* 30–36. Salzburg: Land Salzburg.

————. 2002. *Encounters in Ethnomusicology: A Memoir.* Warren, Mich.: Harmonie Park Press.

————, ed. 1978a. *Eight Urban Musical Cultures: Tradition and Change.* Urbana: University of Illinois Press.

Nettl, Bruno, and Philip V. Bohlman, eds. 1991. *Comparative Musicology and Anthropology of Music.* Chicago: University of Chicago Press.

Nettl, Bruno, and Bela Foltin, Jr. 1972. *Daramad of Chahargah, a Study in the Performance Practice of Persian Music.* Detroit: Information Coordinators.

Nettl, Bruno, and Ronald Riddle. 1974."Taqsim Nahawand: A Study of Sixteen Performances by Jihad Racy." *YIFMC* 5: 11–50.

Nettl, Bruno, and Melinda Russell, eds. 1998. *In the Course of Performance: Studies in the World of Improvisation.* Chicago: University of Chicago Press.

Neuenfeldt, Karl, ed. 1997. *The Didjeridu from Arnhemland to Internet.* Sydney: John Libbey.

Neuman, Daniel M. 1977. "The Social Organization of a Music Tradition: Hereditary Specialists in North India." *EM* 21: 233–46.

————. 1980. *The Life of Music in North India.* Detroit: Wayne State University Press.

Neuman, Daniel M., Shubha Chaudhuri, and Komal Kothari. 2002. *An Ethnographic Atlas of Music Traditions in Western Rajasthan.* New Delhi: Author.

The New Grove Dictionary of Music and Musicians. 2001. 2nd ed. Ed. Stanley Sadie. London: Macmillan.

Nketia, J. H. Kwabena. 1962. "The Problem of Meaning in African Music." *EM* 6: 1–7.

————. 1974. *The Music of Africa.* New York: Norton.

Nohl, Ludwig. 1883. *Life of Haydn.* Trans. Geo. P. Upton. Chicago: Jansen, McClurg.

Obata, Juichi, and Ryuji Kobayashi. 1937. "A Direct-Reading Pitch Recorder and Its Application to Music and Speech." *Journal of the Acoustic Society of America* 9: 156–61.

Olsen, Dale A. 1986. "Towards a Musical Atlas of Peru." *EM* 30: 394–412.

Olsvai, I. 1963. "Typical Variations, Typical Correlations, Central Motifs in Hungarian Folk Music." *Studia Musicologica* 4: 37–70.

Ortiz, Fernando. 1952–55. *Los instrumentos de l musica afro-cubana*. Havana: Dirección de Cultura del Ministerio de Educación.

Osgood, Charles E., William H. May, and Murray S. Miron. 1975. *Cross-Cultural Universals of Affective Meanings*. Urbana: University of Illinois Press.

Owens, Thomas. 1974. "Charlie Parker: Techniques of Improvisation." Ph.D. diss., University of California, Los Angeles.

Pelinski, Ramon. 1981. *La musique des Inuit du Caribou*. Montreal: Les Presses de l'Université de Montréal.

Pelto, Pertti J., and Gretel H. 1973. "Ethnography: The Fieldwork Enterprise." In J. Honigmann, ed., *Handbook of Social and Cultural Anthropology*, 241–88. Chicago: Rand McNally.

Pescatello, Ann. 1996. *Charles Seeger: A Life in American Music*. Pittsburgh: University of Pittsburgh Press.

Petrovic, Radmila. 1968. "The Concept of Yugoslav Folk Music in the Twentieth Century." *JIFMC* 20: 22–25.

Phonogramm-Archiv. 2000. *One Hundred Years Berlin Phonogramm-Archiv*. Berlin: Ethnologisches Museum.

Poladian, Sirvart. 1942. "The Problem of Melodic Variation in Folksong." *JAF* 55: 204–11.

Porter, James. 1976. "Jeannie Robertson's My Son David, a Conceptual Performance Model." *JAF* 89: 7–26.

———. 1977. "Prolegomena to a Comparative Study of European Folk Music." *EM* 21: 435–52.

———. 1978. "Introduction: The Traditional Music of Europeans in America." *UCLA Selected Reports in Ethnomusicology* 3/1: 1–23.

Porterfield, Nolan. 1996. *The Last Cavalier: The Life and Times of John A. Lomax*. Urbana: University of Illinois Press.

Potter, Pamela. 1998. *Most German of the Arts: Musicology and Society from the Weimar Republic to the End of Hitler's Reich*. New Haven: Yale University Press.

Powdermaker, Hortense. 1967. *Stranger and Friend*. New York: Norton.

Powers, Harold S. 1970. "An Historical and Comparative Approach to the Classification of Ragas." *UCLA Selected Reports of the Institute of Ethnomusicology* 1/3: 1–78.

———. 1979. "Classical Music, Cultural Roots, and Colonial Rule: An Indic Musicologist Looks at the Muslim World." *AM* 12/1: 5–39.

———. 1980. "Language Models and Musical Analysis." *EM* 24: 1–60.

Powers, William K. 1980. "Oglala Song Terminology." *Selected Reports on Ethnomusicology* 3/2: 23–41.

Provine, Robert. 1988. *Essays on Sino-Korean Musicology: Early Sources for Korean Ritual Music*. Seoul: University Press of Seoul.

Pulikowski, Julian von. 1933. *Geschichte des Begriffes Volkslied im musikalischen Schrifttum*. Heidelberg: Winter.

Qureshi, Regula. 1972. "Ethnomusicological Research among Canadian Communities of Arab and East Indian Origin." *EM* 16: 381–96.

———. 1986. *Sufi Music in Pakistan: Sound, Context, and Meaning in Qawwali*. Cambridge: Cambridge University Press.

———. 1999. "Other Musicologies: Approaching a Hindustani Treatise." In Cook and Everist 1999, 311–35.

———. 2000. "Confronting the Social: Mode of Production and the Sublime for (Indian) Art Music." *EM* 44: 15–38.

Racy, Ali Jihad. 1971. "Funeral Songs of the Druzes of Lebanon." M.M. thesis, University of Illinois.

———. 1976. "Record Industry and Egyptian Traditional Music, 1904–1932." *EM* 20: 23–48.

———. 1991. "Historical Worldviews of Early Ethnomusicologists: An East-West Encounter in Cairo, 1932." In Blum, Bohlman, and Neuman 1991, 68–91.

———. 2003. *Making Music in the Arab World: The Culture and Artistry of Tarab.* Cambridge: Cambridge University Press.

Radano, Ronald, and Philip V. Bohlman, eds. 2000. *Music and the Racial Imagination.* Chicago: University of Chicago Press.

Radcliffe-Brown, A. R. 1952. *Structure and Function in Primitive Society.* London: Cohen and West.

Radin, Paul. 1963. *The Autobiography of a Winnebago Indian.* New York: Dover.

Rahn, Jay. 1983. *A Theory for All Music: Problems and Solutions in the Analysis of Non-Western Forms.* Toronto: University of Toronto Press.

———. 1996. "Turning the Analysis Around: African-Derived Rhythms and European-Derived Music Theory." *Black Music Research Journal* 16: 71–89.

Ramazani, Nesta. 2002. *The Dance of the Rose and the Nightingale.* Syracuse, N.Y.: Syracuse University Press.

Ramnarine, Tina K. 2003. *Ilmatar's Inspirations: Nationalism, Globalization, and the Changing Soundscapes of Finnish Folk Music.* Chicago: University of Chicago Press.

Ramseyer, Urs. 1970. *Soziale Bezüge des Musizierens in Naturvolkkulturen.* Bern: Francke.

Reck, David. 1977. *Music of the Whole Earth.* New York: Scribner.

Redfield, Robert. 1930. *Tepotzlan, a Mexican Village.* Chicago: University of Chicago Press.

Reese, Gustave. 1954. *Music in the Renaissance.* New York: Norton.

Reinhard, Kurt. 1956. *Chinesische Musik.* Kassel: Roth.

———. 1961. "Das berliner Phonogrammarchiv." *Baessler-Archiv, neue Folge* 9: 83–94.

———. 1968. *Einführung in die Musikethnologie.* Wolfenbüttel: Mosiler.

Reyes, Adelaida. 1999. *Songs of the Caged, Songs of the Free: Music and the Vietnamese Refugee Experience.* Philadelphia: Temple University Press.

Reyes Schramm, Adelaida. 1982. "Explorations in Urban Ethnomusicology: Hard Lessons from the Spectacularly Ordinary." *YTM* 14: 1–14.

Rhodes, Willard. 1952. "Acculturation in North American Indian Music." In Sol Tax, ed., *Acculturation in the Americas (Proceedings of the Twenty-ninth International Congress of Americanists)*, 2:127–32. New York: Cooper Square.

———. 1958. "A Study of Musical Diffusion Based on the Wandering of the Opening Peyote Song." *JIFMC* 10: 42–49.

———. 1962. "Music as an Agent of Political Expression." *African Studies Bulletin* 5/2: 14–22.

Rice, Timothy. 1987. "Toward the Remodeling of Ethnomusicology." *EM* 31: 473, 1987.

———. 1994. *May It Fill Your Soul: Experiencing Bulgarian Music.* Chicago: University of Chicago Press.

———. 2003. "Time, Place, and Metaphor in Musical Experience and Ethnography." *EM* 47: 151–79.

Ridley, Matt. 2002. *Nature via Nurture: Genes, Experience, and What Makes Us Human.* New York: HarperCollins.

Roberts, Helen H. 1936. *Musical Areas in Aboriginal North America.* Yale University Publications in Anthropology, no. 12. New Haven.

Roberts, John Storm. 1972. *Black Music in Two Worlds.* New York: Praeger.

Roberts, Warren E. 1958. *The Tale of the Kind and the Unkind Girls.* Berlin: de Gruyter.

Robertson, Carol. 1974. "Music as Therapy: A Bio-Cultural Problem." *EM* 18: 31–42.

———. 1977. "Tayil as Category and Communication among the Argentine Mapuche." *YICTM* 8: 35–52.

———. 1989. "Power and Gender in the Musical Experiences of Women." In Koskoff 1987, 225–44.

Rosenberg, Neil V. 1993. *Transforming Tradition: Folk Music Revivals Examined.* Urbana: University of Illinois Press.

Rouget, Gilbert. 1985. *Music and Trance: A Theory of the Relations between Music and Possession.* Chicago: University of Chicago Press.

Rouget, Gilbert, and Jean Schwarz. 1970. "Transcrire ou decrire? Chant soudanais et chant fuegian." In Jean Pouillon and Pierre Maranda, eds., *Echanges et communications: Melanges offerts a Claude Lévi-Strauss*, 1:677–706. The Hague: Mouton.

Rowell, Lewis. 1992. *Music and Musical Thought in Early India.* Chicago: University of Chicago Press.

Royce, Anya Peterson. 1977. *The Anthropology of Dance.* Bloomington: Indiana University Press.

Rudolph, Lloyd I. and Susanne H. 1967. *The Modernity of Tradition: Political Development in India.* Chicago: University of Chicago Press.

Russell, Melinda. 1993. "Undergraduate Conceptions of Music." In Livingston et al. 1993, 159–74.

Ruwet, Nicolas. 1966. "Méthodes d'analyse en musicologie." *Revue belge de musicologie* 20: 6"5–90.

———. 1967. "Linguistics and Musicology." *International Social Science Journal* 19: 79–87.

———. 1975. "Theorie et méthodes dans les études musicales." *Musique en jeu* 17: 11–36.

Sachs, Curt. 1913 (1964). *Real-Lexikon der Musikinstrumente.* Berlin: Bard. Rev. ed. (1964), New York: Dover.

———. 1929. *Geist und Werden der Musikinstrumente.* Berlin: Bard.

———. 1930 (1959). *Vergleichende Musikwissenschaft—Musik der Fremdkulturen.* Heidelberg: Quelle und Meyer.

———. 1937. *World History of the Dance.* New York: Norton.

———. 1940. *The History of Musical Instruments.* New York: Norton.

———. 1943. *The Rise of Music in the Ancient World, East and West.* New York: Norton.

———. 1946. *The Commonwealth of Art.* New York: Norton.

———. 1948. *Our Musical Heritage.* New York: Prentice-Hall.

———. 1953. *Rhythm and Tempo.* New York: Norton.

———. 1962. *The Wellsprings of Music.* The Hague: Nijhoff.

Sahlins, Marshall D. 1960. *Evolution and Culture.* Ann Arbor: University of Michigan Press.

Said, Edward. 1978. *Orientalism.* New York: Pantheon.

Sakata, Lorraine. 1976. "The Concept of Musician in Three Persian-Speaking Areas of Afghanistan." *AM* 8/1: 1–28.

———. 1983. *Music in the Mind.* Kent, Ohio: Kent State University Press.

Salmen, Walter. 1954. "Towards the Exploration of National Idiosyncracies in Wandering Song-Tunes." *JIFMC* 6: 52–56.

———. 1960. *Der fahrende Musiker im europäischen Mittelalter.* Kassel: Hinnenthal.

Sambamoorthy, P. 1967. *Tyagaraja.* New Delhi: National Book Trust India.

Samuels, R. 1995. *Mahler's Sixth Symphony.* Cambridge: Cambridge University Press.

Sarana, Gopala. 1975. *The Methodology of Anthropological Comparisons: An Analysis of Comparative Methods in Social and Cultural Anthropology.* Viking Fund Publications in Anthropology, no. 53. Tucson: University of Arizona Press.

Sarkissian, Margaret. 2000. *D'Albuquerque's Children: Performing Tradition in Malaysia's Portuguese Settlement.* Chicago: University of Chicago Press.

Scales, Christopher. 2004. "Powwow Music and Aboriginal Recording Industry in Canada: Media, Technology, and Native American Music in the Late Twentieth Century." Ph.D. diss., University of Illinois.

Schaeffner, André. 1932. "D'une nouvelle classification méthodique des instruments de musique." *Revue musicale* 13/129: 215–31.

———. 1936. *Origine des instruments de musique.* Paris: Payol.

———. 1956. "Ethnologie musicale ou musicologie comparée." In Paul Collaer, ed., *Les colloques de Wegimont,* 18–32. Brussels: Elsevier.

Schering, Arnold. 1926. *Musikgeschichte Leipzigs.* Vol. 2. *1650–1723.* Leipzig: Kistner und Siegel.

———. 1936. *Beethoven und die Dichtung.* Berlin: Junker und Dünnhaut.

Schinhan, Jan Philip. 1937. "Die Musik der Papago und Yurok." Ph.D. diss., University of Vienna.

———. 1957. *The Music of the Ballads.* Durham, N.C.: Duke University Press.

Schiørring, Nils. 1956. *Selma Nielsens viser.* Copenhagen: Munksgaard.

Schmidt, Wilhelm. 1939. *The Culture Historical Method of Ethnology.* New York: Fortuny's.

Schneider, Albrecht. 1976. *Musikwissenschaft und Kulturkreislehre.* Bonn: Verlag für systematische Musikwissenschaft.

———. 1979. "Vergleichende Musikwissenschaft als Morphologie und Stilkritik: Werner Danckerts Stellung." *Jahrbuch für Volksliedforschung* 24: 11–27.

———. 2001. "Sound, Pitch, and Scale: From 'Tone Measurements' to Sonological Analysis in Ethnomusicology." *EM* 45: 489–519.

Schneider, Marius. 1934. *Geschichte der Mehrstimmigkeit.* Vol. 1. Berlin: Bard.

———. 1951. "Die historischen Grundlagen der musikalischen Symbolik." *Musikforschung* 4: 113–44.

———. 1957. "Primitive Music." In Egon Wellesz, ed., *Ancient and Oriental Music,* 1–82. London: Oxford University Press.

Schünemann, Georg. 1923. *Das Lied der deutschen Kolonisten in Russland.* Munich: Drei Masken Verlag.

Sebeok, Thomas A., ed. 1977. *How Animals Communicate.* Bloomington: Indiana University Press.

———. 1994. *Signs: An Introduction to Semiotics.* Toronto: University of Toronto Press.

Seeger, Anthony. 1979. "What Can We Learn When They Sing? Vocal Genres of the Suyá Indians of Central Brazil." *EM* 23: 373–94.

———. 1988. *Why Suyá Sing.* Cambridge: Cambridge University Press.

———. 1992a. "Ethnography of Music." In Myers 1992, 88–109.

———. 1992b. "Ethnomusicology and Music Law." *EM* 36: 345–59.

Seeger, Anthony, and Louise Spear. 1987. *Early Field Recordings: A Catalog of Cylinder Recordings at the Indiana University Archives of Traditional Music.* Bloomington: Indiana University Press.

Seeger, Charles. 1941. "Music and Culture." *Proceedings of the Music Teachers National Association for 1940* 64: 112–22.

———. 1950. "Oral Tradition in Music." In Maria Leach, ed., *Funk and Wagnall's Standard Dictionary of Folklore and Mythology,* 2:825–29. New York: Funk and Wagnall.

———. 1953a. "Preface to the Description of a Music." *Proceedings of the Fifth Congress of the I.M.S.,* 360–70. The Hague: Trio.

———. 1953b. "Toward a Universal Music Sound-Writing for Musicology." *JIFMC* 5: 63–66.

———. 1958. "Prescriptive and Descriptive Music Writing." *MQ* 44: 184–95.

———. 1960. Review of *New Methods in Vocal Folk Music Research,* by Carl Dahlback. *EM* 4: 41–42.

———. 1961. "Semantic, Logical, and Political Considerations Bearing upon Research into Ethnomusicology." *EM* 5: 77–80.

———. 1966. "Versions and Variants of the Tunes of 'Barbara Allen.'" *UCLA Selected Reports of the Institute of Ethnomusicology* 1/1: 120–67.

———. 1971. "Reflections upon a Given Topic: Music in Universal Perspective." *EM* 15: 385–98.

———. 1977. *Studies in Musicology 1935–1975.* Berkeley: University of California Press.

Seetha, S. 1981. *Tanjore as a Seat of Music (in the Seventeenth, Eighteenth and Nineteenth Centuries).* Madras: Madras University Press.

Shankar, Ravi. 1999. *Raga-mala: The Autobiography of Ravi Shankar.* New York: Welcome Rain.

Shapiro, Ann Dhu. 1975. "The Tune-Family Concept in British-American Folk-Song Scholarship." Ph.D. diss., Harvard University.

Sharp, Cecil J. 1932 (1952). *English Folk Songs from the Southern Appalachians.* London: Oxford University Press.

———. 1965. *English Folk Song: Some Conclusions.* 4th ed. Ed. Maud Karpeles. Belmont, Calif.: Wadsworth.

Shelemay, Kay Kaufmann. 1994. *A Song of Longing: An Ethiopian Journey.* Urbana: University of Illinois Press.

———. 1998. *Let Jasmine Rain Down: Song and Remembrance among Syrian Jews.* Chicago: University of Chicago Press.

———. 2001. "Towards an Ethnomusicology of the Early Music Movement." *EM* 45: 1–29.

Shepherd, John, Phil Virden, Graham Vulliamy, and Trevor Wishart. 1977. *Whose Music: A Sociology of Musical Languages.* London: Latimer.

Shiloah, Amnon. 1970. "The Aliyya Songs in the Traditional Folk Literature of Israel" (in Hebrew). *Folklore Research Center Studies* (Jerusalem) 1: 349–68.

———. 1974. "The Status of the Oriental Artist." *Ariel* 36: 79–83.

———. 1979. *The Theory of Music in Arabic Writings.* Repertoire Internationale des Sources Musicales series B, vol. 10. Munich: Henle.

———. 1992. *Jewish Musical Traditions.* Detroit: Wayne State University Press.

———. 1995. *Music in the World of Islam: A Socio-Cultural Study.* Hants, England: Scolar Press.

Shiloah, Amnon, and Erik Cohen. 1983. "The Dynamics of Change in Jewish Oriental Ethnic Music in Israel." *EM* 27: 227–52.

Silver, Brian. 1976 "On Becoming an Ustad." *AM* 7/2: 27–50.

Simon, Artur. 1972. *Studien zur ägyptischen Volksmusik.* Hamburg: Wagner.

———. 1978. "Probleme, Methoden und Ziele der Ethnomusikologie." *Jahrbuch für musikalische Volks- und Völkerkunde* 9: 8–52.

———, ed. 2000. *The Berlin Phonogramm-Archiv 1900–2000: Collections of Traditional Music of the World.* Berlin: Verlag für Wissenschaft und Bildung.

Simon, Artur, and Ulrich Wegner, eds. 2000. *Music! One Hundred Recordings: One Hundred Years of the Berlin Phonogramm-Archiv 1900–2000.* Berlin: Phonogramm-Archiv Ethnologisches Museum. 4 CDs and book.

Simpson, Claude M. 1966. *The British Broadside Ballad and Its Music.* New Brunswick, N.J.: Rutgers University Press.

Singer, Milton. 1972. *When a Great Tradition Modernizes.* New York: Praeger.

Slobin, Mark. 1976. *Music in the Culture of Northern Afghanistan.* Tucson: University of Arizona Press.

———. 1992a. "Ethical Issues," In Myers 1992, 329–36.

———. 1992b. "Micromusics of the West: A Comparative Approach," *EM* 36: 1–87.

———. 2000. *Fiddler on the Move: Exploring the Klezmer World.* New York: Oxford University Press.

———, ed. 1996. *Retuning Culture: Musical Changes in Central and Eastern Europe.* Durham, N.C.: Duke University Press.

Sloboda, John. 1985. *The Musical Mind: The Cognitive Psychology of Music.* Oxford: Oxford University Press.

Slotkin, J. S. 1952. *Menomini Peyotism.* Transactions of the American Philosophical Society, new series, vol. 42, pt. 4. Philadelphia: American Philosophical Society.

Small, Christopher. 1987. "Performance as Ritual: Sketch for an Enquiry into the Nature of a Symphonic Concert." In Avron Levine White, ed., *Lost in Music: Culture, Style, and the Musical Event,* 6–23. London: Routledge.

———. 1998. *Musicking: The Meanings of Performance and Listening.* Hanover, N.H.: Wesleyan University Press.

Smith, Richard Chase. 1971. "Deliverance from Chaos for a Song: A Preliminary Discussion of Amuesha Music." Unpublished paper, Cornell University.

———. 1974. *The Amuesha People of Central Peru: Their Struggle to Survive.* Copenhagen: International Work Group for Indigenous Affairs.

Society for Ethnomusicology. 1974. "Special Ethics Issue." *SEM Newsletter* 8/1.

———. 1975. "Ethics Committee Report." *SEM Newsletter* 9/6: 8.

———. 1977. "Ethics Committee Report." *SEM Newsletter* 11/1: 8.

Solie, Ruth A., ed. 1993. *Musicology and Difference: Gender and Sexuality in Music Scholarship.* Berkeley: University of California Press.

Solis, Ted. 2004. *Performing Ethnomusicology: Teaching and Representation in World Music Ensembles.* Berkeley: University of California Press.

Solomon, Maynard. 1989. "Franz Schubert and the Peacocks of Benvenuto Cellini." *Nineteenth-Century Music* 12: 193–206.

Song, Bang-Song. 1980. *Source Readings in Korean Music.* Seoul: Korean National Commission for UNESCO.

Spear, Louise. 1978. "The Archives of Traditional Music: An Interview with George List." In Caroline Card, John Hasse, Robert L. Singer, and Ruth M. Stone, eds., *Discourse in Ethnomusicology: Essays in Honor of George List,* 1–40. Bloomington, Ind.: Ethnomusicology Publications Group.

———. 1991. "An Interview with Frank Gillis." In Nancy Cassell McEntire, ed., *Discourse in Ethnomusicology 3: Essays in Honor of Frank J. Gillis,* 1–36. Bloomington, Ind.: Ethnomusicology Publications Group.

Sperber, Dan. 1975. *Rethinking Symbolism.* Cambridge: Cambridge University Press.

Spindler, George D., ed. 1970. *Being an Anthropologist: Fieldwork in Eleven Cultures.* New York: Holt, Rinehart and Winston.

Springer, George. 1956. "Language and Music: Parallels and Divergences." In Morris Halle, ed., *For Roman Jakobson,* 504–13. The Hague: Mouton.

Stam, James H. 1976. *Inquiries into the Origin of Language: The Fate of a Question.* New York: Harper and Row.

Stauder, Wilhelm. 1967. "Ein Musiktraktat aus dem zweiten vorchristlichen Jahrtausend." In *Festschrift Walter Wiora,* 157–63. Kassel: Bärenreiter.

Steward, Julian. 1955. *Theory of Culture Change: The Methodology of Multilinear Evolution.* Urbana: University of Illinois Press.

———. 1967. *Contemporary Change in Traditional Societies.* Vol. 2. Urbana: University of Illinois Press.

Stewart, Milton Lee. 1973. "Structural Development in the Jazz Improvisational Technique of Clifford Brown." Ph.D. diss., University of Michigan.

Stocking, George W., Jr. 1968. *Race, Culture, and Evolution: Essays in the History of Anthropology.* New York: Free Press.

Stockmann, Doris. 1966. "Das Problem der Transkription in der musikethnologischen Forschung." *Deutsches Jahrbuch für Volkskunde* 12: 207–42.

———. 1979. "Die Transkription in der Musikethnologie: Geschichte, Probleme, Methoden." *Acta Musicologica* 51: 204–45.

Stockmann, Doris, and Jan Steszewski, eds. 1973. *Analyse und Klassifikation von Volksmelodien.* Krakow: Polskie wydawnictwo muzyczne.

Stockmann, Erich. 1972. "The Diffusion of Musical Instruments as an Inter-Ethnic Process of Communication." *YIFMC* 3: 128–37.

Stokes, Martin. 1992. *The Arabesk Debate: Music and Musicians in Modern Turkey.* Oxford: Oxford University Press.

———, ed. 1994. *Ethnicity, Identity and Music: The Musical Construction of Place.* Oxford: Berg.

Stone, Ruth. 1982. *Let the Inside Be Sweet.* Bloomington: Indiana University Press.

Stumpf, Carl. 1886. "Lieder der Bellakula-Indianer." *Vierteljahrschrift für Musikwissenschaft* 2: 405–26.

———. 1911. *Die Anfänge der Musik.* Leipzig: Barth.

Sturrock, John. 1979. *Structuralism and Since.* Oxford: Oxford University Press.

Sturtevant, William. 1964. "Studies in Ethnoscience." *AA* 66, pt. 2: 99–131.

Sugarman, Jane C. 1989. "The Nightingale and the Partridge." *EM* 33: 191–215.

———. 1997. *Engendering Song: Singing and Subjectivity at Prespa Albanian Weddings.* Chicago: University of Chicago Press.

Sullivan, Zohreh T. 2001. *Exiled Memories: Stories of the Iranian Diaspora.* Philadelphia: Temple University Press.

"Symposium on Transcription and Analysis: A Hukwe Song with Musical Bow." 1964. *EM* 8: 223–77.

Szabolcsi, Bence. 1959. *Bausteine zu einer Geschichte der Melodie.* Budapest: Corvina.

———. 1965. *A History of Melody.* New York: St. Martin's Press.

Tappert, Wilhelm. 1890. *Wandernde Melodien.* 2nd enl. and corrected ed. Leipzig: List und Francke.

Tarasti, Eero. 1994. *A Theory of Musical Semiotics.* Bloomington: Indiana University Press.

Taylor, Ronald. 1991. *Kurt Weill, Composer in a Divided World.* Boston: Northeastern University Press.

Temperley, David. 2000. "Rhythm and Grouping in African Music: A View from Music Theory." *EM* 44: 65–96.

Temperley, Nicholas. 1998. *Hymn Tune Index: A Census of English-Language Hymn Tunes.* Oxford: Oxford University Press.

Tenzer, Michael. 2000. *Gamelan Gong Kebyar: The Art of Twentieth-Century Balinese Music.* Chicago: University of Chicago Press.

Thompson, Stith. 1946. *The Folktale.* New York: Dryden Press.

———. 1953. "The Star Husband Tale." *Studia Septentrionalia* 4: 93–163.

———. 1996. *A Folklorist's Progress: Reflections on a Scholar's Life.* Special Publications of the Folklore Institute, no. 5. Bloomington, Ind.: Folklore Institute.

———, ed. 1950. *Four Symposia on Folklore.* Held at the Midcentury International Folklore Conference Indiana University, July 21–August 4, 1950. Bloomington: Indiana University Press.

Tokumaru, Yoshihiko, and Osamu Yamaguti, eds. 1986. *The Oral and the Literate in Music.* Tokyo: Music Academia.

Tokumaru, Yosihiko, Makoto Ohmiya, Masakota Kamazawa, Osamu Yamaguti, Tuneko Tukitani, Akiko Takamatsu, and Mari Shimosako, eds. 1991. *Tradition and Its Future in Music: Report of SIMS 1990 Osaka.* Tokyo: MITA Press.

Tomlinson, Gary. 1993. *Music and Renaissance Magic.* Chicago: University of Chicago Press.

Touma, Habib Hassan. 1968. *Der Maqam Bayati im arabischen Taqsim.* Berlin: H. Touma.

———. 1975. *Die Musik der Araber.* Wilhelmshaven: Heinrichshofen.

Tracey, Hugh. 1948. *Chopi Musicians: Their Music, Poetry, and Instruments.* London: Oxford University Press.

———. 1954. "The Social Role of African Music." *African Affairs* 53: 234–41.

Tran Van Khe. 1977. "Is the Pentatonic Universal?" *WM* 19/1–2: 76–84.

Treitler, Leo. 1974. "Homer and Gregory: The Transmission of Epic Poetry and Plainchant." *MQ* 60: 333–72.

———. 1975. "Centone Chant: Übles Flickwerk or E Pluribus Unus?" *JAMS* 28: 1–23.

———. 1986. "Orality and Literacy in the Music of the European Middle Ages." In Tokumaru and Yamaguti 1986, 38–56.

Truitt, Deborah. 1974. *Dolphin's Porpoises: A Comprehensive Annotated Bibliography of the Smaller Cetacea.* Detroit: Gale Research.

Tsuge, Gen'ichi. 1970. "Rhythmic Aspects of the Avaz in Persian Music." *EM* 14: 205–27.

———. 1974. "Avaz: A Study of the Rhythmic Aspects of Classical Iranian Music." Ph.D. diss., Wesleyan University.

Turino, Thomas. 1993. *Moving Away from Silence.* Chicago: University of Chicago Press.

———. 1999. "Signs of Imagination, Identity, Experience: A Peircian Semiotic Theory for Music." *EM* 43: 221–55.

———. 2000. *Nationalists, Cosmopolitans, and Popular Music in Zimbabwe.* Chicago: University of Chicago Press.

Turino, Thomas, and James Lee, eds. 2004. *Identity and the Arts in Diaspora Communities.* Warren, Mich.: Harmonie Park Press.

Turner, Victor. 1974. *Dramas, Fields, and Metaphors.* Ithaca, N.Y.: Cornell University Press.

Turner, Victor, and Edward M. Bruner, eds. 1986. *The Anthropology of Experience.* Urbana: University of Illinois Press.

Tyler, Stephen A., ed. 1969. *Cognitive Anthropology.* New York: Holt, Rinehart and Winston.

Tylor, Edward B. 1871. *Primitive Culture.* London: Murray.

———. 1889. "On a Method for Investigating the Development of Institutions." *Journal of the Royal Anthropological Institute* 18: 245–72.

Vander, Judith. 1988. *Songprints.* Urbana: University of Illinois Press.

Vansina, John. 1965. *Oral Tradition: A Study in Historical Methodology.* Chicago: University of Chicago Press.

Vargyas, Lajos. 2000. *The Musical World of a Hungarian Village: Aj, 1940.* Budapest: Planetás Kiadó.

Vega, Carlos. 1966. "Mesomusic: An Essay on the Music of the Masses." *EM* 10: 1–17.

Vennum, Thomas. 1989. "The Changing Role of Women in Ojibwa Music History." In Richard Keeling, ed., *Women in North American Indian Music,* 13–21. Bloomington, Ind.: Society for Ethnomusicology.

Vikár, László, and Gábor Bereczki. 1971. *Cheremis Folksongs.* Budapest: Akademiai Kiadó.

Villoteau, G. A. 1809. "De l'état actuel de l'art musical en Égypte." In *Description de l'Égypte.* Paris: Commission des monuments d'Egypte, 1: 609–846.

Viswanathan, T. 1977. "The Analysis of Raga Alapana in South Indian Music." *AM* 9/1: 13–71.

Voget, Fred W. 1975. *A History of Ethnology.* New York: Holt, Rinehart and Winston.

Wachsmann, Klaus. 1961. "Criteria for Acculturation." In *Report of the Eighth Congress of the International Musicological Society,* 139–49. Kassel: Bärenreiter.

———. 1971b. "Universal Perspectives in Music." *EM* 15: 381–84.

———, ed. 1971a. *Essays on Music and History in Africa.* Evanston, Ill.: Northwestern University Press.

Wade, Bonnie. 1998. *Imaging Sound: An Ethnomusicological Study of Music, Art, and Culture in Mughal India.* Chicago: University of Chicago Press.

Wade, Peter. 2000. *Music, Race, and Nation: Musica Tropical in Colombia.* Chicago: University of Chicago Press.

Waengler, Hans H. 1963. "Über Beziehungen zwischen gesprochenen und gesungenen Tonhöhen in afrikanischen Tonsprachen." *Jahrbuch für musikalische Volks- und Völkerkunde* 1: 136–45.

Walin, Stig. 1952. *Die schwedische Hummel.* Stockholm: Nordiska museet.

Wallaschek, Richard. 1893. *Primitive Music.* London: Longmans, Green.

Wallin, L., Björn Merker, and Steven Brown, eds. 2000. *The Origins of Music.* Cambridge, Mass.: MIT Press.

Ward, John M. 1980. "The Hunt's Up." *Proceedings of the Royal Musical Association* 106: 1–25.

Warwick, Donald P., and Samuel Osherson, eds. 1973. *Comparative Research Methods.* Englewood Cliffs, N.J.: Prentice-Hall.

Waterman, Christopher A. 1979. "The Effect of Western Functional Harmony on Persian and Sub-Saharan African Music." Unpublished paper, University of Illinois.

———. 1990. *Juju: A Social History and Ethnography of an African Popular Music.* Chicago: University of Chicago Press.

———. 1991a. "Juju History: Toward a Theory of Sociomusical Practice." In Blum, Bohlman, and Neuman 1991, 49–67.

———. 1991b. "The Uneven Development of Africanist Ethnomusicology." In Nettl and Bohlman 1991, 169–86.

Waterman, Richard A. 1948. "'Hot' Rhythm in Negro Music." *JAMS* 1: 24–37.

———. 1952. "African Influence on American Negro Music." In Sol Tax, ed., *Acculturation in the Americas,* 207–18. Chicago: University of Chicago Press.

———. 1956. "Music in Australian Aboriginal Culture: Some Sociological and Psychological Implications." *Music Therapy* 5: 40–50.

Wax, Rosalie H. 1971. *Doing Field Work: Warnings and Advice.* Chicago: University of Chicago Press.

Weber, Max. 1958. *The Rational and Social Foundations of Music.* Carbondale: Southern Illinois University Press. First published in German, 1921.

Weber-Kellermann, Ingeborg. 1957. *Ludolf Parisius und seine altmärkischen Volkslieder.* Berlin: Akademie-Verlag.

Werner, Heinz. 1917. *Die melodische Erfindung im frühen Kindesalter.* Akademie der Wissenschaften Wien, Phil.-hist. Klasse, Sitzungsberichte 182, no. 4. Vienna: Akademie der Wissenschaften.

Wertheimer, Max. 1909–10. "Musik der Wedda." *Sammelbände der internationalen Musikgesellschaft* 11: 300–304.

Widdess, Richard. 1992. "Historical Ethnomusicology." In Myers 1992, 219–44.

White, Leslie. 1949. *The Science of Culture.* New York: Farrar, Strauss and Giroux.

Wieschoff, Heinz. 1933. *Die afrikanischen Trommeln und ihre ausserafrikanischen Beziehungen.* Stuttgart: Strecker und Schroder.

Wilgus, D. K. 1959. *Anglo-American Folksong Scholarship since 1898.* New Brunswick, N.J.: Rutgers University Press.

Wilkens, Eckart. 1967. *Künstler und Amateure im persischen Santourspiel.* Regensburg: Bosse.

Wiora, Walter. 1953. *Europäischer Volksgesang. Das Musikwerk,* no. 4. Cologne: Arno Volk. English trans. by Robert Kolben, *European Folk Song: Common Forms in Characteristic Modification.* New York: Leeds, [ca. 1966?].

———. 1956. "Älter als die Pentatonik." In Zoltan Kodály and Laszlo Lajtha, eds., *Studia Memoriae Belae Bartok Sacra,* 185–208. Budapest: Academia Scientiarum Hungaricae.

———. 1957. *Europäische Volksmusik und abendländische Tonkunst.* Kassel: Hinnenthal.

———. 1965. *The Four Ages of Music.* New York: Norton.

———. 1970. "Das Alter des Begriffes Volkslied." *Musikforschung* 23: 420–28.

———. 1972. "Reflections on the Problem: How Old Is the Concept Folksong." *YIFMC* 3: 23–33.

———. 1975. *Ergebnisse und Aufgaben vergleichender Musikforschung.* Darmstadt: Wissenschaftliche Buchgesellschaft.

Wissler, Clark. 1912. *Social Organization and Ritualistic Ceremonies of the Blackfoot Indians.* American Museum of Natural History, Anthropological Papers, no. 7. New York: American Museum of Natural History.

———. 1917. *The American Indian.* New York: McMurtrie.

Witmer, Robert. 1973. "Recent Change in the Musical Culture of the Blood Indians." *Yearbook for Inter-American Musical Research* 9: 64–94.

———. 1982. *The Musical Life of the Blood Indians.* Ottawa: National Museum of Man.

———. 1991. "Stability in Blackfoot Songs, 1909–1968." In Blum, Bohlman, and Neuman 1991, 242–53.

Wong, Isabel K. F. 1991. "From Reaction to Synthesis: Chinese Musicology in the Twentieth Century." In Nettl and Bohlman 1991, 37–55.

World of Music. 1991. Special issue on improvisation. Vol. 33, no. 3.

Wulstan, D. 1971. "The Earliest Musical Notation." *Music and Letters* 52: 365–82.

Wundt, Wilhelm. 1911. *Völkerpsychologie, eine Untersuchung der Entwicklungsgesetze von Sprache, Mythus und Sitte.* 3rd ed. Leipzig: Engelmann.

Zemp, Hugo. 1979. "Aspects of 'Are'are Musical Theory." *EM* 23: 5–48.

Zonis, Ella. 1973. *Classical Persian Music: An Introduction.* Cambridge, Mass.: Harvard University Press.

Index

321; on culture distribution, 345; field experience of, 184; introductory anthropology text by, 221; on natural areas, 331
Krohn, Ilmari, 123–24
Kulturkreis school, 322, 323
Kunitachi College of Music, 384
Kunst, Jaap: on gamelan tuning, 108; on Javanese scale systems, 108; on the Pontic migration, 325–26; on the term "ethnomusicology," 11; on transcription, 74–76
Kurath, Gertrude, 417
Kurds, 426

Laade, Wolfgang, 167
Lach, Robert, 65, 184
Lachmann, Robert, 58, 162
Ladysmith Black Mambazo, 286
Lakota language, 282
Landon, H. C. Robbins, 275
language: as determinant of music, 345–46; and music, 48–49, 51–52; origin of, 266; universal, 42, 49
languages: families of, 51–52; as symbol systems, 310
Lassiter, Luke, 242
learning of music: life cycle in, 389; significance of, 388–92; typical of most cultures, 391; in Western culture, 390–92
Lebanon, 178
Leipzig, 237
Lesure, Francois, 275
Levant, Oscar, 122
Levin, Theodore, 242
Levine, Victoria, 85
Lévi-Strauss, Claude: on myths, 239; semiotics of, 306; structuralism of, 44; on symbols, 305
Lewis, Oscar: on comparative study, 63–65
Library of Congress, 162, 168–69
Lieberman, Fredric, 202, 318, 443–44
life cycle, 389
Liliencron, Rochus von, 331
linguistics: approaches to symbolism of, 305, 308; as basis for music analysis, 310; and origins of music, 264
Linton, Ralph, 246
List, George: as archivist, 162; on oral transmission, 291; and spectographic analysis, 86; on transcription devices, 87; transcription methods of, 83–85

litigation, musical, 202
Lockwood, Lewis, 304
Loeb, Lawrence, 337
logogenic music, 267
Lomax, Alan: analytical methods of, 102, 107, 123; as archivist, 162; cantometrics of, 66, 79, 100–101, 128–29, 231; on folk music style, 368; on the fundamental function of music, 247, 253; on gender differences, 412; musical areas of, 330; on music and culture type, 247, 283; on preservation, 161; on singing style, 71; on social organization, 349; on a universal analytical method, 102, 107; Universal Jukebox of, 329; on use of statistics by, 72. See also cantometrics
Lomax, John, 162
long-distance communication, as origin of music, 262
Longfellow, John Wadsworth, 42
Lord, Albert B., 294, 410
Lorenz, Alfred Ottokar, 57, 288
Lowie, Robert H., 232, 323
Lowinsky, Edward, 275
Lundquist, Barbara, 402

Ma'aroufi, Musa, 296
Maceda, Jose, 210
Madras. See Chennai
Magrini, Tullia, 413
Mahillon, Victor-Charles, 383
Mahler, Gustav, 182, 215, 278
Mahling, Christoph-Hellmut, 285
Mahour (Persian mode), 317
mainstream ethnomusicology, 449
major-minor scale contrast, 316
major second: as universal interval, 46
Malinowski, Bronislaw: culture concept of, 224; on fieldwork, 135–37, 145; on gender, 410; on three kinds of field data, 36
Malm, William P., 100, 235–36
Mande, 104, 242
"Man I Love, The" (song), 122
"manly-hearted" women (Blackfoot), 422
Manuel, Peter, 72, 188, 285
Mapfumo, Thomas, 285
maps: construction of, 326–29
Maraire, Abraham Dumisani, 319
marginal survivals, 331
Mars, ethnomusicologist from, 17, 190–91

BRUNO NETTL was born in Prague in 1930 and immigrated to the United States as a young boy in 1939. Educated at Indiana University (Ph.D. 1953) and the University of Michigan, he began teaching at Wayne State University and the University of Kiel, Germany, joining the faculty of the University of Illinois at Urbana-Champaign in 1964, where he has been ever since, teaching ethnomusicology as a professor of music and of anthropology. His main field experience has been with the Blackfoot people of Montana; in Tehran, Iran; and in Madras (now Chennai), India. He is the author or editor of several books, including *Theory and Method in Ethnomusicology* (1964); *Blackfoot Musical Thought: Comparative Perspectives* (1989); *In the Course of Performance* (1998); and two other books from the University of Illinois Press, *Eight Urban Musical Cultures* (1978) and *Heartland Excursions* (1995), as well as the original edition of this work, in 1983. Formerly president (1968–70) of the Society for Ethnomusicology and editor of its journal (1961–65 and 1998–2002), he holds honorary degrees from the University of Chicago and the University of Illinois and is a Fellow of the American Academy of Arts and Sciences.